Mary, with love and
admiration,

from

Michael Halsted.
16. ii. '60

and Rosemary.

Round the World in Forty Years
A British Council Life

THE
BRITISH
COUNCIL

TRUTH WILL TRIUMPH

Round the World in Forty Years
A British Council Life

by

Michael Halsted

A SQUARE ONE PUBLICATION

First published in Great Britain in 1999 by
Square One Publications
The Tudor House, 16 Church Street,
Upton on Severn, Worcestershire WR8 0HT

© 1999 Michael Halsted

ISBN: 1 8999 37 2

British Library Cataloguing in Publication Data is available
for this book

Typeset by Avon Dataset Ltd, Bidford on Avon B50 4JH

Printed in Great Britain by Biddles Ltd, Guildford, England

Contents

Preface

I saw the following on an exhibition show-case in the British Library:

> Historical documents can be any type of text: a note scribbled in
> a church calendar; a letter; a bill; a diary; a handbill for a meeting.
> What makes us single out particular texts as historical documents,
> and view them sometimes as treasures, is our own changing per-
> ception of the importance of the people and events with which
> they are associated.

It was my mother who pointed out to me the interest and possible value in
keeping photographs and texts carefully dated and captioned – certainly
to the family and maybe to history. My father-in-law felt the same. So I
thought I would write about our unique experiences in the service of the
British Council overseas.

I put my idea to Enid Castle, a former, much respected headmistress of
Cheltenham Ladies College, my mother's old school. Miss Castle replied:
"You must write your book, Michael, because it is history." What I have
produced over six years, with the help of Rosemary's and my letters
home, may not be history, but at this stage who is to know? At any rate, I
have particular satisfaction in being told that the British Council will put
my complete, pre-edited text and material in the Council's archives in the
Public Records Office at Kew.

Michael Halsted

Not forgetting what is owed:

Thanks to faithful Jenny Hedley, who typed cheerfully and accurately for four years from a script akin to Sanskrit.

Then to the staff of Prestoprint, Cheltenham, who often under pressure from other clients have taken much trouble to reproduce Jenny's type-scripts and my illustrations.

And to Dr J.M.B. Harley, a former editor of a scientific journal, for valuable early comments and corrections.

Gratitude to Sarah Scott, who, with her expertise has produced an admirable Index.

And most especially my thanks to Fiona Hollom, my felicitous Editor, who did her utmost with patience and good humour to reduce the mass of recollections. She proves that it is the editor 'who really rights a book!'

Acknowledgement

My thanks to

Imperial War Museum; H.M.S. Enterprise; Professor Bayley; Iris Murdoch; Peters Fraser & Dunlop Robert Byron; Picador, Andrew Lang; The Lord Mancroft; Royal Scottish Country Dance Society; BBC Wildlife; The British Library; Readers Digest; Newspaper Publications PLC; Paul Strachan, Burma; Mr G. Abbott, Burma; British Institute of Persian Studies, Map; Mary S. Lovell; Richard Burton; A. P. Watt. Hassan. (Flecker); Schott. Hungarian drawings; ILN Picture Library; HarperCollins Cartographic; E. J. Brill, Leiden, Netherlands; Anne Marie Schimmel, and to all who have provided contributions to this book.

Reflections in Gratitude

"Happy is the man," wrote Lord Mancroft, "who has a wife to tell him what to do and a secretary to do it for him." This accurately sums up my life of thirty-three years in the British Council's Overseas Service, from 1947 to 1980, twenty-seven of which were with my wife in seven different countries.

I write in special gratitude to my wife, and to my secretaries; and to all Council wives overseas, who devotedly played vital supporting roles.

In our British Council Overseas Service it was a pleasure to have like-minded, zealous, and congenial colleagues, and their wives. We had brave, loyal, and efficient local office-staff; and faithful and willing domestic servants. We became attached to many of both categories, and hated to leave them each time we moved on.

Our conditions of living improved increasingly over the years. We were well housed and furnished, and given good pay and allowances, adequate local leave, and generous home leave. The London Office departments looked after our welfare with a sympathy which gave us confidence. Those at the very top earned our gratitude. They worked desperately hard to keep the British Council in being and, thankfully, they managed to keep the countries in which we served adequately provided with funds. We had excellent support from our British Embassies or High Commissions.

My mind's eye contains a kaleidoscopic image of bright memories and lasting friendships, and absolutely no regrets. Everything was for us. I firmly believed in what I was doing. The variety of work and experience in the various countries was absorbing and exciting. We had the rare opportunity to meet many distinguished British men and women who were sponsored by the British Council, and gave unstintingly of their own well-earned holidays.

It was rewarding to be wholly concerned with educated men and women of the countries in which we served, and to support their aspirations. We were happy and lucky; and we thoroughly enjoyed the varieties of leisure activity open to us, and our contact with country folk. We only experienced one revolution, which was almost bloodless, and the edge of two hurricanes. We were never in danger from riot, war, flood, earthquake or other 'Acts of God'.[1]

The major bonus for me was having a job in which my wife could share. In fact Rosemary was a vital half of the team. She had a tougher time than I did. While I was in a cool class-room or air-conditioned office, she had to cope with the hot, wet tropics for seventy per cent of our service. She had to manage all kinds of servants, a variety of languages, and deal with insanitary markets, dirt, dust, mould, smells, insect pests, pi-dogs, crows, and chaotic and lethal traffic.

Rosemary became friends with numbers of local professional contacts and their wives. She coped with all varieties of British visitor (official Council or other) and the escorting and hospitality they required. She was ready to assist with film-shows, art or book exhibitions, concerts, or country-dance groups. Rosemary was a sound adviser, sensitive and resourceful. In fact she was an unpaid Council assistant.

When Lord Ballantrae, a British Council Chairman in our time, was going over my career with me one day, he hurrumphed and said: "Hand of Death, Michael". These words were not spoken entirely in jest: Hungary, Pakistan, Ethiopia, Iran, Burma, Fiji, Guyana, and Morocco – all except for Morocco have had their crises since we left! But unless one had been a success in the Mafia, one could hardly descibe this comment as an accolade from the Chairman of the British Council after one's thirty-three-year career from 1947 to 1980 in eight countries.

This is not an official account of the work of the British Council. It is more about people and places through the lives of this staff couple in the course of work and leisure – over twenty-seven years!

Michael Halsted
31 July 1998

---

[1] Nor kidnap, as happened in 1998 to the brave Mitchell family in Yemen.

Bradfield

Amateur schoolmaster: junior commando

I wrote *Shots in the Sand* to acknowledge the part played in my life by friends of home, school, college, and regiment who made my life memorable and happy. When I returned from the British Army Staff in Washington D.C., in the summer of 1944, I was patched up a bit more in a former asylum in Radlett, Herts, after the rigours of life on the east and west coasts of America. Then I was pushed out into a dim world for Staff Captains, Grade B. (Med.), while the regiment was in Italy.

I went straight down to my old school, Bradfield College, Berkshire, of which I was very fond, particularly to see my staunch friend, Lt. Col. John D. Hills M.C., the headmaster. John felt I could be more use to him than in some dim depot, so he applied to the War Office, who agreed to release me. So again, something just happened to me without my efforts. When I took up residence in September 1944 as an Assistant-Master on £300 p.a., I was more frightened than when I joined the Queen's Bays in 1941. I knew nothing of the geography, English and history which I was required to teach. But it turned out not to matter.

I had friends among the members of staff, whom up to 1938 I had addressed as 'Sir', such as Joe Wilson, my former housemaster and lifelong friend. I taught geography in the familiar Geography School. I enjoyed what I had to teach; and the bright thirteen and fourteen-year-old Shell scholarship classes astonished me. All I had to do was organise a scheme of work, and they taught themselves and me in the by-going.

I regained my nerve. I could usually manage to keep order. I had a certain cachet in being back from the war, and at the age of twenty-four I didn't have to exert much authority. Most of the disorder, according to members of the staff, was caused by me either in class or out of it. It was the greatest fun but something was missing. Reflecting that I did know something about weapons and warfare, I realised that I might be able to enthuse others with my love of weapons and explosives: I had my Private Army at last.[1]

With the total support of the headmaster, and thanks to the kindness of the Commanding Officer, O.R. Jones and his other officers, I was allowed

[1] See Vladimir Peniakoff, *D.S.O., M.C., Private Army* (Jonathan Cape, London, 1950).

1

The S.C.R. Bradfield College, 1944–46. Most of the staff are
identifiable, including one known as Hank.

THE CAPTAIN

A Captein was ther with us for the nones;
Ful byg he wes of brawn and eek of bones,
And in a schule taughten Geographie;
Wel colde he dresse hys takel capteinly
For in the warre had he ben in Tankes
In Egypte, Libya, and eek wyth Yankes
At Washyngtoun and Yorke, wir he was looth
To shew the spytte and polyshe of in sooth.
Woonded he hadde ben upon hys face,
And wes wel thyrty yere of age I gesse.
In Felde-dayes ther colde he muchel helpe, ·
And rage he colde, and call a man a whelpe
Whan that hys ryfle dropt, or scrap's hys bote;
He was wel hard to plese, that I woot.
A blake patch he boor upon hys eye,
And colde for hys loonche bangyrs frye.
Certes he wes lowly and servysable,
And dynnertymes he sate at the High Table.

W. J. Mizen.

I have always treasured and admired this class exercise effort on the
Chaucerian sonnet by W. J. Mizen

to form a Junior Commando Unit within the O.T.C. The Government provided camouflage jackets for the school contingent anyway; the school bought us green berets for which John Hills designed a silver, metal badge consisting of the school's St Andrews Cross with a sword running through it. My father (Papa), who was Vice-Quartermaster-General at the time, was, I believe, useful when I applied in person to Army Depots for help with equipment. We received motor-cycles, assault boats, thunder-flashes, smoke bombs, live .303 and 9 mm ammunition, unlimited blank cartridges, even gifts such as gelignite and cordtex explosive, and an assortment of useful bits and pieces such as cable, rope, pickets, and the like.

The boys and I built a scaffolding and timber assault course, with obstacles wired up to electrically-fired charges bought from Standard

From

THE HEAD MASTER   BRADFIELD COLLEGE

BRADFIELD 3.   BERKSHIRE

30th October 1945

My dear Oliver,

    Having taken onto my staff a wild man from the Bays, I have to allow him to stimulate initiative amongst the more senior ranks of the J.T.C. This he does by sending them on whole holidays (you will doubtless connect Nov 1 with All Saints!) on various missions, trying to trace film stars or generals. Two of these are after you. Will you please initial the envelope, accept my apologies and good wishes and note that the J.T.C. has found something new to do.

                     Yours ever

                     John Hills

Lieutenant-General Sir Oliver Leese.

3

Fireworks, who also provided lovely maroons. I sat in a command tower and pressed the buttons, one being for the underwater charge below our twin-cable, river Pang bridge. The boys were volunteers. Some may have hated me; most were happy, they told me later. I obtained a blank-firing attachment for the school's Vickers Gun, and mounted it facing backwards on its tripod on a little, open, Morris 8 truck, with a crew of two or three on an old car-seat. I drove the van myself, reversing slowly round a corner to allow bursts of fire against our enemies and then accelerating away. For battle simulation I had my father's 2 pdr. muzzle loading cannon.[2]

We had forced marches with ambushes; whole day exercises, even against Sandhurst O.T.U.; and, at times, quite tough, night exercises among ourselves. I taught the chaps a good deal of battlecraft, during which they learned to earn their green berets. For the real thing I found an old chalk-pit in which my 'men' could fire live with Bren gun, rifle, sten-gun, and Browning pistol. I trained them to crawl flat across the pit floor while I fired live rifle rounds over the top of them. No parent complained; if they ever knew. We had no casualties – apart from the parish church roof. I was blowing up a tree stump with gelignite, and part of the stump rose into the air in a beautiful parabola, and crashed through the church roof. The rector was generously Christian about the incident. John Hills referred to me as the 'Explosives Master'.[3]

For school field-days I introduced two secret weapons, which for safety's sake I fired myself. Mark Dinely of Bapty and Co., suppliers of arms to the film world, produced for me a shoulder-fired, sixpenny banger rocket-launcher. I produced a thunderflash mortar of a stopped-off length of heavy piping held up by a wooden tripod.

Quarter-Master Painting, a W.W.I veteran, coped cheerfully and admirably with all the extra work. But some of the staff were not always so cheerful. We were fairly noisy, and were most unpopular with one member after choking his dinner-party guests with smoke on a night exercise. I told him the wind had changed. Less stressful exercises for the staff's nerves were the Initiative Tests. Pairs of commandos were given sealed instructions such as "Obtain Diana Dors' signature". Nearly all were achieved if the subjects were reasonably accessible.

Then the atom bomb was dropped and V.J. Day came. I was lucky again. Unselfishly, Lt. Colonel O.R. Jones allowed me in his place to take a Bradfield contingent to London to line part of the route. I found myself and the cadets by one of the great lamp-standards in the fountain circle outside Buckingham Palace. It was a thrilling chance. Soon the regular

[2]See photograph in *Shots in the Sand*, p. 120.
[3]See Evelyn Waugh's letter to his wife 31 May 1942; George MacDonald Fraser, *McAuslan and the Sheikh*, (Barrie and Jenkings, 1974).

Bradfield

AN ACTOR WAITING IN THE WINGS OF THE CCF

JOHN BENNETT (C 43-46) explains how the Corps helped him discover his vocation

THE NICK CLARKE INTERVIEW

From the Old Bradfieldian Society
Newsletter of Spring 1998

IN THE LAST YEAR of the war, a group of boys in battle-dress and army boots could have been seen one day taking lunch at the exclusive Berkeley Hotel in Piccadilly. It was perhaps the most unlikely end to a Bradfield Corps Field Day in the history of that august organisation. Each boy had completed an initiative test of his own devising, and the lunch was their commander's way of celebrating their success.

John Bennett had chosen a particularly appropriate adventure: to acquire the autograph of one of his heroines, the actress Anna Neagle. 'I discovered that she lived in Borehamwood, and simply went to her house and knocked on the door. She was charming, and I soon returned in triumph with my prize.'

Like all school cadet foreces in wartime, Bradfield's Corps was a preparation for the serious business of soldiery. It was under the command of the impossibly dashing Michael Halsted, the host of the Berkeley lunch. He was an Eighth Army veteran with an eye lost in action and Bugatti sports car. Bennett remem-

bers him with the awe usually reserved for movie stars. 'He was the most glamorous figure you can imagine, and his car was the ultimate in one-upmanship. We all adored him.'

The was was always in the boys' mindes. Their prefects left for active duty and never returned. They tracked the progress of the Allied forces by radio, and learned the names of every aircraft they ssaw in the sky. And eventually, on VE Day, most of the school simmply decamped, without asking prior permission. Bennett headed for his home town, London, and joined the celebrations in Trafalgar Square. In this obsessive atmosphere, Halsted had no trouble enthusing his young charges with a sense of military purpose. Although Bennett left school in 1946 as a private, he decided nonetheless to opt for a commission in the Royal Artillery, and served out his two years' conscription in the Middle East, proudly wearing the star which marked his Cadet Corps service. Only then did he enrol at drama school.

See 'SIND' January 1976. John Bennett actor and former 'Commando' of mine, came out leading a Royal Shakespeare Company Group. I had often wondered how the boys had really felt about my tough regime. Now I am happy to have at least one favourable view!

Bradfield staff who had survived the war were ready to return. I was happy to hand the Geography School back to Basil Johnson (Lt. Col., O.B.E. T.D.). I had to think about my future. I enjoyed teaching but I could not bear the thought of remaining behind while I had to say good-bye each year to another generation going out into the world. Once again, my future fell into place with no conscious effort by me.

I spent my £180 army gratuity on a skiing visit to a Swedish school-friend, Arne Flygt, in the company of our headboy, Johnny Trickett. While in Stockholm, I came across the British Council in the person of Patrick Meade on its staff who had been at Oxford with me. When I told him I was on holiday but looking for a job, he thought the British Council, of which I knew nothing, would be just the life for me. I applied on return and, to my delight, I was called for interview at their headquarters in London at 65 Davies Street.

The interview date coincided with a day's holiday for the school, and therefore my Initiative Tests were on. I gave one pair of boys the instructions, "Follow me and report on return". I didn't see them during my journey by bus to Reading and train to London; nor in Swan and Edgar's where in the men's room I put on a clean, stiff, white collar; nor even when I entered the British Council.

Oddly enough, I was not nervous as I sat before the Board. There was a cheerful and encouraging atmosphere with some mystification and humour when I told the gentlemen that I had taken my degree from St Edmund Hall and St Hugh's – the latter had been requisitioned as a military hospital for head injuries, from where as a patient I was subsequently able to sit a War Degree.[4]

I remember nothing of my interview except that I emphasised my interest in people; my desire to be of service to any colour or creed; and of my pride and confidence in Britain. I suddenly dreaded the effect of any of the board spotting one of my Initiative shadows! I shall never know if they did, but I expect so. I left by a different door and glanced round the corner in the passage. There was No. 1 commando on the shoulders of No. 2 peering over the transom. I crept away. A few days later I found myself accepted in the Overseas Service of the British Council with effect from 1 January 1947, and appointed Lecturer in English on the Council's staff in Budapest, Hungary. I was hugely excited, but even so I could not imagine the highly satisfying, happy, and fascinating life which was to follow for the next thirty-three years.

I had a five-day induction course back at Davies Street. Departmental officers gave me succinct briefings on Visitors, Music, Libraries, Education and Science, Films, Accounts, Personnel, Pay and Records, and more. I was based on the old Cavendish Hotel, and between and after hours I purchased and packed madly. How often does one not need the 'musts' one buys before a journey to a new destination?

[4]See *Shots*, p.166.

6

An Englishman in Hungary

Journey to Budapest: January 1947

On Sunday 19 January 1947 I boarded the Golden Arrow at Victoria Station. Now I was on a train myself, and waving goodbye, although not actually to anyone. I had maintained that it was a situation preferable to remaining on a platform and waving goodbye to departing friends or relatives.

My, was I green, or a long-way throwback! I had eleven pieces of baggage. (I see why the Romans called it 'impedimenta'.) Mine included a shot-gun, a light rifle, a full magazine of 12-bore cartridges, and a wooden box of books, paper, and a typewriter. The Southern Railway clerk was appalled at the weight, and charged me £6 for it all as far as Paris. "It'll cost you at least F.4000 more from Paris on. How many francs have you got?" "F.2000." "Well, I can let you have another F.3000." What a kind, official attitude. I couldn't pay the £6, let alone buy his francs. I had to dash back to the Cavendish to cash a cheque, and all was well.

At the Gare du Nord a small man held up a large placard on which was written: 'BRITISH COUNCIL'. It was Mr Collins to look after me. I immediately felt cared for. So it was to be for the next thirty-three years. Because of my weapons, a gendarme announced himself as my escort to the Gare de L'Est, and came in the Council car. When he had seen it all registered through to Vienna, he left with a smile, cigarettes, and F.100. I had to wait for two and a half hours on a cold station. Mr Collins took me to a bar near the station, but there was no food. He told me to give the bartender a good tip because he lived on tips. He had to pay the owner for the privilege of running the café. Food was still scarce and costly. Fuel was even more scarce. The streets of Paris seemed so dim because they could only be half-lit; and different sectors had regular periods of complete black-out.

The Arlberg Express came in at 21.15, and I had had no supper. There was no food on the train. I had been misinformed. This was serious. I was hungry. Ah, the buffet! But coupons were required for the measly bread and ham rolls. I explained that I was English (superfluous no doubt and not necessarily wise: a colleague escaped from an Egyptian mob in 1952 by persuading them he was not English but Scottish). I got a ham roll for

7

KÉZIRAT GYANÁNT

COLLEGE NEWS

SÁROSPATAK
HUNGARY

THE ENGLISH COLLEGE

VOL. VIII.   **EASTER 1947.**   **No. 2.**

F.34 instead of F.28. With courage mounting, I asked for another and paid the same price.

I had to share a couchette with a Russian businessman. He never stopped asking questions about England even when I was shaving the next morning. I was polite, and of course informative, thus I survived my first British Council exercise.

The daylight journey from Zurich, with wonderful lake and mountain scenery, was breath-taking. There was a long halt on the eastern frontier at Buchs. We were not allowed off, but we could buy chocolate and 'mandarinen' from a barrow man. The 3.000-foot climb through the snowy Arlberg was a joy.

Then we halted at Innsbruck in the evening. I stamped up and down the platform in the biting cold, eyeing the crowd of poor, harassed, would-be travellers in their motley garb. Then on nearing Vienna I had some good coffee and rolls on the train without realising how lucky I was.

An Englishman in Hungary

I was bewildered when I alighted on to the bitterly cold platform in the general scramble, and a porter whisked off my light baggage and guns, I didn't know anything about my registered baggage. I had no German but a phrase book. However, a very kind Hungarian waiting for his Russian clearance to return home, came to my rescue in passable English. He asked me back to his flat. What a spirit, and with no ulterior motive! We had a depressing trip in three different, crowded, elderly trams; but a flat-rate of a five-Groschen fare made it easier.

We first went to a café in Schwartzenbergplatz. It was cold inside and the clientele looked miserable. There was nothing to eat. I ordered a coffee. It was made of acorns and tasted horrible. The Hungarian's flat was freezing. The Austrians had no fuel at all. Of course, there was nothing for me to eat. The British Council office, when contacted, sent a car and a driver's mate, who took me and all my baggage to the R.A.F. Transit Hotel Astoria. I soon got fed and warmed. I am very lucky. I have never suffered yet.

At the Council office I was efficiently administered, given local currency and the British Armed Forces paper and cardboard currency known as Bafs, for use in British-run canteens to try to end currency speculation by our troops and the locals. I was told that I could not continue by train because my fare had to be paid in unobtainable Hungarian forints. So I filled in papers for an R.A.F. and Russian-authorised Air Transport Command flight. I was then moved to the once-grand Sacher Hotel, to await clearance. Thus I had a free holiday in Vienna, and a stay in an historic institution redolent of Empire days.

Remembering Polonious, the first thing I did was to obtain a British telephone-book to see if I could find a friend: "The friends thou hast and their adoption tried, grapple them to thy soul with hoops of steel".

I found a good friend of my father's: the Deputy High Commissioner, Major-General Winterton, who had been in I Corps B.E.F. with Papa and ran the evacuation from Dunkirk. He was a diplomat of distinction as well as a soldier and a linguist. With Vienna partitioned, the Russians adopted an extremely hostile attitude to their allies, and they required firm and tactful handling. "On one occasion, Winterton was held up at gun-point by Soviet soldiers, but gave them such a tongue-lashing in Russian that they stepped aside. He demanded and got an apology from the Russians."[1]

General Winterton sent his Mercedes for me, and gave me lunch at his lovely house. Then he took me back to his headquarters at Schonbrunn Palace, which he said he had been determined to seize before the Russians reached it. He took me round the palace, and showed me how the elegant great porcelain wood-stoves were fuelled by servants passing along the double-walls. I did not visit all the 1,444 rooms, but I noticed how tiny

[1] *The Times* , Obituary: 18 December 1987.

9

and swallowed-up the entire British staff appeared, whose task it was to help Austria on to her feet again.

The General's support gave me a rare insight into the Vienna of 1947. As I moved about, I saw a population trying to live on very little food amid the part ruins of their beloved city, in a temperature well below zero. My Hungarian befriender had only two meat rolls to last him all day. He had no form of heating, and the gas for cooking lasted only a short time. The younger people, and others with any energy and luck, could be seen trudging back to the city with sacks bulky with firewood. I saw poor, pinched, old people staring at meagre menu-cards pinned up outside half-shuttered restaurants. Most people received their allotted daily calories of food in their registered shops. They could read the amounts in the daily papers, but deliveries were unreliable. Little children were well wrapped-up and pulled along by their mothers on sledges. The most moving sight was two old ladies scrambling on the pavement for fragments of coke from a supply being unloaded into the cellar of a British military building.

Life for the Allies was comfortable and warm: with adequate food (the British supplies came mostly from Italy); constant hot water; and servants, who scraped plates clean and shared out scraps. There were lovely houses used as quarters. It was a pleasure to wander through gilded, panelled rooms, with huge, ornate chandeliers; and in some houses to see original paintings and tapestries intact. I could easily project myself into the past, to the days of the Congress of Vienna in 1815; and before that to an earlier century when Prince Eugene's victorious campaigns against the Turks in 1718 brought Austria great territorial gains.

Austria became a great power, and Vienna the diplomatic centre of the world. I received the strongest feelings of those heady days when in the Palais Kinski, which had become the British Officers' Club. There were two Viennas. The Vienna Symphony and the Philharmonic Orchestras were keeping up tradition and spirits in the two great concert halls (the Konzerthaus and the Musikvereinsaal), with concerts every week for those who could afford to attend. The State opera was completely destroyed in 1945, but seventeen theatres survived. The art collections were being rehung; and I was able to see marvellous Breughel in the Hofburg, another palace of former splendour.

There was general depression and a lack of initiative in coping with the destruction. It appeared to be left to the Allies to clear the streets. Meagre rations seemed to prevent the energetic tidying-up of eyesores. The cold bit deep and the threat of typhus was felt. All the cats had been eaten, and there were very few pet dogs. I was saddened by everything I saw and felt. But I could detect hope: for instance in Sacher's three musicians playing *Tales from the Vienna Woods*, as they knew it should be played.

Russian air clearances came through quicker than expected for us passengers: two American business men; an official of the British Political Mission, Budapest; Captain Pratt (1914–18 War), the King's Messenger; Roma Saunders, who was also for the British Council; and myself. I was hot and bothered at my suitcases, guns and ammo being 240 1bs overweight. My other trunks I had sent on rather anxiously by rail. But the R.A.F. said it would have been all right if I had asked! The R.A.F. 'bus took us to the grim, bomb-damaged Schwechat airfield, and deposited us in a large, warm waiting-room containing a Security Office and a N.A.A.F.I. shop. We tucked into sausage rolls, jam rolls, and large cups of tea. Then we boarded our Dakota, after a bitterly cold drive.

I didn't like the sound of one engine when the pilot tested for take-off. I was relieved when he announced that we should change planes. So we had more rolls and tea, and more time to chat and pick up useful information. What rankled with the crew was that they were never allowed by the Russians into Budapest, but had to remain by the aircraft on the airfield. I went for a walk with Captain Pratt, who told me about his strenuous flying life. It was not a life for me, although the title 'King's Messenger' sounded glamorous.

Now we had a more luxurious aeroplane: canvas seats with back-rests. Learning every hour, I found it is not easy climbing into and groping up a steeply sloping, aluminium body. Luckily it was a smooth flight over flat, icy country and without warm up-currents. It was thick over Budapest, and the pilot couldn't at first find the airfield (Budaors). It was no wonder: on landing I could only see from my window an expanse of frozen snow, and a few crumpled, concrete buildings, with girders twisted and hanging by threads. This place was even more desolate and cold than Schwechat.

The door was opened and a captain in the Welsh Guards could be seen below with a pathetic-looking Russian soldier who had a business-like tommy-gun. We were keen to get out, but the Guards officer called out: "Stay where you are, and do what I tell you, or we'll be here for ever". So we each came to the door as instructed, and called out our names. When these had been double-checked by both the British and the Russian we were allowed to jump down.

How we miserable group of people stamped and shivered in the icy air! The signing of papers was done inside a car for protection from the cold. An English girl in a fur coat, hat, and boots handed an outward bag to Captain Pratt, who climbed aboard again. The R.A.F. blew on their hands to clutch tea and buns. Our luggage was loaded onto a 15 cwt. truck, and we piled into a Wolseley Saloon with a tin Union Jack on the bumper. We were driven away by an R.A.F. corporal to the Park Club in the centre of Budapest. Members of the Council staff greeted us with brandies. The palatial and once-prestigious Park Club of the aristocracy was now the Anglo-American Club for mission staffs. The food was excellent, the service outstanding; both free on Reparations! The waiters came from the great hotels along the Danube. Drinks were cheap, limitless, and of amazing variety. Roma and I lunched with our new colleagues in the former ball-room. We had arrived – in Budapest and in some style!

After the euphoric luncheon at the Park Club, I was driven to my accommodation in the old-world Astoria Hotel. I was happy there: I had heat, light, food and drink, and gipsy music; retreat from the intense cold of the 1946/47 winter; and I was insulated from the miseries of the poor people of Budapest, who were reeling under the problems and sorrows of the recent conflict. There was heavy snow, but the streets were kept remarkably clear by a corps of energetic elderly men and women in straw boots, with spades and brooms. Buses and trains were running well, and there were ancient 'sit up and beg' rectangular saloon taxis available, with seemingly square wheels. Public transport was free to us on production of an Allied Control Commission identity card, which was valid until the Peace Treaty in September 1947. I was shocked on my first short journeys to see the widespread destruction throughout the attractive capital city. The once graceful suspension bridges drooped into the great Danube. The main damage to buildings in Pest on the left bank was slight compared to the shambles on the right bank of the former palace and the noble edifices on the Var, the old fortress hill of Buda.

Luckily for me I made lasting friends of the aristocratic owner of the Astoria, Edmund de Unger and his beautiful wife Eva, who under the 'new regime' were forced to work on their property. Their wise words helped me to understand Hungary's problems, and how not to get friends, or myself, or the British Council, into trouble. The lovely Countess Szechenyi served at the bar. It was a question of work or starve. The dishes at the Astoria were memorable. I ate their goose-liver risotto and chocolate flan nearly every day. I didn't have to pay for my food. Owing to the currency fluctuations throughout Europe, we were on the same system of calculating allowances as in France: the Paris Model. Receipted bills for one's actual meals were repaid; drinks were not included, but baths were paid for as part of living under such circumstances.

In the current circumstances – the need for economy, ease of communication, and safety, the British Council office was housed with the British Legation in the old Bank Building, 6 Harmincad Utca (street) on the ground floor. This arrangement was ideal for us: our offices were behind the glass screens above counters on three sides of the marble floor, which were perfect for exhibitions and displays. The wide, clear floor-space was fine for lectures, recitals, or Scottish country dancing.[2]

[2] See my "Reeling Round the World" in the Royal Scottish Country Dance Society Bulletin, No. 65, October 1987.

An Englishman in Hungary

The atmosphere in Budapest was oppressive, impersonal, and terribly sad due to the destruction, dust, dirt, and general dingyness around. The poor Hungarians were in a state of shock, and extremely wary of each other, and of the tightening grip of the Communists through their deadly efficient secret police. All needed friends, but who were they?

This was my first post and I found, as in every country in which I served, admirable, congenial colleagues in the Council and in the Diplomatic Service. Our boss in Hungary (called the Representative) was (Major) Robert McNab from New Zealand. He was rough and gruff, but with a big heart. He lined up his staff and taught us the Maori war dance, the Haaka, with frightful grimaces. He gave us a good example. He married Constance, a Hungarian nobleman's beautiful daughter. He bet me £50 I would marry such a girl, but I did not want to prejudice my transferability by marrying a foreigner. I somehow managed to escape. Robert was at heart very sensitive, and the strain of the horrors around us while he battled on hopefully with our work forced him to give up. But he showed me the way. So did his deputy Robin Duke (and his wife, Yvonne); Peter Davies[3] of my Oxford college Teddy Hall was a very sound and cheerful support. He arrived at Budapest Station in true British fashion with bowler hat and umbrella.

John Ford, who came to Hungary as Third Secretary, became my close friend for life. After Hungary he achieved a knighthood, an ambassadorship, and finally became High Commissioner in Canada. He proved to be a rock with his valuable qualities: his brain when things got dicey under the Communists; his wisdom in handling persons and situations; his hospitality when I was at a loose end; his spirit of adventure; his energy and resource; and his co-operation when I had a bright idea.

From early experiences in Hungary I found that by being a British Council member and not an official of the British Government I had more freedom of movement than a diplomat, who often had to get his journey cleared with the host government before leaving the capital. But in Hungary we were under suspicion as spies, and our contacts took considerable risks in associating with us. It was a terribly uncomfortable feeling that one might cause disaster to befall a new-found friend. There was surveillance everywhere, and there was sometimes anxiety that a Hungarian associate might be loyal to the Party and report anything that was said.

In the British Council we were rightly forbidden to discuss politics or religion. Thus I was not so well-informed but I could listen. I believe that

---

[3] His daughter, Jessica, followed him to 'Teddy Hall'. After he retired from the Council, he worked selflessly for Anti-Slavery International as Director from October 1980 to the end of 1987. He died too soon – on 9 Ocotober 1993 – really, I think, from his punishing travels and the climates involved.

my job, which was to make visits, to handle British specialist visitors, and to run cultural activities, gave our Hungarian contacts a feeling of not being forgotten, and gave some hope for the future. We were a window to the West. We certainly helped a large number of teachers of English to improve their knowledge of English, and their teaching efficiency. Our most effective and economical English language schemes all over the world were the teaching of teachers to teach teachers to teach. All nations soon realised that higher studies, and thereby national progress, needed English.

Stephen Spender came out to meet poets. He was delightful. I asked his advice on the art of writing poetry, and he said: "The key to poetry is imagery". On the music side I also had the pleasure of meeting Zoltan Kodaly, and helped him hear examples of British music. I particularly enjoyed assisting the Budapest State Opera, in a small way, in their first production of Benjamin Britten's *Peter Grimes*. Perhaps the most effective field of our work was in medicine. First with the supply of up-to-date copies of *The Lancet* and of the Council's own *British Medical Journal*. Of medical visitors there was Arthur Porritt of New Zealand, later knighted, who came with an operating team, and it was great to serve them. McNab of course knew Porritt. Over the years around the world I was to find that I had more to do with the medical profession than with any other. This suited me as I owed my life to this profession.[4] What a success everywhere our medical men were; how they were welcomed; what inspiration! They were all dedicated, selfless, and hard-working, even when they might have been resting from their demanding work at home. Throughout my career I found the medical profession to be the most independent of politics, and the bravest. Governments of the left tend to respect medical men.

As I came to know Hungarians I began to understand a little of their back-ground and outlook, and the extent of human suffering which surrounded me; and which, unlike bomb-damage, could not be repaired. The bomb-damage was closer at hand when I was fortunate to get a flat up on the Var in Buda. I was delighted with the life I was able to lead, but I was a powerless and horrified, albeit remote, observer of all that now went on under the Communists.

In March 1944 Germany had ruthlessly occupied Hungary, and in July of that year Russia, always keen to swallow up Hungary, entered the country to oppose the Germans. From December 1944 to January 1945 there was the terrible siege of Budapest, with the almost total destruction of the Var. By March 1945 there was the complete Russian occupation of Hungary, and even free elections. The Communists got 16% of the votes, and the Independent Smallholders 59%. The period March 1945 to

---

[4] See *Shots in the Sand*, p. 160.

September 1947, during which time I arrived on the scene, saw the full impact of the Russian 'Liberation'. The Russians held fresh elections over which they made no mistakes. I saw a little of what went on. There were false electoral rolls, lorry loads of mobile, plural voters, etc., and, of course, a Communist landslide.

The fortress hill of the Var was a very old site with castle walls dating back to before the Turkish occupation of the sixteenth century. Until the winter of 1944 here was the Royal Palace and a centre of high society life around it. Nearby were minor palaces, various elegant empire mansions and imposing military buildings. Here survives the Coronation Church of St Stephen, the first king of the tenth century Arpad dynasty.

Once established in my flat, I wrote to Papa as follows:

There are street lights once more and a few of the original gas lamps burn fitfully. One or two inns survive. The Var steps can be used, but go carefully where shells have pushed them awry. Some of the original cobbled patterns on the streets remain here and there, but much of the way is pitted with shell-holes. The exteriors of some lovely houses still look picturesque; but in the wind, tattered shutters bang on window frames, and there are no rooms behind. There are piles of bricks and masonry along the streets, rusty sections of war equipment lie about awkwardly, and here and there is a grave crudely marked. The Palace is a monstrous shell, broken and gutted. In what was the main ballroom (and I walked warily), a few huge chandeliers swing like corpses from gibbets, swinging in mockery, hanging by impossible threads from a roof that is almost not there. The only sounds today come from tiles clashing down in the wind, or lumps of clinging plaster banging against iron struts.

The front of Diz-tér 12 where I live is a big double-arched doorway to a courtyard in the remaining lower half of a wall. The one side is half-a-room, with half-a-floor and half-a-ceiling; and on the other a door opening into space. On one side of the front entrance is a figure of Atlas only supporting a shell, but there is a stout beam from the pavement thrust against his nose to keep him there at all.

To right and left are arched shells of rooms, and an entrance hall piled high with broken, dusty furniture and household effects. Somehow, somewhere there the caretaker and his wife and a maid manage to live. Through wide double doors is a reconstructed set of rooms in the surviving third face of the courtyard, once the kitchen precincts. Here lives my landlady, the Countess Kendeffy with her son (10), and her daughter (14). She is young and very charming. She somehow manages to keep going despite what she has been through, including imprisonment by the Germans. The main spiral staircase just leads up to the open air. Another stone stairway leads up to the first floor where the balcony still runs most of the way round. At the undamaged end of the house are two very nice flats. I have one and Joan Cranmore has the other.

My flat was efficiently heated by a tall, mottled-green porcelain wood-burning stove, in the Imperial style. With the then standard European double-doors and windows we escaped the bitter cold experienced in England in that 1947/48 winter.

Joan had been my father's treasured wartime Staff Secretary in the South Wales District. She was a jewel: level-headed, efficient, and enormous fun. She had a small, shaggy, black Hungarian puli, called Polli. Pulis are delightful dogs, with not quite dread-locks. Joan came out as governess-companion to David, son of Air Attaché Wing-Cdr Wilfred Bisdee and Mary. They were great assets too.

We both had maids. Mine was Bugyané (Mrs Bugya, pronounced Boodya-né). Her sixteen-year-old daughter was a great help at parties which we usually gave jointly. Mrs B. had been a housekeeper at the Palace, and was very sweet, I wish I could have understood Hungarian properly and heard her story of the siege.

My daily journey to the office was a perfect way to go to work. I wrote home:

> My light breakfast from 7.55 to 8.10 is timed to listen to the B.B.C. General Overseas Service News; this was vital in order to receive an accurate account of contemporary events. Bugyané thrusts an enormous cheese roll into my hands. I trot off across the square and down the nearest steps. My ears resound to the sound of falling masonry and clinking bricks as the demolition parties shovel and pile the ruins. The air is full of dust and very uncomfortable when blown by the wind.
>
> At the bottom of a series of steps I am at the Danube by the ferry-boat landing-stage, and the little white ship is often waiting for passengers to Pest. The river is always interesting here with the rebuilding of the Lánc Hid, the first suspension bridge in Europe, built by a Scot, Adam Clark. One crossing cost 50 filler (23d), and a book of ten tickets 4 forint = 1/8d. I go straight into the bows however cold it is, and revel in the turn and run downstream, and the swing upstream to the Pest bank. If the boat is waiting on my side, the whole journey takes eighteen minutes.

I was just settling down to office and city life when I was told to go to Sárospatak College to teach English. Sárospatak, meaning Muddy Brook, was a little town in the north-east near the Russian frontier, at the meeting point of the north-west highlands and the Great Hungarian Plain. It was situated by the river Bodrog, which joins the Tisza. There was an eleventh-century castle, which was a natural strongpoint against invaders and became a favourite residence of the Arpad dynasty, and Sárospatak was made a royal town. In 1531 Peter Perényi, Governor of Transylvania, founded an Academy here which expanded into a number of disciplines, and Sárospatak became a stronghold of the Reformed Calvinist Church. John Milton praised the learned men of Sárospatak in a speech to the British Parliament in 1644.

Under the Jesuits in the seventeenth century there were expulsions, imprisonments, and sale into slavery of Sárospatak scholars. The Academy finally achieved independence under the Protestant Church in the eighteenth century with the joint action of the Swiss, Dutch, Prussians, and British. Louis Kossuth, who led the 1848–49 War of Independence against Austria, had been a Sárospatak law student. The boys and girls I set out to help with their English were extremely proud of their tradition.

The Keleti (Eastern) Station was crowded and I searched anxiously for a seat. I was suddenly greeted by a cheerful group of young men who had appropriated a whole carriage. There was mutual recognition and they invited me to join them. I had heard tales of grim conditions up the line, but now it didn't matter. It was a strange journey. The stops were haphazard and lasted for anything between five minutes and an hour. At one moment we would be freezing, crammed into a third-class carriage with a troupe of pedlars. The next minute we would be sweating in an over-heated, second-class carriage. When the train was travelling very slowly some of the boys chose to run alongside to warm up.

A number of boys could be heard muttering or declaiming: and I discovered that they were learning parts for a performance of *Julius Caesar.* I was happily surprised. Suddenly we found ourselves clinging together and shivering on the platform between two carriages with our luggage piled around us. Darkness came, but there were no lights along the train. I managed to get into the guards van with some other boys, and stood with them the rest of the journey. We sang from the *Oxford Song Book.* They knew more words than I did. The journey put me in close rapport with many of my pupils, which was better than facing a class from cold.

When we reached Sárospatak, Maller Sandor,[5] a young teacher of

---

[5] I called him Sandor, his Christian name, which in Hungarian custom comes second. When Hungarians come to be in our Western milieu, they accept that we put their Christian names first, to avoid misunderstandings, e.g. Zoltan Kodaly and Bela Bartok.

English, met us with a party of boys and servants with sledges to pull our luggage home through the snow. I was taken to rooms in the Angol Intézet, the English Boarding House.

This had been set up in 1931 for 135 boys, with day-girls from the town, and two English-born teachers. Geoffrey Tier was recruited in 1939, but forced to leave in 1941. He and his wife Zita escaped internment thanks to an influential Sárospatak parent. But they spent seven weeks in a cellar on the Var during the 1944/45 siege. Then they were allowed to return to Sárospatak. The school was lucky to have such a man: he spoke Hungarian; he was a scholar, a dedicated teacher; a musician and violinist, who won the respect of the gipsies. He fell under the spell of Hungary and its people, especially Sárospatak, as I did. He wrote of the gipsies: "What a wonderful ear they have. They cannot read a note of music, but will play, absolutely correctly, anything they have heard only once."

I met Geoffrey and Zita only after I retired. We three loved Szabo Gyula the Head of the Angol Intézet. His innate kindness shone through, and I knew I had a staunch friend. I came to value his quiet words of advice; his unobtrusive help; his wisdom and courage under the Communists; and his realism, optimism, and humour. The school survived. So did I, very well, under the guidance and companionship of Zsindely Endre, a senior boy assigned to me by Szabo Gyula. He was of a fine Budapest family, and an ordinand. He taught me a great deal about Hungary and her people's problems. He introduced me around the town, and took me sight-seeing and exploring the beautiful, varied countryside, up and down the lovely little river Bodrog. He helped me face the realities of life more easily with his humour. His reputation and popularity assisted in my gaining acceptance by the school and the parents.

In the school there was no running water and no electric light, as the coal train had not got through to the power stations. Fortunately there was plenty of wood for the stoves. Everyone was amazingly cheerful and energetic despite having to live on what to me was very short commons. Meals were apt to consist of nothing more than a piece or two of brown bread, and a plate of soup, or noodles, or ground rice. Luckily for my pupils, their meals could sometimes be supplemented by milk and eggs from the countryside. I was never allowed to go short and I was tremendously touched by what must have occasioned a sacrifice somewhere. I became embarrassed when boxes of extra supplies were sent up to me from the N.A.A.F.I. in Vienna, but I could share some of it. Teaching is pretty demanding and one is giving out all the time. I managed, and the job was fully rewarding, I was treated so kindly, but my self-esteem was shattered, once, when the back row of senior girls continued unconcernedly knitting.

One thing none of us lacked in the school was wine. We were on the edge of the Tokaj country, and all Hungarians had drunk good wine from birth. My relations with the different classes became less formal, but no less firm, after my 'initiation'.

One day I was invited by some neighbouring parents, the Asboths, to their cellar at about noon. I let my pleasant wine-sampling experience run on past the school lunch-hour. Well, I became oblivious by 1 p.m. When I realised the time I hurried from the cold up the fifty or so steps into the warm open air; the wine hit me. I had to reach the High Table. All eyes were upon my every step because the whole hall knew where I had been; all were smiling. I reached my seat with a mumbled apology to my headmaster, but I could hardly remember doing so.

After a few light-hearted weeks we all had to concentrate in earnest on the play of *Julius Caesar*, because a performance had been promised by the school to all around. I volunteered to produce alongside a talented artistic director from the Hungarian staff. I was greatly heartened by the complete response of the cast, and the backstage staff, and the surprisingly talented scene and stage-design executed by the boys. They also handled property provision, lighting, and make-up. The performance in the Mudrany Hall on 29 March 1947 went off very well, so well that two representatives from the Ministry of Education told the headmaster that they would like the performance to be repeated in Budapest. These men, who were obviously 'on our side', had the courage to seek permission for us to go to Budapest, and the school received an official invitation.

The transfer of the whole performance, scenery, costumes and all, by public transport was calmly and safely achieved without great expense. The Madács Szinház (theatre) in Budapest was allotted to us and posters were all round the town. The cast of thirty-three was initially a bit overawed by their surroundings, but it rose to histrionic heights. The stage staff did a fine adaptation with our limited scenery and props. The performance on 9 June won the approval of the Hungarian and foreign members of the audience, and of the British Minister, Sir Knox Helm. Mallor Sandor told me that this was the first student performance of Shakespeare in English in Budapest.

And then I was recalled to Budapest. It was a shock to be back at my desk in 6 Harmincad Utca, but I enjoy administration. After all, my father had at one time been Alexander's Major-General of Administration! I soon learned that the key to efficiency is retrieval. Hence the importance of files and a good system. That was before sophisticated electronics. But filing cabinets don't break down, or wipe off data. I was glad to have Bugyané's cheese rolls as a defence against Hungary's other secret alcoholic weapon, barack (apricot brandy). Workers take a shot or two for breakfast, and good management has a bottle handy in the office for visitors. I had many visitors.

On the one hand, it was a relief to be back among European and American friends, and under the close protection of the British Legation. On the other hand, there were horrors all around, but the suffering was hidden.

There were many deaths and many cripples, both army and civilian, from the actual war; and these tragedies were borne by the survivors with a shining stoicism. Family losses were treated with dignity, and major misfortunes and supreme sacrifices were accepted as being in the cause of peace and freedom. But the deliberate deaths and disappearances now inflicted on brave, loyal, and determined citizens were crushing. These people were innocent except for status, or birth, or occupation; or for the crime of associating with Westerners.

I was frightened by the attentions of the 'powers of law and order'. But I was raised above such weakness and could keep going because the people were so wonderful. They showed me how to endure real suffering, perpetual fear, sudden arrest, torture, death, imprisonment, concentration camps, the enforced witness of torture inflicted upon dear ones, the ruin of their homes, the spoilation of their country, and the uncertainty of the future. People I knew were living examples of George Orwell's comment in *1984*: "They can make you say anything, anything; but they can't make you believe it. They can't get inside you."

My heart went out to all such Hungarians because they were strong in the teachings of Christ, the principles of our form of democracy, and they were allies of the Western Powers. Powers? That word was a mockery, we felt.

Fate, geography, and race have all contributed to the Hungarian character. Centuries of slaughter and depopulation through the ebb and flow of foreign forces over such valuable, vulnerable land have produced unrivalled powers of survival. This, with a high intelligence, and a strong, wry humour, have contributed to the outstanding success of Hungarians at home and abroad; from the explorers Count Teleki and Aurel Stein to Kodaly, Koestler, Kaldor, Professor Kurti in Oxford, Mikes, Biro, and Rubik.

But all the circumstances of history have inevitably bred in the Hungarian character, suspicion, mistrust, guile; the inability to combine together, unhappy jealousies; unfortunate indiscretion. However, danger and disaster are borne with unmatched gaiety, and all Hungarians have undeniably irresistible charm. There is an enviable resilience in the Hungarian character which makes them so admirable. Given the opportunity of a glass of wine and a song, Hungarians will respond, even when under the shadow of arrest and oblivion.

I wrote home:

It is on the Hungarian women that so much depends. They are very hard-working and able to adapt themselves to new circumstances. They carry most of the burdens. They have little money but they somehow manage to keep up appearances. They fight so hard to keep family life going for their children according to Christian principles, in the face of Government anti-Christ school propaganda; suspension from work for their husbands; possible imprisonment; or deportation for crimes no worse than lack of sympathy for the regime. Hungarian women-folk are not only brave, they are extremely attractive, capable, and vivacious. They grow old gracefully.

Yet I thought I saw the continuance of certain unenlightened feudalism. In the late-nineteenth century a few far-seeing noblemen such as Count Szechenyi realised the necessity for a complete change, but no-one listened. Some members of aristocracy took some interest in their huge estates, but in the main they became cosmopolitan wanderers who were preoccupied with sport, drinking, and dancing. The aristocracy set the tone of the capital, Budapest, which became known throughout the world as the centre of gaiety. Such men and women were assisted by the upper-middle class who could afford such pleasures on a small scale, because the national temperament lent itself to carefree living in spite of more serious matters. This attitude existed throughout all sections of the population. By the 1930s Hungary was ripe for a revolution; and an upheaval on the lines of the French Revolution would have had a salutary effect. Unfortunately, this did not come about, and Hungary suffered a much more radical change after 1944.

I wrote at the time:

> The aristocracy were quickly dispossessed and eliminated. Many escaped from the country, many were arrested and sent to concentration camps. Some still survive by earning a living in a humble capacity. But they are always in danger because through their birth they are continually suspect and strictly controlled. Many are not even allowed to earn a living. The sale of valuables helps to keep them alive, but this cannot last indefinitely. Their children are even prevented from studying and making progress at the universities. What is life for the children of such parents? Their fate is uncertain. But they still remain loyal to their parents and their beliefs.

Now it is the turn of the middle classes to suffer. For them it is 'turn Communist or starve'; but even then it is not so easy as it was to enter the Communist Party. Every effort was made to cut them off from contact with the West, and finally the British Council, their one remaining link, was closed down. Hungary has always been western in outlook and never eastern, although Hungarians have a streak of Eastern temperament.

I went on:

> At my level, to my intense sorrow, friends lost property and even the right to work. Others suffered banishment to the country or imprisonment; upper-class children were denied education; acquaintances suddenly vanished and never reappeared; other friends of mine, with their children, managed to escape further repression, and made successful careers abroad.

Events closer at hand had greater impact upon me. One day, so I understand, the Legation radio-operator was crossing the road on foot in the city when he was bundled into a car by the AVO (Secret Police), and taken off to their notorious Headquarters in Andrássy ut. Here he was forced to watch his Hungarian girl-friend being beaten up, which was harder to bear than being beaten up himself. Diplomatic pressure got him transferred, but we did not know the poor girl's fate.

Something similar happened to us. One of our secretaries was a Hungarian girl, Lusztig Anna who worked for my wise and humorous colleague Peter Davies. Anna had been in England visiting relatives. She was stuck there during the war and was able to serve in the A.T.S. as she spoke excellent English.

With great courage she explained to Peter how she had been picked up by the AVO and forced to act as the AVO's informant within the British Council and, if possible, within the Legation. She was threatened with the direst threats to herself and to her mother if she divulged what she had been ordered to do. The AVO had chosen precisely the wrong person to try to 'turn'. Anna was a person with a strong moral sense, repelled by the regime headed by Rakosi and with the strongest affection for everything British following her wartime experiences in England. She was also a devout Catholic.

The Legation under our new minister, Sir Geoffrey Wallinger, went into immediate action and Anna was booked on the first plane out of Budapest for London. So in August 1949 Anna found herself back in England. The Council looked after her splendidly, and she worked with the Council until her retirement in 1977.

Nevertheless, in the midst of all this and worse, such as the disappearance of staff from our office and the arrest of several British and American subjects, we had a delightful time. The Hungarians, the brave ones who said that they didn't have much to lose, introduced us to that special quality of human spirit found nowhere else in the world. In town there were the little restaurants on the Var, and in Pest, where the irrepressible gipsies poured out their music and song. I love Hungarian song and dance. I learned to sing 'Az a szép' (You are beautiful), or 'Csak egy kislány van a világon' (There is only one girl in the village). And I just about mastered the csárdás. My collection of 78 r.p.m. records of Hungarian gipsy and folk songs is now in the Budapest Music Institute. Zoltan Kodaly used the gipsy cymbalom and many folk tunes in his modern, unconventional works which are strongly national in spirit. Both Franz Liszt and Béla Bartok used such folk tunes. The name gipsy is a corruption of Egyptian, but they come from India. They are a most interesting people and worth studying. They pose a problem today: their talents, temperament, and way of life do not make them biddable, hard-working citizens, and their numbers are increasing.

We couldn't just be gloomy. We had fun. I was able to run Scottish country dance sessions for anyone, and Hungarians came. There is a photograph of us dancing in the Royal Scottish Country Dance Society Bulletin of October 1987. Upstairs were living the Minister, Sir Knox, and Lady Helm, who were great sports and ready for fun. But I can't remember why I am to be seen as an old-style, top-hatted tramp picking his pocket. I certainly recall later our Hermaphrodite Party to which guests were invited to attend as one of the opposite sex. John Ford made an outstanding Hungarian secondary schoolgirl. But some of the ladies made even better men.

There weren't many activities outside our houses because, apart from John Ford, we had no cars. I had a rare break out of Hungary. The sporting Geoffrey Wallinger had to go back to London on occasions. His route was by car to Bratislava, then train. Once he told John Ford that he and I could go with him, and bring the car back to Budapest, discreetly and without undue mileage. It would be through some of beautiful Slovakia. This was luckily just before the Russian take-over. After which, Donald Brander, our regional man in Bratislava was shot point-blank, with a small-calibre pistol one evening when he answered the door-bell. He survived. Nothing seems to have been done about his assailant.

Two good Hungarian friends, now living in Switzerland, are Gyula and Margit Groh, both chemists.[6] Gyula introduced me to amateur photography providing me with free developing and printing. He was also a grand, country guide, mostly to spots on the Danube, for picnics or meals at river-side inns. After the failure of the 1956 uprising, Gyula and Margit escaped into Austria with two children: at the frontier they found an

[6] Envelopes are now addressed to 'Dr Julius Groh'.

unattended steam-roller with steam up. On it they crashed the barrier and safely reached Austria!

Until the regime got its hands on people of all levels, life at weekends was delightful. The visits to families in their small country places, some with vineyards attached, were idyllic. The good wine, toasted kukoritza (corn-cob), or delicious pork fat on sticks, with such cheerful company are unforgettable. It did not seem fair to return to security, and to leave them to their fates.

Two other official visits beyond Budapest are memorable. I had a very fine picture-exhibition on British education, which was even more vital to present to a Communist regime whilst a chink in the curtain remained open. I took the set to Kecskemet, an attractive agricultural town that was famous for its *barack*. I had our Humber station-wagon, driven by the dear, silent, gentleman refugee, Horwath, and with me my assistant-cum-interpreter, Baroness Dioszeghy, a fine, talented woman whom I had no chance to get to know well, because she just disappeared one day.

I also took the exhibition to Eger, a striking baroque town in the hills to the north-east, where the red wine Bika Vér (Bulls' Blood) is produced. Eger had a beautiful minaret, remaining from the Turkish occupation of the country from 1526 to 1689, which both began and ended with a battle at Mohács. Our reception was friendly but wary. We knew what was happening in Hungarian schools, but we should have been more confident that these young spirits would never be cowed.

Assignment in Pécs.

To my delight I was next sent to Pécs[7] under the Mecsek Hills, just west of the Danube, near the Yugoslav border. My main task was to help the doctors, professors, and medical and voluntary students of the university to regain command of English. I went by train, and was put up at the Nador Szálló (hotel) on the main square. Here stood the small, rectangular, domed Turkish mosque of Jakub Ali with minaret. There were two fine secondary schools for boys and girls in Pécs, as well as a four-towered cathedral and a bishop's palace. Out of the town was agriculture (sun-flowers and oil mills), and beyond in rolling, open countryside was a great, traditional market area. Here I enjoyed wandering about and photographing the gatherings of peasant groups in traditional costumes with their horse-drawn waggons. The men were in Hungary's standard black and white; but most numerous and striking were the Sokat women

---

[7] Pronounced Paitch; but we won't go into Hungarian pronunciation!

in highly colourful, complicated costumes, coiffes, masses of petticoats, and thick stockings covered in bobbles.

My first night at the Nador Hotel, was one of extreme discomfort and revulsion due to bed-bugs. Next morning I reported this to my friend Mr Hegedüs, and asked him the Hungarian word for bed-bug. I thought he said "Piroska". This sounded correct because *piros* means red. I went to the desk, got hold of the manager, and complained loudly and firmly that I had had *piroska* in my bed. There was a shocked silence. The manager summoned the porter, and said sternly: "Fetch Piroska". He returned with the first-floor maid whom I recognised.

The manager loosed off a crackle of high-voltage Hungarian at her, to which the girl looking very hurt, replied (so I was told): "I'm not Piroska, I'm Ilona." The immediate acute embarrassment was mine! I tried to explain with a drawing. "Oh, you mean *poloska*." That was the first of three contretemps in Pécs.

I was now on my own, away from the comforting proximity of the British Legation, the Council office and my friends. I felt alone and afraid. I knew I was surrounded by sinister men, and a ruthless political system. I was in a small town and almost the only foreigner in it, immediately visible and immediately audible. I was there by permission of the Party, and in a privileged position considering the great suspicion directed against America and Britain. I was a British Council lecturer and only that. I was to work through officialdom and not on my own, as that would have invited suspicion. I had to be extremely circumspect in all I did, in whoever I met, and in whatever I said. I had to explain the British Council to the citizens of Pécs. I made it clear that I was not a British Legation information officer dealing with the general public, nor a government official, but a non-political British Council officer working with the professions. I stressed the English teaching role of my mission which I described, and still do, as 'professional interchange'. The point was soon grasped, and from then on I received as much support, co-operation, and friendship as circumstances permitted.

The English teaching at the university was straightforward and enjoyable. It is pleasure to teach adults who have the incentive to learn English and the readiness to pay. English is in itself fun to expound, except when one is frequently asked for rules which often do not exist. It is easy for foreigners to communicate very simply in English, but proficiency requires solid application. I could only teach in the university or give a lecture in the evenings because there were no day-time periods for such study. The earlier part of the day was up to me.

I had to channel all my Council ideas and activities through a Hungarian-British Society. I was able to lecture on aspects of British language and literature with picture exhibitions. 'Daddy' Wordsworth and

Rydal Mount and a host of golden, bloody daffodils – but they were black and white in those days. I have discovered that students of English world-wide must have Wordsworth. He simply wouldn't go away. I grew to love him.

I gradually began to meet a small number of citizens, rather than officials. I had been able to move into very nice digs. This made it easier for friends to visit. The hotel had been hopeless: it had been under constant surveillance. Unfortunately, my digs were opposite the prison, and the comings and going were most depressing. The Party's administrative grip tightened as the months went by, and that meant a large increase in police, so that more people were frightened to ask me to their homes. There were one or two aristocratic families still in Pécs whom I just briefly met, but I couldn't associate with them for their sakes. There were others, whose society I greatly valued, who said they didn't care, they had nothing to lose and the police had nothing against them. I prayed that they were not to be disillusioned, but after I had left I was told in Budapest not to write to my friends in Pécs.

Was I any use at all? I think so. It was amazing, and cheering, to be told that the mere fact that I was an Englishman officially residing in the town gave Hungarians confidence and hope that they would not be forgotten by Britain. I was struck by the pleas of parents that whatever we had and were allowed to offer was vital for the children of Hungary. They wanted the young to have the influence of just a few ordinary English men and women who could be among them as friends; who could convince the children that learning English was worthwhile, and that England has something real and vital to offer their country and themselves. This was even more of a responsibility for me, and I began to feel the strain of sensing the constant tension in the town. Whatever was said, and however much I sympathized, I was in the role of an unwilling observer of suffering, and was powerless to do anything to alleviate anyone's misery.

I had to observe a rigid mental discipline in order to survive. I did not compare or criticize. I never appeared secretive, I did everything openly. People were still curious to know about me and my activities. This was good when they could believe me and join in what I had to offer. There was the odd individual who would ask me provocative questions, but I learned not to rise to the bait, and not to comment on or criticise the regime. The answer was simply to behave as an Englishman standing for true freedom; to speak of life in Britain in a matter-of-fact way. I asked London for an exhibition on the life of an average Englishman to back me up: childhood, education, home life, hopes and aspirations, opportunities, leisure, and what the state would provide; but the London office couldn't help.

A form of breakthrough came through the local director of education, who supported whatever effort I could manage. Now I was under an official umbrella, and not attempting to operate on my own. I was to be with teachers and children, just as the parents had hoped. I was permitted to organize English classes for twelve or so senior teachers of English. I received from Budapest books and materials to present to teachers for their pupils. I was also told by the authorities that I might visit English classes in progress in schools. This improved my morale tremendously, and put me in touch with the principals and teachers of the leading schools. I met fine people: brave men and women.

The speaking standards of English were not high then, but a few senior boys had learned some English as prisoners of war of the British or Americans. I think I helped to speed up progress, but no teachers or pupils could get to England or go abroad. Later the Council did manage to run its own English courses for teachers in Budapest, and there was a tremendous response.

Nearly all the schoolchildren saw through any attempt by teachers to eulogize communist doctrine, which they were often compelled to do. There were occasions when for everyone's safety, teachers had to beg pupils not to demonstrate or boycott official parades or interrupt in class. The majority of university students also were solidly anti-communist at heart. The Independence Day celebrations on 15 March in Pécs were a mockery in town and country. I was at a school centre and the atmosphere was funereal.

Suddenly I was able to make a breakthrough – with song and dance! It began when I helped some teachers with English songs. Songs and poetry are excellent for appreciating the rhythm and improving the fluency of speaking English. One day I was in the Commercial School for Girls and came across their folk-dance group. I was moved to dance a few bars of pas-de-basque and the odd fling step, saying that I could teach them Scottish dances if they cared. The task the teacher was given for the forthcoming Workers' May Day celebrations was to produce some form of display from the five girls' schools in her charge. Now she wondered about a Scottish country dance? I was delighted, and the mistress selected 'sets' of eight girls from each school. The girls were very quick to pick up the rhythm, steps, and formations. The only problem was that I fell in love instantly with one of the senior girls of the Kereskedelmi Leány Iskola, who was a natural dancer as well as beautiful. Our eyes met when her set had been put together. I was lost but I managed to concentrate on the performance to come. Two hundred, lovely, Hungarian schoolgirls in blue berets, white blouses, tartan-pattern, pleated skirts, and white knee-stockings danced 'Strip the Willow' in the sports arena to a 78 r.p.m. Jimmy Shand record suitably amplified on Party equipment. The triumph of my career, and so early on!

The dancing spirit blossomed further in Pécs. The only criticism of the May Day performance was that there hadn't been any boys. Happily, two heads of appropriate schools put this right, and a keen 'Scót Népi Tánc' (folk-dance group) was soon in being, and the young men and girls rapidly became proficient enough to include Scottish dances in their performances.

I sent out the invitations to the first performance but my wording in Hungarian stated that it would be held at the Leány Kereskedelmi Iskola (not at the Kereskedelmi Leány Iskola). There was great merriment round the town, but luckily no-one took offence. My changing of the word order meant 'At the School for Commercial Girls'. Communication with the leading girl Vali was solved by my using what German I had. It was the second language of Pécs, which was once called Fünfkirchen.

Feeling my way cautiously, I gave the odd party and found these to be popular. It struck me that the best way I could make my presence felt was to give more parties, as far as money would go. Beneath the surface the Hungarian independent spirit bubbled away. Hungarians were just the people for a party. A number of us did go out to restaurants once or twice but we stood out, as most people preferred not to be seen around, nor could they afford meals out.

I found a particularly fine, senior friend in the wise and cautious Dr Donhoffer Szilárd,[8] a university professor of pharmacology. He and his family had a very small vineyard on the edge of the upper town, similar to an allotment. Parents and daughters worked hard on it, and at the time of vintage I was invited along to help. It was the greatest fun.

In Pécs an official occasion was the cause of another *faux pas*. The British Minister came down for the day, and brought with him John Ford. After a generous municipal luncheon in the Nador Szálló, we trooped off to visit the cathedral and the museum. Conscientiously showing intense diplomatic interest in the contents of two opposing display cases, John and I leaned rather blithely, after our good lunch, on the glass from opposite sides and our elbows went straight through with distressing sounds. A grim, shocked silence followed. H.M. Minister was about to apologize before sacking us, but our hosts immediately forgave us. The Hungarians really are sporting.

Before I left Pécs, I felt I had to visit the sites of the two battles of Mohács, being reminded every day in Pécs of the Turkish occupation from 1526–1689. There was a second mosque in the town as well as the main mosque/church with its minaret. In the course of a trip organised

---

[8] Oh dear, he has just died, on 12 January 1999 in his ninety-seventh year. We've had a memorable, long correspondence.

28

by my brave friend, Ivan Jilly, he was able to interpret and to explain to all the folk we met, who were curious about me and asked when the Britain that they respected was going to help them.

It was hard to leave Pécs and my numerous friends. I wrote to my father in April 1949, but not by open mail:

> Our friends get less and less in number. Many have escaped to Austria and some continue to try via Yugoslavia also; some are lucky, some are not. Ivan Jilly was one who had disappeared, but he was found in a prison hospital, badly hurt after being beaten up at the frontier. His family are allowed no contact. The brother of another friend of mine was just taken away from his university lodgings and no-one knows where. The sixteen-year-old daughter of a doctor who had studied in Aberdeen was expelled from school for 'being reactionary-minded'.
>
> My Pécs landlady was recently taken to the police station and forced to give a list of those persons who had visited me, and to describe all that went on. I was begged not to go near the house. I have occasional visits from Pécs friends, particularly one girl-friend; that is how I know. But I cannot risk writing to her nor to anyone else; nor they to me.
> Life changed after I left and I heard the town was full of political police.

Szeged

The only way to get the true feel of any country is to stay put for quite a time in a small town, and to resist all the world-famous attractions of the capital. So I was particularly delighted to be sent to the important agricultural university town of Szeged on the great river Tisza, with its bridge built by Eiffel.

My arrival here was different. I had been told in Budapest to report in Szeged to the town commandant, so I rolled up at the Town Hall to find a Russian sentry on the door. "Davai!" he said, and motioned me inside with his tommy-gun. 'Davai' (come) was an all-too familiar command in Hungary in those days as I had heard from friends, so I 'davaid' promptly into the interior where I handed over my calling-card, my passport, to an officer who had appeared. He pointed to a chair and left. An armed guard then stood over me. I was not in danger, but when one is a long way from one's own people and in the hands of an unpredictable military, albeit willingly, one may perhaps be forgiven a little tremor. I sat as directed and smoked my Dunhill pipe. Finally a less stern Town Major returned with my passport and bowed me out – more or less. "Spasiba," (thank you) I said.

Szeged was very different from Pécs, owing to its geological situation affecting its history, and the ancestry and character of its people of that region formed over the centuries. The inhabitants of this much larger town were not so closely knit as in Pécs, and consequently I met fewer people, but I made several close friends among the teachers of English, whom I had been sent to help.

Thanks to a charming pupil, Herczegh Klára, I was shown famous Hungarian nineteenth and twentieth-century painters, in the town's Museum of Fine Art: Munkácsy, Rudnay, Lotz, Pal, Molnár, Csontvári, and others. Luckily, I was able to buy a village scene in oil by Várady, who was a skilful disciple of Nyilasy Sándor. Klára and her family took me around. In town and roundabout I enjoyed good meals and even better gipsy music and song, since I had someone to translate intelligently for me. 'Részeg vagyok rózsám.' (I am drunk to the top my sweet-heart.)

It wasn't easy to get out of the town of Szeged, due to lack of transport, but I did reach the lovely, marshy, lagoon area called the Fehér-to (White Lake) which was famous as a migratory sanctuary for water-fowl. Unfortunately, I couldn't lurk anywhere there with my camera without courting arrest by the Russian army.

The Russian army in Hungary

In the course of my two years in Hungary I was given a vivid, if superficial, impression of the Russians by several Hungarian friends; particularly the impact and effect of the front-line troops of Marshal Tolbuchin's Third Army from their arrival in 1944.

The rank and file were peasants who were used to a very low standard of living. They were all fear-ridden and they acted in the manner of dumb robots in response to orders – making a very formidable machine. Their behaviour in situations in Hungary was naive in the extreme. The reactions of the ordinary soldier were unpredictable; some led to laughter, others to tragedy. It was a fine balance between life and death for any Hungarian in any contact. In the early days of the Russian occupation in the Budapest area there was the wanton destruction of homes with cries of 'Bourgeois! Bourgeois!' I cannot vouch for all the stories I was told, but none surprise me. Many Russians had never seen a bicycle before, or didn't know how to ride one. A Hungarian cyclist was pulled off his machine by a soldier who wanted it. But he couldn't ride it and blamed the owner for obstructing him (or bewitching him!). He menaced the poor man with his tommy-gun. It took time and a cool head to convince the soldier of the truth. Maybe one or more luckless riders were shot.

The other ranks were fascinated by clocks and watches, and many watches were forced off wrists with threats. In certain houses there were reports of near, if not actual, disaster concerning common items. A timer went off in someone's kitchen, and a burst of fire preceded explanations. These peasant soldiers could behave like children and were ignorant even of plumbing. I heard that a Russian who had got hold of a bowl of goldfish put them down the 'loo' for safe-keeping. The disappearance of his fish, which he subsequently discovered, so incensed their new owner that he demanded their immediate return. The householder's life now hung by a thread. A demonstration of the toilet and much shrugging of shoulders and helpless gestures saved him.

The Hungarians recognized that these Russian soldiers were peasants at heart, like the Hungarian and other peasants the world over: peace-loving and wishing to be left alone to cultivate their own lands. So when, for instance, an off-duty soldier, or a small unit, arrived at a house seeking loot or food and shelter, they could be handled by a strong-minded, courageous person with a firm manner, if they were not drunk.

Dick Sturgess, a humorous and rollicking character, came to Pécs as an Foreign Office language student. One night when returning late to his digs, he found a Russian officer occupying his bed. Dick got him out of it and onto the sofa.

The Russian soldiery could be amicable unless they detected mockery, or distaste at their presence, or any attitude of superiority. They were quick on the trigger; deadly action was often taken through imagined self-preservation and not from aggression. One important positive quality of these poor, machine-like creatures was that, like all Russians, deep down they had soft hearts. They were not sadistic, or innately ruthless. They also had the quality of remorse, for any severe action that proved unnecessary – or for any tragedy they may have come across which was not of their making. My friend Groh Gyula was at the receiving end of their unpredictability. An army lorry was rounding up people from the streets, and Gyula was one such victim. He was told at the end of a gun to 'davai' pretty smartly up into the back of a truck. The order 'davai' was often followed in Hungarian by 'kicsi robot' (a little work) which meant forced labour of unknown destination, duration, or severity. Gyula and fellow passengers were driven to the outskirts of the city to a barn with wide-open doors. "Get down! Get down!" they were instructed. They got down, and were propelled into the barn. Here were long trestle tables and people eating. "Eat," they were told. They ate – for fear of offending!

The presence of the Russian army gradually faded from the scene after the September 1947 Peace Treaty. But then the grip of the Hungarian communist leaders and their apparat was felt more strongly and tightened remorselessly. The regime increased the fear of victimization, if not martyrdom, for overt sympathizers with the West, which made our work increasingly frustrating. Teachers no longer dared to bring their pupils to our centre in Budapest or to exhibitions in the provinces. But many teachers of English were marvellously courageous in attending seminars in Budapest and our two Summer Schools at Sarospatak.

Sarospatak Summer School, 1948.

Three summer vacation weeks of 1948 in Sarospatak for the Summer School, for which I was the admin. man, were almost the happiest days of my career. Here we were in this ancient, venerated town, in charming countryside; a dozen visiting English and Hungarian 'professors' or teachers of English, with one hundred keen and courageous men and women from all over Hungary with a common purpose. An even stronger sentiment than learning bound us together: a safely suppressed common detestation of the regime. There were informers among us, as our teachers knew and as I have since learned.

For us life was easy; and in such a place we staff and teacher-pupils all got on splendidly. We almost bathed in Tokay. Demi-johns the size of carboys shuttled in and out of the school compound daily. 'English as she is spoke' was our aim. We divided our pupils into small groups who would study different subjects in turn. For instance, a vineyard, or a tennis court, or a castle, or on the banks of the Bodrog to swim or row. Or in the evening to an inn for supper with gipsy music, wine and English songs.

For drama I suggested the Council invite Cecil Bellamy, a Bradfield housemaster and brilliant Greek play and Shakespeare producer. The Council sent him, and he was a great success. His *Twelfth Night* talks and scene productions were brilliant; and so Cecil kept the play alive in the hearts of many Hungarians. He loved it all, and the adulation of the Sarospatak girls and the teachers of English.

The Summer School course ended with a concert. I have a bound, illuminated edition of the libretto: *A Few Course Stanzas* composed by the Angol Tanárok (English teachers), with Fred at the piano. Fred was to become Dr C. F. Cushing, Professor of East European languages and literature. My field has been 'The Speaking of English'. Here is a verse from the teachers' parody of the subject:

> Exercise the glottal stops, and watch the vowels and glides,
> Purse your lips and blow your cheeks, and other things besides.
> Mark the stress and alternate the intonation curves,
> And give the dental fricative the attention it deserves.

The last verse of parody of the song "Come Landlord fill the flowing bowl," etc, began: "Oh Halsted hands us out the wine and sees that none is wasted," and contained admirable advice on a non-curriculum activity, under 'Welfare' I suppose:

The man who goes into the park without a girl beside him,
Is missing half the pleasures that Dame Nature can provide him.

Our brilliant, elderly, E.L.T. pioneer was Tom Beach. He was most helpful to me as a new teacher of English, and he was very funny. He told us stories of his earlier careers. He was once a tour courier, an occupation which he ended when in charge of a particularly tiresome group in North Italy. He told us that he tied all their passports in a bundle, threw them into Lake Como, and left.

My birthday at Sárospatak.

I am a believer in celebrating birthdays, but not in paying attention to the number of years. One of my own most memorable birthdays was at Sarospatak Summer School. The start struck my heart and remains for ever there. Three little girls dressed alike in white tops and short white skirts came from a parents' house in the town bearing a generous-sized iced cake with twenty-eight candles on it. I was entranced, and fell in love again – with Peti, the little one of the Asboth family who had pretty well saved them all when the Russians came over the border in 1944. The soldiers descended upon the bourgeois houses, but Peti charmed them by her simple presence and trust, while her father and elder sister played the violin (and had to go on playing for days).

The birthday programme for me was a swim, then lunch and tennis later. In the evening I gave a party at one of the inns, for staff teachers, parents, and Council colleagues: dinner, wine, and gipsy music as before. It all cost me £10.

One day back in the Budapest office I opened an ordinary British Council envelope from London. The letter posted me to the Karachi Office as Functional Officer (Visitors and Programmes) with effect from October 1949.

I finally left the Western Station (Nyugati Pályaudvar) by the Orient Express in tears, clutching a large, red-ribboned demi-john gift of wine. I had fallen in love all over the place, but I had experienced other deep emotions for the first time. There was so much to admire in the Hungarian spirit and character: their physical bravery; their faith in Christ and moral courage; their resilience in adversity; their ability to improvise; their intelligence and skills; their artistic achievements; their love of beauty, of art and music, and wine and song.

Edmund and Eva (from the Astoria) gave their young friends, English and Hungarian, unforgettable Sundays at their Tahi country home. They bravely kept from us the horrors which they knew were being perpetrated by the regime. Thank God they were able to escape to the West. I kept in touch with others with whom I safely could. I set my heart on returning. I did, but only after thirty-two years.

END. "VÉG" (in Hungarian)

An Englishman in Hungary

AN ADDRESS FROM MY STUDENTS IN PECS.

Words which express so poignantly
the anguish and the joys
of life in Hungary
at the time.

LAST ENGLISH LESSON IN PECS AT THE UNIVERSITY ON 6th DECEMBER 1948

MIXTURE

You are happy
we are sorry
that you go home

You have peace there and quietness
    you have harmony and freedom!
Oh! You don't know what that means
    but only those who have to miss
    and desire them in vain.
People who grew up
    and live there without friends
without loving brothers
    in their land.

You gave us knowledge
    in colourful sounds of your soul;
jolly good ideas, dancing and drink,
    and 'honey words' in your lovely poems.
Thank you for all these Beauties.

But we are poor
    and couldn't bring you more
As we have.
    Our treasures are humour,
cheer and laughter
    on the surface.
Inside - you can find
    all other things:
just what you will.

God save us and you, and
    "support us all the day long
of this troubleous life".

Yours faithfully,

STUDENTS.

35

Invitation for a
Csárdás.

János and his puli.

Vintage rest.

Tug of War
or
Not Amused.

Pakistan

Karachi 1949–1951

This chapter comes mainly from my News Letters of the period –
with little hindsight.

On my posting to Karachi from Budapest I had my first dose of culture
shock, and a severe one. This malady would hit me and my colleagues in
varying degrees on reaching a new post. I was in ignorance of what lay
ahead. I knew that Partition had taken place in 1947, but I had been
grappling with the Iron Curtain at the time. However, Papa was pleased.
He had loved his time in Cawnpore in the thirties and had told me a good
deal. Now I could 'argi' (get on) – when told – and 'jaldi' (quickly). I can
still hear Papa growl out to the tune of the Camptown Races:

> Let's take a chukka round the old reed bed,
> Let's take a chukka round the bog.
> Put up a snipe or two and shoot him dead:
> Somebody fetch my dawg.

I was pretty firm on my British Council feet after Hungary. I was convinced
I had a job worth doing. My colleagues and I felt that, despite economic
stringency, we mustn't lose sight of the canons of civilisation: education,
art, music, and literature. Indeed, I had seen enough of the Communists to
know the potential danger of the power of those who faced the exact
opposite: the negation of innate talents and all sincere expressions of truth
and beauty. The new country of Pakistan needed all our help. Apart from
official briefings, I took Papa's advice to heart: "If you are in a good job,
stick to it." Colonel Bill Williams' (Elephant Bill) advice was valuable:
"East of Suez if you lose your sense of humour you had much better take
the first boat home." In *Plain Tales from the Hills* Kipling wrote: "Now
India is a place beyond all others where one must not take things too
seriously, the midday sun excepted. Too much work and too much energy
kill a man just as effectively as too much assorted vice or too much drink.
Flirtation does not matter." I was relieved at the last sentence. But my

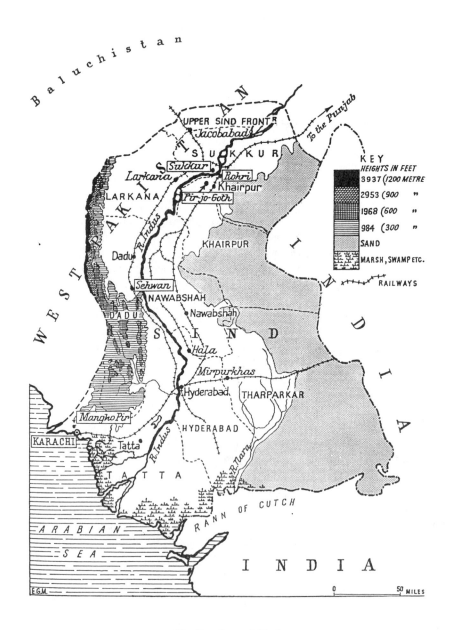

The Province of Sind

absolute standby was E. M. Forster's comment: "In the East the mere asking of a question causes it to disappear".

Maiden voyage

Papa saw me off from St Pancras on the special train to Tilbury, to embark on the P.&O. S.S. Himalaya on her maiden voyage. I was on my own, other passengers seemed to have hordes of relatives to see them off, and I was lonely. I settled into my cabin with my cabin baggage, and trusted that the baggage labelled 'Not Wanted on Voyage' was safely on board elsewhere. To my horror, I had three other cabin mates, but they were young and cheerful and I felt better. But we were tourist-class, vast numbers of us, with very meagre deck-space aft, which vibrated all the voyage. The first-class had three-quarters of the ship and enormous deck-space. We had a small swimming-pool and a few deck tennis courts, but nowhere to walk. I nipped up to a deserted first-class A-deck and read: "Six times round is a mile".

Now I felt more lonely. Everyone seemed to be in pairs exploring the ship. I had tea in silence observing the animated chatter all around. There were strange accents. At boat-drill I spotted a girl who seemed to be apart and she looked more my type. I strolled over to find her reading a German-Russian grammar. I was impressed and commented to her. Heaven be praised! She replied favourably with a pleasant voice, and I now had a companion in Grizelda Heaton-Armstrong. She knew Hungary well. She had lived in eastern Europe all her life, in the Austro-Hungarian society which the Communists had swept away. Her family, half-English, was now settled in England. She was a Cook's Guide having a holiday on her own.

Certain characters

At our table for meals we were three English and one Egyptian, Abbas Shawky. We English had little in common to start with, but we took to our Egyptian at once. He was in his early thirties, very good natured with a constant grin. Abbas, from the Ministry of Justice, had only had three days in England but he could not imagine anywhere more beautiful than Richmond, except Heliopolis where he lived. His hobby was knowing everyone's business. He didn't mind us questioning him or pulling his leg. At Port Said he was up at 6.30 a.m. rushing about, sweating with excitement, humping his suitcases, offering rides in his friend's car which he had spotted. Then he was gone. We missed him. I have always liked the Egyptians I have met. They are cultured and adult.

From the first-class section Rajkumar Bikram Bahadur Singh came into our lives, the brother of the deposed ruler of Khairagarh State. A friend of his knew Grizelda, so he introduced himself to her and, incidentally, to me. Unfortunately, he began to pursue her day and night, and proposed to her. He had a charming wife on board, but wanted another. He was forever making assaults on her cabin, but her sharers, three staunch grandmothers, took it in turns to guard her. It ended by my writing a final note for Grizelda to send him. It worked.

There was a pack of Australian sprint cyclists. They were like huge, noisy children, and were sometimes very funny. Patterson, the Olympic champion, was a natural comic. But we did not enjoy the rough stuff: their being loud and vulgar at meals, or wearing dripping bathing-costumes in the bar, etc. Yet they could play happily together on deck with a toy motorcar. I once found them sitting in a solemn circle with one of their number reading poetry aloud, as they sat absorbed like children listening to a bed-time story.

Friends – one needs friends

My dentist from childhood, J. Draper Cambrook, had given me a letter to Norman Winstone, an assistant-surgeon who had been one of his students. Norman had a well-appointed, first-class cabin and a discerning eye for the girls. He invited me in to meet 'the form' over a gin or two. Through him I met some very pleasant chaps and girls, though every time I had to sneak up from the tourist section feeling like a poor relation.

But the lucky break came. Grizelda found a girl-friend across the barrier and was invited for a drink at the first-class pool café; and I was included. Now I met all the right people. Very well, I am a snob. Well not as much as I was, but I do like to be free to choose. I was asked to the dance that night. My white dinner-jacket got odd looks from my mess-mates.

Here was dancing with a difference, evening dress, and a first-class floor. In no time I had sold my party the idea of an eightsome reel in the Red Sea. We got together with my records and a portable gramophone; and at odd times managed to rehearse in high heat and humidity. The party complained that there was no-one to organise things in first-class. But when it came to their gala night, the Scottish dances were organised!

Life became more congenial among the tourists once I had got to know some of the young better. We had a fine gala night, with Scottish country dances. I got permission, despite initial resistance, from the staff commander and the Tourist Entertainment Committee to bring in the couples from the first-class.

At Malta, off Valetta, on this maiden voyage we circled round to show off to the populace. Then out came three RAF Seafires to 'shoot us up', and three corvettes to salute us. It was cheering. Port Said was smelly and exhausting, but we went ashore. We were crowded in by street-sellers. Two Australians hauled up a camel-skin case from one of the bumboats, and then walked away. The irate vendor hurled up a bottle which broke and cut two passengers, and I saw him draw a knife. The offenders paid up at once at the cries of indignation below and above.

The Australians in my cabin were fine, but their high spirits were occasionally not appreciated. I had the misfortune to be in an upper bunk and the mate below me, would suddenly shout: "Look out, one coming through," and shove a long, British bayonet up through my mattress.

The Suez canal passage was an exciting novelty, with the stark sand on either side, or unfamiliar palm-tree scenes. We had carloads of admirers of our liner driving rather riskily, it seemed, along the side road for thirty miles or so until it got dark. Then we met the Amethyst returning from her epic dash down the Yangtse under the Chinese guns. We gave her captain and crew a mighty cheer. At night I was able to observe the effect of our wash on barges. I saw three mooring ropes snapped by the sucking of the water on our approach at regulation speed; and our wash wave would fling the barges up against the bank.

Out of the Red Sea and sailing east I saw Aden and its 'barren rocks' for the third time. In the evening light the silhouettes were a perfect setting for *The Tempest*. We saw a wonderful dhow, beautifully painted with a high stern, bronzed crew, and rusty-coloured sails. I was taken ashore by Doc Winstone, and we were entertained by his friend, an R.A.F. doctor. They talked a lot of shop, particularly on the effects of alcohol on a hot body in high temperatures. I was saved from wandering round on my own, a helpless prey.

India

Ballard Pier Bombay at 10 a.m. on 20 October 1949 was sweltering and smelly. On stepping ashore I was greeted by Victor Noel Paton (Killick Industries, Bombay Light Horse),[1] who with his wife, Joane, had kindly offered to meet me in Bombay on my way to Karachi, to fit me out and teach me the form. The Council was good enough to agree. It certainly made a lot of difference to my state of being on arrival at post.

I was also met, to my embarrassment, by three members of the British High Commissioner's Office. They gave me the welcome news that I had

---

[1] Later Lord Ferrier of Coulter, by Biggar.

Customs exemption. It was the start of my education. I waited for an hour and a half in a huge, stifling, open shed full of porters who were staggering around with trunks trying to stack separately the luggage of four hundred passengers. They achieved this, but seemingly without reference to the serial numbers hanging from the roof.

I sat clucking on my cabin baggage and waited an hour for the hold staff to appear, and then I got the rest of my baggage stacked round me. Then a declaration form for me could not be found. Was I gloomy? No. I viewed it with a sense of humour, as I had been advised. The man from Thomas Cook came and did a fine job. By 4.45 p.m., leaving guns and trunks in bond and paying nothing, I was away to the Noel Patons' airy flat in Kamal Mahal, Carmichael Road on Camballa Hill.

The Noel Patons were marvellous and despite petrol rationing took me everywhere. I had arrived in the middle of the Hindu Festival of Divali (the Feast of Lights) which drives away evil spirits. For four nights Bombay was lit with all manner of extra lighting: from electric candles to clay oil-lamps. The streets echoed to fire crackers and aerial whizzers, with a wavering background of singing and music.

Victor drove me round the crowded, festive bazaar – quite a feat. I was happily infected by the cheerful, jostling throng, and was fascinated to peer into tiny shops where little circles of shop-keepers sat with their customers, opening their books for a new year. I marvelled at what I saw and began to enjoy my daily V.I.P. treatment. I was taken to the golf club and noted the trays bearing glasses of water and salt pots to cope with the dangerous loss of body salts after exercise in high temperatures. I lunched at the sporting Gymkhana, and in the evening I was taken to swim at the exclusive senior Willingdon Club, under the lights, which in the tropics have to follow sunset so swiftly as there is no long twilight.

I went shopping with Joane in the mornings, which was quite an effort in the humidity. She gave me excellent advice on the tropical kit I would need in Karachi; and it cost much less than in London. I was taken to Kohinoor Cotton Mills, and supplied with high-quality, white duck, which Victor's tailor turned into jackets and trousers in two days.

Through the Noel Paton dinner-parties I learned much from interesting British and Indian guests including J.R.D. Tata, the great industrialist. I found that relations with Pakistan, especially over Kashmir, were very bitter. But if India could take over Hindu Hyderabad with its Muslim ruler, why couldn't Pakistan have Muslim Kashmir which has a Hindu ruler?

The Noel Patons drove a friend and me for a weekend to Poona – 120 petrol-rationed miles. There was a climb of 2000 ft. in only a few miles to the top of the Ghats where we had a picnic lunch, and then a straight run onto the Deccan. I had 'made' the famous hill-station 'Poon-ah' after twenty-eight years. But alas, the town was now a shadow of its hunting and racing days; full of ghosts, yet very attractive.

We had tea at the Kohinoor Hotel, listening to the koel, rightly known as the brain-fever bird.[2] Dinner was with the accompaniment of a little gekko lizard. I slept for the first time under a mosquito net.

Next morning with lower humidity and cool, wholesome air, we set off by car to the end of the road, where Victor engaged two bearers to carry out cool drinks and picnic baskets. We climbed another 2000 ft. to the top of Sinhagarh Fort (4230 ft.), a stronghold of the renowned, sixteenth-century Marhatta Chief, Shivaji Bhonsle. We plodded up the ancient, serpentine, rock-laid path in just over an hour and a half. Around the crumbling masonry we were rewarded with a great view over the Deccan.

Times changed in India with Shivaji at the break-up of the Mogul Empire. Back in Bombay it was a pleasure to visit the museum, in particular the natural history section. I could get an idea of the bird books for Sind. As for the animals, Victor introduced me to Jim Corbett's excellent *Man-Eaters of Kumaon*.

Up to Karachi

Bombay had been a revelation and a reward for the culture shock of the East. It is a great historic, commercial and cultural city with a very sophisticated Hindu and Parsee upper-class, and some stunning women. They were India's saviours against invaders. The lovely women of India simply absorbed them.

I was off on the B.I. Dwarka of 4000 tons with all my baggage around me. I was worried and anxious, suspicious of everyone. It was all so strange. Joane Noel-Paton wisely told me to learn not to worry in the East. I was soon happy in the company of the Lows of Burma Shell. I had a spacious first-class cabin and very good food. There were twenty in first-class, and thiry in second, and five-hundred deck-class passengers resulting in much smell and noise till we sailed. We covered the 500-odd miles in thirty-six hours, sailing close to the coast. The early morning reminded me of the North African desert air.

Ashore – with ease! I saw and heard a camel again, after 1942. It was pulling a four-wheeled, rubber-tyred dray. These are the goods vehicles of Karachi, and the deep, slow, jangling sound of their row of bells became very familiar.

"The Mediterranean," wrote E. M. Forster in *A Passage to India*, "is the

---

[2] See Hugh Whistler, *Popular Handbook of Indian Birds*, (Oliver and Boyd, 1963), pp. 325–327.

human norm. When men leave that exquisite lake, whether through the Bosphorus or the Pillars of Hercules, they approach the monstrous and extraordinary; and the southern exit leads to the strangest experience of all." It did, and this was sadly accentuated by the physical and emotional traumas of Partition. Karachi had been made into a fine and necessary port for Sind by General Sir Charles Napier in the mid-nineteenth century. In 1947 the city had become a federal capital over-night. The population had been swollen from 300,000 to over 1,000,000 – by refugees. From the huge Keamari Docks it all looked pretty grim.

Poor old Karachi had very little character. It was like a war-time camp: sandy, drab, sprawled out over the flat desert along tarmac roads with sand borders. There seemed to be no attractive buildings. Public transport was impossible, so a European needed a car. The alternatives were expensive taxis, cycle rickshaws, or slow, rickety gharries (horse-drawn carriages). We had a staff pick-up stationwagon to and from accommodation, covering quite a number of miles per week. From Keamari Docks one drove to the old city where the main office buildings were grouped round the railway terminus. The crowded streets were chaotic: dirt, smells, varieties of transport, bells, horns, beggars, wailing music, dust, flies, the leisurely movement of pedestrians, and sand. British and Pakistanis alike complained of it all, especially the lack of accommodation. They disliked the presence of the government, the feeling of mushroom-like growth, the absence of historical traditions, the lack of social amenities, the dirt where once there had been famous cleanliness.

I was depressed, despite the solicitous and sensitive administative officer, Martin Skeffington, who met me, when I was told that my accommodation was to share a room at the Beach Luxury Hotel – and this was only possible, after some effort, with a Pakistan Government Requisition Order. Accommodation was at a premium. There were hotel or house rooms only, no houses, not even for ambassadors or for our Representative.

There was no beach, but there was a muddy, smelly, tidal creek behind. There was no luxury to be seen. My 'room', was an open-topped, wooden cubicle, one of a number erected on the first-floor landing, each with two beds, a chair and a chest of drawers. I was in a state of shock. What an exchange for my Budapest flat, the wine, the gipsies, the charm of Pécs, the courage of the people! I went to bed before the 'other-half' returned. He returned late and quietly apologised. Next morning we introduced ourselves.

My room-mate was Roger Macbeth Rigby, (Winchester and Cambridge, Blackdown after me, late 18th Cavalry), General Manager of G.K.N. Pakistan. I was extremely lucky. We have remained close friends ever since. When I dressed for chota hazri (breakfast) I found that the tongues

44

of my shoes had been eaten by rats in the night, but I didn't care. I could face the streets of Karachi, which revealed the aftermath of Partition on my way to the office by car. Every pavement, every island, every rounda-bout centre contained altogether thousands of the poorest and most unfortunate refugees. They were, for a time, forced to live in dirty, mis-shapen hovels constructed by themselves from sticks and sacking. They cooked on dung fires, eating something, sleeping somehow, making the best of life in their new country. There were half-naked beggars and other deformed bodies lying about the streets. These pitiable people were confined to the pavements, talking, smoking, shaving, washing. There was no sanitation, only the hot, dry, day climate. But this was the cool weather, chilly early and late, which was not so good for them. The filth was indescribable.

I was agreeably surprised on first arrival at the pleasant and light office-premises in Sarnagati Building; but this was before I approached it on my own with my eyes open. Heavy gloom returned. I wrote in my diary:

> I walk to the office sometimes. The approach looked fine in photographs, but it was loathsome. Everywhere one goes the countless people stare. I have to pick my way among buffaloes and their droppings. They have even more suffering eyes than cows. I walk past smells and pools of filthy water, along disgusting pavements, beside urinated walls, among beggars and goats, children making patties with dung, flies again, men blowing their noses with their fingers, pi dogs eating goodness knows what, and cows wandering about eating paper and orange peel. I pass men sitting or lying on the pavements, in the squares, asleep, talking, lighting fires, being shaved or massaged, picking lice from their clothes. Some walked about hand-in-hand. Women – walking tents – are totally covered in black or white hoods reaching to their feet with mesh slits for their eyes.
>
> The streets get narrower the further one penetrates, and the open food-stalls grow more numerous, and so the swarms of flies increase, and the cows, sheep, and goats increase, and there are still more flies and filth. Above the hubbub that goes with these swarms of men, beasts, and insects, is the blare of motor horns, but the blowers and the blown at are oblivious of the noise above the traffic. And day and night comes the penetrating wail of Eastern music. It is shocking, but out of the poverty and privation comes a wonderfully cheerful resignation, and above all, dignity. I am humbled.
>
> It is better at night. Deep shadows hide the worst of the misery.

There are strange crowds round curious stalls lit by vapour lamps selling pan, sweetmeats, tea, and other food. There are men sitting on their haunches, talking and gesticulating. There is an air of mystery in the narrow streets and tall, balconied buildings; but there are no exciting cafés, no dancing girls here for us.

The Representative, Bill Owain-Jones, was a splendid man: calm, kind, modest, and experienced. He had spent many years in India, with his wife Mfanwy. He had latterly been the principal of Islamia College, Peshawar, the top public school. Many of Pakistan's senior government men had either been his pupils or knew him well, which was terribly useful. Bill could learn what was going on, and be told what we could do best, in our small way. He had chosen our office, the well-built and cool Sarnagati Building, Pakistan Chowk (circle). It had an open-plan office and library, a wide, flat roof for lectures, films, etc. Situated down-town between bazaar and cantonment, it was easily reached by students. Equipment such as a projector, an epidiascope, Pel chairs, and office equipment, was arriving all the time.

John Elliott, Assistant Representative (with his dear, Spanish wife, Pilar), was unique, and ideal for me. He had been in Hungary before the war and was still under its spell! The specialities of John were age, stature, aplomb, intelligence, humour, and a presence which gave confidence to all who met him. He was the quintessence of what at least some Council officers should be like. Such officers are so effective. But as the years passed I found that such men were no longer in favour as they did not fit the norm. They were not brisk, hard-headed, grey office-men. John would pace the streets; yes, the crowded, filthy, smelly streets too, with his silver-topped ebony cane, sometimes with a French yellowback under his arm. He was not a poseur. He was genuine and persona grata at all levels. He could unconcernedly put his arm round a Pakistani minister, with "My dear man I understand. May I suggest you/we . . . ?" He was a success. But of administration – allowances, scales of furniture, accounts, returns – he cared not a fig. I was only too pleased to pick up the threads for him, and incidentally gain experience.

Martin Skeffington, on the other hand, was highly strung, and given to the vapours over some small disaster or misunderstanding, which was apt to occur. Administration and initiative were not yet qualities of the new Muslim citizens. But Martin's private attitude was his way of keeping sane. He had a big heart, and to my admiration, he was also a natural linguist.

Of the local staff, Mr Rebeiro (of Portuguese extraction, a Goanese Christian) was an admirable administrator. Mr Jaffery was my useful cultural-assistant. We were strengthened and cheered by two English ladies,

Mary Shuja and Helen Ashraf, who were married to Pakistanis. In order to succeed in all we aimed to do we had to rely on our local staff; and this goes for every country in the world in which the Council is represented. I here state my admiration for them and my gratitude.

Here in the East, and in unusual circumstances, I did my best to understand the men who were serving so loyally under me and my colleagues. The old sweepers at the bottom of the social ladder swept with locally made hand-brooms of soft grass, and even fetched or carried chairs, but nothing more. Our uniformed peons or messengers and office-assistants, were pleasant, willing and loyal, but not terribly able. I had to understand that almost everything was a new world to them. No wonder machines ceased to function, or liquids got spilt, or pottery broken! They did their best and then stood around waiting for the next command. They showed no initiative, as I unfairly criticised higher levels too, but not to their faces. Time was not important even to the administrators. I soon learned that we in the West are too much slaves to time.

When a programme or job involved two of our little departments, our staff simply rang bells for peons to carry files, and passed the buck backwards and forwards. No-one would ever take responsibility, which was understandable. That gave a clue to the whole way of life in the sub-continent.

The problems we had running the office in early days were a useful indication of what was happening or not happening in government. The two most irritating aspects of staff behaviour were their inability (or unwillingness) to work together, and their unwillingness to take responsibility. There was no old boy basis of co-operation; no give and take. Offices were rigidly departmentalised. The result of a request "Do this," would be long delayed by the 'executive's' concern with method, order, and precedence. One had to be careful not to become outwardly frustrated, and it was best not to ask when something would be done. Direct questions were seldom answered.

John and I had fun (with good intentions) in insisting on real answers. The poor chaps' real desire was to please, so an answer that will please must be the one to give! John Elliott was admirable with all staff. He did his best to break down the awful hierarchy, and to introduce at least some aspects of team-work. John would treat everyone with the same courtesy. Pakistan needed men with the simplest initiative to begin with, and a new attitude to all those around who were colleagues with the same national purpose. We did at least get our staff not to cringe, but to approach without fear and speak what needed to be said. But we would still overhear how staff could be treated lower down the ladder.

Life seemed terribly complicated for office workers at all levels. This was the way administration seems to have been built: on a system of check and counter-check, and check again. It was clumsy and time-wasting, but it kept each man employed. What he did was another matter. In our office John and I were for ever trying to simplify routine, but the staff did not appreciate our attitude. It meant more time for another job! There was no question of making out a list of jobs to be done, having them all completed, and then on to the next. Even when asked to do a job, the question came back: "How?". Even when told the answer, the staff wanted it all on paper to say that it was authorised.

Imagine how the early government machinery creaked! I knew only the Customs House well. The system of checking, appraisal, clearance, etc. entailed a fantastically complicated system of processes and numbers of signatories for each document. Something which arrived by air or sea could take weeks to appear, but we often needed books or material or parts at once. I knew the form, and went to obtain the release of an item which had been in the process for six weeks. With the help of an Englishman of Thomas Cook's I got it in three hours. The head man couldn't believe it. "How did you do it?" "I followed the papers round." If the papers did not look like moving on, I took them.

I was shaken by the rigid hierarchy which existed. It was Bill who explained that for anyone born in the sub-Continent life was a terrible upward struggle (within one's caste in India). Gain a step upward and then grind down the man on the step below to prevent him overtaking you. My assistant wrote a note to his No. 2, rang his bell, and told the peon to pass it over to the next desk. As No. 2 was not there I had a peep at it. It read "Why are there no pins on my table?" Higher up the scale, a government official was such a great man that lesser mortals sometimes had to bribe the peon on the door to gain an interview. As for a university professor, he was a god to himself and could not unbend. He could not risk loss of dignity.

Bill Owain-Jones and John Elliott did good work at Sind University's sports. When asked to take part in professors' musical chairs, they entered into the spirit of it, fell over backwards and generally played up when a chair was pulled away. The students loved it, marvelled, and came up saying they did not imagine a professor could be so human. Well, there was no-one more human, more kindly, more fitting for his post than Bill Owain-Jones, with his sweet Mfanwy.

In grand terms our work was to help Pakistan to advance, but it wasn't straightforward. It was very sad that certain international concerns mitigated against total concentration on development in areas such as education, housing, industry, etc. They were the menace of Russia; the shadows of war with India; and the Kashmir problem. Bill did his best to make new ministers aware of what administration was for, and what was required to produce desired results. High standards of all forms of work needed to be taught, reached, and maintained, as had been the example of the Indian Civil Service in India.

Certainly Bill knew that the government and its ministers and officials, businessmen, agents and contractors, and tradesmen were all battling on in their efforts to live and work and organise. Alas, we also found contempt for the law, and nepotism. Bernard Budd of the I.C.S. had been asked to remain as anti-corruption officer, but he was soon asked to resign.

We felt keenly the same hopes as the people that Pakistan would flourish; but then some reactions were not encouraging, such as attitudes to practical work which was required of all levels of society, but 'hands on' and 'hands dirty' did not appeal. "We are educated men," some said. "It is for others to to do such work."

We were always campaigning against the over-valuing of written examinations. A Bachelor of Arts degree was the students' goal. British firms in Pakistan found that applicants with engineering degrees had no practical experience at all. Also, I was upset at the power of the students attitudes to professors. They were capable of demonstrating and even confining the Vice-Chancellor to his room if their exams were scheduled too soon. Or they might go 'on strike' if the papers were too hard!

I suffered a form of culture shock working with Muslim students, who were nearly all men. Most of them were awkward and shy but we were gradually breaking that down. They seemed to have an attitude of mistrust. Was it a left-over from the British Raj? Pre-1947 the Muslims did not take as much advantage of the education offered as the Hindus did. Now it took the Muslims a long time to establish their own such institutions.

Before I arrived in Karachi I was anxious about Pakistani feeling towards the British as their rulers, and, our exclusiveness and rigid separation from Indian life. It did hurt the Indians, as I learned slowly from reading. But it was a great shock when a young Pakistani said to Martin Skeffington: "How we loathed your white faces. If you had remained another month we would have cut your throats". But, apart from Amritsar, the British were pretty good at quelling small outbreaks of communal violence without serious casualties by means of our police or soldiers and their stout, brass-tipped staves (lathis).[3] We were grateful to hear acknowledgements of what we had achieved in so many spheres: agriculture, irrigation, transport, communications, law and order, medicine, the preservation of ancient monuments and the armed forces. I was relieved that I arrived after Independence because I hoped that now I might be accepted in the country as a friend.

It was up to me to study Islam: the reason for the creation of Pakistan.

---

[3] Alas, the British were unable to prevent the terrible violence in Calcutta of August 1946. See Francis Watson, *A Concise History of India* (Thames and Hudson, 1974).

In the end I wished that the teachings of Christ held the same position in Britain as the Koran in Pakistan. I appreciate the discipline of Islam but I find it difficult to accept purdah and certain attitudes to women; but I know there are many Muslim women who are happy with their position in the home, and the power it brings.

I understand that the Prophet Mohammed did not order purdah, but only strict modesty. Unfortunately, I found that no girls came to our cultural activities, except some charming Parsees who came to play-readings and country-dancing. A discussion on 'Women's Place in the World' produced an audience of men only. But many of the students were keen for their women-folk to be emancipated. Other strong supporters of purdah were not impressed by Western films. However, it was cheering to read letters in a Dacca paper (the bright Bengalis were a bit contemptuous of their West Pakistan compatriots) saying: "A nation with half its people lagging behind can hardly progress. Our leaders would do well to create such conditions as to enable people to march forward, and one way of doing this is by abolishing the purdah system in Pakistan."

The wonderful Begum Liaquat Ali Khan (who was not in purdah), the widow of Pakistan's first prime minister (who was murdered in October 1951), strove to persuade the women of Pakistan to come forward to work for their country's success and firm establishment. But at the time few women were answering her forceful call.

I admire the unconcern of the Muslim as he goes about his daily punctilious observances. But they don't seem to fit in with modern life. The forty days of fasting in Ramzan, for instance, is far tougher than Lent and, I suspect, much more widely practiced. It was a shock to witness another tenet of Islam, the custom on the Friday holiday preceding Eid-ul-Zuha by which every male adult had to participate in the slaughter of an animal and to eat thereof. One man had to kill a goat or sheep, six could combine to kill one cow, or twenty to kill a camel. There were vast quantities of meat, perhaps going bad, in those times of severe food-shortages.

Australian and Dutch friends in Pakistan felt that there would always be a dividing gulf between East and West, but we hoped there would be permanent respect and understanding. Early on I was alarmed at our Muslim students who saw our magazines and got the impression that we were all immoral. This gave us a talking point. It saddened us to realise that we couldn't hope to share the lives of the people round us.

In my early days in Karachi my spirits would swing suddenly from high to low, though I tried to remain steady. Soon Bill took me off on a round of calls, in his lovely old Wolseley saloon which looked quite out of place, but very gentlemanly. The first call was on the High Commissioner, Sir Lawrence Grafftey-Smith, who was a tough egg but human. He asked:

"What on earth's a Functional Officer?" I replied: "Well, Sir, my job is to arrange occasions for getting people together." Sir Lawrence retorted: "I thought that was the prerogative of God." A sticky start, but I could stand up for myself. Sir Lawrence wrote poetry. On the eve of his departure, Sir Lawrence, U.K. High Commissioner in Pakistan since its inception, sent the following poem to the Karachi newspaper, *Dawn*:

Salute to Pakistan

> You are the dream behind a poet's eyes;
> The voice of steel, defying fate and Kings;
> The fluttering hope that fanned a myriad wings
> Of prayer, of ecstasy, of sacrifice.
> You are a million graves and their bereavement,
> Men bled for you; veins of pure blood are theirs.
> They dreamed of more than cotton, wool or jute,
> To see restored the ancient virtues, soon:
> To stand erect, and equal, man to man;
> To live secure beneath a crescent moon.
> Now that the dream comes true, your friends salute
> This miracle that men call "Pakistan".

In the course of time I met many senior officials, Pakistani and British, who were most cooperative and helpful, even to receiving at once from the hands of the district magistrate a firearms permit to shoot anywhere in Sind with my rifle or shot-gun.

My spirits rose when I discovered another consolation of Karachi: its unexpected close connection with the outside world, and with home. We all loved the wind from the sea, even the Arabian Sea, the sea itself, the harbour, the ocean-going motor or sail craft. Being British and having a great Navy, we didn't feel so cut off. If there was civil commotion or war, we felt that we would be rescued. I spent quite a lot of time at Keamari on board ships which were still the standard carriers for visitors to be met or seen off. These shipboard visits were boon refuges from the dust and dirt and heat.

From Partition to Bank Bungalow

Roger and I were able to break out of our partition at the Beach Luxury pretty quickly. The kind Parsee manager of the local Bank of India and his wife offered us bed and breakfast in their pleasant, spacious, central bungalow. This was fine for a time but there were rats.

One December morning I began to walk down to the Beach Luxury for its concert hour. A European driver coming by spotted me and stopped. "Where on earth are you going? One doesn't walk in Karachi." I explained. "Well, I'm going home shortly, would you like my accommodation?" I was struck dumb. Our need was great. "I'll find my chum." A quick 'shufti' (look around), and we moved straight in. Thanks to Mr and Mrs Whittle, a local family, we now had a first floor 'flat' of latticed verandah and bedroom in Bath Island House, reached by an outside staircase.

My spirits couldn't rise higher once we had shaken down, with the help of Roger's servant, Mohammed. After Winchester and Cambridge, Roger had experience of India and Pakistan, through four years in the 18th Cavalry, and he spoke Urdu and Pushto. He had a company car. He was a sportsman, sailor, Scottish dancer, was well-known and widely popular. How did I get in on the act? I still wonder. Mohammed was calm, quiet, efficient, and discreet, with a sense of humour. "I shan't stay with you if you get married, sahib", he said to Roger. "I couldn't work for a memsahib." To my relief, Roger remained free. I had first worried about the servants in India who could undertake such duties as barman or waiter and be shouted for by 'sahibs'. However, one cannot even hurry one's learning of the East. In due course I understood the accepted rules of behaviour. Mohammed and Roger set perfect examples of respect and caring between servant and master, and taught me much.

Work

The British Council in London did all it could to provide for us financially in our aim to establish professional links between Britain and Pakistan. Once we had overcome the little bureaucratic obstacles to the flow of materials from Britain, for which we had indented, away we went. From now on, I had a delightful time in the British Council all over the world as I discovered that it was never easy to separate work from play, or vice versa.

We had a library as part of our Centre, and a monthly programme of activities, drama, music, lectures, film shows, exhibitions of aspects of Britain, discussion groups, and from the office the handling of specialist visitors. The teaching of English was an important part of the work, both on the spot or at institutions, and mainly to teachers of English. But to the consternation of B.C. staff and visiting E.L.T. experts, we found that the teachers of the sub-continent stuck firmly to certain sentence construction, and to their own forms of pronunciation.

The first major operation was the arrival of a touring exhibition of standard British text and reference books. Once inspected, the Ministry of

Education groaned understandably at the cost of the textbooks and manuals they needed. Next we had a tour by the Norman Marshall Shakespeare Recital Company. Islam is not exactly pro-theatre, so there were no theatres in the Muslim towns of Pakistan. Great improvisation and coping was required on all sides. Shakespeare was and is studied very thoroughly, and the students were amazed and delighted to witness his plays brought to life. The best response was in Dacca where the students' welcome was terrific. The Bengalis are highly intelligent, and literate. Bengal is very heavily populated compared with Sind. For that reason two thirds of Pakistan's population spoke Bengali.

We would only sign up our V.I.P. lectures from Britain in the 'cold weather' since there were no audiences in the hot weather. Some visitors were official, others were grabbed in passing. They took up a lot of time. One of our two cars had to be more or less permanently detached and when two visitors coincided, life became difficult. But they were worth having, and they were so devoted: Dame Katherine Watt, Sir Gordon Gordon-Taylor, Sir Alexander Fleming, Professor Henry Barcroft and H. R. Mills, the scientist. It was thrilling for me to have care of Sir Alexander Fleming. He had met me before: in 1942 when I was a patient in the Radcliffe Infirmary, Oxford, where he used some trial penicillin ointment on me. Unfortunately, my care of him was not so effective; after an official luncheon we both suffered from amoebic dysentry! Conversely, there were Pakistani professionals, doctors, engineers, teachers, and other professional men and women whom we were glad to be able to send to Britain for access to training facilities, or higher studies.

One of our uninvited visiting successes was Lieutenant David Morgan, R.N.A.S., who came out with a sample Supermarine Attacker. He gave an excellent talk with material Vickers had supplied. He was later concerned with efforts by Supermarine Vickers to break the sound barrier. In addition he gave an unbelievable display of aerobatics out at Mauripur. Another hero whom I snared at the Sind Club was Commander Teddy Woodward R.N., who gave a thrilling talk on his part in submarine warfare. Another invitee was Victoria Kingsley, the guitarist. This instrument proved very popular with the students. Sir Eugene Millington-Drake, our former, famous ambassador in Buenos Aires arrived and announced himself! He insisted on giving a talk on English poetry. To my relief, Karachi Grammar School (K.G.S.) were willing to have him. The pupils were beautifully behaved when he declaimed 'Sally in our Alley'.

K.G.S. was an admirable grammar school, with a fine headmaster in Mr Haskell, a seconded missionary. He gave me a pre-certificate class in English: thirty fifteeen to sixteen year-olds, mainly Anglo-Indian boys and girls. They were a tough lot, full of life without repressions. I was fair game as an outside teacher. I tried, as Bill would have wished, to be firm and friendly to make lessons effective but not mechanical. I enjoyed it all, letting them hear a native Englishman speak, and trying to level up the varied standard in my class.

Climate

> In Europe life retreats out of the cold, and exquisite fireside myths have resulted – Balder, Persephone – but here the retreat is from the source of life, the treacherous sun, and no poetry adorns it because disillusionment cannot be beautiful.
>
> E. M. Forster, *A Passage to India*.

The temperature at the end of November was apt to be in the nineties, which was very hot for tennis or other exercise such as reel practices. But within a month the rugger season began and the evenings drew on, giving a feeling of autumn with wistful thoughts of turning leaves and pheasant shoots. One could get out of the dull, uniform whites and wear light suits of one's choice.

The opening meeting of the Reel Club was held in February 1950 on the worst day of winter. A strong, cold, north wind from the desert produced a nasty sandstorm and drove everyone indoors. It was the only evening when Roger and I could not eat our dinner on our verandah-sitting room. It had no glass, only the lattice. We had to retire to our bedroom which had glass windows. But as the days passed, the sun was soon hot enough to try to escape from it.

One missed the marked temperate climate changes of season. But the Indian winter is a perfect climate: warm to hot sun by day, with fires needed in the evenings. Constant hot sun could be boring, but one got along very well by creating a world within a world: the Clubs.

In Karachi Cantt* (the residential area), the Sind Club was a marvellous retreat from the unpleasant side of Karachi, as well as for rest and recreation. There were iced drinks on the verandah from ever-attentive bearers, or one could join the throng at the bar, pick up information, get to know and be known. In the evenings one could give or be invited to parties or receptions, or attend a film show, or accommodated.

The dry heat could be tolerated, but the damp heat of August and September towards the end of the monsoon could be unpleasant and cause prickly heat. On one's bed, under a ceiling fan and one sheet, sweating is not fun but, except for a month or two, the nights were pleasantly cool and

---

* Short for Cantonment: formerly a permanent military town.

the days were not too hot, thanks to the sea-breeze. The old-fashioned punkah still existed up-country: a long flapping cloth suspended from a hinged rod, and activated by a poor punkah-wallah's toe.

A constant fan breeze in an office which runs on paper was very irritating. One had to keep calm and master the disorganisation of always vital loose sheets blowing away, by immediately securing all loose paper with a paper-weight. I preferred to sweat rather than be blown upon by a fan, but I had to give way to the staff and let the fans continue.

If it rained, Karachi could become inundated in a few hours, as on 13 July 1950. It rained again on 4 August. The plight of the refugees was pitiable. Many must have died. Others rioted demanding something be done to house and feed them. Rapid action was taken briefly. Unfortunately, many of the refugees were expecting to find easy forms of work in the city and were not prepared to be put into agricultural settlements. Lighting circuits and telephones failed on such occasions, and Bath Island House's roof leaked badly. We only had a small patch of dry floor to sleep on.

We did very nicely in our new home, but we hadn't reckoned that with no windows there was access to wild-life as well as to breeze. If we were going to be out late, Roger would get Mohammed to leave some sort of supper for us before he left. The first time we organised this, we returned late and found that it had already been eaten. Our first tribe had been at work: cats.[4] Mohammed had no access to a larder or a screened cupboard. The solution was for him to close our suppers in a suitcase. This worked well, and our clothes on trips didn't seem to smell of curry.

The monsoon[5]

In May the power of up-currents of air produce immense towering cumulus clouds and a tremendous sea can be heard for miles inland. Bill and I encountered a monsoon storm on our flight by twin-engined Convair to Dacca on 8 May 1950. Suddenly the cabin went dark and a huge wall of black appeared ahead. "No smoking: fasten seat belts". The aircraft began to dance about like a horse with an itch under its saddle. Suddenly the outside went white, and thin cloud flashed by, hail slashed the whole fuselage. There were violent flashes of lightning, and we dropped steeply a couple of hundred feet in a down-draught. The poor steward hit the roof with several of his pots and pans. A small boy bounced right out of his

[4] Here I must introduce you to E.H. Aitken, (Salt and Excise Department), *Tribes on my Frontier* (Thacker's Bombay, 9th Ed. 1920). 'An Indian Naturalist's Foreign Policy'. 'Birds, insects, reptiles'. He observed all creatures in minute detail, and wrote about them most amusingly.

[5] See Alexander Frater, *Chasing the Monsoon*. Viking 1990. Penguin 1991.

belt. One of the engines sprang an oil leak. We had to spend the night on the waiting-room floor at New Delhi. The farmers need the monsoon, but the precipitation drowns very many people annually.

One of the most evocative aspects of life in Karachi and in other Pakistani cities was the noises: the cries of various fauna, and the street-sellers. There was the crying, bubbling, screeching of the kites ever wheeling in their search for food. Worse somehow was the cawing of ghoulish crows: ever present, assaulting the housewife's nerves. There were the human cries of street-hawkers: some weird and bloodcurdling, others mournful and depressing. Some sounded like death rattles. The gloomiest sound of all was that made by the botli-wallah buying empty bottles from the bearer to re-sell. We paid our servants pretty small wages but, owing to the size of the population, masters had to employ more than one servant to enable more persons to live. By the 'Indian' system, it was one man, one job: sweeper, bearer, dhobi (laundryman), mali (gardener), chowkidar (night watchman) durzi (tailor), kitmagar (waiter), khansama (steward), bobajee (cook), ghorawalla, or syce (groom), and so on.

We had a plague of flying ants, clouds of them fluttering their large wings, obscuring an activity, alighting and running fast rather unpleasantly all over the rooms. I.C.I.'s Gammexane did them in, or kept them out. The well-behaved flies at home fly round and round in the centre of the room, and then stick themselves onto fly-paper. Nothing but death will prevent the Eastern fly settling on one's person.

We were spared snakes, scorpions, and other insects, but not ants. The dining-table legs had to be stood in special ant-proof, up-turned, saucer-like feet. Unfortunately, cockroaches found us. I loathe them. They think, move fast and look horrible. They took to dropping onto my bed in the night, not onto Roger's. Spiders I like, but not centipedes. A four-inch, black-and-yellow horror landed by me as I was shaving. Roger coped. I am ashamed – but I was otherwise engaged.

Six days of Christmas in Karachi, 1949

My Christmas holiday began on Tuesday 20 December with an invitation from the Flag Officer, R.P.N., to witness the arrival of two British destroyers on transfer: the Tippu Sultan (formerly Onslow), and the Tariq (formerly Offa). There was an enormous shamiana[6] under which sat the V.I.P.s, and Helen Ashraf, and I. Beyond was rank on rank of the three services and then dense crowds. The Baluch and Punjab Regiment Pipe Bands marched and counter-marched.

---

[6] An open-sided decorated tentage on poles.

The Tippu Sultan arrived with the Prime Minister and all on board. There were cheers (by a leader) of "Pakistan!" and a roar came: "Zindabad!" (roughly translated: "Up with Pakistan!"). The Tariq arrived and we moved down opposite her, for cheers again. Then back to the Tippu Sultan. She gleamed overall through her Royal Navy crew's efforts. There was a rigid Guard of Honour and her own band to welcome aboard the notables and the Press. I spotted one white face on deck, in brown dungarees, a worried expression, and carrying a big torch. Obviously a Scots engineer. These stalwarts are essential to the running of everything.

When we got on board we made for the bridge, and a very proud young gunnery rating showed us everything for'ard. I then said "Please take us to the Wardroom". We pressed on undeterred at meeting the P.M.'s party. Inside, the sole occupant was the dungareed engineer, transformed into Lieutenant-Commander Engineer Chief. I told him I had spotted him, and we were were invited for a gin! Then in came the officers of both navies, and a good time was had by all on orange squash.

Tuesday of Christmas: I was impressed by the Karachi Glee Singers and the turn-out for the Carol Service and nine lessons at Holy Trinity Church. It was a combined effort by the Protestant, Presbyterian, and Methodist Churches. After dinner at home I was invited to a dance at the Boat Club by the English Director-General of Railways[7] and his wife and daughter. Roger was an active member anyway.

The Boat Club was down on the tidal creek with a mangrove swamp and the sea beyond. It was for rowing, bathing, and social drinking. It was a good spot with a cheery atmosphere and welcome sea-breezes. They put on a very fine, decorated, Christmas show.

On Wednesday night we had a beer in the Club and carols at the 'Gym' performed by the Glee Singers.

On Friday evening at 8 p.m. I went with Bill Owain-Jones to a party at the Jinnah Hospital at the invitation of the Matron, Mrs Finlay. How I came to admire these British nurses around the world! It was a great occasion: decorations, music, supper, presents for everyone, and then performing parrots who stole the show. They were incredible – from driving a pigeon harnessed to a cart, to my favourite, a parrot with a glowing taper in his beak, who on the command 'Fire!' directed it over the touch hole of a cannon. There was a flash, a shattering report, we all leaped into the air, but the parrot remained calm behind his gun. Then we went on to join a party at the Gym.

Christmas Eve was spent well, everwhere. Bed was at 3.45 a.m. How kind people were!

Christmas Day: We were woken by a Pakistan Brass Band rendering

---

[7] The highly successful and respected T.G. (Tommy) Creighton.

Colonel Bogey for the sake of the Christian 'Eid'. I went to church with Roger and we both had lunch at the Shujas. We had dinner at the Sind Club on the Lows of the voyage. I had brought "Cocker", a fellow Wykehamist, together with Roger, which worked very well.

While recovering from surfeits but still on holiday, we had a call from Mr Qutb, the station director of Radio Pakistan. He was suddenly required to put on a feature programme in English using two male and two female voices after speeches by the Prime Minister and Governor-General. Very nobly, John Elliott, Mary Shuja and Helen Ashraf rallied round. We spent two hours sorting scripts on illegible paper in indifferent English; and we just had time for one straight run-through before going on the air. It was a useful British Council contribution, we hoped.

New Year 1950

We had an extra day's holiday in honour of the Prophet's birthday. This gave me a chance to take Himalayan friends out in a bunder (harbour) boat which is an open, small, fishing dhow. Bunder-boating was one of the best pastimes that Karachi could provide: it was restful and entertaining. The boats were smart and clean, well-cushioned, with an agile, willing crew of three; it was roughly £1 per hour across the huge expanse of the outer harbour. The day began with a high wind and a minor sandstorm which covered everything with a film of fine sand, but we were glad of the wind.

The year came in at the house where the Lows were staying. Later at the Gymkhana Club. There was a Pakistani piper. We sang Auld Lang Syne and danced a shambles of a reel. Not any more so, I resolved!

Sand grouse by the Hab River

I now had closer acquaintance with the admirable camel than I had had in the Western Desert. Six of us in two saloon cars and one jeep left Karachi at 7 a.m. one Sunday morning up into the hills. The light was perfect and the sun cast lovely, long shadows. Around us stretched deep wadis, clumps of palms in vague outline, and occasional groups of white, mud houses. We were on a road of tarmac which changed to gravel and then to sand. Driving in sand is an art in which my silent, efficient, tarbooshed Abdul was expert. We were on our way to the Hab River, the border with the little princely state of Las Bela, up the Makran coast on the Arabian Sea.

After an hour and a quarter we reached the flat river-valley, and a village consisting of a collection of goat-infested stick and sacking huts grouped round a Public Works Department dak (staging post) bungalow. The river was only three feet deep, but sixty yards wide. The too keen, impulsive, jeep owners got stuck in it. My camera was at the ready and I shot them: but I had my .256 Mannlicher over my shoulder in case there was a visible crocodile. We needed to find the sand grouse at their early-morning drinking spots.

Suddenly, a camel bearing an angry man appeared in a cloud of dust on top of our bank. "You are in the wrong place," he cried: "Follow me!" He went off west at a fast trot to the next similar-looking village. Here was our bearded shikari, annoyed and anxious for us to obtain results and so keep up his reputation. I had no time to think. I was suddenly up behind our guide on the rear of the camel's double saddle, and told to have my gun ready. I was too new and my William Powell was too precious to have loose to start with, and I got my guide to sling it over his pommel in its case. He thought me very odd. Didn't I want to shoot? If not, why was he taking all this trouble? He was right.

However, I was happy learning the correct technique and deportment on a camel. Fortunately, I had stirrups and a thick cloth under me on the wooden saddle frame. When I rose up in my stirrups to get more comfortable I found it hard to judge when to come down again and every false attempt jarred my spine horribly. I soon discovered that the only way to survive on a camel was to remain quite relaxed and in sympathy with the camel's strange motion. A camel puts both feet on the same side forward together, and when trotting the rear legs do not bend at all. Nevertheless, I soon developed great admiration for the camel. No cross-country vehicle could be so efficient or give one such a good view of one's surroundings. The only thing that upset me was the frightful exchange of oaths going on between man and beast in front of me. Or were they endearments? The camel I rode knelt down when the rider made a sort of hissing noise, but alarmingly needed no command to rise after he felt his 'master' in the saddle.

Francis, another mounted gun, crossed the river behind his driver. The others remained on foot and moved slowly up towards us. We shot four partridges and two sand grouse, which was fun enough. My camel didn't give a hoot when I fired from the saddle, which was obviously the best way to outwit very wary birds. The sand grouse whistled so beautifully as they circled and descended to the water.

The Reel Club

After a month's negotiations, the Gymkhana Club Committee allowed me to run Scottish country dance classes every Wednesday evening. I remember turning up at the hall one evening, plugging in the Council's Deccalian, and putting on one of my 78 r.p.m.s from Rae Mac's in Edinburgh, with the Council's charming Sandy Ross down from Lahore to support me. A few people came out of curiosity. I turned up regularly through every change of climate. Members rose to twenty in March and sank to six in May and June. But George Bartlett, volunteer secretary, and Anne, his Scots-dancing wife, never missed an evening. (In 1998 I still have the file he opened for all S.C.D. material.)

By August we had ten reliable men and girl dancers, and news of our efforts got around, to the extent of the Y.M.C.A. asking for a demonstration. I was underhand and told the dancers that the next meeting would be at the Y.M.C.A. They were angry and horrified at the vast number of people present on what was a special occasion of theirs. But my dancers performed well, and were applauded and thanked. They didn't mind; and were ready to appear at the Scots Kirk Fete when the minister invited my 'troupe' to perform. We had to perform in white shirts and trousers and gym shoes, with the girls in white blouses and dirndl skirts. The effort was well received, especially because the British Commander of the Pakistan Navy boys' training ship had lent us his chief piper and drummer, who made all the difference. I knew we could go further if my dancers would accept discipline and hard practice.

I also knew that to get anywhere with performances, we would have to be properly dressed in kilts and sashes. As a start I got six sashes from Jenners in Edinburgh. Robert Sutherland, a beautiful dancer had his kilt and I mine. We needed four more. The Royal Scottish Country Dance Society H.Q. suggested we borrow from the nearest Highland regiment but this was in Hong Kong! On 9 August the Gymkhana Committee invited us to perform at their Pakistan Day dinner on 14 August. I accepted regardless.

I telephoned Joan Cranmore (see Hungary), who was now in our Glasgow office. She immediately hired six kilts and sporrans from Bambers, had them packed up and handed to the Council driver and driven to Renfrew Airport before Bambers fully realised where they were destined. Then she got them on to a B.O.A.C. freight 'plane leaving at 21.00 hrs. I was horrified to learn on 12 August that the kilts were lodged in Customs. However, on the Sunday morning I was in the Chief Collector's house while he shaved, until he let me take delivery of the kilts, ek dum (at once), from the air-freight strong-room under armed guard, and not to have to wait the usual six weeks. George Bartlett meanwhile had had six pairs of red flashes made in the bazaar; and had negotiated a regular engagement for us with the Police Pipe Band.

We emerged from the trees at the back of the lawn in national dress behind our piper and advanced through the audience into the floodlit dance space beyond. Now the Reel Club came into being, with a president, secretary, treasurer, and committee. I was happy to teach and just to hold membership card no. 1. One of my ambitions had been achieved.

The Commander R.N. who had seen our Scots Kirk effort invited us to dance on the floodlit naval parade ground inside a circle of several hundred cadets. At our performance, on the British Council roof, we had an audience of over 150 Pakistanis and Parsees. After that there was S.C.D. on the Council roof one evening a week: for Parsee lads and lassies and Pakistani lads. The Parsees are a fascinating people originating from Persia, fully integrated into the sub-Continent. They are westernised, very intelligent, extremely capable, brilliant at business, and the women, who are not in purdah, are most attractive.

Commander R.N. then told me he wanted the next Passing Out Parade of cadets to be something special and worth-while. Would I teach them to Scottish dance? I was given thirty-two cadets, over whom I would have complete control so we could try a 'thirty-twosome'! I only knew how to do a Sixteensome, but dear Jean Milligan, Queen Bee of the Royal Scottish Country Dance Society, sent me the details on an air-letter.

This was the hardest task I ever had. I almost came to dread the launch that fetched me across the creek to the naval parade ground. The tarmac and I melted together as I bashed those cadets. Perhaps they dreaded the launch too. At first the complicated evolutions for thirty-two exactly synchronized dancers was a headache to them all. They were not familiar with counting bars of Western music either. But we were all saved because pipe music was native to them – more so than to most British reelers – and they were perfectly disciplined and motivated to be a success, for the sake of their careers.

There was another evening in the week for my dance class at the Karachi Grammar School where I had begun in school time as a visiting teacher of English. So, from February to June, Roger and I were hard at it.

The most enjoyable development was our ability to form an Argyll Broadswords team of four. Some good talent was at hand when approached. Charlie Bennett, who had been at Bradfield with me, was Chartered Bank and a beautiful dancer. When we could persuade him, he would perform the solo sword-dance, Gillie Callum, which was a rare treat. He had been a member of the team in prison camp that had produced the attractive and popular reel of the 51st Division. We got ourselves into sufficient trim to sword-dance at the drop of a hat with the support of the two Punjabi Police Pipers. For instance, when H.M.S. Mauritius returned, we danced at the Union Jack Club.

The Anglo-Indians, the 'Loco', and the S.C.D.

The backbone of the British railways of India were the Anglo-Indians who, luckily for the system, provided reliable, responsible staffs from engine-drivers upwards. They were admirable people, absolutely loyal to 'the old country', conscientious and more patriotic than the British. They desperately wanted to be British, but neither the British nor the Indians (or Pakistanis) would accept them as such. They were not admitted to our clubs.

Early on in the days of the British Raj many Anglo-Indian families originated from the union of certain Indian girls with rather basic British tommies. The results unfortunately produced men with an inferiority complex, a lack of assurance and independence of thought and hesitant reactions to situations. I don't know why, but the dear people spoke with a sing-song 'Welsh' accent. I shall never forget one Anglo-Indian comment as we celebrated Shakespeare and St George on 23 April 1950: "Shakespeare. Immortal bloody words, that man. Isn't it?".

The Karachi Anglo-Indians were based at the North-Western Railway Club nicknamed 'The Loco' and its 'Hall Institute'.[8] The members of the Hall Institute with their families were nearly all employees of the North-Western Railway, which was one of the most efficient bodies in Pakistan.

It was George Bartlett, our Reel Club secretary, who found out that we'd be welcome to hold S.C.D. sessions at the Hall Institute. We responded at once, and the results remain with me as some of the happiest memories of Karachi.

Whenever we went there we found the members' hospitality terrific. Both the Goans, another Karachi community, and the Anglo-Indians were adept at Western music and loved ball-room dancing.

Monday evenings were one slot in the Institute's programme. Volunteers trickled along. We were allowed to put on a demonstration at the Loco's Easter Dance, and unknown to most of the crowd who watched, we produced an Institute team dancing on their own. All who came along, young and older men and women were a joy to teach. They had an enviable natural rhythm and could pick up dances quicker than the Wednesday nighters at the Gymkhana.

The young Anglo-Indian girls can be beautiful. I shall never forget my favourite, Sadie Taylor. She was about fourteen, with a very sweet nature and a lovely face – no figure yet. But she danced divinely in a reel set, or a sinuous solo hula in her little kilt, to such tunes as 'My hula love', 'My

---

[8] John Masters in *Bhowani Junction* (Michael Joseph) captures perfectly the spirit of the Anglo-Indians, their railway connection, and their community life.

happiness' and 'Ever and Ever'. I was bowled flat; Roger and I kept strictly to dancing. Earlier on I had had a letter from my Australian uncle, Hubert, who said "Your Aunt Mossie warns you to be careful of the Anglo-Indian girls who could snare you into matrimony." Older girls very soon lost their early figures, and mothers alas went to fat. We managed to have some of the Hall boys and girls to a party at Bath Island House, with Reel Club support. This was quite an achievement considering their shyness with us. We all had a perfectly straight-forward, good time.

I felt very sorry indeed for the Anglo-Indians after Partition. They were having a rough time. They had held an established position in society before. Now they were despised by the Pakistanis to whom, of course, they lost their jobs. Their only way out, if they had to remain in the country, was to be Pakistani, and to not try to be British, or to emigrate, as many did and by marriage if possible. One of our group asked an Anglo-Indian girl out to a dance, but she was too nervous to turn up. When he went to her home, he found the entire family living and sleeping in one room: such were the straits to which they were reduced.

A dancing match

Thanks to Brigadier Block, British military advisor, an exciting dancing match was fixed for the Reel Club versus the Baluch Regiment out at Malir Cantt. They would perform a dance of the Khattaks, a North-West Frontier people. We would do the Argyll Broadswords. I was put in charge of publicity and invitations.

The Baluch Pipe Band beat the Retreat at 6.30 p.m. and then 400 officially invited spectators were conducted to an enclosure in front of the Officers' Mess, and plied with whisky and curry puffs. It was a magnificent effort.

It was now dark, and we walked back to our seats repositioned into a huge circle. In the middle was an imitation bonfire onto which shone a red search-light, and round it was marked out a wide, white circle.

There was a hush and from far away came the sound of pipes and drums. In came at a smart march a little Baluch band: a leader, two men on double-ended drums, and two playing short, trumpet-ended pipes sounding like the Indian shenai. They wore dark-green shirts (qameez) and pantaloons (shalwar), with red sashes round their waists, and gym shoes.

Their entry tune was their arrangement of 'The British Grenadiers'. Behind them came twenty huge, swarthy Baluchis, and each had a red handkerchief in each hand. The dancers moved into the big circle round the bonfire; and moved to whistle blasts from the leader, slowly bounding and crouching and twisting, round in circles. They held their arms high and fluttered their red handkerchiefs, circling as gracefully as ballet dancers. Gradually the tempo of the music increased, and they leaped and spun with greater violence. They moved perfectly together, but each man seemed proud to show off his own agility and control, and would sometimes utter a highlander's cry as he rose into the air, and sank with perfect balance onto his haunches. We were spell-bound by the power and magnificence of these men until suddenly the lights went up and the men swiftly reformed into parade order. They marched off at the fast rifleman's pace, their heads held high, and with fearsome grins. Then came the sword dancers, to a faster tune, 'The Wearing of the Green'. Each man had two sabres crossed behind his neck. The dancers all moved together with a step, hop, spin, and crouch. Their gyrations became faster and more violent, encouraged by the musicians who followed them round with cries and sudden rapid, rising drum-beats. Then they melted away into the darkness.

Suddenly, four more swordsmen appeared with a bound and a cry. In pairs they leaped and twisted with incredible speed. They whirled their sabres round their heads and bodies so fast that the paths of the blades became a blur. Each man in turn leaped forward almost into the middle of the musicians, who like us were now beside themselves with excitement. Each man seemed to outshine the one before, in his dazzling, almost terrifying display. The leader himself came last, and his performance had us rising out of our seats with amazement and delight, sometimes gripping our chair arms for fear he would cut his own head off. The children sat without a sound. I think it was almost too much for them.

Our turn came. We felt small and tame but we marched on proudly with our glittering swords at the carry. We saluted our hosts and each other and placed our swords down in the form of a cross. We danced over them to strathspey and then reel; bent and picked them up; saluted again and marched off. A dancing match? A dance-over for the Baluchis. But never would we dance in such an authentic scene again.

The joys of Karachi – a Royal Naval visit

H.M.S. Mauritius arrived on a courtesy call with the Admiral of the Eastern Fleet on board with his family. There were parties galore for the officers, lavish entertainments for the matelots. I was horrified to be entrusted with passes to issue to any 'nice girls' whom I could recommend for a Y.M.C.A. dance.

The next afternoon, Saturday, we saw a rugger match versus Gymkhana on the mudflat ground behind our house, hard falling and slippery. There was a good gathering of supporters with their cars disgorging wives, girlfriends, dogs and children, all together in the slanting sunlight. A very English atmosphere. The tweed caps and skirts, and shooting-sticks seemed most incongruous. The Gymkhana won. Roger and I later sank almost without trace, celebrating after I found two of my former Bradfield commandos in the ship's company!

On Sunday morning at the dock I sent my card up to the Officer of the Watch. A tolerant C.P.O. showed us all over the ship and gave us char and wads in his mess. Next day he and the C.P.O. chief cook came to dinner. It was great to meet such men, but we hadn't allowed for how much they would eat and drink.

A moonlight picnic

We found beauty in the day-time in Karachi. The palm trees against the sky and their delicate rustle in the wind; the reds and whites of the Makrani fisherwomen's clothing against the yellow sand. There was blue water and the lighter blue of the dhow hulls gliding across the harbour under their raked sails. The desert cast a strong spell – at sunrise and at sunset; and more powerfully on clear nights with the stars so near, and a brilliant moon. Well, let's have a moonlight picnic, we thought. We had the ingredients: the moon and a calm night; all the available girls in Karachi and their boy-friends. A recce in the desert – to a water-filled, rocky quarry in a new direction; Mohammed to lead out in daylight a donkey man and cartload of firewood; a New Zealand girl to cook; and a Russian to play and sing (Prince George Galitzine); hurricane-lamps, rugs, etc. It was unforgettable: a huge Eastern moon and bright stars, little wind, good company, food and drink, firelight and music with jackals calling in the distance. I had no Panzer enemy to face in the desert dawn ever again.

A stolen home break

As I had been in Pakistan for a year, I was allowed some local leave to get to know more of the country. But I decided to fly home for Christmas at my own expense as I was getting around Pakistan all right. I enjoyed a wonderful Christmas in Edinburgh.

I had to visit Bradfield. I had not lost my talent. I had a sheet of comic songs produced, and was introduced by John Hills in my former capacity as the Explosives Master! At the end of the songs I said loudly, "I shan't need this any more," and I threw the sheet into the fire behind. There followed in a split second, a fairly blinding flash and a loud explosion. I took no notice, but the Bursar had kittens. I now felt I would be safer in Karachi!

The secret? The Chief Constable's Office in Reading produced on loan a .45 revolver and a few blanks. My song-sheet was double with magnesium powder in between. The explosion was created by a boy hidden behind the piano who fired the revolver.

My leave luck continued. A twenty-four-hour take-off delay enabled me to reel in London. Then en route a flock of birds over the Mediterranean cracked the pilot's perspex windscreen, and we had to jettison fuel and put back to Rome. At the airport was the only man I knew in Rome, Colonel Colwill, former M.A. Budapest. A good-free-time was provided! Happily we would meet again – twice more. This *is* hindsight!

Wild pig of the lower Indus

One hundred miles up from the mouth of the Indus[9] lay the large village of Tatta. Ten miles up the west bank were three bungalows of the P.W.D., built of yellow stone on an outcrop of rock above the muddy jungle of the riverside, looking west over scrub and desert. Six of us hired the largest bungalow for the week-end as our base from which to shoot pig. It was an easy two and a half hour-drive. But the last three miles were on the finest slippery powdered sand along the edge of a deep canal. We could only see safely by keeping a hundred yards apart.

It was early spring and the weather only a slightly hotter than a hot English summer. The desert dawns and dusks had their special charm at Luka. At night it was cold enough for fires, sweaters, and heavy bedding.

The 'sportsmen' all had double-barrelled 12-bores, first with No. 5 shot, but later for pig with S.G. or buckshot. It was too dangerous to use rifles.

An early morning chukka with ten locally-recruited beaters, produced three out of four partridges. Even these had to be halal-ed (throats cut) under Muslim law. We returned to the bungalow at 8.30 a.m. for breakfast. At 9 a.m. the Zamindar, the land-owner, arrived in a three-ton truck, dressed in a thick khaki suit, at the head of a fearsome-looking eager body of men, armed with ancient, hammer 12-bore doubles. After a consultation, there followed a tortuous, dusty, and shatteringly uncomfortable trip along the top of a powdered-sand embankment track with a twenty-foot drop.

We arrived bruised but unscathed, deep in the jungle where a large crowd had gathered. Here were more armed ruffians with even older

[9] Read Jean Fairlie, *The Lion River* (Allen Lane, 1975).

weapons. One cheerful, old gaffer had a long-barrelled pin-fire as tall as himself. A huge, moustachioed beater carried a triple-bladed, ten-foot spear. He obviously knew how to cope with wild boar. There were about twenty other beaters, some armed with a useful woodsman's narrow-bladed hatchet on a four-foot wooden handle. They could be useful in emergencies I saw, but they were primarily used for building hides quickly.

The most interesting participants were the dogs. Eight or ten, held firmly with ropes round their necks, were in fighting mood. They were all shades of brown to grey and looked rather retriever-like, but their visages were grim and sour, and they had to be kept apart. Their eyes were half-closed, they had bits of ears missing, some had horrible, hairless scars and looked as if they had fought from the day they were born. One old, brown dog allowed itself to be patted – once, but only after the first kill had taken some stuffing out of it. These dogs were essential hunters, and also our protectors when chasing dangerous game in close jungle.

The guns, and camera-man, me, moved off to the first beat: the far side of a cracked-mud bed of a dry stream. Nothing happened until the beaters were giving up, bunching together and the guns coming out of their hides. Suddenly, two shots came from the right, and another from inside the jungle, followed by the noise of men running hastily into the open.

Then from the jungle came the terrifying sounds of mortal struggle: snarls and piercing screams, and the worrying, chopping sounds of merciless dogs. Woodhouse had wounded the boar and an old shikari had hit it harder. It had left an easy blood-trail for Woodhouse to follow to where the dogs luckily held it down. Woodhouse seized my hunting-knife which I had lent his bearer, insinuated himself into the melee, and stabbed the boar to death. None of the regular Muslim beaters would touch the boar, but word was soon sent to others of another sect to come and remove the beast.

The next beat produced an even larger boar than the first, and luckily a dead one after a double fusillade. The transport of this one was simply done because the official cutter-up had arrived by donkey. Fairhurst and Godwin (the assassins this time) managed to drape this very heavy body over his saddle bow, and away he went.

After our fourth move, two smaller pigs and two piglets were shot by shikaris. On the last beat the Zamindar hoped we could shoot a very large and fierce boar that had been troubling the neighbourhood, but the creature had vanished.

Back at the village all the pigs were laid out under a tree, and the cutter-up got to work. He gutted the six pigs expertly and seemed satisfied with Rs 5. We were now feeling the heat and strain, but we managed to cope with the paying-off ceremony and the usual protests and squabbles. In the end all seemed content and melted away.

By 8.30 p.m. we were monopolising the bar of B.O.A.C.'s Speedbird House at Drigh Road Airport for a pause on our way home. We presented a strange contrast to the well-dressed, pale-faced passengers who came in and out. The caterer to our surprise did buy one pig at Rs 1. annas 5 per pound. Its 80 lb weight almost paid for the beaters.

We were delighted to be able to show off to one of our favourite air-hostesses, who said: "Oh I wish I had been on the spot to do some cooking for you". An excellent idea for another time. B.O.A.C., please arrange the right schedules. Air-hostesses were enviable perquisites of Karachi life. They were around for agreeable stop-overs without commitment, then away, suiting both sexes.

Pakistan: East Bengal, May 1950

1950 was the Wordsworth Centenary: and the Aids and Displays Department in London had sent us a very good picture-exhibition and lecture material on the poet. It was easy to set up in Karachi and Begum Liaquat Ali Khan kindly opened our exhibition. Wordsworth is important to students of English literature all over the world, despite their non-comprehension of the Lake District and daffodils. We could at best bring this drear (to some) poet to life to help them to at least gain more pass marks.

It was the Begum who suggested to Bill that we include East Pakistan, and he agreed. I would take Wordsworth and he would tour the province on an educational survey, despite being warned by the Deputy High-Commissioner in Dacca to curtail his tour owing to the heat.

Orient Airways ran a thrice-weekly, round-trip Convair service to Dacca, which meant we had to be at Drigh Road Airport at 3 a.m. Life begins anew at airports. I found I had to take a large Turkish lady under my wing, for she knew no English nor Urdu, and had sat alone at the airport since the morning, and was a puzzle to the police. But she spoke French. After I had got her some water, she explained through me that she was going to Dacca to get married, which satisfied authority. She sat with me all the way. "This is your safety belt," I explained and later informed her: "No, this is only New Delhi".

I had a marvellous view eastwards, roughly on the line of the Ganges below the fabulous, beautiful, shining, white Himalayas, but I was unable to see Everest. The Bengal landscape was a marked contrast to Sind: instead of monotonous, brown fields there were patches of green, and great waters flowing south. Habitation consisted of small groups of huts and a tree or two perched on mounds, every mile or so. It was very hot and damp. The air was full of steamy clouds and we bounced like the lid of a boiling pan.

On the ground, my exhibition cases were safe, and we were in good hands: Bill would stay with his old friend, Feroz Khan Noon, Governor of East Bengal; and I would stay with Mr L. G. Coke-Wallis, Deputy High-Commissioner.

I was driven straight to lunch to meet him. I had never seen such a profusion of trees and plants and flowers before. The drive from Tejgaon airfield was under an avenue of blazing gul mohr trees. The trees seemed to be on fire. Avoiding the city, the driver took me to Ramna the very attractive, park-like, tree-filled residential area with spacious homes grouped round the maidan.

This part was laid out in 1905 by a Kew Gardens' expert under the direction of the Viceroy, Lord Curzon. Curzon planned to divide Bengal, having Calcutta as India's capital, and Dacca as the provincial one. But the concept was revoked in 1911, and Dacca had to wait until 1947 to achieve capital status. But Partition caused an influx of population far exceeding the most far-seeing early estimates of growth. East Bengal in 1950 contained two-thirds of the whole population of Pakistan.

My stay in Dacca was a perfect example of how work and play were indistinguishable in my British Council life. I couldn't have seen Dacca under more advantageous circumstances. Mr Coke-Wallis's family was in England, so he most kindly gave up time to me, and from his years in India he taught me much.

Dacca was so hot and sticky in summer that activity was limited. It got hot by about 8 a.m., the time for a quiet crawl to the office, hard work under a fan, a return crawl for tiffin (lunch), then a zizz, another crawl at 3 p.m. till about 5 p.m. Then it was possible to play tennis or golf. My 'crawl' was a drive with Coke-Wallis behind a Union Jack in his Humber Pullman.

The High Commission staff were very kind to me, and Frank Mills gave me a desk in his office, every facility I needed, and answers to questions. I received a ticket to a British Citizens' Association musical evening organised by Frank. "Frank, who is that very pretty girl on the sofa, the only one worth looking at?" "She is my secretary. She'll be in the office tomorrow, and will help you all she can." I found another kindred spirit attached to the H.C. in Walter Purcell, a Gurkha major, installed as military A.D.C. in a stone bungalow in the park.

The view from Mr Coke-Wallis's house was like looking across an English park, especially because in the middle of the maidan was a clump of trees with a Hindu temple with a spire, looking very like a parish church attached to the great house. The Dacca Club nearby was homely and well-appointed with tennis, swimming, and golf, and the race course beyond. There were no restaurants in Dacca, so an evening out had to be at the Club, which was very pleasant. Unfortunately, the Club was not yet open to every one; not, for instance, to Europeans of clerical or administrative status. Monstrous!

I was given temporary membership of the Club, which entitled me to three books of drink tickets, so I could repay some of the generous hospitality. I attended a reception given by Feroz Khan Noon and Begum Noon, and was thus very lucky to meet nearly everyone of importance in Dacca and district. It was useful to obtain authoritative views on East Bengal, the last outpost against eastern Communism. I was keen to learn how the British Council might help the province overcome the feeling of neglect, brought about by the great distances involved in reaching her, and the difficulties of communications and transport.

We were out to make personal contacts for the first time with the vast student body of Dacca University. All we could do was to contact the colleges in Dacca, while there were fifty-six other colleges scattered throughout the province.

The reason why most men were living in Dacca was jute, and I was given time off to have a look at this industry. I set out for Narayanganj, some ten miles away and had a frightening taxi-ride. Somehow we avoided crowds of uncaring pedestrians and ungovernable cycle-rickshaws. I had a good geography lesson as a start: how the great rivers run; how the people lived mainly on the water; and how jute was produced.

I learned a little about jute, and admired all the Scotsmen in it, and the tough life they led. Narayanganj had a flourishing Scottish colony and a serious St Andrew's Society. Dacca is famous for its muslin.

In Dacca again, I was priviledged to meet the Governor, Feroz Khan Noon. He confirmed my view that Pakistan was desperately short of technicians, woefully short of clerks, and "men who sit in little cubby-holes and do the heavy, humdrum, grinding office-work," which the Hindu babus made their preserve. He said he had recently taxed Liaquat Ali Khan on the latter point, and he had replied, "We don't breed that type of man". "I told him that they would have to," replied the Governor. I also met a British architect who was working on the 'new Dacca' housing-estate. He was distressed that the authorities would not listen to, or check on, the specifications which he insisted upon. "Foundation depths were only down to half." I was glad to be working on my own terms.

Wordsworth Week was greeted by many smiles in the High Commission. I was known as Mr Wordsworth because the local Press had reported my arrival as such! Thanks to Ronnie George, the Information Officer, Wordsworth was given many columns during the week in the *Morning*

Pakistan

Quaid-i-Azam Mohammad Ali Jinnah and the
Hon'ble Mr. Liaquat Ali Khan

**OUR
GREAT
LEADER**

A TRIBUTE BY THE HON'BLE
MR. LIAQUAT ALI KHAN, PRIME
MINISTER OF PAKISTAN

" . . . . on this memorable occasion* I am reminded of the father of our nation and the founder of our freedom, our Great Leader, our Quaid-i-Azam, Mohammed Ali Jinnah, of revered memory, without whose vision, determination and burning honesty Pakistan might have remained a vague longing and a distant dream, and the reality, of which my humble presence in your august company today is but a symbol, might never have been born. A sincere patriot, a passionate follower of the democratic idea, and a man who saw farther and more clearly than his fellows, he led the Muslims of British India out of their perplexities and frustrations into the open air of freedom, and gave shape, significance and direction to their quest for liberty. All his life he fought for freedom but since he fought for the substance and not for the shadow, for

Pakistan Quarterly, Winter 1950–51, featuring two brave, dedicated, remarkable men, on whom the creation and early viability of Pakistan depended: the one alas died in September 1948, and the other was foully murdered in October 1951.

News and *Pakistan Gazette*. I was given ten minutes on air by Radio Pakistan, and my talk was printed in full in the Press the next day. Nothing quite like our efforts of exhibition, lectures, discussions, recordings, etc. had ever happened in Dacca before. I was welcomed by the University, and a good deal of notice was taken outside also. I was so pleased.

When I found that I needed acres of table-covering for the exhibition in the University Hall, Walter Purcell introduced me to Mrs Blair, house-

71

keeper at Government House, who produced her whole stock of dust-sheets. In the University I was heartened to find Miss Stock, Professor of English, who was obviously a splendid influence. She lived under primitive conditions, suffered much discomfort from the climate and lack of amenities, yet she chose to take on much extra work because of the staff shortage.

I lectured to the students in the echoing Salimullah Muslim Hall. Lumbered as they were with Wordsworth, they were very polite. Humour was luckily introduced by the piercing "uckee! uckee!" of a gekko, which stopped me in mid-speech.

I had three amusing evenings with Miss Stock and her students. Once we had a discussion on the value of poetry, and I cited Lord Wavell as an example of a great man who found inspiration in poetry. I told them about his *Other Men's Flowers*. Some students recited their translations of Wordsworth's poems into Bengali; I found it a musical language.

Another evening was devoted to listening to a programme of music and Wordsworth's poetry on records,[10] which they enjoyed, as had the Kinnaird College girls in Lahore. Encouraged by this, I arranged for Radio Pakistan (Dacca) to have some Benjamin Britten records; and I sent them selections from recordings of *The Rape of Lucretia* and *Peter Grimes*. I had a good response.

On the third evening, Miss Stock and I judged the Wordsworth Recitation Competition for colleges. There were plenty of entries, but not much idea of the meaning of the words or enthusiasm for the poems qua poems. It was the same old story, as Miss Stock said, "Too much dissecting for examination questions, and no time for the spirit".

I was invited to dinner at Government House, and was asked to take Wordsworth with me. Government House was a huge, half-timbered bungalow built by Curzon as a temporary home while building in stone. When it was completed, the great pile was found impossible to live in but served admirably as the Law Courts. Lady Noon was European and a charming hostess. Among the guests was Dr Allinson, doctor cum surgeon for Dacca. He was a most amusing man whom I had been lucky to see quite a bit of. He had been through a great deal as a prisoner of war in Burma. I put on the recital after dinner for the ninth time.

After the trees and flowers of Bengal, there were the people: all three being absorbed into the landscape. But the people numbered millions. After Partition, just three years before, the town of Dacca with its narrow streets and little proper sanitation became dreadfully overcrowded. Thousands of miserable refugees lay about the railway stations and

---

[10] I played them Vaughan Williams' *Greensleeves Fantasia*, Purcell's *Fairy Queen Dances*, Fould's *Keltic Lament*, and Handel's *Berenice Minuet*.

streets. Dacca had become intensely smelly and disagreeable.

I spoke one night to the President of the Chittagong Chamber of Commerce, who had known for twenty years the problems of over-population. He could see no hope for the establishment of birth control, or for the solution to the problem of settlement on the land. The million or so casualties during the Partition movements and riots had not made a scrap of difference to the economic structure of the sub-Continent since there were so many people left.

One of the amusing sights in Dacca was the Bengali. I was tickled by the solemn procession of white, dhoti-garbed figures strolling very slowly down the street carrying open, black umbrellas against the sun. Some umbrellas were so old as to have the green sheen of well-worn academic robes. The bright Bengalis are a definite acquisition for the economy of Pakistan. They have their own problems, being so many per square inch. I heard good reports too of Bengali Muslim students' bravery at Partition in protecting the lives and property of many of their Hindu teachers. One evening a sub-editor of the *Calcutta Statesman* sang an amusing song with a chorus of well-known Bengali names: "The Hoshis, Ghoshis, Mukherjees, Bannerjees, Dhuts, and Mehtas too!"

On the two Sundays I was in Dacca there was very heartening, evening church-going for many of us. The Revd Davies, M.B.E., Baptist Minister, did duty for all denominations. He was a tower of strength in Dacca. He did great work during the war when the Dacca and Comilla region were important supply areas for the Burma army.

From Coke-Wallis's verandah I heard many new bird-calls. They are the most vivid memories which remain. There was the Koel, and the lovely 'tonk, tonk' of the coppersmith bird. I also made the acquaintance of the 'jungle babbler'. These are lively, little birds always to be found in groups of seven, hence they came to be called the satbhai (seven siblings or usually translated as the seven sisters). To quote E. H. Aitken: "They are too shrewd and knowing to be made fun of. Among themselves they will quarrel by the hour; but let a stranger (such as a mongoose) treat one of their number with disrespect, and the other six are in arms at once."[11]

Pakistan: The Punjab and the North-West Frontier Province, 1950 era

The Pakistan Mail left Karachi Central at 7 p.m. every evening and reached Lahore twenty-four hours later. An air-conditioned, Pakistan railway

[11] Aitken, p. 56.

journey was a real pleasure. At every tiny halt there were spruce, uniformed men at attention with their flags, proud to be in such a responsible job. The porters, with their red shirts and turbans and their shining, brass number-plates, crouched in a long, orderly line on the platforms as the trains came in. They were eager and efficient, I was astonished at the number of pieces of luggage they could balance on their heads. Platforms seethed with all manner of folk at every station. One was tackled by a procession of beggars; but there was always time for a stretch, a smoke, or a chat with one's neighbour. There were no corridors. Every time one opened the compartment door, flies swarmed in, and had to be slain when the journey was resumed. Good curry meals were served in the dining-car. Bearers would bring tea, or whatever, to one's compartment at any stop at any time. Water would be carried along by pani-wallahs and proffered in little, throw-away, earthenware cups.

In Lahore I went to Faletti's Hotel and liked the atmosphere at once. It was situated in its own grounds with a central, bungalow section and wide verandahs in front of the suites of rooms. It was like being back in an Oxford College, except that the rooms were very high with a fan in the ceiling and the doors had wire-mesh. The architecture reflected the winter-summer differences of climate up here and made a lovely change from Karachi, but lacked the sea-breeze in summer. Alas, the Punjab was now dry, and life at Faletti's was dead. The fine bar, grill room, dance floor had all gone to waste. The Hungarian manager was disconsolate. I applied for a permit to possess and consume foreign liquor.

In my time, Lahore was an ancient and dignified city in which one felt a sense of ease and spaciousness, a green city in which grass, trees, and flowers abounded. The entire land of the Punjab round Lahore was fertile and prosperous: from the fruit farms of Okara to the large holdings of Montgomery. Lahore had wide roads with clean, red pavements and huge, shady trees. The residential area had the canal running through it; sharp cut banks and old stone bridges. The fine residences and bungalows had large gardens. It was a good sight to watch the race-horses having their morning dip near the Mall Bridge.

The Mall ran from the old city through the European shopping-centre and five miles on to the cantonment. I went straight to one fine, old building which contained the offices of *The Civil and Military Gazette*. On the wall of the back verandah was a dull, copper plate with embossed lettering, saying: "Rudyard Kipling worked here from 1882–1887". Thanks to Mr Vanter, assistant editor, I sat in what was thought to have been Kipling's office, and wrote a short piece for the paper.

Beside the Mall stood a formerly reviled statue of Queen Victoria. Now her days are seen in true perspective, and the old Queen-Empress is again an object of veneration. Her statue was not removed for the visit of the

Shah of Persia, but cleaned and renovated. Having been brought up with cannons, I hurried on to near the museum where Kipling's father was curator, to inspect 'Kim's Gun' Zam-Zammah. No wonder Kim loved her. "Zam-Zammah, 6372 miles from London," as a sign said. The gun had a "shining, decorated, brass barrel, 12' long, 3 sets ornate lifting handles: bore 12" muzzle 5' from ground, barrel supported between two very large, brass-bound wheels, with a single centre wheel in the trail." The brass plate on the front of the carriage says: "Zam-Zammah or Bhaginn-Wali Top, made in Lahore 1761 A.D. or 1174 A.H." I was told it was used in the Sikh War. The Moghuls and their power and influence are fascinating.[12]

One of my favourite Moghul buildings is Jahangir's tomb in Lahore. The low, rectangular building has four, beautifully proportioned, short minarets, and wide steps up to the tomb chamber. There is a mosque nearby, and both buildings are enclosed by a high solid old wall of dark, yellow-grey stones, with living quarters in it nearly all the way round. Aurangzeb, the last famous Moghul, was the son of Mumtaz and ruled from 1658–1707. He had a daughter called Zeb-ul-Nissa.

I quote a description of her:

> Zeb-ul-Nissa, the talented daughter of Aurangzeb, used to sit in this marble pavilion (in Shalimar Gardens) and enjoy the scene of the waterfall. Here in her shady retreats, surrounded by the Royal Princesses, and attended by a host of damsels all in the bloom of youth, she composed her sweet and charming odes; the lovely scenery and the beauties of nature all round being specially adapted to her vivid imagination and poetic genius. Here the ladies of the King's Harem walked free and independent. Here the songs of the northern lands of the Punjab, of the hills of Kashmir and the Vale of Kabul, were sung by the female attendants, and country dances held to amuse the Royal visitors.

Another beauty was Anarkali (Pomegranate Blossom) one of the favourites of Akbar's Harem. One day the Emperor saw in a mirror that she smiled at Prince Selim (Jahangir), and ordered her to be buried alive, which she was, upright. Jahangir later had her placed in a huge tomb in a beautiful, marble sarcophagus inscribed with the ninety-nine attributes of God and a Persian couplet composed by Jahangir:

> Ah, could I behold the face of my beloved once more, I would give thanks unto my God until the day of resurrection.

[12] Bamber Gascoigne, *The Great Moghuls*. (Johnathan Cape, 1971).

Akbar's suspicions had been right!

There was one Moghul Emperor after Aurangzeb: Bahadar Shah Zafar. He was not a 'Great Moghul' and was exiled to Rangoon in 1857. Lord Wavell could never remember the names and order of the great Moghuls, except by this mnemonic: "Best Horses and Jockeys Seen Ascot." (Babur, Homayun, Akbar, Jahangir, Shah Jahan, Aurangzeb).

I was in Lahore thanks to Wordsworth, and here I found understanding and co-operative bodies in Forman Christian College, Government College, and Lady Kinnaird College for Women. All had lovely buildings with excellent facilities and enthusiastic staffs. At Kinnaird I was ushered into a large, light, and airy, but empty hall. Within a few moments in filed sixty lovely young ladies in white shalwar and long, close-fitting, patterned qameez, with flimsy muslin dopattas over the head and shoulders. They sat down gracefully and demurely on the clean coir-matting. I had dreamed of Zeb-ul-Nissa's Court, and here they were. Pakistani women really are beautiful, with a special poise and refinement about them which gives them an extra essence of femininity. From now on there was a general aim among families to abandon purdah. The girls particularly enjoyed a programme of Wordsworth's poetry and music, and asked for more music – which Sandy Ross was able to provide.

I met with great kindness at Government College. The young professor of English, Dr Ashraf Ali Khan, bore down upon me with a flapping gown and a broad smile of welcome. He organised a bearer party of students and appointed Talat Farouk as my assistant. I lunched with the principal, Siraj-uddin, his beautiful wife, and his sister-in-law. We had lots to say about Oxford days. Here in Lahore were people who mattered and had vision. I am glad they were in the teaching profession.

Talak Farouk suggested I go to the art exhibition which was showing the work of Chugtai, a leading Pakistani painter of his day. Roger and I were impressed. His draughtsmanship was exquisite, reminding me of Aubrey Beardesley (without his darker side) in a neo-Persian style. We also saw high-quality photographs of very fine pottery, brass-work, silks and cottons, woodwork, silverware, and the like. We did our best then, and later, to disseminate the latest British design magazines.

Lahore Gymkhana, to which we repaired, was a very fine, Sandhurst-like building in a park with ornamental gardens. There was space for every sort of sport and indoor occupation, and it had a vast, ornate ballroom. In this I attended a Lahore Reel Club session. In the course of time they asked me to teach them a new dance or two. They taught me a 'modern' reel.

Another day I was luckily invited to the Gym on a dance night. It was tough going. I had never seen so much whisky on view before. There was a profusion of lovely Pakistani girls dancing with officers in blues, imparting a martial atmosphere. This was not surprising since some of the best soldiers in the world come from the Punjab, and there was war in the air. One of the legacies of the British in India was the army. There were still British serving officers on both sides of the frontier, and the thought of them having to fight each other did arise. But on the North-West Frontier, the Pakistan army was permanently on active service, just as the British army had been before them.

Another Gym member of twenty-three years service out there told me that the canal system was the best legacy of the British. Their extension was still going on to transform more barren wastes. Unfortunately, the source of all the water was in Kashmir where the great rivers rose, and the big barrage on the Ravi, nearest to Lahore was at Jogindernager in India.[13] In 1948 India cut the water off and gave the Pakistanis a taste of what enmity might bring about.

British gifts to the sub-continent were the railways and roads. The British way of life was on offer, with its sense of proportion, sense of civic duty, and of one man to another, a belief in honesty and in public service, ideas of fair play, uncorruptible justice, and of a fair deal for the little man. Now I learned how our apartness and colour-bar were hurtful and resented, but cricket was embraced. Some of our attitudes, behaviour, and customs were never understood.[14]

Rudyard Kipling at the age of seventeen became a member of the Punjab Club known as The Pig; and he enjoyed it greatly. This Club was another huge building, full of interesting portraits and relics of the Raj, with dark, panelled walls covered with mildewed *Spy* caricatures. Kipling wrote:

> . . . and in that club and elsewhere I met none except picked men at their definite work. Civilians, Army, Education, Canals, Forestry, Engineering, Irrigation, Railways, Doctors and Lawyers – samples of each branch and each talking his own shop. It follows then that that show of technical knowledge for which I was blamed later, came to me from the horse's mouth, even to boredom.

That is a pretty good list of the many ways in which we served India. I can now add 'the English Language' – and I was cheered to learn of a ministerial statement announcing that it was the intention of the Pakistani Government to retain British influence in education. The Punjab Club

[13] See below, p. 494. 19 July 1974 – Good news.
[14] Do read *Punjabi Century* by Prakesh Tandon, an account of family life in India from 1847–1947, under the British. In Book List.

rules were still very exclusive and reactionary by 1950. I felt it had nearly had its day.

From such thoughts I went back to Mr Vanter of the C. & M. G. with a special request that I might be allowed access to its archives. He led me to a corner of the compound walls in which was built a small shed. It was very dusty inside, but there to my great delight, were the tall, dirty, leather-bound tomes of back-numbers. I found a volume dated 1887 in which there were editions containing *Plain Tales from the Hills*. I was most excited, but I could understand how these tales in printed columns would not have impinged much upon the European readers of the time.

To the North-West Frontier: A memorable local leave.

Sandy Ross, our congenial Regional Representative in Lahore, had to drive to Peshawar to select scholars, so he kindly took Roger and me with him. We set off up the Grand Trunk Road which runs from Calcutta to Peshawar. It was a lovely morning for the drive: the countryside glistening after heavy rain and the air temperature was perfect. We crossed the Ravi, one of the Punjab (Five Rivers), which looked small, but we could see how far apart were the monsoon bunds (embankments).

Everyone seemed oblivious to noise. Pedestrians dreamt their jay-walking way along, or diagonally across, the road and seemed oblivious to cars. A hoot might register, but there was a long, delayed reaction. Motorists were slap-dash, and drove pressing their horns all the time. Cyclists were dreamers too and had little control or sense of balance. Four-wheeled gharris, two-wheeled tongas, three-wheeled cycle-rickshaws, all laden with bodies or baggages, filled every piece of road. And everyone had a horn or a bell to blow or ring constantly.

We saw many lovely birds out in the country: the blue jays (or Oxford and Cambridge bird); two kinds of kingfisher, and many busy green parrots. Another was the dark, graceful drongo with its long, forked tail. And there were always kites or vultures about, circling under perfect control with motionless wings, the tips of which were like feathery hands with a strip of white across them.

We passed through Gujranwallah near the site of a battle against the Sikhs. We were slowed by the procession of sugar-cane-laden bullock and buffalo carts on their way to the factory. The beasts plodded patiently on, pulling great weights of carts. The wooden wheel-rims alone were nearly a foot deep, and there were no axle-end bearings. The wheels were fixed on to the axle ends, and it is the axle which turned. From the Grand Trunk Road we could see the extent of the canal system and the huge amounts of controlled water compared to the size of the rivers.

After Wazirabad we had our first sight of the hills. Then we crossed the Chenab with its chocolate-coloured water, and stacks of railway sleepers on the banks, made from timber floated down.

Once we had reached Flashman's Hotel at Rawalpindi we had driven 170 miles. Prohibition had killed hotel life, which made this very agreeable retreat a sad one. We walked through the bazaar to the town's edge and saw the heartening sight of the snowy peaks of the Pir Panjal. In the evening all we could do was go to the cinema. Somerset Maugham's *Quartet* was on. Maugham was singularly popular with foreign students of English, they seemed to have no difficulty in understanding him. A real tribute.

After Rawalpindi, which was formerly a great military centre, we pushed on to Peshawar, just pausing to view the site of Taxila, where Alexander the Great founded a university, and which was near the limit of his brilliant campaigns eastward. We also paused at the little pass in the hills on our way up to the frontier, to read the inscription on the monument to Brigadier General John Nicholson. At the age of thirty-two he had become the conqueror of the Punjab over the Sikhs and he was to die aged thirty-four relieving the siege of Delhi in the mutiny of 1857.

Thence on to Attock where the great Moghul fort guarded the crossing of the spectacular Indus Gorge below the confluence with the Kabul river. Over the bridge we were in the North-West Frontier Province, and in Khattak country, where the dancing Baluchis came from. Nowshera was the next town, the Armoured Corps Centre of Pakistan.

Now we were in the delightfully green, fertile Peshawar Vale. The Grand Trunk Road here was shaded by dense cedars, as it was by trees nearly all its length. We drove by the thick, round, red walls of Peshawar Fort, in which everyone lived before the construction of the cantonment. To enter Peshawar Cantt. one had to pass through 'the wire', the military barrier against tribesmen from the Khyber. The road gates were closed at dark.

Roger took me to view the Khyber from the north edge of the Cantt., and to see his old bungalow, near which a mali had murdered two R.A.F. officers who had sacked him. We could see Afridi country to the north-west, and to the north-east the snows of the Hindu Kush. Movement onwards from Peshawar Fort to Jamrud Fort at the Khyber entrance was across the Kajjuri plain which was a sort of tribal no-man's land. Planted in the middle, and always respected by the tribes, was Islamia College – the public school in which Bill Owain-Jones taught for many years. He loved his tough Pathans who had chosen such a seat of learning. There were still blood feuds among the tribes, but boys at Islamia of different tribes put aside any enmity just for the term-time. If a boy did not return for the next term, he was probably dead.

We went to the Peshawar Club at 7 p.m. It was delightful. Everything was right: the grounds, the buildings, the facilities, and the famous Horseshoe Bar. The English secretary made us welcome – at any time. There was room. During the entire evening there were only six people besides ourselves at the bar, which still functioned in the N.W.F.P. I enjoyed looking at the portraits of all the Masters of the Peshwar Vale Hunt, the last of which was of Lt Col. J.D. Crawford. The Peshawar Vale Hunt was prestigious; it flourished from 1870 to 1946, hunting both the plain and hill jackals.

By happy chance Colonel Hearne, an old Bradfieldian, appeared at the bar. He was helpful in smoothing the way for us to obtain passes to visit the Khyber. He rang up Captain Peter Came of the Khyber Rifles in Landikotal Fort (in the middle of the Pass) to lay on lunch for us. What luck!

Next morning we drove out through the spiked gate across the Kajjuri Plain, which looked flat but was full of hidden wadis. We could see several of the mud forts ahead strung along the foot of the bare, menacing hills. It had always been the policy of the British Government to hold the Khyber from inside, on the hills. At Partition the troops were withdrawn, and as a result the tribes were soon down menacing Peshawar. A big action had to be fought by the Pakistani army to put troops back on to the hills.

Jamrud Fort stood brown, squat, and solid on the right of the road, with only a chain across to mark the entrance to tribal territory. We showed our passes, signed the book, and escaped from the throng of lorry and 'bus passengers, whom we discovered were returning tribesmen. We were careful to keep to the road which was neutral for five yards on either side only. No vehicle was allowed to be on the road after dusk. We were carefully timed in and out, otherwise a search would be sent out, which was reassuring.

The Khyber Pass was neither beautiful nor majestic. It was grim and awe-inspiring within bare, broken, towering rocks. The first section, which was one third of the length and climbing to 3000 ft., was the most imposing of the whole twenty-five miles to the Afghan border. It was quiet now, but we knew enough to realise its grimness, and the sacrifices made to achieve its full purpose. There were forts everywhere: big forts, little forts, block houses on pinnacles, forts with square, steel, corner projections, with narrow rifle-slits leering at one.

Next came Shagai, a huge, rectangular, red-brick fort built 1927–1928 which looked like a prison. It could contain a whole battalion of 800 men. Let into the rock at several points along the road were stone crests of regiments which had served in the Khyber.

Now the road, after running along the river, climbed a little more and twisted again, and the big, stone fort of Landikotal appeared. Further on was a check-point guarded by efficient-looking Kassidars, armed tribes-men in government service but not subject to military law. Here was a breath-taking view for the two miles down to the Afghan border, and up again to the far snow-peaks of Afghanistan.

A voice from a house said: "Good morning". It was the Passport Officer who invited us to join him and his companion, the Customs Officer, on their verandah. 'Passport' said he collected stamps as a hobby, but 'Customs' appeared to do nothing. Actually the word hobby and its connotations seemed to be barely known or understood in the East. Life was too serious a struggle for survival for there to be time or money spent on outside interests. The British in India were always doing something after duty: sport or special interests, which were beneficial to science. And they carried on regardless of climate except in the very hot weather. If only cholera could have been understood and combatted . . .

We motored back to Landikotal up to the outer, steel gates on the perimeter wire, and were halted by a smart M.P. of the Khyber Rifles, wearing a green beret, a grey shirt outside grey, baggy trousers, beautifully polished belt and chaplis (sandals) soled from old motor-tyres. He took my card and in a few minutes we were allowed to drive through even bigger steel gates up to the Mess building. Captain Peter Came met us and took us past single-storey quarters, their roofs forming a platform up to ramparts with loopholes, and on beyond to a yellow-green lawn. The colonel and several officers were sitting together and we were invited to join them.

The colonel said that the people of the province were desperately poor, hungry, and suspicious, having been the victims of conquerors over the centuries. They had very strict ideas of conduct, and could be most hospitable, but there was a rigid line drawn somewhere beyond which it was not possible to go. I asked Peter Came if the job of the Khyber Rifles was a very specialised one, and he said: "No, one must be fit and able to speak Pushto: that's about all". That was modest. Frontier Force officers and Scouts were picked men. They lived a hard life but drew the highest pay in the Indian Army. With nowhere to spend it, their messes were renowned for good living, and for having fine silver and cellars. Peter said that their duties were all police-work.

Of the Frontier units, the Tochi Scouts were as tough as any. Their officers had to move from fort to fort every ten days to draw their full travelling allowance. They rarely lost an officer. Two days after our visit the Tochis fought an action further west at Mir Ali against the infamous Faqir of Ipi, who was a professional trouble-maker and in anybody's pay. The Tochis killed twelve men and had three men wounded.

The doctor at Landikotal, who was present in the circle, said that he was very pleased to find himself almost persona grata with the Maliks (tribal leaders). He had had to cope with an outbreak of typhus; and now the tribes were gaining confidence in medicine, and many persons came in to him. I was glad to hear that the tribes were also becoming interested in education.

Before we left for Peshawar, Roger and I were given the privilege of signing the Visitors' Book, now in its second volume. We saw Wavell's and Auchinleck's signatures twice, first as captains.

Back in Peshawar I was first introduced to carpets by Roger in the Saddar Bazaar in the cantonment, in the rooms of two old acquaintances of his. In the end I bought a little (three-and-a-half feet by two-and-a-half feet) Afghan rug, which survives well. I began to realise the variety and beauty of Bokharas, Kermans, Kashans, etc., and how good rugs can be constantly gazed at in rapture. I was then shown some Kashmir shawls in pashmina wool (from the neck of lambs), with the finest stitching, and a ring shawl so fine that the whole will pass through a finger-ring, but the making of which made children blind. We couldn't visit Kashmir itself. But we took a day off to see the Himalayas. We hired a car to Murree, a hill-station north of Rawalpindi in the attractive, green foothills of the great mountains beyond.

Murree, 159 miles from Kashmir looked like a boom-town after the Gold Rush. It was empty of visitors: hotels and shops were closed, but we got lunch at the highly reputable Sam's. The two big schools survived: St David's for boys and the Convent for girls.

We walked to Kashmir Corner at 7389.92 ft. The air was cool and keen. The pine trees gave off heavy scent, and there were patches of deep snow in shady places. It was silent except for the crows. There was little wind to stir the trees, but there was the faint sound of falling water below us. A troop of brown, furry monkeys crossed our path. We looked up to the horizon and saw the continuous line of the snow-covered Pir Panjal range with swelling cumulus cloud above the 17,000 ft peaks in Kohistan and Muzaffarabad. We could see through to further remote snow-peaks, hoping one was Nanga Parbat (Lady of the Clouds: 26,666 ft.). Up there was the watershed of the rivers of the Punjab, Beas, Ravi, Chenab (also the Jhelum which is not strictly one of the five).

We returned to Karachi, our home for the present. We had plenty of work; and many good friends.

Port Sudan

where cats come in handy

July 1951: A birthday interlude

In Karachi I submitted to Bill Owain-Jones my annual Postings Preference Form, in which I said I wanted a home posting next. He was surprised as he thought I was doing all right. But he agreed to support me when I told him that I wanted to get married, and that I wanted to marry a British girl, possibly a Scot, because according to British Council Regulations marrying a foreigner prejudiced one's transferability. General Slim at a reception in Karachi said he had a wonderful wife who was a Scot, and Scotswomen make wonderful wives. In fact, I found myself posted to Scotland as Director, Edinburgh International House. Was Fate on my side again?

Before I left Karachi at the end of June 1951, I got in for a *bhakshee* (free) party I never forgot. I received an invitation by the agents Messageries Maritime to a reception on the Polish S.S. Batory. The fare was champagne cocktails (one third brandy, two thirds champagne), ham, butter, and cheese on French bread. (I recommend this for many an occasion.)

I embarked on the Anchor Line S.S. Circassia, of 11,000 tons, plying between Liverpool, Karachi and Bombay, with freight and room for 300 one-class passengers. We went to Port Sudan to pick up more cotton. The Circassia had to use the fog-horn in a sand-storm which filled the ship. Port Sudan was a fine, modern port, worked by the fascinating fuzzy-wuzzies, the hill-men of the Sudan. I wanted to know more about the country, so I approached an Englishman in a dinner-jacket who had come aboard and was making use of the cheap bar facilities. He was Mr Powell, a member of the District Commissioner's staff, and he got the D.C., Mr I. C. Rose, to join us. He was a most affable Scot. We had a entertaining time until the bar closed at 11 p.m. Then Mr Rose invited the ship's nursing sister, Shirley Frazer, the ship's engineer, Powell and myself to his house. We drove away from the ship in a large Ford, flying the Union Jack and the Egyptian flag. The Sudan was a condominium. The party lasted until 3 a.m. – three hours into my birthday.

Port Sudan was built to replace Suakin, which became too small a port for the modern ships and volume of traffic. The entire population moved as well, and so Suakin became a ghost town, except for the still maintained Governor's Rest House, and a rich merchant's palace of 365 rooms. The white population of 150 seem to enjoy themselves. They could swim, sail, fish, play tennis, dance, etc. When told that the unmarried proportion consisted of thirty bachelors and two nursing sisters, my horror at the desperate state of affairs raised a laugh. The beauty of Port Sudan was off-shore and under water. Even a rowing boat, in lieu of a glass-bottomed boat, gave us a view of many different coloured fish, and coral. The trip was a relief from the heat of the day. It was 95°F when we left our cabins. We slowly walked ashore; it was the hottest place I have ever experienced. Mr Rose said he wasn't a fisherman until posted to Port Sudan. He had to talk fishing, which was the main topic of conversation with visitors: rich men who came for big-game fishing from their yachts; scientists; and deep-sea divers.

"How much power do the British have here?" someone asked. "All," was the reply. The Egyptians did not have much say except to approve the Governor-General, who was British. They might not wish to have another. The Sudan Government was in Khartoum, 600 miles south-west. There was a twice-weekly train to Khartoum; the journey took two days. But Port Sudan had the top-quality Sudanese Political, Medical, and other services, and the Sudan Defence Force, all with the highest of reputations. From what else we heard I was amazed at the power and responsibility held by the D.C.: power of life and death too. He was required to attend all executions. There had been four; he had not enjoyed them. However, he was a believer in capital punishment, especially in such a country. He felt that our government was "a bunch of sissies". He meant in terms of firm, colonial government.

As we got back into Mr Rose's car to return to the Circassia (on which I soon got some Scottish country dancing going), we admired the clusters of beautiful bougainvillea growing up the walls of his house. "How do you do it in such a desert?" asked Sister. "Cats," was the answer. "When I planted it all out, I asked the sanitary engineer for forty dead cats. We always use cats for fertiliser in Port Sudan."

Edinburgh 1951–1953

Vital Interlude: and a wonderful unknown

I arrived home, eager to take up my post of Director, Edinburgh
International House, but I was first put into the London headquarters.
Here I never wanted to be posted, to become a commuter, a sub-fusc ant
morning and evening. And what a waste of time and money on trains and
tickets! Even now luck was on my side. My accommodation was to share
the Crown Flat of my superior, Donald Wort, in Duke Street, St James's
for £5 per week. Nancy Parkinson, head of Home Division allowed me to
pursue my complaint that the British Council had no adequate public
relations set-up. I was proud of the Council's work; and no-one at home
knew what we were doing. They still don't. But I was shortly moved to
Edinburgh.

Edinburgh International House (E.I.H.) was jointly run by the British
Council, which provided the Director, and by the City of Edinburgh,
which provided the premises and funds. It was a cheap, non-residential
club mainly for foreign students in Edinburgh, with a pleasant atmosphere
in which they could relax, meet each other, and also meet British members,
who joined ostensibly with an interest in student welfare and in other
countries. There were ideal first-floor premises on Princes Street, looking
across to the Castle. During the Edinburgh festivals E.I.H. was open to
visiting artistes and foreign lay visitors. The club's informality and genuine
atmosphere of welcome made it a popular rendezvous, and gave us a
profit. One festival duty and perk which devolved upon E.I.H. members
was to provide a corps of liaison guides to assist foreign orchestras,
musicians, actors, and the like with the ins and outs of their assigned
theatres and halls, even down to an interpreter for the Yugoslav ballet
stage-hands. In return we had rover passes to any show.

I was suddenly ordered south again. I was sent to be temporary Area
Officer South-East, based on Guildford. I had a little office near the
market, Joyce Minns as an invaluable assistant, and Jean Homer as a
steady secretary. We three kept an eye and an ear open for all foreign

students in Kent, Surrey, and Sussex. Joyce and I got around in our official Morris 10, and achieved a good deal: from cold-storage research at Rothampsted, via French assistants in schools to overseas Sandhurst cadets. I never knew what I might be asked to do when I got to my desk in the morning. I might be required to find accommodation, arrange visits to places of interest, obtain theatre tickets, or help students or scholars with their course-work through their respective institutions. My own accommodation in Guildford was solved by the kind Thompsons, the parents of an old Bradfieldian I had taught.

I had to find the right landladies for all foreign students. Accommodation for African students wasn't always easy to find. One landlady I specially liked took in a senior Nigerian scientist, a charmer, "How's it going Mrs Taylor?" "Oh, very well thank you. Mr Mubutu (shall we say) is ever so nice and so polite. But it's just at meals when he offers to cut the bread. I just can't bear his big black hand all over the loaf."

The hardest job in my in-tray one morning quite close to Christmas was a request by the Pakistan Government for sixty-five air apprentices to be looked after over the holiday period. Rotary International took the whole problem off my hands, fortunately, in Worthing and Eastbourne. They helped too with many a lone student's welfare.

My most agreeable duty was to visit an Austrian surgeon, a British Council scholar, at Queen Victoria Hospital, East Grinstead. When I told the staff that I was an old boy, they welcomed me in. They took me over the new wing, and insisted that I should view an operation from the germ-free, new theatre designed for normally clothed visitors.[1]

The greatest fun for the Area Officer was arranging weekend or vacation courses for our H.Q. Student Welfare department, such as 'Life in an English Village'. The perfect village of Shere co-operated beautifully, and 'The Cinque Ports' was another weekend title I chose. This brought me into the debt of mayors, town clerks, antiquarians, vicars, and other local worthies. How good everyone was!

Another side of the work was handling foreign visitors, such as a Nigerian Education officer, a Norwegian professor, and unexpectedly an entire Burmese Education Mission. I had Israeli U.N. fellows to take round art schools, and Indian prison commissioners to visit prisons. It all gave Joyce, Jean, and me true job satisfaction.

I arranged and advertised a Christmas vacation course from 27 December to 5 January 1952 at Brighton, thanks to the Mayor and his Council. I was limited to £7 a head, and students could attend for £5 a head. Thirty-three men and women from sixteen different countries ranging

[1] See *Shots in the Sand*, p. 165.

from Iceland to Siam seemed to enjoy themselves.

Apart from little local visits, we made a popular visit to Greenes Sponge Mixture, and to an official mayoral reception and tea in the Royal Pavilion after a conducted tour. We were given a New Year's Eve Ball in the magnificent Royal Pavilion, which the Mayor himself attended! The municipality, unknown to me, brought a piper down from London, put us together in the Red Drawing Room, and told us to get on with the Hogmanay part. That was no trouble. We had a procession at midnight, then the Gay Gordons, the Dashing White Sergeant and a Highland Schottische. Anyone can do these after a few bars, especially if there is a leaven of those who already can. And then I returned to E.I.H.

Roger Rigby and I drove up in Papa's fine, black, Austin Ascot saloon, CXB 508. Papa was marvellous to me. I was delivered to digs in 34 North Castle Street, near E.I.H. I was soon fortunate in being offered a flat in Rose Street, behind Princes Street. It was handy for the sometimes late hours at the club. I was gaining various experiences, such as prizing lovely Scandinavian girls and their African escorts apart from one another at closing time.

I needed a car. I could not have another Bugatti, but I found a very adequate, modern substitute in an Allard, (Sydney Allard's brilliant concept) an inexpensive sports car with a reliable Ford engine (thus having an efficient power to weight ratio) and with good road-holding.[2]

Life in Edinburgh gave me the dance and drama I love. I was able to learn the basics of the simplest Highland and sword dances. I even tried the solo sword-dance, Gillie Gallum, over a poker and tongs in my Allard's garage where Jimmy Shand happened to be sitting yarning, still with his accordion. I managed to get away to St Andrews on a Royal Scottish Country Dance Society instructor's course. And in Edinburgh there were plenty of private reel parties.

On the drama side, being at E.I.H. and under city administration, we were given access to a stage in Princes Street Gardens, once to put on 'Folk Dances of Europe and Scotland'. As well as reels and strathpeys, I could reasonably perform a Hungarian csardas in costume, and my Scots partner, Rosemary Harley, a member of E.I.H., picked it up very quickly. On another occasion I produced an act as part of a variety show. It was an episode in the life of Rob Roy McGregor. Cornered near his base at Balquhidder by a section of Butcher Cumberland's Red-Coats, he managed to slay his opponents, including me, and escape. Having been a fencer at school and university, I welcomed this chance to stage an Errol Flynn type of sword-fight: there was no swinging from chandeliers, but at least some

[2] See Alan Corps, *The Times Car Supplement*, 6 September 1997.

jumping up on furniture and kicking over of tables, and the like. Later on, I graduated to stage a Hamlet v. Laertes sword and dagger fight in a Royal High School production.

Rosemary's parents were E.I.H. members who had much interest in overseas students through their years in India, and they had suggested that Rosemary join. She often came from her Guild of Service office in Frederick Street for an inexpensive lunch. Mrs Harley was a Digby, and an artist of distinction, specialising in child portraiture. She stayed with her brother Kenelm (Bengal and Nagpur Railway) in Calcutta, and in the course of a field-trip in Kashmir was met by James Harley on a walking tour from the Y.M.C.A. in Lahore. One of 'Mum's' portraits in the field in camp is of Sarah, daughter of the then Colonel Dunsterville (Stalky).[3]

When the Great War came, the young marrieds could not return to India, so they remained in Edinburgh. James Harley became a Classics Master at Watson's. I was a strange creature to Rosemary, with my southern and army background, but not so strange to Mum, I felt. I managed to win over Rosemary's father, her four brothers, and finally Rosemary. A girl friend of hers had seen the Allard at the Harley house, and said: "Bait".

Rosemary didn't fall for that, but I fell further for my passenger who wasn't scared, and who proved to be a very fine map-reader, even at speed. When we were at Morar, I gave her a go with my Webley .38, and she did fine. I knew I couldn't live without her. But before agreeing to marry me she said that she wanted to be absolutely sure. "It's so important." It was indeed. We sat silent by the Falls. If she said "Yes," her whole way of life would be totally changed. I sympathised.

In May 1953 I opened a letter from the Personnel Department with trembling fingers, such as I became accustomed to do over the years. I was to go as Second Master to the General Wingate School, Addis Ababa. As Papa taught me, I never refused a post, I never volunteered, and I went where I was sent. It paid off, as I learned later.

The stakes were now higher still. I told Rosemary the news, and asked her to marry me. She accepted. Now I write in love and gratitude. For the next twenty-seven years she was my great support, and an uncomplaining, but a sometimes suffering, unpaid servant of the British Council. Rosemary needed no references, but her great-great-aunt was the Lady Jane Digby of the four nineteenth-century, famous heroines of Leslie Blanche's *The Wilder Shores of Love* – not a bad title for our lives.[4]

I had to tell my Personnel Department quickly of my change of status. I was proud to show her off; and she was keen to see the British Council

---

[3] It can be seen in black and white in the *Kipling Society Jounal* of December 1985.
[4] See also the admirable, family-approved biography of 'Aunt Jane': Mary S. Lovell, *A Scandalous Life* (London, 1995).

set-up. So I took her to our headquarters in London to see the head of Personnel, James Livingstone, a tall, stern, laconic, but great-hearted Scot. He just said to Rosemary: "Your father taught me." (Her father's nickname at Watson's had been Julius Caesar!)

Back in Edinburgh, my happiness was heightened by the committee of the Coronation Highland Ball including me as a steward. It was wonderful with Rosemary; and exciting to experience the thrill of being in the Assembly Rooms as part of two double lines of 64 men and women, (eight sets), all knowing exactly what they were doing, and in their own manner with tremendous verve. Then came the moment which we stewards had been waiting for: the signal to call for 'Hush', to hear the chairman read out the news of the climbing of Everest by Hilary and Tensing. The roar of delight must have reached Arthur's Seat.

We were married from James Harley's house, at Colinton Church on a perfect 8 August 1953. John Ford, my Budapest diplomat friend, was my best man. Our honeymoon was spent at The Swan at Bibury, Gloucestershire. We are near-by again now, after twenty-seven amazing years overseas and a retirement which has allowed us to visit France and Italy at leisure, at last.

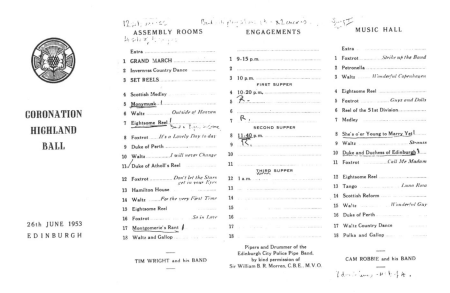

Our Ethiopia

Preface: from Prester John to Haile Selassie

Some two thousand years ago the influence of the great Egyptian civilisation up the Nile Valley was stopped at the confluence of the Blue and White Niles by the natural barriers of the Sudd swamp and the Ethiopian Highlands. The earliest trade was in aromatic spices such as frankincense for religious ceremonies and embalming, and myrrh for perfumes and cosmetics, which was obtainable only in Southern Arabia and Somalia. Transport was by camel caravan through Arabia to the Mediterranean, until navigational skills developed enough to use sea routes. Then a major kingdom arose on the edge of the Red Sea with its capital at Axum (south-west of today's Massawa). This kingdom became the dominant mercantile power in the region, with fleets plying to Egypt, Persia, India, and Zanzibar.

The Christian Church flourished in post-Roman Egypt, and spread south to take root in Ethiopia under the kings of Axum. Frumentius from Tyre was captured by King Ezana in A.D. 341. He won over his captor, who became converted to Christianity, and Frumentius became the first Bishop. Hence forward there were diplomatic ties between Axum and the Empire of Byzantium, although Axum maintained a certain political and religious distance. This was not difficult considering the inaccessibility of the country.

The kingdom of Axum flourished from the third to the eighth century, and laid the foundations of an enduring Christian civilisation. This gave rise to the medieval European legend of Prester John, a powerful Christian protector ruling a mysterious and exotic land.

His exotic land was thought to be in the remote East. But as the years passed, European travellers who explored inner Asia could find nothing but petty Mongol Khans. So they looked for Prester John elsewhere. European travellers in Egypt and Palestine heard rumours of a mighty Christian king who ruled a region vaguely described as somewhere beyond Egypt, India, or Abyssinia. So this king must be Prester John. He was, and an old map seen in the museum in Zanzibar purported to show the kingdom of Prester John, stretching from Nubia in southern Sudan well down the East African coast to Mozambique.

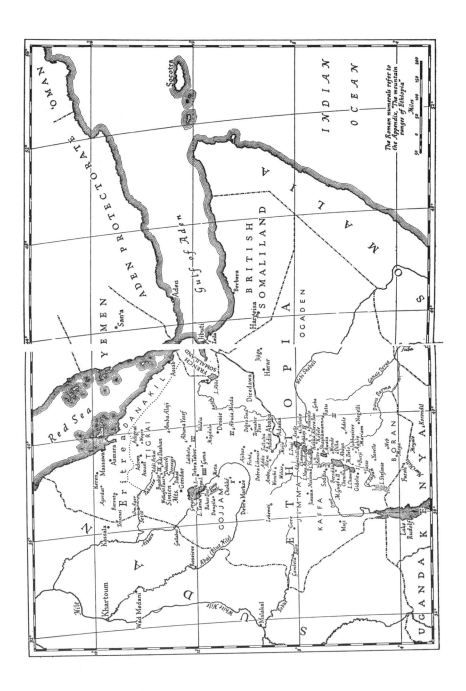

The middle years

The rise of Islam helped the downfall of the Axumite dynasty in the tenth century, but the Imperial Crown continued down the ages to be kept in that city. Two centuries later, despite Islamic inroads from the Nile Valley and from the Red Sea, a new Christian dynasty was established further south in greater safety at Lalibella. In our day Lalibella could only be reached after several days on a mule from a point on the Italian-built, main road north. In Lalibella ten spectacular, rock-cut churches were created in the centuries that followed. The Church of St George, the patron saint of Ethiopia, is carved in the shape of a Greek cross out of a huge block of stone isolated from the surrounding bed-rock by a twelve-metre-deep trench. The block was hollowed out and decorated. The top of the church is level with the ground! Although isolated from the rest of the Christian world for centuries, these churches are still in use, and Ethiopia has retained her distinctive faith and her Coptic rite.

In the fifth century monasticism came in from Syria, and remote monasteries have been flourishing in Abyssinia/Ethiopia for the last fifteen hundred years. Indeed the clergy, both church and monastic, has been fantastically numerous. It was said in our time that one in every five males was a priest.

In 1487 the Portuguese sent Peter de Cavilam to Abyssinia, but he was never allowed to leave. He was met some thirty years later by the next visitor, Alvarez, whose most interesting accounts of Abyssinian life survive.

From the nineteenth century

Four hundred years on, the Ethiopians were tremendously proud of their independence because they had remained unconquered for almost 3,000 years; the longest of any country in Africa except Egypt. Unlike Egypt, Ethiopia had never been under foreign domination until the nineteenth century when the Khedive Ismail of Egypt secured a foothold for Islam in Eastern Ethiopia. Harar became an independent Muslim kingdom until it was reconquered by Ras Makonnen, Haile Selassie's father.

The British made a sad incursion into Ethiopia in 1868, which was expensive in terms of men and money. The Napier Expedition rescued a handful of British subjects held captive by the Emperor Theodore (1855-1868) at Magdala in his mountain stronghold. Magdala was destroyed, and the Emperor committed suicide. The redcoats could only identify his body by the pistol which had been presented to him by Queen Victoria. Theodore had been much admired for his efforts to unify a country that

92

was exceedingly difficult to govern. But Ethiopia's pride was restored when the Emperor Menelik II defeated an Italian invasion at the Battle of Adowa on 1 March 1896. This remarkable victory is the subject of many primitive, bloody, battle pictures by local artists.

When Menelik II died in 1913, he was succeeded by Prince Lij Yasu. He was deposed in 1916 on account of his Islamic tendencies and his dealings with German and Turkish agents. Luckily for Ethiopia, Ras Tafari Makonnen, a cousin of Menelik's was appointed Regent since Menelik only had a daughter, Zauditu, in direct line. Ras Tafari, by his ability and actions established his right to the throne. He was the ruler of a country now fully delineated, and some six times the size of Britain.

So, on 2 November 1930, Haile Selassie I, was crowned Emperor Negus Negusti, King of Kings, in Addis Ababa; and his coronation was attended by *The Times* correspondent, Evelyn Waugh. Waugh wrote about it in *When the Going was Good*. We were lucky to find good going over twenty years later under this enlightened despot.

But for Haile Selassie and his people much suffering was to come first. In 1935 Mussolini carried out a successful invasion of the country. This criminal aggression was accompanied by barbaric cruelty. Mustard gas was used, and 'rebels' were slaughtered after engagements had ended. This was all shamefully ignored by the rest of the world. But the Emperor was rescued by the British Navy in May 1936. (See p. 589).

The Italians administered a severe jolt to the country, and their total occupation brought Ethiopia to world prominence. They managed to plant a whole system of settlement, for their colonists in the first place, of communications, administration, and development. Some of this was essential for British counter-invasion forces after 1939. The country, as we found it in 1953, was continuing from that point in its own way. Some idea of what the Italians fully planned could be gathered from the few remaining copies of *The Italian Guide to Ethiopia*, which was compiled on the lines of Baedeker. It made interesting reading – as a fairy tale.

However, without the Italians there would have been almost nothing for the Emperor to build upon: no roads, no government buildings, no lighting, no water, no telephones, and such like. By all the accounts of the day, Ethiopia had enormous agricultural potential. The land was rich and fairly accessible, and could have become a granary for the Middle East. In our time, there was a world-wide coffee boom which allowed a five-fold increase in Ethiopia's coffee export, which was her rather precarious, major cash-crop. The minerals were there if they could be extracted economically. If only the Emperor could have invited the Italians to assist him. But the Italian invasion had left terrible scars. Apart from the military slaughter, nearly all the few hundred young Ethiopians who had completed their education abroad had been shot. The excuse was their alleged part in the attempted murder of 'the Viceroy' Marshal Graziani. This meant that the Emperor was faced with a particularly serious, long-term problem. He had to build up from scratch a new class of modern administrators. They were needed to supersede the effete, older generation of notables (the Rases, or Chiefs) whose regimes were rigidly feudal.

After his restoration,[1] the Emperor made a remarkable and wise decision. There were several thousand Italian civilians mainly artisans, living in the country and working happily who wished to remain. The Emperor ordered their complete protection, and so these people continued to play an important part in the life of the country. Another asset was the Italian language. The self-styled masters of the country had very sensibly made Italian compulsory. This tongue was a unifying force. Italian became the lingua franca of Ethiopia for all classes; previously only the intelligensia had any knowledge of a European language. Ethiopians high and low, including our man-servant Wolde, who came from Jimma in the far west and spoke a remote dialect, had a touching faith in the ability of an Italian to handle any technical work or to put right any electrical and mechanical equipment.

The language problem arose because the people of Ethiopia are from distinct tribal groups who were limited to their own tongues because they remained isolated in the rugged, mountainous country. The principal language of Ethiopia is Amharic which is spoken by the ruling tribe of Amharas from the central province of Shoa. Amharic has its own script. The inhabitants of the province of Tigre to the north spoke Tigrinya. In the south are the Gallas, and in the South-West are the Gurages with their own dialects. Somewhere to the north are the remaining Falashas, the Jewish tribe which would not accept Coptic Christianity. To the east are the savage Danakils, and the Somalis too. An Amhara would think twice before venturing alone into these still remote parts. The Coptic Church language is Geez, an ancient language of Arabian Semitic origin, developing into Tigrinya, Tigre, and Amharic. Until 1900 the only schools were church schools, in which no foreign language would be taught.

The ecclesiastical head of the orthodox church of Ethiopia, which has its own church at Jerusalem, is known as the Abuna, but the Emperor, an extremely devout Christian, was considered to be the head of the national

---

[1] The story of the restoration of Haile Selassie to the throne and his return in April 1941 makes wonderful reading. See *The Abyssinian Campaigns*, (H.M.S.O.) or W. E. D. Allen, *Guerilla War in Abyssinia* (Penguin Books: 1943), and David Shirreff, *Barefoot and Bandoliers, Wingate, Sandford and the Patriots* (Radcliffe Press, 1995).

church. Below him came aristocratic Rases, the tribal chieftains, and the high-born government officials, all strong in their faith. As the American social historian, John Gunther, put it, Ethiopia was a theocracy.[2] The Emperor was quite sure of his power and divine right since he was the lineal descendant of Menelik, son of the legendary union of Solomon and the Queen of Sheba. This lovely story is depicted by Ethiopian artists in sets of up to forty-four little pictures in strip-cartoon style, on canvas or skin.

The word Ethiopia comes from the Greek meaning 'burnt face'. The people prefer to ignore the old name Abyssinia, because of its Arabic origin meaning 'mixed'. The Amharas consider themselves pure and superior and, of course, are far from black since they are Hamitic and Semitic. The features of the purer stock are markedly Caucasoid, often strikingly handsome. The black-skinned people are mostly descended from former negro slaves from the Sudan, "Is there a colour bar in Ethiopia?" we were often asked outside the country. We had the pleasure of replying, "Yes, but we don't mind".

---

[2] Gunther was the author of 'Inside Ethiopia: Armchair Travelogue', *Readers Digest* (c. 1950).

Our Ethiopia 1953–1957

Our honeymoon was over; taken gently, savoured and never forgotten. Now I was posted to Ethiopia, to the General Wingate School, and Rosemary was coming with me. I was heartened. We studied the Council's 'Record of Living Conditions' and other recommended reading.

Brother Michael from the Gold Coast sent us to Griffiths McAllister, outfitters in the city who specialised in supplying the requirements of missionaries in Africa. "Bicycles, missionary, reinforced. Hats, ladies, double-terai. Khaki drill garments." A blushing assistant measured perhaps his first lady, for trousers. Rosemary began to resemble Ava Gardner in *Mogambo*. I was happy selecting a Blacks tent, bags, mosquito nets, Tilley lamps, water-containers, canvas buckets, all musts for expeditionary needs. Rosemary took charge of specialist selection, such as kitchen-ware, flat ware, insect repellent and First Aid boxes. Our chosen outfitters, F. P. Baker, whom we dealt with ever after, gave excellent service including cards of introduction to specialist firms for cutlery, crockery, cameras, and the like.

In Suffolk, Papa, the handy-man, had made off his own bat slatted crates of Australian iron-wood, beautifully screwed together to protect our light trunks. All our heavy stuff had to be packed professionally in strong cartons because all would be flown to Addis from Aden. A precious piece of baggage was a wonderful wedding present from Roger Rigby: a .275 Rigby Mannlicher sporting rifle.[1] We enjoyed the peace of the Deben estuary, which gave us rest to recover from various 'jabs': yellow fever, smallpox, cholera, typhoid, and also T.A.B. which gave a nasty reaction. All were duly stamped into our yellow International Health Certificate booklets.

I was delighted to find that we were booked on the Himalaya, and first-class this time. Papa saw us sail from Tilbury, and signalled to us by driving his Austin Ascot saloon, CXB 508, rapidly backwards and forwards

[1] Martin Booth in Kenya, on a walking safari wrote in *The Independent on Sunday*, 9 February 1992: "Had this been 1961 I would have been standing with a Rigby .275 in the crook of my arm, But it was 1991, my arm cradled not a rifle, but a camera . . ." I agree with him now.

along a little stretch of riverside. I hated to leave him for a long time on his own; and I was sorry to be taking Rosemary, an only daughter, so far away from her family.

From previous experience I tackled the Chief Steward early, and was pleased that we were put at the table of the First Officer, Michael Donkin. We had a cheery, entertaining voyage. Thanks to Donkin, the galley produced a superb birthday cake for Rosemary, and the table was given champagne at dinner.

At sunset in the Suez Canal the sands and rocks revealed their rare colours of soft golds and rose-pinks, with a contrasting, decorative, straight, blue strip in between. As the sun went down, an enormous moon suffused a motionless, dim sand-scape in a silver sheen. Standing with Rosemary on deck during a three-hour wait in the half-way Lay-by, I found a greater awareness of beauty in nature, and in the works of man. I was now enjoying the desert all the more in luxury, protection, and sensitive company. But an early test of our sweet, newly-married relationship was to have to pack our belongings in a cabin at 93 °F in the Red Sea.

Through the Straits of Bab-el-Mandeb, Aden appeared round the corner. We had asked the piper at our wedding to play *The Barren Rocks of Aden*, a great tune. But we had not envisaged such dark rocks on a bright yellow sand, and the appalling heat. We were lucky. Thanks to the kind Spencer-Cookes, we were swept ashore in a smart Cory Brothers launch, and deposited in the Crescent Hotel, from where Cory's manager, Mr Griffiths, and his wife took us in charge. They provided an example, which we took to heart, of the tradition and extent of hospitality overseas.

Next day we boarded a good old D.C.3 Dakota of Ethiopian Airlines on 'The Wonderland Route'. The port engine would not start; then I saw a gang of rugged Arabs hauling a heavy rope attached to the propeller! I did the wondering, but Rosemary had never flown before, and accepted it all.

On reflection, I confess that I took my wife for granted. I simply expected and accepted without question, her admirable support, care, and attitude to all that happened to us over the years, but especially in Ethiopia. I never knew until later what she went through, or the causes of pain and indigestion from which she often suffered through stress in a life strange to her.

Up and up we went from sea-level to over 8000 ft., via French Djibouti and Ethiopian Diredawa. Here from 1918 was the French-built railway centre of the line from the coast to Addis Ababa, as it reached 2000 ft. on to the plateau from the desert. As we flew on, we could see an enormous, patchwork landscape of all shades of green, with an occasional amba – a flat-topped, isolated hill. We could also make out the deep, narrow, tree-covered valleys, and here and there the mushroom-like clusters of circular-roofed 'tukuls', the village huts.

Our descent was minimal since Addis is at 8000 ft. When we had come to a stop our engines appeared to give up, so we were hauled backwards by a tractor towards our reception committee on the balcony. This, to my surprise, was led by Bill and Nancy Smith, friends from Budapest Embassy days. Then we were engulfed in a welcoming group of Wingate School staff. After half-an-hour in Customs – a mild taste of things to come – we were borne off the ten miles to the school in the little western suburb of Gulele.

We had a pleasant outlook from our temporary flat over a tree-filled countryside, and a compound surrounded by eucalyptus trees. The Entotto hills rose beyond. The track across the top of the compound gave access to our bungalow, but it was also a right-of-way for villagers. The passers-by were fascinating, and never a problem.

At the end of World War II, the defeated Italians, 'conquerors' of Ethiopia, had deprived the country of an educated class which they had ruthlessly slaughtered. The Emperor's first priority was to ask for international assistance in the establishment of a modern, secondary school system. The British Council helped first in 1946 with a school in disused radio huts. Then a British architect was commissioned to build a school for 300 boys. This was opened on 5 May 1951 by the Emperor, with Mrs Wingate present, as the General Wingate School in memory of her husband's Gideon Force's contribution to the Emperor's return. The British Council provided some funding, for instance in the staff salaries of the then headmaster, Alec Heyring, and the second master, myself. There were two other boys' secondary schools: the American-staffed Medhane Alem, and the Canadian Haile Selassie Ist. There was also the Itegue Menen for girls. There was a Lycée under French control, a Greek school and an Armenian School; and the Sandford family's[2] English School, which was open to all nationalities.

There was no lack of pupils, once word got around the country that secondary schools were opening in Addis Ababa. The boys came from every province. Many, even quite small ones, were known to have walked for up to a fortnight from afar to one of the few main roads, carrying their belongings on their heads.

The Wingate staff, whether recruited by the British Council or the Ministry of Education, was cheerful, congenial, talented, and enterprising. Our colleagues' comradeship, support, and humour were the major assets of our Ethiopian days. For newly-married couples the close community

---

[2] Colonel Dan Sandford D.S.O. Leader of Mission 101, a former Consul who survived , and remained to farm, run a good school, raise a fine family. See Book List.

life was reassuring. Rosemary could pop across the compound for advice, or to borrow anything from a primus, to a book, or even a motor-car.

The British Consul soon invited us to luncheon in the Embassy compound a few miles away. The Gills kindly lent us their Morris. When we arrived at the gates we could only engage reverse; so backwards we had to go up the winding drive past a terrace full of astonished guests.

On the staff we had a Swiss teacher and his Armenian wife, and a charming Egyptian bachelor, Badia Salib, who would do anything to help anyone, with a cry of "Ya habibi!", which we still use ourselves. Everyone made his or her own contribution: in music, dance, cookery, or topical information. There were two Ethiopians: the courteous, willing, and indefatigable Ato (Mr) Negeri , the secretary; and the perplexed and perspiring, but solid, Ato Manker, the warden. He, like the headmaster, had to serve two masters: on the one hand, British standards and customs; on the other, the requirements and attitude of the Ministry of Education.

When I got around to up-dating our 'Record of Living Conditions' I was amused by variations in staff outlook on all sorts of aspects of our life. I shall never forget an answer to my query on equipment: "Gumboots are essential but not necessary".

Many people rode where there were no roads. One reason for this was that the country was so impenetrable and wild that for centuries the concept of the wheel had been lost. It must have been known through the Egyptians about 1500 B.C., and then forgotten as impractical. A number of our poorer boys had to stay at school during the short Christmas and Easter holidays because they could not get home and back in the holiday period.

We had 300 boys aged thirteen to eighteen years from all parts of the country and all walks of life. They were all shades of skin too; the very dark boys, probably with negro slave blood, were sometimes mocked as 'blackie'. A large number received free education, food, books, stationery, and clothing. They were a cheerful lot, well-mannered, intelligent and keen to learn. They were a pleasure to teach. They arrived from primary schools with a pretty good grounding in English and major subjects due to the excellent work done by Indian teachers, who deserve great credit. The boys were quite ready to criticise their teachers but didn't attempt to lead them astray. We tried to get the boys away from the slavish following of textbooks, and to think and to question beyond the set texts needed for exams. They were capable of blaming their teachers if they failed!

There were almost no disciplinary problems. The boys respected firm treatment. The worst punishment was to be kept out of class. There were only disciplinary problems out of school. Sadly, the master-boy relationship was tenuous because there was little supervision or contact out of the classroom. There was only a duty master around at meal or shower times. It was the Ministry of Education who were responsible for the boys' welfare and relations with parents. However, a number of our staff couples acted as ex-officio housemasters and wives, which was much appreciated.

Classes were fun. Lessons only ever came to a halt when very heavy hail fell on our corrugated-iron classroom roofs. Then was the time to sing songs, which were good for stress, rhythm, and intonation. My certificate class came to our little house sometimes, to read and to examine our books, magazines, pictures, ornaments, and equipment. Rosemary could never provide enough cake. They usually stayed until they had to be turned out. They were bright and able to pass London G.C.E. quite well. The great responsibility of running this British examination precisely and securely was taken by the headmaster.

The boys' food was standard Ethiopian wat and injera: the first, a very spicy stew was not at all palatable to us: and the latter was a thin, grey, unleavened bread which looked, and to us tasted, like sheets of foam-rubber. The local alcoholic drink (not for the boys) was tej – a potent barley beer. Drunkenness was a sad blight among the people. Their non-alcoholic, honey-based mead, called talla, was slightly sweet, but it was very good with soda.

Addis Ababa (New Flower) was built in 1883 on a plateau at 8000 ft. by the Emperor Menelik (died 1913) to please his Empress. It is high and remote. There were only rudimentary roads in the nineteenth century, which were impassable except by horse or mule. The plateau is intersected by precipitous valleys, so 'Addis' was difficult to reach from any direction. The country seldom had visitors or passers-by. Only when the French built a railway from Djibouti in 1918 could Europeans reach the capital with ease. When you arrive by air you find you are in a world within a world; and much of Ethiopia, as we were to find out, is breathtaking.

In our day the universal form of architecture in Ethiopia comprised low houses of white-washed chika (mud), green doorways, and corrugated roofs. These contrasted sharply with the modern brick, or concrete, or stone-faced houses of the rich and foreigners. The most imposing buildings were Italian-built and were scattered for ten miles around within a eucalyptus forest. Here and there were mud and wattle tukuls of the very poor. The quick-growing eucalyptus, which was essential for house-building, had been wisely planted by the Emperor Menelik to replace the long-gone abundance of acacias and junipers.

Local car journeys were bewildering because of the haphazard spread of the town, and one often had to follow circuitous routes in and out of the hills. Roads swarmed with people driving laden donkeys and mules to the big market on the outskirts. In the market we did not find many souvenirs of good Ethiopian arts and crafts, only two amusing, naive paintings on canvas. As David Buxton later wrote:

Little notice is taken of car horns, as men and beasts wander anywhere along the route, regardless of 'traffic', a new phenomenon! To the north the town straggles up past the British Embassy with a few of its buildings still in the local round tukul style, to the Entotto Hills.[3]

He described the views graphically:

The hills rose abruptly to 10,000 ft. behind the house, and we could never exhaust the charms of their winding paths among gums and junipers, their quiet, grassy glades and rocky bluffs commanding marvellous views over the city and the surrounding hills. But the real glory of this outlook is the vast semi-circle of mountains that bound the horizon to the south. There is Wachacha, the highest of them, to the west, with Managasha, like an inverted basin on its right. Further left is Furi, then Yerrer the most picturesque in form. Beyond all, blue with distance, rises the regular cone of Zukwala, the sacred volcano, impressive in its isolation.[4]

In March 1956 Rosemary got up Managasha, the Holy Mountain (for which a permit was needed): "just so far in the V.W., and then staggered on foot to the hill-top church, monastery, and hermitage. This is of cells carved out of stone into the hillside: and a tiny courtyard dug out in front. The incurably sick are told to stay there so many days by the priest, and to pray. Probably finishes them off."

Rosemary got to the far side of Wachacha in February 1957; to the forest which is an Imperial reserve and which required a permit. It was a lovely place, and unusual for Ethiopia. There were huge, cypress-like trees with silvery trunks, and interesting plants and bushes. The scent of jasmine was everywhere; the prickly and bushy, evergreen variety.

In our day the population was some twenty million: hardy people in a very tough terrain, but with fertile soil. They were fairly easy-going although life was cruel and violent when they were ruled by despotic Rases (head chiefs). The Rases fought each other for the throne and their armed bands lived by pillage and slaughter. The Amharas had fine features and were good-looking. All down to the poorest had an air of assurance and a dignity of bearing. None more so than the stately, white-haired, old men, wearing drill jackets and jodhpurs (an introduction of Menelik's), and a locally-made topee of woven straw.

[3] David Buxton, *Travels in Ethiopia*, (Ernest Benn, 1957), p. 46–53.
[4] *Travels in Ethiopia*.

Some Ethiopians, male and female, wore a shamma as well. This was a generous shawl of fine, clinging cotton with a coloured, patterned band down one side. It was a multi-purpose garment: draped like a stole, or as a wrap at night; as a head-covering; as a handkerchief for tying the baby on the back; or for carrying goods. The women wore white full-skirted dresses. The smart ladies' dresses had the hem-band matching the shamma. They wore their hair in an Edwardian style, on top of the head, standing out covered with a tightly tied piece of bright cotton. Most of them carried black umbrellas against the sun or the rain.

It was fascinating to watch the daily procession to and fro in front of us, to buy or sell in the market. The most numerous were the women carrying huge bundles of eucalyptus branches and leaves for firewood. All along the wide road moved donkeys and mules with loads of hides, and multitudes of drivers. Everyone occupied the road, which was also congested with one-horse gharries. These were hardly more than a board between two big wheels, brightly painted, and they careered all over the tarmac.

In the town-centre men, women and beasts were not quite such a menace. There were good shops, the main buildings being: the Ras Hotel, the Italian Opera House, and the King George (of Greece) Bar, which was that great hub of certain local life – which included the Wingate staff!

The locals appeared very polite to one another. Men passing each other in the street, depending on relative rank, bowed low, doffed hats and offered one or two hands for a distant handshake. When relatives met, the ritual was two kisses on each cheek. It was good to see an important person wrapped in a coloured cloak, mounted on a mule with a red-tasselled, ornamented bridle and saddle. His retainers would be trotting along behind, one carrying his umbrella, another perhaps carrying his fly-whisk – this being a special symbol of authority depending on its size and length. All such persons wore hats, normally trilbys, in various stages of decrepitude. I have seen a gentleman mounted on a mule adding to his dress a black tail-coat and a black homburg. The condition of our comic servant Wolde (from Jimma in the south-west) as he returned for evening work drunk or sober could be judged by the angle at which he wore his hat. This hat was a symbol of status achieved from the wages we gave our servants.

We had to spend some time going into town to get ourselves properly accredited and organised. The far-seeing Thomas Hodgkin wrote in *The Spectator*, "In Ethiopia, the Ethiopian comes first, and the 'ferangi' is kept in his place. In fact, Ethiopians now, as formerly, are firmly convinced of the advantages of their own civilisation."

This was good advice for us to take to heart. It was also useful to read John Adfern of *The Daily Express*, who had an interview with the Emperor soon after we arrived. Adfern was particularly concerned with the impact of modernisation. He wrote that with the introduction of Western materials and methods and the necessary foreign staffs, the ancient administration and its old-style officials simply could not cope. This was true. I sympathised with the government officials who had to cope just with permits and licences. In spite of the tremendous bureaucratic delays, one was treated politely, if one was polite oneself.

I came across foreign teachers who left through frustration, "inefficiency, procrastination, endless papers, etc." Luckily, I had tolerance and patience with officials. One needed lots of 'warrakats', papers of authorisation. Even to retrieve our passports from Immigration took three and a half hours of personal application, over three visits. The only thing to do was to be friendly and come back, for a hunting-licence perhaps, a week later. Then all would be ready, signed, and stamped.

Rosemary made history. She was given a chair, and received a driving licence in twenty minutes. I wasn't given a driving licence at all, in spite of flourishing my International Driving Permit. That was indeed a blow. My one eye was the cause. I owe much to Miss J. K. Watt (later Dame Katherine), a British matron leading a Tsahai Hospital team. Miss Watt had one eye and a driving licence. She badgered the Consul and the authorities until they granted me a driving licence too. We had bought an admirable, second-hand Volkswagen, which was ideal for the road conditions. One had to drive with scrupulous care because of the terribly keen, British-trained policemen. They were ready to pounce on the slightest infringement of the rules of the road, which did not in fact exist. The police were particularly strict at lights; but there was no amber!

Life for us

The climate was excellent: temperate and salubrious. There was a cooler season from October to February; a hot, dry season until June, with the 'little rains' in March to April. In June came the big rains, a convectional rain season, in which we got the crashing hail, through to September. In Addis at 8000 ft. the sun burns, but it is very cool out of the sun and too cold to entertain outside after dark. We didn't notice the altitude in normal life, except when we at first began to run up the stairs to our flat. The altitude affected cooking because the water boiled at 91 °F. The often-needed candle-light was poorer up there, and cigarette lighters didn't work so well.

We could play tennis easily, but preferred doubles. Luckily, we could enjoy Scottish country dancing: we had lovely talent in Jim Marshall, Ronnie Macbeath, and Derek Turner. But when we played hockey against the boys, we could only manage ten-minute chukkas. Even so, when John Rich from the Embassy team came to play us, he began to turn blue during a game, and had to be carried off on a stretcher. He survived, and went on to a distinguished diplomatic career.

The boys played soccer, bare-foot and for full-time games. There was no altitude problem for them. Ethiopians have become world-champion long-distance runners because they have for centuries jogged mile after mile with goods carried at each end of a pole across the shoulders. Leslie Casbon, a great chap, was our sports master. He soon had the boys' soccer up to the best British form, but only after calming down their natural, inter-tribal, aggressive reactions to this form of confrontation. I once had to cope with an incipient pitched battle of sticks and stones. The only way to stop it that I could see was to walk between the rival forces, saying "Tut! Tut!", or stronger. I was scared, but it worked. Later a boy spectator was killed at a school's soccer final, so future matches were played between teams of boys made up from different schools.

It took time to get the boys round to athletics, but Leslie achieved some high-standard results, especially in javelin and long-distance running. The boys were at first apathetic about inter-house sports, but after a few comedy races they saw the point. The obstacle race introduced me to an Ethiopian menace: ants. As I crawled under the tarpaulin I felt ants biting me all over. As I came out the far side I shouted for Rosemary and kept on running home. The spectators thought I had gone 'potty'. We used the altitude as our excuse for all forms of staff behaviour. But this time it was ants. My only chance was to take all my clothes off and for Rosemary to pick off each ant fast, as they kept on biting. It wasn't the only time! Fleas were another menace, as a British Council E.L.T. Inspector discovered, but I was spared. One effective way to catch fleas was to dab them with a piece of damp soap.

Before we left our flat we decided to make it a venue for a bit of fun. It was Hallowe'en, which we combined with Guy Fawkes and had a bonfire party. Tariku, the son of an Ethiopian member of staff, draped in a sheet made an excellent ghost rising out of a packing case on the dark stairs. The boys were fascinated by the goings-on. We took no notice, and let them steal out in their night clothes. They began to think that either we were pagan, or that our form of Christianity had real appeal. Our first servant got over-excited, leapt over the bonfire, disappeared, and was never seen again. We didn't mind. We got our Wolde instead, who was such a lovely character. "Matie" (Madam) he said, holding up the kitchen clock which he hadn't yet been taught to wind, "It's asleep."

The school bell

The 'bell' hung on a wooden frame between the teaching block and assembly hall; but it was the clutch housing of a lorry and was banged with an iron bar. This is not good enough for the Wingate, I thought. Most opportunely, we learned that Earl Mountbatten of Burma on a visit to H.I.M. would come to the Wingate. An idea struck me. . . .

Mountbatten came and gave an excellent address, mainly on Orde Wingate. And "Yes", he would get us a ship's bell. He and Lady Edwina attended a Service of Remembrance at the beautifully kept War Cemetery for the British and African troops. The Africans particularly had been tremendously loyal and brave.

The Earl's A.D.C. related to us at the Embassy Garden Party, that anyone, even the Earl, had to advance into the Audience Chamber in three sets of steps and bows, and on departing repeat the procedure backwards. "A little to port: a little more: a little to starboard, Sir," got them safely out of the Presence. Rosemary commented: "The Embassy is in a lovely setting: sloping and terraced lawns, tall trees, splashes of bougainvillea. Lady M. had a lovely apple-green dress. What bright eyes she had. Michael made an absolute pig of himself on eclairs, as the servants came round so often."

This is how the boys' reported on the visit:

SOME EXTRACTS

from compositions written after the visit of Earl Mountbatten to the General Wingate School, Addis Ababa, 5 November 1953.

Lord Mount Botton is an English nobleman. He came to visit our school. He has got a regular face and his black eyes were shining like a metal in a hole.

When he came to visit our school I saw him with a navy uniform well dressed. The collar of his shirt was shining. His shoes were as clear as crystal. In short I should say Mount Button's talk would melt the heart of a stone.

He has a fair hair with blue eyes and a friendly look which he wore during most of the time of his visit. He is almost an eloquent speaker. He is a ponderous and a valiant Earl. His gentle speech made him lovable and his good qualities made him admirable. He advised us how to improve our knowledge and how to modernize our country. I wish him to get a perpetual life.

Lord Mount Bouton the Admial of the English navy paid us a visit on Monday the 5th November. Indeed we were lost with joy to see such a famous and great man wearing his uniform. He encouraged us to work hard in order to ring the fame of Ethiopia to foreign countries.

The bell arrived the following March, and the Ambassador, Sir Douglas Busk, presented it to us. We had cheerful, clear tollings thereafter for our daily round.

c/o Foreign and Commonwealth Office (Rabat),
King Charles Street,
London, SW1A 2AH.

Her Majesty the Queen,   4 September 1979
Buckingham Palace,
London, SW1.

Your Majesty,

<u>The late Earl Mountbatten</u>

A few weeks ago before you undertook a strenuous African tour you graciously and unselfishly held an Investiture at which I was present. You kindly asked me what my work was, and I replied that I was in the British Council (in Morocco).

I would not have dreamed of writing to Your Majesty if it had not been for the recent tragedy. But as I <u>am</u> writing, I beg to say 'Thank you' on my own behalf: and I ask Your Majesty to accept the deepest sympathy of my family and myself at this cruel and senseless act.

But even in times of mourning there are, I think, moments for a smile and a chuckle of happy reminiscence. It is for this reason that I send Your Majesty a note I made while Second Master at the General Wingate School, Addis Ababa, early in my British Council career.

Staff and pupils were thrilled to have a visit from Earl Mountbatten. He was marvellous on the occasion: spoke splendidly and actually gave us what we had the temerity to ask, a ship's bell for a school bell, to replace a lorry's clutch casing hit by a metal bar.

Those Ethiopian boys were fine material. They were perfectly able to appreciate the qualities of leadership, courage, sympathy and Christian faith, which shone through the sparkling personality of our 'valiant Earl'.

I remain, Your Majesty's humble and loyal
servant,

Michael Halsted.

J.M.G. HALSTED

Ethiopia

BUCKINGHAM PALACE

5th October, 1979

Dear Mr Halsted,

I am commanded by The Queen to thank
you for your kind letter of 4th September
about the tragic death of Lord Mountbatten.
Her Majesty much appreciated your taking
the trouble to write, and was much amused
by the extracts from the compositions
written by your pupils in Addis Ababa
after Lord Mountbatten's visit there in
1953.

The Queen was happy to learn that you
had enjoyed your visit to Buckingham Palace
for the Investiture.

Yours sincerely,

J.M.G. Halsted, Esq., O.B.E.

Then we got away on our first trip, with the Gills. "Where does this
road go?" I asked looking left out of the school gate. "To the Sudan." No,
I decided. We went right in two cars forty-five miles down the railway line
to Moggio at 6000 ft., on the Harar road. We ate at a little concrete box
bearing the grand name of Acropol Palas Hotel. The kind Greek manager
moved out of his room, put us all in it, and fed us very well.

The next morning we set off south-west down the Kenya road. Some
miles were on tarmac, which was not maintained. We lost more height for
we were entering the great Rift Valley. We met thorn bushes and flat-
topped acacia; we were now in the real savannah of the Arussi Province of
the Gallas. The men we met carried spears. The women had hair greased
with butter, in ringlets with a fringe. We made a detour just to see little
Lake Coca, and its monkeys. We were aiming for Lake Elena, but the

right track took time to find and became difficult. Local woodcutters kindly put down logs to help us along, and we came across charcoal burners and their camels for transporting it. The countryside seemed remote and empty; but if we stopped anywhere someone, maybe leaning on a spear, turned up to stare at us.

It was the wonderful birds we came to see. We found hornbills first and as we got down to the water's edge nicely covered by thorn thickets, we found hippopotamuses and crocodiles. There were egrets on a dead tree among a creek's reeds; then black geese with bright red and yellow head-patches; and a solitary, Egyptian brown goose. Now appeared an elegant crested crane. We saw vultures, little waders, doves, and irridescent starlings of brilliant, shimmering blue and others darkish purple-blue. Finally, a huge tortoise, two-foot long and a foot high, came in view. We had had our reward for the journey. Seven spearmen and several women watched us eat lunch, but wouldn't allow photographs. They asked for our tins, for they needed water-containers. The other reward was that we never gave a thought to our safety; and in our time we never had to worry, so well had Haile Selassie created a land of safe travel, and in such a short time. Nevertheless, we were not tempted to visit the Danakils in the south-east.

Immediately after the World War II, lawlessness had been rife in Addis and round about. Locals and foreigners were killed for fun. The task of taming a mixture of war-like races in a wild, inaccessible land made us appreciate the greatness of H.I.M. The worst offenders were hung publicly, at the scene of their crime.

On our way back, we stayed at the new hotel above the deep, crater lake at Bishoftu where the Emperor had his summer palace, which he named Fairfield after his Bath home in exile. Rosemary and I often returned to Bishoftu, and would hire a canoe to glide round the rushy shore and enjoy watching the pigmy kingfishers. Before Christmas, John Rich took us to Green Lake, which was another crater lake nearby. There were lots of

One of Innes Marshall's sketches of Addis Ababa churches which she used as a Christmas card.

108

duck, and a troop of baboons and we were very wary. Baboons could turn nasty, but a group of inevitable, but admirable, small boys dispersed them with stones.

1953 ended well for us. The annual Poppy Day Dance was held in the school hall. The staff sang comic songs and we showed off a Scottish dance or two. At this we began to feel the altitude: but we were fit. This St Andrew's Night is especially remembered for Jim Marshall's undertaking to make a haggis. Rosemary provided the sheep's stomach.

Peter Wingard produced a lively *Gondoliers* in the school hall with a cast of Britons, Americans, Dutch, and Swedes. The cosmopolitan, temporary population of Addis, of many professions, provided much interest, variety, and fun. There were Norwegians, Yugoslavs, Soviet and German doctors, Greeks, Americans, Arab traders, not forgetting 'Auntie', Mrs Abbott, the Russian widow of an Englishman. She was a fiery character with a big heart, who ran a V.D. Clinic. When she lost her temper she cried "Constantinople" so as not to be accused, as in the past, of swearing rudely at her Ethiopian 'hosts', who were often policemen.

According to the Ethiopian calendar Christmas falls on our 6 January. It is a sensible calendar: each month has an equal number of days and the surplus five days are taken just as they come, before their New Year (which falls on our 4 September).

At our New Year the staff gave the boys a party, and Wolde's contribution was 200 biscuits. We introduced the boys to physical games such as musical chairs, spinning the platter, and various forms of relay races. They seemed very happy. Then it was the boys' turn. They were natural actors, and often put on little, topical plays among themselves. Now they staged a Nativity Play. It was a revelation it being far more lively and realistic than ours, and with many more scenes. There was for instance, Jesus being taken to Simon in the Temple, and the slaying of the babies. The chorus intoned passages from the Psalms during the action, and 'King David' sang solos, a very dreary sound. They had gorgeous, red, gold, and purple, brocade cloaks which were long and full, and they carried sumptuous, coloured, fringed, ceremonial umbrellas. All was in Amharic, and the actions were so alive and natural.

There was a wonderful last scene with Mary enthroned, holding the infant Christ. Sparklers were lit in 'her' crown, and angels with swords stood on either side. All Ethiopian angels, as seen in church murals or in naive art, carried swords! More youths came from the church and sang and danced before Mary and the child. The youths were in two lines facing each other and they jigged, clapped, and shook sistera.[5] Two other young men beat enormous, deep drums slung round their shoulders, and

[5] Discs on wires with a handle, which jingled when shaken.

the tempo became more vigorous. The whole play was loudly jubilant and totally unselfconscious. The Christ child was a sailor doll, and Herod was wearing a row of school sports medals.

We discovered that the boys could learn and recite chunks of Snakes-peare, so we decided to stage *Macbeth*. We were not allowed to stage *Julius Caesar*! Our cast was familiar with tribal warfare, so Malcolm versus Macbeth was acted upon with spirit. We dressed Malcolm and his staff in our kilts. They cut down branches of eucalyptus from the trees outside the hall, and Birnam Wood marched relentlessly towards Dunsinane. It was rewarding teaching English literature, drama, poetry and prose. I learned more than ever before.

The Emperor's Christmas party

The occasion of the Emperor's Christmas party afforded the opportunity for the Emperor to be seen in his role of ruler and father of his people. On this day all men of importance, the Rases and their officials, men from the ministries, and priests wore national dress. By 9.30 a.m. every primary and secondary school child had arrived in the Ghibbi (Palace) grounds, and had been arranged by their teachers in twenty lines in front of a long, verandahed building. There was a scarlet and gold canopy for the Emperor and Empress, and in front, long tables piled high with presents of a slipover, an orange, and a big bun with a hard-boiled egg in the middle (a surviving Italian custom). The school children, mainly in uniform, were out in the full sun for hours, but they did not seem to mind. The girls' schools were not in uniform; they were quite dazzling in their white dresses and shammas.

I introduced Rosemary to several of my Imperial Guard English class and they put us to the front when their Majesties arrived. The queues of pupils started moving up. The Emperor handed out gifts to the senior boys, and the Empress gave gifts to the girls. Various members of the royal family spaced out along the verandah handled the rest. It was pretty fast, and it was amusing to see the officials keeping the Emperor supplied from behind. H.I.M. seemed most pleasant and spoke to many of our boys. He even smiled at us when we had the nerve to take photographs.

We enjoyed observing the jostling and hanky-panky going on in the background. Every boy had to surrender a ticket as he received his gift so that he could not come back again. But other hands sometimes went out for tickets; servants were sneaking up trying to pass off their offspring as school children, probably not having the money to buy them presents. Dirty little ragamuffins were hurtling around the fringes of the crowd and being whacked away by police or soldiers of the Guard, supposedly under the command of their orderly officer, a huge man with an ugly face, in riding breeches and boots, who dashed about in a state of panic shouting at everyone and waving a baton.

The handout finished at 12.30 p.m., and on marched three genna teams, who were presented with a ball. Genna is a traditional, inter-village, hockey-type game, but with no fixed number of players and no fixed rules. The one basic aim was to bash a wooden 'ball' (chunk of wood) with any sort of bent stick, into the opposing village. Before the match, the teams lined up, stamping, waving their sticks, and chanting the genna song, which contained insulting verses. On this formal occasion two teams started to play, giving enormous whacks with rough, short-nosed sticks. They were in full swing, when the band suddenly began to play the national anthem. The players froze where they stood, and after the anthem they dashed off singing a war-like chant, waving their sticks in the air.

We teachers now trooped towards a large pavilion laid out for luncheon. The Imperial family sat at a high table, and looked bored. We were among 300 to 400 guests, all helping themselves at a buffet to what they fancied of Ethiopian food. On each table were varieties of European liquor, and tej. We ate wat with curried chicken and enjoyed the tej. When we had nearly finished eating, in marched the duty guard. Each man was given an enormous plateful of raw meat which he ate with grins of satisfaction, standing against one wall. When all had fed, Colonel Makonnen, the Emperor's A.D.C., a charming, long-suffering man in a flowing white shamma with gold edging, gave the signal. We all rose, did a little bow or curtsey to the Emperor, and left for home.

Occasionally we would see Colonel Makonnen riding with the Emperor in his Rolls Royce, with H.I.M.'s little papillon lying behind his head on the back shelf. If we saw that we were going to pass them in our car we would stop, as required, get out and bow.

The Emperor's movements were uncannily sensed by his people. There was no state welfare and no other redresser of wrongs, but when H.I.M. in his Rolls halted somewhere he would descend and be ready to receive written petitions from anyone. The petitioner would come forward at Colonel Makonnen's signal, prostrate himself at the Emperor's feet thrusting his paper forward. The Colonel would retrieve it and hand it to H.I.M., who would read it and give whatever order he chose. I happened to be duty master when H.I.M. made an unheralded visit to the school at lunch time. I took him round the tables of boys. There were no complaints or comments. Everyone seemed satisfied. Then I mentioned to H.I.M. that when he had landed off H.M.S. Enterprise at Haifa in 1936, fleeing from the Italian invasion, my father had commanded the Guard of Honour ashore. I had seen it all on the news-reel at home. H.I.M. again said how grateful he had been.[6]

1954, 1955, and 1956: A pot-pourri of three happy years

Life really opened up when in late January we moved into our little brick semi-detached bungalow. We had to get our fireplace put in, and when a four-oil-drum water 'tank' on a wooden tower had been installed and was working, we moved in. The move was easy and soon completed because my class worked in relays with Rosemary at the flat loading boys' arms held out as they came round. We fed the boys on cake, as usual, and as usual had to turn them out so that we could get on.

The best thing we did in Addis was to engage a bright, personable, resourceful, and totally loyal young man named Melaku Tiruneh. He had walked to Addis for schooling but he couldn't get into a school. Our house was sited in a woodland clearing off the main track through the compound. So we thought: how about a garden? "Take as much as you like," said the authorities. Melaku and I first built a brick path from the front door just up to the track. Then we took a stake each, and Rosemary stood at the front door and as we walked east and west she told us when to stop. Then we both turned north to 'about the right spot' behind. Then we built garden fences, a front-gate, laid down a drive for the car with a double front gate – to keep out hyenas. Then we felt we should have a garage. Melaku and I built an open-fronted one out of eucalyptus. For the walls, Melaku got hold of a 'chika' man. This mud-wall maker dug a pit, adding straw to the loose earth. He worked it together with his feet, adding water to make a thick mud which had to be left a week before use. Then when he approved of its consistency, it was plastered on to our wooden framework. For the roof we bought sheets of corrugated iron which we transported singly from town on a simple, hired, one-horse gharri.

Rosemary did a wonderful job with the garden, which soon came to be admired. I wrote to her parents describing how marvellously she managed house, garden, servants, everything. Apart from being totally in love I now had ample proof that I had the best possible wife for the job, wherever it led us.

As time passed, Matie said "Let there be a lawn." So she and Melaku dibbled in creeping grass on the earth plot after we had consulted Longmans' excellent *Gardening in the Tropics*. Later we needed drainage, so we dug narrow trenches at angles, filled with gravel. Finally, we put up

---

[6] I include extracts from a copy of R.N. Captain C.E. Morgan's report on completion of his task. See p. 589.

a little summer-house. We called it a gaze-bo because we could enjoy watching the passers-by from it.

Of course, to follow custom or common sense we had to employ a zebaniah, a night-watchman. The zebaniahs at the school were on the strength. They had enormous Mauser rifles of something like .500 bore, with which occasional hyenas might be frightened at some risk to the rest of us. These zebaniahs were supposed to be of some insurance against robbers, but ours was a complete comedy. We came back late one night, and he woke up at our approach. He sprang to his feet, saluted, and fell backwards into the flower-bed. Next day I let him try a shot or two with my Webley air-pistol at a wooden box on the lawn. He stood where he wished, but he never hit it. Rosemary wrote home: "Michael loves trying to pass the time of day (if not night) with our zebaniah. Michael knew the torch with which we had provided the zebaniah, as 'batterie'. It was a fine, full moon, and Michael said to him, pointing at the moon, "Ah, tillik batterie"! (Big torch). Whereat the zebaniah replied: "Christos batterie". Collapse of Michael."

Glimpses of medicine

The Red Cross Leprosy Colony was run by a dedicated, young German, Dr Shaller (Edinburgh 1938). There were 1,600 patients in a hospital intended for a tenth of that number. A Wingate boy teaching English there said: "Conditions may be awful, but compared with village life, it is not unusual at all."

The Colony's annual fund-raising fete was held at the Embassy, and there were side-shows, mainly involving gambling. We ran a shove-ten-cent board, but I was not skilled at fixing long odds. I had to pay out to members of the Imperial Guard who were fiends at it. In the evening we ran a Scottish song and dance show at the Y.M.C.A. We had half of Addis looking through the windows, some on stilts.

A British doctor arrived in response to an Ethiopian appeal in our British newspapers for someone to run a hospital. He arrived and was shown a meadow, with the words: "Here's your hospital." He responded with resolution.

Shooting

In February H.E. Douglas Busk very kindly asked me to join a duck shoot. This was a grand start for me to go with a fully clued-up senior diplomat with a cross-country vehicle, and four other experienced guns. A key figure on such occasions was Colonel Sandy Curle, our six-foot four-inches tall Consul. He was a fine Scot, humourous, efficient, know-ledgeable, and a tower of strength to all. Sandy had a well-organised group of keen, young beaters-cum-bearers who met us at our rendezvous near their village. Before they set off beating, Sandy tied one half of an airline baggage label to each so that there could be no argument about payment at the end.

All went well, until suddenly the air became full of locusts. Then the landscape became almost obscured by them; we were pelted by locusts, and they hurt. There were duck still, so Douglas B. pressed on until it became very difficult to tell if a speck at the end of one's barrels was a duck far away or a close-at-hand locust. We had to give up. I did all right with five duck, a goose, and a hare.

Back in the Embassy, Sandy gave us his cocktail 'Garry Horse's Milk': equal parts of real ice-cream and gin, grated nutmeg, and a dash of rum; it had quite an equine kick.

H.E. invited me again in March: fifty miles over Entotto for plenty of duck on small lakes. We were allotted fifty-six duck from the bag. You should have seen Wolde's face when he opened the Volkswagen bonnet and found no engine, but duck! It was a pleasure passing duck round the compound.

A day or two after the February shoot, locusts hit the school. The main body was high, moving north-east, looking like trails of brown smoke; but a large body of stragglers flew low. They settled in patches anywhere, on bare earth or green. There was a roar of wings like a waterfall, and a noise like hail as they fell on tin roofs. Many just fell the last ten feet or so and seemed none the worse. Village boys appeared driving them up again; and in three-quarters of an hour they were gone, except for a few dead-beats. One horrible consequence was the rain of tiny excreta all over the town.

February 1954: Hot springs and guninea-fowl

In February 1954 we got away to Wolleso, a delightful, favourite spot. We drove 115 kilometres in one and a half hours on the Jimma road, losing height across a flat plain. Then up over low hills, west at 6000 ft., into a much greener, pleasant land. Wolleso was a large village in a countryside of thickets, flat-topped acacias, and rounded figs. Here we found an Italian-built, well-kept, well-appointed, single-storey hotel, with a Czech manager, Czech-brewed St George's Beer, and natural hot springs. The water was in two outdoor pools, and suites of rooms with deep, sunken, seven-foot by four-foot baths, each with a huge brass tap ready to gush lovely, hot-spring water at a bearable temperature. There were pleasant walks for us, and we saw birds such as parakeets, blue-breasted waxbills,

114

Bradfield

Lt. Col. J D Hills, M.C., M.A.
Headmaster of Bradfield in my day. A
great friend to have.

Aerial view of Bradfield College, Berkshire.

i

Troop Carrier.

*The 'troops' with QM Painting,
coming away from live firing in the
chalk pit.*

Battle.

NIGHT MANOEUVRES

SIR – The anecdote about Donald Fairclough and Daphne Dodd's boobs was indeed hilarious reading! It prompted another OB a year my senior in A House to recall a JTC exercise known as Night Ops, an event fraught with all manner of shenanigans under cover of darkness. Donald and myself were detailed to crawl into the 'enemy' guarding the bridge over the Pang to reconnoitre. The defendants were G House and there were some stories about how they would pull off bootlaces from unfortunate captives, who were then unceremoniously ejected into the Pang.

My 1928 Type 40 Bugatti with Jarvis Boat Body. It is now in America, according to the Bugatti Owners' Club.

We noted some very sleepy youngsters lying about with heads drooping over their SMLE's and their minds elsewhere. Just as we were about to withdraw, the Adjutant, OB Hank Halsted, roared up in his Bugatti. Not wishing to be caught in the glare of the headlights, we stayed put. Halstead dismounted, had some words with the G House JUO and others and then moved over to the undergrowth where Donald and myself were concealed and asked if anyone was there. We naturally kept silent, whereupon Halstead undid his fly and piddled all over our backs! We were very glad to retreat as soon as Halstead moved off.

BRINSLEY BARNES (A 42–46)
Victoria, Australia

(NOT TRUE: I never took my Bugatti on night exercises!)

Bradfield College – The Greek Theatre in action.

iii

Hungary

Old Sárospatak and the wooden bridge, with Sátoralujhely (!) and Russia beyond.

Sárospatak School (The English Boarding House). The author had quarters here.

Dr Bassola, the brave pro-Western Secretary of Education, visiting us all, and supporting our production of Julius Caesar *in English, in Budapest with students, in 1947.*

iv

The British Council Office and Centre in the very suitable old Bank Building in Harmincad Utca, with the British Legation above.

Hungary

Sárospatak Summer School, August 1948, bringing back memories 'grave and gay' of wonderful, dedicated men and women teachers of English. The great E. L. T pioneer, Tom Beach, is centre front.

*Tony Mann (British Council) and Cecil Bellamy (Bradfield College)
planning programmes.*

The irrepressible Cecil Bellamy with some of his drama students – off duty!

Hungary

*A Sokat peasant couple
at Pécs market.*

*Bacsi ("Uncle")
and his pipe.*

A new bell for Visegrad church, on the Danube.

. . . hoisting the bell into the tower.

Staff all together in Sarnagati Building, 1949 –
our office and library in those early days.

Press Conference in Council Centre, 26 August 1950, issue of our programme
of activities 1 September–30 November.

Karachi

Karachi Docks, after Partition in 1947.

*Begum Liaquat Ali Khan performing the opening ceremony of
an Exhibition of photographs illustrating the life and work
of William Wordsworth in Karachi on April 11th 1950 – his
centenary year.*

Transport in Sind: the camel cart – slow, silent, and steady.

One of the sad casualties of Partition:
an aged Kashmiri refugee.

Karachi

The beaters on our wild pig shoot, Sind.

The beaters and their dogs.

Our verandah life in Bath Island House: Mohammed serving us 'tiffin'.

Rehearsing the Argyll Broadswords with our invaluable Police piper,
kindly loaned to us when required.

Karachi

Tribal dance in formal setting, at Malir.

Zamzamah – Kim's gun in Lahore.

Lahore – The Offices of the Civil & Military Gazette, for which Kipling wrote.

The notice outside Kipling's office at the C & M G.

sun birds, and flashing, unidentified, brightly coloured tinies.

We contacted the local headmaster, Mr Shedad, a cheery Indian, who arranged to take us out next morning after guinea-fowl, pig, and bushbuck. The prospect got us up at 5.15 a.m.; it was still dark but there was a brilliant full moon. With his friend Ato Makonnen and a boy to guard the car, we drove with Mr Shedad some seven kilometres into the bush. It was very beautiful: the dawn light on one side and the moon on the other. We collected a very tall villager who in his shamma looked like a draped telegraph-pole. The trouble with guinea-fowl is that they won't get up. They run some distance fast, and then perch visibly in trees. We advanced, and Shedad and Makonnen were excitedly handling their shot-guns rather carelessly as they rushed up for a shot. "Why doesn't he shoot?" Shedad asked Rosemary. She explained that I refused to shoot a bird on the ground. But one did come back over us and I shot it, thus saving face.

We then went after larger game. To achieve anything we now had to go through every bush and up and down the steep sides of a stream. The sun was now up, and it was very hot. Rosemary left us to it. Shedad missed a dik-dik, which I was glad survived, but we got six guinea-fowl and our recovery in the hotel was delicious.

Feast of National Foods

The Feast of National Foods was a much-looked-forward-to annual Red Cross 'do'. It was held in a large hall; each community from fifteen countries had a stall laden with mouthwatering efforts. It was badly organised with too many people, and all the turns, songs, and dances, and general dancing came before the food, which was not served until after 10 p.m. H.I.M. came and sat patiently after being led round all the stalls. "Then," wrote Rosemary, "there was a dirty dive, especially by Greeks and Armenians, not to mention the Wingate staff. At last I got a piece of lobster, unknown here. Fresh! Joy! From the French stall, of course. Drinks of all sorts could be bought, but no beer which we badly needed . . . What lovely dresses the Indian women wear."

On 10 May Rosemary noted, "I'm getting quite a name for my pancakes which I do on the hot plate. The pile I took over to a tennis tea all disappeared though they had said they didn't want anything to eat."

May 1954: To Diredawa and Harar

We went on the Littorino train, a single-coach diesel. There were no fences along the line, so with a cow-catcher in front and a wonderful horn we went whooping out of Addis, with children, dogs, cows, and pigs fleeing in all directions. Along the way we had to slow down for animals. There were many Greeks with us. They couldn't bear shouting at one another across the tiny compartment, so they all sat on top of one another, leaving a double seat free all the way. Five huge melons rolled about the floor and masses of chickpea got into everything, including my case.

Most of the way there was low scrub and thorn bushes which were green and pleasant after the recent rain. Here and there small acacia bushes were in flower, and their sweet scent was very powerful. The landscape now had striking, volcanic features. We could see the Chercher hills, lava-flows with clean-cut, recent lines, and flat-topped ridges with sharp edges. Near Lake Metahara we went through acres of black volcanic rock with few plants. To the north, near Diredawa, the desert stretched away. We saw gazelle and a long-tusked, wild boar running up a water-course. The journey was tiring – 8.30 a.m. to 6.30 p.m. – so, having seen the country, we came back by 'plane. The Diredawa of the locals was a compact town of white-washed, flat-roofed houses known as the megalla; while the European houses, mainly Italian-built as usual, were built in a grid pattern.

The European section was attractive with masses of bougainvillea, hibiscus, frangipane, and huge flame of the forest trees and roofs of red tiles. The countryside at the foot of the southern hills was dull and flat with thorn and prickly pear, and camels grazing. It was a pleasure to walk around the megalla in the wide streets of mostly neat houses, which had a coloured frieze along the top, and pastel-washed walls.

Rosemary wrote: "The Galla people are much more colourful than our Amharas. We saw groups of women carrying weird-shaped gourds on top of their heads – or a solitary beer bottle! Their hair was in two low buns. They wore arm-bangles, huge amber and red coloured beads, and large, coloured shawls either round their heads, or used for holding babies or goods. Many wore coloured dresses with a very full, patterned skirt a few inches showing below. They are obviously fond of red and patterns. The men wore the usual dirty drill, but in a town with a large Moslem population there were many Arabs in lungis and bright turbans."

We had an introduction to Bill Clift, the American area manager of Sinclair Oils. He seemed to live tied to his transmitter-receiver, but he was so good giving up time for us. He had a spot of bother when a European truck-driver pulled up on seeing a body on the track. On getting out of his vehicle the driver was set upon by several waiting Somalis, one of whom accused him of killing his brother. The truck-driver found himself in the local jail accused of manslaughter.

We gave Bill dinner at the hotel, which was built as an Italian officers' leave centre. The town was unattractive. It was only pleasant to walk about after 5 p.m. "Michael liked it," she wrote, "because of the people we met." True, Bill took us out after dinner in his car on a jolly hyena chase in the dry river between the towns into which the megalla refuse was thrown. Bill chased the hyenas in the headlights for a good look, as they loped just in front of the car. Hyenas were to be seen all over the place; some fighting over a dead cat. They look quite pleasant from the front with their teddy bear ears; but the side view of an immensely powerful neck and crushing jaw is horrible.

The same evening was Easter Eve for the Copts and the Greek Orthodox Church in Diredawa. We were taken by a Yugoslav locust officer to the midnight service in the Greek church. It began in the courtyard with the congregation of Greeks and Armenians carrying lighted tapers, and the priest reading and chanting. At midnight they let off noisy fire-crackers for twenty minutes. The priest continued the service in the church and the people drifted in and out. A number of Ethiopians were spectators.

There were many French in Diredawa connected with the railway and its main repair centre there. There were two British couples in the Cotton Company, and three members of the Desert Locust Survey. One splendid, moustachioed, Jimmy Edwards, ex-R.A.F. type who came to the hotel for a meal seemed glad to have new company, and he told us quite a lot about his job. The team was constantly on the move between Kenya, Saudi Arabia, Somaliland, Eritrea, and Ethiopia. The locusts breed after the rains, and it was best to catch them while they were still hoppers, and the Diredawa area was a favourite spot. The local Issa tribe were unco-operative, and had even speared locust men, so that troops had to be brought in to let the work go ahead. The Issa view was that locusts were friends who gave employment and pay. There might be three to four months' wages, enough to keep the tribe in funds for a year. Chiefs when asked for perhaps forty helpers, were likely to reply: "Employ two hundred or none". Buxton mentioned the Issa with distaste.[7] We were pleased and curious to see several of the fiercer, wild-looking Danakils, with their bushy hair and fearsome, wide-bladed, curved knives. A Danakil warrior is revered by the number of men he has slain, and these are marked by stones in front of his tomb. Our Danakil were quietly leading laden camels, perhaps from their market centre at Beta to the north.[8]

---

[7] Buxton, *Travels in Ethiopia* (Ernest Benn, London, 1957).
[8] See L. M. Nesbitt's marvellous book, *Desert and Forest* (London, Cape 1934). Douglas Busk says: "This records the first crossing of the Danakil desert from south to north. The little-known story of what is in my opinion one of the greatest and most courageous journeys of modern times, which earned the protagonist the Murchison Grant Medal of the Royal Geographic Society." Nesbitt dedicates his book: "To the memory of the men who sacrificed their lives in the endeavour to explore the Danakil country."

Harar

Eighty minutes in a Volkswagen 'bus took us the thirty miles up 2000 ft. to Harar, by an amazing road of steep, hair-pin bends up an escarpment. Some of the steepest slopes were terraced for growing bushes of khat, the narcotic plant which was exported to Aden by air. Once up, we bowled along through green, heavily farmed, undulating country, with quite a few streams, and two lovely lakes. We passed an old, sadly neglected, probably Italian, settlement with fruit and flowering trees, shrubs, and cypresses. The countryside, which was perfect for walks, was the most delightful of anywhere we visited in Ethiopia.

Harar old town was enclosed by a high wall. The houses were built of rough, honey-coloured stone, with roofs of branches and turves. The megalla had only one main street; the rest were passages. Harar was the most unusual town in Ethiopia because it was the capital of the only part of Ethiopia ever to fall under foreign domination. The province had once been seized by the Khedive of Egypt and had become the centre of an independent Moslem kingdom, as the first Europeans found. When it was re-conquered by Ras Makonnen, the father of Haile Selassie, he accrued much respect. The whole area appealed to the Italian twentieth-century invaders, who had plans to make Harar an important centre, the beginnings of which could be envisaged by the wide road layouts, and some completed ground buildings.

Two school boys to whom we had brought letters from our Wingate pupils took us for an enjoyable, long and hearty walk around the upper parts of the settlement. The climate was perfect. We made a couple of visits to the megalla. One very steep street of huge cobble attracted us; it was full of tiny cloth shops where Rosemary got some "frightfully gay striped silk for a cocktail skirt". We had set out to find some attractive, gaily coloured basket-work from a reputedly half-Turkish woman. She was reached up extremely ricketty stairs, and was clad in a too-tight, orange dress, sitting surrounded by girls making baskets and mats. Two babies crawled around; they were disgustingly-covered in flies, poor little things.

We were given dinner by the humorous, well-known British Consul, Gerry Pink, and his colleagues the Lawries from Edinburgh. Gerry told us that forty to fifty hyenas would gather outside the megalla walls at night. He kindly motored us back to Diredawa in his Land Rover, with the flag flying and locals waving everywhere. Then we were in the hands of the Williamsons, a very kind Lancashire couple who ran the cotton mill. People were so kind to us everywhere in Africa.

As Rosemary wrote, "We were welcomed home by the sight of the first flower in our garden, a huge red dahlia, now my pride and joy. It's an enormous plant, I counted 35 buds on it."

Visitors

Visitors were few and far between, but we needed them to keep us in touch with the outside world. Early on, Andrew Martin, an old Etonian and a British pentathlon competitor was driving his Land Rover through to a farming job in Southern Rhodesia. He was a fine, young man, patient and helpful, and the Wingate boys benefitted from their easy association with him. A year later, Ross Charlton and his Oxford and Cambridge Trans-Africa Expedition in two Land Rovers 'dropped in'; there were nine of them who proved to be keen pioneers, good ambassadors, and fun. Tom Pakenham was an entertaining visitor in 1956, who had Ethiopia at heart.[9]

Of the official visitors to the school our Ambasador, Douglas Busk, who was also an an accomplished explorer and dedicated mountaineer, gave a magnificent talk on mountaineering in the Ruwenzori. It was beautifully tailored for the boys.[10] Also Tom Stobart, of the triumphant Everest expedition of 1953, showed his photographs. It was a great chance for us and the boys to see a remarkable story vividly unfold before us. R. R. Stokes M.P. (whom I had applauded in the War, for his campaign for better tanks), spoke well on Ethiopia's future potential, and the part the boys would need to play. The boys were pleased with Christopher Sykes, who spoke on General Wingate. They said to me, "He didn't try to avoid difficult words but spoke to us as if we were English boys."

Dance and drama

The boys wanted to dance our Western way with girl partners; and to meet girls, which didn't happen in their society. So an Old Boys' Dance was arranged. A hundred more young people came than were expected and only a quarter were Old Boys. Great efforts were made to get girls, and many were ferried over from the Itegue Menen Girls' School by Volkswagen bus. There were not nearly enough women, so 'excuse me' dances were very popular. The European ladies here gave up all hope of enjoyment. Rosemary danced with thirty men but she was only able to manage a few steps before another partner took over, each dancing differently. It was all the more exhausting because that evening we put on a proper display of dancing including Scottish country dances and two foursomes; the ladies in evening dress.

[9] The result was in a well-illustrated book: *The Mountains of Rasselas* (London, 1959).
[10] His book on Ethiopia, *The Fountain of the Sun*, is a classic containing delightful paintings and sketches by his wife Bridget.

Our next effort was a staff production of *French Without Tears* for the boys and for the general public. Rosemary was make-up and prompt. But I escaped because I was working for the Ministry of Education on scripts for an English teaching workshop and on a *Manual of Common Errors.* Next a team of four of us had to mark 1100 primary school to secondary school entrance papers. It took us four days.

In June Cecil Curle got us dancing at an evening for the Anglican Church Building Fund with American dancers in the lovely home of the kind, rich, and generous David Nadel. We enjoyed rehearsals and all, finally getting all the dancers to do a 'Dashing White Sergeant'. We made £250.

Precipitation

Now came the heavy rains and hail storms; one lasted twenty-minutes. All the flowers were bashed and bedraggled. But the going was good at the annual Embassy Gymkhana; an All Nations occasion which H.I.M. enjoyed. There was very fine riding by the Imperial Forces. The Wingate stables (a mud hut in Jim's garden) were unplaced. Now we could feast on mushrooms. Hordes of small boys made easy money trailing round selling from bulging shirts or pullovers.

29 September: Maskal Day

The festival of 'The Coming of Spring, and the Finding of the True Cross by the Empress Helena' was upon us, and suddenly, and without fail every year, the bright yellow 'maskal' daisies were everywhere. As Rosemary noted, "The far compound wall is now completely hidden by a thick, long, six-foot-high bank of them. The square in town in front of the main Coptic Church becomes filled by a pyramid of long poles brought by every celebrant of this festival. Every devotee adds his or her long, thin pole with a bunch of maskal daisies tied at the top. The Emperor and his court processed three times round in the afternoon, followed by the archbishop and priests. Crowds trudged cheerfully into town with bobbing bunches on their poles often mixed with delphiniums and cornflowers. Bonfires of the discarded poles were lit all over the town; while other groups with flags and drums processed along singing ho-ho songs. Lovely every year, with everyone so happy."

Ethiopia

A surprise visit

Rosemary also wrote: "Thanks to Sebastian Knowle, a Gordonstoun O.B., we were taken out to the pleasant village of Addis Alem some thirty kilometres to the west. It is set among trees with a church on top of a little hill. This was an unusual church, being square and not in the round, where the priests usually process. But its chief delight were the paintings on the plaster walls. There were gay, flowering trees with snakes in them (the devil?), and smaller trees in pots painted between the windows. One wall had gorgeous, typical Ethiopian paintings. In the middle section there were two groups of leopards and two pairs of lions. The leopards were wonderfully naive, all cross-eyed, and grouped as if posing for a family photograph."

A sudden death

A charming boy from my class died of spinal meningitis. The class took the news hard and all threw up their hands and wept for ages. The lad was buried the next morning in the church-yard next door. The boys, Mrs Heyring, and Rosemary rushed round the garden for flowers, and made huge wreaths. The coffin was laid on the church steps, and priests chanted and sang over it. There was much wailing by local women acting as professional mourners. A priest in colourful robes and swinging an incense burner preceded the coffin to the grave which had been dug by the school servants. As the coffin was lowered, the women and servants crowded round moaning while the priests continued chanting. But the boys who had really known their friend stood apart, quiet and stunned. It was hard to be faced with such sadness.

December 1954: The Emperor's return from abroad

There was a holiday and Caird Wilson got us on to the Mitchell Cotts' balcony in town to see the fun. We clapped and cheered H.I.M. passing in his Rolls, and the crowd made OO-OO-noises. Our real interest was watching the crowds, who for once were not staring at us. There were circles of men jumping up and down with shouts and chanting; a sort of solo verse and chorus.

Then finally came the largest number of Galla horsemen we had ever seen. Their clothes were not grand, but they were a tough, independent lot. They wore topis, or trilbys, or straw boaters and carried a long stick or a spear. The harnesses were highly decorated with red tassels, some straps had brass or silver plates, and there were gaily striped saddle-cloths. Many were bare foot with big toes stuck through the stirrups. Some riders wore baboon-skin head-dresses, with a piece as a chin-strap looking like a beard. One had a bright-red cloak round his shoulders. At the head of the troop rode three men wearing head-dresses of lions' manes. It was wonderful.

Christmas 1954

This Christmas was much more cheerful. We risked a Nativity Play by the staff. We felt we should do this, and it was appreciated. Melaku got us a free Christmas tree after dark. "Where from?" I asked. Our zebaniah commented: "You wouldn't have got it from wherever I was the watchman." The Sandfords gave a memorable dance; and we just remember cheerfully chasing two hyenas down the school drive on our exuberant return. Luckily, they didn't go into our garden. Hyenas sometimes did get in when they were starving, and gnawed the rawhide thongs binding our cane garden furniture.

Our New Year and the Ethiopian Christmas were wet and cold. Four households got together and we had a feast of two roast pigs. At home we laid on a whisky-tasting party, using eight of the many brands on sale in Addis in plain, lab bottles. A brandy which I put in foxed everyone.

We were glad to fly to Lake Tana with the Hamiltons by cargo Dakota; no khat but hides were carried this time. We flew over the vertical-sided gorges and canyons of the Blue Nile. Every shelf seemed to have its houses, but how did the people move about? We made two stops in grassy fields at Debra Marcos and Danghila. Each stop was a great social event in sight and sound. We alighted near the source of the Blue Nile!

Bahar Dar was an ordinary village, with an attractive position on a bay at the south-east corner of Lake Tana and here lay a simple, small, verandahed hotel close to the water's edge. The lake was very large, with a far horizon; but with peace and charm and a view to the further shore of low, wooded hills. We could sit and watch the squirrels in the trees, the fish rise and the kingfishers diving. The variety of almost-tame birds was a delight: herons, divers, toucans, kites, seagulls, wagtails, martins, ibis, egrets, crested cranes. The sacred ibis came in to roost every night in the two great trees at the waterside. We became very fond of these elegant birds.

There was no hotel cook at the time, so we took tinned food. We got milk and eggs, and funny little loaves. The cook-house was filthy, and all our food tasted of eucalyptus from the aged wood-stove. For long, cooling drinks we simply knocked green and yellow limes off the trees.

Ethiopia

To the Blue Nile and Tesseisat Falls

We were lucky in having two old Wingate boys, Deresegn Ayelu and
Yaragal Taffara, now teachers. They were a great help as guides and
translators, and, best of all, they introduced us to the Governor, Major
Yayahired Merid. He was a little man in a homburg hat, who was greeted
by everyone with low bows. We addressed him as Your Excellency. He
most hospitably invited us to a dinner of at least seven courses with
frightfully hot wat and we drank tej. He sent us milk every day, and called
to see us several times. This was kind of him, but rather a strain on our
peace and quiet.

Major Merid organised a trip for which we were happy to pay. We went
in his Chevrolet truck to the huge Tesseisat Falls on the Blue Nile. Mrs
Hamilton and Rosemary were in the cab of the truck. In the open body
were David and I, the Governor's daughter, Yaina Addis, and another lady;
also the priest, His Excellency's friend, and his son, five servants (two
with revolvers), small boys to carry guns or rifles, two live kids for lunch,
baskets of injera, and more.

We left at 6 a.m.: it was still dark and cold. We went two hours along a
track on a grassy plain which wound round clumps of trees and palms. It
was beautiful country with a thick belt of trees by the river, watered by a
huge cloud of spray mist. Hills rose around us up to the plateau above. As
we drove, inhabitants wanting to make requests of the Governor came on
to the track and kowtowed. The lorry parked on the edge of the trees and
we walked to the sound of the falls. We first had to cross several channels
on bridges of branches to reach the wide river, which here flowed directly
up against a hill in front and disappeared. When we got onto rocks in the
middle of the river and looked over a lip we could see the tremendous 150
to 200 ft. falls. At the bottom of the hill the river turned sharply at right-
angles through a narrow canyon. Only David, with the aid of the priest
and schoolmaster, was able to wade further across and see the magnificent
main falls.

The Governor intended to spend the day here. We walked back to
'base', and found everything for his feast, including a table and chairs, set
out under a spreading ilex on a natural dais covered with rushes. The
retainers were busy skinning the kids. Later a fish eagle arrived in which
we showed great interest, so they shot it for us. What a tragedy! After
lunch we walked downstream a little way in a less steep-sided canyon and
looked at the fine, old Fasil Bridge, built for Emperor Fasil by the
Portuguese some 400 years before. It was very solid with the mortar still
sound, but the Italians had blown one end.

Whilst on leave in East Africa we went to the source of the White Nile,
at Jinja, out of Lake Victoria. There we saw the stone block marked

SPEKE, at the spot where Speke could confirm his discovery of the source of this great river. This landmark was soon to be covered forever by the waters of a dam.

At Lake Tana we were fascinated by the reed boats – tanquas – made out of bundles of papyrus. It was exciting to see papyrus growing in masses some ten to twelve-feet-high at the edge of the lake. The spongy stems let the water in and out of the boat, but the tanqua was unsinkable. Goods were placed on a firmly wedged block of papyrus along the boat to keep them dry. Tanquas looked fragile, but we saw one being paddled carrying a full, forty-four-gallon drum of petrol. They were propelled by long pieces of bamboo. It was hard work, and it was surprising that no attempts were made to fit blades to the poles. Rosemary managed a solo voyage very well. A flotilla of tanquas was an attractive sight. We saw thirty-five or so coming to Bahar Dar market in little groups, the paddlers singing and shouting to each other. The market was a solid mass of laughing, shouting, shrieking people, and numerous donkeys. It was mainly a food market: millet, barley, sesame, peas and beans, chillies, coffee beans, a few potatoes, flax seed, maize, and root ginger. All were displayed in straw baskets over which the women sellers squatted under little straw umbrellas. Cotton was being sold by weight, using very primitive scales consisting of a balance of wood with leather pouches for stone weights.

We flew up to Gondar for a brief visit: a provincial capital and an ancient kingdom. It had a gloomy air, and looked as if the war had just finished: houses were uncared for and falling to pieces. But the 'Portuguese' castles built by each succeeding ruler, and dating from the 1600s, were interesting. They were grouped together within a high wall scattered around a grassy meadow. One had been done up as a residence for H.I.M., and we were able to see over it, including the pleasant, simply carved furniture of solid wood with traditional patterns.

With permission from the Provincial Director-General and the loan of a Land Rover, we visited the old Abbey of Quequam. We were able to see the famous Holy Book, on the good works of Mary. A young deacon in a sheepskin said that the priests had gone to town with the keys. But $1.E. was an adequate key for the old book to be produced with the aid of an incredibly old and dirty man. This book was in a leather cover wrapped in cotton, and again in cotton inside. It was laid on a bench, and every local around started turning the pages in curiosity.

We went on to Debra Behan to the Church of the Holy Trinity on a hill outside the town. It was a rare, oblong building, full of lively and colourful paintings of Ethiopian saints on cloth. That was a great joy. Thanks to an introduction, we then had a short drive up to the view-point on the Asmara road where one could look across a fantastic jumble of peaks, pinnacles, humps, needles, cones, and slopes at 90°: the Simian Hills which, alas, we could not visit.

February 1955: Garden Palace interlude

For a few months, from February until our leave in July 1955, Rosemary was governess to Prince Paul the eldest of the three sons of the Duke of Harar, the Emperor's second son. Paul was not easy to get on with and he was very upset at the recent departure of his Scottish nanny. The prince was used to getting his own way; and he was also desperate to get some attention from his father, who was seldom around for him. On the whole, Rosemary got on with Paul, but she still has the mark of a kick on the shin from him! The Emperor soon set up a proper school for all his young grandchildren, so Rosemary's job came to an end. There were sunny patches, she says, and I think she was getting good results.

A car from the Palace would take Rosemary to and fro. She ate lunch with other employees in a sitting-room in the Garden Palace, in a large villa-cum-bungalow built for the Empress. At one luncheon Rosemary was presented to the Emperor, and to the Empress. She found the Empress so nice, despite her normally forbidding appearance. The job gave Rosemary a certain kudos, I suppose. She had to press rather hard to get her salary which was apt to be two months in arrears, a common situation in Addis.

April 1955: Donkey for dinner

Driving home late at night we often saw hyenas in the car headlights, and I wanted to get to know them. The chance came when Derek Turner having been told of a dead donkey had it dragged across the road outside and tied to a steel pylon near which we could park.

We drove out early the next night, but there was only silence as the moon came up. As a lorry passed, I moved our car up to twenty yards from the body. We sat still and silent, and it got colder. Our eyes became tired. The strange light made every shadow move.

The next movement was not a shadow. One hyena came up the road, and disappeared. I could hear my heart beat through my open mouth; and I had to listen for half-an-hour. Suddenly two hyenas appeared, darted backwards and forwards, and finally went at the donkey. There came a crunch and a nasty, rending sound. With a slopping gurgle the donkey's gaseous insides spewed out. The hyenas fled. We had a brief interruption from a school zebaniah just before 2 a.m. After another half-hour four hyenas appeared. They darted towards the corpse and then retreated. The moon was brighter, but occasionally obscured by cloud. The hyenas sometimes appeared ghostly white, or as dark humps. Their dartings and weavings, pauses, and sudden movements took the form of beasts in a weird puppet ballet, joggled by the two strings of fear and hunger. Hunger was winning. We could now shift our cramped bodies quite frequently and with less caution.

We heard a familiar "whoo-oop" in the distance, and then another call nearer. One of the hyenas now gave several, long, rising calls. A lorry came by and the hyenas scuttled off into the bushes across the road. Another lorry passed but the hyenas were back in a few minutes. There were six or seven of them, but in spite of the moon and the lights from Lolivare, the stone-mason opposite, we could not spot a new arrival or get a total. It was now near 3 a.m. and there was another interruption. Lolivare's large black and white mongrel came down the road, stopped, stiffened and let out a 'wuff'. The hyenas scuffled away from their tearing and scrunching. The dog advanced a few trots, gave another 'wuff', and bravely went home! The moon swung over the tall eucalyptus; the cold crept deeper and our bones ached. There was silence – just for a moment. Then in seconds and too quick for us to see, the carcass was surrounded by weaving forms, heads nodding, front quarters rising and dropping, sloping rumps twisting, and pads scuffling.

Then came a soft snicker of eerie laughter: a reckless, excited sound, a merciless sound of savoury anticipation, of drooling jaws. The carcass was now torn and ripped, and lumps dragged clear to be chopped and swallowed in gulps and gurgles, snarls, and yaps. The crunch of bones caused us to tense and shiver at the steel power of those teeth and jaws. We sat still in a state of repugnant fascination, tinged with fear. One small donkey wouldn't go far, and as the last morsels of skin, flesh, and bones seemed to disappear there was a sudden change of mood, and we heard the most chilling sounds of all.

First came a very sinister, falling "woo-oo": a strangled moan of ecstasy, of stuffed satisfaction. Next wilder laughs echoed from the stones and the bank beyond. There was a maniacal whicker of exultation as we watched a dance of dismemberment. In and out, round about they moved, darting, weaving, twisting, swaying. And then we heard them screech a mad, strangled, rasping, cut-off screech, repeated again and again. We had had enough, put up our headlights and drove slowly away. One or two beasts raised heavy heads with swinging heaves. Then all backed away and disappeared into the trees. At 4 a.m. I went back, and no vestige of the donkey remained. Once again the hyenas of Entotto had performed their useful, self-appointed chore.

10 May 1955: the Red Cross Fete

Our Scottish and Highland dance team were over early on Janhoy Meda to take possession of our plot on the huge, grassy meadow. Rosemary wrote out performance signs, and I fixed up the gramophone. We and the Greeks had to use records; the Swedes, Armenians, and Ethiopians had live music. There were tents, enclosures, and temporary buildings covering most of the ground. In no time the different sites containing quack doctors, strong men, American square dancers, cafés, shooting ranges, and games of chance were all thronged by Ethiopians. The sites were so densely crowded that we hadn't a hope of getting near them. And we almost had to fight to keep our grass plot open, but the police helped. We had to dance on grass since no platform could be obtained.

The Emperor opened the festival at noon, and while he and his family lunched on one of the permanent stands, we danced the 'Duke and Duchess of Edinburgh', and the 'Argyll Broadswords' in front of them. We knew we had one ally among them because grand-daughter Princess Sybil had been in the Trinity Reel Club at Oxford and had asked Jim for a polish up to teach S.C.D.s; and Prince Paul had insisted on coming to see us. In the afternoon we danced again. It was terribly hot, but the champagne at the French stall helped to keep us going; and we made no mistakes. We managed to dance again at the fete the next day.

Siafu: The soldier ants

June 15th: the big rains started. The thunder rolled around in the afternoon. One morning Wolde rushed about, this time laying eucalyptus branches on the front and back door-steps. "The Siafu are coming. They don't like eucalyptus." Then we saw them coming in through the bathroom window, a column of soldier ants six-to-seven-inches wide, steadily trekking round the edge of the sitting-room into the kitchen and out through the door. Wolde had snatched up the eucalyptus in time to let them leave. We were able to watch fascinated at a respectful distance. The Siafu were awe-inspiring. In twenty minutes they had passed on, leaving no trace and us unharmed.

On stage again

In early July we had an end of term concert, which was open to all. Rosemary became expert at making convincing, custard-pie missiles for my slap-stick act. Soon the house became full of lifebelts and sailors' outfits. *H.M.S. Pinafore* was upon us. It was beautifully done, and unforgettable. There has never been a Captain Corcoran like Leslie Casbon.

Finally we got away on our first Home Leave. Our home leaves have been precious, and immensely rewarding through carefully planned, intermediate stops homewards or on return to post. Nevertheless, trying to see all the very scattered members of our respective families from Devon to Ross and Cromarty caused me to agree with our diplomatic friend James Glaze[11] that leaves are hell!

November 1955: Back to post and good news

On our return to Wingate, Rosemary commented, "What a difference to step straight into one's own home all clean and ready. I can't get over the brightness of the light." And we learned that Sheelagh Wilson's baby had been christened Robert, and that his mother's horse had won the Emperor's Gold Cup.

January 1956. Timkat

This was the time of the colourful festival of Epiphany in the holy month of Tirr. We spent it at Wolleso. We went up to the local church along with much of the populace to escort the tabots from the church to a tent in a field for two days of rejoicing. The tabot is the same as the Jewish Ark of the Covenant, containing the whole code of religious observance and behaviour. The Ethiopian Church has a full code of conduct for everyday life, though the amount of religious basis is not known. There is not so much emphasis on Jesus, but Mary has a much wider sphere. Its bible has the same Old Testament material as our King James' Bible, but also contains many other writings. Amharic is now used in many services rather than Geez. There were three tabots draped in brocaded cloths, which were carried on the heads of priests who were escorted by umbrellas held over them, and followed by swingers of incense censers, shakers of sistera, holy pictures, more priests, monks, and deacons. Notables under umbrellas walked behind. Women followed, singing and chanting, or ululating. Six officious policemen pushed people around.

The procession followed a winding path through the huts, over a stream, to tents surrounded by a palisade of bamboos which only the priests entered. A service was held within and people came streaming across the field in their best clothes. It was lovely in the golden evening light with

[11] James Glaze was appointed Ambassador to Ethiopia in April 1992.

the rich, green foliage round about, and the snow-white shammas trimmed with bright colours. There was a peaceful, soothing atmosphere in which we 'ferangi' felt welcome.

February 1956: At Lake Helena; hippos, at a distance

We took our staff members Tony Auckland, Eric Hamblyn, and John Fitzgerald, the headmaster of a neighbouring school, into the Rift Valley to Lake Helena. We only reached a campsite after dark because the level of the lake had gone down with the season and we had three kilometres of unchartered new track to negotiate. We camped in an open space a hundred yards from the tangled bush at the water's edge, under large, flat-topped acacia. It was idyllic: there were fewer flies, and there was mauve convolvulus all over the undergrowth. Before getting down to bed we only saw one hyena, and our hunting torches lit the ruby eyes of crocodile on the further reed beds.

During the night, above the ceaseless crickets we heard snuffling and grunts, sighs, splashings, and asthmatic breathing. These were hippopotami; they were sometimes very loud and probably near our shore. We knew the danger of an alarmed hippo finding danger between him and his safe water habitat, but we were too comfortable to think of moving.

The night was full of noises. Rosemary woke up and said sharply: "Michael, you are snoring." I woke up: "Oh no darling," I told my comparatively new wife, "I don't snore". "Well you were. "I was saved from further calumny, for wafting across the water came the snufflings loud and clear. "Hippo darling," I called out. Silence from the other bed – and from across the water. But we found hippo tracks on our shore in the morning.

Our boys were aware of hippo. Michael Powne, who had been a contemporary at Cambridge with Flanders and Swan, had brought with him the score of the very clever Hippo song. The boys loved it; and now we had a new school song with the chorus: "Mud, mud, glorious mud."

We became fond of hippos, but at a distance. The Golf Section of the Nyanza Club at Kisumu on Lake Victoria in Kenya had a hippo head as a badge. Rule 4, on the back of its score-card says: "If a ball comes to rest in dangerous proximity to a hippopotamus or crocodile, another ball may be dropped at a safe distance, no nearer the hole, without penalty."

Rosemary urged us to try harder for game because she was "having a dinner party on Friday". But we never toiled out early enough, and guineafowl ran so fast and far! The bird-watching was more rewarding: silver-grey cranes flew low in V-formation against the dawn sky, leaving the lake for their feeding grounds; many dapper little waders, geese (black and

Egyptian brown), grey and also great white egrets, duck and divers and, our favourite, spoonbills.

A stage appearance

Thanks to all the talent in Addis, I became a fan of Gilbert and Sullivan. I offered to be Private Willis in the next production, *Iolanthe*. I couldn't sing, but I could drill, and Sandy Curle produced a service rifle. I was taken aback to find our poster in the King George Bar in Addis, which featured Private Willis, with EOKA scrawled over it. The Greeks didn't like our administration in Cyprus. I hoped they wouldn't take it out on the cast of *Iolanthe*.

Rosemary hit on the way bearskins are made. Using a stiff, Ethiopian straw-hat as a base, she made split-cane hoops into a dome. Christine Sandford produced pieces of an old fur coat which Rosemary dyed black. Rosemary even 'created' an ermine cape for Lord Tololler, and headbands and garlands for the fairies. There was raucous laughter from husbands in the audience on the entry of their wives and others to: "We are dainty little fairies. . . ." We made £300 net for the Leprosarium.

12 July 1956.

Rosemary wrote: "Rains under way – rather miz. Red Cross Ball in the Opera House: evening ruined by ghastly crush of 3,600 people. We danced again in front of H.I.M. We worked at the Bar from midnight until 3.30 a.m. How they drank."

Leave

During July to September we had our annual local leave, during which time we visited Kenya, Uganda, Rhodesia, Dar-es-Salaam, Beira, Mozambique. Here was one advantage of living nearby!

October 1956: The stage again

We returned to a production of *See How They Run* by Derek Turner. The costumes and prompt were by Rosemary. The boys loved it. So did I, as part of the audience!

Next task for Rosemary – at the Armenian School

Rosemary became visiting teacher for English, history, and geography, in English. "I didn't really want to teach," she said, "but I couldn't have had a pleasanter job. The children were very nice, but regimented, poor dears. When 5 November came the Armenians thought we were crazy to still go searching through Parliament after three hundred years."

The outside world

It was remarkable how supplies and postal services got to us during the Suez crisis (even though Christmas cards came at Easter).

Christmas 1956

This Christmas was memorable for the Sandford's party for eighty people. The new Ambassador, Geoffrey Furlong, complimented Rosemary on her reeling. Later noting her spirited "gamesmanship", he said that he would have her in his rugger team.

For the pantomime we had *Cinderella*. Rosemary wrote: "My wigs were admired. It was quite a feat making a strapless, evening dress for Tony Auckland." As for me, I was blissfully happy. At last I had two perfect assistant comedians in Leslie Casbon and Derek Turner. With them I could put on my long-planned, slap-stick, paper-hanging act.

17 January 1957

We got our first Land Rover. We were able to buy a new, little, red S.W.B. fire-tender, less its fire-fighting equipment because there were no hydrants in Addis. I shared it with Alec Heyring. Now being confident in our vehicle we went off with Tony Auckland and Melaku to the Ghibbi river. Down at 5,000 ft. it was much warmer, and we found a good track used by timber lorries. The scene was now thorn trees and high scrub with tall grass. To the west we could see the river flowing across the plain with small hills and mountains beyond. We were about to pitch our tent when a Land Rover of Yugoslavs from the timber concession arrived, to whom I had an introduction. "Don't camp here, there's malaria," they said, "come and stay with us."

So off we went on an exciting hour's climb up a narrow track, even coping calmly with two laden lorries coming down. We were in a comfortable wooden hut, and fed and drunk on tots of slivovitz and helpings of hospitality. Next day we made a short trip, there were pretty jasmine bushes everywhere, but it was very tiring. We were given a wonderful evening back at base, and learned some Yugoslav, Giveli: cheers! Volim vas: I love you.

On our journey back to Addis we camped back from the Ghibbi river, where an old Italian welcomed us. He was mending the wooden bridge, and he told us that there were only mosquitoes in the rains. It was a wonderful place to remember: lovely, big trees and with nobody to stare at us. At 4000 ft., it was cool by day and very cold at night. There was crashing and grunting in the riverside bushes. I spotted a red eye shining in my lamp beam; it was a small hippo, so we allowed it to gruntle off. There was water buck spoor, but even being up before dawn we never saw one of the beautiful defassa.

24 January 1957

We went wild-fowling with Caird and Sheelagh Wilson. Up at 4.15 a.m. to be an hour along the Asmara road, across the plain by dawn to a little, open lake. There was soon twenty or so chattering, shivering children around us. They were anxious to retrieve birds and earn something, poor things. But they were a nuisance, crowding us at breakfast and bringing all the flies.

6 February

John Rich directed us to the Flamingo Lake, a gently sloping crater in the Bishoftu region. It was reached by a narrow track only passable by Land Rover and it was slow-going, particularly that Saturday against the tide of men returning from market, each driving about ten donkeys laden with the empty sacks and skins. However, it was well worth the effort although there were no flamingos this time. We were amused to observe several canny ladies under a huge acacia dispensing tej to travellers – at a cost.

To Jam-Jam Forest – hunting butterflies!

Liverpool University wanted a swallowtail butterfly variant found in Ethiopia, to study mimetic changes. They wrote to the Embassy, offering £50 expenses. In the absence of any resident lepidopterist, Philip and Eleanor Mansfield organised an expedition with us and Eric Hamblyn. Rosemary and I made the nets at little cost. Jam-Jam was a private forest. A charming Swiss, to whom I had an introduction, welcomed us to his

132

timber concession camp. It was a lovely place, and easy for us all to reach in Philip's L.W.B. Land Rover.

We found ourselves on an escarpment edge in a long, steep-sided, heavily wooded valley. The forest was not too thick because of regular cutting. There were grassy glades and thickets of bramble and wild roses. It looked very English except for the creepers and sudden patches of scarlet allium a foot high.

We had had no idea that butterfly hunting would be so energetic. The swallowtails were strong, fast flyers, and very hard to catch. We made mad leaps and dangerous dashes, with frantic yells of: "Coming your way. Up to the left you fool! Got it; no, it's gone again". It was terribly hard work, but most exciting, and funny to watch the others. We only got one swallowtail. But it was so beautiful: there were no locals, and no eucalyptus, and all home comforts in the camp. It was idyllic.

Next day in another area we ran into a group of larger, faster flyers, and managed to catch three. This was much more fun than hunting beautiful game; and it was an activity useful to science.

We did see beautiful game. At last we saw the striking, black and white colombus monkeys high up in the great trees. Their long, black tails with white, feathery ends hung down like great, house bell-pulls. It is terribly sad that the locals slaughtered them to make rugs, including the popular circular rugs needing eight skins. Rosemary saw an eagle's eyrie across the valley, and we both saw a lovely caracal. I greatly admire all the cat tribe; it is nature's best effort.

12 April 1957: War of nerves again

I learnt that the Personnel Department was posting me to Damascus. Then in June I was told to stay another year. Fine! Personnel now posted me to Birmingham. Imagine the horror of that after Ethiopia. Another letter came: "No, not Birmingham, perhaps Beirut!. Then another: "We can't be certain until you get home." It was very unsettling. A tremendous hailstorm added to the gloom. Roofs were damaged, and the hail lay so deep that Rosemary had to convince her Armenian pupils that it wasn't snow.

28 April: At last to Lake Awasa

We drove down the Kenya road into the Rift Valley past lakes Zwai, Lungano, and Hora Abayata to the crater lake Shalla, with cliffs and hills all round. The country here was so flat and featureless and there were no clear indications as to where to turn off the main road to find one's destination, only vital kilometer stones which must be noted down and remembered! We navigated easily to the hot springs by seeing the steam rising from the sand ahead. It was a scene of awful desolation. There were clear, hot-water pools, and pools of liquid sand plopping and seething. We pressed on through Sheshamana, where the Leprosarium was, to a promontary on Lake Awasa with good views. It had taken us between five and six hours. Thunderstorms kept us in camp; Rosemary cooked under our canvas awning. Our Black's tent was excellent, but its very design became a problem with an integral groundsheet, and zip door-flap closing.

A ghastly, huge, horned beetle walked over Rosemary one night, and we couldn't get it out. Its body alone was three inches long; and it ran very fast around the tent. It couldn't be bashed on the waterproof floor, nor against any solid wall. We nearly had hysterics. Finally it took a bash, and we got it outside, and gave it another bash. We aren't good bushmen. It took us ages to get to sleep. The horror was still kicking in the morning. Ugh!

Cattle were driven down to the lake about 11 a.m., and their attendants would stay and watch us until about 2 p.m. or 3 p.m. The men wore practically nothing except a leather cloak; and the women had thick, brass bangles, lots of bead necklaces, and also leather cloaks with bead patterns, which would have been attractive if they hadn't been black and stiff with grease and dirt. The birds were a joy again: pelicans, skeins of geese flying low over the lake morning and evening, some storks fishing at the edge, and a pair of fish eagles based close to us, with their eerie, piercing cry. The most lovely sight on that grey Sunday morning was a string of pink flamingoes passing across the grey background.

We made our last camp at Lake Helena on our way back to Addis; hippos were grunting and splashing in the reeds at night. Six of them were out in the middle of the lake in the morning. And we saw a beautiful serval cat.

22 May 1957

Prince Lul Makonnen, the Duke of Harar, Paul's father, and the Emperor's second son, was killed on the Bishoftu road. His driver, in a classic error, overtook a lorry through the dust cloud behind it. They hit an oncoming lorry head-on. Full mourning was immediately ordered for at least one month. Many ladies appeared completely in black, and all government servants and office workers wore black ties for the whole period. So did we. The Royal children were quickly packed off to the country because the custom was that royalty could only be informed of a death when in Addis Ababa. "Poor soul," said Rosemary of Paul, "he's so sharp that he's bound to put two and two together." It was a great tragedy because the Duke, although not exactly an angel, was very popular. The Crown Prince seemed a duller character.

The Royal Family now had a tough time because thousands of Ethiopians, diplomats and representatives of foreign groups all came to the Palace to pay their respects. All were received by the Emperor, who spoke to the crowd. The meadow in front of the Palace was full of Galla horsemen. We had lunch on Entotto and saw home-going streams of them riding away across the plain on their gaily caparisoned mules and horses, many carrying shining gold spears and shields. We had a special service in the English Church, as did other churches; and led by H.E. we took a wreath to the church where the Duke's body lay. Days later groups from all over the country were still coming to pay their respects despite H.I.M. asking people not to come from afar, but to pay their respects through their local Governor. In their innate loyalty this was a hard order for them to obey.

The tragedy gave Alec Heyring, our headmaster, who was in charge of the London G.C.E. Examinations much worry. The exams would have to be held on the official dates, but these would be during the forty days of mourning. Despite ancient royal tradition, the ministry, to our admiration and relief, allowed the exams to go ahead on schedule.

16 June: the Queen's Birthday Party

The Q.B.P., as we came to call it, was given by the Ambassador or High Commissioner for British subjects. It had been an eye-opener at our first one in 1954 as to just how many different kinds of British subjects there are: Adeni Arabs, French Canadians, and so forth. The Q.B.P. gave us the welcome opportunity to tell friends and acquaintances that we were shortly leaving for good, including Anthony Besse, whose family provided my Oxford College, St Edmund Hall, with the magnificent Besse Building.

This would be our first re-posting, and I will mention everything involved just this once. First of all there was the regret at not having achieved more, seen more, learned more; then the sadness at leaving a happy home, however strange; and the sadness at having to say goodbye to our domestic staff, and to our colleagues, and to our very faithful office-staff, and to our British and foreign friends.

There was the business of packing separately what we needed on leave, and what we needed to take to our next post; then having all our possessions professionally packed (the whole process not costing London too much); and then selling the car, which required going to the High Court in Addis. We had to make our travel arrangements including planned stop-offs or deviations at our own expense. Thus great chances came our way over the years. Then there was giving and going to farewell parties; the selling of items no longer required; the wondering about our future

To Jim and Innes Marshall

This page is specially in memory of Jim and Innes. After our time they both went on from the Wingate to the University of Addis Ababa, Jim to Mathematics and Innes to Science. Here they remained for forty years or more living dedicated lives in Education and Service among the people they loved and admired. Innes the sensitive, kindly, humorous wife of the irrepressible Jim.

We were happy to be remembered each Christmas by cards(and news and quips)produced by Innes. Her evocative sketches beautifully convey the spirit of the country and the lives of an admirable, proud and hardy people. This card is of a poor little shepherd lad with his pipe and his heavy garments against the cold and dangers in the near-vertical ravines in the spectacular mountains of the north-west.

Jim and Innes both decided to retire in Addis Ababa where they could live cheaply within their means in the style they enjoyed, with five servants who were totally loyal, and find a cheerful social life among a host of friends of many nationalities.

Maybe they thought that they would end their lives there, and this is what did happen. Innes died suddenly in 1992. In time, Jim returned to Scotland, but he did not take to this new style of life. So Addis Ababa reclaimed him, despite the absence of Innes. Then one day in 1996 he was taken so ill that he had to be flown home for treatment. In the circumstances he wished to be allowed to die without more ado. We understood.

The ashes of Jim and Innes lie in the cemetary of the little Ethiopian church in Gulele, next to the Wingate School, and they will be commemorated on a single gravestone.

posting. We did not know where we were going, so we couldn't ask for a Post Report. But where we were finally sent affected our lives very happily, ever after.

Late news

I am pleased to add an encouraging item of 'late news'. The General Wingate School was able to celebrate its Golden Jubilee in 1996 and a copy of a commemorative magazine reached me in 1997. In it there is a very generous article by Mairegu Bezabih, who was a pupil of mine. He writes of a school of very high standard which was "more than an educational institution". He rightly gives very 'high marks' to our headmaster, Alec Heyring, and to Jim Marshall: "the former was disciplined, quiet and authoritarian . . . while the latter was extremely sociable, courteous, affable and even friendly . . . to his students." He pays special tribute to John Adderley, a retired teacher of physics and his wife Laurie, for their loving attitude to one another, and to John for his perfectionism in his teaching and experiments, his dress and deportment. If other Wingate pupils of mine feel as he does about my contribution, and Rosemary's at home, I am happy indeed to have been of value to a people we greatly admire.

Tehran 1957–1961

Posting

Back in London, and installed once more at The Cavendish under the care of Edith Jeffery, I telephoned the office next morning and was told that I was posted to Tehran as English language lecturer at the Institute. I would now be back in a regular Council office with other British staff and wives.

Initiation

We were lucky to be introduced to Iran by Sir Reader Bullard, that great British Ambassador to Iran at the time of the fatal Tehran Conference in 1943.[1] Sir Reader was a very outspoken person, particularly on the Persian character. He summed us up, and became enthusiastic for our future. "Read Curzon," he said, and produced one of the two heavy volumes of *Persia and the Persian Question*, (1892). Formidable works, sound advice. We also met my Representative to be, Dr Derek Traversi, in Oxford on leave at the same time. He was a literary critic and Shakespearean scholar, with a charming Spanish wife, Conchita.

This was our first country-to-country move, and Rosemary got it right with the minimum of fuss and the maximum of skill in what became our standard procedure every few years: the overhaul and purchase of clothing; some items got out of trunks in Martin's Edinburgh store; and any 'leave behind' items put back in listed and labelled cases. Another task was the replacement of items of household, kitchen, or safari equipment. My province was 'the vehicle for the country', i.e. a Land Rover, tools, spares, etc., weapons and ammunition.

28 September 1957: Out to Iran

We flew by the B.O.A.C. four piston-engined Constellation, 'Epicurean'. We weren't too happy as an unsuspecting businessman had recently had the miserable luck of being sucked out of a similar aircraft when a window

[1] See Reader Bullard, *Letters from Tehran* (I.B. Tauris, 1991).

138

Tehran 1957–1961

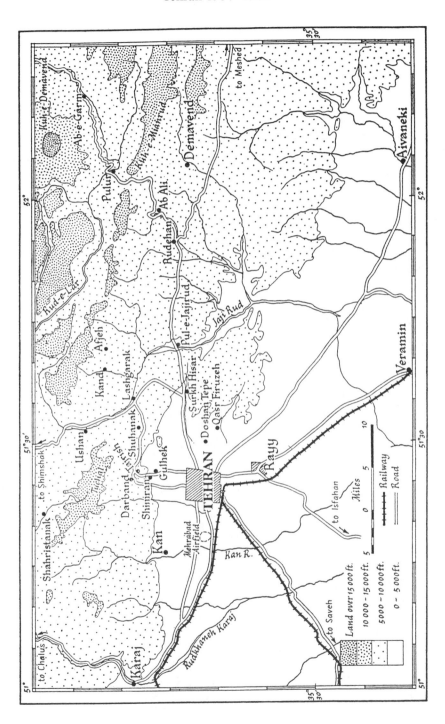

gave way at 30,000 ft. We were over an hour late leaving Paris where we changed planes. It was an hour's flight to Frankfurt, and an hour's wait, then a forty-minute stop at Istanbul at 2 a.m., and then several hours on to Tehran.

We were not in a cheerful mood looking down on what appeared to be a desolate countryside: a mass of dull, grey-brown hills with mountains far away, which were hard to see through a dust-coloured haze. There were dull, grey-brown villages, and hardly any vegetation except near towns where we could make out signs of agriculture. "What do they feed their animals on for the carpet wool they need?" asked Rosemary. (Much of the wool came from Australia, we learned later). At last we saw the great snow-capped cone of Demavend rising dramatically to the east. And when we landed at Mehrabad Airport in the west, we were startled by the vast Elburz mountains rising steeply to the north of the city.

Aileen Maconochie, senior lecturer, kindly met us with Babai, the number one Council driver. We all came to owe a lot to Babai, moustachioed, with a big smile and good English, a typical, loyal Council servant in a job which might not always be secure or safe. We drove across an open, stony plain to reach the city. Then down the long, wide Khiaban (avenue) Shah Reza, edged with trees by running watercourses, the jubes, which were along every street carrying water from the hills, and easy to fall or drive into. We saw a woman washing a carpet in one jube, and a man washing himself in another. It was a shock after Addis Ababa to be in a full-sized, roaring, traffic-filled city. The main streets, which were arranged on a rectilinear pattern, were very wide and extended for miles. There were many large, brick buildings, but most of the streets were lined with a ramshackle collection of two or three-storey houses, of a warm, sandy, pinkish tone. Trees could be seen growing behind the blank walls fronting the houses and gardens. We drove into the centre of the city to Maidan Ferdowsi, where sat the delightful sculpture of the poet Ferdowsi. We turned down Avenue Ferdowsi, past the British Council's blue, metal doors on the left, with its buildings in a Persian garden of trees and a pool, hidden behind carpet shops. Next came the British Embassy on the right, which was entered through a fine, stone arched gateway into a high-walled compound of houses and gardens. Further down was the Hotel Ferdowsi. It had adequate, air-conditioned rooms, and ceiling fans in the dining-room. We were there for a month, being conscious of this expense until we could find the right house.

Rosemary did a lot of sleeping, and then began to explore the main shopping streets. She noted how crowded the streets were, mainly with "men of all ages, just meandering along and chatting. All stare rather. I saw very few foreigners, and only about three obviously foreign women. I suppose they all use cars or taxis." Taxis were cheap, 1/- (10p) for any distance up to 10 kilometres (7 miles). The ordinary taxi is known as a keraye,[2] or group taxi. One calls out to a passing keraye where one wants to go. One with space (just!) and going to, or beyond, would stop. This works very well in Iran."

Rosemary had a shaky start with taxis. Laden with a shopping bag on either arm, she could only signal with her head. So when one appeared she raised her head and chin in an enquiring 'Yes please' gesture. She was always ignored. She finally told a friend, who explained that the Persian gesture for 'No' is to raise one's chin in the air. This is sometimes used in conversation or confrontation, even by a shop-keeper, with a tongue click as a rude, uncaring gesture!

As Rosemary remarked, "The traffic hurtles along these wide, long, straight roads and there's masses of it – all on the wrong side of course! Then every road has deep ditches at both sides carrying streams from the hills, full of paper and rubbish, and not always with water running through them, sometimes so wide that there are little bridges across – definitely a hazard when one is watching the traffic and not the road. The pavements are pretty uneven and full of gaping holes, so what with my proclivities for falling over, one cannot relax much."

On one of her down-town shopping surveys she came across a shop selling items for house interiors, with the sign outside saying "BORD FIBBER". That kept us guessing – answer 'Fibre Board'. Of course "SWEATMEATS" we could all horribly understand. There were few howlers, but they were useful shopping guides, for which reason I explained the errors to the shopkeepers, but suggested they left them in place.

Charlotte Reid, Director of Studies, took us in her car to the residential areas up towards the foothills of the Elburz, a twenty to thirty minute drive with houses all the way. There was always heavy traffic and dreadful driving to cope with, which put us off living in certain elegance and quiet, up in the suburbs of Gulhak or Shemiran. But we came to enjoy invitations to such homes!

In Gulhak there is the British Summer Embassy, now used all the year round, not just for aestivation.[3] It is a lovely place, full of tall, old trees and little lawns, shady and pleasant, with tanks and streams.

---

[2] 'hire, rent, fare' according to Professor A.K.S. Lambton, C.B.E., whose authoritative *Persian Vocabulalry* and *Persian Grammar* (C.U.P.) are two indepensable necessities to the study of Persian. We greatly value her acquaintance and her friendship.

[3] *Concise Oxford Dictionary*: Zoological, in a state of torpor in the summer.

Work

In Iran there had been a steady demand for English classes up to the time of Moussadeq (1952) when, unfortunately, our Tehran Institute was closed. Once the oil dispute had been settled, the Persians were anxious to have the Institute re-opened, and so was the British Council. Aileen Maconochie, who had met us at the airport only the day after she had returned from leave herself, remains especially in our admiration.

Aileen was a woman with the maximum of spirit and the minimum of advantage.[4] By 1957 she was no longer young and not tall, and she walked with a severe limp owing to scandalous medical mismanagement of a hip damaged as a child. Yet she was equal to any man, of any nationality, any position. She was efficient and full of vigour, put down by no-one, and able to achieve whatever her profession required. Her account of the re-opening of the British Institute, Tehran, in 1955 is a revelation:

> The British Institute in Tehran had been closed at the time of the oil dispute when Moussadeq was Prime Minister. Now that the dispute had been settled and the Persians were once more on friendly terms with us they were anxious to have the Institute re-opened so that they could start learning English again. Before we could re-open our doors, however, there was a lot of preliminary work to be done as the building had been shut up for several years and the interior and its contents were in a bad state of repair. New text books had to be ordered from England and local teachers of English recruited in order to help out the two men Council lecturers and myself. While these preparations were going on we were besieged by anxious Persians wanting to enrol for lessons. We announced that no applications would be accepted until a certain day – and that day was one which I and the other Council staff will never forget.
>
> From early morning crowds began to gather round the building and we ourselves could only get in with the greatest difficulty and by slamming and bolting the gates after us. By this time a huge crowd had built up outside in Ferdowsi Avenue, stopping the traffic and preventing all other pedestrians from getting through. We rang the police who turned out in force to try to control the mob. When we opened the gates there was a tremendous surge forward and a living flood threatened to engulf the buildings. We shut all the doors and windows, and with linked arms tried to

---

[4] My senior tutor at Teddy Hall, G.R. Brewis, described Queen Boadacea as a woman with the maximum of courage and the minimum of clothing.

hold the front doors against the pressure of the crowd outside who were now rampaging through the gardens, breaking down trees and bushes and trampling flowers underfoot. Eventually the police got the upper hand and formed the crowd into long queues in the street outside allowing only half a dozen inside the garden at a time. We worked hard all day, giving out application forms and testing the English of the few who could speak it at all. It was a nightmare, for the queue never seemed to diminish and there were always anxious faces peering over the shoulders of those being interviewed. As time went on I noticed that all the applicants who appeared before me seemed to have a small piece of paper with a number on it clutched in their hands. I asked one of the Institute servants what these numbers were and was told that an enterprising policeman at the gate was making a nice little sum by selling places in the queue at so much a head! Eventually worn out by the sheer weight of numbers, we closed the doors telling the disappointed crowd outside to come back tomorrow.

The next day was nearly as bad, though by now we and the police were better organised to deal with the crowds. This went on for nearly a week when we announced that no more applications would be considered and that in due course the successful applicants would be informed when and where to report for classes.

The first night of classes was again bedlam. Every Persian who had been accepted was convinced that his knowledge of English was far superior to the grade to which he had been assigned and every one of them tried to argue this point with us. Then those students who were in a class taught by a Persian teacher insisted that they must have an English English teacher, and at one point I found my own class invaded by members of the class next door who had a Persian-born teacher, and who refused to leave until I promised to teach them some time, too. Gradually we managed to sort out the sheep from the goats and establish order throughout the classes. But the Persians are all individualists and hate to be considered as one of the herd, and we were always having cases of students who sincerely believed that we under-rated their linguistic ability or did not recognise their command of the English language. One gentleman told me that he considered my English was faulty because he could not understand *me* when I spoke to him! I found the best method was to treat them all like unruly children,[5] laughing at them gently when they became aggressive

[5] See p. 146.

and praising them whenever they did well. Fortunately, the Persians, in spite of their many faults, are a kind and courteous people, generous to a degree, and quick to forgive imaginary insults.

Later, when the general evening classes were running smoothly, we started specialist English classes. Most Persian women did not like mixed classes so we ran special ladies classes in the morning. We also had classes for doctors in the morning and I found these most entertaining. All the doctors were busy men and I often marvelled that they found time at all to attend classes, but attend they did, rushing in at the last minute or with their black bags and surgical cases, chattering like children and arguing some point of grammar as fiercely as if it were some medical problem. Often tempers would run high, and I would have to bring them down to earth by reminding them that this was an English lesson and not a debating club.

We also ran special classes for teachers of English and these proved so successful that the Persian Ministry of Education asked us to run a Summer School for teachers outside of Tehran who had no opportunity during the year to improve their English. At the first School, held in Tehran, the standard of English among those attending was so low that we marvelled that they dared to call themselves teachers of English. One of them admitted that he was really a learner and was only one lesson beyond his class. Another always used the present tense because he said he had not got as far as the past or future tenses and the interrogative was quite beyond him!

Down to work

At the opening of winter classes in my second year, I arrived at the office ready to help register new students, but I was apprehensive on finding a mini-riot at Aileen's back, and a few policemen outside the closed Council gates. But I needn't have worried. Aileen was in control as ever. "Let us in first please," she cried in firm politeness, "or you can't be registered for class at all!" Sense prevailed, and calm returned. Indeed, we went on to enrol some 2,000 students, with special classes as Aileen described. We also had classes for the police and for customs staff, both producing very useful friends! We had British qualifications classes for Lower Cambridge and Cambridge Proficiency in English Certificates. We also acted as an examination centre for other bodies such as City and Guilds. I remember invigilating a Flour Milling exam

144

for a sensible and intelligent student, who was looking to his future.

English classes were from 9 a.m. to 1 p.m., and 4.30 p.m. to 7.30 p.m., so my afternoon snooze was safe-guarded. The trouble was accepting social invitations from 6.30 p.m. But in time hosts understood, and Rosemary and I accepted the fact that we would always be late. She nobly changed for the occasion, unbolted the garage door and climbed into the Land Rover without ruining her clothes and drove to a safe and easy parking spot to pick me up. A Land Rover was a vehicle which Tehran traffic respected, which eased my apprehension of danger for her. She always kept her nerve.

Some evenings I had a students' Scottish country dance class which the Council was pleased to support. It was a very popular activity: demand far exceeded capacity. Mothers followed staff imploring them to let their children join our S.C.D. class. The young had nothing to do in the evenings and girls weren't allowed out much. But this sort of activity was allowed at certain levels of Persian society.

On other evenings there was often a rehearsal for a play or a play-reading. Many an evening Rosemary brought 'supper' along to the office for us and at least two others who couldn't get home after work. The atmosphere in our Centre upstairs, and in classrooms everywhere, was marvellous. The place fairly hummed, and it was good fun once one got 'on net with' one's Persian adult students, male and female. The staff-room, with twenty of us and a director of studies, was a good place for a chat, despite – or because – we were very cramped for space.

We had a number of Persian-born teachers of English who were helpful and kind. Our part-time English-born teachers were of great value, and there were also Persian-born teachers who taught English to the very beginners, and translation to and from Persian for the senior Cambridge exam classes. My work was even sweeter when John Mills arrived from Japan. He was destined for Shiraz but to our delight he remained in Tehran as television officer. A business consortium had applied to the Shah to open a television station in Tehran. Permission was given on condition that time was given weekly to English, French, and German language programmes. The British Council suddenly had to take on this form of E.L.T. for the very first time. John Mills made a great job of it with his team of Alan Grant and Ali Samandari. We were asked to join them the following year.

John had to share my tiny office, but he had a great sense of humour and we had fun. John had been in Japan, so he suffered from terrible culture shock when faced with living in an unrefined Muslim society.

People: our job, our life

A reward which I had not envisaged when joining the Council was having an established place in society on arrival in a country. So Rosemary and I were soon meeting Persians and Persian teachers, who were charming. An Embassy secretary invited us to its first seasonal reel evening, and was happy to learn that we had a certain proficiency. His Excellency, Sir Roger Stevens, we were told, was keen on S.C.D. to keep his staff happy. Soon the Morrishes, our administration officer and his wife, did us a fine service by asking us to join a party at an Embassy dance in its new recreation hall, and especially to meet the Shah's pilot, Eddie Makoui, who was a keen hunter. He was to add much to our lives.

Eddie's wife, Leila, was the daughter of the Persian General Arfa and his English wife, who had been a ballet dancer. They ran a dairy farm from their estate at Larak in the foothills. I managed to get a day off one Sunday (a working day for us) when we were invited up to tea. We had difficulty finding our way up the stony wastes, chosing the right track among many. Up behind the Arfa's house was a most striking view of the mountains, which rose steeply in slabs with great crags, all pink and gold in the sunset. Eddie was great, and so kind. We both loved guns and game, but he was the real hunter.

Rosemary found that she was not in a normal Council office. The boss was distant and shy, and his wife was seldom at post. There was really no-one free to show her round, or tell her where to go for our needs. But as Rosemary remarked: "Aileen and Charlotte were splendid, arranging tea-parties at their homes, and helping with everything. Just what I expected and amazing the way they kept it up. It's jolly hard work on the teaching side alone."

But the Embassy was a bulwark. I suppose that from time to time I envied my friend John Ford for his diplomatic immunity and privileges, but I would never have wished to change places. In the British Council we had much greater freedom of action, greater variety of work, and closer contact with the people of the country at many levels of occupation. Although diplomatic privilege would have made life smoother for us, it was worth being independent of government control. Yet we often had it both ways. In Tehran we were very lucky. As Christmas 1957 loomed, all our London staff were invited to the Residence for drinks by our Ambassador and Lady Stevens. It was a happy occasion. Sir Roger was a wonderfully kind, cheerful, ebullient character to whom we were specially grateful. "You must consider yourselves one of the family," he said. That was most encouraging. "I am so glad to be here," I said, "and to be teaching adults again." "Don't you believe it," he said. You should have seen him reeling, with his frizzy hair receding from a high forehead,

146

above a prominent beak, piercing eyes, flailing but organised limbs, and exuding keenness and cheer. A real character, and a real scholar.

Sir Roger produced a *sine qua non* on Iran: *The Land of the Great Sophy* (Methuen & Co., 1962), thus was the great Shah Abbas of Isfahan (1586–1628), a contemporary of Elizabeth I, referred to by the English. (Sophy from Safi, i.e. Safavid, the Persian dynasty.) Rosemary, on our return to Iran in 1966, would go nowhere without 'Sir Roger' under her arm.

Enduring in our memories for their contributions to our lives were certain Embassy staff, George Hiller for one. He arranged marvellous week-end mountain walks, such as the one in October to Emaneh. We travelled by car to Ushan, then took three hours to walk five kilometres at 7,500 ft: and a climb of 1,500 ft to reach Emaneh, a pleasant village in a broad valley covered with orchards. We stayed for lunch and the night. Our eyes were being opened to Iran. By 15 October the snow had come to the mountains. It was cold and sunny every day. We could not see that there were mountains until the haze had gone. Then as Rosemary wrote: "They stand up pure white against the blue sky, while in town the leaves are still green."

Our special friend, as it turned out, who came to the Embassy later was Donald Makinson, once a Frontier Scout. He was extremely capable and knowledgeable. Also Jack Burridge, transport officer, gave me great confidence in Iran by voluntarily keeping my Land Rover up to scratch. There was Leslie Fielding, our humorist, and Martin Berthoud his accomplice (now both knighted!). The Oriental Secretary was Arthur Kellas,[6] whose lovely talented wife was Bridget, daughter of a distinguished diplomat. Our military attaché was Colonel Desmond Phayre, with his wife Biddy. Martin later married Desmond's daughter, Marguerite. At a higher level, there was the formidable minister, John Russell, son of the famous Russell Pasha,[7] a boy-hood hero of mine, as I told John, which pleased him. John later became ambassador in Ethiopia.

The double-act of Fielding and Berthoud remain memorable for one special occasion when they decided to give a lunch party in the spacious and calm Embassy grounds. We had a joyful experience because they had laid on donkey races on one of the lesser lawns. It was a hilarious occasion. But I had to dash back up the Avenue in time for a 2.30 p.m. Lower Certificate Class of some twenty ladies and gentlemen who had paid for good teaching. Unfortunately, on this particular day and hour, and never again, I realized that riding a donkey does not require complete sobriety,

---

[6] See Arthur Kellas, *Down to Earth* (Pentland Press, 1990), on his war in the Parachute Regiment.
[7] See Ronald Seth, *Russell Pasha* (William Kimber, 1966).

but teaching English does. However, the class was very sporting. The students said later that I was not to worry, they had enjoyed the occasion! Even as Muslims they had understood and kindly forgave me my predicament.

In a special Halsted British Council category came the Embassy secretaries, who were delightful girls, most willing to help with British Council activities, be they Scottish dancing or drama. Pamela Hendy, who made a perfect Louka in *Arms and the Man* in 1959; Anne Gourlay (now Mrs Savage), a long-suffering wild-fowling companion; Tish Herrick, who never got the destruction of papers right, and went off to Hong Kong University as a student; Hilary Shakespeare, who later showed great courage in Indonesia in the siege of the British Embassy; Sue Pumphrey (now Mrs Ramus), a very cheerful walking companion, and Hazel Roberts (now Lady Gifford), who was always game for a weekend mountain trip.

We got to know many British outside the Embassy quite quickly. We were also lucky to meet the high-calibre staff sent out to our big contracting firms such as Taylor Woodrow, Costain John Brown, Mowlems or Sir Alexander Gibb, during a period in Iran of steady development of roads, airfields, irrigation, and banking.

24 October 1957: We have a house

How vital the right house is! We had had a long, frantic, and seemingly fruitless search. Derek Traversi gave us one more week to search. We were in deepest gloom until Ali Samandari, a charming, congenial teacher of English, told us that his friends, the Abadis, had a house to let. Rosemary rushed round with him at once and liked it very much. It was in Kuche Bahrami, a quiet, little street about ten minutes' cycle-ride west of the Council.

Mrs Abadi liked Rosemary and most kindly put in all we needed, such as a bath and a water-heater. I arrived back from work next day to find the bath in the middle of the sitting room. I was so happy that I got straight into it. I'll never forget that moment. Number 9–13 Kuche Bahrami turned out to be our happiest home of all.

It was a jewel of an old, traditional, two-storey, thick mud-walled, pale, brick-faced house, comprising gracious living with two twenty-foot-long rooms facing the garden, each with three tall windows, the ground floor opening on to a tiled patio and pool.

In winter we were warm indoors thanks to the 'modern' heating-system, but it needed careful operation and control. We had to live with the smell of paraffin (naft), but the Coleman stoves were excellent. They were free-standing in the rooms with a four-inch curving flue-pipe at the back going out through the wall. In the summer, when we arrived, I couldn't think what all the brass tompions with porcelain knob-handles in the walls were for. We soon learned! We also learned how hard it was to tickle the carburetters just right to allow enough naft in to catch fire from a flaming tow-spill. If they went out one should try again if not hot. If one tried to relight a hot stove there would be a nasty explosion, but usually nothing worse than a shower of soot in the room.

Tehran street cries

Old boys and their barrows were a frequent loud and raucous disturbance. Winter cries in our early days came from the 'Nafti!' who pushed a little trolley of kerosene cans. On a wet day much of the water on top of the cans would trickle into the naft itself, and cause tiresome stoppages. Another winter cry came from men passing with great, wide, long-handled wooden shovels, offering to clear the snow from one's flat roof. This was necessary because the weight of snow could become too much for the poplar beams.

The rounds of the street vendors started earlier on summer mornings. They would cry "peas", or "beans", or "old coats and trousers", or cries of fruit of all kinds on their barrows. When the melons happened to be ready at the time of the month of Muhurram, Rosemary was startled to see the men dressed in their black shirts of mourning.

Real life beginning

A familiar Ferdowsi Hotel face introduced himself as Theodore Burton-Brown, assistant-curator at Manchester Museum. We found that he was the twin brother of Christopher Burton-Brown (B.B.) who coached our Bradfield shooting VIII so well. So at his kind invitation we went with Charlotte Reid and Jeffrey Rowthorn (Cambridge Language Scholarship) to B.B.'s dig west off the Kasvin road. We took a side road across a fairly level plain, which was cultivated but stony.

"How pleasant it was," wrote Rosemary "to find trees planted along the small roads. We drove through two villages and very high, mud walls smoothly finished, with odd alleys stretching away, women shrouded in their shawls carrying pottery jugs of water, trees growing out of the stream along the street, and men squatting outside little shops. Everyone was very friendly and had such nice faces with quite ruddy complexions, and they were not too effusive. Gateways showed large gardens – really orchards– sometimes with a house tucked away at the far end."[8]

We found B.B.'s house at last with piles of shards everywhere, and we were directed to his dig by little boys, some in striped, pyjama-like trousers. B.B. was digging down into a tel (mound) of 4000–3000 BC He let us take some pottery away. It was fascinating to see these ancient objects coming into the sunlight again. Most were decorated with various simple patterns, wavy lines, chevrons, and dicing; some depicted ibex in black or very dark brown on red clay. On our way back we passed several farm buildings with roofs of many small domes. Because local builders were not able to cover a wide flat roof with their only materials of poplar trunks and mud, a series of mud domes or barrel vaults were formed instead. Several donkeys passed carrying straw in great rope nets on either side like medieval ladies' 'earphones'.

The British Institute of Persian Studies (B.I.P.S.)

In the house just down the road from us in Kuche Bahrami was the now famous archaeologist, David Stronach, O.B.E., and his assistant, Clare Gough. In this house he set up as Director of the British Academy Archaeological Expedition to Iran, c/o The British Council. David was very kind to us. We were often in his premises looking at treasures. We began to appreciate and understand the expertise and precision required to identify objects and assemble broken artefacts, pinpoint their location, and build up a whole settlement picture. It was fascinating. David later set up the British Institute of Persian Studies (B.I.P.S.) which flourished in its own building next to the Embassy Gulhak compound, complete with permanent British and local staff, a library and a laboratory.

Carpet washing

We were curious to see the great pool and spring of Cheshmeh Ali, the famous carpet-washing site at Rhey. We often saw women or girls in villages scrubbing away at their carpets in a jube, but to wash valuable ones seemed horrifying. We drove south through the dreary industrial area and the poorer parts of Tehran, to reach Rhey the site of the ancient city of Rhages, where we first visited the hideous mausoleum of Shah Reza, the then Shah's father. The tall windows were paned with slabs of alabaster, and there were many carpets. It was amusing to see the disused, little railway constructed during the last century for pilgrims to visit the sacred

[8] See *The Legacy of Persia*, Oxford Legacy Series (O.U.P., 1953 and 1963), chapter 10 by Vita Sackville-West.

shrine of Shah Abdul Azim over the tomb of Huseyn, the true descendant of the Prophet. We weren't allowed to go near, but we could see our first golden dome. There were also two tiled domes and tiled minarets. The older dome had a fine pattern of soft colours, and the other had strong pattern in the usual turquoise shades. We were beginning to find such quests of ours most satisfying. Cheshmeh Ali was a revelation its own. The spring created a great pool of clear, shallow water under a high, sloping cliff with the ruins of Rhages above. Everywhere there was someone tramping, turning, lathering (with a special, soapy bark), and squeezing the carpets. Carpets of all qualities, sizes, and patterns were brought from Tehran and its environs, often the whole complement of a household. The carpets were placed to dry on the rocky slopes; it made a strange and colourful sight.

An Embassy walk

Rosemary wrote in her journal: "When we could get out again, we took part in an Embassy walk, and it is worth recording. We were driven in three Land Rovers to Lashkarak about thirty or forty minutes away in the mountains to the north-east. We came down into a valley surrounded by steep hills, with snowy peaks behind. There we walked down the valley about five or six miles to a place which the cars were able to reach with our lunch.

"Oh, it was so lovely. The valley was gently sloping on our side and there was level ground near the river with many plantations of trees. We wandered down across little patches of field, with banked up irrigation-ditches between them providing easy paths, and then past lines of trees along stream-banks and round the edges of walled orchards. The colours were superb, as the trees were turning. There were plantations of poplars, probably for building purposes, elegant, slim, little trees with pearl-grey trunks and now a wonderful gold mixed with their green. There were walnuts also with brilliant yellow leaves, many pollarded willows turning palest yellow, planes going yellow and brown, and many different shades among the fruit trees, some a wonderful red. Much fewer rust and brown shades than at home. The river ran among grey stones, very clear, almost greenish, the rolling, low hills behind were bare and stony, a sandy beige colour, with here and there patches of ochre, brown, or green showing.

"After lunch we walked through a much wilder part where the river runs through a gorge; it was not beautiful but impressive. Great rocks had rolled down the mountainside everywhere. It was very stony going, but we were at last rewarded with views of another gentle valley with golden poplars all the way down it. We were picked up by the cars after tea in a Persian teahouse."

Winter work and play

25 November 1957

We were rehearsing for a play-reading of the *Doctor's Dilemma*, which Rosemary was in as Jennifer Dubedat; and we were rehearsing at the Embassy for a St Andrews Night S.C.D. demonstration. We were also starting Farsi lessons with Mr Firoozi. The Persian language is called Farsi because it is the language of Pars or Fars, the original home in the south of the Persians.

2 December 1957

The St Andrew's Ball including our demonstration was voted a success. It was the first Ball since Moussadeq. Part of the success was credited to a self-appointed research committee working in an old Embassy house to produce the definitive Athol Brose. Our happy result was appreciated, and went under the name of Glenniffer because searching for a name I saw it was the make of the old loo fittings in the house! So:

> Dissolve 4 teaspoonfuls of honey in 4 oz water.
> Add 6 oz cream and beat together.
> Add 12 oz whisky (3/4 bottle), and 4 teaspoonfuls of Drambuie.
> Mix together well.
> Finally, add 6 oz porridge oats, finely ground, and mix thoroughly.

This will make a bottle full, from which 22 tots may be obtained by Aberdonians.

Baggage

16 December was a great day for Rosemary – our baggage arrived. So far she had had to manage with the minimum of kitchen items from the Council's pool. "How can I do laundry without an iron?" "I am going to make a Christmas cake in a borrowed bread-tin and no scales." "I have people to lunch tomorrow and Christmas rolls on fast." Poor Rosemary, but she triumphed.

Christmas 1957

The Persians remembered our 'Eid' and with their business acumen suddenly produced a long line of fir trees stacked up against the white-washed, southern, streetside wall of the Russian Embassy. So we had our Christmas tree, at a price!

We were invited to dinner in the Sisters' Mess of the Training Hospital. The matron was Miss Watt and the sister tutor, Eileen Smith, both of Addis Ababa days! They started this hospital until pushed out in the Mossadeq crisis of 1952. These two are tremendous characters, and of course gave wonderful service – and they gave great parties. We were very lucky.

Sundays were our working days but we could get to church on Christmas Day, and on some Sundays, because I was elected to the Church Committee and read the lessons from time to time. We received a valuable and enduring Christmas present in the persons of 'Bax' and Felicity Baxter (Bax was head of personnel, of the Oil Consortium), whom we met on introduction from the father of Alastair Hubbard, who was a fine pupil of mine at Bradfield. Bax was a scholar, and Felicity a botanist and artist of renown. We treasure several of her paintings, which are evocative of Iran. They were doughty travellers, brave and hardy, full of energy and curiosity in their quests for scenes, sites, and specimens. We had marvellous times in their lovely Shemiran house above the city, sometimes when their niece Frances Partridge was left in charge! Another senior oil executive we knew was Roger Varian and his wife, Pam. He was a kind and modest scholar. I remember him well as a Roman emperor at a Baxter party. When he retired he took an ancient-history degree with ease. Felicity years later was once chosen by the B.B.C. gardening expert, Geoffrey Smith, to go on a reconnaissance in Northern Greece for a lily programme. She was game enough to accept the challenge by 'bus, but she couldn't have managed this physically or logistically. So the B.B.C. paid for a hire car for her – which we drove. It was a rare and unforgettable experience.

We had more good fortune. At the Ferdowsi Hotel we met Bob Stigler, a Columbia University archaeologist, whom we took to at once. When he left for home for six months he told us to make use of his Land Rover. It just fitted in our garage. Bob returned in July while we were at Hamadan, but he had to leave again suddenly. He told us to use his Land Rover until ours arrived from Britain and then sell his. He also left us a quality suitcase of books and safari gear (which we still have). What a man!

New Year 1958

The year started pretty badly for some because in early January there was a serious earthquake in Pars. The Embassy arranged an event to raise money for relief, known as the Earthquake Ball. We had to do two Scottish Country Dances in a cabaret. We then had the pleasure of watching a lively song and dance and earthy mime by a Persian couple in the best, exaggerated make-up and costume.

First official visitor

Our first official visitor was Horace Cartledge, E.L.T. inspector from Addis days. It was he who had suffered from fleas at our dinner party and had been very British about it.

Very welcome new staff

Merlin Jones, whom I knew, arrived with Aileen from Baghdad as our new administrative officer. He was and is tremendous chap, an irrepressible Welshman, ex-commando, with great spirit and with no fear, no nonsense. He rose to any occasion with adaptability and ingenuity. We wanted to move far out of Tehran at Now Ruz (New Year), and needed passes which normally took ages to obtain. Merlin composed them, had them typed in Farsi and stamped all over. They worked whenever demanded! He fairly cheered up the office. Aileen was a superb support.

We had somehow assembled a congenial crew, known by Rosemary as the hungry types; Jeffrey Rowthorn, who was one of the best of our part-time teachers; the Finns, Henri and Anya Broms from Helsinki library, studying Persian at the university; and Alan Grant, Glasgow and Cambridge, British Council lecturer in English literature at the university who was pleasant, frank speaking, and an excellent actor. Further cheer came from Dick Sturgess (and Mary) in the Embassy. Dick had been the hilarious, devil-may-care, Foreign Office language student in Pécs.

As Cambridge Examinations secretary, I had just despatched to Britain, 200 correct entries for Persians taking the English exams and of course the money. The term had ended with a students' S.C.D. class open evening, at which they did themselves credit. It had taken them a long time to count bars of Western music easily.

Now Ruz 1958– the Persian New Year

We had the whole fortnight celebrations of the vernal equinox of 21 March. This goes back at least to the sixth century B.C.

Our trip to Isfahan and Shiraz

What a time we had, the Broms, Jeffrey, and ourselves. It was tremendously exciting. Rosemary wrote: "Little did I dream of this when in Addis Ababa last spring I read about ancient Persia to my young Armenian children. I am so enjoying seeing spring again – the long trails of weeping willow and white, blossoming thorns appearing over garden walls." She had permission from our B.C. librarian to take the rare volume of Curzon's *Persia* with her – carefully wrapped up. We had read Wilfred Blunt's *A Persian Spring*. So we went, and so we returned, 1940 kilometres to Shiraz and back, five people travelling together in an S.W.B. Land Rover, who couldn't have been better company. The long drives across boring plains were enlivened by Henri and Jeffery discoursing on the Persian language, or Jeffery reading useless, minute details from the *Guide Bleu*.

Tehran to Isfahan took us just under nine hours' driving, and there we stayed, at the charming old Irantour Hotel for four days. Rosemary recorded: "Isfahan we found most congenial– a broad river running through it, a lovely main street, and a huge maidan. There was so much to see, the wonderfully decorated mosques and remains of the palaces of Shah Abbas the Great. I got so excited by all we saw that I fairly danced along the streets, drunk with patterns. There were mirror mosaics on palace walls, up to the ceiling and all over the pillars; fountains and pools on verandahs high above the ground; painted and gilded marble; huge murals and rich brocade hanging; lovely porcelain bowls in Chinese style; frescoes in the tiniest room of a pavilion; all done to please the fancy and give light-hearted pleasure.

"In the city is the beautiful seventeenth-century theological college with its own mosque and twin minarets, the five old bridges across the river, the Friday mosque, parts dating from earliest times, in plain, honey-coloured brickwork. We saw many examples of Isfahan's silver craft-work, with bowls, boxes, and trays engraved in traditional carpet and tile patterns. Miniaturists working in their little shop-studios, antique shops of old copperware, enamelled pen-cases, carved seals, and pottery. Mosaic boxes and lovely printed cloths. I bought a pair of bed-spreads for 32/- each. They are most attractive with borders of several colours and centres with repeating patterns. In this centre of fine printing we were able to buy some old, decorative printing-blocks. We were able to acquire two lovely old tiles, thrown out when the mosque in question was being restored."

By chance we came across the Church Missionary Society (C.M.S.) people and Bishop and Mrs Thompson on a picnic for his birthday, in an orchard by the river. I went to take a photograph of the whole scene, stepped back and fell into the ubiquitous jube, here soft, attractive and tree-lined. Bishop Thompson was a great man. He led a life of contribution, first as a Royal Engineer in World War I in Persia where he built a road, and in India, where he built St. John's College, Agra. His spirit vitalised the Christian Church in Iran. The example of Bishop Thompson and his family helped us to understand the C.M.S.'s attitudes and aspirations. We were lucky to have friends in the C.M.S. Our special admiration went to the staffs in Isfahan of the Christian Hospital, and of the Blind School.

Our journey on to Shiraz took two days. En route we stayed the night at the 'hotel' at Abadeh, in the public park, which was an ordinary sort of garden. We entertained the public unwittingly by us men shaving at the garden tap, and later with the ladies washing up our lunch things.

Next day the weather deteriorated, and soldiers in a brick fort sportingly let us into their guard-room to shelter from the wind for our picnic lunch. We only managed seventy kilometres in two hours on a muddy, sometimes flooded, road. But we reached Pasargadae, and had a brief look at the lonely, isolated, stone tomb of Cyrus the Great. We stayed in Shiraz in the imposing old British Consulate-General, which was to house the British Council. To have Councils in the place of so many Consulates is an ideal change in the course of history.

We had a four-day holiday after the exertions of Isfahan, especially enjoying the Council's lovely, green garden. Shiraz is much more fertile than Tehran or Isfahan. We visited the tombs of Hafez and Sa'adi and the bazaar, which was full of marvellous gelims (woven rugs) and saddlebags – real carpet bags. We spent a day at Persepolis, the capital of Darius, King of Kings, an ancient royal citadel more complete than any other. Rosemary read from Curzon. Several Persian visitors spoke to her, intrigued by the great book she was carrying. I was excited by the surviving nineteenth-century graffiti on certain flat, marble surfaces, especially that of Arminius Vambery, a Hungarian world-traveller, born in 1832. He reached Samarkand and Bokhara in a Dervish band.[9] We just had to return to Persepolis, and we spent an afternoon and evening with the Gods, heroes, bearers of tribute, and the owls. We were able to spend two days in Isfahan on our way back to Tehran. We visited a Government carpet factory and found that the women were paid about 3/- a day. Everywhere we went British Council students appeared, dying to show us their city

[9] See Fitzroy McLean, *A Person from England* (Jonathan Cape, 1958).

which was exactly what Rosemary didn't want. She wanted peace on her own. It was hard to refuse tactfully, for our attitude was so puzzling for them.

Carpets

The vacation lasted until mid-April, and in Tehran I could go window-shopping with Rosemary, especially to the carpet dealers. It was enjoyable learning about design and weave, and region, from books and now to see the real thing. It was fun visiting the shops of the dealer friends whom we came to know and trust, and having carpet after carpet unrolled for us.

Rosemary has always been admirable at not spending money, so unselfishly at times. But we now know that, with our interest in Iran, we could and should have spent more in Iran on better carpets and objets d'art.

My one illogical regret is that when on leave with time to spare we went to a Sotheby's auction. In Ethiopia we had developed a love of hippos – at a safe distance. In Bond Street we saw a small, jade, Fabergé hippo with ruby eyes. It went for £170: Oh! But £170 was a lot of money for us then.

The pleasure while on the spot was having several rugs in the house at a time on loan, in order to make agreed choices. When we had a personal visitor, such as Jimmy Cumming, ex-Queen's Bays, and now Raleigh Exports, 'our carpet man' would bring a selection to the house and spread them all over the place. Jimmy had spending power! What was also fun and good for our character were the 'carpet parties' that we sometimes had in the community. Some admiration was usually displayed by guests at one another's purchases, but usually more anguish and gnashing of teeth, at the aquisitions of others.

Jimmy got me a Raleigh bicycle through his agent in Tehran, Mr Tavacolipour. Now I cycled eastward easily to the office by cross-lanes. One day a policeman at a main north-south street held up all the traffic for me. I could only raise my hat and bow. However, on using a bicycle my status plummeted in the neighbourhood. I was expected to travel every-where by car, preferably with a uniformed chauffeur, so our maids informed us.

We never met our neighbours, but our respective servants mingled when off-duty. The Persian home is a very private and secure place. Opposite us there were only small, wooden doors in high walls, as the houses on that side were set at the end of gardens. Figures simply popped in and out. We heard that the young man opposite had 'got through' four English wives.

Hospitality

I am sad that we didn't receive invitations in Tehran from Persians. But once a lady student, an Assyrian Christian did invite Aileen Maconochie and us to tea with her family. It was 'entertaining'. She was a nurse in a tough part of town. Mother was a character, short, enormously fat, but very nimble. She kept tucking her legs under her as she sat. She had a wide, ugly face surmounted by fantastic hair, hennaed brilliant orange at the front shading to darkest Titian at the back. Father was shot in 1945 by the Tudeh Party, apparently because of his pro-English sympathies. Her brother and a friend played mandolins, performing Iranian tunes, Russian dances, and more modern tunes. The trouble with visiting or entertaining students is that it had to be done on a Friday, which was our day off!

Happy outings from Tehran

Eight of us went on a picnic in the Karaj Valley, thirty miles west of Tehran, where a dramatic road runs through to the Caspian. As soon as we started scrambling about the rocks and bushes to see the beginnings of a huge dam, a large figure in a blue safety-helmet loomed up, and in the most polite American English, said he was sorry but we were trespassing, and inquired who we were.

We explained with profuse apologies and introduced ourselves. The Being was the safety engineer, Ed Dokoozian, and he offered to show us round. That was pretty big of Ed – who soon became a firm friend – and typical of him. We had a delightful picnic by a little stream under trees; Rosemary and Anya Broms walked up the steep hillside and found wild, yellow tulips, and a tortoise.

A year later we imposed upon Ed's friendship by taking twelve friends out to the Karaj Dam, and Ed showed us all around. The enormous scale was now apparent. It was going to be the fifth highest in the world. We reported this to our friend in Edinburgh, John Bartholomew, head of the famous family cartographic publishers.[10]

This was in May, and we got up into the mountains several times more, once walking very steeply up above a river bed. What paths! They are the only way up to fair-sized villages perched way up. We met rosy-cheeked schoolchildren clambering homewards, as they did every day. Some fruit blossom was still out, and Rosemary picked more tiny, yellow tulips up the screes. They are so elegant with their pointed petals compared to the modern tulips. We saw very few red ones.

---

[10] And we were very kindly given credit in the *Bartholomew Times Century Atlas*!

July: the end of the academic year

"It is sad," wrote Rosemary "all our year's friends are leaving. There are so many farewell parties. We can now eat outside with candles under glasses on tables round the pool. Alan Grant gave us six glass dessert bowls. We floated them on the pool with nightlights in them. The Joneses are being sent to open up Meshed." I had the Cambridge Exams to run from 7.30 a.m. to 7.30 p.m. with a break from 1 p.m. to 4 p.m., and the oral examining of six persons an hour.

The Queen's Birthday Party (Q.B.P.)

Our first Tehran Q.B.P. was terrific. It was held on the Ambassador's lawn in the town Embassy, for 1,750 guests. It was pretty sight, looking across a large, square pool, and seeing people so gaily dressed. We were now allowed to swim in the Embassy pool at stated times; it felt chilly after the Ethiopian hot springs.

Hamadan Summer School, 1958

We eventually arrived by 'bus at Hamadan at 2.30 p.m. after 180 miles, having left at 5.30 a.m. We stopped at a very dirty tea-place for 'breakfast', and luckily Rosemary had provided our own. We bounced over many diversionary roads while Mowlems were building a new highway. As lunch-time approached the driver simply went on and on past several attractive chaikhanes (tea-houses) despite our protests. We gave up and ate our own lunch in the 'bus. The drivers now changed seats – while the 'bus was moving! We finally stopped at a dreary place only thirty kilometres from Hamadan, where we stayed for forty-five minutes!

What a chance to live for three weeks *gratis* in such a Persian city, which Sir Roger described as having "the most illustrious past, the highest elevation, and the finest situation of any living city in Iran . . . It was originally called Ekbatana, and lasted as a great capital for fourteen centuries."

It is quite humbling, and very exciting to be on the spot even with only a few pieces of the past remaining. Persia's past had greater effect on Western life than we are taught in the West. Few cities had so much history or such riches. Hamadan had vitality in our day, as Sir Roger saw, especially in its carpets and blue pottery. Happy memories remain of the work we nine teachers did together with our 150 student-teachers, and of the valuable, but alas fleeting, association we had with those devoted

Persian men and women teachers. Rosemary came as a voluntary librarian. She found in each country that she enjoyed any library work needed, and would like to have had library training, but no-one at home or university suggested it, so she went into social service work.

The Summer School

In Rosemary's words: "We the staff live in the Hamadan Hotel at the Min. of Ed.'s expense. It is a comfortable modern building, but the service poor and the charges for tea, laundry, etc. ridiculously high. We are well out of the Tehran heat of 110 °F, we hear! The student-teachers live in two schools, and classes are held in a third school nearby.

"It's quite fun, but pretty hard work for the staff. There are three morning one-hour classes, then back to the hotel by car at 11.30 a.m. It is just too far to walk. Lunch is at a school at 12.30 p.m. We sit anywhere and mix around each meal. The Iranian food is not bad, but leaves me hungry. The students eat faster than us, and what with answering questions I'm always left eating when the rest get up. Then back to the hotel and nap until a one-hour class at 4 p.m., followed by three to four hours of tutorials or seminars. Then at 6 p.m. one of us gives a lecture, such as English language, or education in Britain. The rest of the staff escaped, but there was supper with students again at 7.30 p.m., followed by "evening activities" at 8.30 p.m., short films, play-readings, Michael's records, Spelling Bee, etc. There isn't much free time as all preparations for lectures, etc. have to be done in the afternoons. And time is taken waiting for cars to fill, or talking to students before and after meals, valuable but most exhausting. One needs to be a walking dictionary.

"I do all right as I'm only the librarian. We have about 100–150 books, and also B.C. pamphlets for sale, and magazines to read. It was quite a lot of work to get it organised as we had to bring everything. They don't really use the library very much, and most can only manage simplified texts of well-known stories. The students are feeling the strain of more continuous effort than they are used to, but all are cheery and amicable. A little group come regularly into the library to talk with me, or chiefly to listen. When any conversation begins several others add themselves to the group at once, just to listen to English as she is spoke. What an effort, my grammar has gone to pot as a result.

"What conditions the teachers struggle in at school! Few have classes of under fifty pupils, many classes are up to eighty. They have hardly any free periods, and non-graduates have to work to supplement their incomes after school finishes – one told me that he gets 3000 rials per month, which is less than a cook's wages in Tehran, and that he has had no increment since he started seven years ago. Living isn't cheap at all, and doctors and medicines are extortionate. How they survive I don't know, but they keep jolly and I enjoy meeting them in this less formal way. Most of the women are quite young, and attractively turned out, and are particularly friendly.

"I find religious attitudes stultifying. The women refuse to go out at weekends by themselves, even in groups. It is irritating how they cluster together and act like schoolgirls. On a picnic they all went in one 'bus, and men in the other three. They do mix up at meals though. But the men's selfishness – always *'me first'* – gets me down."

"It is sad that the local education department has asked us not to hold country dancing as an evening session, and that includes not even Michael and I demonstrating together. Men and women mustn't be seen holding each other. Teachers who came to our Tehran classes have asked for our reels. They don't care. But not in Hamadan. Sad. But Michael was able to wear his kilt for my lecture on Scotland, and caused quite a stir."

Breaks for the Halsteds

One Friday, we went for a thoroughly enjoyable walk from the hotel at the upper end of the town, into the fields and orchards and poplar plantations on the northern mountain slopes. It was so peaceful and we were not followed. We hadn't had a day to ourselves for so long. Family parties were picnicking under the trees; and a little boy was taking his pet sheep to join his group, calling to it all the time and giving it fruit out of a grubby hanky. There were lovely views up to the mountains and across a very wide plain.

Another day we drove eighteen kilometres with our colleague, Ali Samandari, to see the production of the famous Hamadan turquoise pottery. The drive through the ripe corn fields and twisting villages was lovely. The landowner received us in a beautiful, round room made out of a bastion in the old village walls. We drank tea and horribly sweet, iced sherbert, and ate fruit, wondering if it had been washed, and where the ice came from. I was peeling an apricot when the landlord, thinking I didn't know the fruit, insisted that I ate the skin. In this village he helped the potters with land and loans. There was a whole area of 'potting sheds', each potter making something different. The rows of pots laid out in the sun were very attractive. And so was the scene of the distribution of pots which were carefully placed in straw-filled saddle-bags on donkeys. The landlord's firm organised the collection and the marketing, which was a relief for the potters.

16 July 1958

We had heard of the bloody revolution in Iraq, but had no recent newspapers, nor a good radio, even though we were sited on the main road to Baghdad! We had two teachers from Iranian schools in Iraq and they were very worried. Iran's relations with Iraq had been good. Faisal was here in the winter. I thought that if this is the work of Nasser's minions, Iran will be in a tizzy.

We could only get on with our work. Rosemary wrote: "Last night we did a walking play-reading of *Arms and the Man*, which the top class is doing. We could hardly see our books, let alone the cuts in the text we made for the sake of time and simplicity, in the dim hall-light. Michael climbed on to the balcony as the escaping soldier, but got into a fix as he was holding a book and a pistol, and had to light a match as well." But the audience enjoyed the joke. We were gradually finding our feet with acting play-readings, because I found they worked well. Our audiences every-where who were students of English would get a much wider fare as busy, volunteer casts didn't have to learn lines, and staging was minimal. One learns to act with a book quite well.

Our students organised a picnic on a Friday. They set off at 6.30 a.m. without us. We enjoyed looking for them later among the orchards and fields. We joined one teacher and his family in a grassy orchard sloping down to a rocky stream. Two itinerant musicians came along and played for us, and a crowd of other picnickers soon gathered. The men danced, burlesquing the women's dances. Women couldn't dance in public. But the little sister could, aged about eight. I thought she was delightful, but Rosemary wrote, "It sickens me to see a child imitating those sophisticated twists, wriggles, and leers, but one has to clap and smile". But Rosemary was fascinated by the player of double pipes: "an ugly, little man squatting under a dirty trilby. Never have I seen anyone's cheeks distended so far". The other man had a tambourine with short lengths of chain attached to the rim to make a jangle.

21 July 1958

There was still little news from Iraq. What efficient clamping down on communications and frontiers! Not a word came from any embassy or R.A.F. Habbaniya transmitter. The military and air attachés had been here to make plans with the local authorities should any refugees come out this way. The Popplestones from B.C. Tabriz, had been asked to stay for a few days since they had a useful Land Rover, driver, and servants here. The attachés came again and went on to Kermanshah when they heard that the Iraqi frontier was to be opened on Tuesdays and Saturdays. We heard that the British Embassy had been burned down, and one member killed by a ricochet bullet. The British Ambassador was living in a Baghdad hotel. The Iranian Ambassador to Iraq came back here to our hotel for a while. People were genuinely shocked and grieved at the murder of Faisal, who was very popular. Thank goodness his fiancée was out of the country.

When we got back to Tehran, the wife of our Ambassador to Iraq told Rosemary that the Embassy gates were pushed down by tanks so that people could get in. "Hardly a sudden mob as reported in one British paper," wrote Rosemary. The death of Faisal was only called murder in one paper, it seems. We were surprised at the calm way all this was taken at home. Britain seemed to give the impression that the nation was ready to be slapped in the face. However, "Things go on quite well here," wrote Rosemary "with a lightening of spirit as the end approaches". She was reading Freya Stark's autobiography *Beyond Euphrates*. Freya stayed in Hamadan on her first visit to Persia, to learn Persian. Rosemary commented, "How did these people manage to write such beautiful long letters to so many people, and say everything properly? Reading these books makes me feel so fidgety, to be in the same areas and yet to be unable to make journeys on foot and by mule, unable to see the places and meet the people. I long to wander off and see what happens over the horizon at my own speed and in my own way. We are so close to the Valley of the Assassins . . ."

The month of mourning, Muharram, was upon us just as we left. There was preaching by the mullahs every day in the mosques. This period is the annual commemoration of the martyrdom of Hussein, the grandson of the Prophet; his mother being Fatima, Mohammed's daughter and wife of Ali. The Shia Moslems of Iran believe this is the true line of inheritance. Hussein and forty of his followers had been surrounded by the rivals and slowly killed off in conditions of great thirst. To cope with crowds special meeting places were set up all over the town. We came upon a huge canvas roof stretched above a street of little, glass-fronted shops on a raised walk.

We were lucky to hit on the last day on which we could walk around. The roofed area was beautifully decorated with the Iranian lion, Chinese-like medallions and shapes, and angels holding quotations from the Koran. The ground beneath was covered with large carpets, and wooden rails were being put up all round, also to make an entrance passage. Here the very best rugs were hung. The little shops were also being smothered in rugs. All the carpets and rugs were lent by very trusting locals! It was fascinating to walk round with Ali Samandari to learn and compare the different makes and designs.

We were told not to go anywhere near the rites from the following day.

The crowds got very worked up by the tales of the tragedies related and acted out to them. The mourners would weep and wail as they moved along, and beat themselves with short chains attached along a handle to draw blood. Some cut themselves with knives. They could turn very dangerous to any infidel. People had been stoned. We heard that the government would have liked to reduce the fervour.

It is to Aileen Maconochie that we owed the success and pleasure of our stay in Hamadan. She wrote a graphic account of her struggle to obtain the terms and conditions acceptable to her staff and pupils. Briefly, her first journey back to Tehran by car was over the unsealed, narrow, dangerous road as it climbed through the mountains north of Qasvin. On meeting a lorry, the car's brakes failed, and Aileen's driver drove into rocks rather than over the precipice. Aileen was knocked out with a scalp wound. She wrote: "Apart from two black eyes and a swollen face I was back at work in a few days."

Then began a running battle for weeks with the Ministry of Education over the need for proper toilets, wash basins, and showers in the accommodation blocks, which were non-existent at the time. But there were several earth privies, and a large tank of water in the courtyard, Aileen was told; she retorted that this was no answer.

The food for the first few days of the Summer School was so bad that even the patient Persians complained. Nobody could eat the meat. The education official entrusted with the food supply had been buying old and decrepit animals which were dead before reaching the slaughter house. "But I am spending vast sums on your food," he declared. Aileen threatened to tell the Minister in Tehran, and the meat improved. Then she had to battle over the quality of bread, vegetables, and fruit. The official groaned when she approached his office again. "Are all English women as formidable as you are? Now I understand how the British won an Empire."

In Tehran again: Food and drink

Persian dishes are not exciting but pleasant, and good for one, which is a consolation! They are quite different from Indian or Chinese dishes and tastes. Certain of them are common to the Middle East, such as kebabs or dolmeh (stuffed vine leaves).

We enjoyed chelo kebab, meat with steamed, white, fluffy rice and khoreshk, a good stew. Chelo plus, served with raw egg in a half shell and a little thimble of red, ground sumak is a dish special to Iran. But the dish we enjoyed the most was fezanjan: wild duck or chicken cooked in a sauce of ground walnuts and pomegranate juice.

Vegetables were plentiful: onions, aubergines, peppers, spinach, and cucumbers – the little, sweet, juicy ones were delicious. Many Persian workmen enjoyed them with their snack lunches of goat's cheese and bread.

The Persian bread was delicious. The four varieties were the most memorable edibles: lavash and taftun, which were very thin and crisp, nun or nan barberi, which were large, flat, deep-ribbed, oval or round slabs, shaped from the roofs of the mud ovens. Then sangak, which was baked on fine gravel on the floor of the oven – this was delicious as long as the small boy 'de-stoner' outside did a proper job!

Iran is a wonderful country for fruit (miveh). We had strawberries, apricots, greengages, plums for cooking, huge pears, flavourless apples, nectarines, peaches, and grapes. Quinces too, and pomegranates. We had persimmons in our garden. But pomegranates are one of the finest fruits in the world, with lovely, semi-sweet, iron-rich juice. We learned how to drink just the juice: hold the fruit double-handed, thumb over thumb, press and suck.

Liquids. Yoghurt (mast) is used a lot in recipes, and it is good for one! It is said that Genghis Khan, and no doubt his horde, lived on yoghurt – and koumiss too (fermented mare's milk – tartarskumiz) – during their long advances through Mongolia and the Persian Empire, when no other food was to be had. Yoghurt is also used diluted with water, and salt and mint added to make a popular and refreshing drink called dugh; it was bottled and sold as abdugh (ab means water).

In Tehran we ate out pretty well. For me there was the Hungarian-run Paprika restaurant, which had nostalgic Hungarian dishes. The Marmar Hotel above Ferdowsi Square was a pleasant refuge with an English atmosphere and menu, and British draught beer.

For special occasions there was the Beluga and its Caviar Bar, and no music. We most enjoyed visits down-town to tiny premises presided over by a large Russian lady who produced the best Boeuf Strogonoff, with perfect matchstick potatoes. But in order to pay, one had to face a fierce boxer dog which sat under her desk and resisted one's approach. We have cheerful memories of the popular winter and summer premises of the Sheherezade Night Club. And just one memory of the Darband Hotel for the upper-classes in high Shemiran, where we saw a performance by the famous belly-dancer, Nadia Gamal.

But you can't beat good meals at home, especially in hot August in Tehran. As Rosemary remarked, "Our little pool is a great pleasure, but the water is warm being so shallow. John Mills and Alan Grant (the great T.V. team) came to supper the other night, and we first sat in the pool with our drinks."

It is all very well enjoying one's host country food and hospitality, but one should pay careful attention to the local host and guest customs.[11] It took us too long to learn why our guests arrived late: they did not wish to appear too eager! And why they wished to leave immediately after the meal: they did not wish to be thought to be wanting more, nor of not having been fed enough.[12]

August 1958: A trip to the Caspian

We were not able to wait for a get-away near the end of the Persian holiday because registration of students would start in early September, so we decided at once to head for Bandar Pahlevi, the port for Russia at the south-western end of the Caspian, and hope for the best.

Before we left for the Caspian over the Elburz Mountains we read some of Freya Stark's *The Valley of the Assassins.* Her perception and sensitivity and her beautiful English heightened our own understanding and appreciation of just a few of the places we managed to reach, about which she had written so well. We have great admiration for her. She died in Asolo, Italy on 9 May 1993, aged 100. Her obituary in *The Times* of 11 May 1993 is worth reading.

A Land Rover does not foster such sensitivity, or allow one to come into intimate contact with the people of the country. But in our circumstances we couldn't have reached the Caspian without our vehicle. We were lucky to be in Iran at all.[13]

Bandar Pahlevi

The road to the Caspian here was pretty tough. After an initial climb up to the 4000 ft plateau, it was all twists and turns down the side of endless river valleys to 92 ft below sea-level. It was quite different from the rest of Iran. How lovely it was to drive suddenly into grey skies, gentle rain, and green hillsides. The coastal plain looked quite English. I enjoyed the Norfolk-like flatness. There were large trees, many streams, lush greenery, and thatched houses, some town houses had red-tiled roofs. The dullness was that the only crop was field after field of rice.

There was a pleasant atmosphere round our seaside pension. Our meals were outdoors among the cannas, and the floors were covered in sand, but

[11] For a good guide see the introduction by Claudia Roden in *A Book of Middle Eastern Food* (Penguin, 1970).
[12] See Margaret Shaida, *The Legendary Cuisine of Persia* (Penguin, 1994).
[13] A deeper study of the Assassins is found in Professor Bernard Lewis (S.O.A.S.), 'Historical Essay', *Encounter* (Weidenfeld and Nicholson, 1967).

the beds were dreadful and the conveniences were primitive! We had several days of sun, which was not always so common here. The sand was darkish brown and there were even waves in the water, which was extra-salty due to evaporation. Bandar Pahlevi was once one of the chief ports for trade, and for travel to and from Baku which was still possible. There was a good but quiet harbour.

Moving about gently in sometimes tatty and dirty little places, but looking for any flora or fauna, is a very satisfactory occupation. Exploring the dunes to the west we found them inhabited by tortoises. Looking carefully into the creeks we found water-snakes as well as turtles. There were also enormous and fascinating frogs. We discovered that we could row among the abandans (swamps) behind the town and watch the water birds.

Our ornithological architect friend Chris (Kit) Savage told us that Bandar Pahlevi was on one of the migratory flyways, and that the gunsmith in the port sold ten to twenty tons of shot every year to wild-fowlers; and between one and three million duck were shot or trapped every year in the region. Kit described how the hunters would go out at night in poled, or rowed boats rigged with pressure lamps on a frame or a staff, and quietly cruise. The 'crew' had hand-held nets, and one man sounded a high-pitched gong with rapid mesmeric beats. The duck were strangely attracted to the noise.

We went eastwards to Chalus which lies almost at the centre of the Caspian shore in sight of the sea and at the foot of very steep, green hills. There were tea gardens as well as rice fields. There was a very comfortable hotel but which provided poor meals. In Chalus there were fine, tea-drying buildings and a silk factory, part of the developments by Reza Shah who came from those parts. We bought lovely silk for cushions.

We took the most spectacular, direct road home to Tehran through the Elburz. We climbed straight up into the mountains, to about 9000 ft along most dramatic rocky valleys and gorges, with tree-clad hills miles above our heads. In one place we could look down on five different levels of the road in a direct line below each other. In a short distance we were over the top and back to the arid plateau.

Lar Valley camp

To escape from the summer heat we needed altitude, but there were no hotels in the mountains. Therefore, since 1890 the British Embassy had run a standing July/August camp in a spectacular site at 8000 ft near the foot of Mount Demavend.

Leslie Fielding sent round an enticing circular in July, and we signed up at once. I quote from it: "It is a wonderful place for fishing, shooting of all sorts with shotgun or rifle, riding, climbing, and walking. To get to the camp you have to drive to Pulur (sixty miles, two and a half hours), and from there ride or walk to the camp (twelve miles, four hours). Horses and mules are kindly provided by the Iranian army." There was room for twelve persons at a time, good fresh water from a spring, a large mess-tent, and a caretaker who could help with the cooking. The charge was very small for a tremendous return.

Rosemary described the trip: "We set off for the Embassy's Lar Valley camp last Tuesday morning 19th. Pulur is near the foot of Demavend. What a mountain it is! It stands away clearly from the surrounding hills, and is an almost perfect cone, still streaked with snow. The army uses the Lar valley to let their mares and foals run wild during the summer, and so provided us with mounts and baggage mules."

"We saw our baggage loaded into cotton sacks and tied on to the mules, and then we gingerly selected the most sympathetic and exhausted-looking horses [to give gentle rides] and set off up the valley westwards, climbing a pass. Tish Herrick and Stella Kay from the Embassy came with us. The path was steep, narrow, and very stony, and we were an awful melée all the time with four of us, soldier escorts cavorting about, and several loose horses. The horses frequently stumbled on that stony path. In some places there was a steep drop down to a stream or river, so I tried to look at the landscape instead as there was nothing one could do about it. Actually, the horses are very good and much better than expected when you see how the soldiers treat them. We went upwards for ages with huge, forbidding rock walls on either side, and then had a sharp, short descent to a wide plain. Here we trotted a bit, and Michael and I walked several miles beside the horses to relieve our leg muscles. We had to mount again at a large nomad camp because of the dogs. Even their masters chase them off with stones. We entered the Lar Valley between high mountain walls and moved slowly along above the lovely, ice-green river, with unrivalled views of sunset on Demavend over our shoulders. The horses could at last move faster on the plain.

"As it got colder and colder, and darker and darker, we got sorer and stiffer. After four and a half hours' ride the lights of the camp appeared at last. But we had to wait an hour for our supper until the food boxes arrived!

"It is a very fine camp, with those lovely Indian tents that are lined with patterned, yellow material and have lots of pockets and ropes and flys. There was a large communal tent and cooking tents etc., proper tables and chairs, and a spring close by. The camp is set on flat ground near the river where it does an S-bend through a narrow part of the valley. As one saw the site throughout the day with the changing shadows on the rocks and changing colours on the distant hills, it became very attractive.

An excellent place for a holiday as it is so empty, just a stony river, and bare hillsides rising to crags, only four trees, no bushes, no people, no distractions of scenery. Here was a wide, wide landscape in which to relax with only the sun and the wind. It suited me down to the ground.

"In the early morning we were gently woken by the tinkling bells of sheep and goats grazing round our tents. In the evening they came past again. There are numerous nomads in the valley with their black tents. They send most of their yoghurt into Tehran, but when we saw the goatskins in which it is made we refused the offers of a drink as we went past. On our way up we passed a whole group on the move, with dark-brown, hairy camels carrying their tents and goods, and the fat old 'wifies' lolling about on top. The camel bells' deep tong tong was a pleasant bass to the bells of the flock. As well as a long string of bells under the neck, they also had a pair of little strings of bells worn like ear-rings so that they had their own harmony! The sound of distant, soft bells became an integral part of the scene."

We sat around in the sun, walked, and chiefly fished. The river had plenty of fish, but was crystal clear over a stony bed so it was jolly difficult. Spinners were the only thing during the day; flies in the evening. It was great fun, with the best pools very near the camp and small streams to explore. Rosemary wrote, "We got eight altogether, mostly pretty small, one or two half-pounders, but all fun. The others rode. There were free army mounts whenever you wanted them, and there's also a chance of shooting at ibex, mouflon, hare, etc. but very hard work, high up and far."

A surprise one evening was the sudden appearance at the gallop of two middle-aged ladies festooned with gear. They were Felicity Baxter and her sister, Marjorie. Intrepid personalities in the Lady Jane Digby tradition. I know that if I was in a tight spot I would be glad to have Felicity with me. For instance, we discussed the possible danger from the great, zealous shepherd dogs throughout the region, of which Felicity had had experience. The only way to cope she said is to keep poking at your attacker with a stout stick. In fact I always carried (and carry the same today) a stout ash plant, which has two holes bored through it for a sling when on horseback.

We were to see something of her and Bax for the next thirty-five years, in different parts of the world, which was very cheering for us.

Rosemary wrote, "We had four complete days there. The ride down we enjoyed much more, being fresh ourselves. We had only one soldier with us who went to sleep on top of the baggage mule instead of beating our horses as before! It must be a lovely way to travel through these mountains on horseback, as Freya Stark did. How Curzon did it on post horses driving hard, wearing his horrible iron brace, I can't think."

169

10 September 1958: Tehran – visitors

It was hotter than it ought to be. Nights were cooler but late. The evenings were very pleasant for our terrace dinner-parties beside the pool.

Rosemary had been disappointed by the reception we first received in Tehran, and was determined to spend time on any newcomers who needed help. There was the usual stream of people driving to Adelaide or Bombay! Quite a few offered to give English lessons, but they had to have qualifications. However, the Consul got the brunt of visitors, especially if their vehicles packed up. He had many comic stories to report.

A young, bespectacled Englishman breezed into my office one day. With a tremendously keen look he held out his hand, and announced, "I'm Lampel, spiders and scorpions". I was taken aback until I realized that I had an active entomologist on my hands. I am fascinated by spiders and have an awareness of scorpions, so I found his company, when I could get out, very interesting, He was so earnest and nice, but alas he was killed in a motor accident later near Tabriz.

Regrettably, we did not think of asking guests who came for meals, as well as our house-guests, to sign our Visitors Book. We now miss having a valuable, full record.

Michael Holloway arrived as librarian, with his wife, Anne, and a little daughter. They were a fine example of dedicated B.C. staff. At first Tehran library was smartened up; then they dashed about the country on the job in their Land Rover, round the centres, Tabriz, Meshed, Isfahan, and Shiraz, and elsewhere, always ready with suggestions and ideas for the promotion of British books, and the reading thereof. They would drive to and from England on leave, getting the best out of fine cities, telling us where to eat in Arezzo, etc!

Then Michael Biddulph arrived as our new director of studies, and Frances Gladman as an English lecturer. Roger Cooper, of Hungarian exploits, was next to arrive to study Persian for one year.

Mountain partridge in the Elburz

There was a national holiday one Saturday, so we accepted an invitation to join Eddie and Leila Makoui in a party of twelve on an annual visit to a special place in the mountains. Since Leila, who was very useful as an interpreter, could go, Rosemary was also included.

Rosemary described the scene: "What with participants rushing about and having tea Persian-style (in little glasses, no milk, sugar lumps sucked), we left the house an hour later than planned. We stopped to buy water-melons and again *en route* to buy cold drinks, bread, and other food at chaikhanes." From then on the very kind Eddie would charge into the house and sweep us off into his plans, leaving Rosemary without any commissariat details. *"Bereem! Lets go!"* he would cry.

As Rosemary continued to record, "now we got another air-force pilot to drive our Land Rover as we didn't know the road at all, and we drive rather too slowly for these types. We were on the Caspian road of the Firoozkuh (Turquoise Mountain) Pass, which also goes on to Meshed. It was very twisty, up and down mountain sides much of the way. By the time we arrived at the last village on the south side of Elburz it was 8 p.m., dark and chilly, so we stayed the night there."

A villager offered his house and garden, so we all tumbled into the one room vacated by the family, who humped their bedding into the kitchen next door. The party quickly got down to our evening meal, while I put up our tent in the garden.

One of the party was "a dear little General," as Rosemary called him. He produced an enormous pot-full of pilau and other items. Rosemary's minced-meat pie had almost disappeared by the time I returned to the house. I *was* upset!

We were up at dawn and later drove for an hour to the top of a high valley-pass where we saw thick, white cloud pouring over like a blanket from the Caspian side. We were at about 9000 ft as we drove into the cloud. We felt very chilly with the wind and no sun, and made camp in a grassy hollow just below the top. After breakfast we set off in a line on the far side of the valley. It was steep and gullied but not hard-going. The vegetation was low tumps of juniper-like plants. The sky cleared a bit to show us a wonderful view down-valley of huge mountains and far ranges beyond. On one side the valley wall was topped by a grey, saw-tooth crest of tremendous ferocity, and above our heads the mist occasionally parted to give glimpses of lofty, pink crags. For ibex you have to climb up to to the foot of these next crags.

There was fine sport. The partridge were fast and cunning, rocketing off in every direction. I got two birds, and two other guns bagged twelve. We had a stiff climb back after three hours right down the valley. Two guns were still missing. They were very nearly lost in a cloud when Eddie and a friend found them, but they wouldn't admit it.

That afternoon the mist came down and conditions remained miserable for all of us. No fire could be made easily. But in the evening all twelve of us packed into our seven-feet-square, Embassy-loaned, igloo tent. With the bodies and the pressure-lamp we had a good fug. Eddie produced a tasty partridge stew. Then a non-gun played his violin.

We had a chilly night in which our Black's Icelandic sleeping bags weren't quite up to the Elburz requirements. The cloud had gone by after breakfast and we soon cheered up. The bag was small as the birds had scattered and did not move, except one rose at my feet just as Rosemary prepared to take an action photograph. Good luck bird! I was only posing.

T.V. Tehran

Our major event of 1958, (which carried on year by year more systematically) was the start of our English language by television series. This was all in the hands of John Mills, Ali Samandari, and Alan Grant. Periods for situational vocabulary programmes were devised, and Rosemary and I found ourselves to be the situationals! It was great fun but sometimes hazardous. For instance, *Scotland* was our first title. Rosemary used the basis of her Hamadan lecture. Then we danced – reel and strathspey steps, and I did some fling steps. Rosemary caught sight of a close up of her feet on closed circuit and nearly fell over. She remarked: "Michael waved his kilt about rather too much, I felt, when showing the depth of pleats."

I later ran a 'Twenty Questions' programme with students as the team. For another slot Rosemary and I scripted and produced a special vocabulary programme on travel. 'My wife and I are going on holiday' was the start. Properties included posters, air tickets, a globe, passports, health certificates as required then, packing, etc. Our staff was very pleased with it.

An Anglo-Persian T.V. effort

In due course when another situational programme was required, we decided to stick to what we knew about, and put on a 'camping/shooting weekend'. We had our igloo tent up on the studio floor, with beds, bags, lamps, cookers, watercans, guns, binoculars, the lot. We even managed to cajole Madjur, Eddie's very keen friend, to join in. He certainly lent the necessary colour and verisimilitude, *but he didn't speak English.*

While we were acting the evening meal, we put some token soup on the stove, and got down to handing it out. Poor Madjur didn't know it was simply brown liquid, and the gallant trooper downed his mug without a grimace. John Mills came round trailing a mike and lead whilst commentating. He asked Madjur a question in English, but Madjur did not understand it. There was a fractional pause. It was unnoticed by viewers, as we later checked, because sharp Rosemary rushed up, stared through binoculars at the far distance, called to Madjur, "Look Madjur, ibex!" handed him his rifle and rushed him off.

1958, last quarter

Rosemary never had a birthday party in Ethiopia because we had either been away or just returned. But now she could have a buffet supper for twenty, our little Persian house was ideal, just the sort of place Rosemary had envisaged: people being able to float in and out of the French windows; the little pool and candle-lit tables. It took her two days to prepare, but it was a memorable occasion, with dancing on the terrace.

Harvest Festival, Persian-Christian style

There were red and cream gladioli, dahlias, French marigolds, and the first yellow leaves, for the Harvest Festival. At the centre base of the altar there were melons, aubergines, pomegranates, limes, grapes and plums, trails of dates on their branches on the font, and grapes of different shades down the front of the lectern. There was no wheat as it had all been harvested two months ago. The padre asked for rice, tea, lentils, and sugar. It looked very well with flat rounds of local bread, red cheeses, and tall cones of sugar loaf, and sugar crystals on strings, as sold here.

The annual church bazaar

The church bazaar became a duty for Rosemary every year, when she found herself landed with the many ideas she had. For instance, noting the unavailability of table lamps in shops, she obtained local pots, got husbands to provide the frames, and made the shades herself. She also had teas to do, and 200 were served. Our admirable maid Mabanum was at the sink for three hours. I made a doll's bed which Rosemary fitted up, and it was auctioned for the equivalent of £3.10. Rosemary blessed our Land Rover for the carriage of crockery and tables. In 1959 Rosemary helped in a large-scale production of Christmas puddings, and in 1960 the bazaar raised £600. Rosemary's food – shortbread, fudge, truffles, and sugar mice – brought in three times its cost.

Abadan: On the Gulf, home of big brother

1958 saw another 'first': the National Iranian Oil Company's first Cambridge Syndicate English examinations. While Rosemary was on bazaar fatigue, I flew down. We didn't like being separated, but I knew she would be invited out on three of her four solo evenings. I was well received by N.I.O.C.'s Dudley Danby, and pretty satisfied with their E.L.T. set-up. But I was glad not to be in such a milieu. I found it oppressive that everything seemed to belong to the N.I.O.C.: houses, furniture, knives, forks and spoons – the garden gate. There was no escape. And then there was the ceaseless noise of the plant, the whine of the cat-cracker, and a constant unpleasant smell which the whole process involved.

29 October 1958: The Shah's birthday: a public holiday

Our form of celebration for the Shah's birthday was delightful – of course we were with Eddie Makoui. After a previous week's ibex shoot at 12,000 ft, Eddie took us at 7 a.m. up a nearby mountain valley to his family summer home at Fasham. They had a dear, little house set into a steep hillside, with streams gushing all round, and pools full of autumn leaves. We made breakfast there, and then went further up the valley for partridge, just five of us. It was long and steep, which was tiring. However, we recovered over a picnic lunch above the river. The trees were at their best, and it was a beautifully clear and brilliant day, the deep gold of plump walnut trees, pale gold of poplars, crimson apricot leaves, brown and pink hillsides with a spattering of snow on the higher crags. Eddie did all the scoring. He could run after the birds over the rocks like a goat.

Christmas 1958. Rosemary:
"The most social I can remember."

I was thrilled to be allowed to join in the Embassy Christmas show, which was to be a Music Hall this year. After Addis, I now had a new, but equally talented, supporting team. I now had the nail-biting task of planning my acts, obtaining props, and making the necessary preparations. Rosemary complained that she was stuck with making custard pies again, but she's a fine trooper at heart. She noted: "If I find Michael looking glum at meals it's only because he's concentrating on his acts to come."

My act as a conjuror who failed every time went off all right, because I managed to get hold of an old, useless wrist-watch which I could smash up (by substitution). I enjoyed seeing the real watch owner's horrified face when I produced all the bits from under my hammer. I had a lovely assistant in Bina Axford, the Ambassador's niece. Another diplomat lent me his top hat. Bina actually had a live, white rabbit. Rosemary even had a pair of large, white fur gloves. The children were glum when after a lot of crashes and bangs off-stage I could only produce white fur gloves and not the rabbit. Rosemary's custard pies were fine for a fracas in *Lizzie's*

Lay-By. Rosemary noted: "I got the consistency perfect for the first time. It really clung and dripped off faces slowly. Michael missed with the first one which shot off into the wings so that at the end there wasn't one left for me to fling at him. I was cross. However, I gave them all a dose of the soda syphon."

A vivid, Embassy party-piece that remains with me is the elegant, upper-crust Counsellor, John Russell, unbending to recite *The Green Eye of the Little Yellow God* to a delighted audience and great applause.

Christmas itself was great because we could entertain the Regional Representatives and wives who came and stayed, as allotted. They were so good to us when we landed up in their towns, Tabriz, Meshed, Isfahan, and Shiraz. On Christmas Day Rosemary was rather occupied with Michael Lorraine (university lecturer, ex-Kings African Rifles!). He suddenly developed polio and part paralysis, and was in hospital. He had to be got off home from hospital. The Consul swiftly managed his exit visa.

The Ambassador's Dance on Boxing Day, alas, did not see us all with the joie-de-vivre expected of us. But we manfully ate our way through turkey and plum pudding for the fourth or fifth time, and danced our best.

"Faint but pursuing"

In the midst of festivities, Eddie suddenly breezed in and said, "We're off after ibex. Like to come?" We left by his Land Rover in the afternoon for a fast drive north-west to the mountain village of Useboschchai, took possession of the chaikhane, had a good meal and bedded down. I shall never forget these sallies by Eddie and his friends, though I could never catch up with their lines of thought or plans and was always a laggard.

However, by now I more or less had the hang of things, and Eddie was marvellously considerate of my shortcomings. 'Reveille' was before light. Eddie had laid everything on, shikarchi (local hunter-guide), mules, and men. After a ride and a climb on foot, we reached 7000 to 8000 ft and ibex were spotted. It is amazing how sure-footed these noble beasts are, even carrying huge, heavy horns. I had a strapping guide, Ghafar. He kept urging this pathetic *feranghi* upwards. But I couldn't make it. I handed my lovely rifle to Ghafar, and told him in two breathless words "Shoma bala," (You up!) Ghafar got one beast and I was delighted for him. Madjur, Eddie's friend, managed another. Why do I do these things? But I did – we did – the following November.

14 January 1959

Little occasions are remembered as well as the big – such as a picnic lunch with Bob Rehder, a very congenial, young American student from Iowa, and Sergio dello Strologo, an Italian heart-throb and perfect gentleman, who was studying ceramics. We went up a lovely valley to the snow-line. All these valleys feeding the city and the plain with rushing water were dramatic, with their steep sides and craggy mountains towering above against a brilliant blue sky. It was unusually mild and pleasant.

The Tombstoners – an important pastime

I have always loved firearms, and Iran was an ideal country in which to enjoy their use – peacefully. A contradiction in terms I suppose, but I was happy playing with my Colts, Browning, and Smith and Wesson – apart from my William Powell 12-bore from Papa which was far too good a gun to have out in such rough places – and my .308 BSA rifle. Thanks to the first U.S. advisers to Iran, and the U.S. attitude to firearms, the Iranian Government accepted their recommendation that foreigners should be allowed to own and operate up to four weapons each. Charles Sayyad our sporting Assyrian administrative assistant was on good terms with the police. When I mentioned that I really needed more than four weapons, the Chief smiled and said, "You have a wife haven't you?".

I love the Wild West too and, after a visit to Arizona in the War, I became a devotee of Wyatt Earp, Doc Holliday, and such like, of Tombstone, Arizona. There were others keen to try their hands, so I formed the Tombstoners. We moved around in ideal, safe, firearm-shooting country, which looked boringly bare. But after our lunches at which we drank cans of Tennants beer (bearing pictures of scantily clad girls, which pleased the Persians), we then had plenty of empties as targets.

Early Morning Duck Shoots

We could leave home at 4 a.m. and walk the ditches and icy, flooded marshes out Karaj way, just as the sun came up to gild the far mountains and disperse the mist. We only got one or two duck, so as the sharp blue sky appeared we returned to 'our' smoky chaikhane for breakfast – it was a perfect meal. We had eggs fried over aromatic bush and lovely, thick, ridged slabs of taftun bread with our butter and marmalade. We gladly accepted the Persian milkless tea on occasions, but we usually had our gas burners, char (tea) and Starlac milk-powder with us.

It was more peaceful, and fun, going out the night before to our chaikhane, that is the handiest chaikhane to the marshes. The locals in possession were remarkably good-natured and accommodating. We looked forward to erecting our neat safari beds on top of local rugs on a white-washed, brick platform close to the charcoal brazier. Here we could unroll our Icelandic sleeping bags, and lay out our washing things carefully. The thick, mud walls gave excellent insulation, and our beds were hard to leave before dawn.

On top of all these sensations, the most vivid, exciting, and romantic was the rare appearance of a train of Bactrian camels with all the evocative sights and sounds of men and beasts on the Golden Road. The camelteers were taking advantage of a 'good kneel-down' for their beasts, and rest and refreshment in our chaikhane. What magnificent creatures were these very shaggy, double-humped, majestic, huge-footed Bachtrians. They appeared more tractable, and more agreeable than the querulous, bad-tempered dromedaries, and they carried enormous loads.

The night the camels came to town

One night in Tehran we awoke to the unmistakably measured tonk and jangle of camel bells. It was a Bactrian train going south down Pahlevi Avenue. The poetry of James Elroy Flecker is never far from my mind. Where was this train going? I asked, thinking of the *Watchman* in Hassan:

"Ho, travellers," I open. For what land,
Leave you the dim-moon city of delight?

Maybe this land was Persia, but I did not have "the lust of knowing what should not be known".

In Tehran on stage

I was delighted to be part of a B.C. production of *Arms and the Man*. I loved being Nicola (in my Hungarian costume), and I had a super Louka in Pamela Hendy from the Embassy. Rosemary was Catherine Petkoff, Nicholas Barrington, (now Sir Nicholas Barrington, who was High Commissioner in Pakistan to 1994) was a handsome Sergius, and Jim Curran of the American Embassy was just the sort of Bluntschli I imagine. We had full houses on four nights, 200 were turned away. We never had a prompt. That says a lot for the author.

Offstage

It was bitterly cold on 25 February and had snowed heavily for eighteen hours. The city water was cut off for two and a half days. We melted snow for washing-up. It was the coldest spell for ten years. The Caspian road avalanched and fifteen people were killed in an unlucky bus on the spot. Rosemary went to the Embassy pool with our drinking-water jerrycan and other vessels, and filled up. "What *are* you doing?" enquired a passing wife! "It's an ill-wind . . ." There was enough snow at Ab-Ali for four ski-lifts. Many of our young teachers were free in the mornings, and could climb into our Land Rover with Rosemary, who loved it all. She was very popular, and had seven aboard one day.

A special visitor

We had much amusement out of the visit of David Talbot-Rice, Professor of History of Fine Arts at Edinburgh University, specialising in Persian arts. He spoke fluent Farsi, but had never been here before. Our new Representative, Charles Wilmot, with whom we were very pleased, took the professor to the curio antique shops grouped together down Avenue Ferdowsi. Here the professor pronounced nearly all the 2000 to 4000-year-old pottery and later Islamic pottery to be fakes. He left consternation in his wake. "Who is this man?" asked the shop-keepers in awed tones, pretty much in ignorance themselves.

We were proud of David Talbot-Rice. He was a fine example of the depth of British academic intellect. He could point out genuine fragments without hesitation. He took photographs of objects in the old-fashioned style with a piece of black cloth over his head.[14]

Good driving

Thanks to some special English classes we had friends among our police students, and they gave me the opportunity to talk to a group of senior officers on 'Good Driving'. I had studied the subject more than some perhaps, thanks to my cousin Robert B. Peters who ran The Institute of Advanced Motorists. He sent me much useful material to help my efforts. I was upset by the totally selfish and suicidal driving around Tehran, and all I could do was talk. I was very nervous driving to the venue, but, and this was very much in my mind when Rosemary was driving alone, taxi

[14] See his piece, "Persia and Byzantium," (Oxford Legacy Series, Persia, 1963).

drivers and others were respectful of Land Rovers. Persians respect those in power!

Now Ruz 1959: To Khurasan

We took the Golden Road to Samarkand, but only as far as Shahrud on the way to Meshed. We were on a grim road with little traffic, because of the parallel railway, across a flat, howling wilderness. We could not stop in Semnan, which has wonderful eleventh and thirteenth-century buildings, nor in Damghan, a city of great history, but it was a thrill just to be there. Ten miles west of Damghan lay the remains of the great Assassins castle of Girdkuh. The Mongols took it after a siege of over ten years.

A few miles south of Damghan is the site of one of the principal Greek settlements founded by Alexander the Great. It was a Parthian capital 200 B.C. to A.D. 200, which was important at the time of the Arab conquest (642) and had one of the first mosques in Iran. It was sacked by the Mongols (in the 1200s) and the Timurids (1300s to 1400s) and the Afghans (1723). Dr David Bivar of SOAS. told us that this site was discovered by the modern technique of topographical archaeology. That means painstaking research into every possible source, written, chiselled, or hearsay, and then testing out on the ground any mention of distance in measurement or time.

Our eastern aim was Shahrud, a pleasant, modern, little town. Here we were put up by Mr Taslimi and his wife. He was a congenial teacher of English whom we had met on the Hamadan course. This was a rare and precious occasion for us. They lived in a typical, small, Persian town-house of single-storey and verandahed rooms round a courtyard. There was a central, circular pool for washing, and also for some washing-up it seemed. Our kind hosts allotted Rosemary the bed. Then she had her pillow and sleeping bag. John and I had our safari beds in another room. This was a lovely spot to wake up. We were given a perfect breakfast of fried eggs, taftun, butter and jam and tea.

Before descending northwards by the Pass of the Chehel Dokhtaran (Forty Daughters) down to Gurgan, we made a detour of some eight miles off our road to see the ancient town and fortified complex of Bastam. There was a lovely series of mud-brick and coloured-tile-decorated buildings, domes and arches. This was the Seljuk capital (A.D. 1000 to 1100) of the whole region south of the Elburz. There were some beautifully proportioned buildings in honour of a renowned Sufi who was born here and died in A.D. 874. Such Persian architecture we find extremely satisfying, because it is entirely indigenous with a brilliant technical use of natural materials.

In Gurgan (formerly Astarabad) which was frequently destroyed by the

Mongols, we were happy in the hotel. But what awful things must have gone on all over the country, as historians relate, pyramids of heads, baskets of eyes . . . After further devastation, by an earthquake in 1928, Reza Shah had the town sympathetically rebuilt, and it was very pleasing. We were in green-grass land again, on the edge of the Steppes! At the very edge was Gonbad-i-Qabus the tomb of Shams el Ma'li Kabus, King of the Zurarids, who died in 1012. The tomb is an amazing concept, built in 1006, and still in good repair. It is a 150-ft brick tower of sharp flanges with a smooth, conical dome. It was an exciting moment to see "one of the great buildings of the world," (Sir Roger quoting Robert Byron).

We were delighted to find colourful, friendly Turkomans. Old and young showed us round their village, and took us to one of their yurts – a portable, wooden-framed, domed, felt home. We saw fine-looking horses in the market that day, and some high, solid, two-wheeled carts. The Turkomans also showed us rug-weaving on horizontal looms. Many men and women had Chinese-like faces. The little girls were sweet, un-shy, and colourfully dressed. The men wore huge, tapered, black, fur hats of karakul, the Persian lamb. Some had wispy 'Chinese' beards.

We put John on the train to Tehran from Behshahr, which travelled up the fantastic, twisting, German-built track which doubles back and back at least four times. Behshahr is an attractive, Italianate town with cypresses and houses with red-brown, heavy tiled roofs, deep eaves and white-washed, vine-covered walls. Westwards at Babolsar on the Caspian shore, we stayed at the Pension Paniantz of Monsieur David. Of all holiday stops this remains in our minds as one of the most perfect. There was peace and beauty all round. We were given caviar for breakfast and orange-petal jam, and we paid £1.75 each a day, all-in.

Rosemary wrote in her journal: "The Caspian coast was lovely with blossom out, and a few oranges left on the trees. Yellow daisies grow along the tops of all the mud walls and on the red-tiled roofs. If contrast is a good recipe for a holiday, this was it. Our route back to Tehran was by Shahi and the Firuzkuh Pass. There were grape hyacinths and violets lower down. We found celandines and dwarf wild-iris growing everywhere, and tiny, pale, pale crocus."

Rosemary the tribal guide

Ann Porter of J. Walter Thompson came out to see if she could follow the Qashgai tribe on their spring migration up into the mountains from their grazing near Shiraz. She asked her brother in the Embassy for someone with local knowledge for company, and he thought of Rosemary.

They were away for four days, and Rosemary returned home exhausted after early morning starts to see the tribes on the move, and late nights. As she recorded, "We went to a party in the hotel for the Ambassador on his first visit to Shiraz. We met Freya Stark (Chanel-outfitted), and lesser eccentrics. Altogether very amusing.

"The tribes on the move were fascinating and impressive, when one stopped and realised the vast numbers surging past, though each group was quite small. Everything was loaded onto camels, horses, and donkeys. There was a wonderful medley with women clutching children or calves, while little boys nodded along with small creatures such as puppies, or even a baby donkey, in their laps. They stopped at midday for some hours, erecting temporary shelters. We visited some of these and had to drink fermented milk offered by the women. But my Farsi wasn't up to conversing."

June–September 1959: Home leave

During our home leave we were able to let our house, to avoid 'nugatory expenditure', to Mac McCormack, who came out to head Cooper Brothers, which was opening in Tehran. Rosemary left me in the responsible hands of our maids, Mabanum and Batul, and was happy to go off early on a sailing cruise from Oban. I found company with Alan Grant. With his man-of-the-world air, we managed to take out a pair of delightful English chorus girls who were working at the Night Club Shookoofeh Now. We were surprised how normal they were. I wonder what they thought of us.

I later left for home via Switzerland to be reunited with my close friends from Budapest who had made a remarkable escape in 1956 and settled in Fribourg. On our leisurely return to Tehran, Rosemary became my guide, and from then onwards opened my eyes to the unrivalled cultures of France and Italy. These visits made up for all that we were missing at home.

This time I was introduced to Milan, Cattolica, Urbino, Florence, San Gimigniano, Siena and Rome. From Cattolica we made a sad trip in a hired car to where C. Squadron, and in particular my 4 Troop were all but destroyed in a suicidal attack on a strongly held ridge, as the Germans later described it too! We spoke to a local farmer who had seen it all. We stood in silence and sorrow as we read on a specially built memorial at the start line, the names of my comrades who had died[15].

---

[15] Read John Strawson, 'The Italian Campaign', Secker & Warburg, 1987.

Back in Tehran

Once back in Tehran, I was put in charge of the Institute, and I found I had a very calm and willing new comrade in one David Harper. At home we could now get together with our temporary resident bachelor, Mac. He was large, quiet, generous, and dependable. Mac had nine staff out, not all at once. He fed them and looked after them, and we found them good value.

Mac did not remain a bachelor for long. He fell for Verna, nanny to the children of Desmond and Judy Harney in the Embassy. He had met her at our Reel Club, at which we chalked up four marriages!

Action!

It was a pleasure to have acquired enough know-how of life in Iran, and to be available to visitors of all varieties! The first ring of the door bell one evening was Roger Cooper, who announced in his usual nonchalant manner, "I have two bloody Frenchmen here". They were a poor French couple after a motor accident, bloody but not bad.

One other autumn evening, we received a visit from the Polish Count Krasicki, an experienced and knowledgeable, big-game hunter. His aim was to shoot a Caspian tiger. He swore they still existed, and had photographs and documents to prove it. We could only put him in touch with Eddie Makoui, and give him a copy of the laws of the Game Council, forbidding the shooting of tiger (Babr) until 20 March 1960.

We never heard further, but we did enjoy his company. Fancy discussing the future of the Hyrcan tiger! "Approach thou like the rugged Russian bear, the armed rhinocerous, or the Hyrcan tiger," as quoted in Major R. L. Kennion's *By mountain, lake and plain; Sport in Eastern Persia* (William Blackwood & Sons, Edinburgh and London 1911). Kennion shot Hyrcan tigers. Poor, beautiful creatures, let them live, as long as they are not menacing man.

Our most prized visitor whom we were fortunate to meet was Rear Admiral Paul Furse, a delightful famous botanist and plant-collector. It was to Rosemary that he was directed. We were to help him later in a small way, from Isfahan. I told the Admiral how I admired his expertise, and his land travels in his real (?) life. He replied, "Well, yes, but a Land Rover full of scientists is harder to control than a battle-cruiser". Alas, Paul Furse died in October 1978.[16]

---

[16] I recommend his second obituary in *The Times* by Patrick Syme, dealing with his travels and plant-collecting, after his distinguished naval career.

Scottish country and highland dancing

My Council class had nearly fifty dancers. It was hard work but good fun especially having Mac McCormack and Frances Partridge, the Baxter New Zealand niece to help us.

Now I had a willing Argyll Broadswords team, Mac and David Harper, David Millar (Chartered Bank), and myself. I had two real broadswords for ceremonial, but we needed swords with flat hilts for dancing over; and I was able to buy four Iranian Officers' dress-swords quite cheaply. Rosemary wrote, "It's quite a mental exertion as well as physical, the steps being so complicated". Mac and I were properly turned-out escorts to the Haggis with my basket-hilted broad-swords at the next St Andrew's Night Ball. Rosemary noted: "190 sat down to a lengthy dinner till midnight. Then we danced".

Once again Alan Grant and I managed an Oxford and Cambridge Dinner, with thirty-seven in attendance. Rosemary made very nice dark and light-blue favours. We had an even better dinner the following year. Rosemary reported, "Michael came home at 1.30 a.m., and wouldn't stop talking all about it for three hours. I had been at another party, and was only just in bed."

Now even Rosemary took on teaching a middle-level English class, to ease the pressure. She had between twenty and twenty-five in the class twice a week, with a Persian translator for the third period. She wrote: "I find them rather frightening, but we are becoming more friendly. I went too fast at first, and one said I was too 'sharp'. Oh dear!" Her class contained a university professor, two army officers, bank and railway officials, two secretaries, several teachers, and a few students. This was a good way to get to know a cross-section of Persians, and to be known. Rosemary did not have an E.L.T. qualification, but she had gained teaching experience in Addis Ababa, and was able to use my favourite class-books with confidence and sympathy. She also gave private lessons to John Mills' friend, the Japanese Counsellor, and his wife. She then took on a Persian dentist, and the French military attaché.

One afternoon our Japanese Counsellor was twenty-minutes late, and Rosemary was very surprised. Then his card was handed in at the door – we have it still. A message on the back read, "I would like to ask you if I could have no lesson today. I couldn't help rejecting an invitation by a Vice-Minister of Iran. I drank so I feel it not polite to meet an English lady. Please allow me." On the front he had written, "I am in front of your door" but he had gone by the time Rosemary got there.

6 November 1959: Final go at ibex

I was fated never to get a shot at an ibex. On this occasion it was the elements which interfered, not the altitude. We went in our two Land Rovers with Eddie, Madjur, and Azadeh, a Bakhtiari Khan! There was a good place at Macheen an hour beyond Kasvin (west of Tehran). Here we turned north into a maze of Scottish Border-like hills, but the right track was hard to identify. It was now 5.45 p.m., and the muddy routes were almost impossible to find. After several hours we finally reached the village before our destination. The headman (khadhoda) invited us to stay, but we had to go on, so he gave us a guide. Even the guide became lost because he was now going so much faster than he was used to on foot. But he finally got us up a series of bare, rocky ridges to our village.

It was now 10.30 p.m., but even so, the khadhoda welcomed us into his house, and we ate our provisions while he and his sons and friends watched! There were six samovars in the room so there was blessed tea in abundance. Their bedding was in rolls along the wall, tied up in gaily coloured cloths, with bolsters on top which were comfortable to lean upon. Then our hosts left the room which Eddie insisted on giving over to us, while Eddie and company slept on the porch.

Next morning the rain returned, but we managed to drive to the top of the pass. We looked down upon rounded hills, all alike. No wonder one gets lost in such terrain. Eddie went with Madjur to the left and kindly sent Azadeh with us on the right, which had been the best area on a previous occasion. We crept along the crags until they fell right away, but we saw no game. The others saw a herd of forty and Madjur got one. "It wasn't hard work," wrote Rosemary, "it was just wonderful to be up in the hills, looking across to the Caspian mountains. We could now see our village at the bottom of the valley. It was very pretty, with a good stream and fruit trees." Soon the hillside was covered with flocks of sheep, even cows and little boys appeared. There was no chance of ibex now.

We returned to the village for lunch, and the khadhoda honoured Rosemary by eating some of her fruitcake. Then it began to rain again, and we all became worried about the state of the tracks between us and the main road. Eddie said: "We go home." The drive was the worst I have ever undertaken – a constant slide in mud and slither past boulders, being guided by splendid Rosemary constantly out in it all. I wondered at what angle a Land Rover fell over; and so did she.

Dark descended, and with it heavier rain. Our two vehicles got separated, taking different tracks, and I had a puncture. But we arrived at Kasvin in time to find some supper and reached Tehran at about 11 p.m. "What a trip!" was Rosemary's comment later. "I don't think I have been scared frequently for so long." Nor had I, but my faith in Land Rovers became boundless.

Christmas 1959

20 December. There was so much happening both publicly and privately. There were visits by Ayub Khan and Eisenhower, and the Shah's wedding. We were not involved, but we were close enough to walk to see the processions, and what went on in the crowds. The poor children had been lining the streets since 7 a.m. Ike didn't come until after 9.30 a.m., and it was very cold. Few wore coats and half hadn't even gloves. They and their teachers were so good, and not irritable at all.

'A Christmas Stocking', at the Council.

I put on a stage show for the students to give them an idea of what Christmas was all about, but I kept it informal and cheerful like a Christmas party. There was a speaker on the origins of Christmas, carol singers came in, poems were read, the tree was explained and decorated. Father Christmas distributed presents, and filled a stocking at the foot of a little boy's bed. Then Rosemary had her dinner table ready which she spoke about, candlesticks, crackers, and the menu, pudding, cake, and mince pies, etc. The Mummers play *St George and the Dragon* followed, and we finished with the *Twelve Days of Christmas*. It went down pretty well, and was a useful try-out. I had enthusiastic assistants in the younger members of staff, and some of the part-time teachers. All enjoyed it. In the course of Christmasses to follow I was able to produce a definitive version.

The Embassy Review

This year I had the chance I longed for: my offer to put on my Addis act. 'The Art of Redecoration' was accepted, and I had two good, slap-stick, volunteer assistants. We trained to make a hilarious bog-up using planks, trestles, 'glue-pots', paper, buckets and brushes. No-one was injured. Nor was I hurt in the second act: 'Killer Kelly from Khorramshahr', i.e. the Oriental Secretary, Arthur Kellas, a Scot, a perfect gentleman, full of humour – and tough! The idea of the skit was that a young sprog (me) takes on the professional at a fair, and somehow manages to knock out both the barker and the prize-fighter, and walk off with the cashbox.

New Year 1960

Rosemary and her fellow Scots, Mac in particular, with his excellent cook, Mohammed, saw to it that the New Year should be properly sung and danced in. "This, despite," wrote Rosemary, "my lack of proper upbringing re seeing the New Year in, and so not having all sorts of quaint little Scots customs ready. These bachelors [mainly from Cooper Brothers] are apt to have generous tastes and lash out far more than I would, so we had a salmon!" I agree with her that dancing on tile floors causes awful leg ache next day. We had to suffer this discomfiture all over the world – despite dunlopillo in my pumps.

Deserts and gardens

Rosemary wrote in her journal: "In this barren land everything that grows belongs to the person who planted it, so one goes very far afield to pick anything. Two of our garden fruit trees have passed on from old age. As a result the landlady Mrs Abadi, arrived with six trees, a Japanese quince, and labour, and proceeded to stick them all over the place despite my protests." But later Rosemary realised that we were only temporary 'owners' of the garden, and that Madame Abadi as a Persian took a special interest in trees which would need the best sites and be productive for many years.

Gardening on concrete on T.V.!

After 'much hard labour' we produced an English-language, situational-vocabulary programme on gardening. As Rosemary wrote, "You should have seen Michael pushing a mower up and down the concrete studio floor, and me planting seedlings in the same. We had tools, flower-pots, seeds, bulbs, the lot, and a slide of your [her mother's] front border to show what an English garden is like." A Persian garden is very different, as is described beautifully by Vita Sackville-West in *The Legacy of Persia*.

The Persian character

It was a pleasure getting to know Eddie's hunting friends. They were good enough each in turn to invite us. When they came to us for dinner with their wives we nearly had a riot when we played shove-2 rial pieces. They couldn't bear to be beaten, and they cheated whenever they could. Oh the noise, the arguments, the ugly passions, and the heat it engendered though they were good friends!

On a broader front, Michael Leapman wrote an accurate, historical analysis of the Persian character in *The Times* of February 1981, which is worth studying. For instance: "The long Iranian history of instability and insecurity put a premium on self-preservation. This resulted in an almost total pre-occupation with self."

But the Persians deserve sympathy for all the times they have been overrun, and admiration for the way in which they have coped. I quote a wise, but unattributable, remark: "The Persians have long since learned how to come to terms with their conquerors." One way was through the Zurkhaneh: the old Persian gymnasium, where exercises which were developed to produce fighting men are still performed in the traditional manner. The Arab invaders realised what was going on, and tried unsuccessfully to abolish these Zurkhaneh. The original buildings are still used. To preserve secrecy they were built to resemble mosques which have no windows.

Rosemary described a visit:

The Zurkhaneh

"A special building is used – the one we patronised was rather like a mosque, a large, arched and domed chamber, highly decorated with tilework, mirror mosaics and painting, with benches rising all round. The athletes perform in an octagonal pit sunk about three feet in the floor. The variety of types is fascinating – huge, burly chaps with dapper mustachios; thin, agile types; a famous Iranian wrestler (sort of guest star); an enormously tall freak; and a snowy-haired gent reputed to be aged eighty – all wearing breeches of patterned, local cloth. The exercises are accompanied by a drummer, using his hands and beating out various rhythms, and interspersed with the odd prayer, or invocation to, or blessings on Allah, to which all reply, audience included. At the beginning the exercises were done in unison – side rolls, arm swinging and press-ups – the length of time they continued doing press-ups was amazing. There must have been hundreds of them. All those patterned bottoms rising and falling in unison! Then more space was needed for later exercises which were solo, while the rest leant against the pit edge and appraised.

"One obviously ancient martial exercise was swinging an enormous metal bow across the head from shoulder to shoulder, or till each arm was outstretched in turn. Instead of the bow-string there was a metal chain with yet further weights attached to it. It must have been extremely heavy.

It made a wonderful jangle as it was hefted over at a good speed – one hand on the bow, one on the chain."

Another superhuman exercise was hefting a great, wooden slab with a handle at the back, from side to side, even while lying supine. These were to simulate forbidden shields. Rosemary continued: "The 80-year-old hefted his shield longer than anyone else, out of sheer bravado? He was absolutely beetroot under his snowy crown at the end. Then there were spinning jumps, and club swinging and throwing. It was quite a thing to send clubs up to the roof – from a horizontal position. Each man's clubs (substitutes for fighting maces) were proportioned to his strength. The owner and leader of the place had huge, black, shiny ones. It was the eve of a religious holiday, so there was a Koran recitative (plainsong-like) by one of the athletes, and it ended with long speeches by the owner, chiefly of welcome to some Iraqi visitors. The whole thing has quite a religious basis, and a very firm place in Iranian life – a sort of club. Most of the spectators were fairly ordinary types, with some women and children."[17]

We later acquired a local and very funny painting on cloth of characters in a Zurkhaneh showing off their muscles. Underneath (in Persian) was the revealing motto:

> People who are strong are truthful.
> People who are weak are crooked.

March 1960: Broadswords on T.V.

It was two years after Rosemary's T.V. talk on Scotland that we felt sufficiently confident to put on a Scottish dance programme, beginning with the four-man Argyll Broadswords. Rosemary recorded: "March on with swords at the carry, salute in line, form square, salute each other, lay swords down. The swords fairly flash on the screen. After march off and a two-minute breather we all eight then danced 'The Duke and Duchess of Edinburgh' which has some very pretty figures. Michael had got all the music from several different records, with appropriate pauses, put on tape. Very near the end of *The Duke and Duchess of Edinburgh* the technicians cut the music suddenly, with us in mid-step! Hastily glancing at the screen we saw we were still on the air looking dumbfounded, so we marched off as smartly as we could.

"Now I have my T.V. appeal for the Blind School tomorrow night, at last. I don't expect anything much will result from it but it's an experiment

---

[17] See the *National Geographic Magazine* January 1961, containing a picture of the same zurkhane as we went to, in its article on Iran.

that should be made. Tonight Michael is 'lecturing' on John Gilpin. He is talking about Cowper and the poem, and then showing the delightful Ronald Searle cartoon film."

Now Ruz 1960

In accordance with the Muslim calendar, Ramazan[18] (Ramadan), the month of fasting, had been going on for three weeks. It was not so fully observed in Tehran, but the tempo of life did slow down, and it was difficult to get anything done. Most upper-class Persians and many servants didn't observe it. But our maids did and they became wan and stupid and increasingly slower. Mabanum's alarm clock didn't wake her one day for her pre-dawn meal, so she couldn't and didn't eat for twenty-four hours. Then there were several days of special mourning for Ali, with all cinemas, restaurants, etc. closed.

Now Ruz was followed by four more days' holiday, giving us nine consecutive free days. This suited us in a way, but became a bore. Owing to the shifting Muslim calendar based on the moon, each year's combination of holidays being on different dates made a pleasant, seasonal variety for us, but it could upset the plans of infidel visitors based on a mainly fixed calendar.

We planned to drive to Meshed with Kit Savage, who would obtain passes for us to enter a special, unpublicised reserve for ibex and mouflon, and stay overnight. We would loop north-east through the forests of the hyrcan tiger near the river Arak. Alas, the mild weather reverted to winter snow and mud, which was too much for us, so we went the 600 miles by train in comfortable German coaches on shaky rails that ran alongside the road we had taken to Shahrud at Now Ruz in 1959.

Meshed (place of martyrdom), has been an important place of pilgrimage since the ninth century for Shia Muslims to the shrine of Iman Reza. Pilgrims, who annually numbered over 100,000, were the city's main source of income and prosperity. The pilgrims were accommodated mainly in large caravanserais. The city is the capital of Khorassan, a frontier province bordering Russia and Afghanistan. Hence a British Consulate-General was here.

The Consulate premises were now the British Council's, headed by Merlin Jones and Aileen. It had been opened in 1949 by James Grimes and his family. The past hung so strongly about everything in this tremendous place. It was sad to wander round the huge grounds past the former homes of the Vice-Consuls, Oriental advisers, doctors, hospital

---

[18] See *Whitaker's Almanac*, Time Measurement and Calendars.

staff, and the quarters and stabling for a hundred Seistan Levies, the Consulate-General's Guard. I was excited to see some Levy medals which Merlin had found in a drawer.

The Joneses had an up-hill task, with ceilings falling in and everything fading. Mud didn't last long on roof-beams eaten through by white ants, and weighed down with winter snows. No official body within our Ministry of Works, nor the Indian Government to whom the premises first belonged, nor the Pakistani Government had made any repairs. The only habitable building was the Consul's house, a large, rambling, verandahed and pillared edifice, which was repaired by the British Council. The Joneses had made a charming place of it, using downstairs for functions and film-shows, etc., and living upstairs. The rooms were very large, with each bedroom having an enormous bathroom leading off, as is customary all over India and Pakistan. The Consulate garden was lovely in summer with tall trees, green lawns, looking very English.

Some of the far, ruined, mud buildings gave ex-Commando Merlin and I a lot of fun practicing 'house-clearing' on flower-pots placed inside rooms, as targets for my favourite little .38 Colt Police Positive Special.

Rosemary wrote, "Meshed is a fine town, well laid out and with a prosperous air. Everything revolves, literally as well as metaphorically, round the famous Shrine over Imam Reza's tomb, and the beautiful Gawhar Shad Mosque next to it, because a huge, circular street has been made around these buildings, and all the ancillary halls and courts and approaches. Parts of the bazaar are in this circle, so one gets sudden glimpses from the bustle of the bazaar of lovely, blue-patterned arches and sunny courtyards. The chief features, a little further inside, are the golden dome of the Shrine made by Shah Abbas, and two golden-sheathed minarets near it. They can be seen miles away gleaming brightly. Near them is the mosque's lovely green-blue dome. Alas, we can never see them properly as no infidel may enter, and one gathers that even a halt in the approaches isn't very welcome.[19] All you get is a sudden view of the two domes rising from the jumble of bazaar rooftops.

"The street crowds are fascinating, as there are so many types from all over Iran. Turbans are common here, unlike the rest of the country, but usually in dull colours, often white, and many worn with a long tail of cloth hanging behind. There are a number of mullahs about, in flowing black or brown robes, and seyyids (Mecca pilgrims), with their henna-ed beards and green turbans or cummerbunds.

"We were allowed to visit the Shrine museum, which is full of wonderful things such as 500-year old carpets, Chinese vases and bowls, many

---

[19] See *The Road to Oxiana*, Part V, in which Robert Byron describes his and Christopher Sykes' brave, or foolish, entry into the mosque.

brocade and embroidered hangings which use similar patterns to those of the carpets. There was one incense-swinging censer, gold-plated and liberally studded with stones of all colours. There were strips of gold leaf from a tomb, beautifully engraved with pieces of the Koran on them, lovely calligraphy. The real treasures must be the room full of manuscripts, with Korans richly decorated by miniaturists, with gold and silver-embossed covers, miniature paintings, and very old books in earlier scripts. There were also man-high manuscript pages with giant lettering, framed separately. What hours of work are represented in that one room!"

We had eight days in Meshed. One day we drove to Nishapur through wind and rain to see Omar Khayyam's memorial next to a lovely little mosque with a blue dome, and flower-patterned tiles.

Another day we visited Tus, an ancient city laid waste by the Mongols. We could see the foundations of the city walls and the citadel in the midst of a great sunny plain. We came to pay our respects to Persia's greatest poet, Ferdowsi, who alas lies in an ugly modern tomb. He was born in the tenth century, and wrote the wonderful *Shahnameh*, or Book of Kings, which Persians still revere. Illiterates are able to recite from this work, in the great oral tradition of the East.

Beyond Tus, near the Iranian-Soviet border lay the vast, natural fortress of Kalat-i-Naderi.[20] Turquoise was mined near Nishapur, but in order to buy some we had to go to a dealer in Meshed. A sunny old boy produced packet after packet of stones in folded pink paper, and we looked at hundreds of different sizes, shapes, and colours. The colours were astonishing – from palest sky-blue through common turquoise colour to sea-greens. Some were clear, some with matrix. There were sheets of paper with sets of stones glued on, in the form of necklaces, bracelets and ear-rings. Some were huge chunks of brilliant blue.

Our last few peaceful days were spent pottering in the bazaars. Meshed was a great place for 'poshteens' (skin coats), and Rosemary bought a lovely, long one with sleeves, brown fleece inside, and Persian-lamb collared and cuffed, for £4, and also a Kabul-style waistcoat with beautiful embroidery in dark-yellow silky thread. They are both in good repair after thirty years – and they don't stink! We walked through the carpet street, where we found chiefly Turkomans and Bokharas, but most were cheap and gaudy with analine dyes.

---

[20] See the *Illustrated London News* of 24 June 1967, reporting the successful visit to the fortress by Sir Denis Wright, our Ambassadaor in Iran from 1963–1971. Lord Curzon had reached it, but had been refused entry.

9 June 1960: Our first moonlight picnic

We had accepted a lot of summer entertaining from friends living in lovely houses up towards the mountains: informal buffet suppers and a little dancing. We felt we could repay some of our hosts in our own way – by a traditional Persian picnic. I reminded Rosemary of the ones Roger and I had out in the desert from Karachi, and now it was full moon again!

Looking for a picnic site took us at least two Fridays bouncing about in the Land Rover exploring the little villages and orchards along the foot of the mountains. That was great fun and we found all sorts of picturesque corners to remember, and little valleys not far away, by driving by eye to patches of greenery, or driving up village streets till they petered out. The venue had to be close, easily found and reached in small cars, sheltered, with a view over Tehran lights, with running water if possible. We went up at night to try out one of two and eventually found the perfect site, Abdullahbad.

This was a little cherry-orchard owned by a Doctor Hashtroodian in town, who gave us permission to hold the picnic. It was up a track to a tiny village. There were trees planted near a pool containing huge fish and superb roses round it. The custodian cum gardener spent his days by the pool with his wife and young children. We enjoyed writing precise, clear instructions for the guests. They had to have no trouble finding the spot or parking.

Mac's cook Mohammed was indispensable. He heated soup on the spot, built two low walls from bricks around, tipped charcoal between them and laid skewers across. Rosemary had provided mutton, liver, bacon, small onions, sausages, and mushrooms, tomato salad, fruit salad with condensed milk, and Nescafé. Mabanum had been a great help at home. Our Tilley lamp was needed for the cooking, but the light didn't spoil the scene because we had a good fire. People brought blankets and cushions but it wasn't very cold. It was lovely with the full moon climbing up in front of us, and the mountains towering behind. The crowning touch was John Killick from the Embassy,[21] who played his guitar and sang beautifully. We were all very happy to listen.

After dinner I announced a chase, thus, "Rosemary has gone off into the hills, and there will be a reward to the first couple to find her. She will flash a torch every thirty seconds." She belted up the hill, down the next, round the humps into little valleys flashing as she went. Rosemary recalled, "It was so bright I could see every stone and plant, and any wolves that

---

[21] Now Sir John G.C.M.G. Ambassador to Moscow 1971–73, Deputy Under Secretary of State, F.C.O. 1973–75.

might choose to come. It was so bare that walking was easy. As there was practically no cover at all I was soon winded, so I finally ended up in a patch of shadow.

"The first person to find me was Mohammed the cook! He was horrified when he realised that I had gone off into the mountains by myself, and rushed off after me far faster than the rest, clutching a skewer! He then stood near me with his glaring white shirt, so I was soon found. We all settled down to more music until 1 a.m. or so.

"We sat by the fire until 3 a.m. watching moonlit thunder-clouds over Tehran and forked lightening, and the shadows moving across the mountains. Oh how lovely it was! The rain never reached us. We had put up our tent complete with beds, etc. near the fire to give a safari touch, and there we stayed until the morning."

Back to the Embassy

Lady Harrison was a very fine support to Sir Geoffrey. We admired her firm hand and creative, organising capacity – so much so that one day when our telephone rang, and Rosemary answered it from her stool, I heard her say "Yes, Lady Harrison," as she sprang to her feet. She was needed to 'pick brains' to create an exhibition in the autumn representing (British) women's contributions to society in a Women's Week exhibition at Amirabad, north Tehran.

This year's Q.B.P. was a huge affair with 1100-odd British, enlivened by the Black Watch brass band from Cyprus – 'very tiddly' in white jackets and kilts. The Black Watch also appeared on television and beat a Retreat on Friday evening in Sepah Square. There was a crowd of about 60,000 as there was generally so little public amusement when out for a weekend stroll. The onlookers had to be convinced that the band wasn't composed of women. They only understood when it was explained that the soldiers were from our tribes, like their Bakhtiari and Qashgai!

The friends thou hast ...

Donald Makinson arrived at the Embassy as press secretary, and he became a friend for life, alas only until June 1990. I admired him tremendously: he was knowledgable on any subject, a competent handyman, a keen shot possessing a L.W.B. caravan-equipped Land Rover. He had been in Iran before, and was once in the South Waziristan Scouts. He spoke Pushtu as well as Urdu and Farsi. He gave me complete confidence, and much more.[22] Donald and his wife, Lois, made me god-father to their elder daughter, Lucy, who became a wonderful friend as she grew up.

Donald and Hazel Roberts, a very sweet Embassy girl, led us on a perfect, two-night break way down into the bottom of the Lar Valley gorge, which curls round the east end of the mountain. It was a dramatic route as we crept in our Land Rover behind Donald's along the lip of the gorge, and we were still going uphill when night fell. Then we descended a fearful zig-zag road into the gorge, in the dark, down and down, with a few lights shining way below us. I wouldn't have driven down on our own if I had first seen how far the river was below.

There were engineers working on a new road, and a Persian directed us to a good camp-site by the river. The next morning we found that the place was ideal. It was a little meadow at the river's edge, with a line of willows under which we had camped. There was a superb view up and down stream, of dramatic cliffs and mountains, with a huge, craggy rock sweeping up a thousand feet just in front of us.

Demavend breathed out sulphur. Unfortunately, the attraction of little villages down below such as Ab-i-Ask, was off-set by the horrid smell from sulphur springs. Nevertheless, people went there for bath cures because the streams ran clear. There were lovely old houses above a bend in the river, perched on a rock. They had finely latticed windows and paintings on the walls and rafters. This occasion gave us the happiest of memories, in a lovely climate, sunny but cool, with ideal companions.

August 1960: A British Council month

The Tabriz Summer School for teachers of English was on, and all the other London-based, English-language staff were involved except for Halsted who was put in charge of the British Council while the Representative went on leave. I appreciated the test which I couldn't have managed without the imperturbable administrative officer, Dick Edwards. After the first rush of reading up the files on current Council topics, which were quite unfamiliar to this English lecturer, and taking action where necessary, I enjoyed the variety of it all. Rosemary reported home that I came back exhausted after six hours' non-stop in the office. Part of this was due to all the visitors, whom I was nevertheless happy to welcome.

Luckily, Dick and the Consul coped with an Oxcam expedition when one of its Austin Champs blew up near Kerman. There were Persians

---

[22] You will get an idea of the expertise and bravery of those men by reading Charles Chenevix Trench, *Frontier Scouts* (O.U.P., 1986).

194

aiming at courses in Britain, either applying for an English test and certificate, or wanting information on entrance qualifications to British institutions. In Tehran the British architect of the new 'public school' had to be assisted with his many daunting difficulties with the Ministry of Education.

All along I had been attending Ministry meetings with my American and European cultural/educational colleagues to provide an agreed standard form and level of English-language test which would-be students to Britain, Europe, or America would have to reach before being allowed to leave Iran. Fortunately, we all agreed and at once recruited examiners from our staffs.

```
                                      19th June 1960

More than dearest, Sir, J. M. G. Halsted,

Respectfully, I do not know how express my
gratefulness to your Excellency.
In the world over which prevails the
jungle rules, still there are individuals,
to whom The Almighty has endowed kind
heart and leniency.
They seek pleasure in others tranquillity,
even if it may cost them trouble.
They have found out a trace to eternity,
and have comprehended the paradise belongs
to those who enrapture a sombre heart.
Thank God I have met one of them, I am
very proud of the chance that luck has put
on my way.

With much regards and best wishes for your
future time.

             Very faithful to you.
                M. S. Monajemi
             English teacher
    Iran Sanandaj, Gorwah, Hafiz Secondary
                                     School
```

The Ministry informed my American colleague and me that there would be 150 candidates for the English examination. Good, I thought. Two days before the date fixed, they rang to say there would be 750! That was not so good! But everyone rallied splendidly. An easily corrected and eliminating examination paper was devised and roneo-ed, and a team of eight correctors found. The Ministry arranged the examination very efficiently, and by 1 p.m. the same day we had corrected and graded the lot. From now on the Ministry, having the basic material for future tests, could examine and send abroad whom they wished, and we were relieved of the invidious responsibility of selecting candidates.

Other commitments

Parents of school-children out for the summer holidays wanted Scottish country dancing on Saturday nights. Rosemary and Mac ran these splendidly. We also had our Tabriz couples, the Popplestones and the Joneses from Meshed, to stay to meet their children, and to advise on where to go and where to shop in the big city, and, of course, to offer to take them by car. All this was nothing to what they suffered from visitors at their posts.

New official 'visitors' of ours then came out ahead of the new academic year – lecturers for Shiraz, Isfahan, and Teacher Training College. As Gladys Fraser, Rosemary's friend in Edinburgh, said of all visitors: "They must all be cherished on arrival". Ours certainly needed cherishing and a good deal of guidance in such a strange and rather formidable city as Tehran. Some 'planes landed at Mehrabad very early in the morning and had us up; and some visitors need to stay around for a day or two.

Next came very official, but unofficial, visitors in a parliamentary party of M.P.s on their way to Tokyo. One member wanted to see the Council at work, which he did next morning. As Rosemary wrote home, "It couldn't have been a more impressive day. It was the first day of registration for new students for classes, and there had been a queue in the street since 6.45 a.m. There was controlled bedlam all morning. I saw some of it. People everywhere were asking questions. Michael was tearing about with ten people trying to talk to him. He wasn't doing the registration and examining, but had the M.P. to look after and some Germans, the Governor-General of Khorassan, some archaeologists, an Imperial Institute lecturer who couldn't get on a 'plane to Colombo, and students badgering him to get into classes to mention only a few! Persians always want to see the top person, and will not take 'no' for an answer even the seventh time!" I lost my M.P. sometimes in the throng.

196

More S.C.D. September/October 1960

There were probably groans at turning out for dancing again. But however tired one feels, the moment one is on the floor, in a set, or instructing, energy returns with the output, and with the need to be bright and sprightly! It was now great fun running the Embassy's weekly Scottish country dance night in its hall, which was open to all British. We had the usual shortage of men but the Embassy secretaries gradually found partners to join in, and some husbands who at first wouldn't dance, joined in not liking to be left out.

I was helped by Rosemary's admirable attitude: "Our house seems to have been a calling point for everyone in Tehran. There are so many new arrivals about. Anyone on the spot with a little local knowledge can help so much, and make such a difference to arrivals' problems that I feel I must help as much as I can. But it is wearing trailing around and takes up most of the morning."

New Deputy Representative

We were very cheered when Michael and Ursula Everett arrived by Austin Gipsy. We were out to meet them on the Karaj road, Rosemary with a St Andrew's flag. Michael E. was intelligent, calm, humorous, active, ready to take part in anything worthwhile. He played the French horn – partly because he had been born without a right hand. Rosemary and I both had friends in common with Ursula, and she was just the person Rosemary needed for mutual support and company.

She did her best to help Ursula settle in. Rosemary met other wives who needed her help, by going shopping with them. "One woman," she reported home, "blew into the Council and asked Michael if she could go and talk to his wife. A complete stranger. One must do what one can. It is so difficult for people who for instance have to furnish from scratch, and have no Farsi." I was proud of her.

Rosemary put on her first big party, which was for the Everetts to meet the people with whom the Council works: Embassy staff, people from the Ministry of Education, U.N.E.S.C.O. and C.E.N.T.O. specialists, and others.

This description of hers typifies such occasions: "I was terrified, as we had only had small, informal parties in Ethiopia. Seventy-seven including wives were invited, and fifty-three turned up. I hired two Embassy servants and had one from the Council, so that the maids could do the background work. The food was enough and complimented, but I hadn't had time to make two items which the dry climate requires to be made at the last moment. I am always seized by panic and gloom at the beginning of parties, thinking it will go dreadfully, and rush to the safety of the kitchen. When I must, I return in a 'do-or-die' mood to find it's all alright! Poor Michael."

Not so, not so. I basked continually in her support, unrealising, and unconcerned.

The run down of 1960

October

We took in lecturer John Green, who was ill for a week. He didn't get better as fast we we hoped. After two days' progress he had a bad go of chicken pox. It was only awkward because we had so little guest space. Luckily his Persian girl-friend came and took him into her home. They were married later, and set up in a flat, unfortunately over a brothel. Rosemary said, "Last week was so busy it was grim, no time to think more than an hour or so ahead."

November

For once we did our own thing, in our own way, and loved it. With Mac and Mohammed, his cook, we took the Firoozkuh road to the Caspian, and stopped high up in the mountains in the big Nimrud river valley at 6000 ft. The scene was very beautiful and it was warmer than when we were here before with Eddie and Leila for partridge. We were able to drive off down to the river.

"Michael wouldn't take the Land Rover across the icy river because of the risk of a later rise preventing return," wrote Rosemary. "So we camped on a grassy track through a poplar grove; and the donkeys with their loads of fuel for the winter went past several times a day. The trees were just at their loveliest, the air was so clear, and the mountains wonderfully grouped. I meant to lie about, but the mountain air made me feel fine, and I walked up hills happily, I love wandering about the little fields and copses down by the river. By 5.30 p.m. it was getting dark and cold. My Meshed poshteen was a great comfort. I was never out of it till the sun was well up. If one has a pressure-lamp in a tent, it soon warms it up, and a little whisky helps too. We managed to have a fire the second night, as it had taken time to find anything to burn."

The river bent sharply at one point to cut through a huge, rock rib running down to it, which seemed to close the valley. We reached the top of this and looked beyond. There was a little village tucked away directly below us. We sat there in the sun glimpsing all the life of the village – how the houses were built in a seemingly haphazard ground-plan, noting how the houses were built room added to room round a courtyard. From ground level one sees only mud walls and alleys, but up here we felt like birds over the village, because the rock we were on was sheer below us. Looking back up the valley we could see the snowy peak of Demavend.

The Shah has a son and heir!

Thus Rosemary reported on the event: "The town was well lit – they use neon light strips a lot, in different colours, tied like fences round lamp-posts, or fan-wise on a facade, or merely stuck at odd angles in the branches of a tree. There were necklaces of lights across the buildings too. We went to look at the arches of chrysanthemums near the palace. There were carpets and flowers on the road. All the old crones of the city had been waiting for days near the hospital, to see the poor girl's pain as she was taken in. There were gold coins for all the hospital staff but not so much rejoicing in the streets – it was a bit chilly dancing in some of the main squares. People seem pleased, as always at the birth of a boy, but they don't really care, I think."

4 December 1960
Mountains for Michael: Isfahan for Rosemary

Charles Wilmot came back from leave, and let me take a few days off. At that very moment Eddie asked me on a trip. I accepted at once because Rosemary had been invited by the Gayfords to go to Isfahan.

Rosemary had a 'prophetic' time in Isfahan, because we found ourselves posted there in 1966. She joined in Nan's weekly ladies coffee-morning for English conversation, and took part in a play-reading. "Rather too like work," she wrote. She spent a useful time at the Blind School, and took photos which could be used for the publicity of this fine institution among the Tehran communities. She also visited the bazaar.

"There's an amazing diversity of things made there," she reported. "I am really happy wandering along those high-vaulted, crowded lanes with dusty beams of sunlight spot-lighting the wonderful variety of passers-by."

Rosemary demonstrated here her astonishing ability to find her way anywhere in any complex, or on any terrain. Bazaars were never a problem to her. Her map-reading in town or countryside is fast and accurate. I just drive.

199

"There are not only shops along the alleys, but here and there through an arched doorway you see surprisingly large workshops, extremely dark, with human figures moving about in the gloom and steam, stirring, pounding, kneading, haggling, banging, weaving, and everything you can think of. Giggling little urchins were weaving the cotton carpets by hurling the ball of thread along between the upright warp threads without a shuttle. The men printing the cotton cloths by banging the wooden blocks on to them are quite a tourist sight now. A lot of dyeing goes on as it's a textile centre.

"My chief target in the bazaar was the tile-making, for which Isfahan is famous. If I'd gone there first, I could have had whatever I wanted made to order. In order to see the designs they had, one chap took me back through the maze of little rooms behind his open shop-front, past all the different processes, and through a tunnel under the oven, across a lane, and into even more workshops till we finally reached the man painting designs onto unglazed tiles.

"It was a true assembly-line: chaps dipping tiles in glaze, stacking them, pounding large blocks of rough glass for glaze into fine particles, stoking furnaces and so on. My curious mind revels in it as I love to see how things are done. At one place I asked what was in a huge, shallow, copper tray. The man was cutting white stuff into beautifully regular diamonds entirely by eye. It was halva and I was given some of the best I've ever had."

At the British Council John Gayford taught sixteen hours a week, ran the office and activities, met and handled visitors, or danced in attendance; V.I.P.s and everyone downward travelling to Iran visits Isfahan. There was a luncheon for the Japanese, which was was not as formal as expected, and Rosemary had a chance to talk to the Crown Prince about Edinburgh, and also to make suggestions as to what they should ask to do on arrival in Ethiopia which was their next destination. Rosemary described the Crown Prince as "exceedingly plain, but the Princess is very pretty and has charming gentle ways."

Christmas 1960

20 December 1960. Rosemary was soon back in Tehran on the Blind School job, again helping to provide food for teas, and items for sale. The Bazaar made £1,400 to £1,500, and 800 people came.

Rosemary had a day ski-ing, and then she coped with another 'Wives' Invited' clay-pigeon shoot, cooking kebabs with Mohammed. As Rosemary noted, "He gets such good meat, and soaks it in cream or yoghurt or something."

Eddie and his fighter 'planes were now stationed at Dez, or Dizful, on the Plain of Khuzistan. He had a little house and invited us down for Christmas. We were in balmy weather at only 500 ft. We went down by train. Ed Dokoozian was now on the Dez Dam and had us all to lunch. That was a pleasure. A German girl married to an Iranian pilot gave a party on Christmas night. My splendid quartermistress took down tinned Christmas pudding, brandy butter, mince pies, fruit, sweets, etc., which she "produced at intervals, so we did well".

Rosemary reported home: "The pilots have all known each other for years and were always dropping in. We had a few meals in the mess, and did for ourselves otherwise. The comic, conscript batman couldn't cook. Eddie went of at 6 a.m. so we got our own breakfast, which suited me much better as Michael insists on porridge and all kinds of un-Iranian things. We stayed around in the mornings with Haji. In the afternoons we went out shooting, always in the plain which Michael preferred.

"A lot of it is cultivated very fertile land and we walked through the winter wheat and the plough, getting partridge and hares. It was so easy, as we only had to drive up to thirty minutes on a beautiful, new, tarmac road. What a difference from the distances and energy required to shoot from Tehran. It was beautifully warm and sunny with lovely skies.

"One day we were beside a river with russet scrub along its banks and reeds in the river. In the open fields there were flocks of wild geese and cranes. It was so flat that we could drive almost anywhere after them in the Volkswagen. The technique was to drive slowly right round the flock in ever-decreasing circles, and at the right 'sprint' distance turn sharply in towards the birds and go hell for leather. It was hair-raising and exciting tearing along at between seventy and eighty kilometres per hour bouncing up and down, with someone hanging out of the passenger window trying to get a shot with a semi-automatic Browning as the birds took off, and someone else trying to shoot from behind the driver, and the retriever trying madly to leap out, and spent cartridge cases hurtling into the car while we were swerving and jinking and jolting and oh, the noise! Most unethical, I'm sure, but it's the only way to get anywhere near them as there's no cover at all and we were shooting for the pot. We charged several times and did get three or four. Then home to pluck, clean and cook – straightaway!"

I was excited next morning when Eddie said, "Let's go over to Shush," (ancient Susa and Shushan of the Bible) which was quite near. We quartered the area of Susa, the ancient capital of the Elamites, and the site of the winter palace of the Achaemenians of Persepolis. Susa is probably one of the most ancient inhabited places. It is a famous archaeological site and has been quite cleaned out for museums, with just holes and a few broken columns left. I was moved to be on such a site, and felt sad at slaughtering some of the beautiful 'black' partridge, with white spotted feathers, and the odd hare.

End of 1960: Tehran

Rosemary wrote, "We drove out to photograph the exceedingly tall minaret in the north-east of the city. It is called the Camel Drivers' Minaret because there was a light at the top to guide in caravans. One woman in a family group sorting cotton for carpets offered me some of her children!"

I was busy with external examinations, and the pleasant task of writing a talk with colour slides on 'literary Britain'. In my spare time I was coaching a diplomat's young son to shoot clay pigeons, but the wind was a bit fierce for a true picnic atmosphere. Our attempts at self-preservation against invitations had been fairly successful, and the spate of invitations which we could not refuse was nearly over. Snow had now reached town.

February 1961

Rosemary wrote home, "Ab-Ali, the ski-place, is so busy on a Friday that it's hardly worth going, but one can ski down a long, gentle valley from Ab-Ali to a village at the head of the next valley which has a decent road. I got a party of six together and we had a wonderful day, although the snow was really too soft. When I fell over trying to avoid Ursula, who had fallen on the track ahead of me, I went to the side and fell full-length myself. The result was that when I finally extricated myself I had broken the end off one ski! I *had* to go onwards.

"I managed to get across to a beaten pathway where I could walk. For hours it seemed I walked towards a village and it never came any closer; the clear air here was so deceptive. Finally I made it. I found most of the village women were out on their rooftops gaping at the rest of us ski-ing round the village. There was great excitement and calling out when I tottered through. I asked for a boy to carry my skis, and got an nice, old chap, and his donkey, which I was urged to ride. I had a terrible job getting on to it, as they use a huge, wide pad as a sort of saddle. They often sit cross-legged or kneel on it. There was a wonderful view of distant mountains with cloud shadows on them. Finally Michael met us outside the village. He had only just arrived as the other car had got stuck in the mud and he'd had to tow it out. We were all very, very weary. My legs were sore for three days."

Visit of the Queen and Prince Philip

When the Royal visit was first announced there was quite a flurry among the ladies, sending home for hats or what not, or hastily putting outfits together.

We didn't go to the airport as we thought it would be more fun in the crowd, near the university. But it wasn't. The police were a bit edgy and started using their truncheons. By dint of slipping sideways and pointing out that she was our Queen, we reached an empty stretch of pavement kept for children, and waved our little Union Jacks, shouting like mad. Farah with Philip waved from a tiny carriage, but the other Royals were too preoccupied with the coaches just starting! These hadn't ever been used, nor had the mounted escort. But everything went like clockwork, down to the army of street-sweepers brandishing their shovels and spreading grit for the horses.

Rosemary noted, "There was pretty heavy security since the Shah had once been shot (only through the cheek)." The 'heavy security' reported by the foreign press was partly due to the fact that people were not falling over themselves to oblige the press because they daren't ask the Shah's officials for, say, the colour of Farah's dress or what was on the menu.

Our Queen caused a big impression on the ride in, and she looked terrific. The next day was an appallingly busy one for the Royals, but nevertheless Philip came to the British Council in the morning. He spoke to some students in the garden on his way in. Then he came into the hall and took his hat off. Now we could see him realising that there were a lot more people to meet, and that remarks must be made. We noticed the effort he made to pull himself together. He looked very tired, and we felt sorry for him. In fact a feeling of sympathy was the prevailing one among the British.

We were all introduced by Charles Wilmot, and the Prince's standard line was "What do you do?" followed up quickly by extremely direct and penetrating remarks and questions. Rosemary wrote home: "Do look in the photo, Michael's thumb is straight down his trouser seam." I told Prince Philip that I taught English, and assisted in the running of the English Language Institute, and gave the occasional lecture. Philip remarked: "Not Shakespeare I hope? I could never get on with that man." I replied, "Oh yes, Sir. Shakespeare certainly. We have a number of very intelligent students."

Rosemary wrote, "This was really rather funny, and we were all laughing. In fact we were all ready to be relaxed and informal, so it became very jolly. Philip asked John Mills if they did any television lessons on Shakespeare, and John, preparing such a lesson at the time but losing his nerve, said "No". "I should damn well hope not," was the reply.

But I knew Prince Philip had acted in Shakespeare at Gordonstoun, where my brother John was a contemporary."

When it came to the Embassy banquet (a lot of food and flowers had to be flown out from home), Lady Harrison kindly left the dining-room curtains open as long as possible so that the Embassy girls could look in from the verandah. The Embassy servants were beside themselves next day: "Me! I served two kings and two queens!"

We got in for the Reception in the Golestan Palace. Rosemary wrote in her journal: "This is a wonderful Victorian affair replete with pillars, mirror mosaic, priceless rugs, fantastic chandeliers, rather delightful. Michael and I shot around the huge dining-room so that he could see some of the fabulous presents to the Shahs over the centuries." [The most desirable, I thought, was a pair of beautifully engraved Bland 12-bores, from Queen Victoria, in one ivory veneered, double-fitted case] "We went on into the dining-room, and had about forty minutes of great fun chatting to everyone from Embassies and Cento and Oil and Business, and trying to think of nice things to say about their appearances. What wonderful saris there were. We were served with tea in beautiful blue and gold cups, with gold teaspoons. That made my day!"

The Queen came in very quietly, and an awful hush descended. How grim to come into a huge, silent room, except for Rosemary bravely trying to keep things cheery. There were presentations at the door. Then the Queen walked slowly round the oval of people, speaking to persons here and there. What a quiet way of speaking, and so tiny and slim. She wore a simple dress of a pretty apricot colour, with a very fetching flower petal hat in pinky, peachy tones and a lovely diamond brooch. One girl produced the right word – so very *humble*. Philip came round more slowly, still firing off questions. Christopher Dalley of the Oil Consortium, said he was really grilled by the Duke on current problems such as the Shatt-el-Arab, and this was quite awkward with so many people listening.

"When the Royal couple were due to leave their apartments," Rosemary wrote, "Pat Calder, Anne Holloway, and I hung out of the very high windows overlooking the garden. As the Royals drove away beneath us we couldn't bear the silence and yelled out, "Good-bye". The Queen looked about her, then finally peered up out of the car window and waved specially to us. The nicest bit of all, I thought."

Mazanderan

John Gilroy, son of the famous Guinness artist and an original Tombstoner, took us to Babolsar very comfortably in his company Ford station-wagon. John is a very easy quiet person, a good companion, interesting and interested. We stayed at the Babolsar Hotel. We walked along the sands and among the attractive, thatched cottages, freshly white-washed at Now Ruz, now buried deep in blossom and orange trees. We picnicked for lunch every day, finding somewhere safe for John and I to fire his .22 pistol at our lunch tins, which kept us happy. But what kept other guests of ours happy as well as us was a Sirram Volcano kettle. It consists of a cylindrical jacket of water round a flue, set on a base bowl with side air-openings. It can be fuelled with anything. One starts it off by filling the base bowl with paper and twigs, but from then on, twigs or any other combustible material scrounged from round about are simply dropped down the chimney. The volcano boils water very quickly. It acts like a samovar, and we explained to intrigued locals that it was a "samovar farangi" (a foreign samovar!).

Rosemary recorded in her journal: "We had a boating trip in heavy, wooden punts hired from a Mohammed Mohammedi, on one of the flooded marshes. The coast there is a wide plain known as the Abadans where cotton and rice are grown. At exactly the time of the Boat Race at home, one Oxford and one Cambridge punter vied with one another. Our only audience were milliards of croaking frogs and distant duck. [Cambridge won, I'm afraid.]

"We visited the Caviar Station. There are depots all along the coast where the netted, caviar-bearing fish (four kinds) are hurriedly taken and the caviar whipped out. They reckon to have it in tins in ten minutes – cleaned, graded, and salted. We saw some of the priciest 'golden' caviar – a form of albinism.

"We were also taken into the refrigerator rooms where the fish were stored until they were exported. It was nightmarish in there, the fish were placed according to size in circular heaps, tails in, heads out, lying on their backs so that the yawning gashes of mouths, dogfish-like underneath, all seemed to be reaching out at us as we cowered in the entrance. The bigger ones were nearest the door – about five feet long. They didn't give us special warm clothing at all, as at other stations, John said."

I am very fond of caviar, good caviar, fresh or well-tinned. In Iran, caviar was packed in either a blue tin, or a pale-green tin. A chap used to come round the office with a nondescript bag of green tins at a very good price. This was the black market supply. "Don't eat that stuff," said someone, "you'll be poisoned." I did and I wasn't.

From the sea, we cut inland and then along to Gurgan, away from the sea in the great plain running alongside the north-east frontier mountains. We stayed three nights in Gurgan, and had a good look at the Turkomans. The first day we drove two hours further north-east to Gonbad-i-Qabus, a rapidly growing village in the centre of the plain. Here we stared up again at the wonderful, 950-year-old tomb tower of Qabus, and bought some attractive woven Turkoman bags. I'd seen a horse with a lovely, rich red-patterned nose-bag (toubret), and was delighted to buy the same for about seven shillings. We had lunch on top of a tepe which a British team, all friends of ours under David Stronach, had been digging in the autumn. Its side has been sliced away by a river, so they could easily see that the lower levels were rewarding. How we revelled in the green grass, the wild flowers, the balmy air, and the great, green plain all around with snowy mountains behind. A few horsemen riding decoratively across the green, and some grazing flocks were all the distractions.

As Rosemary described, "The second day we went to another Turkoman village near Gurgan. In Gurgan there's a lot of cultivation now, there is wonderful soil and many tractors. We wanted to see the real steppe (uncultivated land), and drove north over to some yurts and got out to watch a family group milking their sheep inside a wattle fold. The old boy in charge, complete with Turkoman hat and white beard, though not with a slit-eyed kind of face like many of them, received us amazingly warmly. He announced himself as Khan Molla Chafour Toumach, then to my astonishment he presented me with a lovely, white lamb! What were we to do? We each nursed it in turn, then treating the gift as a kind of traditional gesture, handed the lamb back with due ceremony, explaining we had nowhere to keep it in Tehran! He didn't speak much Farsi, but his young son did, and the driver spoke Turki, as many people here do, so we got on fine.

"The Khan invited us to have some tea. I was longing to see inside the yurt. They had three yurts grouped together. There were other families nearby. While we waited for the samovar to boil, we were led over to the lowest yurt and found, to our surprise, three more female members of the family inside, who were extremely busy weaving a carpet. It was laid flat along the floor; in fact the far end was outside the tent. It seemed a large one to us, but they assured us it would be finished in a month, although only eight inches or so were done. Then the family will move nearer the Caspian. The girls were unmarried and so kept their silk shawls pulled well over their bent heads. How fast they worked – no pattern guide, nothing. Their own wool too, all red, black, and whitish. The minute Michael and John left the tent, up came the heads to have a good look and now lots of gold coins and all their jewellery were revealed!

"When we'd sat down on the felt mats inside the tent – quite tidy and pretty clean – they also produced lump sugar, round, thick loaves of bread and bowls of gooey, yellow stuff. The latter horrified us, as our last sheep's butter had been revolting. But this turned out to be excellent and we dived in, Michael murmuring happily 'just like Devonshire cream'. We also had our tea in bowls, with fresh, hot milk. It was the first time I've had it with milk in an Iranian house. The two old chaps and the two sons sat and chatted with us, but didn't seem particularly curious or interested. One couldn't help feeling that either they'd had lots of foreign visitors or were blasé. Meanwhile a young wife (I didn't dare ask if she was the only one) sat behind and pumped what seemed to be the cream separator, a remarkable piece of machinery to see in such a place, but very sensible. They seem pretty well off, these nomads, with plenty of sheep, butter, cheese and skins to sell, and the women making perhaps several carpets a year. As we left we pressed a tin of pears on them, with explanation. It was at least a rare item up there."

The road to Tehran from here was the shortest and most dramatic, and I had to get back fast for my Oxford and Cambridge dinner. In Tehran diplomatic receptions in other Embassy residences did occasionally come our way. We were not diplomats but the Council staff were under our ambassador for guidance and protection, and we were sometimes kindly included as friends. We thus learned that neither we nor Embassy staff could leave such functions until His Excellency had left. This could be a little tedious when we did not have affairs of state to settle. So I introduced our younger diplomats to simple brain games to wile away the time, such as Pairs. Unfortunately, at one tedious occasion H.E. came over to find out what interesting topic we had found. I had to confess, and he was not amused.

Term began on 25 April, and we began to rehearse for an open-air production of *A Midsummer Night's Dream* in the Gulhak compound. I was so happy to be back as Oberon, whom I had been in my final year at Bradfield, in the Greek Theatre, in 1938.

8 May 1961: Fate steps in again

I opened just another Council letter from London, and learned that I was posted next to Visitors Department, London. This was a shock, but it would give me H.Q. experience and the stimulus and responsibility in handling interesting men and women of calibre from overseas.

But M.N.D. and the visit of our Director-General, Sir Paul Sinker, filled our minds until he left on 5 June.

The Director–General's visit and A Midsummer Night's Dream

To us at that stage of our career Sir Paul Sinker was remote. But we had heard a great deal about him from London staff, who spoke of him with admiration and enthusiasm. We now know how much we owe him. He took over from Sir Ronald Adam in 1954, one year into our time in Addis. We bless the body which appointed him. For, had he not taken charge then, and gone forward in his unique way, the Council might have been reduced to a non-body, and we would certainly have been 'cut'.

We knew little of this at the time, but he was obviously our saviour and a man to follow. Now I am drawing on his obituary which James Edmondston, one of our senior London staff wrote in our office bulletin of 8 March 1977:

> With his background of Cambridge don, war – and post war Civil Service Administrator, he seemed to combine the qualities needed to re-invigorate an able and willing staff in danger of losing heart. He was able to re-affirm the Council's identity, and to lead it in the discharge of the new responsibilities the Government now confidently foresaw for it. A Government now prepared to invest more in Britain's presence overseas.
>
> His greatest gift was to enforce his high standards of pro-fessionalism on the Council and to get its expertise recognized at home and abroad. Headquarters staff found him austere, somewhat remote. His mind worked rapidly as well as profoundly, and two of the cardinal sins were to waffle and not to "have done one's homework". But people serving overseas, once they had success-fully identified a mountain for him to climb, could enjoy his company, and that of Lady Sinker, whose presence with him on tour made it much easier for him to reveal his warmth and humour.

Now we had the Director-General with us. Sir Paul's day off (our Muslim Friday) was to be a mountain picnic and our responsibility. Our several reconnaissances into the Elburz foothills, sharpened by a sense of duty were most enjoyable. We found the perfect site, by a small river, with some shelter from the wind, and a flat area for parking and eating. We had prepared clear sketch-maps, which was Rosemary's forte, and we got all species of London staff there on time. I was even provided with a little free kudos when a Persian family got their saloon-car stuck in the river, and it was easy for Rosemary and I to pull them out with our tow-rope and an exhaust-pipe extension tube.

Rosemary wrote: "Play-reading rehearsals (*Macbeth* – for students at the Centre) must be after the big Saturday party for the Director-General. Oh, what it is to marry the job! Our people in the provinces have to continue teaching, and give luncheon and dinner-parties all the time, with so many included or they would be huffed. The Tabrizis are having 160 students to tea, and thirty-five nobs to dinner the same day."

When Merlin Jones in Meshed was driving the Director-General out into the mountains, he asked for a comfort stop. The irrepressible Welsh

Merlin stopped, waved his hand, and said, "A loo with a voo," then realised whom he was addressing.

June 1961: Midsummer Night – real and dream

The last full moon before we were to leave Iran was a few days ahead, so Rosemary decided that we would have another moonlight picnic up at Vanak. The picnic was successful, though not as warm as last time. We devised another game which luckily warmed the guests further than the fire could. I had placed nightlights in jars in odd corners, creeks and gullies below the rounded hills, and by each jar was a token (a wrapped sweet) to be collected and counted towards a win. It worked. It was fun for us mooching about in the moonlight listening as the guests either sped by, or simply went for a romantic stroll. Rosemary recalls, "We were warmly dressed and got no colds. We slept there again, and oh it was lovely when we woke, all the huge roses round the pool."

"The play's the thing" – in the Gulhak compound garden

The play presented no problem, except that it was an anxiety to be performing in front of the Director-General and Lady Sinker, and as Rosemary noted, "It's been pretty hot, and rather trying for a couple of days at a time with high winds and dust. We're in the 90s daily now, low 70s at night."

There was a lot of fun earlier in the casting. I was allowed to choose my Titania. I chose the beautiful Judy Harney, wife of Desmond in the Embassy. I chose the fairies from a number of very attractive, young things, both Persian and European. All the other members of the cast, in the attached programme were well-known colleagues and friends. But the whole show rested on the professional expertise of the producer, Ian Calder, of our staff, and his wife Pat, who was a delightfully lively Puck, as well as a tower of strength to producer and stagers.

I quote Rosemary: "The play was a tremendous success – the setting, at night was really lovely, and the lighting put so cleverly in overhanging trees. A stage was built with ramps leading up to it, and with only the trees as backing. So you could see the actors coming from far back in the wood, the fairies flitting about just as they should, Theseus and the court preceded by torch bearers, and Oberon and Titania first revealed by the glitter of their sparkling head-dresses.

"Michael wore a shot-silk cloak, and as he moved fast back down the black ramp off stage with small steps, his cloak would lift up, and he really seemed to fly as he disappeared. I got more and more alarmed each night that he'd get too excited and ambitious and leap just too far! Titania had long, floating, nylon 'wings' of two colours, grey and mauve over a green dress, and she seemed so floaty and ethereal next to Oberon's shining magnificence. I was there several nights to help with costumes, a lot of waiting about and most time-consuming, particularly when one is packing up to leave the country."

Sad, sad, and yet?

Rosemary began to pack, and to sell household items. I managed to sell the Land Rover, luckily to a colleague to be sure of the money. We loved our house. It was so attractive and in such a nice street. Rosemary commented: "The garden is lovely now. We are eating supper outside again. We were so happy, and we hope our friends who came in were happy too. Bless Ali Samandari, such a wonderful friend and member of staff." "Oh yes," I said, feeling very sad suddenly. But we had our home leaves and foreign visits to look forward to. I liked to boast that I always spend my birthday on Torcello, the perfect island. In fact we managed it twice in twenty-seven years.

Departure from Tehran, a memorable journey

Packers came in on 17 June. Chaos reigned, and it turned stinking hot – 90 °F in the house. The men took three days and under-estimated the total weight badly. A lot of hurried re-thinking of the most economical freight routes had to be done. The last two days were the big Shia mourning days for Ali, so it was difficult to get jobs finished, rubbish collected, etc.

Rosemary recorded, "We were given a number of farewell parties, just the kind we like. There have been none in the mourning days, so we creep off to bed rather quietly and sadly. But morale is good, and the last two days have enabled us to recover a bit." We moved up to Mac's house for what remained of our last night, when one has to get up at 3.30 a.m. for the 'plane.

Luckily, we did not remain concerned over Mabanum (it is always a wrench leaving such servants) because Mac took her on as office cleaner, where she also had more social hours to look after her family.

"Away for we are ready to a man . . ."

We flew with Mac to Istanbul, to the Pera Palas Hotel, where the rooms had three brass bell-pushes, "chambermaid," "valet," and "groom". Then we flew to Athens and embarked on the Italian Adriatica Line M.V. Barletta, for Crete, Corfu, Brindisi, Bari, Dubrovnik, Split, Katacolo for Olympia, and Venice.

Here Mac's younger brother was waiting with Mac's 25/30 1936 Rolls Royce, and his mother. In it we all drove in a manner 'dignified and stately' through Italy and France – to "fresh woods and pastures new".

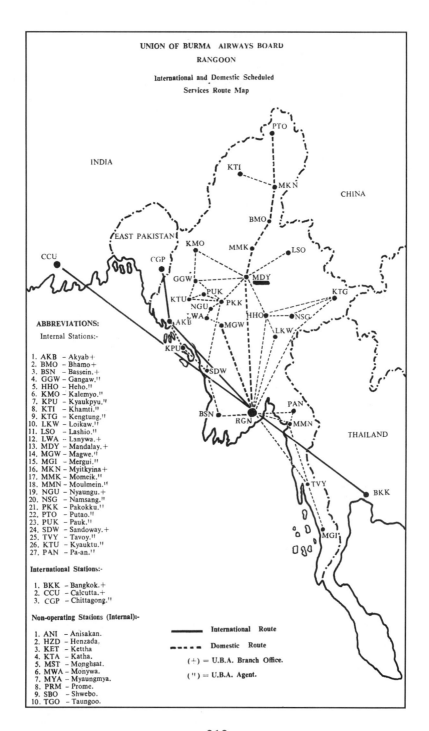

UNION OF BURMA AIRWAYS BOARD

RANGOON

International and Domestic Scheduled
Services Route Map

INDIA

CHINA

EAST PAKISTAN

THAILAND

PTO
KTI
MKN
BMO
KMO
MMK
LSO
CCU
CGP
GGW
MDY
KTG
KTU
PUK
NGU
PKK
LWA
HHO
NSG
AKB
MGW
LKW
KPU
SDW
PAN
BSN
RGN
MMN
BKK
TVY
MGI

ABBREVIATIONS:

Internal Stations:-

1. AKB – Akyab+
2. BMO – Bhamo+
3. BSN – Bassein.+
4. GGW – Gangaw."
5. HHO – Heho."
6. KMO – Kalemyo."
7. KPU – Kyaukpyu."
8. KTI   – Khamti."
9. KTG – Kengtung."
10. LKW – Loikaw."
11. LSO – Lashio."
12. LWA – Lanywa.+
13. MDY – Mandalay.+
14. MGW – Magwe."
15. MGI – Mergui."
16. MKN – Myitkyina+
17. MMK – Momeik."
18. MMN – Moulmein."
19. NGU – Nyaungu.+
20. NSG – Namsang."
21. PKK – Pakokku."
22. PTO – Putao."
23. PUK – Pauk."
24. SDW – Sandoway.+
25. TVY – Tavoy."
26. KTU – Kyauktu."
27. PAN – Pa-an."

International Stations:-

1. BKK – Bangkok.+
2. CCU – Calcutta.+
3. CGP – Chittagong."

Non-operating Stations (Internal):-

1. ANI   – Anisakan.
2. HZD – Henzada,
3. KET – Kettha
4. KTA – Katha,
5. MST – Monghsat.
6. MWA – Monywa.
7. MYA – Myaungmya.
8. PRM – Prome.
9. SBO – Shwebo.
10. TGO – Taungoo.

――――― International Route

- - - - - Domestic Route

(+) = U.B.A. Branch Office.

(") = U.B.A. Agent.

212

Burma 1961–1963

We thought we had left Iran forever, so we were very sad. But we had had an uplifting journey home via Istanbul, Knossos, Olympia, Dubrovnik, Split, Venice, Padua, Grenoble, Burgundy, and the Loire. I was not looking forward to a London posting. On reaching home I decided to attend a Staff Association party for our departing Chairman, and there met Controller 'B', the great but unassuming A. J. S. White of the I.C.S. in Burma, 1922–37, and early British Council fame 1940–1947. I told him of our last Christmas shoot in Khuzistan, and he recalled his days after jungle-fowl in Burma. He said he had a job for me, but *they* didn't agree. Now Fate intervened.

When I reported to our H.Q. at 65 Davies Street to meet my Director, and squeeze myself into a shared hutch of an office, I was called outside by the laconic Scot, James Livingstone, Head of Personnel. We walked round the block, and I was offered the post of Assistant Representative, Burma. I was thrilled. 'A.J.' had won! As *The Times* (14 February 1991) wrote:

> But for A. J. S. White, the infant British Council might not have survived the Second World War and become so far reaching a national agency for cultural relations.

Kipling described Burma in 1887 as "a very new land – a land where people understood colour – a delightfully lazy land (because it is so fertile) full of pretty girls and bad cheroots . . ." It sounded good, but on his approach by sea he called the Irrawaddy "the River of the Lost Footsteps – the road that so many many men of my acquaintance had travelled, never to return, within the past three years"[1] which gave a clue to a violent history.

We had an excellent briefing in London. This included a short course at the School of Oriental and African Studies (SOAS), a lunch at the East India and Sports Club, and free tickets for *My Fair Lady* to accompany a Burmese parliamentary delegation, which thought the show was put on

[1] R. Kipling, *From Sea to Sea*, vol I.

for its benefit. Next day at the Visitors Bar of the B.B.C. I discovered that the delegates were all keen 'hunters', and had been buying guns in Belgium.

Leah Kitchingham, our efficient and supportive Regional Officer, took us to a meeting of the Britain-Burma Association at the Royal Overseas League, and we had our first view of rubies: beautiful jewels worn by an elegant, young Burmese mounted in gold cuff-links. Rubies came from Mogok, where there were also dacoits who were not to be ignored.

> A foolish young man in Mogok,
> Thought the silly old bandits a joke.
> But they shot him one day.
> Now his mates kindly say,
> "He wasn't a bad sort of bloke."

Leah put us up for membership of the Royal Overseas League which has proved to be of permanent value.

We left for Rangoon by sea from Liverpool on the Bibby Line, S.S. Warwickshire, 10,000 tons, semi-freight. The atmosphere among the seventy-five passengers was cheerful, and we found extremely useful and life-long friends in Darley Tanner and Betty, who were returning to his Rangoon Chartered Accountancy business. During the voyage the Captain, E. V. Thompson, taught me a number of poker variations, but failed with Mensa-type mathematics. First Officer Douglas Hine was a very funny part-time companion.[2]

The chief engineer was a Pop-eye double, with a tiny, shrunken, jutting jaw. A foul, metal-stemmed pipe, barely supported by ill-fitting teeth, added to his incomprehensibility. He was a dear but he wouldn't turn on the air-conditioning. We had two young Burmese British Council scholars, U Thaw Kaung a librarian, and Nwe Nwe Tun, a post-graduate botanist from St. Andrews. We became instant friends. I spent longer in Burma than Kipling and would have risked telling him: "Never underestimate Burmese girls". Maybe he didn't. Nwe Nwe learned Scrabble from us and won every time.

In Port Sudan I could introduce Rosemary to my old acquaintants, the terrifying, mop-headed Fuzzy-Wuzzies. In Aden again, the British Council Representative, Elwyn Owen. did us proud, and took us everywhere. In Colombo we had our first experience of the beautiful East: the spectacular plants; the people; the Buddhist monks; the bullock carts loaded with fruit; the animals, including elephants, in the lovely zoo; attractive, old

---

[2] He taught me the very best gin sling: 4 of gin, 1 of D.O.M., 2 of Cherry Brandy, 2 of lemon juice; mix and add soda or lemonade to taste.

Dutch houses, emerald rings from Siedls. Dock-handling problems enabled us to leave for up-country. We were very happy to be invited by disembarking fellow passengers, the Swaynes, to visit them on their estate at Kaikawela, twenty-two miles out of Kandy.

We had palatial accommodation and a wonderful opportunity to visit the Royal Botanic Gardens at Peradinya, which are particularly famous for their orchids. We then went to Polonnarua, the eleventh-century capital of Sinhalese kings, to undertake ascending the almost vertical, crumbling, iron ladder fixed against the huge rock of Sigiriya (the Fortress of the Sky) safely past the swarm of guardian bees, to see the life-size damsel frescoes in the cave, with colours undimmed. It was an unforgettable experience.

We sailed up the Rangoon river in the early morning. The Burmese passengers had been rushing about since 4 a.m. Dawn was lovely: the wide, brown water, the little, sharp-prowed boats, the flat and shadowy landscape, and a small pagoda silhouetted against a pale, pink-tinged sky. As we moved slowly up to Monkey Point, the first rays of the sun picked out the huge, gleaming, golden Shwe Dagon Pagoda. This was Kipling's view:

> Then a golden mystery upheaved itself on the horizon a beautiful winking wonder that blazed in the sun, of a shape that was neither Muslim dome nor Hindu temple-spire. It stood upon a green knell, and below it were lines of warehouses, sheds and mills.[3]

We were met on Sule Pagoda Wharf by our Representative, Bill McAlpine, an ebullient Irishman, and his wife, the highly-charged Helen. Some forty cases of our baggage, including my shotgun, a .375 magnum rifle and a couple of pistols were all spirited away by our cheerful, confident staff; and no duty was paid.

After only a few minutes in the car, I was being shown into our upstairs offices in Lewis Street. I had never had such an office to myself before: with my name on the door, an air-conditioner, modern reproductions on the walls, a carpet. It had a good view on two sides: up to the thick, green-treed rise of the distant, residential suburbs, and down to the harbour quay. The famous Strand Hotel nearby was pointed out to me. The British Embassy, the G.P.O., the Hong-Kong and Shanghai Bank were all near at hand. It was comforting after Addis and Tehran to be in touch with the sea again, even by the muddy Rangoon river.

We were kindly put up by the McAlpines until our house was ready. Their house, 19 Windsor Road, was quite close to town. It had a very large

[3] R. Kipling, *From Sea to Sea* Vol. I.

central hall, which was ideal for British Council gatherings. Life did not proceed for us in the orderly manner expected. We floated along on a tide of discovery and sensation. That very evening we were bidden to the Embassy Ball for Princess Alexandra so we had to unpack our evening clothes immediately.

What a welcome party at the Residence, a lovely house – formerly that of the general manager of the Irrawaddy Flotilla Company. A dance floor had been put down on the tennis court with a striped awning above. There was an R.A.F. band, and a steel band from Singapore. The food exceeded normal standards. The Princess was elegant in bright red chiffon, but a bit out of scale among the tiny Burmese women. It was an odd feeling for me as a complete stranger to be whirling round in the dances, responding to the welcoming gestures of guests who knew of our posting, and trying to reach them to ask who they were!

The next evening was the McAlpine's official welcome party for us. Number 19 came into its own at once. I had to bone up on an expertly-produced, wide-ranging list of ninety-seven Council contacts, from foreign bodies to Burmese departments of education, medicine, business, culture, the zoo, the press, music and drama, etc. That was good training for me, and it was most heartening to realize that we had such a ready-made niche in Rangoon society. This was a great help in overcoming culture shock.

Life and work we found to be at a fairly leisurely pace. This was partly due to the Burmese temperament, and partly, I am sorry to say, owing to the scope of our work being slowly reduced by our host government. A fact which we were forced to accept as guests of the country, as in every British Council post abroad. All we could do was to redouble our efforts within the framework allowed. We were very lucky to be in Burma at all. It was wonderful to be among such lovely people, hence my compulsion to write at some length of the life in which we found ourselves.

The day after that party, we had to attend a Burmese Government garden party for Ben Gurion. The grounds of the President's palace were ideal for stalking helpful officials or professional contacts. But the effort to remember new Burmese faces was bewildering.

There was another shock to follow. We had arrived in the middle of Council rehearsals for a forth-coming production of *Twelfth Night* in the Residence garden, and I was to have a walking-on part, which grew to several!

Bill and Helen were thus too preoccupied to help answer all Rosemary's questions about settling into our home, so we were in limbo. But the play was fun. The setting was perfect. Raymond Adlam, our senior university lecturer, actor, singer, conductor, well-versed in the East, was an admirable Feste. The rest of the cast remain a blur. I only remember the pleasure of being made up for four nights (one night at University College for an

216

audience of 800) by a beautiful Anglo-Burmese girl, Marika Barrington. I just went into a swoon, and left it to her. The Anglo-Burmese were quite different from the Anglo-Indians in Pakistan. The Anglo-Burmese mix produced a specially bright, attractive people. They had no chips on their shoulders, and fitted in easily anywhere.

The McAlpine's had chosen a house for us with great care and effort. It was a modern bungalow on a small rise in Inya Myaing (meaning swamp), near Inle Lake, which was now an unobtrusive, small residential area of neat, modern houses hidden by thick hedges, and shaded by beautiful flowering trees: laburnam, gul mohr, padauk, and frangipani. The roads were narrow and sunken, but as there was very little traffic they were no problem, and they helped to preserve the atmosphere of quiet retreat.

We had a kindly Indian landlord, U Ba Aye, who was in the leather business. He did all he could for us by replacing with white paint the Indian taste for bright-blue, sick-green, and dirty-pink walls. He gave us a new tile roof, but during one night in February, it unaccountably rained without the new tiles being in place, while half a mile away at the university it didn't rain! We had dirt and chaos before restoration, and it put our official entertaining back a bit. But the house had pluses. It was very secure, with thick bars on the windows and expanding metal-grill gates front and back. When the window bars were painted black they hardly showed by day, and not at all by night. I obtained for the grills a set of matched Chubb padlocks and a master key. Burmese thieves oiled their almost naked bodies, to slide more easily through small openings, and to avoid capture. They used rods and lines to remove items of clothing – often finding keys or money in pockets. Some carried a dah tucked into their longyi folds, a heavy, elongated, triangular Burmese chopping-knife which they were prone to throw. Fortunately, we escaped attention.

It took us eight months to get our house absolutely right for an all-purpose base for us and our eventual successors. Rowe and Co. made us London-approved furniture of lovely teak items, Chinese crafted. Teak is a perfect wood: a very pleasant colour, easy to cut and work, but resistant to changes of temperature or humidity. Before the export regulations, foreigners would buy a house-set of teak furniture, and ship it home in selected teak-plank packing cases. The excellent local textiles in lovely colours did well for curtains and covers. The local cane and basket-work was fine for small items, including strong, waisted stools called morahs. The final requirement, for which the landlord paid on seeing our need, was a second gate to the garden, so that guests could be driven up, under our wide, rainproof porch, and chauffeurs could drive on out.

In Burma we first met the tropics. The 'hot weather' was exceedingly hot, and in the monsoon it was very wet. I was employed around the house fixing things. The smallest effort left me saturated in sweat. Tools could go rusty overnight. Leather objects developed mould if left for a short time. In some months bare arms stuck to paper. The one air-conditioner was in the bedroom which in the monsoon we had to use as our living-room. Despite metal mosquito and fly-screening I had to wear mosquito boots in the evenings, and Rosemary would wear a long dress.

We suffered from ants.[4] The tiny ones got into anything that was not hermetically sealed or protected by moats of water. The legs of wire-meshed food cupboards had to be stood in bowls of water. The larger ants inhabited electric light switches and plugs, and piles of bodies caused shorts. We had invading, almost choking, swarms of flying-ants in one season and green-fly in another.

If a screen door was left open, the hall could be visited by the odd toad. We never had a snake in the house, but a Russell's viper killed an oil company employee in camp one night, which made us wary. The monsoon rain washed the scorpions out of their holes so we never wandered about bare-foot, and always shook out our shoes before putting them on for fear of them. Cats would play with live scorpions.

We now suffered a fairly severe attack of culture shock. The climate was tough. Even in the dry season the sun was too hot for country picnics. We were living in Rangoon on a narrow, laterite ridge amid hundreds of square miles of paddy fields. The nearest beautiful highlands were four hundred miles away. There were no tracks for Land Rovers, and nowhere to go at weekends. Life was rugged for Rosemary. We got used to the heat and damp, but it was still pretty tiring for her as a housewife. I worked all day in an air-conditioned office.

Buddhism preaches tolerance of all creatures, even pests, to the extent that the taking of any life will not help one on The Way. Where the city corporation was lax in the removal of rubbish, crows were useful scavengers, but thousands of hideously noisy, maddeningly insolent, cunningly wary crows made daily life round the house wearisome.

As a shopper, Rosemary had to suffer pretty unpleasant conditions. The covered meat-market was the worst. There was heat, humidity, smells, dirt, and horrible crows in the rafters. 'Ordinary' shopping was difficult due to the climate, and because there were no recognisable shops specialising in European foodstuffs. The pi-dogs were another problem. They were not aggressive as we feared, but pitiful creatures, emaciated bitches and mangy curs, and they were everywhere. At night they howled, a weird, spine-chilling moaning. We had come to terms with hyenas in Addis Ababa. But Rosemary never got used to the pi-dogs, and their sudden howling bouts. Something would set them off, another dog, a

---

[4] And had to put up with a number of the 'tribes' mentioned by E.H. Aitken in his book *Tribes on my Frontier* (London, 1904).

pagoda bell, or a durwan's (a doorkeeper's)[5] tong-tong of the hours on bits of rail or car part. But for me the bells or watchmen's gongs were pleasant, all-night, reassuring sounds. They never struck together, but one would follow another's lead, always in double beats for the even hours, like ship's bells.

During the day the peace of Inya Myaing was shattered by loud Burmese music coming from the radio in the Sino-Burmese house opposite. We just had to get used to it, but the family went to bed early, so we weren't troubled in the evenings.

We soon recovered from our culture shock, for Burma offered us many compensations. We found we had delightful neighbours in Colonel Freddy Shaw, our military attaché, and his wife Mary, whose proximity made us feel more secure. Other friendly neighbours, whom we met quite regularly, comprised a Swiss with a Burmese wife, a Yugoslav couple, an ex-prime minister of Burma, a Burmese barrister, and Doreen de Glanville and her three lovely, Anglo-Burmese daughters. It was a cheerful contrast to our Tehran neighbourhood.

Bill and Helen clearly had found an ideal house though it was a little small for parties indoors. We had no trees that shaded so it was too hot to use the garden in the daytime, but at night in the dry season we could have lovely parties, official and private, on our spacious lawns lit by a set of Council lights.

I had qualms about the lunch and dinner parties we Europeans are accustomed to giving for business and pleasure. But we stuck to our custom. The Burmese would get up about 5 a.m., and go to bed about 9 p.m. They wouldn't give cocktail parties, or meals such as we give. They would love to provide an early morning breakfast for a group of pongyis (monks). Then all the family would turn to, cook for hours, and dress in their best for the occasion. I believe that some of the Burmese, who were all extremely courteous, came to our parties despite having eaten their own meal beforehand.

To avoid embarrassment, we soon learned not to hurry out to meet a Burmese male guest getting out of his car, but to give him time to open out his longyi and retie it more firmly before stepping forward to greet his host and hostess!

Thanks to Betty Tanner, we had marvellous servants and our household in Rangoon was for us very happy: Saw Maung, our portly Burmese bearer was a perfect gentleman's gentleman. He began by unpacking our heavy baggage. It was all safe, except for three Persian, Chinese-style plates (packed with their hanging wire backs on: a warning!). Saw Maung

[5] See *Hobson, Jobson, A Glossary of Colloquial Anglo Indian Words and Phrases* (Routledge, 1985), and Philip Howard in *The Times*, 18 April 1986.

was our alarm clock. He would normally call us every morning at half past seven, but eight o'clock on Sundays. If I wanted calling at 4 a.m. to go shooting, he would call me just as easily. A tap at the door: "Come in." Soft footsteps entered. Saw Maung would open the curtains, throw up the mosquito-net, move quietly between the beds, remove the iced-water jug and glasses, and set down the orange juice. "Good morning Saw Maung." "Good morning sir." "Scrambled eggs please Saw Maung." "Very good sir." When I emerged at 8 a.m. on a work day, there he would be with the breakfast ready and the newspapers on the table, *The Nation* for madam and *The Guardian* for master.

Saw Maung was the head of the domestic household who managed the others firmly and impressively – when in earshot. He lived peaceably in the servants quarters away from the house with his wife and small daughter called Tutu. He had a teenage son of whom he was proud but who seldom appeared except at high speed on a bicycle. Saw Maung was a man of property and some substance – in both senses. When dressed for a party in gaungbaung, gingy (jacket) and silk longyi he resembled one of the guests. In fact, on one occasion, he approached a foreign ambassador to ask him for his choice of drink, but the ambassador shook him by the hand and murmured that he had not seen him for some time, which was true. The ambassador's mistake was an easy one to make for there was, happily, little outward social distinction among the Burmese. They all appeared to be cheerful, easy-going people who preferred to live simply and quietly without being materially acquisitive.

Saw Maung always seemed to be about. He seldom took time off. His English was excellent and he was honest, loyal, and invaluable. He was there to deal with every situation. He fetched and carried, cleaned and polished. There was a lot of furniture rubbing to be done, especially in the monsoon which caused much extra work: every week all the books and many other items had to be carried out into the garden and aired during sunny periods. His knowledge of Rangoon was extensive and his common-sense considerable. He guarded us against intruders or importunate callers. He would be there in the morning to put things into the car, and at the door in the evening to take things out of it. He was ready on the dot of six o'clock with the whisky and the ice. He served meals deftly and at the week-ends served us tea on the lawn. He locked up the house at night, and if we were going out, stood at the door with a button-hole for me and made sure we had a key.

He was also fond of animals. Helen had given us a tiny kitten soon after we moved into the house, and Saw Maung, who had a cat of his own, looked after our beautiful Burmese-Siamese cat with loving care, so we could go away at any time with confidence.

Our cat, for whom we could never find or agree on a name, was a source of constant joy. Pussy was a very beautiful, mid-brown and coffee cream, with a long, expressive tail. She was full of personality and had an infinite variety of easily distinguishable moods. Pussy ruled us: we were her slaves.

Pussy had her meals in the kitchen given by Ananda, our Muslim Mugh cook from East Pakistan. He was a pleasant but rather taciturn individual, though a very good cook. He made wonderful curries on Sundays with the finest paratas, puris, or chapattis. His curried prawns were unbeatable. He was excellent at parties – under Rosemary's tutelage. He wouldn't clean or polish, not even the tiles on the kitchen floor. Unfortunately we couldn't lay on a hot-water tap for his dishes. No house had this facility, it seemed. Ananda was expected to wash his dishes from a cold tap near the floor above a lead-lined drain space. When extra help was needed in the kitchen, he could always bring in another cook friend because he belonged to a close fraternity of Pakistani cooks who saw each other nearly every day.

Another member of the household was Khin Saw, a Karen Christian 'wash nanny'. She was a young, cheerful, sometimes scatter-brained creature, but she gave valuable, loyal service. She did all the clothes-washing, ironing, and floor-polishing. She was graded in local household society as a sweeper, so she swept – no higher than the skirting boards, for above them it was dusting and therefore Saw Maung's job. Khin Saw also carried out the rubbish bins. A lot of sweeping and polishing came her way, because like most Rangoon houses ours had good teak parquet flooring, and the house floors were the housewives' pride. Before we bought an electric floor-polisher, Khin Saw used coconut husks, a half in each hand. We now miss her noisy giggle and chatter. We shall not forget her cheerful, willing service, nor her almost square feet.[6]

Once we were invited to a Karen New Year party, outdoors on a tennis court on bamboo mats round low tables. The Karens had a wonderful dance like a sword or rapper dance. Long bamboos were laid on the ground in pairs, a man grasping each end of the pairs, three pairs one way and three pairs laid across them, making a large square. The clash of bamboos was exciting. Then four girls did a dance of varied steps in and out of the squares, very like a sword dance.

Mongalu, our mali, who came with the house, was agile and willing to be instructed. He never stopped work and always had a cheerful smile. Saw Maung often had to interpret for Rosemary, but later on she and the mali appeared to be a close team. Rosemary loves gardening, and in two

[6] It was very sad to read in *The Times* of 28 January 1995, of the Burmese government' s crackdown on the Karens. The girl in the photograph published reminded us of Khin Saw.

years had really achieved much, with the compost heap, the placing of the flowers and shrubs, the care of the many and varied pot plants. It was hard for her to leave that garden in 1963. Poor Mongalu was put in prison while we were on leave. He had two wives. The young and pretty one was living with him in the quarters, but the wife of the mali opposite enticed her into the arms of another. So our mali stabbed her – with a knife which I had given him. She soon recovered, but he was put away for three years.

Saw Maung next produced his son, Maung Chit, to be the fifth member of our household as driver and handyman. He had the makings of a mechanic, and he soon learned how to drive our 1961 Ford Consul. He would wait at parties too, always with a broad grin. When we came to leave we got a very good price for the Consul, because it was a good model, and because there were no modern cars in Burma.

The Rangoon we knew was a slow-moving, uncrowded garden-town. My drive to the office every morning took twenty minutes down good roads fringed with thick, green foliage which sometimes bloomed into white, red, scarlet, or yellow. There was no traffic problem, and from the position of our house in Inya Myaing there were several ways to go which made the routine even more pleasant. Everywhere there was colour, cheer and charm: the Burmese men in longyis, and the Burmese girls with blossom in their hair. Not far from our office was the tall, graceful Sule Pagoda at the heart of the city not far from the Sule Pagoda Wharf. The Sule Pagoda was reputed to be 2250 years old, and built to house relics from India.

The whole town of Rangoon had a disorganized, dilapidated air. Along the river's edge Strand Road was densely built-up and bustling, and the passers-by were fascinating and colourful to watch. The centre was the same but the pavements remained in a war-time-shattered, uneven state. The library was near our office, in the attractive Phayre Street, which was one of the few arcaded streets of Rangoon. It appealed to me that in the arcade by our library door was a young catapult seller's stall. Phayre Street was named after an early British administrator of renown. His direct descendant of today is Colonel Desmond Phayre, who was our M.A. in Tehran. We are happy to still be in touch with such a friend and his wife Biddy. They visited Rangoon in the eighties, and Desmond took the chance to urge our ambassador to lobby for his ancestor's statue to be re-erected. And it was – a charming Burmese gesture.

When I got down to work I discovered that nowhere before had I been so well served by our locally-engaged staff. Our Director-General, the admirable Sir Paul Sinker, said in a speech at a staff convention that too many people had the idea that administration was a waste of time, and so it was sometimes neglected; but Sir Paul reminded us that administration must go hand-in-hand with the rest of the work to make a proper, balanced whole. Conversely, administration was not an end in itself.

My work was nearly all administration, and I loved it. I enjoyed learning the game. Everything came through me: London and local staff, including three British Council-appointed university lecturers, and our man in Mandalay, Wilfred Kirkpatrick and his staff. I soon learned from Bill about our man in Mandalay. They were on the same intellectual wavelength. Wilfred found administration a bore, but he was a delight and I found myself enjoying his letters and willing to respond at once to whatever he asked, which was little. He used to write apologetically, diffidently about such matters. Much of my daily administration was to do with the library. I sometimes muttered to myself at every fresh flood of demands from the band of ladies and their attendant peons headed by the indomitable Joan Frank. But I appreciated their efforts highly, and both we and the Burmese benefitted from it.

Joan we can never forget. She was so alive, bright and active, efficient and fun. Hers were the first eyes I caught at Princess Alexandra's Ball. She was an organizer of the Monsoon Madness Tournament. She introduced me to Bix Biederbecker. Joan was highly strung, and alas committed suicide when working as British Council librarian in Rome. I am glad we had visited her there during a home leave. The British Council library in Rangoon was our one remaining presence when we left. I loved my work for our libraries overseas, and their dedicated staffs.

Joan's number two was the charming English lady, Monica Mya Maung, who had been married to a well-known Burmese for over twenty years. She was full of kindness and good works. The other Burmese girl assistants couldn't fail to be good at their jobs! In the office Mrs Achard, the Representative's secretary was young, efficient and had been long with the Council. She was Anglo-Chinese-Burmese? Mrs Janet Aukim, whom I took on, promised well. Young Maung Tin Win (Indo-Burmese) made a pleasant, efficient, and willing clerk of all work. Our Indian Swami ran the McAlpine's house after hours, and in the day-time was the office wizard who could produce, find, buy, make or repair anything required, from a picture-frame to a gardener or a cocktail party for sixty. He could drive the office car or show films – what would we have done without him? Our real strength was on the accounts side, where we were lucky to have George de Souza. He had been with the Council for years, a calm, confident, long-experienced accountant, highly spoken of in London for his model accounts. I soon learned in the Council that one cannot make mistakes with money or accounting regulations. In the fluctuating financial situation in Burma, George was the ideal man to handle it all.

Christmas in Rangoon 1961

Christmas was a peaceful season, unlike in Tehran. In Rangoon we enjoyed rest and reflection after so many official functions. We had four days' holiday and we could get on with home jobs. The sung Eucharist at the almost full cathedral was uplifting. The English bishop was there, the dean was Anglo-Burmese, as were many of the congregation, and there were Burmese and Karens too. All the Burmese clergy were barefoot. The choir was magnificent under our Raymond Adlam. In the evening, Raymond brought a small group round to Freddy and Mary Shaw's dinner party, and they sang carols beautifully.

Lewis Varley, a bright spark of Bombay-Burma Company, gave a 'Roman Evening': "Dress accordingly and come by chariot". We were too new and unadventurous to do more than dress up. We shall never forget the lovely sunset scene. Coming along a quiet road enclosed by high palms, was a line of double-yoked bullock carts with native drivers, bearing exuberant Romans in togas and their ladies in becoming classical dress.

A valuable asset to our work was John Dawson, English language lecturer at the Teacher Training College. He was an admirably qualified, sympathetic teacher and examiner of teachers of English. I learned a lot from him, as did the devoted and attractive Burmese band of mainly women teachers of English who were regularly under his care, many voluntarily. His measured tone of voice and his lucid explanations made him a star. Under U Nu, in our early days, competence in English was regarded as an important asset to the Burmese people. They understood this, especially the women. John's wife Victoria, was Greek and a perfect match. They met in Salonica where John was teaching. They had four small, beautifully brought-up girls: Athene, Ariadne, Daphne, and Anna.

Our Ambassador, Sir Richard Allen, was a good sort, and great fun, with a most attractive wife. She was especially kind having the cast of *Twelfth Night* all over her garden, for numerous nights. Sir Richard was a keen and bold sailor. I have memories of him dashing about under a tight sail, or whatever one says, in the wide, but craft-crowded, breezy Rangoon river on which few ventured. He had an old alarm clock tied to himself by a piece of string, for time-keeping; and an Embassy secretary who was a brave and experienced girl crew.

The Allens thoughtfully invited us together with the Dawsons, who were also newcomers. Tea is a sensible Scots practice, and is a good occasion to entertain lightly and converse at a reasonable hour, without the hostess having to work in the kitchen, and without everyone having to be careful about drink. Sir Richard and John got on fine. I enjoyed their penchant for limericks and sitting-down games.

This is John's:

There was a young lady of Πατρασ (PATRAS)
Who made an agreeable ματρεσ (MATTRESS)
So soft were her αρμσ (ARMS)
And less evident χαρμσ (CHARMS)
That all the young men of the neighbourhood
Left their villages and gravitated to Πατρασ (PATRAS)

"Dear Michael," wrote Sir Richard on 9 July 1962. "Thank you very much for your letter of July 6th with some charming verses to remember and John Dawson's comments. I enjoyed this pleasant alleviation of our bureaucratic boredom! Try the British Council instead."

English is an easy language to pick up for simple communication, but it is tricky to learn – and to teach – any further. Problems can arise, for example: "I wish to thank the Council for its unspeakable hospitality". "The gen of your transfer to Fiji has suddenly killed me with surprise. But I sensely see it in British Council Overseas Service." Some errors which occured in notices are worth keeping as sign-posts for customers. The Rangoon Laundry had an entrance up three steps; and on the third rise it said: "WATCH YOUR STEP". But Gerry Abbott in *Back to Mandalay* (Impact Books, 1991) rightly informed the Burmese Tourist Office that they should change their pagoda notice which read: "LADIES MUST NOT WEAR BRA-LESS".

Burmese is a tonal language and was classed as very difficult. But we enjoyed our lessons with U Tin Aye, in the company of Gerd Lee, the charming, humorous, Danish wife of Tony, the Oriental Secretary. (She once offered us "whisky on the stones", and is never allowed to forget it). Here I pause for a moment to remember Tony, a great companion, later killed in a motor-accident in upper Thailand. Gerd was luckily able to return to the Danish Foreign Office. She remains our friend.

A year in Rangoon: 1962

Each day took me morning and evening past the towering, gold Shwe Dagon Pagoda on its hill, a never-ending source of pleasure to look at in all the different lights and season, 'the greatest of all' Burmese pagodas, a lovely symbol of the Buddhist faith. It is perhaps best seen at a distance in the evening across the waters and palms of the Royal Lake.

The gaudy, glittering, ramshackle, cluttered, and jumbled atmosphere of the Shwe Dagon itself took some getting used to, after the perfectly proportioned, satisfyingly shaped, and exquisitely tiled mosques of Iran. But the more often we went, the more we became absorbed in this essential part of Buddhism and the Burmese way of life. The two aspects of Buddhism which affected us most were peace and tolerance. The Burmese built pagodas as acts of piety, in the sense of achieving merit. Most Burmese were practicing Buddhists and regularly visited the pagoda of their choice, but two pagodas were shrines for all, since they contained relics of the Buddha.

All day and every day the Burmese came to worship at the Shwe Dagon. They climbed the long, steep, covered flights of steps to the main platform. Here was an array of smaller shrines at which the faithful performed private acts of worship at the shrine appropriate to their birthday and day of the week. Here they were away from the world, and could relax in peace. All men were welcome to share in the beauty and peace all around, provided they conducted themselves in a seemly manner, and observed the one rule, 'Footwearing Prohibited'. Fortunately, there were coir runners round the platform because marble flooring in the sun could become very hot.

All the way up the north, south, and east steps were stalls and shops at which a truly remarkable range of objects could be bought; thus the approaches to the pagoda were a delight in themselves. Many stalls sold offerings such as real flowers or skilfully made imitation sprays and decorative motifs in gold paper and wire, held on little canes. There were lacquer shops selling boxes, or ducks, or owls (the bird of good omen) in black and gold; and also the sacred bird, the Shwehintha, in gold lacquer 'bejewelled' with green or red or white specks of coloured glass. There were ivory carvers producing replicas of the great Chinthé (the mythical beasts which guard the entrances), and workers in tortoise-shell or mother-of-pearl. There were iron-mongers, booksellers, gong and drum makers, and makers of ingenious toys in painted bamboo. There was a constant procession of people of all ages going up and down these steps – a happy spectacle in itself.

The Shwe Dagon became part of our lives which we shall always miss. In Buddhism we found a tolerance of other faiths, which hardly exists in Islam. We found peace too at the pagoda, and often friends to whom we could quietly talk. They might even be smoking cigars. We became caught up in the atmosphere, and some of the strangeness in the architecture and sybolism became comprehensible. Buddhist festivals at the Shwe Dagon were fascinating, such as Ktain, the presentation of gifts to the monks, or the Festival of Light, best seen at dusk. So many and varied were the gifts brought by the devout (which seemed to be everybody) at Ktain, that the whole surrounding area looked like an itinerant bazaar, with displays of cloth, flowers, rice, aluminium utensils, and a great, wooden tripod covered in enamel teapots. Full moons were beautiful, satisfying, happy times, at which we could have the fun of finding and gazing at the huge ruby set at the very top of the gold 'hti' or ornamental umbrella (parasol) which crowned the point of the pagoda. This ruby could only be seen when lit by a bright moon, and then from only one spot on the platform.

Independence Day was on 4 January. There was a huge parade which we did not attend, but we were invited to the President's garden party. In Rosemary's words: "One is bidden at 4.30 for 5 p.m., lounge suit or uniform, hats and gloves for ladies. One clambers out of the car on to the lawn in front of the former Government House, now the President's palace. It is a monstrosity. The British architect must have felt this was his big chance and so crammed in and on one building every fashionable style from pepper pots downwards. The lawn grass is rather rough and spongy and ladies teeter about on their high heels, sinking in frequently. Then the President, Prime Minister and retinue emerge from the palace, and there's a general move to the tea-tables at the far end of the lawn. One stands and gobbles away. It is a good tea, and so is the iced coffee.

"Then there is a surge back again while the President et al move about; and we go to sit in front of a stage for a cultural performance lasting about an hour. The stage is set up in front of trees and it is lovely watching the sunset sky changing behind, and then see the coloured lights coming on. There is an orchestra in front. The dancers' costumes are the old court dress – long longyis for the women trailing round their feet, which have to be kicked back in a sort of irritated reflex-action time and time again. The women also wear little organdie jackets winged out at the base. The men are wonderfully swathed in silk, folded most skilfully around their legs and in front; and all glitter with necklaces and embroidery. The movements of the dances are very stylised with much finger positioning and arm twisting, less static than the Indian dances. The group dances we enjoyed very much, especially one about two peacock brothers gorgeously dressed and having glittering bluey 'breasts'. The colours are always tasteful, apricots, creams, and whites predominating.

"The orchestra was very strange in tone and tune but always enjoyable, comprising mostly woodwind with different drum arrangements. One man squats inside a tiny, circular palisade of drums of carefully graded sizes hung round inside it. Another man has a huge drum suspended below a prancing dragon, all glittering with gilt and 'jewels'on a wooden frame.

"Sitting in the palace audience it is pleasant looking across the dark heads of the women in front, with their neatly coiled hair often wound round a comb stuck through the centre knot, and with fresh flowers, or plastic ones, or jewels tucked at the base of the knot. On such occasions the men wear their gaung baungs; this is an irregular, domed hat-frame of cane, covered with pastel silk, knotted at one side. There is a triangular, loose end fluttering gaily at one side. The men buy them ready-made.

227

"Burmese dress is very attractive in its good taste and simplicity, particularly the men's on such occasions. The longyi is stiff silk, usually plain or with a pattern in the weave only, and usually in a pleasant, unobtrusive colour: dull greens, light browns, soft apricots and yellows, seldom gaudy. Over their shirts goes a neat, collarless jacket, very Chanel-type, reaching just below the waist and cut straight, but not very loose. Across the front are frog fastenings of the same material, small and neatly made. Often the jackets are white or cream sharkskin, silk or similar, but many wear black or grey. They look so nice and cool, always freshly ironed.

"The advent of nylon has rather spoiled the women's dress, in European opinion. From being very modest people, always decently covered up to the neck and with long sleeves, their little blouses are nowadays made of nylon and most revealing. It is odd the way they have gone overboard for such material. They of course all wear white-cotton, embroidered bodices underneath. The broderie anglaise blouse is the nicest. The women wear too many pieces of jewellery, the blouse buttons usually being jewellery on such an occasion. And they wear stoles which spoil the line. Anyway they are charming, tiny, delicate creatures, so intelligent. But I could never quite get used to the grey/white thanaka paste (from a tree bark), which the ladies put all over their faces for their complexion, and leave on in public, quite unconcerned."

Music and pwe's

Burmese music appeared to consist of crashes and bangs interspersed with woeful, nasal intoning up and down a very wide scale of semi-tones. It was usually very loud because the Burmese seemed to have a passion for using high-wattage loud-speakers which they rigged up with great skill against all the canons of electric wiring. The noise (not music to us!) could be hellish and prolonged.

Pwes remained a curiosity for us, but the Burmese orchestral instruments were interesting to study. The drums were called saiwan, the big drum a panma, the little drum a sekon, the xylophone was a gyi waing. The pwe is the main form of Burmese popular entertainment. It is an open-air, all-night performance, and as Gerry Abbott describes:

A sort of masque resembling in its lighter moments pantomime and music-hall or vaudeville, and in its more serious episodes rather more like ballet and opera except that it is perfectly in order to chat to friends, get up and buy something to eat or drink and even to sleep during any part of the performance.

228

We loved the pwes we came across and would stay awhile to watch and listen. It was charming the way they built their temporary covered stages (mandats) at a convenient spot in town and filled the trees with coloured lights. The programme would contain song and dance, instrumental items and slap-stick cross-talk. The audience would happily squat for hours on their woven mats, often in the street itself. They smoked huge cheroots and would remain fascinated, guffawing away but not applauding. Children would wander in and out among their parents, or sit hopefully beside the food-and-drink vendors who were also in the audience.

On a cold, pre-dawn drive on our way to a rendevous for a jungle-fowl shoot, we went through one village and the pwe of the previous evening was still in progress. The village audience of whatever hour since the start were there motionless, rapt, huddled in such warm cloths as they could muster.

Holidays

I was cheered to learn that the Burmese year would give us 105 official holidays, but I was disappointed when I found out that nearly half were Buddhist sabbaths, which were only observed by government offices and schools. The day of the sabbaths varied from week to week, which complicated administration.

Unfortunately, we did not receive many British specialist visitors, who in most countries were important catalysts in our work in many subjects needed by the host governments. But here we could support the Burmese medical profession, for whom I have had the greatest admiration. The Burmese doctors and surgeons were as highly skilled as one could find. Many were British qualified. They were all deeply dedicated to their calling, and in Burma were brave, disregarding politics at some danger to themselves. In February 1962 we were invited to attend the Burma Medical Association Conference Dinner and Ball, which proved to be a fine occasion.

We enjoyed meeting our distinguished British men and women visitors. It was rewarding to be given the simplest facts on a variety of specialist subjects. For instance, we appreciated Professor Stuart Harris, known as 'the great immuniser', for the work he was doing combatting rabies. The medicos gave a great party for him, as they did for others, and kindly included us.

Conversely, we sent whom we were allowed to send to Britain for training or study. U Khim Maung went to Britain to study hospital laundry services. The spin-off was good, for on his return he ordered a wide range of British equipment.

I didn't succeed with the postal services. I paid a semi-official visit to the main Rangoon post-office to see if I could find a potential trainee of sufficient seniority who on his return to Burma would be able to make the post less erratic. Oddly enough, to emphasise my point of complaint, I spotted a British air-letter lying in the middle of the sorting floor, and picked it up. It was from Papa to me!

A new Sittang bridge

The Sittang is a wide river east of Rangoon crossed in its lower reaches by only one bridge. In 1942 the British could only hope that Rangoon would be given enough time to prepare for the southern advance of the Japanese if this bridge was blown. The British were in retreat, and after causing 2,000 Japanese casualties, blew the bridge. But this was a disastrous move. A large part of 17th Indian Division, the 46th Infantry Brigade under Brigadier R. G. Ekin,[7] was cut off, still on the east bank, losing all its heavy equipment. It suffered many additional casualties among those who tried to swim across the swift current, but luckily not the commander. And Rangoon wasn't ready to resist the Japanese. This was another ghastly episode in that cruel campaign of the 'Forgotten Army'.

In 1962 the bridge was to be replaced, and our Representative and our librarian were invited to see the second span being floated into place. As they were unable to attend, I was given leave to go in their place. The librarian was invited as a gesture of thanks for organising our Book Box scheme, which supplied little isolated communities with returnable collections of books and magazines in locked boxes. The chief engineer of the bridge and his staff were on our list of recipients.

Rosemary and I were borne away one night in a special coach attached to the Moulmein Mail, which was used as accommodation by senior railway staff. Our coach was very comfortable: with kitchen, bathroom with shower, bedroom with two proper beds and cupboard, screened from the passageway by a curtain. And we had a sitting-dining room with two fold-up couches. We were under the care of the friendly and informative deputy-chief engineer and the deputy-chief of signals. We had our meals on board, and our coach stayed at the site for the night.

A new bridge was being built of six cantilever spans on piers. The first span was in position and we were invited to watch the second span being placed on its piers. This was five miles above the old bridge and would provide both a road and rail link to Moulmein in the south. The Burmese Railways were building this bridge without foreign help, showing pride

---

[7] See his obituary in *The Times*, 19 March 1990.

<u>COPY</u>   Shwebo

                                                14th February 1962.

Dear Miss Frank,

    It is something like finding an oasis in a desert
when I receive your book-box. I cannot find suitable words
to thank you. On receipt of your letter, railway receipt and
keys, I sent out my peon to the railway station and took
delivery of the box. The contents are checked against the list
and found correct.

    I am glad to announce you that we have successfully
formed our reading club among our staff and I was elected
Chairman, being head of the department. So I shall be very much
obliged if you kindly register our reading club, and send any
kind of reading material which were issued on free service.

    I beg to request you to send the box monthly until
further notice. If possible please include Film Magazines and
books written by Navil Shute, Earle Stanley Gardner, and
Agatha Cristie in next box.

    With many many thanks,

                                        Yours sincerely,

                                Sd/- KHIN OO (Manager)
                                State Agricultural Bank,
                                        Shwebo.

and ingenuity in improvising with such materials as they had, and never
having built such a bridge before. The only foreigner was the chief
engineer, an Anglo-Guyanese.

That evening a ceremony took place below the veranda of the chief
engineer's office hut. The head watchman had asked if he might once
more propitiate the local river Nat (spirit) with little gifts of fruit and
flowers. The chief engineer was in an awful state of nerves about the
crucial operations due next morning, which depended so much on the tide
and the unpredictable wind. So why not? In Burma there are Nats: so we

were ready to attend. Long before the time of Gautama Buddha the peoples of Burma and their eastern neighbours were animists. They believed that there were spirits everywhere in the land: in trees, rivers, caves, lakes, hills, and mountains. Houses had more personal guardian spirits who nevertheless needed propitiating.

According to legend, a man once felled a tree and made the tree spirit homeless. Thereafter, where there are trees, tree-spirits require propitiation at least with gifts of fruit and flowers for the offended spirit. When Burma's greatest king, Anawrahta, came to the throne in Pagan and became a devout Buddhist he was upset by the prevalence and strength of Nat worship. But he achieved a compromise by including Sakra, the king of the gods, as the chief guardian of Buddhism.

The propitiation of the river Nat had been particularly successful over the floating in of the first span. A special weather report from Rangoon forecast high winds, and strongly advised against floating the second span that day.

At 9.30 a.m. next morning we spent a long time looking round the site listening to the eccentric chief engineer explaining his problems. He wept when he heard that Rosemary was Scots. He was so happy to meet one of his father's race. His mother was Guyanese. His companions were his pets: pigeons, a monkey, snakes in a cage, a deer, jungle-fowl, and half-grown wild pigs.

The first span was firmly in place; now the second span had to be floated in on three pontoons. Each span was 350-feet long, and this was high above our heads. It had been assembled on temporary trestles along the river-bank upstream.

The nature of the tides made the job very tricky. It was timed for the spring tides, but the river varied so much that there was no complete certainty that the river would fall low enough to get the pontoons under the span. A wind the wrong way could adversely affect the required water level. The current here was very fierce, and the tide rose in only two hours. It was a swirling flood of water which sped the fishing canoes past at a great rate.

The Commissioner of Railways and the ex-Commissioner arrived on the bank with the wives and children of the 2,000 men on the payroll, and the pongyis too! At the river bank the wind was blowing hard, but the propitiation ceremony went ahead. At the right point of the tide-level, the wind dropped completely. The order for floating in was given, and was successfully achieved in complete calm. Then a strong wind blew again.

Now those concerned began to operate the ten winches on each pontoon with cables to the shore and to buoys moored mid-stream. It took four and a half hours to float the whole construction out into the river and swing it round downstream into position on to piers. We were in the crowd on the open end of span one, and it was thrilling to watch the huge mass being moved into place. It hung seven inches above its seating and was delicately moved inch by inch to the correct spot on to which only the falling tide could drop the great span. The operation was entirely successful.

The walk along the first span was rather alarming. Wooden platforms were laid along the centre, but most of the floor level consisted of views of the river a hundred feet below. Boats were everywhere: the high-sterned country boats, launches; myriads of fishing canoes; a few motor boats; and a small tug. In the midst of the excitement of the closing stages, the chief engineer slept head on arms at his office desk worn out by a sleepless night and nervous tension.

The daylight journey back was across entirely flat, almost featureless, paddy fields. This view was only broken by the huts and trees of villages. When we told Saw Maung back home about all this, he was horrified, and hastened to explain that he being from the vastly superior Upper Burma was a pure Buddhist and didn't believe in Nats.

2 March 1962: A coup d'etat in my absence

On the night of the shots in Rangoon that heralded a coup d'etat, I was up in Mandalay with Wilfred Kirkpatrick at a Burmese wedding party. Rosemary slept through whatever happened, but was then informed by Saw Maung's wife of an army take-over. She had heard the early-morning radio news. We did not know why this intervention had happened. We heard that there was possibly some Shan trouble brewing, with the rumour that Shan leaders were under arrest. There had just been a seminar on federalism and the position and progress of the Burmese states in relation to Burma proper. The different states wanted more decentralisation but the army didn't. One poor fellow was killed unintentionally. He was the son of a Shan leader, and the first Union President. Later we heard that the popular Chief Justice had been arrested. We were all fond of him. However, the general opinion was that the army seemed to be getting on quietly and efficiently without causing unrest. Rosemary was pleased to learn that beef cattle might be slaughtered again, as she was very weary of pork. We did not know then, nor could we read in *The Times* what else was to come.

April 1962: Bad news

The British and American Summer Schools were cancelled by the new military Government. British Council scholarships were stopped. Ford and Asia Foundations' work was at a standstill; only government to government aid, such as the Colombo Plan was allowed. A second lecturer for Mandalay, previously sanctioned, was not now permitted.

But we made the acquaintance of the Rangoon River, and that was cheering. The first occasion was an invitation to a private dinner and dance on a little, flat-topped, two-deck river-steamer. We had the works: food, the dance band, the lights, the guests, the chatter, the gaming machines, which the Burmese cannot live without; and I learned to dance 'the twist' to such pieces as Chubby Checker's 'At the Top'. We went for several hours up and down the river, past the lights of Rangoon and the shapes and sounds of the river traffic, enjoying the breeze this created. It was tremendous fun, and was fortunately not our last 'voyage'.

We experienced a day's trip by river-steamer organized by the Australia-Burma Society. We went through the delta cuts and creeks to the Irawaddy itself and to the town of Maubin and back. There was constant interest in the country boats going with their produce, mainly vegetables, to Rangoon with the tide. There was a surprising amount of traffic on the swift and muddy water.

The Boat Race 1962

We were very pleased when my Desert Army Scottish friend, Jimmy Cumming, who was with Raleigh Industries, could pay us a visit after a tour of Japanese markets. He was a Cambridge man and although very tired, happily attended the Boat Race Dinner which I was glad to be able to arrange in yet another country for an Oxford and Cambridge Society. Luckily the zone time interval allowed us to listen to the race over dinner. We had to borrow evening clothes for Jimmy, but he could not conceal his brown shoes from the appraising eyes of His Excellency. There were between thirty and forty of us gathered in a garden.

Besides this annual dinner the Oxford and Cambridge Society quietly flourished through regular outdoor tea-party meetings at a member's home. We greatly looked forward to these since in Rangoon we could really get to know fellow members.

To Sandoway

Our constantly kind friends, Betty and Darley Tanner, laid on a memorable trip to the beautiful Arakan coast to the west, during a five-day festival. One hour's flight by Dakota from Rangoon took one to Mazin Airfield within sight of the sea, five miles back down the track brought one to a group of two-bedroomed bungalows among the palms. To us Sandoway beach surpassed all others we have ever visited. The coconut palms were massed along the shore, mixed with other exotic vegetation. The sands were golden yellow and very clean. There was lovely greenish water of a delicious temperature.

The huts with high-pitched palm-frond roofs were on stilts, and were adequate in such a climate. They had a teak frame and teak floors, with walls of split bamboo woven into sheets which had an attractive texture like an enlargement of woven tweed. There was a large verandah in front, a passage and two bedrooms, and two bathrooms behind with slatted floors. We enjoyed the washing system. Each bathroom has a huge, Ali Baba water-jar on the floor and one baled out water over oneself, letting it pour through the slatted floor on to the dogs and chickens below. We had bare feet all the time, and just swept the sand out occasionally. There was clean sand all round the house and we were only ten yards from the beach proper.

There was more surf at this time of year and one had to be careful. There were also more people at festival time. There was a rocky part nearby where the Tanner children sailed their boats, and we had fun using goggles. We knelt on the rocks, holding our breath looking at the fascinating fish: dark-blue, round ones, so thin head on; white ones with tiger stripes, tiny, brilliant-blue, striped ones. There was not a great variety as it was so shallow, but that amount of under water suited me. We slept out on camp-beds on the verandah at night. It was lovely looking at the early sun among the palm fronds hanging over the roof. It was a bit stuffy when the breeze dropped later on.

We had several walks up and down the beach and through the village. There was bay after bay of lovely beaches, all were different. Shells worth collecting were hard to find as the locals collected them all to sell. The countryside behind was most attractive – little, wooded ridges between flat paddy fields, which were bone dry just now. We found a beautiful scene when we ventured further. We reached a little port where several country boats were unloading rice in baskets which were carried down the steep gang-planks on the heads of most graceful girls and women. Each basket was poured onto great golden mounds, to be shovelled into sacks. The bright colours of the longyis made a delightful contrast with the trees and vegetation around, and the blue-green sea beyond. There were hundreds of small crabs along the beach at night, and bigger ones round the house, ready to pop down their holes when we came near. Rosemary recalls: "Michael dropped some broken glass down a hole and a large red crab popped up to see what was happening. There was mutual astonishment!"

Back in Rangoon: Easter

Rosemary noted: "Easter morning was made memorable by my first mango, and the flowering of the tall padauk tree opposite our gates. Immediately we got out of bed we saw that overnight it had become covered in rich, golden-yellow blossom – a magnificent sight. They were very pretty racemes of little flowers, with a pleasant scent. All over the town the same thing had happened and people were carrying armfuls to their friends, while most women had some in their hair. The flowers fade by night. The flowering will happen again, and after the third time the rains will come."

B.C.S.A.

We gave a dinner-party for the British Council Scholars' Association. It seemed to go well. They were easy to talk with because they spoke such good English. We remembered that the Burmese liked to go to bed early so we didn't try to prolong the evening. On large or semi-formal occasions when the Burmese had nothing particular to say, they were quite happy to remain silent, which was so refreshing.

April 1962: Mandalay and Maymyo

I travelled by train to Mandalay for the first time. I intended to look for staff and pupil accommodation for a Summer School for teachers of English in the cool hill-station, Maymyo. I loved these Summer Schools; they were such fun. There was a marvellous rapport with keen teachers, and delightful extra-curricula activities. But I soon heard the bad news. At 5.30 a.m. I was met by Devi Dass, the Council's Indian factotum/driver, who was another fine example of our loyal local staff. The ancient Land Rover needed all the 'help' we could provide!

I had been looking forward to meeting Wilfred Kirkpatrick. He was a delightful man, kindly and modest, an Arabist and scholar, convivial and clear-sighted, who was totally devoted to his students and his studies. Administration was certainly not his forte, but it is impossible in Council service to escape from such mundane details as weather-worn fly-screens, Land Rover parts, tape-recorders, or ridiculous correspondence when read in abstract, such as: 'may one buy a bath?'. But rapid solutions make for peace of mind, and efficiency. In Kirkpatrick's out-post position he coped with everything with humour, and I was ready to help him all I could. He was very close to Bill McAlpine, whose creative energies he admired, and he sympathised with the present frustration Bill felt. Bill showed me a letter Wilfred wrote from Mandalay on 6 July 1962, which ended thus: "Sometimes when even that (work on his novel) fails to lift my spirits, I play at being Michael, I switch on the B.B.C. newsreel – where they are always changing the Guard or following the Queen to Ascot or something equally boring – I stride up and down the balcony, knock back (rather than sip) my whisky and soda (I'd much rather have absinthe) and say to myself: "Now old man, remember you are British". Having twirled my moustache and made sure that all bolts and bars are in apple-pie, I then climb into my flannel pyjamas and go to bed with – a copy of last December's *Sphere*."

Mandalay suffered extensive damage in World War II and in the civil war which followed. I found it a sprawling town, very dusty and dirty with stagnant water lying about. I did little sight-seeing, but one could not fail to observe the mile square, crenellated walls of the old fort and palace (which was destroyed inside and then occupied by the army) surrounded by a wide moat. Mandalay Hill was impressive, with covered stairways all the way up, and pagodas here and there. The main entrance was guarded by two enormous white Chinthé. (The outline of a Chinthé became a very appropriate badge for Major-General Orde Wingate's fabulous force The Chindits.) I had read Field-Marshall Sir William Slim's *Defeat into Victory*,[8] and I turned again to his account of the storming of Mandalay Hill by British and Gurkha troops on 9 to 10 March 1945, which was dreadful to read. I did not have time to see the remains of Fort Dufferin in the city where Theebaw's Palace had been destroyed and Government House 'sadly battered'.

In Rangoon we were once taken to meet a 'royal lady'. She was Daw Su Su Khin, a grand-daughter of King Thibaw and Queen Supayalat,[9] and she was living in a very dark, wooded area in a spooky, Charles Addams type of house. She was aged, but dignified. It was fascinating to contemplate her ancestry. Conversation, alas, was perfunctory.

I stayed in Maymyo next, with Wilfred at his week-end retreat not only from the heat of Mandalay but from the demanding pressures of university life. It was a nice, little house only one and a half hours' away from work.

When Wilfred was in Mandalay he never had his house to himself. University staff frequently called on him, and students who treated him as one of the family would wander in at any time of the day or night and make themselves at home, a compliment which was not entirely ap-

---

[8] The Four-Square paperback edition of 1958, at 3/6d. is the best value book I have ever bought.
[9] See Tennyson Jesse, *The Lacquer Lady* (Heinemann 1930; Virago 1979) and also A.J.S. White's article, most of which is quoted in Appendix I.

preciated. They treated his magazines, books, drink, and even servants as their own, almost ignoring his presence. Even when he was ill they invaded his privacy, not understanding our meaning of the word. Sadly, they tired a lonely, bedridden figure. They were hardly a comfort but he was so patient and good with them. He had to escape to Maymyo to prepare lectures, mark papers, and write.

Additional British Council lecturers were refused by the new regime, and Wilfred's future was uncertain. The Rangoon coup of 2 March was to cause his later transfer to Peshawar. The take-over government now subjected staff and students to irksome and ridiculous regulations.

May 1962: The garden

Rosemary reported: "Some of our orchids are flowering. What magnificent things they are. Our Indian doctor always has different ones in his waiting room. He grows them on pieces of plank hanging from a wire, and he brings new blooms along to his surgery every day. Gul mohr trees are now flowering and the one at the end of our lane stops one in one's tracks."

Mandalay and Maymyo

Now we could have some local leave in Mandalay. Wilfred being there would make our stay so much easier. The staff of the Burmese Railway, in the tradition of the great Indian Railways, after fifteen years of Independence remained imbued with the same esprit de corps as elsewhere in the world: from the Chattanooga Choo-Choo to the (North-West) Frontier Mail. I recalled later the bravery of the 'Anglo' engine drivers and other staff aboard who kept their trains running despite insurgent attacks. We were happy to board the Mandalay Mail which left Rangoon at 8.30 p.m. and arrived at Mandalay gently next midday. This was the best and effortless way to enjoy and appreciate one's surroundings; although not when dacoits were blowing up trains, which thankfully was not in our time.

This time Wilfred met us with Devi Dass and took us to lunch in his attractive wooden bungalow. He had so much to say about life in Mandalay, and then he was ready to tell us about his earlier life in the War in the Sudan, and afterwards in Cyrenaica and Iraq. His true vocation was in the Arab world, and with his knowledge of Arabic he became much admired by students and professors. He showed us round his house explaining what his various books, pictures, and trophies meant to him.

Mandalay had had its first rain that morning, which kept the temperature down, and which made our drive to Maymyo more comfortable. On the way we encountered a horseman glittering in the court dress of olden times, all peaks and wings, and gold and scarlet, carrying a lance. He was the vanguard of a cheerful procession taking a golden Buddha to present to a pagoda. There were more characters in costume on foot, and ladies shrieking and giggling on two elephants. The rest were heaped up in jeeps and on a lorry which bore the idol shielded by gold paper parasols with flowers massed around. What delightful people!

Maymyo was at 3500 ft. We started across irrigated country along the bottom of the hills, then we climbed fairly steeply, up through wooded country. Another rise and there we were in a hill station with only glimpses of distant hills, it was not hilly itself. It was most attractive park-land with large trees. Beyond the town-centre the housing was spread out for considerable distances around. Each house stood in large grounds. The countryside beyond was light jungle, and one could walk in it, while being deafened by cicadas.

The town (myo) was only a century old. It had begun as a British army base under Colonel May of the Bengal Infantry[10] who had been posted there to pacify the area soon after the annexation of Upper Burma. A prosperous town developed a decade or so later. The British put in a comprehensive, asphalt road system which extended through the suburbs. Our one-inch map, a rare and valuable 'acquisition', showed many rides through the jungle, and all were named.

The houses in the residential area were very similar. An architect with a turret fixation appeared to have designed most of them. We stayed in a large house belonging to the Bombay-Burma Company. The house with its loyal staff of former years would have made an admirable Summer School centre.

Despite the lateness of the season, the quality of the flowers outshone those of Rangoon. "The greatest joy," wrote Rosemary, "were the wild, pink crocuses growing in the house grounds but mainly in masses along the wide, grassy road verges, zephyranthes, larger than ours and opening out more. There were various amaryllis lilies, some peach coloured." She took samples back to Rangoon and they flowered in the rains.

The Maymyo of the old British days was now a ghost town, but thriving in its modern form. There was a Defence College and I took up a British presentation of a collection of books on the war in Burma, which were fascinating to thumb through, but were dreadfully sad. Many important Burmese had houses in Maymyo now, which helped the atmosphere, and the golf course was popular. As we drove slowly round the quiet roads,

---

[10] See G. Abbott, *Back to Mandalay*, (Impact Books, 1991).

Maymyo seemed to have the atmosphere of a crumbling Camberley. Indeed, General Slim described it as being very like Surrey, with imitation Tudor houses among the trees. The houses still had English names. All were well kept up. Even the old street names remained: The Mall, Club Road, Commissioners Road, Forest Drive, and so on. Burmese signs were less common. Apparently, Government House was burned down during the Karen 'insurrection'.

We walked with much pleasure, enjoying the refreshing, early rains. It was quite chilly, and we even had a log fire twice. By lucky chance we ran across Ted Stevens of Bradfield whom I had known since he was a small boy. He was now a C.M.S. missionary, teaching at a theological college in North Burma.

Ted took us to Aneskan, a series of lovely waterfalls right down in a gorge. The 1000-feet scramble down the very steep sides through sparse jungle gave us some idea of what the Chindits had gone through.

Our Travel Scrabble came into its own on the train and in our Maymyo home. But we were not much alone. We met a number of the resident Anglo-Burmese, the headmaster of the school, the dentist, and others, including the local hunter who came in to discuss prospects. But I had not come up 'armed'. Luckily, we could spend as much time as we wanted in the bazaar; the only one we have ever seen all hung round with orchids on sale. There were some wonderful faces, especially the old people. "The older women," wrote Rosemary, "look so serene and confident. They wear the lovely, big hats from the Shan states. I got one to use as an umbrella when gardening in the rains. The vegetables are so good that I bought huge baskets and filled one with vegetables and the other with 110 best mangoes. What with two other boxes of plants for people, the Shan hat, and two cane sleeping-mats our compartment was bursting on the homeward journey."

We had an evening in Mandalay, and drove round the great fort. The wide moat had large areas of lily pads. There was the whitewashed gateway and the watch-towers with many tiered roofs along the dark-red walls. We didn't feel like going on to Mandalay Hill, with such grim memories, but we looked into a little wooden palace with heavily carved and gilded decorations and pillars. It was full of gilt cabinets, furniture, and Buddhas. Some pongyis (monks) were living there, their few personal belongings tucked away among all the magnificence.

Rangoon

Our future was not yet settled. There was renewed confidence now that the new Government had had time to study the facts. The university had been tidied up under a firm hand and the Government had issued a rather vague policy statement with much emphasis on self-discipline, marching forward on a united front, and so on. Most of our British Council contacts seemed to be out of favour, and Burmese friends were unwilling to comment. The implied absence of elections would be a shock to those who were educated for years to regard parliamentary democracy as the goal. More Indians were leaving. "Theoretically there was little place for them here now," wrote Rosemary in 1962, "but I wonder how long it will be before the powers realize that other elements in the community have their special gifts and talents to offer? The Burmese don't really take to trade." Her remarks were prophetic.

But our life and work went on. We enjoyed performing in Raymond Adlam's serialisation of *Wuthering Heights* on the English radio programme. We heard that the serials we undertook were much enjoyed, and were said to have about the highest listening figures of any of the programmes. We had already been in Raymond's version of *Alice in Wonderland*, in which Rosemary and I were very happy. We were supporting cast to Bill McAlpine, Joan Frank, and Raymond himself, who were excellent.

June 1962

A Muslim festival caused the arrival at the house of two plates of raw beef with visiting cards laid on top: one was from the landlord and one from the painting contractor. The humidity was very high. There had been several thunderstorms with heavy rain, but the real rains would be next month. Lots of flying things had come with the rain despite the screens. The scorpions were washed out of their holes, but they were easy to kill. One bag amounted to five in two evenings, two in the kitchen. There was never a dull moment!

The large, outdoor parties of the dry season ended with the advent of the rains, since our houses were not large enough to hold them indoors. Entertaining now consisted of small dinner-parties, which most people preferred. We didn't know many Burmese well enough to ask them on their own, though we had enough specialist contacts who were pleased to come to meet doctors, or writers, or other professional visitors. We enjoyed our first meal in a Burmese home, with the parents of a young woman doctor who was very jolly and friendly. We looked forward to some real Burmese food, but they had Chinese food brought in. None of them were great conversationalists. It was a relief to find that this European urge was not a Burmese one. The Burmese didn't natter at meals, they enjoyed the food.

241

Food

Living in Rangoon gave us the widest choice of dishes of any of our postings. We could enjoy the most delicious food of Burma, India, and China through skilled native cooks, and pretty good English food too. Our cook Ananda's specialities were prawn curries and such like from his native India. Many Burmese recipes owe much to India – Balachaung for instance. The ingredients were: 7 oz. prawns, 6 oz. sessamum oil, 1½ oz. shrimp paste, ½ cup of cold water, 20 cloves garlic, ½ teaspoon saffron powder, 6 dried red chillies (optional), salt to taste.

Burmese dishes were otherwise not terribly exciting. They often contained rice flour, coconut milk or flesh, and noodles, which were more or less the ingredients of one of their well-known 'kaukswe' dishes. For variety we were happy to repair to the Chinese Hai Yuan restaurant close behind our house. There we could also enjoy Mandalay beer.

The range of Chinese dishes was vast. To partake of a meal at a Chinese home was a memorable and testing experience. I remember a particular dinner at the home of a well-to-do, Chinese cigarette-merchant. Each course as it was presented looked as delicious as the last. How much of each should one take, and how many courses were there going to be? There were sixteen courses at our dinner. We could not refuse any, and somehow survived.

July 1962: Chauk, Pagan and Taunggyi

We flew up to Chauk in the oil company's ten-seater plane, flying over flooded paddy fields and floods along the river banks. We landed on the 'wrong' side of the Irrawaddy and had to cross a swirling current of yellow water on an old launch. We were lucky to have cloud and cooler weather than usual and to see fresh green on the trees and shrubs that could grow there. We stayed in the General Manager's house on a bluff over the river. The new General Manager was on the same 'plane. It was rather hard for him to have guests immediately, but we had met him in Rangoon. He was a very fat Burmese, almost Buddha-like, and was very cheery and friendly.

We were delighted that he'd already arranged for us to go straight off to Pagan after an early lunch. The security officer, who took all visitors, turned out once more with his Land Rover, and we bounded along the twenty-one miles of sandy, bullock-cart track. It only took an hour and a half. We saw rather attractive, gently rolling country, which was mainly flat with glimpses of the Irrawaddy and mountains beyond. The road and fields were edged with a prickly cactus on the point of flowering.

Edinburgh

Edinburgh International House, Castle Street. A good vantage point in which to make overseas students feel at home.

Demonstrating Pas de Basque . . . The Daily Graphic 2 Sep 1952 was kind:
Another popular Edinburgh rendezvous is the International House, run by the
British Council. In charge is Captain Michael Halsted, who lost an eye while
serving with the 1st Armoured Division in the Desert. He served with the
Council behind the 'Iron Curtain' in Hungary from 1947 to 1949 . . .

The Allard – with my 'intended'.

Edinburgh

Princes Street Gardens. International Dances by members of E. I. H. including two imitation Hungarians!

Men's Highland Class at the Summer School, St Andrews, 1951.

Ethiopia

*Emperor Haile Selassie in exile, 1936, off HMS Enterprise,
and arrival at Jerusalem.*

A Lion of Judah, cast in silver.

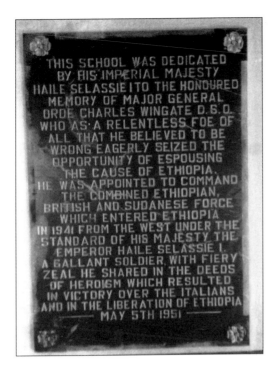

School Dedication plaque.

Staff and senior boys, General Wingate School, Addis Ababa 1954/55.

xxi

My G. C. E. English class.

The old School bell being rung by a Prefect.

The new School bell from Lord Mountbatten.

Ethiopia

Wolde and Melaku with our firewood man, bringing the invaluable and universally used eucaluyptus. Addis Ababa could not have existed without this quick-growing tree, coppiced after five years; it had been introduced by Emperor Menelik.

Boy playing a kerare – the sound box is an enamel bowl.

Seniors in the school library – avid for books.

The School from our garden.

Kate Regan, wife of John on the staff, running the sickroom.

Ethiopia

Boys admiring the Macbeath's blonde baby girl.

International Red Cross Fair, on Janhoi Meda, 7 May 1956. We danced the 'Duke & Duchess of Edinburgh' before His Imperial Majesty and family.

The sword dancers salute His Imperial Majesty and family.

The Emperor's grandchildren:
(Back, left to right) *David, Miss Chamberlain, Sean, Mrs Zammen and Jacob.*
(Front, left to right) *Paul, Mary and Michael.*

Ethiopia

April 1955. Rosemary keeping me in the style to which I was accustomed, on her palace salary.

A not unusual scene out shooting.

Tehran 1957–1961
Hamadan

Hamadan Summer School 1958. Teachers correcting test papers on the first day: Aileen Maconachie, Director of Studies, Iran, Dorothy Reid, British Embassy wife & Mrs Hodgson from the London Office.

Harold Popplestone (based in Tabriz), John Mills (Tehran), later our first TV Officer, student teachers and administration staff.

Picnic for all at Malayer. Only men could dance in public so I could do my bit!

Hamadan 1958. Rosemary and Harold Popplestone studying design in a carpet workshop.

Tehran

The Tombstoners on an outing.

Tehran March 1961. 'Shakespeare Defended'. Prince Philip amid Council staff.

Tehran in December. "Christmas trees" along the wall of the Russian Embassy for sale to the Christian communities.

Pagan was an ancient city of Upper Burma, 92 miles south-west of Mandalay on an inside bend of the Irrawady. It was founded by King Pyinpya in A.D. 849, and served as Burma's capital until it was sacked by Kubla Khan's barbarian hordes in 1287. For at least two hundred years it was constantly enriched by pagoda and temple building of all kinds, involving craftsmen and ideas from all over Burma and India. Students found it a living source-book of the history of religion, art and architecture and the interplay of different influences, all within a few square miles.

Bells and gongs

A number of pagodas still had their lovely great bells suspended from solid wooden frames. It was a pleasure to follow the example of countless pilgrims and pongyis and sound the bell by means of a heavy, wooden stave. The beautiful, long-lasting, soft-toned reverberations spread one's prayers far and added to one's merit (kutho).

The Burmese were obviously highly skilled, bronze-metal workers. Their gongs (chee-zee) had lovely tones. There were many sizes and weights, and thereby tones, but all were of the same shape. A good example was the gong of the begging recluse, in the turn of the century painting in *Silken East*.[11] A gong measuring seventy millimetres would weigh a mere thirty-six ounces and the largest we brought back weighed thirteen pounds. The different tones that size and thickness would produce, again from a tap by wood, were charming and evocative.

We drove from pagoda to pagoda: the guide chose an excellent variety. We would arrive, clamber out, remove our shoes, often walk painfully over grit, perhaps pick our way through bat-droppings, and return over a wall or a parapet, replace our shoes and get back into a hot car. We did this at least thirteen times. Twice we went to the rest house to recover for twenty minutes.

Rosemary wrote: "We also visited the lacquer works there; it was too late to see people working, but we were able to buy some items. I'm told they are really heat-resistant and very hard wearing." And so they have proved to be.

In 1965 I was left by my collector cousin, Walter Fuller, a handsome, large, gold-ornamented, circular lacquer box, which was purported to have been part of the British loot at the fall of Mandalay. It probably contained jewels or regalia. I was glad to be able to return it to the Burmese Government.

The General Manager took us on a lovely drive to Mount Popa, a very

[11] See V.C. Scott O'Connor, *Silken East* (1904, repr. Kiscadale 1993).

holy hill about twenty-five miles away, 'the Olympus of Burma' where the chief nats also lived. It was used for retreats. The country was very attractive and we saw it at its best, all green with very red soil. We only had thirty-six hours here before we flew off by Burma Airways to Taunggyi. It was lovely to get up high again, and we found it more satisfying than Maymyo, with more hills and good views. We landed at the delightfully named village of Heho, and drove for an hour across two valleys and up to a plateau shelf beneath a great crag where Taunggyi lay at 4700 ft. To us it seemed so familiar to be back on a school compound and in the funny, little house of the British Council-appointed headmaster, Tim Slack; it had so much more atmosphere than ours in Rangoon. Roses were blooming on cuttings brought a year ago from Britain. The bazaar was full of wonderful types, including the hill people in their weird, dark-blue clothes, including little gaiters, and the Shans in their baggy trousers. The women with a series of brass rings round their long necks weren't far away.

Taunggyi was the capital of the South Shan State. It was now rather in abeyance, yet it was a thriving cheerful place after Maymyo. Almost anything would grow there, so the people could be well off if they could be bothered to work hard! What lovely country too! We drove beyond to a spring and pool, Hopong, which hadn't been safe to visit six months before. There were two checks on the road, and much army traffic. The army had stopped gambling, so a lot of dacoitry has decreased on that account alone. There used to be huge gambling meetings once or twice a year for several days at a time.

The highlight was a trip to Inle Lake, well known among the Burmese as they have few lakes. It was in the valley below Taunggyi, and the country was so flat that it was all marsh and creek around the lake. The villages were on stilts. In a little creek we got a narrow, canoe-shaped, forty-foot boat to which an outboard had been fitted. I was surprised how many outboards were around; of course they needed boats to get about. The paddling canoes often comprised a whole tree-trunk, beautifully shaped with double points at the stern where the paddler stood on one leg, hooking the other round his paddle on the back stroke. These chaps were famous. If he had help, a wife perhaps, she knelt on the lower platform at the bows and paddled normally. They made a charming picture together.

We went by outboard for three miles through the creeks, it was a convenient but noisy way to travel. We slowed down to pass little boats – which seemed to contain everyone of all ages – some with goods, some with women returning from market, holding up their umbrellas against the sun, some deep laden with smelly weed for the gardens, and one boat moored under a water tap with an old lady filling a row of pots. We crossed some miles of open lake to the main villages at the far end where there was a bazaar in boats in the village 'street', and some shops which opened onto the water. We visited a pagoda whose little Buddha was so covered in gold that it was just a ball without human shape. There was also a silk-weaving factory which made lovely longyis. On the way back we were lucky to find five gaily decorated boats taking little boys to their initiation ceremonies – one boat was the orchestra, another had an enormous, wind-up gramophone with the biggest horn I'd ever seen.

Back in Rangoon we enjoyed putting together and performing a programme in the McAlpines' spacious house: Poetry and Music of the Four Nations. The audience was a cross-section of senior Burmese and some diplomats. We could but try to keep spirits up. We had a good response from our audience, but they were friends and not the general public.

Crackdown

Unfortunately, the next weekend was most unhappy; and our friends were faced with sinister political developments. On the Friday night there were student protest disturbances against new hostel regulations at the university. Then on Saturday a fairly rowdy demonstration took place in the vast university compound, which included hostels and staff houses. Police arrived to arrest the leaders of Friday night's troubles, but they were driven back. Then at 6 p.m. from our garden we heard bursts of Bren and rifle fire very clearly and for too long. That stopped it all, and road blocks were put round the university. Next morning at 6 a.m. we were startled out of bed, as was most of Rangoon, by an almighty, sharp explosion. We heard next day that the army had blown up the Students' Union which was labelled as "a meeting place against the government."

All the students were sent home; there were twelve thousand of them. All universities and colleges were closed. Rangoon University certainly was unwieldy – almost anyone could gain admittance. The constitution of the proposed new, single party was now published. An Austrian friend recognised the format of Nazi days.

Our work went on. When the McAlpines went on leave we became involved in additional, but enjoyable, official entertaining. We were still able to entertain, on our own account, particular Burmese friends: the professors of mathematics and history and their wives, and the leading anaesthetist and his wife. We found the Burmese so easy to get on with. I couldn't help thinking of the way we had behaved towards them, pre-independence.

Thanks to the Tanners, we used to go to the Pegu Club to play tennis or have a drink. We met a senior Burmese official there one evening. He said to me with a smile, "You know, in your day, I wasn't allowed into this 'prestigious' Club. This exclusiveness certainly riled the Indians and antagonised the Burmese, who were already particularly hurt at being ruled from India by Indian Civil Service men, and not by a separate Burma Service. Kipling had quite a lot to say about his visit to the Pegu Club in *From Sea to Sea* Vol. I, No. 11, 1887–1889. He made particular reference to members coming down from Upper Burma in the aftermath of the Annexation War of 1885, and fighting the resistance which continued after the fall of Mandalay.

The Reel Club at the Strand Hotel was going strong, and I didn't run it. I was glad. It was so humid that we would go with towels to mop ourselves between dances. I took a towelling jacket to wear afterwards so as not to get a chill from fans or air-conditioning. The monsoon was at its height now, with steady rain and cloud for the past two weeks. Rosemary wrote: "Now we can't put anything outside to air. I go round wiping mould off suitcases, belts, shoes, dresses, and ties even. The floors are an awful nuisance. They go blotchy and pale if not rubbed or polished frequently. French polish can't stand up to life, so we had to use wax polish which doesn't stand up to mould so well.

"The garden survives the rain very well, being largely shrubs and trees at the moment. The only flowers are balsam, zinnia, and gladioli which do very well. The coreopsis and African marigold should have been good but failed. It's hard to find flowers for parties; cannas luxuriate but the gardenias are finishing. What a fine plant they are: our bushes are all over six-foot tall and glossy, dark green, and the flowers have such a lovely scent. I've planted one bed of all the curious foliage plants that flourish during the rains: caladiums and spotted, striped, or veined marantas. What solid clay it is; much compost is needed."

Waso

One full moon of the Burmese calendar was a special festival, Waso. It was raining gently. We went to the Shwe Dagon pagoda to see the crowds who came to pray, offer candles, wander about, sit and eat food, or listen to sermons. We met several Burmese friends and walked around with them. Then we we were met by a pongyi U Way Pon Hla, whom I had met at Wilfred's house in Mandalay. He was studying English to become a missionary, and was delighted to practise speaking it. He and his great friend, U Zargara, lived in a small, decorated, green pavilion on the Middle Way, a path circling the mound between the main steps' entrance to the pagoda and its platform. Here there were resting houses, servants quarters, and store rooms.

U Way Pon Hla seemed to be privileged as the main monasteries were further down. He had a room on the ground floor, open to the pathway, with tables and the usual deckchairs, a glass-fronted bookcase, a transistor radio, a glass jar of cheroots for visitors, and piles of carefully folded, spare, yellow robes. Some other pongyis came to look at us; we stayed about half an hour and enjoyed the conversation and surroundings. They begged us to come again with friends. They both spoke English and were keen to keep in touch with the outside world. But we resolved not to make them a Shwe Dagon sight. They offered me Burmese cheroots, but alas I had to refuse them as I couldn't get on with them. This was a pity when Scott's Imperial No. 2 from that long-established firm were 8/6d a hundred. It was always amusing in towns and villages to see stalwart ladies in odd corners rolling cheroots by flat hand on fat thigh.

September 1962

We were losing our popular Sir Richard Allen. The Embassy party held for him included a skit on him giving a British Council lecture. The Council's farewell gesture took the form, on Rosemary's suggestion, of a poetry and verse programme at the McAlpines' house with Sir Richard as the theme. He had previously taken part in several himself.

The Council's party was on a fine and hot evening, so we had drinks out in the garden and then moved into the hall for an hour of reading and songs. Raymond sang Figaro's farewell advice to Cherubino, which put the audience in the right mood. "Here's an end to the life that was gay, lad, here's an end to your games with the girls." His Excellency was well known for his interest in pretty girls, so we were all rocking with laughter. The hilarious finish was an extract from Lawrence Durrell's skit on diplomatic life: *Esprit de Corps*.

Rosemary had to slip off early because we were giving the Allens dinner. All this Rosemary felt was "part of the happy atmosphere of Rangoon life which alas was evaporating under the new regime." What fun it was to work together with one's staff and sponsored lecturers in an effort to give pleasure and new experience to international audiences. We later had a bigger 'do' for the Allens at the request of the B.C. Scholars Association. This time we hired a pair of Burmese women to play the harp and sing. Burmese harps are small enough to be held on the lap. The one for this occasion was of red lacquer and glass, gilded, with red tassels on the ends of the strings. It had its own gilt stand and a red satin cover.

Monsoon Madness

The foreign communities organized an annual tennis tournament called 'Monsoon Madness' when the rains were still in full force and one was pretty well 'confined to barracks'. The weather was cooler, so Monsoon Madness tennis was possible, and cheering. There was a motto on a badge issued to volunteer players: 'For fun, not for glory'. Anyone on declaring his or her standard was paired with someone of any nationality of opposite standard better or worse. It *was* fun; with matches on courts all over the city giving enjoyable variety. I didn't last very long, but I didn't mind when one of the organizers suggested I commentate. So I did my best and learned just how much expertise was required. But the players were amused to hear their games 'on the air'. The festivities at the conclusion of the tournament were a delightful riot. A king and queen of some sort (they were hobos one year) were elected, and crowned, and they eventually would present the cups. Next came some 'crazy games', viz. three-legged tennis, ladies doubles (four players each side), mixed doubles (two men and one lady each side), mixed doubles (couples tied back to back) and tennis on 'horseback', mixed doubles! Finally the band, if there was one, led all to drinks, dinner, and dancing.

Shikar

I was delighted to receive an invitation from an elderly British resident and a keen shot, Pip Palmerino, to go snipe shooting. Pip had for years retained villagers in various areas to report on game of various sorts and to act as beaters. He was pretty strict with the guns he invited, commit an error and you didn't get asked again. Pip and I and two military attachés did not have to go more than ten miles along the main road north, which ran straight and high across a great plain of paddy with only regularly-spaced, wide, spreading trees breaking the monotony. Having picked up Pip's 'Swami' and his boys on the way, we parked at the roadside and followed him along a wide ditch. Then we moved in line across the wet paddy.

Rosemary recorded: "The water isn't deep, about four to six inches, and the mud goes down about the same again, but you walk on the little bunds where possible. When they did one large sweep I stayed behind, and was soon all alone in the midst of acres of paddy, perched on my shooting stick. On the far edge were masses of trees where the villages are, and the white spires of pagodas. The bunds aren't good walking being clods of muddy earth. They do several drives, only two or three guns, moving a mile or two along the road in between. On other drives I stayed with the cars, with a grandstand view, while old Palmerino tells the most fantastic yarns, and catches the odd bird coming away over the road. Poor chap is very arthritic and can't walk far. The bags weren't large, Michael doing not too badly, but the birds are quick away. This snipe and muddy paddy would soon bore me, and snipe aren't anything special to eat. Anyway its grand to get out a bit."

The Light Festival

As Rosemary reported: "We've just had the Light Festival at full moon at the end of the rains, and the end of Lent. We went up to the Shwe Dagon on Friday evening, and watched the wonderful sunset among the huge cumulus clouds – pink cloud and gold spires and dusky blue sky make a wonderful combination. Then we wandered right round the whole tiled platform at the base of the main spire, where the main and minor shrines are. In various quiet corners the country people were settling down for the night, spreading their sleeping-mats near huge bells, and heating up food on little fires behind shrines. Some associations were feeding all who came around. The Medical College Buddhist Students' Association, for instance, had one hall spread with mats, crowded with students and called us in to have coffee and sticky sweets. We chatted a few minutes and admired their long row of tiny candles on the low wall opposite, with the red and gold small shrines behind and then the towering bulk, all gold, of the main spire. There were many children about as it was early. It was funny to watch the tubby tinies falling on their knees all anyhow and making a sketch of a reverence, hands clasped in front of face, and then bowing head to ground, scrambling up all smiles and going on round. The women clasped their hands holding long bunches of flowers, charming, all silhouetted against the flickering candles. The full moon rose in brilliance, but we were too early this time to see the great ruby at the top-most tip of the spire, which is only visible from one spot, at full moon.

"Then we drove around a Burmese village cum suburb admiring the lanterns in front of the houses; some had rows of tiny candles along the verandah rail, up and down, others had lanterns around the garden. All the children were enraptured, gazing with pride at their own display. Even the tiniest hut had a few candles. How dull our area of large houses seemed afterwards."

Chinlon and broadswords

U Way Pon Hla and U Zargara invited us in November to an annual Chinlon Festival at the East Steps, which was promoted by the stall-holders. Teams were invited to demonstrate their prowess in this popular South-East Asian sport. The teams, comprising circles of five men, had to keep a light, open-weave cane ball, six inches in diameter, in the air with their bare feet. This was hard enough in itself, but if the ball should be kicked out of the circle over someone's head, they were actually able to kick the ball into the circle again over their backs. At whatever angle a ball was fed into the circle, an incredible contortion of backward and upward kick would keep the ball inside the circle.

And then we watched a schoolboy who skipped on one foot over a rope swung by assistants, and kept a chinlon ball in the air with the other. At the same time he passed a flaming hoop over his head, and out past his feet. There was a huge crowd, and we sat among them with our friends and their friends. It was all very jolly and a lovely atmosphere in which to serve. How can such delightful Burmese be so tough and cruel to one another?

Set-backs

There were officially 'no restrictions', but the university staff had to deal with foreign bodies through the Burmese Foreign Office. The result was long delays in presenting books and journals. We received no reply to our request to resume one-day seminars for teachers of English. Those arrested at the take-over were either at the army cantonment or, like the Shan leaders, in Insein Jail for questioning. We had friends amongst them. They seem to be well-treated, with visits by relatives allowed. No length of detention was announced. The ex-President kept cheerful by cooking, which he had always enjoyed. The Student Union was abolished. Now the students had no means of representation.

At Inya Myaing

Rosemary went off to make notices of donkey rides for the cathedral fete. There had been an evening plague of greenflies from the paddy fields. They were larger than aphids and could bite. One could see them in great masses under the street lights, which became pillars of flies. They were all around the house and poured in to the lights. I couldn't use my desk lamp despite the mosquito screening.

Burma 1961–1963

Our new Ambassador

We went out to Mingaladon Airport to meet Gordon Whitteridge, a small man with a large panama hat. We soon discovered that he had a larger heart. We were very taken with Mrs Whitteridge whom we were lucky to meet at their dinner for the Singapore Minister of Culture. She was a tall, slender, charming Katherine Hepburn style American.

I have reason to be specially grateful to Sir Gordon, as he became in 1964, because when I left Burma they would not let me take out my beautiful William Powell 12-bore, No. 1 of a pair. Sir Gordon was able to take it out of Burma, and two years later when he returned home from Kabul, he cleared the gun himself from the Customs Bond, as the Customs required. This was just one indication of the fine man he was.

We rightly felt he was going to have a rather sad assignment in Burma. But we were hardly affected. We had to carry on as best as we could. Sir Gordon had had terrible sadnesses in his life, but he remained so calm and kind.[12]

Faux Pas. An embarrassment never repeated

Rosemary got dressed up for the Russian embassy reception on the forty-fifth anniversary of the Great October Socialist Revolution. We 'swep up' under the great porch, and Rosemary descended gracefully to be greeted by four smart, short-haired, young men. One of them came up, and said very nicely: "I'm sorry, but this is for men only". My error has not been forgotten.

Remembrance Day

There was a military cemetery at Taukkyan out near Mingaladon, in beautiful surroundings. What a peaceful place; but what horrors remembered all around; twenty-seven thousand Commonwealth war dead. The simple ceremony here with a speech by the Counsellor was particularly moving.

---

[12] See his obituary, *The Times*, 1 March 1995.

The Rangoon Sailing Club

The Tanners kindly introduced us to the Rangoon Sailing Club. We thoroughly enjoyed its ambience if not so much the sailing. It was situated on the lake just behind our house. Members had 'tindals' on the Club staff to look after their boats and get them ready. It was a good place to meet like-minded Burmese – and to admire Rosemary's talent at the helm: the lake could produce quite tricky wind changes.

The Second Light Festival

We set off to the Shwe Dagon to see what we could of this Light Festival, before the early sunset of 5.30 p.m. There were big crowds and all sorts of activities going on. In one hall a traditional weaving contest was just starting to weave a length of orange cloth for a monk's robe in one night, the first finished robe was to be presented to the pagoda. There were five looms, each with a pair of girls, and an orchestra below crashing out an encouraging pace on drums and cymbals.

All over the pagoda platform there were tables specially set out with offerings of flowers, fruits, sweets. The fruit was often beautifully and elaborately peeled, and all gaily lit up. Some groups, from districts or factories, had collected enough money to buy the one-foot squares of gold leaf, the form in which gold is put on the pagoda. These were displayed on special stands, where young girls stood with large, silver bowls calling out to passers-by for further donations. There was an orange afterglow behind the palms and fretted storied roofs of the shrines, and the great spire was gleaming gently against the deepening sky, while a full moon rose beyond. It was almost too thickly laid on! In the glimmer of thousands of candles we watched many groups settling down for the night in quiet corners, and other family parties came to offer, pray, and walk about to stare – then this time we saw the brilliant, red gleam from the huge ruby at the very top of the spire.

Shikar jungle-fowl

I was lucky to be invited on a jungle-fowl shoot. This was a small affair, so I suggested to Dick Harland, our visiting auditor, that he might like to come too, with my host's agreement. I fitted him up with the right garments and footwear, and we were up at 4 a.m. We returned at 2 p.m., very tired, and very hot and sweaty. It was fascinating to be in the teak forest with beaters and guns for company. I shot a jungle-fowl with Dick beside me, and we saw a barking deer. The red jungle-fowl cock (gallus gallus spadiceus) is a very beautiful and sporting creature.[13]

These lovely jungle-fowl can be dangerous – to the guns, but more so to the beaters. The birds tend to rocket along 'at nought feet', and it is no use in the jungle trying to turn and get a going away shot. They will have gone – through the trees. So one has to take them in front, at what can be a dangerously low angle for the advancing beaters. On one occasion Keith Colwill, our friend, the Australian military attaché, had the misfortune to pepper a beater, but not seriously, and the beater was more pleased with his reward than upset by his wound.

At the same time we guns also ran an extra risk because there were leopard about. I kept an S.G. cartridge in my left barrel. That didn't matter because I wouldn't have had time for a second No. 5 at a jungle-fowl.

Wives at work – unpaid!

Rosemary was now well integrated into Rangoon life. For instance, she had been invited on to the board of governors of a private diocesan school. She was asked to be a judge at the Anglican School Elocution Contest, and she was teaching some Y.M.C.A. Club leaders some Scottish country dances.

Hong Kong

What with all this, and the Caledonian Ball, we were glad of a break, and an exciting chance to visit Hong Kong. It was great. We felt very country-cousin-ish when we were pitched into the rapid street hurly-burly, after the slow Rangoon pace. We stayed at the Repulse Bay Hotel, which was good for watching Chinese Society. We had wonderful shopping and I made use of the fast expert tailoring. More than that we had our good Tehran friends, David and Jackie Millar, now in the Chartered Bank Hong-Kong, to take us by the hand. That included a sail in Hong Kong harbour in their yacht, with air liners flying in and out of Kai-Tak Airport just over the mast-head.

Christmas 1962: Memory round the tree

We put up a Christmas tree and below it assembled all the presents. One of the presents was a very good replica of a Thompson sub-machine gun,

---

[13] See Bertram E. Smythies, *The Birds of Burma* (1953).

which we had bought in Hong Kong for the then little thug, Gordon Tanner.

The guests included our retired Burmese neighbour, U Nyo Tun. After Gordon had opened his present, and was mowing us all down, our Burmese neighbour seemed upset, and took me by the arm. Gordon was calmed down by Darley, and U Nyo Tun held the floor. "I'm afraid," he said, "that Gordon's present brings back terrible memories." Silence. "Yes, I was Secretary to Cabinet in 1947, and after Aung San returned from London we were in session in Parliament Building. It was then that the men burst in with machine-guns and began to mow us down swinging along the line of men at the U-shaped table. I just had time to fall under the table before the bullets reached me, but seven of my colleagues including Aung San died." That was very sad to hear, and our wassail became muted in respect. What we never knew until then was that Aung San in spite of his early record of antagonism to the British, had been surprised by the warmth of his welcome in Britain, and was very taken with Attlee, Lord Pethick-Lawrence, and others, to the extent that he might well have decided to keep Burma in the Commonwealth.

New Year 1963 was memorable for another occasion, this time very cheerful. We were at dinner with some of our Scottish dancing friends when we heard, to our amazement, the sound of the pipes quietly and tentatively played in the garden. "Who is it, Saw Maung?" "Sir, it is a Nepali." "Bring him along please." And in came Rifleman retired, Nar Bahadur of the Gurkhas. And away he played, wonderfully, just out on the verandah. His arrival made our evening and we had to dance.

A river-steamer to Twante

To our delight, we came across a lively and charming Italian-American friend from our Tehran days, Sergio dello Strologo, a ceramics expert who had come as consultant to a new university project. "He already," said Rosemary, "knows all the attractive European girls in town."

We were soon able to take him with Bill McAlpine on a river-steamer to Twante about sixteen miles away across the delta. It was a big pottery centre, a spreadout village or township, where the many different potters' premises were grouped together. Sergio had a chat with a leading pottery owner, the purpose of the trip being to get him to make modern sewage pipes out of pottery – which were unheard of in Burma – for the new university buildings.

Another memorable river trip was to a village with V.S.O. (old Bradfieldian) Raymond Busbridge from the Chittagong Defence College. We found an amazing little pagoda full of statues of elephants, horses, and tigers, and crocodiles as balustrades. There were also replicas of highly decorated rafts full of courtly figures and Nats floating on imitation oil drums, marked 'B.O.C. Engine Oil'.

The next plague: Flying ants

We were delayed going out one evening by an eruption of flying ants in the bedroom. It was an amazing sight. Within seconds of the few fluttering noisily round the lamp, hundreds more came. They are horrible to be among. We sprayed D.D.T. hard at the cracks we found, and finally stopped them coming out of the tiniest, little slits. In a few minutes they came out of the bank below the bedroom wall, clouds of them, large, with bodies up to an inch and a half long and with wide wings. There was a tremendous concourse of screaming crows swooping down on them. Then it was all over. Our floors should have been teak blocks which they don't eat.

February 1963: A sticky patch

No active measures were being taken against foreign cultural and aid bodies, but new restrictions and regulations caused problems for us by the delays in obtaining the new permits, licences, passes, etc., frustrating our normal support for professional and academic bodies and individuals. The Tanners saw no future and were leaving for good. Oil business men did not expect to remain much longer. In the circumstances we were thrown more among ourselves, and we appreciated such closer contacts. For instance, it was a pleasure to get to know our Third Secretary, Nick Fenn and his wife, Sue. We admired their ability, and knew they would go far. Indeed, Sir Nicholas returned as Ambassador in 1982. At a Press interview in London, he said: "Burma has immense, untapped resources, and near self-sufficiency. But economic development has a lower priority than the maintenance of her distinctive society. She has a long Chinese Frontier, insurgents in the jungle, and the most charming people on earth."

Our work was faltering, but we still had Burmese friends and we could go shooting. Being involved with the shooting fraternity, as we found in Ethiopia and Iran, was a very good way to get to know the countryside, and something of the lives of the country folk. We also enjoyed real camaraderie with our patient hosts.

A nine Buddhas party in Rangoon

A Buddhist ceremony in which we could join was a nine Buddhas party in Rangoon. For the party a shrine was arranged in an upstairs room, the centrepiece being a small Buddha surrounded by eight golden statue disciples. On either side there were statuettes representing the planets by the figures of the associated animals: bear, rat, elephant, etc., and also representations of the Nat spirits. There were flowers in vases, and paper decorations, and the numerous shiko-ing Burmese guests coming and going. Our hosts explained that such parties were incumbent upon good Buddhists to give, but that they could only be afforded every five years because two hundred or more guests were the norm to be invited.

Guests in their best longyis and with flowers in their hair would come at any time between 5 p.m. and 9 p.m., would sit at one of the many tables filling the lawn to eat some food – noodles with spicy sauce, sweets made with coconut – and would move round very informally to chat to friends. There was a constant coming and going, and changing of places to view the shrine and leave. No wonder the Burmese find our parties a trial where you get stuck next to people and have to make conversation.

Welcome friends from Iran

Felicity Baxter, a botanist, artist, and the wife of L. H. Baxter (head of N.I.O.C. Personnel) came with her cousin Isobel to paint. She loved the Shwe Dagon where she always had a good audience, whom she found "very polite and restrained on the whole".

With Rosemary we all flew to Heho airfield, and went straight to Inle Lake. Rosemary wrote in her journal: "We were lucky to find that it was big bazaar day at the far end, on dry land. The families looked so charming in their gay clothes all in a line in their low, black canoes amongst huge baskets and jars and heaps of recently bought vegetables, with one or two paddling and all were smiling." She was able to buy a number of attractive, practical, and strong Shan shoulder-bags to take back to Britain. Ours are still in use.

I enjoyed myself in Taunggyi doing a lot of walking and seeing the people I'd met before, especially the Principal of Kanbawsa School, Daw Mi Mi, who was an old friend of the Council's and ours. Alas, the school was definitely becoming a state school next term in the new academic year, which meant a great lowering of standards. Daw Mi Mi would leave, and so would those who could afford to do so. It was their last sports day which I attended. It was all very informal and gay, but it was strain for Mi Mi. Her husband was one of the imprisoned Shan leaders. There was no sign of his release. The Shans were a delightful people. Their chiefs, the Sawbwas, and their upper classes were particularly elegant, graceful and charming.

26 February 1963: Nationalization

We had said that soon we would only have foreign diplomats and bankers to talk to. Now we lost the bankers. The Chartered Bank became the People's Bank, No. 1, and the Hong Kong and Shanghai became the People's Bank No. 2. Army officers took over. Our bank friends had to work desperately hard before moving out and returning home. I was foolish enough to remark to H.E., who was very upset and pressed, "Bang goes my Argyll Broadswords team." The poor man reacted pretty sharply, and I apologised.

Of course problems arose for foreign bodies and their staffs. We were told not to bring in any more sterling but to live on a local overdraft pro tem. Thank goodness, George de Souza was our accountant. We also heard that all private schools, which were mainly mission schools, were to be nationalised.

But we could still dance; and we gave a tea-party with a S.C.D. performance and general dance in the garden. It was a great pleasure to see the white dresses and vivid colours of the sashes and kilts in one's own garden, charmingly lit by the porch spotlight. I managed to get a number of guests to dance the Dashing White Sergeant, and I made sure of having the Sawbwa of Kentung's sweet wife on one side of me.

16 April 1963: The monsoon again

We'd just had our first big rainstorm, with thunder and lightning. I bravely killed an enormous scorpion which was lurking gloomily in the garage.

Thingyan. The Water Festival

This ceremony of propitiation came at the hottest time of the year with four or five days' holiday when work was difficult. It was a restful break for us since we could let the servants off much of the time and have the house to ourselves.

So here was Thingyan. It was quite amazing the amount of hard work and energy the Burmese produced for the water-throwing rituals. Households, societies, groups of friends, and the like would set up a water-throwing point (a pandal) at the roadside, preferably near a tap or better still, a hydrant. There they would make a bamboo-mat shelter, perhaps decorated with a few palm leaves, and furnish it with tanks, oil drums, even old baths, and plenty of bowls and cans. Some of the grander pandals had teams of identically dressed girls. Pandals could be anywhere, on any road. There were also enthusiastic children lined up with buckets, stirrup pumps, garden sprays, water-pistols, the works, hoping to catch the odd, unwary pedestrian or driver. Then the rest of the population, it seemed, climbed into jeeps, Land Rovers, minibuses, old buses, lorries, some highly decorated, and drove endlessly round the town. Some dressed up a bit, but nothing elaborately for at each pandal they would pause and let the people throw, pour, squirt, and spray water over them while they beamed and yelled, or maybe recited or sang a song. When all the water-throwing stopped, they would mop themselves with streaming towels and go on to the next pandal. The Burmese loved it, and would continue doing it all day for three days! We made a rather rapid tour round once with all windows tightly shut, and never stopping.

The water battle was pursued not so gently either. Rangoon had a bad reputation for being rather rough. Fomerly people used silver bowls to sprinkle scented water over each other decorously, but we saw a bus of ordinary passengers being drenched with hoses even aimed inside the bus. No-one was immune except the monks.

Thingyan was the cheerful, traditional, letting-off-steam time. Formerly the cracks, ballads, and skits performed on the floats could be anti-government, and were pretty strong at times, but not this year. No one dared now. We were told that it was not a patch on the previous years' festival, as there was no organized procession of floats for prizes that were given by the municipality. Instead, the Government were going to have a workers' festival, circuses, fairs, etc. on 1 May in the grounds of the old Race Course. The Turf Club had been closed the previous month. It had been one of the best equipped in the East. It was an old established institution, much cherished by the Burmese who kept it going in traditional style. They loved gambling, which was now forbidden. I'm glad they had this annual let-up of Thingyan, because life here was getting more depressing daily.

Not wanted

John Dawson our teacher-training college lecturer, who was so highly regarded and popular, had to wait with his young family for six weeks for a re-entry visa just when he should have been on home leave in order to be back on time for the next academic year. Should they wait to be told their future and be ready to go with all baggage by sea? No, they went by air, and we were later told that John was not wanted back. It was very sad.

Luckily we had a farewell party for the Dawsons before they left. They said they would like to play games, and still invite their Burmese friends. Yes, we would give them a last fling of defiance. We would play everything:

blow-football, drawing clumps, flower-pot race, tug-of-war. And guests were asked to come dressed as the opposite sex, which they did. The Burmese responded marvellously. It was easier for Burmese men because they wear longyis like the women.

A river trip – the last

The Burma-Britain Association was good for a show of solidarity; or something to take their members' minds off their problems. And they came on a Rangoon river-trip. The B.B.A. hired a 150-person boat, with a Chinese caterer, and a cheerful amateur band which played in the stern. It is amazing how people respond to a different environment, and this was no ordinary one. Everyone chattered away and seemed to have a good time.

The doors were shutting

There were endless pep-talks on radio, and on loudspeakers, given by army officers. The cutting-off of foreign contacts continued. Re-entry visas were harder to get. The outside showing of films stopped. Our unit had been giving two or three film-shows a night in the Rangoon area at clubs, hospitals, and schools. Specialist book presentations stopped. English programmes on B.B.S. stopped: it was all very sad. There was no weekly E.L.T.; no language problem discussion; no set-book dramatic serialisations; no 'Books on the Shelf'; no music programmes. But Bill McAlpine refused to give up.

22 April 1963

The Queen's Birthday Party was great as usual, but it was very hot and damp. His Excellency made Rosemary's day by complimenting me on my primrose-satin, Royal Armoured Corps cummerbund. She had bought the material in Hong Kong, and had finished making it that morning.

30 April 1963

Our librarian, Joan Frank, and our university lecturers, Raymond Adlam and John Dent-Young, had left, with no return. None of them knew where they were going next. But our re-entry visas were granted. For the first time we advertised in *The Lady* and *The Times* to caretake someone's house in England for a period while the owners were away. It worked very well and we did this again before another home leave, with equal success.

A wedding

We were now invited to a most impressive Muslim wedding reception for nearly a thousand guests, the ceremony having been performed two days before. This was a glorified tea-party in the big new air-conditioned hotel. We sat at small tables, while the second-class guests, poor relations, servants, etc. were in an ante-room.

It was a wonderful sight. The Burmese wore their best silks and brocades; their hair and blouses glittered with jewels. The couple processed in, followed by three bridesmaids in blue saris and three young men, and the parents. The bride looked terrific in a wonderfully supple, gold-brocade sari with a huge, golden ornament hanging high on her forehead. They sat in state on a dais while a cleric read from the Koran, then two men recited, or rather sang, their own compositions in honour of the occasion, one in Burmese, the other in Urdu. Then there was a speech in English in our usual style. The different styles were very interesting. The great event was the presence of the groom's father, U Raschid, U Nu's Minister of Trade, one of the detainees since February 1962, who was in 'protective custody', as the revolutionary government were pleased to call it. He looked much aged and thinner as he'd been ill, but he seemed to be in good form as he went around to speak to his many friends and the wives of his fellow captives. He had to go back that evening. What an amazing state of affairs!

Rosemary wrote: "Rangoon is really rather attractive now with a lot of fresh green coming out, and the gul mohrs at their most brilliant. They spread out so gracefully and contrast sharply with the enormous, hanging sprays of the big Indian laburnam. At home the frangipanis are flowering, and the gardenias are early this year though not so showy. With some pink cassias and purple crépe tree, and the remains of bouganvillea, we are very gay."

The Full Moon of Kason Festival

Rosemary recorded: "The big storm yesterday nearly spoiled the Full Moon of Kason festivities but cleared up enough for the afternoon programmes to go on. This is the festival when the Bo trees are watered, vendors set up shop with a myriad little bottles of sandalwood or some essence to add to the water. Various associations staged processions round the Pagoda platform, following close on each other's heels and halting every 200 yards or so to give a performance of dancing or suchlike. One group of mobile musicians amused me, the percussionists stood in the middle of the usual heavy, wooden circular frame slung round them, in which their instruments were arranged. At a halt they would squat down and begin to play, but at the go-ahead, they would have to stand up willy nilly and shuffle along in the middle of their instruments.

"There were lots of gold-and-white umbrellas held by little boys, who implored each other to hold their umbrellas while they dashed for a free drink of an improbable green colour being dispensed by some other association. Of course, the number of rigid umbrellas one child can hold is very limited so there were problems. We met our pongyi friends and had pale Burmese tea, bright yellow slices of 'cake', and white segments of cold semolina at their sub-monastery, all this before our breakfast! But we do enjoy going along at these festivals."

Home leave 1963 – in Kashmir first

This home leave was particularly memorable because it was the golden wedding year of Rosemary's parents, James and Bertha Harley. It was great fun to visit the Kashmir scenes which Mum had painted, and to take back to her our impressions and colour slides. For a golden-wedding gift we were able to obtain at a very reasonable price a lovely Burmese embossed gold-lacquer casket and include in it an ode which I wrote, and which amused them:

Colinton. 26 July 1963
A fragment or figment of *The Ballad of the Harleys*

When James Glen Harley strode across the Himalayan peaks
Bertha Digby quickly sought what every young girl seeks,
While J.G.H. the valleys roved from Leh to Katmandu,
Bertha put her easel up and lightly sketched the view.
No matter where that young man climbed from Pindi to Pahalgam,
Bertha blocked the only route with canvas, paint, and charm.
When James the Christian gentleman paused gravely to enquire
If she and her duenna were not courting fate most dire,
Bertha answered airily, "It's such a lovely view —
Pish and tush to danger; don't you see I'm courting you?"
He did, but rode his bicycle right up into Ladakh:
Then scared the bears with whoops of joy as he free-wheel'ed back.

261

With Bertha on the saddle-bar, and chaperone behind,
Jim rode them right into Lahore, and neither seemed to mind:
How could they be but happy with a man so straight and kind?
A gorgeous shamiana was put up at Shalimar
For the munshi sahib's tamasha: still the talk of the bazaar.
In forts beyond the frontier, tribal maliks called a parley
To celebrate the union of a Digby and a Harley.
They were sad to hear the wedding was at Cambridge, Inglistan,
But sent as representative a most respected khan.
Then up into the hills again James Harley took his bride,
Far far beyond the Hindu Kush, beyond the River Clyde.
And that was fifty years ago, right to this very day:
Fifty years of happiness and many more we pray.[14]

We made unforgettable side-trips at very little extra cost to us. We stayed outside Srinagar under the great chenars on Nagin Lake, and glided by shikara gently about the waterways, visiting the Shalimar Gardens and Nishat Bagh. Then we travelled by 'bus up to Pahalgam where our houseboat owner fixed us up with tents, equipment, servants, and ponies to trek a short way up the East Lidder Valley. It was magical. We were relieved to be told, maybe a fairy tale, that bears, if alarmed or on the defensive, can easily run uphill but not down!

I returned from home leave ahead of Rosemary, and routed myself back via Peshawar, Lahore, and Karachi. It was a delight to be back in much loved surroundings which I had left in 1951, and to catch up with local staff, and to meet one or two friends from elsewhere in their new posts in Pakistan.

My priority was Wilfred Kirkpatrick from Mandalay. He had only been in Peshawar as Regional Director for ten days before I arrived. I was looking forward to guiding him here and there in an exciting environment which I was happy to explore further. But Wilfred seemed to have been in Peshawar for ages because he already knew so many people and was fully accepted. His house was already full of his treasures old and new, particularly his collection of Burmese gilt wood-carvings and gold-lacquer ware. He was obviously sad at having left Burma, but he knew he could not have continued as before.

"I must go to the office," said Wilfred next morning, "but where do you want to go?" "To the bazaar, please." Soon we set off by cycle rickshaw. Wilfred did his best to converse with many shopowners in a mixture of

---

[14] In truth, Dad had simply ridden the first bicycle in Leh, as a demonstration after helping a local merchant put together the cased contraption he had ordered 'on spec'.

Urdu and Farsi. They couldn't quite understand our Persian, but our knowledge of it raised our *izzat* (standing, as of the educated class!). The great bazaar of the tribes of the north was new to Wilfred, but he appeared to be quite at home. I soon felt that *he* was taking *me*.

Wilfred spoke nostalgically of Burma. I knew that he had made a great success of his post at the cost of his own privacy, but he told me he had cried on leaving Mandalay. Sad to say, we never saw Wilfred Kirkpatrick again. He was murdered in Peshawar on 6 April 1965 in the hotel room in which he was staying for the night, before flying off on home leave.

The news caused widespread grief in Peshawar and elsewhere. His funeral was attended by over five hundred students, headed by the Vice-Chancellor. Many of the Muslim girls in purdah attended, having spent the morning making wreaths and crosses. Lord Kinross paid tribute to Wilfred in *The Times* of Thursday 8 April 1965, concluding with these words:

> In Peshawar, a place used to the British Proconsul of the imperial days, whom the Pakistanis could respect, he was well on the way to creating a legend for himself as his antithesis, whom they could also love.

October 1963

After a wonderful leave which included visiting Pompeii, Ravello and Arles, we had to go straight into a Scottish country dance display in a U.N. Day programme at the Rangoon City Hall.

Unfortunately, our English language work was curtailed, now that our lecturers had been forced to leave. But at least I could fill some empty hours with school work, adult education, and teacher-training with my E.L.T. experience. I saw my chance to get closer to a few more of the very pretty Burmese girls around. So I put it to Mother Rose Virginie, Mother Superior of St Philomena's Convent that I was free to do a little English language and poetry teaching with any senior class. She smiled and took me on saying that she knew perfectly well that I would put my heart into my job! It was great fun and my class was lovely. But St Philomena's was soon nationalised.

"What charming people the Burmese can be," wrote Rosemary. "The women especially are so pleasant and easy and un-selfconscious. We are unlikely to find another country where it is so easy and enjoyable getting to know the women." In *From Sea to Sea*: Kipling wrote:

I will always walk about with a pretty almond-coloured girl who shall laugh and jest too, as a young maiden ought ... She shall look at the world between the eyes, in honesty and good-fellowship, and I will teach her ...

The Dead Hand

Social life now became noticeably quiet. People came to the office and house, but government employees were being questioned about their foreign friends and connections. People were becoming unhappy at the increasing nationalisation of all sides of life. The numbers of plays at religious festivals were controlled. Many private firms were going out of business. There were shortages and there was confusion. Bazaar prices were rising, and there were reports of unrest up-country.

November 1963

November was a melancholy month. I was posted to Fiji as Representative, which was promotion, and a relief owing to the state of affairs in Burma. Acquaintances who were remaining envied our departure. The situation was worsening so rapidly. The new income tax was crippling. An elderly Englishman retiring to Britain found that his gratuity and capital savings were taxed. Very few Burmese or foreign residents were allowed to travel abroad, not even a wife who wished to have her baby in Europe, although the fare was being paid in foreign currency.

Farewell

We planned a big party to show our appreciation of Burma and our gratitude to so many Burmese. We intended to hold it outdoors, trusting that the rains were really over. Then we heard the appalling news of President Kennedy's assassination. We didn't feel like having a party. Burmese and foreigners alike were stunned and incredulous. We went to a memorial service in the American Ambassador's garden. It was so lovely and peaceful. It took place on a lawn over-looking the lake, with the evening sunlight catching a few sails. Our Embassy was in mourning for a week. We discussed our party with His Excellency. He sensibly said, "Go ahead, as long as there are no coloured lights, music, or dancing."

On the evening none of that mattered. The companionship was quite sufficient. The Chinese caterers were marvellous. They lit the drive and the garden with tiny naked-flame oil-lamps. A large number of guests came wearing lovely silks and jewels. Everyone seemed to enjoyed the party. The last guest left at 11.30 p.m.

Luckily there was plenty of food left over which the bearers were pleased to bear away. The party had been a pleasure and a strain for us because many expressed how sad they were at our leaving. Such good-byes occurring in our lives weren't enjoyable. Yet this was definitely the right time to leave Burma. We felt particularly sorry for the Anglo-Burmese and the Anglo-Indians, who could see the last links with Britain being broken. Saw Maung, who loved cats, simply took our 'puss' on his strength.

Other lively parties were given for us, one was a Scottish dancing evening, in addition to the Caledonian Ball which we managed to attend. There was also a poetry reading of 'Comic and Curious Verse' angled at us: "The Professor of English was teaching his staff some of the limericks this morning, we hear."

We were overwhelmed by the unprecedented and unexpected number of gifts we received from our Burmese friends on our departure. Was it partly due to local custom, and partly because the Burmese realised the doors were closing? Most of the gifts were welcome items that we did not have. There were beautiful examples of almost the whole range of Burmese crafts. I especially treasure an ivory Chinthé on a plinth with a silver-plated inscription from the British Council Scholars Association. The table mats and trays we were given, are in daily use thirty years later.

We were even more overwhelmed when U Way Pon Hla came and insisted we accompany him to the monastery. There we found U Zargara with food especially prepared for us, and more presents: a gold-leaf-covered lacquer box for Rosemary, and a finely painted walking-stick for me.

We thought we didn't know many Burmese well, but it seems they knew us better. Dear people. Fare Well.

Fiji 1963–1966

It was hard to leave Burma, but such was our life. The Director of Agriculture, Suva, wrote that no cat may be imported and the Commissioner of Police informed us that no guns at all were permitted in Fiji. Oh well . . .

At Djakarta Airport on our way to Fiji we met by chance the Council Representative in Indonesia, who had opened the Council office in Fiji. It was a useful encounter. In Sydney I was able to meet and introduce Rosemary to several members of my family, headed by Uncle Frank aged 84, who had been in the Boer War. We flew on to Wellington, New Zealand, where we were met by Richard Hollyer, British Council retired. We were fortunate to find such a person conveniently placed to look after our interests in Fiji in the unavoidable absence of a Representative, and who could brief me on my duties.

We flew on to Auckland, past Mount Egmont, the famous, snow-capped, volanic cone. In Auckland we met more of the endearing side of the New Zealander: we asked the way, and a flood of help followed. We learned not to criticise anything. We discovered one or two other traits. In the hotel we had to sit where told, even with people at the only other occupied table. And we had to be prepared for staff to enter our room at any time without knocking!

On 15 December 1963 we sailed for Fiji on the S.S. Tofua, a comfortable ship, and we had a spacious cabin. We appreciated the rest we got, and enjoyed the quay-side singing and dancing by islanders sending off friends, all of them dressed in bright clothes. Music, either guitar or piano, continued the entire voyage. The dinner menu included "Burma curry and rice"!

It was suddenly daylight and we were docking in Suva, Fiji, in the middle of the Pacific, 11,590 miles from home. No-one had told us to be ready for immigration at 7.30 a.m., and the crew were cross when we didn't come at once. Then bang, crash, in walked an energetic little lady without knocking! Rosemary, who was not yet dressed, was pretty short with whomever it was. In fact she was to be my P.A., Mrs Merle Benyon, an Australian. She had come to welcome us – but *not yet, please!*

Subsequently all went well, and we found ourselves installed in the

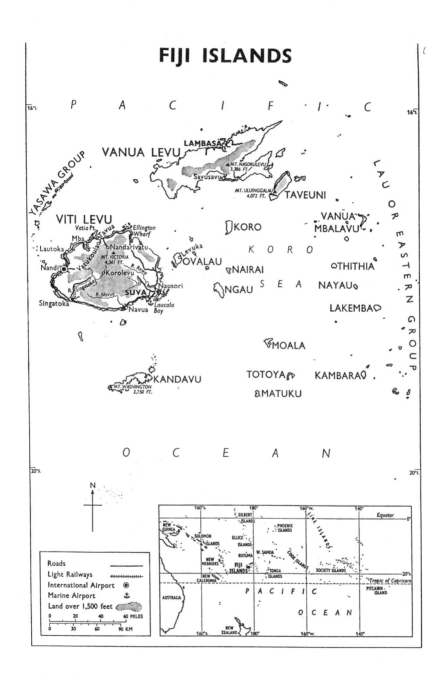

FIJI ISLANDS

splendid old Grand Pacific Hotel along the shore from the arcaded, little streets on a road lined with palms and great fig trees. It rained hard, and didn't stop, and we were a bit sore at being faced with a strange Christmas away from all our friends in Burma. But Merle was a great help, and Christmas in the Grand Pacific was actually fun: it was better than being lonely in a bare semi-furnished house. The sun shone, and we had our first view across the bay – of reefs and white breakers, with green mountains piled up beyond. The Bishop of Rangoon had alerted the Dean of Suva, to make sure we were entertained, so I wrote to my former Lord Bishop:

> Hail Victor Rangoon, and farewell.
> Read book, hold up candle, ring bell.
> The shade of your crozier
> Made life so much rosier,
> A step nearer Heaven than Hell.
>
> The prayers of John Polynesia,
> Have made our inception much easier.
> We are sure he will prove a
> Great blessing to Suva,
> No island, nor Bishop was breezier.

To which he replied:

> Dear Michael
> So glad you've discovered a nook,
> In the shade of the sheltering crook,
> Of your new local prelate
> (Don't broadcast or tell it:
> I've stored my bell, candle and book).
> It must be terrific
> To span the Pacific,
> A sort of benign Thomas Cook,
> Amazing what bounc'll
> Come out of the Council
> For giving the world a new look!
> Blessings on you
> Yours V.R.

That helped a lot.

One fact we had to master was that we were living almost on the International Date Line. As Rosemary wrote: "The Far East is to the west of us, and the Far West to the east of us. It is best not to think about it."

268

Fiji 1963–1966

The Archdeacon of Polynesia wrote in his succinct and outspoken little book, *The Moon and Polynesia*, "It is quite possible to take a midnight Christmas service in Suva, then fly four and a half hours eastward to Samoa, and take a similar service that same day." The 180° Meridian actually passes through the little village of Waiyevo on the Fiji island of Vanua Levu. Once upon a time the people there found they were living on different days of the week depending on which side of the street they happened to be. So the Date Line was officially bent to take in Vanua Levu and the Kingdom of Tonga 600 miles to the east. This Tonga is pronounced with a soft g, Tong-a. (A tong-ga is an Indian two-wheeled, one-horse vehicle.)

One of our Fiji scholars, who was asked to report to our London office on a Friday, unsuspectingly left Nadi International Airport on a Thursday, but he arrived in London still on Thursday after twenty-five hours' flight via Los Angeles. Of course his accommodation wasn't ready! The Date Line had its uses. We left Nadi on home leave one Saturday morning, and arrived in San Francisco in time for a drinks party being given by our Tehran friends, the Millars, on the *previous* Friday evening. The *Fiji Times* rightly announces that it is the "First Newspaper in the World". We also learned quickly that we were in Melanesia, 'the black islands', a rectangle containing the Fijis, New Caledonia, the New Hebrides, the Solomons, the Bismarck Archipelago and New Guinea. The Polynesians (dwellers in many islands), in the triangle of Hawaii, Easter Island and New Zealand, including the Tongans, have straight hair and lighter skin and, to us, have more attractive features than the frizzy-haired Melanesians.

Gaugin wrote of one of his models and lovers that she was not at all handsome according to our aesthetic rules, but that she was beautiful. In fact there are very few pure-blooded Polynesians left, because extensive inter-marriage with many other races soon produced refinement, and beauty. I never met any Tahitian-Chinese girls, who I heard are the most beautiful of all.

We were happy in Melanesia. Viti Levu, the main island of Fiji, is a beautiful 'high island', as opposed to a flat, coral atoll, and the Fijians were delightful. For the first time we found ourselves in a British Crown Colony, and not one annexed by force. From the mid-1800s the Fijians had been under pressure from slave traders, and with internal jealousies and strife, a growing population of European traders needed protection. It finally became impossible for one chief, known as the King of Fiji, to establish proper law and order. After the considerable reluctance of the British Government to create another colony, and the resignation of Gladstone, Disraeli saw that King Cakobau[1] needed British assistance.

[1] Pronounced Thakombau, see p. 275.

The King and his people finally agreed to cede his country unconditionally to Britain, as he said "in the best interests of his kingdom for internal peace, stability and progress," and the Deed of Cession was signed on 10 October 1874 in the old capital Levuka, on the island of Ovalau. As the Archdeacon wrote in *The Moon and Polynesia*:

> We are trying to wipe out something of the infamy of a serious blot on the history of European contacts in the South Pacific. The Slave Trade, known as 'blackbirding' was the most infamous. It led to terrible cruelty, and the upset of ancient island societies. After the martyrdom of Bishop Patteson bravely opposing the slavers, we sent British warships to stamp out blackbirding.

Much of Suva is on a very hilly promontory with lots of ups and downs to explore. I was sad that there was no indigenous wildlife on Fiji. No fauna from any continent reached so far on its own accord. There was only the mongoose brought in by Indian indentured labour. There were no snakes. There were few large birds; some protected duck, the occasional heron, dove, and parrot.

Our base of operations was 89 Princes Road, Tamavua. It was an admirably sited house in a suburb rising steeply up from the harbour. In our area there were no fences and few hedges, so all the gardens were open stretches of tough, reed grass. This was reduced to passable lawns by the industrious mowing contractors, the Indian Hanif brothers. Nowhere else would equal our view across the rolling lawn, through palm trees down to the turquoise blue ocean, beyond the bright, white reef water and the narrow harbour entrance.

At the bottom of our open slope we had a stream to the seaward side fed by almost constant rainfall. The water then dropped vertically several hundred feet down among the thick vegetation. I never went near the edge! Along the stream grew clumps of luxuriant cannas, and upstream more on the land-ward side was a group of golden palm trees, which was occupied at night by a quarrelsome colony of flying foxes, or fruit bats. They sensibly went to sleep at 'lights out'. There were masses of hibiscus everywhere in Suva and in our garden. In January the gardenias flowered magnificently, the bushes were white with them. There was less bougainvillea as it was too wet. "Everything washes away here," wrote Rosemary. But she managed to build up an attractive, new flower-bed round the house using lumps of coral off the reef which adhered to itself well. As Rosemary found "it was full of interesting shells and things."

The house was built out from a steep, grassy slope over a flat driveway, with steps up and round to the front door. It was essentially a one-floor house with two small bedrooms against the slope, and a large sitting-room cum verandah. It was a good house for entertaining. There was glass in the windows on the land side, but on the other two sides there were large, wooden shutters which were outward and upward hinging, supported on poles. It was easy to keep guests happy simply by indicating my X20 prismatic telescope in the far front corner.

The house needed a lot of scraping, scrubbing, and varnishing of the basic internal woodwork. Rosemary had high humidity to contend with in all she did, and found it sapping. I have often referred to work needed on our rented houses, but I just repeat our need was to have a sensible representational house in which to entertain. We received fine support from our London office, which trusted us to be reasonable with requests for furniture and furnishings.[2]

Rosemary had particular problems in Fiji when it came to entertaining. Fijian girls were very agreeable, but made the most irritating and baffling servants we had ever met. It was very difficult to find and retain a good servant girl, however nice she might be, and however much we would try to accommodate her. One reason we discovered was that the Fijians were not consumer orientated. Nor were they money-grasping. Servants in Suva had no sense of service as we had known servants elsewhere. From their very way of life they didn't need to work unless they felt like it! When we needed to make a special effort for a visitor, overtime payment didn't tempt them to stay. This is a refreshing outlook in the world today, but it would not help the Fijians' advancement.

One of their age-old customs is known as keri-keri. If a member of a family, or close tribal friend, came into possession of a covetable item, such as a cassette-recorder, another member of that unit was entitled to take possession of the item simply by saying "keri-keri". It even applied to services. One unusually go-ahead Fijian tried to run a taxi-service, but failed because so many of his journeys had been keri-keried by relatives.

As was customary with each "move", Rosemary had to learn a new shopping routine and to recognise new types of local products, such as dalo,[3] yams, new types of shops, and new prices in new currency. This turned out to be pretty straightforward. The enormous Fijian meat-cutter at the butchers gave her frissons of the Fijian past! I was very anxious for the coconut sellers. They sat with a stout, sharp, pointed stake between their legs, and with both hands dashed down the whole husk to split it. Then the extracted nut would be held fast on the palm of one hand, while

---

[2] See its letter Fiji/221/3 of 21 November 1966, p. 315.
[3] Dalo (taro): a starchy tuber (colocasia asculenta), a staple food of the Pacific Islands.

chopping down on it with a nasty looking panga. The sound "shuuh" was followed by "Have a drink".

The Colony of Fiji

We didn't have a particularly warm welcome to this miniature colony, which in time we found intimate and interesting. To begin with we had to face up to an expatriate community largely of New Zealanders, Australians, with a few English and Scots. The Colonial Servants were nearly all British and early on were remote from such as us. We had no colleagues, and there was no British Embassy or High Commission staff to give us a cheery welcome. The Education Department basically comprised New Zealanders, because New Zealand had a remit to assist Fiji by providing officials and teachers whose conditions of service required them to teach outside their own country, in Fiji and New Zealand dependencies. There was a feeling that we were poaching on antipodean preserves, and what was I doing in Fiji?

I had to make it clear quickly that because Fiji was a British Colony, the duty of the British Council was to act as a cultural and educational link with Britain, and to provide a shop-window on what teaching aids were available and what opportunities there could be for training or undertaking post-graduate studies in Britain. In my position I needed to meet the Chief-Justice, the Attorney-General, the army and police chiefs, and the heads of the government departments of agriculture, fisheries, power, and transport. But I was not getting to meet such people because we were not being invited, as we had been used to through the British communities elsewhere. There were no business parties and only the Governor had an entertainment allowance. So I simply went round Suva finding out who did what and introducing myself. I was rewarded.

We were saved by my predecessor's good friends, Robert Kay, a Scot, and his wife, Gillian. Robert headed a leading firm of chartered accountants. The wide knowledge of people and events which they both had was of great value to us. The Kays really cared for the British Council, and for us! They introduced us to many useful people. We were also saved in a sense by my uncle, Townsend Halsted, who had been in Cable and Wireless in Fiji in the thirties. He kindly alerted the chiefs, and also Maynard (and Moira) Hedstrom, head of the great Pacific firm of Morris Hedstrom. He was good at cricket, playing for Fiji, and at tennis, and was a popular, social bachelor. He was also a friend of the sporting young chiefs of the future. He had told me he used to entertain them at his home, and give them the beer they loved, but which they were forbidden by law to drink.

In C. P. Snow's *Cricket Heroes* there is reference to the Fiji team's

272

impression on the New Zealand public on their first tour there: "figures in gleaming white shirts and skirts, with noble heads of hair, shiny bronze legs flashing in the sun, brilliant white teeth, radiating natural goodwill."

I brought a letter from my uncle to Ratu Edward Cakobau, who when younger had played cricket with my uncle and who was now a senior chief. We met him at the home of Robert Knox-Mawer, the Puisne Judge and humorist, and his wife June, the author and broadcaster. We took to Ratu Edward at once. He was the greatest fun on many an occasion.

I was now interviewed by the *Fiji Times*, and by the Fiji Broadcasting Corporation; then Rosemary was interviewed by the F.B.C. for the Women's Hour programme. Rosemary's interview focussed on where we had served and on the role of the British Council wife. I was very glad of the publicity for her, and the emphasis on the unpaid devotion of our wives. I came to know the F.B.C. well.

In due course I found that I was to spend three evenings a week at home writing scripts for the serialisation of set books for schools, which I enjoyed producing and broadcasting. I loved Gerald Durrell's *My Family and other Animals*, and never tired of it. I also gave talks on some of my favourite books and on those that were available in our library. I also prepared programmes on poetry. I discovered that the ultimate test of a first-class poem was for it to come through unscathed from a class-room mangling, and still be loved. 'The Lady of Shalott' is one.

Rosemary went into realms beyond me, and gave a series of talks on the development of sonata form to accompany piano and violin recitals, to help listeners comprehend classical music. Through the radio we discovered just how keen the people of the Islands were to hear about the outside world, even from us 'small-fry'.

But then I thought, I'm not such small fry. I am the British Council Representative in the Pacific! I'm a form of British ambassador, as the translation into Fijian of who, or what I was, conveyed to people outside Suva. I exchanged letters with Charles Wilmot of Tehran days, who was now Representative in Canada. I wrote that my representation was the largest in the world, though I kept quiet that it was mainly ocean. He replied smugly that his was larger, but that a lot of it was tundra. Mine extended to the Pitcairn Islands. I could have paid them a visit, but it would have taken me two months to travel there and back! But luckily Pitcairn came to Suva one day.

Sir Derek Jakeway, the new Governor now arrived. We were bidden to his swearing-in ceremony. "Hat, gloves, stockings, and all. Oh dear!" wrote Rosemary. Sir Derek was in full white fig, with a lovely, white-plumed, cocked hat. Lady Phyllis sat demurely beside him. (I got a shock when I saw the same scene used in *The Independent on Sunday* of 19 April 1992 to illustrate "Dressing up in a Shrinking Empire".) My short start ahead of his arrival was a help to me, and even to him. When Sir Derek and I got to know one another, my job became much easier. He knew my position, and he gave the British Council his full support. I had never met a Governor before, let alone a young one. I gradually learned to be less in awe. He was good fun, but I remained respectful.

'Our Fijians'

The Fijian physique as exhibited in their rugby team, huge thighs, legs and torsos, belied their normal gentleness and kindly disposition. But their war-dance gave a different impression – one of awe! When these huge men, dressed in the traditional costumes of the long, narrow leaves of dracena or cordyline, and carrying spears or clubs and huge palm fans, stamped, roared, rushed, and clashed, it was hard to believe that they were really gentle and friendly. There were many Fijian men wearing the sulu, which was more like a kilt with side pockets than a skirt. It was calf-length, wrapped across the front, was tailored to the waist and hips, usually in dull trouser colours, but it was very becoming. When Ratu Edward and Ratu Mara (who became Fiji's first Prime Minister at Independence in 1970) were in London, they kindly came to luncheon with Papa at the United Services Club. It was splendid to see these two huge, genial men, beautifully turned out in their 'town' sulus and jackets striding along Pall Mall together.

Many women were pretty large too. Rosemary found it rather alarming interviewing possible maids who towered over her. "I miss the neat, graceful and elegant little Burmese terribly," she wrote. Culture shock. It wore off! Nowhere else did we have an office char who scrubbed the floor singing excerpts from Handel's Messiah! She typified the sunniness, willingness, and the culture of the office staff. We certainly appreciated the wonderful Fijian choirs, who sang so well in English or Fijian at home or abroad.

In the late-nineteenth century the islanders were taught English hymns by members of the London Missionary Society, and so were led into other forms of English music. The Fijians showed innate fine understanding of rhythm and tone, and the ability to imitate and reproduce these skills. The girls' school choir singing of the now famous Fijian farewell song of a man to a maid, 'Isa Lei', and also the beautiful Water Lily Song, displayed a charming mixture of cultures. I have the record. The original Isa Lei goes back to Fijian legend, but the words and music of today we owe to Lieutenant A. W. Caten, a former bandmaster of the Fiji Defence Force.

I suppose that these earnest missionaries, who I think were wrongly motivated, supplied many strange, 'good' concepts for the lives of the

Fijians. Indeed, in time the Fijians exhibited great Christian faith and (sometimes!) behaviour, and a sense of community belief and worship. Unfortunately, the early missionaries upset the traditional indigenous ways of life which had produced a stable, albeit cruel, society. The missionaries preached against nudity, and insisted on their women converts wearing ridiculous cotton cover-all garments known as muu-muus. They had to wear their muu-muus even when out on the reefs collecting shells for food. In constantly damp garments many suffered from tuberculosis, and some succumbed. These garments greatly inhibited their ability to swim, so they began to lose this valuable, sometimes vital, art.

Another Wesleyan contribution was a system of orthography to reduce the Fijian language to writing. Some of the letters of the Latin alphabet were used to express sounds common to the Fijian language but which are quite different from the sounds of the same letters as used in English. This was unscientific and confusing.[4] Ratu Edward's surname was written Cakobau but pronounced Thakombau, as originally spelt. The international airport was pronounced Nandi, but written Nadi. We went to the island of Beqa one day. But the notice on the quay said that the boat was going to Mbengga!

Fijian is an agglutinative language. It sounds rather like a light machine-gun, as short syllables follow one another. So a Fijian gentleman might introduce himself: "I am Sitiveni Tamanikairukurukuiovalau." It is quite easy once one is accustomed to such syllable sounds: Tamani-kai-ruku-ruku-i-ovalau.

Fijian customs

The Grand Pacific Hotel had a prize specimen of a Fijian as commis-sionaire, smartly dressed in a blue sulu, white shirt, and red jacket. His main job was to greet new guests in a much modified Fijian ceremonial fashion. One would be offered a half-coconut bowl of yanggona, and one should pause, gravely sip it, and bow in a friendly manner. If one was going to make any visit or any project a success, it was vital to have the Fijians on one's side. It was therefore most important to know the forms of yanggona ceremony and their significance, and to go along with them respectfully and patiently.

The proper yanggona ceremony is a sacramental ritual and is still faithfully observed. To attempt to brush the trappings aside when meeting Fijians would cause the gravest offence, but not death today. It would certainly preclude Fijian co-operation thereafter.

[4] See R.A. Derrick, *A History of Fiji* (1963), p. 72.

Yanggona is the powdered root of the shrub *piper maethysticum*. It could be bought in shops. The proper custom was to cut the green root into small pieces which were then pounded or grated. The result was then steeped in water and thoroughly mixed in a large wooden bowl on legs (the tanoa). In the old days the roots were chewed by village maidens to make them more soluble. Next an attendant squatting on the ground would strain this mixture through a bundle of hibiscus fibre. When the master of ceremonies acting on behalf of the guest of honour was satisfied that the mixture was right for drinking, the cup-bearer would come forward bearing the bilé (half coconut shell), and with much ceremony and respect present the guest of honour with the first bowl. The yanggona was then poured into the guest's personal cup held out with both hands before him. When the guest had drained the bowl in a single draught, there would be the cry of "maca (maathaa) – it is drained," accompanied by the clapping of hands. Then on to the next guest and so on, one of the host group drinking after each guest. When all the guests of rank had been honoured, the ceremony would be declared over, and the magiti (feast) would follow. Yanggona tastes rather dry and is slightly numbing.

At these ceremonials a thick rope of coconut fibre embellished with white cowrie shells, called the Tui-ni-Buli, would protrude from the tanoa, and would be pointed towards the guest of honour, who could be seated cross-legged on the ground – although the Governor always had a chair. During the ceremony no-one, on pain of death, might cross this rope. During the ceremony there might also be a group of chanters singing to the rhythm of small, hollowed log drums (lalis). The Fijians taking part would wear the traditional skirts of grass or leaves, with the upper parts of their bodies bare, and their faces blackened. Every part of the procedure was conducted with a slow and dignified grace. It could be very impressive indeed. It could also be extremely time-consuming – for the British administrator or businessman. It could not be avoided; and no kind of discussion could take place until after the ceremony.

A special ceremony rarely seen today, only perhaps for royalty or head of state, was the presentation of a tabua, or whale's tooth, as the mark of highest respect. Formerly a tabua was a token of fealty on the visit of a chief. Earlier still, a tabua was offered as an act of propitiation before undertaking hostilities, or the planting of crops, or house building. These teeth came from the cachalot, or sperm-whale, and were beautiful, highly polished objects. They were generally suspended from plaited coir ropes – for hanging round the necks of chiefs, or their daughters when given in marriage.

Any ceremony could be called a meké, such as one consisting of songs or a dance, or both. The wild war-dance was still considered to be a meké. Mekés were terribly popular for young and old, and were more intricate to produce than would appear. They were great fun to witness and to listen to, Fijian singing being very pleasant. There is an abundance of poetry in the language on many subjects so there was no lack of themes for a meké. The men and women performers dressed elaborately in leaves and flowers. They had frequent rehearsals to make sure that the drill movements of heads, arms, and legs were in perfect unison. Percussion could be by lali or by thumping pieces of thick bamboo of different diameters and lengths, on the ground, thereby producing different tones. This was most effective and the singing very moving, particularly Isa Lei when sung by a large choir at the departure of a big ship.

The Fiji Defence Force was a most impressive unit. Its parades and official gun salutes thrilled me. The dress uniform comprised a red jacket, a white sulu with a deep serrated edge, and black, polished sandals.

The Fijians are natural soldiers. The first disciplined force was raised by the then newly recognized King Cakobau in 1871, and armed, trained and commanded by British officers. Being accustomed to the precision of their old war-dances, the warriors took easily to drill, and when used against the hill tribes of Viti Levu (who had been responsible for the murder of the missionary the Revd Baker, in 1867), the authorities realized how good they could be at jungle fighting. There was only a Labour Company in France in the First World War, but Fijians' hard work and discipline were second to none.

The centre of Viti Levu, the main island, was an ideally tough training-ground for Fiji commando units raised for the World War II campaigns against the Japanese in the Pacific Islands. They proved to be terrific, an absolute match for the Japanese in toughness, resistance to climate, bravery and skill in silent jungle movement, tracking, and attack. A battalion went on to serve in Malaysia from 1952–1956 under Lt. Col. Ratu Edward Cakobau O.B.E., M.C., and also Lt. Col. Ratu Penaia Ganilau D.S.O. It eliminated over two hundred terrorists. In our day the Commanding Officer and certain other specialists were from New Zealand.

Beating Retreat

We were once invited by the C.O. to a Friday Beating of Retreat at the F.D.F. base. We took along an aged Brigadier fishing friend of Papa's who had called in on a World Tour. Imagine all of us – the Bishop and other V.I.P.s, wives, chums, R.A.F., and hordes of children – spilling over a long verandah at Government House, with rain threatening. In front an asphalt drive, beyond a very green parade ground, with guns and a flag-pole on a bluff at one side, and in the distance the sea and coastal plain. Against this were the vivid colours of the dress uniforms topped by beaming, black faces. Fijians love singing in harmony, so after the brass-band items, a quartet sang Swing and strummed guitars.

Then there was more colour: bobbing spears behind a canvas wall turned out to be a group of the gaudiest warriors – grass skirts in cherry, or purpley blue with fluffy bands of raffia round wrists and ankles, and flower garlands on the biggest of thugs! They did a wonderful dance in two opposing groups – lots of confrontations and threatening waving of spears and warlike attitudes and threatening cries, all to a very brisk rhythm and singing and shouts from the band behind, on this occasion using Fijian instruments, especially the thumping of big bamboos on the ground. The movements were amazingly complex with subtle, spear wrist sinuosities and cunning foot-work. Maximum enjoyment was gained by full audience participation, shouts of joy and laughter – probably from all the relatives. The warriors did one dance sitting in line and using hands to mime verses of the song which sounded rather risqué judging by the audience's howls of delight – also because it was really a women's dance. Everybody enjoyed themselves, and the music and the dancing were first class.

The warriors went on to march up and down and beat Retreat in proper fashion in a steadily increasing downpour. Whenever they stamped to a halt or turn, water squirted up their sulus from the soggy ground. Afterwards we went to the Mess for drinks and the old Brigadier was delighted to meet the young Fijian officers recently returned from Malaya.

A sudden shock!

I received a letter to inform me that Sir Paul Sinker, our Director-General, and Lady Sinker proposed to visit Fiji in a month's time. This meant that I had to learn a great deal more about Fiji as fast and as accurately as possible. I knew there was to be no flannel and no hearsay. From our experience of his visit to Tehran in 1961, I had to include topography in my survey. "What is that huge conical rock or hill beyond the harbour, known as Joske's thumb?" "It is a volcanic plug."

Rosemary and I got away to the west with our young driver, John Mohammed, in a fine Council Ford Zephyr Estate. John was educated and experienced, and a good guide and adviser. He was one of the rare persons of mixed Fijian-Indian parentage. I don't remember meeting any other whom I could recognise as such. The mixed race we met were unfortunately known as Part-European. They were dear people, but somehow lacked the better qualities of both bloods – unlike the Anglo-Burmese.

We had a four to five hour twisty 133-mile drive to the towns of Nadi and Lautoka. Short stops at the best beach hotels on the way made pleasant breaks. We inspected these for future V.I.P.s or visitors, and for the Director-General. The tourist literature described the drive as "a fascinating journey along a coastline with glorious vistas of the Pacific Ocean, up and down soaring mountains, and through verdant green valleys." There were very few good beaches; the coral reefs often came right up to the shore. In other places there was mud from the rivers and impenetrable mangrove swamps as additional deterrents. The winding road was very tiring. Yet we were never bored by the ever-changing scenery.

The guide book continued: "Fringing the road, sometimes close together, sometimes many miles apart, attractive Fijian villages, dotted with picturesque thatched dwellings, give glimpses of the Fijian people in their natural environment." We were lucky to be paid to see all this; and perhaps the Fijians were lucky in their lives here too, if they were left alone, and not dragged into the twenty-first century. Unfortunately, there was the threat of relegation in their own country by the Indian community descendents of the original indentured labourers of 1879, whom the British brought in to produce sugar. Quoting the Archdeacon again: "Of the two hungers of the Indian population, born in Fiji and with a right to take a leading part in the land of their birth, the first is for land, and the second is for education."

In fact, my visit to the dry western sugar-growing zone turned out to be principally to Indian Institutions, starting with the Rama Krishna Mission, which had built up a very good school and library. I met the Indian member of the Legislative Council, and heard what their Swami (religious leader) had to say. Thank God there was no bloodshed in our time. I had heard hot-headed Fijian mutterings in Suva.

A further half-hour's drive took us to the Western Region capital of Lautoka. It was a fine town, almost totally Indian, with branches of the big firms of Burns Philp and Morris Hedstrom. There was a small, Chinese (controlled) immigrant settlement of some 5,000 in Lautoka. The settlers lived quietly and effectively, in business as store-keepers, restauranteurs, and as wood-workers. I found an excellent Chinese cabinet-maker in Suva who did a number of jobs, until he was recruited by a Canadian immigration team and went to Toronto! We were kept busy in Lautoka, meeting provincial commissioners, headmasters, British Council scholars in education, churchmen, businessmen, travel agents, book-sellers, and even an Anglo-Burmese friend from Rangoon, Dr Kenneth Minus, who had wisely left Burma while he could.

It is the British Council library work which we have enjoyed as much as anything in each country. Rosemary could help in this work along with our professional staff. Our books, periodicals, and newspapers were useful to the locals, and to British visitors. Our libraries attracted all manner of persons inside, whom it was easy and rewarding to meet. In Fiji it was necessary to support educational and cultural development by the written word. In Lautoka it was essential to keep the economically richer Western Region in touch with Britain. For this reason, the Overseas Development Administration in 1962 had provided £20,000 towards the colony's Lautoka library building fund. I was very pleased to meet the O.D.A. funded librarian here, Bob Pearce. He was an ideal development officer, who knew his staff and was able to manage his building, book-stock, and clientele with cheerful confidence. Book presentations in both towns and districts were made easier through the British Government subsidised English Language Book Society, which made available cheaply an excellent selection of titles for lending or for sale in many subjects.

Upon our return to Suva we found that our baggage had at last arrived. We quickly unpacked and were surrounded again by our tools of trade for creating an instant home: crockery, cutlery, pots and pans, clothing, books, pictures, rugs, ornaments, records, a clock or two. We were now ready for the Sinkers. Then came a Qantas pilots' strike, and the Sinkers had to overfly to Sydney. A shame. We cancelled the dinner-party for them, but carried on with the cocktail party for 140 guests at the Council, which was centred round an exhibition of all that the Council could do for Fiji. In spite of our absent V.I.P.s I did all right by having the honour, instead of Sir Paul, of handing to the Governor the British Council's £6,000 topping-up cheque for the Western Region library. The Governor's Dinner was not cancelled, so we left the staff in charge of the guests on the Council premises and went on ourselves. On our way home from Government House at 11.30 p.m., we were alarmed to see a light still on in the Council premises. We investigated gently, and then crept away. The staff were happy after their hard work and causing no harm. John, the driver, was dancing 'the twist' with the assistant-librarian.

The local staff

One aspect of Fiji life which caused me no concern was my local staff. Merle Beynon as P.A. and book-keeper was good and reliable at her work. She knew everybody, which was so important. When she left after a year or so to return to Australia, Dorothy Lloyd, who was English and the wife of the Director of Lands, made an admirable and congenial replacement.

The other local staff, headed by Semi, were reserved, not terribly bright, but they were so nice. Semi was absolutely reliable, and was splendid managing with his assistant the particular and exacting effort of our Book Boxes, which could include records and films. These were greatly appreciated by communities far and near; and Semi was known all over the islands. He could also rise to the occasion for a function, once he had arranged the flowers to his satisfaction.

All the dear Fijians in the office seemed to me to have the same characteristics. They didn't have sparkle or drive, and couldn't be precisely efficient. They continued quietly in their own way, which was pretty good and often earned praise.

We lost our locally appointed librarian after a year, and Rosemary gallantly took over despite all her other jobs. I was delighted because she understood that the library was the main front for our work. She could pick out people who came for information or to use the library. Readers and visitors were met cheerfully and intelligently, and sometimes firmly! She would keep me informed and would perhaps get me out of my office to talk. She encouraged staff who tended to be diffident, to talk with her. This wife often did extra hours while waiting for me. She had to have time off sometimes for cooking, when we had Very Important People to dinner! She was invaluable to me, and to the Council. London backed us up over the need for a smart, efficient library, and gradually we received excellent furniture and flooring. Our stage was then set for whatever came along.

Rosemary suffered from an almost inexplicable departure of maid servants. "They won't tell you what's wrong, as servants do elsewhere." There probably wasn't much wrong really, but I think they preferred to be at home. But Rosemary had a new compensation in Fiji, which she didn't have in other foreign countries: the clubs. There was the Gardening Club, the Y.W.C.A., the Fiji Women's Corona Society (for Colonial servants and their wives), but only later did she find her real delight in the Shell Club.

Now that my position was understood I could go anywhere and be welcomed by an Indian or a Fijian, a Colonial servant, or a kai-viti for whatever I had to offer. The travel was pleasant. On land it was all much the same: palms, sugar or copra, and mission stations. The 'island hopping' was much more fun. I had confidence in Fijian seamanship. Our living conditions in Suva were excellent, and accommodation everywhere on tour was good. We had a big task: our contacts needed so much help.

Suddenly I was summoned by Sir Paul to meet him in Sydney. What's an ocean to a Director-General? It meant another free ticket to Australia and a welcome break! It was really very fortunate for me to meet such a fine man in a relaxed, one-to-one situation. We had a good deal to talk about. I was extremely impressed by Sir Paul's detailed knowledge of Pacific affairs, his views on having Council representation in the Pacific, and on the appointment of Rosemary and me as a 'strong team'. He understood our difficulties in view of the Australian and New Zealand strengths and influences. It was useful to be able to look objectively at one's work from a distance of 2,000 miles.

Sir Paul and I had one day at the beach. I'm not a *plage* type but I was glad to be around because Sir Paul was an energetic man, and I felt I had to keep an eye on him out to sea. I didn't want such a good Director-General to be chewed by a shark.

After a day's leave with the Halsted family, I flew back to Nadi Airport in the west, and took the chance to see a bit more of Bob Pearce in his library.

After a few months my view was that Fiji was a colony, but not one prepared to follow the already established pattern of progress towards independence. Many Fijians did not seem to want independence. They were intensely loyal to the Crown and they did not want to be hurried. They hoped to rely for some time to come on the British Colonial Service, under the terms of the Deed of Cession, and to retain control of their lands. Some would criticize the British for having spoon-fed them, and for not giving them opportunities for self-advancement soon enough. Yet they did not appear very ready to grasp educational opportunities, and often lacked the drive to make the best of what the future offered. The Fijians, oddly enough, appeared to be shy and retiring when in the company of other races, and tended to lose heart in the face of competition. They were of the opinion that they did not have a sufficient number of qualified people to maintain a balance in any future form of government.

I thought the Fijians were much happier in their villages where they were at their best. I sympathized with them for preferring to keep to age-old customs which served them well for survival. Yet, as the Archdeacon wrote, there was a drift of young Fijians to the towns where they were much in need of guidance. Unfortunately, the Fijians by nature remained unreconciled to continuous purposeful hard work; and their adherence to ancient customs tended to prevent any success in business.

There simply had to be a breaking-down of old customs, and an earnest, continuous drive to produce a higher percentage of qualified men and women. Firstly, a higher standard of English language proficiency was needed. This was only possible at secondary school level, which was expensive for the government, and for parents whose primary school children only spoke Fijian at home. In Lautoka I could see how the Indians were getting ahead in all fields. Even its population was overtaking the Fijian. Of course, my staff and I treated both races alike. However, it was very difficult to bring such deep differences of race and culture together for social and cultural activities. But Harry Charman, Cockney, boxer, castaway (as I understood it!) managed to do so in an admirably conceived Charman's All-Races Sports Club. We went to a show for the new Governor – boxing bouts, judo, gymnastics, guitar quartet – with 'all races' taking part. It seemed to work.

Fiji 1963–1966

Adi Cakobau Girls' School

I thought the Adi Cakobau Girls' school was the finest institution in Fiji. Its success was largely due to its New Zealand headmistress, Frankie Charlton. There are surely hundreds of Fijian women today who remain grateful and affectionate towards this small, cheerful, highly intelligent, and commonsensical lady. She was brilliant at synthesising the best of Fijian customs with the needs of a modern secondary-school pupil. This included plenty of practical work and the care of the grounds and the orchards.

Frankie Charlton included us in their annual 'Do' and Old Girls' Day – a magiti: a feast! It was a sumptuous, very well-run occasion. A shelter of corrugated iron on bamboo posts was put up on the big lawn. It was decorated with palm leaves, flowers, and trails of plant leaves. There were five double lines of guests down from the 'top table'. The table cloths were banana leaves laid on mats such as those on which we sat. The food was ready laid out: dalo, yam, crab-meat in their shells cooked with coconut, 'parcels of leaves' with cooked vegetable mixtures in them, chicken, pork, water melons, and pineapples. We drank green coconut milk from a reed stuck through the eye of its shell.

Ratu Edward and I once attended a luncheon at the school given by the home economics class – intended to prepare the girls for Western life. It included palusami, i.e. corned beef in dalo leaves with lolo, which is a tenderising coconut milk. I said: "Ratu. This is an anachronism. What did you have before corned beef?" "Human flesh," he replied, with a smile of relish.

The early Fijians were cannibals. The last missionary to be eaten was the Reverend Baker in 1857. His boots remain. The index to Sir Alan Burns' *Fiji* (H.M.S.O., 1963) reads:

Cannibal,
    forks, 27.
    Isles, 27.
Cannibalism,
    Europeans eaten, 27, 48, 53, 59, 76, 85.
    examples of, 50, 53, 61 103, 140.
    Fijian reputation for, ;5, 27, 35, 45, 140.
    practice of, 12, 27, 29, 61, 81
    stopped, 73-4, 78, 100.

I'm afraid there is the story of Ratu Edward on his way to England by P. & O., saying to the steward "Take that menu away, I'm feeling peckish. Bring me the Passenger List."

Floods of March 1964

One night we listened to the rain belting down, and the thunder rolling in the hills, and the floods came. Poor Ratu Edward, who had been at a party, was Commissioner of the badly flooded Rewa Delta area near Suva, and had no rest.

Suva, which was on a promontory away from rivers, didn't suffer at all. But twelve miles away at Nausori, the chief Rewa delta town, there was a lot of flooding. Loss of life then known was only two. Further up in the tributary valleys, which were mostly long, winding and narrow, the rivers rose forty to fifty feet in some places. Houses were washed away. Many of these were fairly easily replaced. Many villagers just tucked their possessions up in the rafters and went up the hill to a neighbour. Reports said the people affected by flooding were pretty cheerful and getting down to work again with a will. The Fijians would be cheery about anything. But the serious aspect of such occasions is not so much the loss of possessions as the damage to crops and agricultural land. Hundreds of people in every valley had nothing but jungle berries to eat and so needed to be fed, once they could be reached.

Within a day communications were completely disrupted, except by telephone. The circular road, which ran near the coast and crossed the rivers at their widest points, was completely blocked in several places by major landslides. Two of the most important bridges had been put out of action. For a few days, with the two Suva airfields flooded and at Nadi too, there was no movement by land or air beyond Suva.

The Red Cross and government and other agencies had worked out a disaster-relief scheme some years ago and went into action most efficiently. We were best out of the way. We were very impressed by the radio reports, hearing of co-operation everywhere, such as P.W.D. lorries taking Royal Suva Yacht Club members and their outboard launches to the flood areas to evacuate people – those boat owners worked for days on end. They were mostly New Zealanders and they were terrific.

Until very recently the R.N.Z.A.F. had a Sunderland seaplane base at Luthala Bay. But alas the Sunderlands were superseded by the land-plane Orions. This was very hard on the distant islanders. They had been able to rely on the Sunderlands to land on the sea to pick up sick or injured cases quickly. Now there was no such air-sea rescue service.

A break for Alma Mater

Despite the aftermath of the floods we were told we shouldn't cancel our first Fiji Oxford and Cambridge dinner chez nous. Even the Governor managed to come, which was fine support for us and for the fourteen eligible local members. Everyone was pretty flood weary, but all stayed past 1.30 a.m. to hear the direct broadcast. Rosemary commented: "Fancy having a husband who invites the Governor to one's first dinner party in a place with no servants at all."

Don't go to your dentist on a Monday

I went on a Monday to my excellent young New Zealander. But "Agh! Agh!" I said, as he lent on a tooth which gave an ominous crack. "I'm so sorry" he replied. "I'm so tired after having to swim after my boat yesterday when the mooring slipped. "How long are you going to work here?" "Oh long enough to make enough money to go on to London and buy a Jaguar."

The Royal Suva Yacht Club

We were delighted to be accepted as members of the Yacht Club thus to enjoy its fine premises. But the Club atmosphere appeared hard and there was much beer-drinking. I am no sailor. Rosemary was disappointed, but the Pacific ocean, even inside the main reef, with its hidden currents and underwater snags is not a playground for a novice.

Living on the ocean

For those who were brought up with the ocean, as are many New Zealanders and Australians, Fiji is an ideal posting. The New Zealand-born Director of Education in Tonga went further than many, literally. He and his family built a trimaran in their garden, and at the end of his tour of duty, they sailed back to New Zealand in it.

My only experience of the Pacific occurred early on when I was invited on a fishing trip by the Presbyterian Church Group. There were about eight hearty colonials and one rather anxious 'pom', who all set off in a sturdy motor-fishing craft to the edge of the reef to moor and fish with hand-lines.

After an hour or so the motion of the moored boat began to have its effect and I no longer cared whether I caught a fish or not. In due course there was a winding in of the lines, and much activity below. Primus stoves were lit, and with great gusto mixed grills were fried and beer handed round. To me the smell below was dreadful, and the ocean swell seemed worse. I reached out miserably for a piece of bread and tinned sausage, managed to get it down, and then make an apologetic surrender.

Worse was to come. Owing to the impending state of the tide the skipper had to navigate over the outer reef, and come in by the main channel. I became prostrate and green, vowing 'never again' would I accept such an invitation, while attempting a hearty thank you and cheerio.

The loss of a passing sail

A charming, classical-educated Englishman, Bill Procter, came through in his twenty-foot, self-built ocean-going yacht, Popey Duck (the Cornish for Puffin). We liked him so much. He was a nice, gentle character. With the *Iliad* and Greek plays for reading material, he was on his way westward round the world. Alas, after Indonesia, contact with him was lost, and no trace of him was ever found. His wife at home went on hoping for a long time that he was living on some remote island . . .

A bit of ourselves

Our social life may have been dull, but I had a great deal more to do than in Rangoon. I enjoyed being stretched. Rosemary wrote: "He wakes me up in the morning bursting with ideas, comments, and queries. He's writing so hard, every weekend for weeks, and every night we are at home." London supplied us with some ideas. For Shakespeare's quarter-centenary, we were able to get together a cast to perform *The Rose Distill'd*, an essence of Shakespeare devised by Dorinne Ingram.

Rosemary did much more physical labour in the garden than in Rangoon. The garden looked wonderful, with its golden coconut palms, hibiscus, frangipani, poinsettia, and ginger plants. The heavy rains could make gardening difficult, but the toads were happy. We got tired of ushering them out of the hall so we fixed a plank as a toad barrier across the front door-step at night. Pot plants, such as ferns or African violets were in sections of tree-fern trunk as there was no local pottery, nor plastic pots then.

Bau (Mbau)

The little island of Bau lies a few miles up the east coast from Suva and about half-a-mile out, but it can be reached on foot at low tide. It remains the extremely important chiefly base of the ruling Cakobau family. One can go there by invitation only. We were particularly lucky to be able to go to Bau on duty at the invitation of a good friend, Senimili Kikau, a teacher at the primary school, and secretary of the leading group of women's clubs. She is a fine person (teachers on Bau have to be of chiefly rank!). She had been to Britain as a British Council bursar to visit Women's Institutes. What puzzled her and amused us, was that whenever she was invited into the English countryside she was expected to admire the view. She couldn't understand this, as she hadn't known what a view was! But she learned to respond enthusiastically.

Our visit to Bau was a model of organization. I have my copy of the typed programme: "3 p.m. at the landing. 3.20 p.m. arrive Soco – met by Senimili. 3.30 p.m. arrive up at the school. 3.31 p.m. Flag ceremony. National Anthem, 3.36 p.m. Guests of Honour to be seated" – and so on. I wish the Queen could have come instead. The Fijians *would* have been thrilled.

The island was delightful, but it had a bloody history. A hundred years before there were tribal battles here, and the murder of ships' crews and of some settlers. And it was usual to kill and eat one's prisoners. The Fijians had special wooden forks for eating human flesh, as 'it wasn't done' to eat it with fingers. They had horrible practices such as burials alive and the strangulation of widows and old people. But in our time the houses were set in green grass under palms and spreading trees. There was a bathing pool and a huge, grassy space for ceremonies, and even a concrete cricket wicket!

The Council of Chiefs' great, reed-thatched buré meeting-place had a huge, old Methodist church alongside it. This building was once a temple and the font in the church was originally the old chief's killing-stone on which the victims' brains were dashed out – supposedly the most merciful form of death. We visited the Cakobau family burial-ground which was an 'enchanted' spot on a cliff-top. By the time we returned to the school for a meké, the children neatly dressed in blue and white had reverted to spear-shaking savages in grass skirts and bark cloth. First the boys danced to the girls' singing, and then vice versa. I now knew the standard of school materials that I should try to send over. Some months later we were on Bau again for a District Parents Day; but after a long wait, and frequent beating of the lali, only twelve parents came. They were reluctant to contribute to the upkeep of the temple building. Alas, the marvellous Melanesian powers of survival and adaptation to land, and especially to the sea and climate, which was centuries' old, no longer counted in the march of time. I felt that the Fijians simply had to advance, and by means of education.

I must pay tribute to Freda Gwilliam, an outstanding Education Adviser to the Secretary of State for the Colonies. She inspired her staff everywhere, and also the local ladies in the Fiji Education Department. I also pay tribute to Marjorie Stewart of the South Pacific Commission Community Education; to Ruth Roberts, (N.Z.) Women's Interests, Ruth Lechte of the Y.W.C.A. and Mrs Elizabeth Eden, F.A.O. Home Economics; also to Sister Ram Samuj in Public Health. We were most impressed by their successful way of raising standards of health and hygiene through the women of the villages. There was also Anne Soper of the Red Cross. She saved many lives by travelling round the islands with her inflatable dummy, teaching resuscitation.

These ladies covered everything to do with village life thoroughly and patiently, including how to run meetings and the making of simple, effective, cement water-closets by means of easily constructed moulds. But above all, the Fiji women had to ensure the co-operation of their men! One of the incongruous spin-offs was the provision of sponge cakes to visitors even in remote parts, which were up to the high-class, home-baking standards of New Zealand.

A change from text-books

A British Council travelling exhibition of 'Recent Artists' Prints' which was returning via Fiji from New Zealand to Britain made a welcome change from the usual text-books. Rosemary wrote notes on the thirty-eight examples for the benefit of adults and schoolchildren. She also provided drinks and snacks for a preview. We were assisted in setting it up by the Fiji Arts Club through Ken Bain. He was a New Zealander in the Fiji Government and a member of the New Zealand Arts Council. We were glad to work with him for the establishment of a Fiji Arts Council, which came into being through local enthusiasm and with the help of experienced New Zealanders. We did all we could to encourage and help local bodies to arrange concerts and exhibitions.

I took the Artists' Prints on to Lautoka, where Bob put on a splash, funded by Council funds. We had an encouraging variety of viewers, for many of whom Western art was new.

It was now the cane-crushing season, and we were given an excellent introduction to the industry by the manager and staff of the sugar-refining company. Sugar cane is a tough crop to handle, and the smell in the factories wasn't pleasant. But we were amused by the transport of the cane to the factories by means of a miniature steam railway.[5]

There were birds everywhere, pecking at pieces of cane which had fallen off the flat, open, iron trolleys. People working here were happy

[5] The lovely, ancient engines were soon all sold to outside enthusiasts.

because owing to current Cuba troubles, sugar was fetching twice as much as two years before.

The Kingdom of Tonga

The Kingdom of Tonga was called The Friendly Islands by Captain Cook in 1773. They were discovered by Tasman in 1643. I was delighted to make my first official visit to Tonga at the end of May, and to take Rosemary. Her costs were allowed by the British Council for trips to far-off islands in order for her to meet, cheer, and interest isolated wives. But Charis Coode, our hostess, the wife of James, the British Resident Adviser, was far from isolated. The charming and popular Coodes were never without delighted visitors.

We had some 600 miles of ocean to cross in one of the little four-engined, fourteen-seater Heron aircraft of Fiji Airways. Aft of the pilot's cabin on the port side was the navigator's table, and I looked over the navigator's shoulder with interest, and then with apprehension. He seemed to be peering down to see where he was. Then he unzipped a soft pencil case, and a couple of dice fell on the table. Oh dear! I thought, but we reached the capital Nukualofa on Tongatapu safely.

The Coodes had a huge, rambling bungalow with a fine wide verandah all round. The side facing the sea was 'carpeted' with lovely Tongan mats. The sea was just across the road beyond a grassy verge lined with casaurinas. At low-tide people wandered about on the reef looking for shell-fish. Queen Salote's little palace was nearby. It was built of white-painted wood with fretted balconies and a red tin roof. It had a Royal Chapel almost as big as the palace, perhaps because the Queen was head of the Free Wesleyan Church of Tonga. Only a low wall surrounded the buildings. There were no security problems as the area was sacred. Late one moonlit evening we wandered along by the palace, and found a little group seated at the bottom of the back-stairs playing guitars and singing a royal lullaby in harmony. Another evening we heard two of the Queen's musicians playing their nose-flutes as a lullaby, making soft, sweet sounds.

Nukualofa was a very small, well-laid-out town with a lot of grass and trees. Most people walked everywhere, and seemed to know each other. The 300-odd Europeans enjoyed the village atmosphere and had a host of activities such as Red Cross, Hospital Week, and Vestry Committees.

The royal tombs were not far away. They comprised heaps of rock sanded over and close together, forming a large mound of about 150 yards square. There was a grassy area all round which was tabu to the locals. But the Queen gave permission for the Europeans to play golf there.

We had hoped for an audience with Queen Salote. I had seen that splendid, smiling figure in the Coronation Parade of 1953. She had driven along the route famous in her open carriage regardless of the rain. They took no notice of rain in Tonga. The Sultan of Zanzibar sat beside her, and was referred to by some ribald bystanders as Queen Salote's lunch! But now, alas, we heard news that Her Majesty had hurt her foot and could not see us. The Queen took a great interest in Tongan affairs and was always thinking of ways of stimulating her rather lazy people, who had an easy life, to maintain correctly their crafts and traditions, and to make improvements and progress.

The Crown Prince, Tungi,[6] was a great support to his mother, and undertook much of the direct rule. Everything was very feudal and personal rather as in Ethiopia. Tonga was a British Protected State, self-governing, under a Treaty of Friendship. The people were very well-behaved with a strong social code.

Prince Tungi and Princess Mata'aho came to lunch with the Coodes one day. We enjoyed the occasion immensely, especially since they had the most cordial relations with the Coodes, who were obviously ideal for the responsible post of the link with Britain. Prince Tungi was a vast man with a huge, jolly face and a bright twinkle in his eye. The Coodes were not small themselves. The Prince was very shrewd and intelligent, and full of enthusiasm for the latest projects, such as audio-visual teaching aids and new maths systems.

An attractive natural product produced by the women is tapa, or masi, the bark cloth. Tapa is made from the inner bark of the *broussonetia papyrifera*, the paper mulberry tree (masi) which is cultivated expressly for the purpose. The bark cloth is used for many purposes, such as house partitions, mosquito curtains, bed covers, decorations, a couch covering, as a presentation at a ceremony of birth, death or marriage, as a covering for a grave, and for ceremonial dress. The making, dyeing, pattern-making, and application of pigment are fairly complicated, requiring considerable skill and application. It was fun watching the ladies at work.

The main island of Tongatapu is a flat, coral atoll just a few feet above the sea. On the more exposed east and south sides the land ends in a small cliff about twenty feet above sea-level. Ten yards or so further out is a lower shelf against which the sea breaks. This coral shelf is much eroded underneath and right through in places so that when the great rollers come surging in unchecked there is an almighty boom and rush of surf as the breakers crash down upon the shelf, and then comes a woosh as hundreds of huge high jets along the coast are forced up through the coral cavities. The sea on this side drops abruptly down into the Tongan Deep, to 35,000 feet. The backwash makes new waves which mount nearly as high as the

---

[6] Now King Taufa'ahautupou.

breakers. "Superb," said Rosemary, who missed breakers in Fiji. "Awe-inspiring," said I.

The British Council could contribute something to education in Tonga. I had some money for the purchase of text-books and for teacher-training expenses, and for the building up of libraries, which I was able to discuss with departmental staff and teachers. I thoroughly enjoyed visiting schools and talking to such lovely children. And so did Rosemary, who showed slides of Britain to the Girls' Secondary School. Tonga required more help than Fiji. The people needed to understand the value of modern textbooks in teaching, and the value of library books themselves. There were many mission schools as well as government ones in Tonga: Wesleyan, R.C., Anglican, Seventh Day Adventist, and a huge and expensive Mormon establishment with good classrooms and a good standard of teaching. The Mormons happened to think that the Polynesians were connected with the Israelites, and so felt a special duty and sympathy towards them. We felt an urge to help the Tongans – just because of themselves.

Back in Suva

The cooler and drier period in June was ideal for the Queen's Birthday Party, and this one was very different from others. There was a splendid F.M.F. parade in the morning. The Governor with fluttering plumes walked some distance with care and attention to inspect the ranks of Her Majesty's Troops, who were finely turned out in their scarlet jackets and white sulus, and perfectly drilled. The police were in blue jackets and white sulus. All these colours were on the brightest and greenest of grass with a glimpse through the waving palms to blue water and white surf on the reef. The afternoon Garden Party in the spacious grounds of Government House was an attractive occasion, with great terraces of flowers rising up, and the scarlet band perched up on the slope, and the guests smartly turned out. They later toiled up the slope to watch the beating of Retreat on the flat lawn beyond which we could see the mountains and the sunset clouds.

I was off to Tonga again later with the Science Textbook Exhibition, accompanied by our new, professional librarian, Mary Thornhill, the wife of Jack Thornhill working under Aids to Commonwealth English (ACE). She was excellent, particularly when we had a special topic to plan such as the setting up of a Tonga public library, which was so worthwhile.

I had a great time in Tonga, chaperoned by Mary some of the time, and there were many delightful young Tongan secondary school girls ready to help with the book exhibition. I had already discovered on my previous visit how attractive the Polynesian girls were. But they tended to grow rather large, requiring rather large men to cope. I was content to admire at a distance.

I soon felt a certain warmth towards a senior Tongan girl of a fine family, who was ready to give intelligent help. She told me that the less sophisticated boys and girls were apt to treat a book in itself, apart from its contents, as a means to school success, even by offering it to God by placing it behind the altar in the chapel! The Tongan girls 'en masse' were great in song and dance. The distinctive timbre in their singing appealed to me. I paid a visit to the Pacific relay station on the subject of possibly supplying material from the B.B.C., and I was given as much taped Tongan songs as I could ever want. The songs are so evocative of our lives in the Pacific, but of course they sounded the most exciting on the spot.

Rosemary was rather pleased to be on her own for a bit, but her peace didn't seem to last, what with long suppers out, guests in, a Y.M.C.A. meeting, and the music committee of the Fiji Arts Club.

A stroke of luck!

We heard from London that the renowned Oxford Clarendon Laboratory low-temperature physicist, Dr Nicholas Kurti, was about to go to Australia and New Zealand to lecture. He was famous for having achieved one degree above absolute zero in his laboratory. He informed the London office that he would welcome a five-day break in Fiji on his way, and would be willing to give a "light-hearted chat" entitled 'Science for Profit or Pleasure'. I was thrilled to accept the offer especially since he was a Hungarian, and I concentrated at once on the publicity. My nightmare in any country was for a V.I.P. to stride to his lectern only to find himself facing an audience of a few cajoled friends and B.C. staff.

The requests for free tickets soon, to my surprise, almost reached our hall capacity and I became anxious. But I needn't have worried, I was allowed to use the town hall across the road. What a relief! I owed much to the Mayor.

Dr Kurti and I strolled together across the street from our office and we found the town hall packed with a well-behaved, eager audience of old and young. Dr Kurti's lecture was fascinating. We were intrigued by his section on low-temperature and living creatures. He believed that one day scientists would be able to freeze a human being, place the body in a container with instructions that the occupant was to be thawed out on a certain date in the future! He then told the story of the gerbil which he

THE BRITISH COUNCIL

65 Davies Street London W1   Grosvenor 8011

Reference GEN/360/2 D-K   24th March, 1964.

Dear Dr. Kurti,

Halsted has written from Fiji on 16th March, which will have crossed with your letter to him of the 18th. As it is amusing, here it is:-

"Many thanks to Dr. Kurti for being willing to give a talk (light-hearted chat) entitled "Science for Profit or Pleasure". I will lay this on for Wednesday 18th: also a convivial evening (I hope) afterwards.

I think Dr. Kurti's own travel plans are just right. If he would have sufficient rest by staying with us he will be most welcome. He will have a reasonable bed, his own study and telephone, some bathroom inconvenience but all the mod cons are there, a lovely view, and a car and wife at his disposal - if he sees what I mean. Or I can book him at the Grand Pacific Hotel which is undoubtedly very pleasant.

To save delay I will make his Korolevu and tour bookings, and 'plane to Suva on Tuesday 16th June and hire of car to Korolevu (18th), and Suva hotel booking if required, as soon as you or he confirms.

I think that all this will be enough without going to Tonga, since Dr. Kurti has not indicated a special reason for going there."

You will, perhaps, write direct.

Yours sincerely,

C. N. P. POWELL,
Deputy Director,
Specialist Tours Department.

Dr. N. Kurti, F.R.S.,
Department of Physics,
University of California,
Berkeley 4,
California,
U.S.A.

cnpp/js

To remind you of the beginning of our friendship, 26 years ago.

Nicholas and fiana.

froze quite stiff as part of a demonstration, stiff enough for its body to span two uprights. At the end of the occasion, they unfroze the living creature, but its ears fell off. The staff were all very upset. How had it happened? The eventual answer was that the visitors were so intrigued to see this poor little thing in such a state of totally suspended animation that they could not resist touching its ears which developed gangrene as the body unfroze.

Dr Kurti stayed with us, and we had a splendid time. "He enjoys his food,"[7] Rosemary wrote home, and was a perfect guest. We were sorry when our brilliant, cheerful, and vibrant professor left. Later his admirable, congenial wife, Giana, came from Australia and stayed with Rosemary while I was away.

The next excitement, was a visit by the pianist Dennis Matthews with his wife, Brenda. They chose to stay with us and were model guests. Dennis gave a radio interview, and was happy with whatever time was free for him to practice in peace. Rosemary had charge of flower arrangements at the F.B.C., who were broadcasting the recital, and sharing the cost with the Council. She begged hibiscus from her friends. It is a dramatic and amazing flower, often four to five inches across and is now bred in many colours But it only lasts one day, and without water, closing in the evening. Rosemary noted: "We kept them in a fridge all day to slow down their closing, and then stuck them on the thorns of branches from a lemon tree, with a background of 5ft. yellow-and-green-striped stiff sword blades off an aloe plant, with huge, dark-green oiled leaves at the base. All this went on a kind of stand which didn't fall over."

To my relief, we didn't have to charge the 120 people we could get into the studio for the recital. "It was a great joy," wrote Rosemary, "to hear such gorgeous playing once more, and all the earlier composers whom I prefer." Brenda told us that Dennis liked to unwind afterwards in company, so we asked a few up to our house for a drink. After most of the audience had left, Rosemary found to her horror that I had asked the Governor and his party also; and that they were already on their way. But our house was still locked up. We tore home, and found them inside! The Governor had given his A.D.C. a leg-up through the lavatory window.

Dennis was very pleased and kept us up until 1 a.m., telling clever, punning stories. Next morning they slept in. Then Rosemary shot them down to see the market and so on; then back to meet a few more people for drinks before lunch, then lunch at home and off to the airport. Rosemary nearly fell asleep on the way.

---

[7] As we saw from his television appearances and his book, *But the Crackling is Superb* (I.O.P. Publishing, 1988). Alas, Nicholas died in March 1999.

Fiji 1963–1966

Vanua Levu

It was our first visit to Vanua Levu, the other large island which lay north-east of Viti Levu. It has a dry side with sugar cane, and is much hillier than western Viti Levu. We stayed in the capital Labasa (Lambasa) with the Provincial Commissioner. I did my best at the school by showing a variety of slides of life in Britain, including some of my own. It was to interest teachers and children, and to talk with them, and find their needs. Rosemary spoke to the members of the Women's Club, who were mainly European, on our other countries. Next day we met our friend from Suva, the talented ex-school teacher and choir master, Fijian District Officer, Joshua Rabukawaqa. He later went on into the Legislative Council. He took us for a drive to Bua Bay, where early traders had denuded the area of the valuable sandalwood through shameful exploitation.

We next stayed at Natuwalu, the district centre, where it was strange to see Caribbean pines on the dry shore, while coconut palms flourished not far away on the wet side. We were lucky to enjoy some of the week-long, all-Fijian Methodist celebration which marked the independence of the Fijian church from the Australian branch. In Natuwalu we had a close view of the finest Fijian ceremony and dance by sitting with the Roko Tui, the senior Fijian area official, and his wife. There were story dances by village after village, some were exceedingly funny. Our penalty was having to drain half-coconut after half-coconut of yanggona, or else cause grave offence. When Rosemary became awash she asked the Roko's wife if she might refuse any more, and received a firm "No".

Our call next day was to be at Savusavu on the south coast. There was no road, and the D.O. thoughtfully sent us round in his launch so that we could sleep on board that night, and not get up for the 6 a.m. regular boat next morning. Rosemary wrote: "For all the peace we got we should have stayed in the Rest House, because the crew seemed to return at intervals throughout the night, and each deciding to brew up on the primus, making an awful row pumping, and clattering tin mugs about!"

"The next boat in early was full of people still singing after the meké, and pounding yanggona root! But later the five-and-a-half-hour voyage along the coast was a delight, looking at the lovely mountains rising blue from the sea, and I had my best view yet of flying fish as they skimmed away from our bows. Mercifully it was very calm as some of the sea route had to be outside the reef. Coming into Savusavu was pure tropical dream. We sailed along a finger of land heavily fringed by coconut palms with small, steep, green hills above, and great, spreading rain trees smoothing over the gullies. We could see an idyllic island off the shore, and the sea here was oily calm."

The small community had been busy with a cruise ship calling in, and

295

was tired. We stayed at the little, informal but grubby hotel, and met the people we needed to see who might take charge of the films and book boxes and see that they were sensibly used. We enjoyed meeting some of the local characters, who were nearly all planters. They had been there for a generation or two and were regarded as a breed apart, with some odd ideas bred of isolation. But they were very decent to us as we were doing our best to enliven lives, and to help their teachers and children.

To the New Hebrides

On our return to Suva I packed up an exhibition of British textbooks, and made a nine-day trip eight hundred miles west across the ocean, again in a little Fiji Airways Heron. I put my trips and dates in the *Fiji Times*, to publicise my activities. I went first to Vila, the capital of the condominium of the New Hebrides. This make-shift concept is both curious and comic. There are two languages, English and French, and two of everybody it seemed, certainly two policemen working together with two sets of laws. But you can't have two rules of the road!

Fortunately, I was greatly helped by Jennifer Kennedy, a very competent and charming U.N./V.S.O. She organised my contacts, spruced up the only possible display room, and helped me throughout. I felt that the Fijians were further advanced than these islanders. I learned a bit about the local Cargo Cult and its strange leader John Frum.[8] I also met a talented, locally based artist, Michoutouchkine, and his man, Pilioko. His paintings did more than justice, if possible, to the wealth of natural island beauty.

New Caledonia

I flew on to New Caledonia (Nouvelle Caledonie). In Noumea I went to study the work of the South Pacific Commission in relation to the aims of the British Council. The S.P.C. was a development body with its head-quarters in Canberra. I was able to make them aware of what was available, and how to gain access to up-to-date teaching materials, and I became better informed. Nouvelle Caledonie, an overseas French territory, is volcanic and very rich in minerals, even on its barren mountain surfaces, and its valleys are very fertile. A pretty ruthless extraction seemed to be going on everywhere, with little cultural contact with the locals. But I was given fun.

Captain Cook discovered New Caledonia in 1774, but he simply could not have taught the natives cricket. However, this is what I found them

[8] See P. Worsley, *The Trumpet Shall Sound* (2nd edn, London, 1920).

playing. The game was played most enthusiastically by goodness knows how many players in each team. There were wickets and bats of a sort, but balls were just uneven lumps of rubber which bounced anywhere. Fielding was therefore a taxing acrobatic exercise: and one could never be quite sure of a successful field. Runs were, therefore, more easily come by.

I never identified a scorer, but it didn't seem to matter. I wrote it all up and reported it to the M.C.C.

Back in Suva

I was supporting an amateur production of Christopher Fry's *A Man for all Seasons*, and found Rosemary busy making a red velvet Elizabethan dress, which she described as "rather gorgeous with Indian sequinned silver-braid round the neck like jewels; and grey satin facing in the long, pointed sleeves, so that they could be turned back with heavy, red embroidery on it." Performances were well received. Our cast party ended at 3.30 a.m., even though we had got wise to cast parties and started them late. This one at 11.15 p.m! "They don't usually go on so long," said Rosemary "but I had filled them with solid food, and the result was that they all perked up."

Sadly for us, our excellent maid, Selai, left us. Fijian girls were quite used to service in the households of the chiefs. The chiefs were held in such esteem and respect that all persons below them in status could never appear physically above them. Servants would crawl to and from their presences, and work from behind their thrones. This was not required in our house when we had a chiefly guest. On one occasion one of our maids would not even come into the presence of a certain chiefly guest. We wondered why.

An unusual charity effort

Rosemary took part in a successful charity ploy: an 'Exhibition of Personal and Historic Treasures', laid on in a lovely old house where people were invited to lend items of interest and value for display. A most interesting selection of objects came in, reminiscent of today's 'Antiques Roadshow'. The best of a number of silver items was an Edinburgh-made, large, silver tea-kettle presented to the Revd Lewis Balfour (R. L. Stevenson's grandfather), on 28 August 1856, by the parishioners of Colinton to mark the fiftieth year of his ministry, and his thirty-third year at Colinton. (We were married in that church in 1953.) The exhibition was well attended and raised £160 net.

Governor's dummy

The District Officer, Rewa, John Deverell, became a good friend. He was in charge of one of the toughest territories west of Suva. His district included mountains of the interior, hunched and crumpled, dark-green matted peaks, and volcanic plugs rising to 4,000 ft. His job meant knowing intimately the people and their lives in every village. Many of these villages could only be reached by laborious journeys on foot or on horseback, after travelling quite dangerously up fast-flowing rivers in heavy, narrow, outboard-powered boats called "punts". John was able to cope with everything in his District including hurricane relief, and occasional earthquake tremors. But his sang-froid ebbed away when the new Governor announced his intention of visiting the interior of Viti Levu, and penetrating deeper than any Governor before him.

John felt that to be sure of keeping his job he would have to make a detailed reconnaissance – but to get it right he would need to employ a stand-in for the Governor. "Quite so," I said. "True. Very sensible." "Well, you're coming as H.E.'s stand-in." "But I'm not a Colonial Servant, and all I've recently done is to sit on a led pony in Kashmir." "Oh come on," said John. "You're always moaning about no shikar, whatever that means, and you'll deteriorate if you sit any longer on your ass." (Real friends are tiresomely valuable!)

Day 1: up river

We were away for two days. The first day was spent in exciting and brilliant 'punting' upstream, interrupted by proper Fijian yanggona ceremonies at the various key villages. They could not allow such an important official with his British guest simply to pass through.

The ceremony at the top village of Lasalevu turned out to be my most memorable yanggona occasion: the remoteness of the setting, the soft, pressure-lamp lighting, the dark shadows emphasising the craggy faces of the tough-living villagers, the atmosphere of proud respect in the squatting figures, the dignity of the elders, and the solemn presentation of the bowls.

Day 2: the ride down

A local woman brought us hot water early, so that we could shave. We were soon ready to enjoy her fried eggs, dalo, and tea. Then I had to pack my baggage round the horse's saddle without impeding my position. My horse looked fit and business-like, and gave me a not unkind stare. Then we were off, John, and I with our guide, Ratu Qoro from Lasalevu. The idea was to keep close to the river, but in some parts the horses had to climb very steep tracks to make any progress. We reached the village of Matainasau perched on a spur, but could not spare the time to stop for yanggona. In the village of Lutu we had yanggona but nothing else.

I had never imagined such difficult country. At 2 p.m. we stopped and ate our lunch of large lumps of buttered scone and hard-boiled eggs out of Ratu Qoro's belongings! A flask of tea revived us. The vegetation became more and more remarkable as we went on. Everything was giant-sized: vast clumps of bamboo and stems up to a foot in diameter; plants with enormous leaves; towering tree ferns; anaconda-like creepers; ferns the size of peacock's tails; huge, red ginger heads; outsize orchid blooms; wild dalo the size of elephant ears. There were no mammals, only two species of bird, a grey-green parrot with a raven-like comment, and a barking dove which we never saw. It sounded like a jackal high in the hills. The next part of the track was the trickiest. The dark, gluey mud scattered with rocks and laced with tree roots changed to clayey sand, through which the track cut its way every now and then in narrow, sheer-sided defiles. These were almost too narrow for horse and rider. We went on until we reached the village of Naivuthini with its lights already showing through buré doors and windows. Would we stay the night? No, we must go on in the dark. We had yanggona without ceremony and then hot, locally grown cocoa, a recently established crop. Our guide was on horseback accompanied by a boy with a torch, who sometimes rode pillion.

After the third fording and an hour in the saddle there were the welcome lights of Serea high up on the far bank. The horses slid down the near bank, and we followed our guide upstream to the last crossing. We reached Serea at 8.35 p.m. There stood our faithful driver, John Mohammed, who would have waited there however many days it took us to arrive. We had been twelve hours in the saddle; and we had covered over thirty miles, not the sixteen which John had forecast. I had developed a great affection for my horse. He stood there muddy white with the same patient, long-suffering, superior look in his eye. I patted him and made a little speech. I hope he understood.

Oh yes, John kept his job. The Governor's trip was re-scheduled to take an extra day. It was voted a great success. [See Postscript, District Officer, Rewa.]

23 August 1964: A visit to Levuka

We much enjoyed our visit to the old capital of the Fiji Islands on the island of Ovalau. We travelled for an hour and a half by road to the jetty and then for over two hours by the daily launch service to Ovalau. It was here that on 10 October 1874 the Islands were unconditionally ceded by King Cakobau to Britain. We were touched to see the stone monument on the spot where the Deed of Cession was signed.[9]

Rosemary wrote: "Ovalau is as one imagines the tropics: though small the island rises steeply to fantastic-shaped mountains, and from the sea one has lovely vistas of deep gorges and amazing cliffs and volcanic plugs all thick with greenery toppling over palm-fringed beaches, with sunlight below, and clouds catching on the peaks. Levuka is packed into a tiny fold of the narrow coast, and many houses are only reached by countless steps up through thick tropical plants and perfumes. Its older wooden buildings and pleasant little bridges over the creeks give it much more personality than other towns. In its heyday there were fifty-two hotels and pubs along the water front. Recently it has become more of a ghost town, but a Japanese deep-sea fishing fleet with freezing plant is changing that."

"The comic old wooden hotel with all bedrooms opening on to a large common verandah had some odd types in it. It is very Somerset Maughamish, and said to be the setting of *Rain*. Michael and I met the library committee, who are making valiant efforts to start a children's library. As there are only twenty adult subscribers to the little township library, they reckon it is not much use making an effort with the adults, but the children are keen. Michael presented 800 books that have been going around as an exhibition of textbooks, and added children's Readers too. There was much joy. We visited four schools, and Michael spoke to the children about the new library and who and why he was. We talked with the staff to find out what help the B.C. can give: teaching aids, films, records, book lists, and so on. So many teachers are thrilled that there is someone interested in their problems who can find out things for them."

29 September 1964

A holiday – at last! To Wakaya Island.

Taking with us lots of tinned food, fruit, and vegetables and beer, we drove to the ferry on the east coast, left the car at a school, and awaited the launch. As Rosemary recalls, "We were able to take the weekly copra cutter, which was much cheaper than hiring a launch. A copra boat, like

[9] See *The Times* article 'The Annexation of Fiji', 21 November 1874.

all coastal boats here, has lots of bits added on the deck and was very top-heavy. I sat on top of the cabin, while Michael stood forward in the wheelhouse. My, how we rolled – huge, blue, Pacific rollers coming down the channel unchecked by any reef and with the wind behind them. I felt not too bad with sunshine, dolphins, and seabirds to look at, but Michael found the sight of me wheeling across the skyline very alarming and kept telling me to come down – but it rolled too much for me to move! He survived, but was not at all cheered by the sight of the clock in the wheelhouse with no glass and no hands."

"Wakaya is only four miles or so to the east of Ovalau, which fills its horizon, After one and a half hours at sea we came at dusk to a lovely bay with a sandy beach and the water so clear that one could see right down, even in deep water. Round this bay are the copra drier, the labourers' huts, store sheds, and the manager's house. Across a flat neck of land under coconut palms were the visitors' burés – near enough for visits and servicing, but far enough away from noise."

"In front was a very good beach with the outer edge of the reef about 200 yards out, and, unusually, a 'bay' or two in the coral so that one had plenty of swimming space. At so many beaches, as on Viti Levu, the coral comes right up to low-water mark and one can't swim well, although it looks lovely. There were palms round about and steeply wooded hills behind."

"The island is four to five miles long and there are tracks all over it. It is now owned by the Native Lands Trust Board, who run it as a plantation. One private owner in the past introduced deer, which have now multiplied exceedingly, also some goats and cattle gone bush. So they shoot them regularly for food. Michael went out only once with the headman but couldn't bear it. They are only allowed a far too light .22 rifle. The headman simply wounded two."

"Michael had got me a mask and snorkel and I spent happy hours peering about the edges of the reef at low tide – when it was only ankle-deep – or walking about on top of it. It is so beautiful. I saw fish in every conceivable combination of colour or pattern. They grouped themselves round certain types of rock or coral. If we'd had had experienced company with us we would have been more venturesome. One can get nasty infections from coral scratches and there is always a fear of sharks, and other horrors. But the colours were superb and the water amazingly clear. We fished one night outside the reef at dusk catching small barracuda with hand lines. Alas we had to return home after five days as the only boat was leaving, but we spent one day in Levuka."

Our V.S.O.s. October 1964

The hot season had begun. Rosemary managed a picnic for eight V.S.O.s on a private beach an hour's twisty drive west. She was fussing around, wisely trying to stop them getting burnt, and making sure they were properly shod on the reef against the odd danger, such as the beautifully camouflaged stone-fish, whose spine if trodden on would inflict terrible pain, if not kill.

We enjoyed being the "overseas arm" of V.S.O., offering excellent young people help or hospitality. In Fiji they came under the Department of Education, some to teach, some to work on community projects – health, sanitation, construction or agriculture. I worked with the department staff on the difficult job of finding and evaluating the potential of new projects. Not all were successful. It was good to keep in touch and to hear of their comings and goings, and to learn from them what real life was like for the people with whom we were all working.

They got up to all sorts of adventures, especially in the sea. Thank goodness we had no casualties. But we had one V.S.O. who was teaching on the Isle of Rotuma, annexed by Fiji in 1881. This young man and a Polynesian girl of his class became quite attached to one another – in a perfectly honourable way. However, such an association caused a rumour in the community that they were going to marry. "This," said the headmaster, "was rather awkward". Indeed things looked tricky. But the headmaster achieved a brilliant face-saving solution. He gave out that there would be no marriage because the parents were unable to agree on appropriate settlements. Everyone was happy. They were familiar with this formula.

At home in Suva

Selai now came back after Rosemary had sent a message, but said she was pregnant. Rosemary was surprised because Selai was thirty-five, had children aged fifteen, sixteen, and nineteen, and was separated from her husband, "and seems very respectable". But in the Pacific, despite missionary strictures, it was and is quite normal for babies just to appear and be looked after by the community. Our concern was to see that Selai herself was looked after. A fortnight later her replacement, Asenaca, disappeared leaving all the laundry to be done.

Science textbooks

My undaunted wife nevertheless bounced back into action. We had six hundred titles selected by London for this area, packed into eight light Revelation suitcases, and we took these books round the island, setting them up in exhibition form in school after school, sending information, publicity and display instructions ahead. We had additional commitments: school meetings, an old pupils' dinner to attend, and the D.O. Lautoka to meet, with whom to discuss possible bursars, or scholars, or visitors to Britain.

Then we got a beach cottage for a holiday weekend. Rosemary described it as an "interesting reef. You could walk about right on the outside edge next to the breakers, as if on a pavement." She enjoyed snorkelling so much, and peering into chasms of gaily coloured fish. One was in another world of peace in a moment. I preferred to keep an eye on Rosemary as she floated along. It annoyed her, but I didn't care about that.

A surprise visitor – and friend

We were delighted to find that the Brigadier in charge of 'Fire Brigade' operations round the world, who arrived on tour, was my childhood friend, Micky Collins, the second son of my god-father, Lt. Colonel Neville Collins of the Loyals, the North Lancs. Micky's job was to have a force ready to help British subjects caught up anywhere in the world in local civil commotion or war. The existence of this precaution was reassuring for those stationed round the world. Very luckily we never experienced serious trouble in any country; and none directed at the British or the British Council. But violent anti-British action has occurred in countries from time to time with the British Council library a target for attack.

Christmas 1964

Christmases are important, and noted yearmarks. It was a pleasure to be in our house for this one. I took Rosemary and a friend for a trip up the Rewa river with the punt crew John Deverell and I had been with on our Governor's dummy run. I was glad to revisit the village of Korosoli and they laid on a fine yanggona ceremony, and an unavoidable 'royal' progress up to the school. We had a picnic on the bank further up under a huge tree; and then swooped down-stream to Serea again, catching up with two rafting families on bamboo bili-bilis. These rafts could only be used down-stream, and then were broken up. It seemed such a waste, but it was practical in such a rich land.

Other aspects of this Christmas remain in our memories. One was receiving from Mum a King's College Chapel Christmas Service record ARGO.RG 33, 1962. We don't think it has ever been successfully superseded. The choir was directed by David Willocks, and the selection of carols is marvellous: Personent Hodie, Torches, Lute Book Lullaby, Myn Lyking and Ding Dong Merrily on High. I have often used them in my Christmas programmes. Our first effort in Suva wasn't much appreciated. But the next year our performance with a 'Miscellany of Music and Poetry, Myth and Mummery' in the Cathedral was greeted with acclaim.

We were lucky with our lively Australian neighbours: the gynaecologist Dr David Lancaster and his wife Shirley. Rosemary went off to Levuka for the night with a friend, during which Selai had her baby at her home. Her elder child rang David at 12.30 a.m., and he coped at once. The Lancasters were great people and gave us much pleasure and fun. I obtained copies of *Let's Stalk Strine* and *Nose Tone Unturned,* two works on the Australian way of speech. It is very clever, but unless you are a Dinkum Aussie, the text is hard to read. When we had English friends in and we spoke of Australia, we would ask David to come over and read some Strine to us.

More passing lecture talent was welcomed. Rosemary was happily reminded of home by a lecture given on the construction of the great Forth Road Bridge by Mr J. A. K. Hamilton, consultant engineer, who was passing through. Then came Rosemary's brother, David Harley, of the British Meteorological Office, to Suva for the South Pacific Air Transport Council. He and two other delegates kindly gave us a magnificent symposium on 'World Meteorology and Aviation: Forecasts and Warnings, and David talked on 'General Aspects and Climate'. The town had never had such free and first-class talent available before!

Hurricane

The Christmas quiet had been suddenly shattered by a hurricane which swirled round the north and west, and the south-west of our island, Viti Levu. No-one gave parties outside: the weather was too unpredictable. Gale and downpour and flooding ruined or upset many a Christmas. We could hold our staff party later and it was fun. Our staff members were learning to unbend with such games as blow-football and pat balloon.

9 February 1965

The North Yasawas were finally in the direct path of the hurricane, and we felt the effects, which spread over more than a 100-mile radius. From Sunday morning when we received a 'final warning' we battened all down, and put up hurricane shutters or verandah shutters. This made the house so dark. The wind really got up on Sunday afternoon and blew a full gale until midday on Tuesday, during which time it rained almost non-stop, battering on the glass window side, and the force of the wind blowing the rain up under the windows, so we spread rolled hand-towels and strips of old sheet along the window sills and wrung them out frequently. We moved about restlessly, staring out at the lashing trees, the palms with their skirts blown over their heads, whilst listening to the hourly radio reports about flooded roads, and rising rivers. And all to be repeated in Fijian and Hindi, and messages from the D.O. Suva and police reports about missing people.

"It's really not been too bad in Suva," wrote Rosemary, "being partly sheltered from the full force. Trees are down everywhere, including four of our ornamental coconut palms. In coconut areas on Vanua Levu thousands of trees are down, and new cocoa trees too – an attempt to establish cocoa as a second cash crop was well under way."

"Lambasa, the main town in Vanua Levu, had twenty-one inches, three months rainfall, in two days, while the gauge near the top of the hills on this island read thirty-one inches in twenty-four hours. The rivers are already up to last year's mark and still rising and it is still raining. In one long, narrow valley it was up sixty-seven feet at midday. What is so distressing is there is so little one can do, but keep out of the way of those who do know what they are doing, and get on with one's job."

28 February 1965: The aftermath

The Government of Fiji had some funds from the last year's Flood Relief Fund, so it did not appeal again. It was also anxious not to sap the will to self-help of the villagers. Tents and food came through rapidly from Australia and New Zealand. Mercifully, although many homes had been destroyed by the gales very few lives were lost, mostly Indians who couldn't swim or wouldn't leave their homes. The Fijians on the other hand have great survival power and can endure amazing hardships. A fishing party who had been catching crabs survived two days perched up in the mangroves. A 100 people reported the previous night to be on the church roof turned out to have been *in* the roof! A very anxious District Officer found them at first light perched in the rafters with two primuses and a guitar going, and all were cheerful. Great Fijians!

Villagers were expected to dig up their damaged root crops and eat them up in the first week, then rations would start, but there was a tremendous supply problem. The New Zealanders, who comprised the majority of foreigners, were marvellous, and so were the Australians and Fijians, who were all out in the motor launches and other outboards at once, regardless of conditions. In an emergency New Zealanders are the greatest. I learned this from the war. You can absolutely rely upon them as fearless, disciplined fighters.

It was the long-term effects which were the hardest to redress – for instance the loss of cash-producing crops such as coconut palms, stock, chickens, pasture land, whole chunks of good land were washed away.

The financial year

31 March was the end of the financial year. There was always an anxiety getting the current year's expenses, repair costs, fuel, everything neatly receipted and not carried over. It was not always possible to do this, however much one begged for work to be completed and bills presented before 31 March. It was tempting (and not unknown) to pay the bill in the current year before the work was done, so as not to face the expense in the next year's budget. I was sent a kind private letter from London. In Fiji I was boss for the first time, and I had a lot to learn. What the kind senior officer said was "Don't be too precise in reporting everything that is not quite in order. It is not likely to matter, but if you did report it, London would have to take action, which they would rather not." That was a great relief!

1965: April onwards – very agreeable

My work days and many evenings on our 'cannibal island' were fully occupied. They were not dull. There was more for us than Sweeney, in T. S. Eliot's 'Fragment of an Agon', explained to Doris. *We* weren't bored in our little world apart.

A George Cross award

A Fijian in a fishing party rescued a man who was severely mauled by a shark after all the rest had fled ashore in a panic. Alas, the injured man died, but it was agreed that so much courage deserved the G.C. There was a charming presentation ceremony on a grassy hill-top with a fine view westward over the sea to the islands where the act had taken place. We sat on chairs in rows on the grass, and loved it. The Governor was in full fig. His white feathers fluttered as he presented the medal. The Girl Guides served afternoon tea. The first Fijian dance team performed with verve. The Fiji Military Forces Band beat Retreat. And a little, toy, blue and white police detachment marched along the skyline and lowered the flag.

Valuable friends from home

The Baxters, Felicity, who had been in Burma with us, and now Bax himself came on from New Zealand with slides and paintings of great beauty and interest.

L. H. Baxter, a double-first in Classics, was a guest and a help at Government House for a famous Oxford and Cambridge Boat Race Dinner. We had over thirty members in the great drawing-room, which was large enough for a dry Boat Race. Crews of eight and their coxes took a bit of argy-bargy in the selection process, but we finally got each crew member seated on the floor close up to the one in front, legs down each side and arms round waists. A break in the arm links counted as a sink in choppy water. Just imagine Fijian chiefs, which they were, in their sulus, and with ceremonial tapa cloths round their waists, bumping along the floor, with their wives applauding alongside, apprehensive of revelations! Later we had relay races which I put on the programme. "What are they?" asked the eligible ladies present. "You are being relayed!" I replied.

A party of islands

Work which was especially fun was a 'do' at the Council for twenty men from various Pacific islands on a co-operative officers' training course, and twenty girls from the same area on a home economics course, under the South Pacific Commission. I invited any Fiji residents who were interested in meeting them, or might have some connection with them professionally. We were over ninety people at the party with nineteen different speakers who described their islands, including Australia, Pitcairn Island, and the Isle of Man. Some speeches were a bit dreary, but other contributions were delightful like the song in Pidgin English given by a very black Solomon Islander, and a roof-raising dance performed by an enormous, square Western Samoan. It was particularly interesting to meet a young Mr and Mrs Christian from Pitcairn Island. They were true Somerset – showing amazing purity of descent. I asked them what we

307

could do for Pitcairn and they said there was a need for D.I.Y. books. So with the help of our Libraries Department in London I was able to send them a small library of these. We showed a few short films. Rosemary gave a deliberately biased and outrageous talk on Scotland which made people laugh. The party went on until 11.45 p.m. as everyone seemed to enjoy the occasion.

Rosemary had been horrified at the local Suva catering quality and prices, so she tended to take it on herself. Shortly afterwards we had a 'do' for the Fijian Force Unit, who were going to the Edinburgh Tattoo and the Royal Tournament in London. We showed films of Britain and asked returned Fijians to speak. We were luckily on home leave at Royal Tournament time, and were thrilled to be given tickets by General Nelson, G.O.C. London and the Household Brigade, for the chairman's box on the night our Governor was taking the salute.

Home leave now

Being on the Date Line we had the choice of direction when flying home. We chose eastward out, and westward back. The extra mileage via San Francisco, to join our Tehran friends the Millars, cost us only £24 each. Our return flight gave us a free trip to Greece and to Hong Kong. We valued such travel perks, which were especially possible from far away Fiji.

A new look at Fiji!

Now that we were back out of the world's hurly-burly, we could reflect on our good fortune and write home: "This does seem a nice place to come back to. The weather is fine. There has been a dry 'winter': the garden and the house are fine. Of course one cannot suddenly come to terms with a new country after several years in another. When we first came to Fiji and were installed in our beautifully sited house, looking across the lawn and palm trees to the great cruise ships as they steadily made their way out into the ocean through the narrow gap in the reef, we would envy all on board going back to the big world. But now we would gesture to them to go back to all the frenzy and complications of life on the continents, and leave us in peace on our 'cannibal isle'."

St Andrew's Night

In 1965 the Jakeways took a hand in a slap-up St Andrew's Night, with no less a guest of honour than the Chief Commonwealth Scout, Sir Charles MacLean of Duart. He was a most amusing, talented, delightful, and unassuming man. "Always having too much to do," he is quoted as saying in 1990, "is probably the secret of life". I believe him. We were summoned to help with the guest list and dancing. The Thornhills ran the guest practices. Rosemary and others planned and organised the food and decorations.

The party went like a bomb from the start. Cheerful Indians, leading Fijian chiefs and their wives, and the odd antipodean all joined in and tried a few dances, even Scottish and English traditional. Rosemary remarked "It was a wonderful sight looking down the long room at huge Fijian chiefs with tapa cummerbunds whirling round in 'Strip the Willow', all apparently chaotic, but in fact quite orderly, gazed upon by the black-and-gold-framed Queen Mary and King George V at either end of the room. In the middle of the rammy in burst our Puisne Judge, Ronald Knox-Mawer, impersonating his forebear Dr John Knox, castigating us all for such lewd, devilish practices. We had our retorts! No doubt the Athol Brose of which I made four bottles, straining oatmeal and so on, helped to keep up our energy." Rosemary wore her wedding-dress again: "not quite such a tight fit as in Rangoon. It was much admired." So was the wearer.

Our cats

In due course we had the confidence of residence to embark again on cat partnership after Rangoon. Our two Fijian kittens were six weeks old when they came, and were a complete delight until we had to leave them behind one sad day . . . They played together constantly and slept together – first on the upstairs verandah where they were meant to be, but subsequently in Rosemary's garden basket on top of shoes, trowel, fork, and secateurs.

They would tear about the house after each other, or rush after a ping-pong ball which they could dribble fast and neatly. A second later they would be out for the count on a chair or under the sofa. Hours were spent scrapping and biting each other, and taking it in turns to be the bottom one. They were vastly entertaining, and beautiful and obedient. They were very good with people too. They loved the wide, unfenced gardens and would come when called. Their survival capacity was up to standard. One fell off the back stairs: the other into an empty oil drum.

1965 into 1966

Christmas was quiet in Fiji. Servants went home, so entertaining was kept to a modest level. This year there were no obvious waifs or visitors to ask, except the V.S.O. from Rotuma. Of course we had an office party.

We were glad to relax after a round of attending school prize-givings. We enjoyed a co-operative dinner-party for about twenty. Our new maid Losanna was away, and then her little cousin who came to help Rosemary walked out without a word. It transpired that she had never been away from home at Christmas before, which was fair enough.

Rosemary had long wanted a proper party in our house, so the New Year was our chance. Decoration was helped by our 'gold' items from Rangoon flowers (leaves beautifully made in paper), and by well-chosen items sent out for Christmas from the family. Guests came as required: "Dressed to express your suppressed personality." Some were simple but clever. A glamorous wig quite transformed one girl. The Jakeways did splendidly. They had been to an earlier function, but soon reorganised themselves in our bedroom. Sir Derek appeared as a Chinese dragon because he wished he had a dragon's power to get all he wanted done. Phil bounced out as a marvellous St Trinian's girl, complete with catapult. It suited her! She regretted she normally had to behave beautifully all the time.

Visitors

We never had to say 'next please' – visitors, friend or Council, just came. John Watson, an Australian diplomat friend from Rangoon, decided to be a helping hand on a copra boat. But he sailed barefoot, and his burnt feet caused him to be returned to us on a stretcher.

Ron Pickering came to coach on behalf of the Fiji Amateur Athletic Association. He was a really special visitor: large, easy, enthusiastic for the Fijian physique, and a popular success. Just the sort of visitor whom we would only meet through our job. He gave us great delight – but also problems of beer supply.

We were both at our desks in the evenings, bedevilled by kittens racing around trying to catch a few of the myriad moths and beetles that abounded in the hot evenings. Unlike in Rangoon, we had no window-netting.

Hugh Carey of V.S.O. was a visitor who gave us confidence. When we took him up river, he was respected enough to be given a full Fijian yanggona ceremony, whale's tooth and all. He then went off to the Gilberts, and returned for a trip to the Nausori Highlands looking at the scope for V.S.O. in the settlement of new farmers.

Fiji 1963–1966

Visit of the Queen Mother

April 1966. A very superior, live, female dummy was now required, and June Knox-Mawer was chosen as stand-in prior to the arrival of Her Majesty the Queen Mother off the Britannia. June performed the role perfectly. Everyone curtsied to her. She inspected the Guard of Honour, planted the tree and all. She said she felt very gracious for several hours afterwards.

It rained for two weeks. Roads and bridges were flooding, but the police ensured access for everyone. The Britannia sailed in through the passage, scarcely visible because of rain.

From our verandah telescope we watched proceedings. Guns banged from the wharf, and were whisked away to make room for dignitaries. We watched H.E. going out first in the 'barge' with plumed feathers fluttering. Then a load of high Fijian chiefs sailed out on the same beautiful craft, looking incongruous in their tapa and leaves and oiled skins. They had to perform their special on-board ceremony before Her Majesty could disembark. Then we rushed off to the grounds of Government House for the main ceremonies of welcome. The Fijian chiefs were not going to be pushed into any R.A.F. hanger. They would perform their ceremonies properly, however wet they got. Mercifully the rain cleared.

The chiefs gathered, dropping by ones and twos to sit with the rest on mats some forty yards from the dais, some in jacket and sulu, some in full Fijian dress – huge, fat men with wonderful whale's tooth necklaces or bone 'breastplates'; the yanggona bowl was brought to its appointed place. Ratu George, the chief of chiefs, fussed around in a long, black 'grass skirt'.

Once the Queen Mother had arrived, the leading Fijian ladies appeared in stately fashion in an unusual slow march in two long columns. There was no sound at all – silence signified respect. Two of the most senior ladies then came up to the canoe representing the ship on which H.M. had arrived, one clutching a bundle of large leaves from which she suddenly emptied water over the bows, and the other placed a whale's tooth (tabua) on it. Then there was the yanggona ceremony, conducted with tremendous solemnity. H.M. managed to drink off her dose, after which the motionless rows of chiefs could permit themselves a wriggle and a grin. Then a huge roast pig and basket of vegetables came out. There were more speeches, then a file of warriors clutching armfuls of beautiful mats as gifts which they piled up. After the ceremonies there was a mime dance performed in lines by a huge group of men and women from the Lau islands. It was more Tongan in character and jollier than the Fijian. Then came an excellent spear dance. The Queen Mother, who seemed so pleased by all she saw, made a little speech, and asked H.E. questions.

We went home to get ready for an evening reception on Britannia. Half-way to the quay the heavens opened. We were driven by Mohammed right to the foot of the gangway, but many had to leave their cars some distance away, and arrived on board drenched.

Rosemary recorded: "We had to line up on the narrow side-deck and process slowly aft, wondering where to put dripping umbrellas on such an exquisite boat, and mopping each other drier. We went up a very steep and wet gangway all covered with awnings, but still the rain came in. At the bottom we had to wriggle between a steward holding an umbrella under the worst leaks, and the remaining drips! I was a bit demoralized and only realized halfway up that I would meet the Queen Mother almost immediately at the top and would have to curtsey. I had never thought about this! Michael, who had inexplicably been very nervous about the whole thing, went first, and H.E., who was standing with her, said he was British Council. H.M. murmured faintly "How interesting". I thought she looked a bit dazed and, on moving on, saw why – there were well over 150 guests."

"Being old party hands we stayed where there was more space and air so we talked to Lady Jean Rankin, the senior Lady in Waiting, whose home was at Ford, Midlothian. We also talked to Admiral Morgan, and found we had met him in Tehran when he was naval attaché for Turkey, Iran, and elsewhere. The reception took place on a sun-deck which was covered with awnings, and dripped along every sag, so conversation was a little erratic as people concentrated on adjusting their stance to a new pattern of drips!"

"The Queen Mother and the Governor moved around and talked to many people, but alas not to us. She is Colonel-in-Chief of Michael's regiment. A Muslim friend later told us that her questions to him were so penetrating, covering such issues as the problems of modern youth in Islam, that if it hadn't been for H.E.'s help he could hardly have answered. And he was an able young lawyer! The officers were very friendly and good at chatting. It was such fun to be with the Navy again; they do know how to do things well. But never have we had such strong drinks at a party before, rather dangerous we thought. So rain drips apart, all went very merrily until a yellow light lit up on the wall: H.M.'s departure signal, and ours too."

"The next day the Queen Mother went to church, and lunch at Government House, and that evening hosted a dinner on board. The ship sailed at 11 p.m. There was a big crowd down at the wharf, light rain again, but the respectful Fijian silence was most worrying to us expecting crowds to join in the songs which the band are playing. As usual, a massed Fijian choir sang hymns! Sir Derek and Fijian guests then came ashore, and the Queen Mother stood alone under a spotlight so her tiara and crystal-embroidered dress glittered. H.E. couldn't bear the silence and got the band leader to call for three cheers as the ship drew out. This was unprecedented but they responded. It was very touching, the brightly lit little ship moving off into the misty night with the one tiny figure waving and waving."

Shell collecting – a wonderful experience almost too late

Rosemary saw a Shell Club promotional display in a shop-window, and was very struck. She got in touch and went out with the Club. She described the outing: "I have been out once with the Shell Club. A comic looking group in all sorts of old clothes to keep off the sun but very short so as not to get wet, topees and straw hats and all, with gumboots or canvas shoes below. They choose a Saturday or Sunday about once a month when there's a very low tide and go out to a reef two hours before low tide and stay until two hours after. You wander along looking in crevices and turning over any loose pieces of coral. Very sharp eyes are needed, as some have mantles (the 'foot') which almost cover the shell, and some have husk-like growths or deposits on them. We have 'viewers', round tins with a handle and glass bottom, which are excellent. I picked up everything I found, but the more discriminating members just take an odd one or two leaving the ones I got excited about. But I found one of the best shells of the day, an unusual, pretty cone shell which several experienced members didn't have in their collections. It was poisonous but dead, and in good condition."

Prior to her arrival in Suva, the Queen Mother had boarded Britannia from Nadi airport and spent two nights and Good Friday near a large island south of Suva having a rest. Apparently they picnicked on an islet in a lagoon and she gathered shells for Margaret. Hearing of this on her last night Ratu Mara, one of the Fijian chiefs at the farewell dinner on the Britannia, shouted orders over the side to a henchman who sped to his home, and half an hour later H.M. was presented with a rare golden cowrie for Margaret, We hoped she realised its value: between £50 and £100. Ratu Mara only possessed two himself.

Bows and arrows

Meanwhile I had joined the Archery Club. This was a small group well run by Geoff Moller of the Bank of New South Wales and his team, who had a highly professional attitude to the sport. Papa had always been intrigued by the bow and its use in war, and I had had a light bow and arrows for a time as a boy. Here since no guns were allowed, now was my chance to shoot! I tentatively applied, and was so pleased to be welcomed as a complete novice.

I was presented with a bow of only 30lb pull, but it took me three days before I could string it! I never got anywhere in competitions, but it was fun trying to improve my performance, I found it much harder than with a rifle. Luckily the curving open slopes of our garden border with our co-operative neighbour, allowed me to hold archery parties at home with club members, shooting from our lawn across at targets placed on his side of our dividing gully. When we came to leave Fiji I was presented with a beautifully framed, embroidered blazer badge, and a citation signed by all the members.

A shock in May 1966

In May I learnt that I was to be posted back to Iran, as Regional Director, Isfahan. This was terrific news, but we had become fond of Fiji, and had asked for two tours at least. Now to have another mid-tour move was hard on Rosemary. The house, the excellent new girl, Sarah, "the boat, the Shell Club, the garden, the sea, the view, the cats – to have all this snatched untimely from one is very hard," she wrote. In Fiji we had good food supplies, medical facilities, security, and no corruption. Life was so simple and straightforward. Now we would return to the constant alertness needed in Iran, the attitudes of the Persians, and Islam. And as Rosemary had seen from Tehran, the wife of a Regional Director is one of the hardest working jobs for a Council wife. But there it was, and in reality I knew we'd love to be back in Iran. Fancy being paid to live in Isfahan. Fortunately, our cats found a sympathetic and caring home with Gordon King of the F.B.C.

Bad news followed. I was not goint to be replaced, and the Council's operations in Fiji were to be closed down: but I was not to announce this until told to do so. The University of the South Pacific was about to open in Suva . . .

There was little time to philosophise. In July we had to pack urgently in order to get the baggage to a ship which would dock at Bushire in time for our arrival in Isfahan by air in the near future. The pace of life began to hot up. We had two friends visiting from New Zealand, and Rosemary took them out of Suva for a break.

She came back early to put on a book exhibition on Taveuni Island for me. Next she had the four appreciative Swedes of the Kyndel Quartet to look after: to administer their three concerts and to take them sight-seeing and shopping. The Fiji Arts Council was in business!

THE BRITISH COUNCIL

ᴍᴴ

Albion House   59 New Oxford Street   London W C 1

Covent Garden 2468

Reference   FIJI/221/3

21st November, 1966.

Dear Mr. Halsted,

Representative's House, Suva

It was so nice to receive your letter FIJI/0300/2 of the 12th November, 1966 and to read the kind things said of Supplies and Despatch Department.   I feel sure such remarks act as a spur to my staff to continue acquiring all the knowledge they can and thus be better qualified to help in the selection and purchase of suitable furniture and equipment.   I will therefore ensure that all concerned see your letter.

With thanks,

Yours ever,

F. A. JENNINGS,
Director,
Supplies and Despatch Department.

J. M. G. Halsted, Esq.,
The Representative,
Suva, FIJI.

faj/ad

Now came an exciting stimulus for us at such a time but which was not our responsibility. The Indian Kalekshetra Ballet arrived from Madras, a very professional, lively group. The dancers performed beautifully in a programme of dance dramas based on ancient tales. We never learned what the Fijians thought about the very different Indian culture in their midst.

315

Paper-Hanging Again!
The best at Harry Charman's All Races Club

Now sloughing off so many responsibilities, I was delighted to play the part of M.C. in an Old-Time Music Hall at Harry Charman's Club. Remembering the Fiji Arts Council's production of South Pacific, I knew that there was plenty of talent available to put on a reasonable entertainment. On the stage I loved telling dreadful jokes and taking part in a rapid succession of short, lively acts of double-entendre. And, best of all, I had a super team for 'Paper-Hanging' again.[10]

---

[10] I sent Papa a photo of me on stage on the floor balancing a glass of water on my forehead, a trick learned in hospital. He couldn't make it out at all, and pasted it vertically in his scrap-book!

Work-wise I had to visit a school at Sigatoka and to make an encouraging speech at the Teacher Training College in Suva. (For such an occasion I found Gilbert Highet's *The Art of Teaching* very useful.) With matters under control, Rosemary and I managed a short break on Wakaya again. We went over in the estate longboat on rather a rough crossing. Half-way over the engine stopped. I went several shades greener from mal-de-mer and apprehension, but it was "only water in the fuel". After this visit I had a triumph for the estate. The Commissioner of Police allowed the manager a BSA .308 rifle, to prevent further cruelty to animals wounded by their .22.

Sydney again for me

Dr J. de Beaux thought I ought to have a proper medical check before returning to sandy deserts. The British Council was slightly shocked, but it was understanding about my old wounds, and agreed. So off I flew to Sydney. Cousin Des and Lesley met me and took me along to the War Memorial (Veterans) Hospital in Birrell Street, where I was admirably looked after.

I had first-class attention from Peter Duke, the leading ophthalmologist who had studied under Tony Palin in Bristol, my ophthalmologist from war days in Oxford. Duke would remove a cyst. I was also examined by the orthopaedic surgeon Dr Hodgkinson. He decided that the best way to cure the pain in my left foot was to fillet out the bone in one toe.

Two operations? Oh dear. Luckily, the Sydney surgeons agreed to my suggestion and operated on me at both ends while I was under the one anaesthetic. All went well and the nurses were terrific. I have all their names! I listened to The Beatles for the first time ('Yellow Submarine'), and to The Seekers whom I always loved, especially their singer, Judy Durham, who had such an appealing timbre.

I now had another of my life's strokes of luck. Keith Colwill, formerly the Australian military attaché in Rangoon, was now based in the beautiful Victoria Barracks, Sydney, and he and his family of three girls, took me in to recuperate in their spacious quarters. I shall never forget the film of *Dr Zivago*, to which I took them.

Meanwhile, Rosemary, who remained in Suva, with Merle Beynon coped splendidly with a visit from the high-powered William Clark (I had fixed his programme): Head of the Overseas Development Institute; on the Council of the British Council and V.S.O.; T.V. paneller; and Foreign Editor of *The Observer*. The Council was withdrawing but there were more V.S.O.s coming, whom Rosemary enjoyed meeting and helping: "such lovely pink cheeks," she remarked. The Vienna Trio came next: "Oh what a joy to hear Schubert played by Viennese," Rosemary exclaimed.

She was next asked to help put up the annual flower show. Then a new V.S.O. came to stay. Rosemary was now asked to assist in cataloguing the new Pacific Theological College Library. It was a shame that she would have to miss the job.

I returned to Suva to enjoy sick-leave with a three-day trip, generously given by the Kays, cruising with Rosemary round the Yasawa Islands. The Yasawas are a string of mainly high islands to the north-west, with many lovely beaches. This was a strange time for us: it was sadly wonderful since it would be our last; the sea was calm and we revelled in the sunshine.

Everywhere we visited Rosemary swam and snorkled. The water was perfectly, excitingly clear.

In the early evenings up in the bows I would look out for dolphins which often appeared and swam in beautiful curves along with us. I blew a triton shell which I could use to try to call them. Maybe they heard me, and therefore they came? I could blow this 'horn', as a flute is blown. I learned where to tap a hole, and managed to tap one myself. Every hole tapped in a triton shell comes out square. Why?

The triton has another connotation for us. The senior, well-loved Chief of the Islands died. He was the father of Ratu Sir Kamisese Mara, later the first Prime Minister at Independence in 1970. Throughout the days of his lying-in-state, in Suva, relays of retainers sat at the corners of his coffin and blew their triton horns, keeping a deeply traditional sacred rite of continuous sound. It sounded very mournful at night.

On our return to Suva we had the sad task on 'Black Monday' of announcing the closure of the British Council, and getting on with the whole business of it. H.E. had returned from home leave and was upset at the Council's decision, but he was most supportive of us in the painful process.

The announcement shocked the people of Fiji, especially the British residents. Many refused to accept this as a permanent closure, and most were very sad. The hardest part was losing our loyal local and household staff, and having to put it about that they needed re-employment.

It was Black Monday for the Fiji Government too. All Government Departments were reeling under the shock of a budget with drastic cuts. The boom of the last few years was over. The world prices of sugar and copra had dropped, and production was reduced for six months by the drought conditions following the two hurricanes and floods.

At least Rosemary got away for a bitter-sweet last reef visit and a picnic on an island with five V.S.O.s in two rowing boats from a Fijian village. Then came kind farewell invitations from our friends; our own large cocktail party at the Council; and later having special friends up to the house before leaving Tamavua for the Grand Pacific Hotel again.

Rosemary went ahead of me to fly home to Edinburgh to collect, pack, and bring out our warm clothes. Her flight to Prestwick luckily allowed her a stop-over in Montreal, where her brother John was a Professor of English at McGill University's Institute of Education.

I was 'removed' from the hotel by H.E. to Government House for a couple of nights. I remember clearly the beautiful walks which Derek and I took round the lovely, palm-treed grounds of Government House and beyond. His kind gesture softened the blow. I flew to Sydney for a final check-up, and to buy over the counter a beautiful, new, light .222 Brno. rifle.

On I went to Tony and Gerd Lee (of Burma days) in Hong-Kong, thence to Calcutta, Karachi, and Tehran for briefing before flying down to Isfahan. Isfahan – 'Nesvi Jahan' – Half the World. It has remained so for us. "But Fiji," Rosemary wrote, "was a very pleasant place to live. The Fijians are so endearing."

District Officer, Rewa

John Deverell was promoted to be Commissioner Central and he later distinguished himself in Intelligence. It is a pleasure to be in touch at home with friends made in one or another country. But John we shall never see again.

He was one of the Security Service victims of the Chinook helicopter crash on 2 June 1994. He had been due to retire the following month. His obituary in the *Times* states: 'His particular affinity was for district administration in which he worked with outstanding success as a District Officer'. So I well remember . . .

To Isfahan, Iran, 1966–1970

December 1966

Posted to Isfahan! I could hardly believe it. Rosemary solved the mid-tour clothing problem by flying home from hot Suva and getting lots of warm clothes out of store in Edinburgh and air-freighting one suitcase to me in cold Isfahan.

In Tehran our Representative, Stephen (and Joan) Bach, kindly put me up. I could not have served under a better man: he was fair, sharp, and understanding. He was a Persian scholar and a Farsi speaker. His personality and sympathy for Iran made a great difference to our life.

One evening I was borne off to the birthday party of Miss Palmer-Smith, a well-known and loved Tehran character.[1] She was a former governess to a British Ambassador's children, and then to a number of Persian noble families. She must have had quite an influence on Persian affairs in her day, judging by the manner in which she was revered. The English Governess abroad was a sterling figure.

I spotted a tall, serene lady standing alone and I introduced myself, asking who she was. "I am Lady Wright," she replied, looking me in the eye. I met Sir Denis Wright later. He was British Ambassador in Iran from 1963 to 1971, and was first class. Sir Denis was well aware of the pressures on the B.C. man in Isafahan (and on his wife) and that streams of visitors made for this beautiful city. He was careful who he sent to us, or to whom he mentioned our presence out of the many official visitors who called upon him and desired a break in Isfahan.

I flew down to Isfahan in excitement, to take over from James Mandy, who had been with me in Queen Alexandra's Military Hospital during the war in 1944.

A surprise safari

Before Rosemary arrived I was whisked off by Sir Denis and Stephen Bach in the Council car, driven by Babai (still our senior driver from

---

[1] Vita-Sackville West wrote of her: "Palmer-Smith defies description. She must be seen to be believed." *Vita Sackville-West's Letters to Virginia Woolf* (Hutchinson, 1984), p. 1.

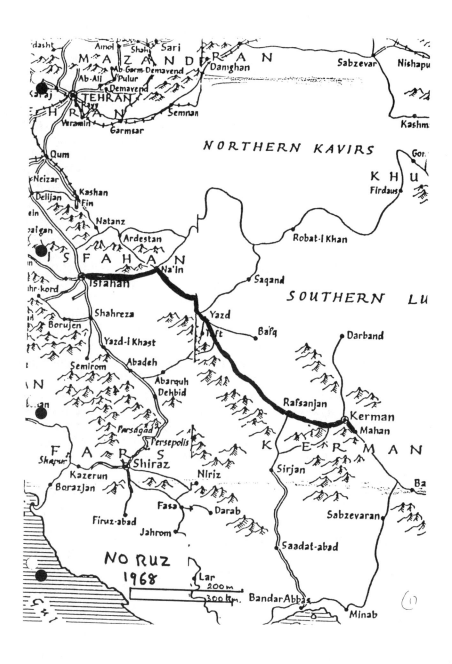

Tehran days), to the desert in the south-west to see at Cham Gordan the site of the Russian steel mill, and the Persian railway link from the south. Babai turned out to be our host as well. He drove us to his house in a village not far away to spend the night. His family welcomed us with typical Persian hospitality.

Persian houses and life in them are not quite the same as in the West. Houses may be of one or two floors, and consist of a series of rooms opening one into another. There is usually a deep verandah in front, and a flat roof on which to sleep in hot weather. There would be an outside pool, and the whole house would probably be contained within high mud walls. There are no bedrooms as such, no beds and few, if any, chairs. For bedding, Persians rolled out light mattresses and quilts or blankets straight onto the carpets in one or another room depending on the household state at the time. Sir Denis, Stephen, and I were allotted a downstairs room in which to lay out our bedding.

I made myself as inconspicuous a junior as possible. There was a loo, but washing facilities were pots, jugs, and bowls filled from the pool. As we lay down to sleep Sir Denis looked sternly at us, and said "I hope no-one snores?" "Oh, no, sir!" But someone did.

After Stephen Bach, Sir Denis Wright was the other main character in our happy life. He had been Chargé and Counsellor in Tehran from 1953–1955. He was perfect for the job.[2] He is a scholar and Persian speaker, and a fellow Aularian ten years before me. He and his wife, Iona,[3] have both given us great support and friendship from these days on.

On our first arrival in Tehran in 1957, we had been ignorant of the influence of Persia on the West. partly due to the narrowness of British school and college syllabi. But we soon grew to appreciate the great beauty of the country. We learned enough Farsi to go anywhere where we could go with confidence in our Land Rover, especially in what was a perfect climate for much of the year.

In Fiji in 1964 I had written a letter home, without an inkling of a return to Iran:

> The inner rewards from service in a country such as Iran remain memorable and unmatched. In spite of certain aspects of life in Iran such as the political and student unrest, the tribal problems , the corruption and the poverty, the whole country was completely satisfying to the soul. Hardly a day passed on which we did not revel in the whole atmosphere of ancient history and culture, the

[2] On 13 June 1991 Sir Denis Wright, G.C.M.G. lectured to the Royal Society for Asian Affairs on 'Ten Years in Iran – Some Highlights'. See Appendix I.
[3] See her *Black Sea Bride* (Square One Publications, 1997).

beauty and grandeur of the scenery, the contrast between bare mountain and green river valley, the glories of architecture, and the excitement of travel.

Our friends were Persian, British Embassy and British banking and commerce of the highest quality. They all responded to the country and were alive and stimulating. We shot and climbed and ski-ed and drove and danced and sang with the nightingales in a mountain orchard.

Now we were returning to Iran in excited anticipation to a city known throughout the Persian world as Half-the-World, Nesfi-Jahan. We felt a little dampened down by the responsibilities ahead of us.

Early Isfahan

Isfahan was on the route of the great trade caravans from China and India, as they passed between desert and mountain on their way to the west. The city lies in an oasis on a 4–5000 ft. plateau, on the banks of the only river of the region, the Zayandeh Rud. The river rises in the Zagros mountains to the west, and disappears into the desert in the east.

The Seljuk Turks ruled Iran between 1037 and 1187, and built the great new dome of the Friday Mosque in 1086, an amazing feat of architecture then. The Mongols under Genghis Khan destroyed much of the city, so did the Timurids, but both also built splendidly.

In 1499 Shah Ismail saved the region from chaos, and became the founder of the Safavid Dynasty 1499–1736. His son Shah Tahmasp unified the country over his fifty-year reign, and became known as a powerful oriental ruler with whom the West was able to trade. In fact he gave time for Persia to regain the fame lost with the fall of Darius.

Shah Abbas the Great ruled from 1586 to 1628. He secured his frontiers and moved his capital to a central site at the provincial town of Isfahan. He left it the equal of Cairo or Constantinople, i.e. one of the greatest cities of the world, the fame of which spread to all the courts of Europe.[4] His grand design included some of the most beautiful religious buildings in the world. He also built an imposing pavilion known as Chehel Situn (Forty Pillars), for the state reception of foreign ambassadors and emissaries who came to admire and learn.

Another aspect of the Shah's greatness was the improvement of communications, which included the establishment of fort-like caravan-serai every twenty miles for the safe sojourn at night for travellers and

[4] Wilfred Blunt, *Isfahan, Pearl of Persia* (Elek Books, 1966).

traders, and their camels and pack animals. We enjoyed visiting the remains of such buildings as we could reach.

At home at night in Isfahan we occasionally heard a camel train passing. We also heard one once from the chaikhane in which we were staying on a shooting trip. Our hearts would beat faster on hearing the steady, deep bells of the great Bactrian camels, evocative sounds swelling and dying as the beasts padded past.

> Come to the wells, the desert wells!
> The caravan is marching down:
> I hear the camel bells.
> > J. E. Flecker.

One caravanserai does survive in Isfahan, a great central edifice, which was restored as a first-class hotel: the Shah Abbas. We found it most heartening to experience a form of the original atmosphere, and to appreciate the faithfully reproduced examples of Persian decorative art of many periods.

Shah Abbas also undertook public works and irrigation projects to the point of attempting to channel water from the Karun river, which flows south from the mountains in the west to the Persian Gulf, to flow east into the valley of the Zayandeh Rud.

Shah Abbas even resettled peoples to pacify his country, for instance Kurds were moved from the west to Khorasan in the east as a defence against the Uzbecks. He brought Armenians from Georgia to Isfahan to provide skilled labour. They are still here, across the river in Julfa. He brought European and Chinese craftsmen to practice their skills, and no doubt to instruct in fresco painting, pottery, and tile mosaic. The Chinese influence is clear in many early Persian works of art.

Art and architecture

Without Robert Byron's illuminating work *The Road to Oxiana* (John Lehmann, London 1950), we would never have been able to appreciate as much as we did in the time we had in Iran. What he wrote cannot be equalled and stands as a perfect introduction to Islamic art and architecture, and from which I quote here:

> It will soon be obvious to you as you gain closer contact with Persian art and architecture, that the Persians have an intense love of beauty in all forms. Life is grim for many who live in stark surroundings and suffer from heat and cold; and the real lives of

324

Decorative use of calligraphy

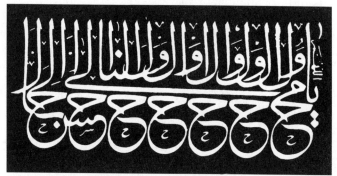

Prayer in Thuluth, playing on the letter *h*; Turkey, probably 19th century.

Praise of the Prophet Muhammad, written by the Ottoman Sultan
Mahmūd II (Turkey, around 1810).

ar-rizq 'ala'llāh "The sustenance is upon God" in the "flame-script"
invented by I. H. Baltacioglu, Turkey 1955.

a great many Persians are reflected in the fatalism and pessimism of parts of their literature – such as Omar Khayam.

This love of beauty, which exists in all classes and is an instinctive joy, is revealed in a thousand years of wonderful pottery, metal-work, carpet-weaving, miniature painting and unexcelled designs for carved stucco, calligraphy and tile-work. Of course, the passion for colour in the Islamic art of Iran, which, as you will soon appreciate, achieved such an intensity and harmony, was generated by the landscape.

. . . light has always been regarded as an element of the divine, and of good, opposed to the evil of darkness. In Persian art, both light and clarity are sought, echoing the intense brightness and clarity of the light in the country. The turquoise, dark blue, yellow and green tile-work on flat or domed surfaces is dazzling, and perfect. Balance and symmetry are strictly observed, and there is never a sense of conflict of colours.

Islam feared a return to idolatry, and the priesthood was against any representation of the living form, so the artist transformed his inspirations into ornament of line and colour. The devising of every kind of floral and geometric design was a challenge to his imagination. The most successful compositions could be found both in mosques or on carpets. However complex the pattern, the effect was always tranquil to the eye.

14. THE TWO BASIC TYPES OF KNOT USED IN PERSIA

1. TURKĪ (TURKISH) KNOT   2. FARSĪ (PERSIAN) KNOT

used by weavers of   *used by weavers of*
Turkish or Kurdish race   *Persian race*

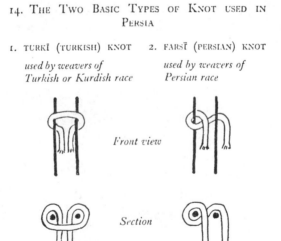

Front view

Section

From that classic book *The Persian Carpet*, by A. Cecil Edwards, repr. 1960, Gerald Duckworth & Co. Ltd., London.

The great Isfahan bazaar was one of the finest in the world, only surpassed by Fes in Morocco. It handled much of the goods of trade caravans from China, Central Asia, and India which passed through Iran leaving a lasting influence on the arts and crafts. In the same way the arts of Iran had a profound influence on Western culture.

The most colourful interest in the Isfahan bazaar was that it was a manufacturing bazaar. Everything was made by hand, off broad, high-arched domed passageways. Of principal interest were the printers of textiles (qalamkar) using hand-held wooden blocks carved in ancient motifs. We have an old, worn one in boté, which is known as Paisley pattern! We loved the tile workers and their beautiful colours and patterns, even produced to one's requirements. There was everything one could imagine being made – from taps to copper trays, which one could order. Felt was another special product: for tribal hats, carpets, horse-coverings, rugs, blankets, cloaks and coats. Isfahan had its own sweetmeat made in the bazaar, called gaz. It came in little, flat, wooden boxes containing white lumps of a very hard form of jaw-sticking nougat with nuts. Edible oils such as sesame were also processed in the Isfahan bazaar.

Our treasured memories are also of an ancient people who were hospitable and congenial and in Byron's words, "with great powers of survival under the most fearful circumstances: having a philosophy we could well emulate, in which beauty has a particular place even for the hardest of lives."[5]

James Elroy Flecker during his short, sad life must have been inspired by the East to write *Hassan*. In it the poet Ishak, threatened with execution at dawn by his capricious 'friend' the Caliph, speaks these words which to me are so evocative of our happy years in Iran:

> Thy dawn, O Master of the world, thy dawn;
> The hour that lilies open on the lawn,
> The hour the grey wings pass beyond the mountains,
> The hour of silence, when we hear the fountains,
> The hour that dreams are brighter and winds colder,
> The hour that young love wakes on a white shoulder,
> O Master of the world, the Persian Dawn.

Life begins

On 19 December 1966 Rosemary joined me. She wrote: "I arrived at the airport after a wonderfully smooth jet flight, to find Michael, James

---

[5] Byron, *Road to Oxiana.*

Mandy, the Hamburgers and the Prince all waiting. I nearly passed the others as I never expected them. It was a beautiful morning to arrive, everything bathed in miraculous light which is brilliantly clear and luminous without glare. The silvery trunks of the chenars and poplars stood serried against the pale-blue sky. We took a little drive yesterday and it was lovely to be out again in the brown and blue and green. There are many 'edifices' to visit, and exciting mountains and shapes, the whole more sympathetic and congenial than the north." I found that the extreme, dry, cold air on the 5000 ft. plateau quite hurt my nose as I breathed.

One of the splendidly loyal and indefatigable characters on my staff was Eric Hamburger, Colonial Magistrate in Central Africa, Lieutenant-Colonel, R.A., in Burma, and a former C.M.S. administrator. He was an excellent teacher of English literature up to Cambridge Proficiency, and was appreciated and respected in Isfahan. You can imagine his retort when I accused him of destroying the beautiful Fort in Mandalay, the ancient Burmese capital. But he was a totally reliable second-in-command.

His wife Ellen was a jewel. She had been a nurse. She was cheerful and full of humour, patient, generous, and highly competent. She played a big part in the British Council, whilst also working for John McDouall, being in charge of staff at his Iran-Tour Hotel. I was happy to be in the Iran-Tour again after eight years; there was no change except for the better. John is English-Armenian. He was a very special person to us, and to many Isfahanis. He was always a saintly supporter of the Christian Church, the Mission and the hospital. He lives in England now. His wife, Arax, alas, died in 1997.

The other vital personage in our life and work was Prince Jahangir Massoud, known as Shazdeh (Prince). He was a descendant of the family of the last Qajar Governor who lived in Isfahan, and who owned property in the Hezar Jerib (Thousand Acres) across the river from the city, which now contained the British Council Centre and residence. He acted as librarian for which he wasn't trained, but he did his best, and Rosemary, who enjoys library work, helped him when she could. When I first met him at his desk he was in the process of sorting a collection of rifle and shotgun ammunition. An excellent portent, I thought. He was elderly, tall, thin, and elegant, a unique treasure who made our lives so much easier by smoothing our paths through the Isfahan maze. He was thereby invaluable to the British Council.

In the days of the 'Great Game' there were twenty-three British Consulates in Iran. The British Council later came to replace Consulates; and certainly to occupy the lovely old premises of two of the former Consulates, Meshed and Shiraz. The British Council is non-diplomatic and we had no consular status anywhere. I was not a diplomat, but a British Council officer. I am not sure that the authorities everywhere believed this, which was tricky. Shazdeh for instance had earlier been in British Consular Service. Now he was on our staff, and he liked to play his former role, and keep up our status as he saw us; but it had to be as we saw ourselves, and we had to treat him gently. However, Shazdeh was our guide, philosopher, and friend; and the Council did not suffer. There was, however, the odd occasion in which I had to act in a consular capacity. There was a problem when two English cabaret girls were stuck in Isfahan without having received any pay, and of course they came to me. Luckily Shazdeh sorted out their problems; he knew everybody. He was especially useful for ensuring that I did not unintentionally ignore a senior official at some diplomatic function.

Our lack of a working knowledge of Farsi and its script was a handicap and left us in ignorance of what was affecting the lives of all around us; but we had never had a chance to specialise. However, Shazdeh kept us informed. Our handicap reinforced the fact that the British Council never became involved in politics or religion.

Shazdeh could organise a mouflon or sandgrouse shoot, or introduce me to Governor Parsa of Isfahan, or to General Partow, Chief of Police: or act as interpreter when meeting Isfahani worthies, such as in fine arts or antiquities. General Partow was a delightful character with whom we got on well. One day he said to us: "My job is not easy". "No," I said, "I can imagine that". "But," said the General, "I really need one policeman per Persian: and even then I can't always trust the policeman." I got quite a shock one New Year's Day when I received a personal telephone call from General Tagavhi, the head of Isfahan Savak – the secret police. I gulped. The voice said: "A Happy New Year. I hope you enjoyed your picnic?" I relaxed – perhaps audibly. I had no guilty conscience, but I took note – that he knew everything.

On our own in our new home

Rosemary had only two hours with James Mandy discussing domestic matters before he left for England. We took over the very attractive, if not entirely practical, establishment across the river from the city. There was a lovely irrigated orchard garden, and a two-storied, typically Persian house, with an imposing, tall, pillared, open, raised verandah. The office and library were on the ground floor. The classrooms were adjoining, and in out-buildings. We lived in a sort of flat on the first floor. This was not very convenient, but it was agreeable. From our elevation we had a good view of the garden, and also an inspiring outlook down-river to a range of pink-grey hills.

Mohammed was our cook and house-servant. As he started with a tray-full of crockery and food up the long, steep stairway, Rosemary would shudder as she heard the familiar Persian cry: "Ya, Allah!" which was used as an encouragement; here as a prayer not to drop the tray – he never did.

We inherited three Massoud servants: Hassan, who was short with a bushy, black moustache and a proprietorial air, was our ferash, our messenger and general factotum; and Seyed Hussein, our elderly, benign gate-keeper and watchman. The Council paid and uniformed these two. The third, Abbas the gardener, an original Persian of the soil, was still in the employ of the Massouds. He dressed in a loose coat of any old, heavy material; and baggy, black, cotton trousers of standard village dress; heavy, cotton shoes (ghivé); and a brown, pudding-basin, felt hat. I gave him my old British warm which he cherished. At irrigation time we and any guests from the tropics were fascinated to see him clearing channels and directing the flow of water by temporary earth dams.

George Alexander, an Armenian, was our accountant. He had a very talented pianist daughter. Young Ruhollah Moslemi was my bright, conscientious and essential administrative assistant. Nasser drove the office, green Land Rover well.

Christmas

Christmas 1966 was upon us. The climate was perfect: cold, night frosts, still air and bright sun almost every day. It was pretty quiet. Rosemary found it more trouble to adjust to the 5000-ft. altitude than I did. But this gave her a better chance to sleep, and to sleep off the exertions of the move, both mental and physical. There was a C.M.S. party one night, and carols to listen to the next, and a great lunch by Ellen Hamburger after two church services. Guests included three C.M.S. hospital volunteers, and to our delight, Ralph Pinder-Wilson from the British Museum. He is a Persian scholar, charming, and tremendously interesting. This retiring, gentle man has patiently shared his knowledge with us over the years.

Work – for us both

As British Council Regional Representative my main task was to organize the teaching of English. This remains a popular subject of study every-where since a knowledge of English is a stepping stone to higher studies and to getting on in the world. The demand for English classes by adults and senior students made the whole atmosphere of our life in Isfahan even sunnier. In a couple of years I got the nominal roll up to 700. Having seven hundred Persian pupils was pretty taxing, but of course some classes were particularly rewarding and often fun. Teaching adults who pay to learn is a different matter from teaching schoolboys.

Eric Hamburger and I were able to reward ourselves respectively, with Eric taking the Senior Cambridge Proficiency Classes for English literature, and I the Use of English paper. For my texts I was able to get cheaply from the B.B.C. multiple copies of *The Listener*. Eric of course had his set books. One or two of our pupils were the children of French construction executives. Such families made a pleasant leaven in Isfahan society. When all the students had departed at the end of the teaching day, at about 7.30 p.m., we did sometimes breathe a sigh of relief.

Obtaining top-class teachers was my headache. They had to be good enough to satisfy British Council standards, and our pretty choosy pupils. All the teachers, except for Eric and myself, had to be locally-employed. The teachers already recruited locally, and those whom I took on, could only be paid in local currency, the rial, for the hours they taught. The British Council could not afford to allow me to give any of them contracts. Those who were the British wives of Persians or of other nationalities, or British residents such as Mission staff, did not need contracts, nor support beyond their salaries. My teachers were a fine team: Mr Faghighian and Mr Zandy were the Persians teaching beginners: Miss Aidin and Miss Eardley of the Mission taught the third and fourth years; Elizabeth Ramsay, out on a local mission contract, and English-born Mrs Christine Chalian taught the fifth year. These residents were less of a worry to me than the young British teachers whom I was very glad to employ if they were qualified or experienced, such as Geoff Squires from the Isfahan University Department of English. All who came except Geoff had to manage to live from the fees for the hours of teaching English which I was able to allot them. This was unfairly precarious for such loyal and keen young people, especially when the examination results they obtained were very satisfactory.

I was very fortunate to have in my second tour two young Cambridge graduates, Sebastian Cleaver and David Marshall whom I had interviewed in London when on leave. They came out and coped very well together. In fact it was Sebastian who interviewed me – at the Ritz, as he suggested!

And then in Isfahan out of the blue I received letters from Hilary Torrance and Elizabeth Kessler, both Oxford graduates, who wanted to come out together to teach. From their C.V.s I told them to come at once and I rejoiced when they did. I soon gauged that both were ahead of me intellectually. They made the very best of life in Iran.

Husbands and wives

It is in these one-man posts such as Isfahan, Fiji, and Guyana that Council officers' wives are stretched to the limit. Rosemary was essential to me, and was willing and able to play an active part from morning to night in many aspects of my life and work. One of her regular tasks here, apart from household chores, was running a ladies' conversation group once a week in our living room, assisted when possible by Ellen Hamburger. I know this was appreciated by the ladies who took part, and certainly by me because most of them were wives of eminent Isfahanis, whom the British Council was glad to help. We often met them at functions and we enjoyed their hospitality too.

Rosemary's association with any of these very charming ladies could never go beyond these group occasions. She was well aware that we had to distance ourselves from politics and the problems of individuals. So it was inadvisable, owing to the smallness of Isfahan society and the Persian nature, to make particular friends with anyone. Another task for Rosemary was to act as relief librarian on occasions, which, luckily, she enjoyed.

Wives on parade: Guests of Isfahan city

We were touched that the Isfahan authorities regularly invited us to join their official Receptions for foreign crowned heads and other dignitaries. This usually meant Rosemary and I, Eric and Ellen, and Shazdeh, (but not his wife, as they were Muslims), parading in morning dress in the airport lounge. We only had one top hat between us, and that was Shazdeh's! We had no limousine, but we looked as dignified as we could in the Council Land Rover. At least we had a respectable uniformed chauffeur in Nasser. It could be fun. It could be very cold. But at least the occasions were like morning, drink-free cocktail parties at which one could make useful contact with resident diplomats and Persian dignitaries, until we were taken out and lined up along the red carpet on the tarmac. On one occasion a jet turned too close too soon, and blew our red carpet away.

Unofficial guides

A major wifely task was taking charge of specialist visitors when I was working or teaching and the specialists had the time they needed to relax and sightsee. Rosemary revelled in this guiding task. She soon knew her way around the whole bazaar, and had mastered the facts the visitors needed to know about the famous buildings and bridges. She managed all of this on top of organising dinner parties for these men and women and their opposite numbers. How rewarding and appreciative our visitors were.[6] At the Council she would on other occasions without a murmur turn to help me and the staff with touring exhibitions. At Christmas time she would arrange student parties as well as occasions for our own guests. She would play an essential part in play-readings. When we had proper plays put on by our Tehran staff, she acted both as stage hand and hostess! Sometimes she would assist me with one of my talks by operating my slide projector. She knew exactly which picture I needed, and when.

One of my jobs: Propping up the premises

Persian vernacular buildings were made of the only available materials, mud and wood. Our class-rooms were flat-roofed with thin, poplar trunk beams and mud brick. Collapses would come after years of the roofs being annually re-surfaced with more mud with stone rollers after winter snows, and the roofs finally becoming too heavy for the beams. When a classroom roof collapsed it needed replacing very quickly, to keep the classes going. We later came to need some accommodation and toilet facilities for young British travellers whom we were very ready to help, but not in our living-quarters! I found an unused ground-floor room which I was allowed to make into an extra bathroom. Unfortunately, I couldn't spend money on lovely Persian bath-tiles.

Our situation

Rosemary wrote "We have only to go across the Si-o-Seh Pol, the thirty-three arch bridge, and we are in the Chahar Bagh, the Four Gardens of Shah Abbas, now the main shopping street. The river bed is seldom covered with water, there are just blue channels among golden grass, but wide. It is one kilometre from our gate to the far side of the bridge. But it is fun walking all the way over with the changing vistas through the side arches." We never failed to enjoy the shifting scenes in the city streets, especially the wonderful portal, the twin minarets, and the dome of the Theological College.

---

[6] See the kind letter I received from the House of Commons, appendix . . .

Isfahan society

For our own satisfaction and for our visitors, we learnt as much as possible of local art, architecture and history. In these subjects we were greatly assisted by Dr Lotfullah Honarfar, Director of Isfahan's Department of Antiquities, with whom we fortunately had cordial relations. He was a key figure in Isfahan. He was the Oracle summoned to guide crowned heads, princes, politicians and V.I.P.s of many nationalities who were accorded the Isfahan treatment by the Persian Government, or by foreign Embassies. This task he loved and did so well. He had an authoritative presence, but was the most courteous of guides. We were lucky to enjoy his hospitality in his treasure-filled home, and hear of fascinating discoveries of art and architecture.

We met Isa Bahadori, Head of the Fine Art School, and a particular friend of Shazdeh's. We learned quite a bit from Bahadori when we visited his school about the training of future classic Islamic artists and craftsmen, which seemed to consist of copying again and again patterns of the past to perfection. This seemed soulless, but as Titus Burckhart wrote:

> Islamic art is far less a way of expressing emotion than a science. A Muslim artist will willingly subordinate his individuality to the, as it were, objective and impersonal beauty of his work.[7]

Then there were Caro Minassian and Dr Sepanta with their scholarship, and rare collections of ancient artefacts. Caro's son, Carlyle and his comely English wife, Lindy, ran an excellent little hotel. We were introduced to all these worthies by Shazdeh. They in turn told us from whom to buy our own treasures. We never spent enough money, which with hindsight after our Tehran days, we should have done.

In my working day I often had contact with university professors from the Vice-Chancellor down. For instance Mr Z. N. Davidian of the Department of International Relations was particularly helpful and knowledgeable. The most charismatic character was Dr Nawab, Deputy Dean of the Medical Faculty. He was a genial, lovable poet of distinction. He would recite from his works on official occasions, which would draw loud "Bah! Bah!s" of Persian approval from the assembly.

Dr and Mrs Sedigheh Rastegar, she of the Massoud family, were very supportive of us. Another good friend was the architect Mohandes (engineer) Ali Asghar Bakhtiar and his sweet wife, Lili. He had studied in London and has served his country with distinction and sensitivity.

On our side of the fence were some particularly fine C.M.S. men and

[7] 'The Nature and Role of Sacred Art', *Art of Islam* (World of Islam Press, 1976).

Form of Basmalah

In the shape of a stork.
Turkey, 19th Century

The invocation, "Bism Allah al-rahman al-Rahim" (In the name of God, the Compassionate, the Merciful) is known as the Basmalah, from 'Bism Allah . . .' which stands at the beginning of anything written. The forms of the arabic letter for these words allow them to be used by the artists who are inspired by the prophetic, "He who writes beautiful 'Bismillah' obtains innumerable blessings" to create the most fanciful patterns and shapes.

women headed by Bishop Hassan Dehqani-Tafti and his wife, Margaret, daughter of the famous Bishop Thompson. The Bishop's secretary, Dora Udale, who was a missionary of long-standing, became a good friend.

There was the Mission Hospital headed by Dr Peter Wild, a dedicated and very wise man, and his wife, Mary. Then there were Drs Ron and Molly Pont and their children, and nurses such as Ena Burke and Sue Hargreaves. They gave us friendship and confidence. Luckily, we seldom needed treatment. For dentistry which I did need, my Persian dentist, Dr Khalili, was expert.

Another fine Mission Institution was the Blind School for girls, run by Dorothy Shillaker. Augmenting the staff was a series of excellent young English girl volunteers. They were usually too occupied to join in our activities but they were an asset at parties.

A little way out of town were the boys' and girls' Mission secondary schools: at the boys' Carr School there was the headmaster and Doris Sedeghi, with young Andrew Brooks and Peter Iliffe. At the girls' school was the wonderful Mary Isaac.[8] She was a memorable example of the very best of missionary spirits. I valued her opinions.

On the foreign side, there were the French Consul, M. Banel and his wife and daughter, and a succession of American consuls, particularly the Allens. He was an orchid enthusiast. The very congenial Bob and Bonny Pugh succeeded him. Bob had been a U.S. Marine, and was happy to join my Tombstoners.* There were two American couples in the Iran-America Society, and twelve Yorkshire men in the local textile mills, some with

[8] See her obituary in *The Times*, 8 November 1986.
* See p. 372.

families. There was also a number of agreeable young American Peace Corps, some married, who were usually stationed out of Isfahan, whom we got to know pretty well. They were happy to join in our centre activities. We made some good friends among them, especially Dennis Marino. He opted to return to his Italian roots, and teaches English with the title Professore, in Milan.

On my birthday one year we invited several Peace Corps, among others, for supper in the garden. At one moment a Confederate flag was unfurled and a seditious speech was made, and a tin of tea tossed into our pool!

The most talented group of foreigners and the most entertaining were the Italian planners, restorers, and technicians, under U.N.E.S.C.O. We specially remember Eugenio Galdieri, Camillo Bonanni, Signor Ferranti, Roberto Cerubino, and Roberto Guia, a lighting expert. Theirs was a tremendously responsible job to preserve and to save from future damage or even vandalism, priceless monuments of the heritage of man's civilization. I remember one very tricky discussion on how to save the Maidan-i-Shah from the increase in commercial traffic, perhaps by putting in an underpass. A neat idea but the foundations of the exquisite Lotfullah Mosque would probably have been upset. What certainly was achieved was the restoration of the beautiful but fragile Chehel Sotun, Shah Abbas' Pavilion of Forty columns. There were twenty delicate, tall, wooden columns (the other twenty being their reflections in the long pool in front). Each column had its wooden, segmented casing opened down its length, and a steel core inserted, then recased with the original wood – a concept brilliantly achieved, and interesting to watch being implemented.

28 December 1966

Our heavy baggage which had not been seen for six months had arrived in Bushire, on the Gulf. I had to go down myself to clear it during the four days' post-Christmas holidays, but I had to return before classes started on 4 January. Rosemary accompanied me. The journey was novel and fun. We arrived in time to see our crates opened. I was nearly driven frantic by a customs officer needing a list of our books. Some of the books were taken to the security office, but were later released!

Our journey down and back became a saga. Bad weather halted our flight from Shiraz to Bushire, so we had to spend the night in a hotel. We flew down the next morning, arriving too late to do business, and the next day was an Iranian holiday. The 4th January loomed. Next day we made a big assault on the customs office and almost finished the business in time to get the afternoon 'plane back to Isfahan. But the notary public, who had to give our agent power of attorney to customs, was so slow that we

336

missed the 'plane. The 'plane we took the following day got us as far as Shiraz, but Isfahan was closed because of snow. We got home next day in time for classes, having enjoyed a glimpse of Shiraz and of our colleagues the Pettersens.

Even more satisfactory was the fact that we had got to know staff and pilots on the Bushire, Shiraz, Isfahan run. By providing well-iced, cold boxes, we received regular supplies of prawns at very low cost. Wonderful!

A further three weeks elapsed before our baggage arrived, maybe at such speed in response to our choleric telegrams burning up the wires. Well, the packing in Fiji was the best we had ever had: nothing was damaged, there was only a bit of mould and rust. In the middle of the day our verandah, on which we had to unpack was quite warm. But where were we to stow a Suva house-full in our Isfahan flat?

Two welcome visitors

Rosemary wrote: "English visitors last week weren't official, but we were asked to help, and they were so interesting and pleasant that we enjoyed their two-day visit. One was Graeme Shankland, an architect/town planner with his own business, and the other Jack James, Chief Planner, Ministry of Housing. They fell hard for Isfahan; not only is there a great deal to see but all the little things are so fascinating to those with eyes to see them, which these trained people have. I mean the subtleties and skills of construction, the use of materials and colours, etc. It was very interesting to hear their comments."

"I went," Rosemary continued, "to the most important (architecturally and historically) Friday mosque with Graeme and the ex-Director of Antiquities so that I could learn about it properly too. Then on Friday a local architect took us forty kilometres to an eleventh-century Seljuk mosque at Barsiun which is specially fine. It was a lovely but dusty drive. The fertile areas round Isfahan are enormous, which makes it so different from Tehran. The minaret of this mosque was built of very sturdy brick, with no tiles at all, only patterns in the brick dating back to 1098. We climbed up inside with an attendant flock of small boys. Small boys were so close behind me coming down – I was the last of the party – that I thought if one slipped we'd all go. So I asked if they'd ever counted the steps – no – so go and do it! To my amazement they all belted up to the top again and left me in peace! Minutes later a steady chant could still be heard coming from the minaret as they came down, and I was proudly told "110"!" [9]

[9] Graeme took a great number of professional photographs which could be very valuable for future studies. But he died not so long after, and we have so far not been able to trace his collection of slides.

Rosemary wrote: "Our driving licences are approved at last so we are independent of Nasser, the driver, and can hire the Council Land Rover. We had a little run out this morning, and ended up walking through endless alley-ways trying to get near enough to photograph a stork on the village pigeon tower. We had much help from everyone, but they frightened it off!"

3 February 1967

Rosemary wrote: "Michael is out praying for the Shah. This is the anniversary of an assassination attempt some years ago, and is now remembered by ceremonies all over the country. The P.M. has come here to assist; besides today's ceremonies (on our free day), Michael should go to three more tomorrow – the Army, the Medical Faculty, the Arts Faculty, and so on. Other recent 'invitations' have been to the laying of a foundation stone, the opening of a new hospital wing, and a reception for the Chief of Staff. Very time-consuming but it is difficult to know where to draw the line. It shows the confusion in everyone's mind as to our real identity."

Tehran after five years' absence

Rosemary wrote: "We are just back from the Regional Directors' conference in Tehran, and feel quite tired after all the excitements. We nearly didn't leave Mehrabad because of heavy snow falling, but Isfahan was clear and our 'plane finally took off."

"We had a very social time, with the Representative and the Ambassador giving cocktail parties, and a lunch at the Canadian Ambassador's. It was nice to slip back into the old ways, meeting people at these parties and then going on to dinner at a small restaurant afterwards, which had not been possible in Fiji. We met several people from before whom we didn't know were around, and had meals with them, and visited others. We saw our dear little house again (1957–1961), still in Council hands."

Our first 'Do'

We had to rush back for a concert that we had decided to put on. The performer was an Australian violinist, Ronald Woodcock, whom I had invited after he had told me in Fiji the previous year that he'd be in Iran. He was accompanied by an old friend, who was now our television officer in Tehran. They didn't arrive until 7.15 p.m. for the concert at 8 p.m. We

338

were just choosing records to play to the audience until they would arrive. What a panic! To our relief the recital was well attended and much enjoyed. There were very few concerts of Western music in Isfahan. We had people in afterwards to meet our guests.

Surgeons and hospitality

Rosemary wrote on 13 March: "Most of our preoccupation has been with visitors, particularly this last week. Wherever we are, they seem to come in largest numbers in March and April. There were two official B.C. visitors, both surgeon specialists from London, one specializing in kidney transplants, and the other in livers. The first had his wife with him and was three days here so I was able to go around with her while her husband was busy lecturing and visiting hospitals. Then after two days came the other. I was less involved as he had no wife, but we were invited out almost every lunch and dinner for them by the local doctors. We gave our first biggish parties for them in return, two buffet dinners for about twenty each time. The servants work well on these occasions, but I was pretty fussed before the first one until I could see all was well. I like to do a lot of the cooking beforehand as the cook is untrained, but I can leave him to cope at these times at least, such as to do a big dish of rice and some Persian dish. This room is really too small for that number, not a large figure by local standards. Now the Vice-Chancellor of Warwick and his wife, Jack and Doris Butterworth, are coming on Wednesday for the night!"

Introducing ourselves in Isfahan

Rosemary again: "Then in the breathing space in the middle we finally had our grand 'introductory' tea-party, which had been postponed several times until the Governor-General could come. But only seventy-odd of about 140 invited turned up. The Iran-Tour Hotel did it all, and made our big hall look very smart with carpets from a bazaar merchant all over it, and hired armchairs. All I had to do was the flowers, as usual only carnations were available, but they looked so good in front of the red-velvet stage-curtains that I was asked to run a flower arrangement class! It is almost impossible to do so here with the scarcity of materials, and I know very little really."

"It's most exciting, we have daffodils in the garden, I haven't seen them for fourteen years growing naturally! The Gayfords planted them, bless them. There are masses of violets too along the edge of the paths on the banks of the water channels. It was so warm last week, but it is cooler again now."

"The Persians here are in a great tizzy because their New Year, the annual holiday is next Tuesday, 21 March – Christmas, Easter, and New Year all in one. All housewives are making goodies and cleaning the house and carpets, and buying new clothes, and no one will do any jobs! I hope we have some servants. Meat is already scarce, since so many Persian holiday-makers come to Isfahan."

Our first Now Ruz

On 26 March Rosemary recorded: "We have been having a nice holiday period, with the Persian New Year last Tuesday and all the days holiday that follow it, two more odd ones to come next week, let alone Easter Sunday today! I went around in Isfahan with friends, the Atkinsons from Fiji, over three days. It's rather hard here to send people off on their own when a little Farsi can make such a difference. Prince Massoud asked us out to his village to see the blossom, a party he has annually. But the very strong wind, common at this time, made it so cold that it was an effort to go."

"We did finally stagger out and picked grape hyacinths under the almond blossom and wandered through the village. One persistent old crone managed to invite us in – this is the season of calls. We sat on a quilt on a little arched porch and ate toffees and nuts, while her three villainous-looking menfolk stood grinning down at us, all very affable. They had a carpet loom in an open room at the side of the courtyard and demonstrated the technique."

"Now we had to make our Now Ruz calls. Michael went to the Governor's 'Salaam' ceremony in the afternoon, and to the General's in the evening. Then the next morning the Hamburgers, Prince Massoud, and we 'did' the Governor General, the District Governor, the Mayor, and the Chief of Police; and we and the Hamburgers did two more in the afternoon. These people spend the day 'sitting' at home to receive, in a drawing room stuffed with chairs round the walls, and with all the occasional tables laden with huge dishes of biscuits, sweets, nuts, and fruit. Relays of servants or young relatives stand by to serve glasses of tea and the refreshments. One makes conversation, eats something, and downs a glass of tea, and then leaves just after the next arrivals (if they didn't come too soon) – all very painless. Actually, I thoroughly enjoyed it all. It was much less formal than I'd expected, and we had some good talk. Inevitably, one meets the same people several times as you trail each other around. Now Ellen and I must 'do' some of the lesser lights who come to our conversation group."

"Isfahan has been bursting with people: half of Tehran seems to come here, and the streets are crowded with family groups parading up and down, and making calls."

V.I.P. visitors!

Rosemary continued: "I wanted to try Mohammed at cooking but not in the midst of a flood of visitors! I haven't enumerated them all. We had one buffet dinner on Tuesday last for Jack (and Betty) James, Chief Planner, who was back here lecturing, to which I suddenly found that the Governor-General was coming! I had everything very plain and simple and got very bothered as it wasn't grand enough!" [And the Mayor, General and Mrs. Vaghdanian, came too! It was splendid.] "Then we have another dinner on Sunday night for the Cambridge Professor of Biochemistry, Dr Young, who is Master of Darwin College, and the Bachs, who will also be here that night with Lady Riches, the Ambassador's wife from Beirut. And the same day the Professor of Economic Science at Edinburgh comes, to lecture the next day! He's called Youngson![10] Life isn't usually like this at all, and Tehran do their best to avoid us having pile-ups, but there are so many V.I.P.s around. Each said the situation was out of control! Tehran is quite a conference place these days."

"Sir Stanley Unwin is great value, we all enjoyed him. He is tiny, slight, and bearded, with a little gold tennis racquet with a pearl ball on it in his lapel. He still plays! A very clear and interesting talker, and his comments on people though not freely given, were dry and devastating."

Islam's month of mourning

"We are now in the month of Muharram when the Shias mourn the martyrdom of the Imam Hussain." The helpful, annual circular distributed by the Embassy stated:

> The ninth and tenth days of Muharram, Tassu'a and Ashura, are the anniversaries of the eve and day of the martyrdom of the Emam Hussain. Hussain was the second son of Ali, the son-in-law of the Prophet and principal saint of Shi'a Islam. In A.D. 680 while making a journey with a few followers, Hussain was surrounded near Kerbela by the troops of Yazid, a Sunni, and the rival Ommayed Caliph.

[10] A.J. Youngson very kindly gave us a copy of his great book, *The Making of Classical Edinburgh* (Edinburgh University Press, 1966).

The troops of Yazid cut off Hussain's and his followers' water supplies from the Euphrates (this episode is symbolised by the free water booths in the bazaar area during Muharram). After ten days Hussain rejected an ultimatum calling on him to surrender and he and several of his followers were murdered.

Tassu'a and Ashura are thus particularly holy days of mourning and two of the most important Shi'a religious anniversaries: day and night processions take place and religious emotion runs high. This year they fall on 17 and 18 March. Members of the staff are advised to be circumspect in their movements on both these days and on the evening of 16 March, particularly in the neighbourhood of such places as the Bazaar, South Tehran generally, the Saveh road and Evin in which large processions take place.

Ostentatious parties should not be held on 17 and 18 March or on the holiday Arba'in on 26 April which is the fortieth day after the anniversary of the death of Emam Hussain.

Rosemary noted: "Isfahan does it in proper style and keeps it up for two months! Dark clothes and no public parties; the drink shops closed! At least it means the restaurant band next door will be silent. We always took care to keep out of the way of religious processions."

5 May 1967: Royal visitors!

Rosemary wrote: "Our social life remains at a high level. Last week Isfahan had a day's visit from the Thai king and queen, Bhumibol and Sirikit. I've always wanted to see her. But what agony we had to endure first! It was one of our windy days, very chilly though sunny, and as usual they got us out on the tarmac almost an hour early – to hold the carpets down? At times we could hardly stand still. We had our backs to the wind. Michael and Prince Massoud divided time between keeping a topper on or having their hair blow in their eyes. All the University academic robes were flapping and filling! A full turnout, as the Shah and Queen Farah came too. We had an excellent view as they had to come right past us; and we were introduced to the Shah and Farah the next day when they departed, the Governor being less flustered."

"Queen Sirikit is enchanting – very tiny and slim and beautifully dressed – by Balmain in Thai silks of course! With her long, thick hair she can wear these attractive little chignon hats that just sit on the back of the head – gorgeous carved coral jewellery with a deep coral dress and jacket. Queen Farah was very cheerful and unsuppressed, looking very tall."

To Isfahan Iran 1966–1970

A surprise visitor and an unexpected thrill

"Two nights ago we were summoned by the Governor to meet an English V.I.P. at a dinner in the Shah Abbas Hotel. We couldn't elicit even from the Governor who he was, but he turned out to be Lord Rupert Neville! "It was a very interesting evening, which finished with the Governor taking us all to see the newly-installed flood-lighting of the Shah Mosque in the big Maidan. The great thrill was being able to go through into the mosque, just us with the huge, dark courtyard glimmering with lights reflected from the illuminated dome and minarets – wonderful! Especially the reflection in the huge pool. Lovely shadows everywhere, all the tile colours being softer than by daylight."

"We were lucky to be invited to the local theatre the other evening, by its leading actor/manager, Mr Arham-Sadr, who had earlier received a British Council Bursary. He put on his Persianised version of Scrooge. It was terribly funny even to us with our very limited Farsi, and the audience was delighted. The main reason being that the theme of meanness is well understood here, Isfahanis being the Aberdonians of Iran. Michael is well but still very busy. However, he managed a catapult match with the gardener's grandson this morning."

13 May 1967

Professor Hunt, physiologist from Guys visited us and it was a pleasure to get some of our medical acquaintances together for a good reason, and also Ena Burke from the C.M.S. Hospital, and Pauline Hill, a V.S.O. nurse. I have a very great respect for the medical profession, and admiration too and gratitude for what they have done for me. So I welcome anything I can do for them.

This week's event was several showings of the film of Olivier's stage performance of *Othello* which made such a hit last year. The B.C. was given a special concession. We had two invited audiences, and another student showing, and one for Mr Arham-Sadr and his group. As it was two hours and fifty minutes they didn't all last out!

"After a bit of pressure," Rosemary wrote, "I gave a demonstration about flower-arranging last week. I tried frantically to remember what I could of the meetings I attended in Fiji. About twelve Persian women came. I got rather carried away and went on for more than one and a half hours! Of course one can spin it out for days if necessary. I must get myself some books on it."

25 May 1967: Five Finger Exercise by Peter Shaeffer

It was a welcome surprise to me to find how audiences, in any country it seems, are willing to overlook actors performing a walking play-reading, as we first learned in Hamadan in 1958. This production included three students, one being Christine, daughter of Andre and Micheline Rivoire of SOGREAH, (Water Engineering), a charming family from Grenoble. Christine gave us a new word in our current vocabulary. She had to say Phooey!, and to our amazement and amusement, out came a loud PHOO-HAY! She never really mastered phooey!

Great sadness

At this point we heard that Rosemary's very dear mother had died suddenly. Rosemary needed an exit permit in a hurry, and this was where Shazdeh was marvellous – even though I had made his job more complicated by having arranged earlier for Rosemary to have my extra weapons on her passport.

Rosemary meanwhile in spite of her distress continued to play her part in *Five Finger Exercise*, and to entertain the cast, as I asked her to do. I thought it would be better if she continued to keep her mind otherwise occupied.

June 1967: War news

While I was about to make my way up to Tehran prior to joining Rosemary for our home leave, the horrible Iraqi Revolution broke out. One result was the expulsion of British diplomats from Iraq. They came out by road to Hamadan. One of them was my great friend Bill Stevens, a grandson of the founder of Bradfield College. We were able to meet. I had known Bill as a tough, little four-year old while I was still a boy at the school.

1967 home leave

We spent June, July, and August at home in Britain. September was spent in Switzerland and via Hungarian friends in Zurich who had escaped in 1956. We went on to Italy. We flew to Milan and thence to Genoa. We took the bus to Pisa and up to Florence – seeing the aftermath of the terrible flood in 1966. Then we hired a Fiat 600, and drove to San Gimigniano. Imagine our surprise and delight to find John Ford there from the Rome

344

Embassy with Mr King, Speaker of the House of Commons, whom we had missed in Isfahan! On we went to Siena and got in for an extra special Palio for a Scientific Congress. Thence to Perugia and Rome Airport.

1 October 1967: Return from home leave

As Rosemary wrote: "After only three days back, leave already seems remote." One pleasant surprise is that my predecessor, James Mandy, had returned, by local request, as English lecturer in the University. I was not at all embarrassed as some people thought I might be. James was a good friend and totally neutral. He provided pleasant social company for Eric, Shazdeh, and me at the Iran-Tour at lunch time.

House-hunting

Housing problems had developed for us, and it became imperative to move out of Hezar Jerib. Our classes had happily increased in number to the extent that I was forced to convert our spare bedroom, luckily reached by outside stairs, into a class-room, and also to turn our first-floor landing into a class-room, thus immuring Rosemary for a lesson period in either our bedroom or sitting-room. Rosemary was not altogether delighted at my success: "Michael has gone all ruthless."

We had fun designing an ideal house for ourselves which our landlady Mrs Massoud was willing to build, but that would have taken too long. So far Rosemary had seen over twenty houses in the town, but no Persian house had plain interiors or a design of rooms on the European pattern, nor the atmosphere we needed.

We found nothing as nice as Hezar Jerib despite its drawbacks. It took nearly a year to find the right house, and then it was one offered to us!

In town and out

I was pleased when the local cinema manager, no doubt encouraged by the peronality and reputation of Arham-Sadr, agreed to show a series of English films in English. Good British Council stuff. I was invited to attend a showing of *The Taming of the Shrew*, but it began at 8.30 a.m. on a Friday, my day off! I remained awake to notice a good attendance of locals.

We took courage and began to run Scottish country dance classes. We thoroughly enjoyed the relaxation with our European friends. Alas, few Persians came, unlike in Tehran, but that was not surprising.

November 1967: The Shah's coronation

Every day sees more of Isfahan disappearing underneath a load of flags, bunting, and electric lights draped and swathed everywhere.

The coronation period

Rosemary wrote home: "This has been a very busy two weeks. We were asked to many parties, mostly official ones given by provincial departments of government like electricity, agriculture, the Mayor, Iranair, and so on. Some were social evening gatherings of hours standing around talking to the same people, while a too-loud band played. Other occasions were ceremonies with speeches; elsewhere there were theatrical entertainments (very lengthy usually), and a couple of parades and sports shows. Michael was very assiduous in attending, but luckily wives weren't included in all of them. It was pretty tiring really."

"The highlights were two ceremonies in the reception rooms and great verandah of Shah Abbas' Pavilion, the Chehel Sotun. Coronation Day was the Shah's birthday when there is always a Salaam ceremony with the Governor-General as the Shah's representative. This year it was held in the Chehel Sotun; the whole area was covered in carpets, with a choir in Bakhtiari dress and an old-style orchestra. Servants were in colourful eighteenth-century uniforms. Morning coats and uniforms were de rigueur, and there were speeches, and an ode by our local poet Dr Nawab, Deputy Dean of the Medical Faculty. It's a charming facet of the Persians, their love of poetry. At several parties all stopped to listen to a few lines tossed off by someone. There was great attention and applause."

The second ceremony was an after-dinner party also given in the Chehel Sotun by the Governor-General. First some of us had dinner in the Officers' Club nearby. This had been the home of Shazdeh's family. Shazdeh Jahangir Massoud, was in his element, and at my elbow. He introduced me to Lieutenant-General Minbashian, A.D.C. to the Shah-in-Shah, and to the local C. in C., the charming General Hatam. I met them all most happily, thanks to Shazdeh. General Hatam wanted to know all about malt whisky.

Then, as Rosemary described, "we walked up through the garden to the Chehel Sotun, softly floodlit, right along the huge pool in front of it, which was edged with candles in old, brass candlesticks with glass shades. In the rooms, which are magnificently frescoed with scenes of old feasts and battles, cushions and blankets had been spread along the walls, and charcoal braziers in wide, brass containers stood here and there on copper trays. Servants, complete with scimitars lined the steps;

346

tables groaned with fruit, European drinks, and eats."

"It was most amusing to see the men we knew well as modern lawyers, doctors, and so on, sitting against the walls and round the braziers cross-legged, telling stories and eating nuts, looking absolutely at home and normal as they would have done 400 years ago, despite their dinner-jackets. Next came night-club singers from Tehran; the choir again, and some dancers entertained us. Since everyone would stand up and crowd round to see them, it did get rather tiring. But all was a memorable sight, and it was most exciting to be there. In two corners of the outer area they had arranged on banks of shelves all the pretty old oil lamps and candle glasses with prisms and coloured glass that could be borrowed from the antique shops. This was just the way they used to light the Pavilion."

1967: Out in the country

Whenever we could we got off in the Land Rover into the lovely surroundings of Isfahan, to the countryside of the plateau villages. The plateau of 5000 ft., was largely desert, but broken up by agricultural oases irrigated from the Zayandeh Rud river, or by water via underground channels (qanats) from the mountains.

There were small fields of cereals, melons or tobacco and plantations of poplars for building, and productive trees in mud-walled orchards of apricot, almond, walnut, and pomegranate, which were particularly beautiful in spring and autumn. There was no monotony because here and there were isolated little ranges of hills, and rocky mountainous outcrops of strange shapes. The area was criss-crossed by well-worn tracks which could peter out, or be cut by open water-channels, so a Land Rover was essential.

It gave us the greatest pleasure in such a lovely climate to explore the countryside in autumn, winter, and spring; and it added spice if we could have a visitor or two with us. There was no other facility for visitors to see rural Persia.

Our first picnic was in mid-February 1967. Rosemary described the occasion: "We found a lovely picnic place just above the river, but it was sheltered, so it was quite warm. It looked across the greeny blue water through silvery, pale tree trunks to the mud curves of village roofs, the reddish hills standing up sharply against a brilliant blue sky. Everyone is working hard in the fields just now, preparing for spring sowing. Lines of men in black, baggy pants and little skull-caps can be seen digging with long-handled spades in a fast swinging rhythm. Donkeys with loads of manure are being urged along, and other men are cleaning out irrigation ditches. The fields have little bunds like paddy fields. The villages are attractive with fine water-courses running through them." There were often lines of women and girls washing pots and dishes along the banks. Rosemary's paté went perfectly with Persian bread, spring onions, little juicy cucumbers, and Persian melon (such as praised by Marco Polo during his travels to Iran), and beer, often the local ab-i-jou (water of barley), and coffee made with hot water from our Volcano kettle.

Out in the country there are many ancient works of man to be seen. There are tombs and mosques with delicate tile designs, occasionally with small turquoise domes, blending with the green fields and trees, beckoning us so beautifully. On that first picnic we were alerted to the treasures we might discover in Iran by finding a shrine with lovely areas of stucco patterns, which I had not come across before, and a few of its original tiles of alternating blue and turquoise in a sort of patchwork pattern. Outside is a rock with a hole in it made by the hoof of the horse of Ali, son of the Prophet. We were at Linjan. Where next?

The Head of Antiquities of Isfahan, Dr Honarfar produced an admirable, little pocket *Guide to the Historical Monuments of Isfahan* (Tehran, 1967). We found it invaluable in the course of our peripatetic pilgrimage, specially for the lesser monuments which can be found for quite a distance round about Isfahan. When we came to a little village to reach a religious site we could just negotiate the narrow lanes between houses and gardens in our short wheel-base Land Rover – short for getting round village corners or on mountain twists and turns! Our width was the same as that of a double-panniered donkey – ergo we could get through!

The shrines or tombs we found stood out as beacons to us, and no doubt to the faithful. Freya Stark wrote sensitively on the special significance of tombs in Islam, in her book of essays: *The Zodiac Arch* (John Murray 1968). There is a feeling of safety which the devout feel in proximity of the shrine of a particularly venerable holy man. In a savage world she felt that "the happiest perhaps were the poor and the old who gathered from the corners of Asia, lived round their ark of salvation, in attendance on a future in which their faith was secure." This is one reason, she felt, that strangers or dissenters are watched with fear or anger, even forbidden entry. However, Freya wrote: "This fierce feeling of safety and exclusion melts into what we think of civilisation, when we leave the holy cities of Iraq or Persia, and step under the azure domes of Isfahan . . ."

On our Land Rover journeys into the country we didn't have the personal contact or the language which gave a hero of mine, Edward Browne,[11] such enviable rapport. But we met some marvellous-looking characters with whom we could exchange a few remarks and questions. For instance,

[11] E. G. Browne, *A Year Among the Persians (1887–1888)* (A. & C. Black, Rep. 1959). See pp. 97 onwards.

the miller at Linjan who welcomed us into his minute, low-built, mud-roofed mill on a very small water channel. We also came across the new motorised generation of village dwellers, on light motor-bikes, or riding and driving load-carrying tricycle-vans (all Japanese) known as 'taxi-bars'. They had problems when water channels crossed their track, which donkeys or camels don't have, and sometimes we were on the spot to help.

Pigeon towers

One day far from Isfahan we had a great piece of lasting luck. At a petrol station we found David Stronach with the French archeologist, Audran Labrousse, and the charming Elizabeth Beazley, A.R.I.B.A. What a joy her friendship has been to us, and that of her husband the retired R.N. submariner, Captain David Walters. Associating with her and her work on Persian vernacular buildings has opened our minds to the visual pleasure to be found in Persian villages. This is what she wrote:

> Between ten and fifteen years ago, the plateau villages held a huge legacy of fascinating and often very beautiful buildings. In another ten years time, most will have crumbled. They are disappearing rapidly for various good reasons:

> 1. They are no longer needed. Twentieth-century innovations have made them redundant, E.g. modern refrigeration, chemical fertilisers, new sources of power and the internal combustion engine have overtaken such buildings as ice-houses, pigeon towers, mills and caravanserais.

> 2. They are chiefly built of mud-brick (unbaked) whence their fine sculptural form. Any mud-brick building will deteriorate rapidly without constant maintenance; this ceases once a building is no longer useful.

> 3. Their huge number has made them seem common place. Few people have been concerned that they are disappearing.

> 4. Iran has such a wealth of architectural and artistic treasure that few Iranians or visitors have had time or inclination to look at the villages.

This is terribly sad. Luckily there is a consolation in Elizabeth Beazley being able to produce, with Michael Harverson, an indispensable reference work on the subject: *Living With The Desert, Working Buildings of the Iranian Plateau* (1982). One great enjoyment was driving Elizabeth out and about looking for specimens of pigeon towers for her to photograph, measure and log; pigeon towers large and small, plain, or decorated. These huge, circular buildings are like giant pepper-pots or chess castles, others are tall, narrow towers. Many are fancifully castellated or painted with amusing red and blue designs of birds, flowers, and faces.

The pigeons were kept for their dung for fertiliser which was caught in great nets suspended inside the towers. The classic interior and function of a pigeon tower is well described and illustrated in the pamphlet 'The Dunster Dovecote'.[12] While photographing a pigeon tower one day, we claim the first known recording, but not the discovery, of a largish, ruined, and roofless mosque, with a marvellous, carved plaster prayer-niche of the early-fourteenth century. Someone knew of its existence because its wall had been buttressed, but it wasn't in Honarfar!

Wildlife

From Isfahan we were able to range beyond the sharp-outlined, bare mountains back into further flat, green, wooded valleys still watered by the Zaindeh Rud. But, alas, we only saw the occasional jackal or hare. Once I saw a porcupine quite close to Isfahan, popping back into its deep hole in a sandbank. On our way to Shiraz near Yazdekhast we actually saw, with some excitement, two wolves. We never saw wild pig alive. But it was a shock one day in Isfahan when a party of Massoud hunters dropped a couple of carcases off into our Hezar Jerib compound. The hunters didn't care that pig is unclean. Only Mohammed of our strict Muslim staff would go near these gifts to cut them up for the table.

Alas, the ibex (wild goat) and mouflon (wild sheep) live high in the Elburz mountains and remain only in our Tehran memories.

The only birds we could recognize were snipe and storks. There were no wild duck out round Reza Gholi's farm, but further afield with him in the desert we saw sand-grouse. Small flocks together feed on seeds in the nearest cultivation. But their downfall comes when they fly regularly morning and evening to water, and are easy to find and shoot. Reza Gholi took me to a water-hole in the desert further east, and I did get some shots. But never again. They are so charming.[13]

---

[12] Obtainable from Dunster Church or the Priory in Somerset.
[13] See Richard Burton in Harar, in Mary S. Lovell's 'A Rage to Live', Little Brown & Co., 1998. He never shot a sand grouse again when one bird going to water, as he knew it would, saved their lives thereby.

Hugh Whistler, who served seventeen years in the Indian Police, wrote the wonderful *Popular Handbook of Indian Birds* (Oliver and Boyd, rep. 1963). He had a happy knack of putting into words the salient characteristics of a species which enables them to be readily recognized in the field. He describes sand-grouse perfectly.

Back to work: an exhibition to handle

Rosemary recorded: "What has given us so much work recently is a British Council exhibition of university textbooks, which has already been to Turkey, Lebanon, and Israel. This is its first showing in Iran. Luckily our librarian, Struan Bell, came down from Tehran for several days to help. There was a great deal of work, 2,000 books to be checked and arranged. The sort of work the local staff can't help with much. Special stands had been made in Britain, but we had to find more tables. The librarian and ourselves worked flat out for several days. Our exhibition stayed open for ten days, and attendances were quite good. But there probably won't be many orders to local bookshops here, as there is little teaching in English. Shiraz and Tehran should do best. It is good for teachers and pupils to sec and handle these admirable productions. They are backed up too, by a very good catalogue. There will be some prestige in the scope and size of the exhibition. Added to this, the ever-keen Michael decided to show the medical section of our text book exhibition at the medical faculty since many of the doctors hadn't managed to get to it while it was on display in our hall. Then they wanted physics, chemistry and biological sciences as well, so this was all quite a chunk. Only we could do the sorting and selection. Michael said he'd never before had to work so hard physically for the B.C., packing crates of books, etc."

In addition to the book-work Rosemary put on a party to present Lower Cambridge Certificates to twenty-two successful candidates. On another day she gave a tea-party for the English Teachers' Association to which I was lecturing.

20 December 1967: A Christmas stocking, revised version

As Rosemary noted in her diary, "Two of the gloomiest religious Days of Mourning of the year with a Friday in the middle, most hampering just before Christmas. We had our Christmas show last night, so now I can recover gently and organize our own affairs."

"It was a show Michael devised for Tehran, called *A Christmas Stocking*, with about five or six people speaking in turn, with short accounts of Christmas customs and their origins, interspersed with suitable poetry. "Christmas" by W. H. Davies was especially good. The whole event was enlivened by the entry of a group of carol-singers from the Mission, who joined the party on the stage which was set as a living room, and sang carols. Father Christmas (Eric Hamburger was perfect) came in, and filled the stocking of a child in bed in a corner of the stage – a six-year-old who 'slept' beautifully and then Father Christmas gave presents to our staff's children. The rest of the programme was rather disturbed by children examining presents! I talked about a housewife's part, and produced our Christmas dinner, I had a table with four seated at it and pretended to feed them. There were roars when I produced a 3 lb. chicken and spoke of huge turkeys. There was a Christmas pudding borrowed, flaming, and mince-pies for all on the stage, and even some for those members of the audience who were agile enough to catch one – or more! We had made forty-five! Otherwise, I played bits of suitable music on the gramophone. The highlight was the Mummers' play, with Michael, as a saucepan-helmeted St George, and Slasher, the 'heathen knight', having a great sword-battle, followed by St George bashing a wonderful dragon. The hall was packed out. All sorts of people came. It was much enjoyed I think. We certainly enjoyed ourselves, and there was mulled claret afterwards for all the cast."

Our own Christmas 1967

Rosemary's diary entry of 7 January 1968 records: "Our Christmas went off very well, but only by our own efforts! We were nine for dinner – the Hamburgers and James Mandy, and five young people who were on their own and rather lonely. It was the best turkey we've ever had – one of the specially bred ones. We roasted chestnuts and had candles on the tree. Then on 27th we had a party of twenty-eight, inviting some of the livelier Persians, the Bishop, and Mission doctors, some Americans, etc., We had to use wrapped boiled sweets for the Bean Game. We were able to use the library downstairs and a classroom as well as our rooms, but all the players tore at it so hard that they finished very quickly. It was successful though. I have a happy memory of the Bishop mooing gently (cow team) over a 'bean' in a potted plant on the stairs long after the main flood had passed. We were gentle with them after that – a game of blow football for volunteers. My Christmas was made by a German girl saying she hadn't seen a tree with candles since leaving Germany many years ago; and by the expression of the night watchman's son (aged seven) taking his first blow on his mouth organ! Oh, we also made the guests come wearing headgear to represent someone well known. Dr Peter Wild came with a smart stainless steel bed-pan 'helmet', i.e. Peter Pan! Two of our guests were the admirable Arnold (Arnie)[14] and Raphael, the new American Vice-Consul-General, and his wife, Myrna. He didn't realize how informal we all were together, and was a bit anxious about his dress and attitude and reception. He soon succumbed!"

[If you don't know the Bean Game: strew beans so they are just visible, high or low all over the house, large white dried beans. Choose team leaders, get your guests into teams, and give each team the name of a farm animal. If you are a cat, off you go; and when you find a bean you stay by it, forbidden to touch it, and miaow until your team leader comes and collects it. We have never known the Bean Game to fail when played properly, and not mucked up by the host beforehand – see Christmas '69.]

24 January 1968: Two special lectures

Rosemary wrote "After the New Year lull we have been kept busy with two special lectures, followed by dinners for eighteen or so. This was the only way to ensure there would be some audience! Last week's was on 'The Historical and Archaeological Background of the Ancient Elamites' by Professor Max Mallowan of Nimrud fame: 'Sir Agatha' to us! He had offered to lecture for us in Isfahan as Cecil his brother was our man in Meshed, and Sir Max was Chairman of the British Institute in Tehran. We could scarcely refuse him. We cajoled our friends, etc. and got quite a good turn out, including the Governor-General, who came to dinner."

"The Mallowans were here three days so we saw quite a lot of them. We were fascinated to meet Agatha but we didn't dare mention her side of their life at all. I tried one feeler and the atmosphere became chilly. I actually asked her if the attractive girl in *They Came to Baghdad*, a book with an archaeological setting was a particular person, and she said "No", which quite surprised me."

"They had been visiting a dig at Siraf down on the Gulf where the staff live in a fort with very steep steps. She said it took two young men to get her around it, one to push and one to pull. We got on well, but she didn't really 'give'. She must have had to protect herself, being so famous. I think Max does what he's told. She *would* buy some badly painted, modern tiles. He thought so too, but soon shut up. With us he was a very friendly little man."

I had an anxious time before the lecture. I took Sir Max into our hall,

---

[14] Arnie was the senior American diplomat in Pakistan some years later, and sad to say, he died with General Zia when the general's 'plane crashed.

and on to the stage. Agatha came in too. She sat at the back and said clearly just where Sir Max should stand and where I should set the lectern, lighting, etc. I was nervous. However, I very much enjoyed hearing about the Elamites whom Sir Max seemed to bring alive.

Shortly afterwards, one of our two local academics whom I mentioned, Dr Suzangar Sepanta offered to lecture on Edward Browne, the late nineteenth-century Pembroke College (Cambridge) don. Browne was a remarkable scholar and Oriental linguist specialising in Persian, and his book has its place among the classics of life and travel in foreign parts. He not only understood what was said to him and obviously was able to reply perfectly, he could remember conversations verbatim. Sir Denison Ross in *A Memoir of E.G.Browne* wrote

Edward Browne was a genius no man could deny, and his genius was of two distinct kinds; he not only fulfilled the condition of possessing the capacity for taking infinite pains, but also had genius which reveals itself in the inspiration of the spoken word.[15]

I am grateful to Edward Browne for recounting his journeys with amazingly acute observations. We found our journeys fascinating. As we drove south to Shiraz or beyond, Rosemary would read me extracts from *A Year Among the Persians*, to entertain me and keep me awake.

A musical effort

We sent out an invitation to an evening as follows:

THE BRITISH COUNCIL

Tuesday, 20th February, 1968, at 6.30 p.m.

"HARMONY AND DISCORD"

Arnold and Myrna Raphel, Dennis Marino,
Rosemary and Michael Halsted play recordings
and argue about the appeal of different kinds of
music from the earliest forms to the most modern.

---

[15] Sir Denison Ross, *Edward Granville Browne, A Memoir* (Cambridge, 1949).

We had quite a successful, lively, music discussion evening with lots of audience participation. We were glad to have a number of the new generation with us in Isfahan, and on that evening. I was totally out of touch with what was going on at home – the social revolution, liberation, protest, and all that. But thanks to the young I came to like Bob Dylan and Joan Baez, without a chance to realise their status and social contribution.

Shades of Everest!

We were lucky to have a visit by James (now Jan) Morris and Elizabeth, sent to us by Leila Makoui. They were the greatest fun. We had a hilarious dinner upstairs outside at the Sahara Restaurant across the river. I admire Jan's clear-sighted, sincere, and accurate writing, whether it's cats in Venice, or Sydney N.S.W. – let alone her definitive work, *Pax Brittanica*.

The Russian steel mill

As Rosemary described, "We had plenty of wind last Wednesday at a rather unusual occasion, when bus-loads of guests from Tehran and Isfahan, all dolled up, were driven twenty miles into the middle of a howling wilderness, where we sat for four hours; all in aid of the Shah's breaking the ground for the new steel-mill complex the Russians are putting up. We had to leave here at 7 a.m. – the Tehran people, staff of the head company and from various ministries concerned were up at 3.30 am! It was two hours before the Shah came, in a helicopter from Isfahan airport. They gave us plastic bags with cake and fruit! No tea, no lavatories. We sat in rows beneath a sort of shelter, without much roof, and it was very pleasant till mid-morning when the wind got up and blew sand everywhere, and manure-dust from a few newly-created flower-beds. Every time a vehicle passed it became a real sandstorm. We got well tanned."

"It was quite pleasant in a way once one had resigned oneself to it. When we got back to Isfahan there was a huge lunch party in the big hotel, and a tea party. We talked to some Russians; one an interpreter but who was really a teacher of English. He was desperate for English books, and was excited to hear about our library. I was interested to see if he would come to it."

He did, but only for a couple of visits; I believe he was forbidden to do so again.

Now Ruz

Our own Land Rover at last! Thanks to Charles Sayyad, our man in Tehran (an Assyrian), our beautiful, new, white, S.W.B. Land Rover with all the necessary extras (jerrycans, etc.) arrived just four days before the Holiday. The Iranian licence plates were to hand on the very morning we left – with Teresina Saetti, an Italian-Armenian teacher whom we had known before in Tehran and who was easy to get on with. She spoke Farsi and needed a break from a trying home life. Our plan was to see the south-east as far as Kerman and Mahan via Nain and Yazd, towns on the western edge of the the Dasht-i-Lut (sand desert), the central desert proper.

We were able to make three memorable Now Ruz trips in our time. This one, in 1968, was along the edge of the Sand Desert; in 1969 we travelled in the south-west of Iran towards the Persian Gulf; and in 1970 we visited the 'classical Province of Fars', in the south-east of the country.[16] So much of the excitement and enjoyment of our ideal form of holiday in Persia was in 'the going'. For many hours a day there was just us, the road, and the fabulous scenery to be negotiated.

In the words of Kinglake's 'Eothen':

> But travel in the East is a mode of life. If you are wise you will
> not look upon the long period of time occupied in actual movement
> as a mere gulf dividing you from the end of your journey, but as
> a period of moulding one's character – one's identity.[17]

27 March 1968: Back in Isfahan

Term began for Rosemary with the Ladies Conversation Group, and for us both with Scottish Country Dancing, so we were soon well away again. A good deal of rain alarmed us that our mud roofs might suffer.

24 April 1968

Rosemary wrote, "Here it's been a real merry-go-round with a sudden flood of visitors, friends, and friends of friends, official, and otherwise. Some of the flood was the side-effects of a large congress of scholars on Iran, now called Iranologists. I was hoping to meet some of these well-known names and was sad that their time here was so short. However, our

---

[16] Accounts of each trip exist – 'for the record!'
[17] Quoted by Vita Sackville-West in *Passenger to Tehran*, (Hogarth Press, 1926).

former Ambassador, Sir Roger Stevens, and his wife, to whom we were so grateful when we were in Tehran, were here for several days and we much enjoyed them now that they aren't official any more". Sir Roger signed our copy of his book, *The Land of the Great Sophy* and wrote: "Hoping Sophy will continue to give pleasure". It still does. He was then Vice-Chancellor of Leeds University.

Then came a Hungarian friend of mine, Edmund de Unger, now resident in London. It was astonishing luck meeting up with Edmund de Unger again: not seen since Budapest days, '47–'49. We did not know that he was already a respected authority and collector of Islamic art and architecture. He was a great sport, and on his frequent visits from London he would bring me out a couple of very heavy boxes of .38 special revolver ammunition or 9.mm. automatic (unobtainable in Iran) for the Tombstoners' activities.

Rosemary wrote, "Edmund was leading his Islamic Art Circle. We took a group of them out on Friday to see two unpublished mosques of considerable interest. It is most rewarding to be with people who really know what they are talking about. Wilfred Blunt, author of, *Isfahan, Pearl of Persia* (Elek Books, 1966) was in the Circle.

"We have also had David Holden of the *Sunday Times* and his wife, who was recently the editor of *Harper's Bazaar*. Then we had an ex-headmistress of Croydon Girls' School, Dr Marjorie Reeves, and the great Sir Maurice Bowra, to lecture on 'Graves, Omar, and Fitzgerald'; and a publisher or two, all in a week and a bit. It was very stimulating and great fun, but we are rather on our knees now! However, everyone enjoys Isfahan so it is easy to keep them happy.

"Sir Maurice was rather a worry. He was preceded on the stage by a Persian character of prima-donna-ish tendencies, which may have unsettled him. Then Sir Maurice's way of speaking was so English and ironic, and in such "in" language that it wasn't easy for even us to follow!" The Persians were so polite over it all. Here is a note from Dr Sepanta – a charming gesture and an honour from the Persians:

As March 1959 is equivalent to 1337 of the Persian year, and almost coincides with the centenary of the publication of the translation of the famous quartets of Khayyam, into the English language by Fitzgerald, the English poet, it was decided in Tehran that a young Persian rose bush should be taken from the resting place of Khayyam and sent to England to be planted on the grave of Fitzgerald.

Easter

Rosemary recorded, "We went to part of the Grand Mass in the Armenian Cathedral in Julfa, on Easter Day; a magnificently rich sight, the church interior and the priests all glittering and lots of incense, and the courtyard bursting with the overflow, all in new clothes and cracking coloured eggs."

6 May 1968: Smaller monuments reconnaissance

Rosemary wrote: "At last this week we are having a breather from visitors, having spent the last three Fridays – our day off – taking people around in or out of Isfahan – which was amusing, but not the relaxation we needed. Last Friday it was David Stronach, the Director of the British Institute of Persian Studies, a friend from before, who blows through occasionally. He was lecturing with a Swan tour, and wanted to see some smaller 'monuments' outside Isfahan."

It was always a pleasure to see David Stronach. We learned so much each time, and he was so cheerful and keen – and understanding. I have a lasting mental picture of us out in the country to the south-east in our Land Rover: David standing on the bonnet to get a better view of any likely looking mound to excavate.

We now had a Home Economist from London University, Miss Walley, around for several days. I accompanied her on some of her visits to training courses, etc., here.

We were happy when our visitors had time and energy off-duty, to take them around the city monuments or better still out into the country. Next came Mrs Spurgin, J.P., and the pathologist, Dr Ian McIntyre, who were inspiring and thus, in a sense, tiring. Then came Dr David Howson of Knutford House, (CREDO – Education Development Overseas), who lectured at the University on mathematics; he was fascinating. I wish I undertood maths, and the poetic aspect of this discipline: and how mathematicians are often musicians, or vice versa.

A farewell moonlight picnic

We fancied moonlight picnics in those days in Iran. So, when our Peace Corps friend Dennis Marino was due to leave, we gave him just our kind of farewell party. Once we had obtained the permission of a Mr Kazerooni, the owner of a classic Persian 'garden' close to the Pol-i-Chum, we could go ahead. The invitation was couched as from the

To Isfahan Iran 1966–1970

Isfahan Bird-Watching Society, planning an escape from tiresome species, such as Blue-jeaned deadbeats, Starry-eyed mosque-gazers or Bemused bazaar-shoppers.

24 May 1968: To Khonsar for flowers

We had a really good outing to Khonsar, a charming small town in the hills, a hundred miles west of Isfahan, at about 7000 ft. Much of our delight in being in Isfahan, lay in the landscape near and far. I particularly enjoyed a trip if it had a goal, and this one did.

Our unusually wet spring made everything look terrific this year. Snow was still lying in the northern gullies. We drove through low, rolling foothills to stop for coffee beside a stream, exactly as in the Borders! Here were fritillaries, buttercups, cranesbill, grass! Then down to Khonsar with its cool air and abundant streams. We ate our lunch on the verandah of the same house as the previous year, just above rushing water, all rather Kashmir looking – flat roofs, old, fretted, wooden windows. We walked to the springs, and to buy honey. The sky became grey and cloudy now, and we returned to the 'Border' pass and a valley running right to the base of the 11,000 ft. mountains. We had noticed cars there on the way in. We saw why; among low bushes along a little valley were huge masses of the handsome Crown Imperial fritallary about three feet tall, with a cluster of red bells surmounted by a tuft of leaves. But now almost every one had been picked. I went right up to the base of the mountain before I could find an area untouched.

Someone else was also around: I was quietly mooching along on my own, and I suddenly caught sight of several odd little creatures, sitting up and then popping back into a hole. This was the first time I had seen wild hamsters!

I grew to love Khonsar, by far the most attractive village in the Iran of our day. Old Khonsar lies in a steep, little wooded valley of walls and gardens and narrow paths. It is a village of tumbling streams fed from a great spring that gushes from the foot of a mountain. The spring is first led to fill an ornamental pool in a terraced garden, then it makes a steep, underground drop to another pool through which the water flows through many 'musical' arms among, or under, the mud houses, with their little, first-floor balconies.

Above is the 'New Town' consisting of a wide, asphalted main street with a Tourist Inn above the roundabout at the top. We were its first visitors when we made a last visit one June to search for more *fritillaria reuteri* bulbs. We had found them easily enough when they were flowering. But now the goats had eaten the stalks into the earth. For the same reason there was no trace of the dark, chocolate-purple iris which we had picked so easily in May.

The valley just short of Khonsar is well-known to hunters too, because packs of partridges gather up at the high springs fed by near perennial snow; and nearer by are my golden hamsters nipping in and out of their holes. Beyond Khonsar is a farming area round Turjan which has unusual, square, pigeon towers. Further is Golpaigan and its ancient Friday Mosque.

End of Term

Activities consisted of two play-readings of the set books *Twelfth Night* and *Androcles and the Lion*, and on 13 June a garden party for 300 students. For me that was great fun, to be able to meet very many more of 'my' students out-of-class, and with a bit of leisure. It was rewarding to find out a little about their families and circumstances. It was such a pleasure to teach adults, especially when they had reached an adequate conversation level in English – far above my level of Persian. I enjoyed talking with 'Mrs Temptation' for instance – a lady of charm, which she knew. In class one day she said "Mr Halsted, what is this word, 'temptation'?" She enjoyed hearing my answer.

25 June to 26 July 1968: Tabriz Summer School

Luckily for us, this year's Summer School for about 100 teachers of English from all over Iran was held in the ancient northern town of Tabriz which we were eager to visit. Now we could do so officially, and we could have a great drive to it. Our route was to Hamadan for the night (our 1958 Summer School venue), via Najafabad, Daran, Aligudarz, Azna, Darud, Borujerd, and Malayer. Next day we drove on to Kermanshah founded in A.D. 390 by Bahram IV, the Sassanian.

Thirty miles before arriving at this provincial capital we visited the rock carvings of Bisitun. A huge, cuneiform inscription, in Old Persian, neo-Elamite and neo-Babylonian, occupies an area of vertical rock, some 150-ft. long and 100-ft. high, celebrating Darius' triumph over the magus Gaumatas.

Sir Henry Rawlinson was engaged in 1839 in training the troops of Mohammed Shah. He succeeded in climbing the rock 500 ft. above the plain. He let himself down by ropes, copied the inscription, and eventually de-ciphered what was neo-Babylonian script. His brave and far-seeing action laid the foundation of studies on which much of our present knowledge of early Mesopotamian history is based.

360

There are many lesser ancient remains in the area, but we had no time to visit them. South of here is ancient Media (the land of the Medes). Today it is Luristan, the land of the Lurs (ancient people). Their beautiful bronzes are very valuable. A little beyond the town of Kermanshah is a little garden watered from a nearby spring. Within, there are wonderful examples of early art from the fourth to seventh centuries A.D. relating to famous kings: Ardeshir, Shapur, Khosrow II and his favourite horse, Shabdaz.

26 July 1968

We continued northwards into Kurdistan, heading for the Kurdish capital, Sanandaj, through a fine, rolling, grassy landscape, but with a somewhat remote feel. The Kurds are traditionally tribal and pastoral nomads, but they are now mainly settled in villages and small towns. They are a grand people. Our hearts have bled for them ever since. They are predominantly Sunni, which doesn't help in Shia Iran. They also feel they have a right to large areas of land westwards in today's Iraq, and north into Turkey.

At once we could identify distinctively clad Kurds: baggy, black trousers, wide, white shirts, dark jackets, but bright, floral, fringed shawls wound round the waist as a cummerbund, and black and white ones round the head as turbans, with the outer fringed end down the left side. We drove into the yard of the Hotel Ra'uf, and were immediately intrigued by the comers and goers and their proud bearing. Many wore bandoliers of ammunition and pistols in holsters. We could see that we wouldn't last long as enemies of the Kurds, so we smiled and nodded and saluted cheerfully all over the place. Alas, there was only a little verbal communication, but we felt the spirit of the Kurds.

27 July 1968

We continued northwards through Jafarabad and Saqqez to the village of Bowkan. Here we stopped to have a walk round the market, and we were welcomed. Our shopping consisted of buying me a complete Kurdish costume; and a hilarious, open-air fitting-out ensued. I still have my costume which has often come in handy for parties, and it reminds me of the Kurds. Of course we travelled the world with an acting box.

The next excitement was the town of Maragheh, the first Mongol capital under Hulagu Khan. The octagonal Gonbad-i-Kabud (Blue Dome) of A.D. 1196 still has its amazingly fine brickwork. West of here is Lake Rezaieh. Maragheh was a peaceful place in which to spend a night. And so on to Tabriz, the beautifully situated capital of Azerbaijan.

All that remained in our day was the Arg, an empty, dilapidated, built -over citadel, and a crumbling Blue Mosque. It is so sad. A seventeenth-century traveller likened part of this city of the Mongols to Fontainebleau! Earthquakes have been the main destroyers.

Two views of our Summer School

For my part, I had very satisfactory teacher contact. I can only hope this was reciprocated. I had fun with a little party piece: the text of John Gilpin handed out and discussed, then backed up with the B.C. stills film of Ronald Searle's illustrations. I also had a great time with 'far-flung' British colleagues who were assembled there.

Rosemary described her view: "I am perched up on the fourth floor of a modern hotel in the centre of Tabriz, on a noisy street (which includes a record shop always playing local music loudly). Tabriz is mainly single-storied, mud-roofed houses so I can see across to the smooth hill-line to the north, an amazing red colour, with a greeny-yellow ridge lying alongside further north still: very odd."

"To the south-east tips of a large mountain, Sahand, appear, still streaked with snow. This is unfortunately one of the few Persian hotels outside Tehran that doesn't have a garden. We can brew up in the bathroom on our gas burner, and save by having snack lunches. I also brought my iron and do the laundry on top of a suitcase! The B.C. doesn't pay for me and we have to pay our Isfahan servants so it's quite an expensive exercise!"

"Lots of beer gets drunk out of working hours, and we much enjoy normal conversation and laughter – in Isfahan society there is usually only stilted conversation. I natter with Maria Campbell (Spanish), wife of the Regional Representative, swim with her children, look at the Bazaar and sleep late, lovely."

Before we left we found the grave of dear young 'Spiders and Scorpions Lampel', who called on me in Tehran. The gravestone read: "George Peter Lampel, B.A. Oxon, 6 October 1961. 26 years." Rosemary wrote on 17 July 1968: "On the last day of the summer school the little jobs I brought to occupy myself remain undone. Somehow time has flown by thanks to the American Consulate here (Tom and Margaret Greene) we could use their lovely pool and tennis court. H.E. presented Certificates of Attendance. The final official dinner was in a most unusual setting – the huge, grandiose, modern railway-station!"

362

Return to Isfahan

With time to take a different route back, we were able first to drive 150 miles east to Ardebil, in a remote area rarely visited by travellers. We were rewarded by its one great monument which was well-preserved – the shrine of Sheikh Seifuddin Ishak (d. 1334). From him the Safavids (1500–1700) get their name. We were excited by the fifteenth-century architecture, and the tomb of Ismail, the first Safavid king (1499–1524). We were especially pleased by the rare, brown-and-yellow-glazed tiles used in parts. These with a dazzling blue, and the pale-red brick of the first courtyard go well with the trees and flowers. We found good accommodation for the night at the Arya Hotel.

The road we chose to take from Ardebil was to Astara on the Russian border, and it meant circling south round great Mount Savalan (16,781 ft.). The Astara road rises slowly across a dusty plateau, and then in front of the bonnet was a 5,000 ft. drop into a great, green chasm. Below we could see a series of wild valleys. To the left, wooded mountains, and Russian look-out towers on the frontier. To the right, in Iran, broad views of steeply descending, arable land. We were glad to get down.

We stayed by the Caspian near Rasht slightly inland, after travelling 283 kilometres, and it felt very hot and humid. So we moved next day to Ziba Kenar, which Rosemary described as "a rather comfortable place by itself on the beach for complete relaxation. We returned to Tehran by a shorter route than originally planned, Chalus to Karaj. It was good to see this again, as it is really very dramatic." The Elburz mountains are very fine.

Tehran

As Rosemary related, "We attended a grand dinner-party in Tehran at the Ambassador's summer residence at Golhak, in a large garden full of fine trees. We were the only ones not in black tie but that was no great worry. The house has no very large rooms, so a huge square tent is erected in the garden all summer, hung inside with printed Persian hangings like Indian tents, and lit with pierced brass lamps. I had always longed to dine in it, so was very pleased. I believe the tent was a present from a Bakhtiari khan to a former ambassador."

17 August 1968: Mouflon with the Prince

Jahangir very kindly invited me out for a weekend mouflon shoot, based on his house and garden at Hadjiabad, west of Isfahan. We loved going there anyway. I was glad to take along my Winchester .308, lever action rifle – which was ideal for a left-eyed, and perforce left-shoulder, shot. It had an Austrian Kahles vari-power telescopic sight too, a very cleverly designed, short, small-diameter instrument, unlike other heavy, bulbous lens jobs.

Rosemary recorded the trip: "For the first time we slept outside under the full moon on the roof. In the middle of the night Michael asked if I was warm enough, I said "Yes". A few hours later when it got chilly I reached for the extra blanket to find he'd taken it. He had three. I was so cross I pulled it off him! Out in the morning, mouflon were seen but not hit. Thanks to the good spring rainfall, they are more in evidence in that area. The last few years have been very poor for hunting."

It was a lovely day out with an assortment of guns and scouts and stops in rolling hills and mountains behind. An area easily reached by Land Rover, and well driven by Prince Jahangir. Alas, I never got a shot, "amma eib nadarad" – (but it doesn't matter).

12 September 1968: A new house!

Colonel Matin, a man of property and a good friend of the Council offered us 81 Kutche Bakhtiari, Khiabani Pars. This meant a great change in our lives. It was a splendid house situated in a nice tree-lined street, opposite the Mission Hospital. The house lay at the end of a walled garden, with a garage at one front corner, right in the centre of the town. It just needed some alterations and additions – when 'father' had been moved out. Poor old boy. That's what happens to the old.

Rosemary recorded: "Michael went partridge shooting last weekend: lots of hilly miles covered and not very many partridges. I had my suspicions so mercifully I didn't go." In fact it was a lovely, cool, pleasant day: and I was glad to get to know Jahangir's brother, Reza Gholi, who organized it. He was a very charming, modest, quiet, calm, (unusual!) Persian – a fine aristocrat. This turned out to be a significant occasion.[18]

[18] See p. 378–9.

17 September: Another earthquake

We had reports of a very severe earthquake some three hundred miles east of us at Tabas in the middle of the desert. Unlike earlier occasions, trust in the efficiency and honesty of national and local aid bodies was growing, and tremendous amounts of money had been raised. With the mud and wooden-beam construction of houses it is extremely difficult to dig anyone out of the rubble, but happily one child was found alive – after nine days!

Shiraz Festival for Rosemary

Rosemary wrote: "One bright spot has been a three-day trip to Shiraz for me for the Festival. Michael couldn't come, but I got a lift with American friends; it took only six hours in an American car. What comfort after the Land Rover! That night we were out at Persepolis to hear the tiny, little, black and white Rubinstein play against the stupendous backdrop of the famous, carved staircase, and the huge, remaining pillars soaring cream-coloured into the night sky. Chopin and Lizst, beautifully though they were played, were hardly up to the setting.

"Queen Farah was there, and lots of very smart dresses from Tehran, so there was interest on all fronts. Afterwards we could wander about among the flood-lit ruins, before pacing down the great entrance stairway.

"The wonderful feature of the various stairways, set against the high, stone slabs of the edge of the great platform of the Apadana (Palace of Audience of Darius), is that they contained the most remarkably preserved and accurate reliefs of those who will have gone up and down the staircases, from palace servants, officers and soldiers, to the different races in their costumes bearing tributes of Empire.

"Then," continued Rosemary "we went to a quiet party in the garden of a recently restored, nineteenth century mansion, also superb, with long channels and pools all lit with fountains playing, palms, orange trees, and brick arcades. At the end the huge frontage was subtly lit, and a room of mirror mosaics sparkling as the first owners never saw it."

Burglary

On the night Rosemary returned to Isafahan, a thief broke in. He took a valuable piece of silver and some beautiful copper items. He sliced, with an evidently very sharp knife, a wide piece of a heavy curtain in which to wrap all the swag. The police were helpful, but nothing was ever found.

We heard afterwards that probably the same thief was disturbed in another break-in, and stabbed the poor owner. Perhaps it was as well that neither we nor the watchman heard the thief. We were lucky in that we were not burgled anywhere else in the world.

Fortunately our insurers accepted the word and valuation of Edmund de Unger, whose trained eye had earlier noted Rosemary's family's silver items, such as a Georgian tea-caddy, and we received more recompense than we had imagined. But it did hurt.

However, the year 1968 went out with a flourish. It was all most exhilarating being surrounded by friends and visitors. We couldn't have been better placed than in Isfahan for the life and work in which we revelled – though sometimes we could hardly pause for breath. No matter!

Unforgettable visitors

On 5 October 1968 we were visited by Mr and Mrs Alistair Wallace. He was a plastic surgeon and the Secretary of the Burns Society. He told us that plastic surgeons in Tehran (mainly cosmetic) earn as much in a month as he did in a year. And then there was Dr Hugh Jolly, a paediatrician from Charing Cross Hospital, and his wife Geraldine.

On 3 November we had more visitors, both official and unofficial. Stephen Bach came to sign the lease of our house, bringing with him Reg Wright, the occupant of the new post of English Language Officer for Iran, whom it was very useful to meet. We now have 700 students and classes six evenings a week. Finding the teachers was a worry. Luckily, one English graduate turned up 'on spec' – by car with wife and child. He took a great risk, but I took him on. Next in importance of the unofficials was our friend from Burma, Mark Dodd, head of B.B.C. Overseas Broadcasts. Rosemary recalled "The rain has cleaned the summer dust off the trees and domes. We took Mark on a picnic lunch down the river today – really lovely after the rain, trees just turning, honey-coloured bridge, blue jagged mountains, and white geese on the river. It was very cheering to hear that the B.B.C. gets a tremendous response in letters to their comparatively small Burmese programme." Oddly enough, Bill and Helen McAlpine, my Burma Representative, and his wife came for a day or two, en route from Norway to Ceylon. We were happy to do what we could for such friends whom we met around the world.

In mid-November Sir Denis and Lady Wright came down officially, and with them came John Cloake (Commercial Counsellor) and his wife, Molly. It was good to have just this special four to talk with and to listen

366

to. John has written a fine biography: *Templer, Tiger of Malaysia* (Harrap, 1985).[19]

We made several visits with them, the highlight being a grand lunch party given for them by Sarem-ed-Dowleh (the senior remaining member in Isfahan of the Qajar Dynasty) at his great house and garden of Bagh-i-Now (New Garden). There were silver plates for every course; one solid-silver plate for each of the twenty-four people. We were all peering at the hallmarks surreptitiously. When Rosemary told an Iranian friend about it later, he said: "Oh, didn't you have the gold service?"

We laid on a British residents' cocktail party in our hall for over 100 guests for H.E. and Lady Wright. I had very many occasions to bless Mrs Massoud (our landlady, Sarem-ed-Dowleh's sister) and James Mandy my predecessor, for our hall.

V.I.P.s thick and fast

Sir Ben Bowen Thomas and Mr Glyn Davies of the British Council's Welsh Panel were in our hands for the day. Sir Ben had come to Fiji, and it was good to meet him again. It was a bright day, a picnic luncheon down at Pol-i-Chum, and they were lovely people, ideal guests. Glyn Davies got quite frisky when we spread out the cloths and the bread and wine, and he had two 'thous' to look after him. One was Rosemary and the other Rickie Peterson, the comely wife of David who was in the Peace Corps based on the tiny town of Abadeh.

24 November: We're in!

"At last we have moved," as Rosemary wrote on 4 December, "after many frustrated weeks and unbelievable delays. We are so enjoying the space and the pleasant proportions. Other people seem to like it too. One morning we had about fourteen workmen around at one time, three or four different lots, all calling for me, "Khanum (Madam, Lady), come and look". Then you must go quickly to check their work, or they slide off fast, If one can make them laugh they are willing enough to try harder and to humour me! I am still making curtains (doing the main rooms myself) and odd items like lampshades. We had so many visitors earlier on that I could never get on with it. I seem to have been doing nothing else for months. I look forward to leading a normal life without grudging social time, some day

[19] Major Templer was in my father's regiment, The Loyal North Lancs, and already a high flyer in Palestine when Papa was at H.Q. Jerusalem, 1936.

367

soon. The move itself went well without casualties. I haven't been so tired for years."

I was well-off with a dressing-room and a study. Here I was allowed the bottom half of an old, built-in cupboard, and George 'Nadjar', our admirable carpenter/joiner, put in a rack in which to stand my rifles and shot-gun. My successor thought it was for umbrellas.

December 1968

We staged the 'Christmas Stocking' show again. In this Muslim country we had to keep to the above title. After last year's success the student audience arrived wise and expectant. Several students way-laid Father Christmas (Eric Hamburger) and tried to get at his sack before the show had started!

We were visited by John Bartholomew and six cartographers returning from an international geographical congress in New Delhi. John has been a very cheerful, life-long friend of Rosemary's family, and he stayed with us. We had a great time. Rosemary recorded,"They were such a nice group, and so easy and co-operative – usually in a group that size there are one or two awkward people. We had a small drinks party for them and on Friday took them on a long drive round the outskirts to see the type of country, and the route of the new railway. We had the office Land Rover and ours, nine people in all and were out from 11 a.m. to 5 p.m. bumping around. John took photos incessantly. What a kind person he is, he brought me the most beautiful piece of Indian silk."

Christmas and New Year 1969

This season was a trifle hectic after our move. We had a 'do' for the geographers, followed by a large drinks party as a house-warming: fifty-four people including the Governor-General came out of the seventy who were invited. We were happy.

Of course we had the office staff for drinks and presents. Also a Christmas dinner for thirteen. Drinks for Dr Malcolm Smith of CENTO Science Section. "Christmas," Rosemary wrote, "was a little low on parties – in other people's houses!" Struan Bell our Tehran librarian was staying, and after three days rest, she and Rosemary spent a week stock-taking and clearing up problems. It then dawned on them that the Persian staff did not know the order of the Latin alphabet. Big ABC guide labels were put on shelves.

Boxing Day Mission Breakfast – waffles, and the Bishop's Games

Party. Rosemary noted, "New Year's Eve saw us asleep – library stock-taking is very hard work."

Just when we had Mr and Mrs Harold Malcolm (gynaecology) with us, I was in bed for a day (the only time I can remember during twenty-seven years). Rosemary was struck occasionally, but seldom took to her bed. But she did suffer from a lack of a balanced diet, such as good milk to give calcium against osteoporosis. I just this once had a swollen tennis elbow cleaned out by Ron Pont across the road, after a whiff of pentathol. I gave away no confidences, but felt groggy enough for bed.

We had our first snow, about eight inches. One had to worry about flat mud roofs and get them scraped off by men who trudge the streets with huge wooden pushers, touting with loud cries for the clearing jobs. Walking along the streets is quite dangerous. No cries of 'gardeloo' from above. Our servants had had to walk all the way to us, but they came. What loyalty!

1969

What a relief for Rosemary to be in our new home: we had all mod cons twice over. The situation was perfect for visitors: we had a sunny guest-room, plenty of heating and hot water, the kitchen easy to keep clean and in which to produce good food. Rosemary's parents would have loved Isfahan, knowing India so well, and Mum having a true artist's eye for form and colour. Rosemary wrote: "Even on a short walk there's so much of interest to see, and all much cleaner than India."

It was a joy for us now to be able to stroll from home straight into the centre of the city onto the Chahar Bagh. We were always fascinated by whatever we saw at every step, maybe a cloth shop, a shoe-maker, a silversmith's, a craft shop of glass, copper, or tiles, or the window of a miniaturist.

To us the most familiar Safavid building, and the most attractive, is the Madrasseh (Theological College) of the Mother of the Shah, built in 1714. It has a perfect, turquoise dome with curling arabesques and wonderful tilework. This dome could be clearly seen from our house.

Vita Sackville-West in *Passenger to Tehran* expatiates in rapture and philosophic images upon this Madrasseh:

> By far the most lovely thing I saw in Isfahan, one of those things
> whose loveliness endures as a melody in the mind . . .

Rosemary made a tremendous job of furnishing and decorating our home, using local craftsmen and materials, and doing a good deal of chair covering and painting of woodwork herself. Rosemary wrote: "We are behind-hand with our entertaining, so we are having a regular Monday night buffet dinner for twenty or so, and next week the Lower Cambridge passes will receive their certificates, with hospitality and some ceremony for their efforts!" It was a very pleasant change for Rosemary not to be so tired and worried as she was in the old house with its awkward layout and all the activities going on around. That house had been attractive and conveniently situated, but gradually we were pushed out of the house by the number of students.

14 February: The passing of Prince Jahangir Massoud

As Rosemary recalled, "We have been very taken up these last three weeks or so with the severe illness and finally the death of our dear, old Shazdeh, Prince Jahangir Massoud. He had Asian 'flu after the New Year, recovered a bit, went hunting, got snowed on, got double pneumonia and complications."

"His invalid wife and his son were very hard hit. He was such a character, we will miss him very much, for his geniality, tales of Iran, and helpfulness – and many other things, though he exasperated us often. His job was becoming a problem. He had too many functions; but who could replace him?"

Jahangir Massoud was the most loyal and devoted man I have ever met. Even on his death bed, which was the last time I saw him, he was as conscientious as ever, clutching a rubber-banded bundle of British residents' passports that needed to go to Tehran for visa renewal.

At his funeral I had an inspiration. Remembering last year's mouflon shoot, I appointed his brother Reza Gholi in his stead, a retired banker whom I had come to admire and trust. I never regretted that action, he was an ideal replacement.

Rosemary wrote, "The funeral took all morning, first in the house with wailing coming from upstairs, then to the cemetery with several different rituals – I didn't go there. Then on the third day, a huge, three-hour memorial service in a mosque (9 a.m. to 12 p.m.), come and go, tea and cigarettes, preaching, for the men. In the afternoon Ellen H. and I, completely dressed in black including scarves, had to call on the widow. Entering a room of women all swathed in these black chadors (veils) weeping and moaning and sobbing, was shattering. A mullah was delivering a eulogy of Jahangir, and working them up. Then he ceased and left the room for a period, while they recovered and drank tea and whispered. We only stayed a short while."

"Three of our Tehran staff were about to present their production of

Burma

Rangoon – the catapult seller, and a maybe buyer in the arcade by our library entrance.

Our 'household', distinguished by the tools of their trade.

Our devoted teachers of English attending one of John Dawson's Teaching of English Seminars.

John Dawson's Demonstration class.

Burma

The staff of St Philomena's Convent, Rangoon, plus a part-time teacher of English.

Top left; Our two pongyi friends, U Zargara and U Hwe Pon Hla at their
quarters in the Shwe Dragon complex.
Top right; Up on the Shwe Dagon a throng at one of the many annual festivals.
Bottom left; Festival of Boys' Initiation – Little girls dancing and,
right; the walking percussion takes a break.

Burma

Bullock cart in Mandalay.

Ladies in Mandalay – note the front girl and her shan bag which everyone, man and woman needs – no pockets in garments! Ours are still very useful.

On Mandalay Hill. Chinthes guarding the entrance to a pagoda stairway.

Our family of lacquer owls, lovely in gold!

Fiji

The new Governor, Sir Derek Jakeway, receiving his respectful welcoming bowl of yanggona.

Sir Derek receiving his very special gift to a High Personage of a tabua, (whale's tooth).

A village in the interior of Viti Levu.

Fiji

Our own Party of Islands, 1965.

The British Council – Fiji.
15th May 1965.

The British Council Representative in Fiji (Mr Michael Halsted) organised a get-together of Friday night at the British Council Centre at Suva. More than 20 countries were represented. These included England, Scotland, Wales, Ireland, Australia, New Zealand, Pitcairn Island, the Solomons, the New Hebridies, New Caledonia, Tonga, Western Samoa, the Gilbert & Ellice Islands, Rotuma and Fiji. Some of the representatives are in this picture.

Among those who spoke was Mr E Christian of Pitcairn Island, who is visiting Fiji with his wife.

Mr Halsted said he had organised the gathering to give those representing Pacific Island territories attending courses at Suva an opportunity to meet people of other races.

Photograph: The Fiji Times.
(Free use for all British Council purposes.)

xli

John Mohammed loading the car with suitcases of our travelling Book Exhibition.

Fiji

School children at one of our travelling Book Exhibitions.

Sitting with the Roko Tui, i/c the Province, and his wife, at a school mekè, a song and dance occasion on the northern island of Vanua Levu.

Fiji

Spectators at the meké; childrens' families plus!

Christopher How, V.S.O., with some of his pupils on the island of Rotuma.

Fiji

John Mohammed (left) our driver and handyman, helping staff to clear up our garden after the hurricane damage – February 1965.

A couple of cats – peace reigns!

Pinter's *The Caretaker* on Thursday, but were able to postpone it for a week, so we shall have all of them staying. At least one problem was solved as they didn't coincide with Sir Derek Jakeway's visit."

"Sir Derek had finished his term as Governor of Fiji in December the previous year. We much enjoyed having him for two days, and it was good to hear more about Fiji from the top, and now off the record. He had the High Commission in Dehli astonished by coming off a long-distance bus to a special seat at the Republic Day parade, as a gesture arranged by the Indian Community leaders in Fiji."

"We are still hanging pictures and fixing things as time and money allow. Chaos these last two days as we are being at last connected to the city water supply and sewage system, everything is out of use, we have a guest in house, and seven coming to dinner!"

24 February

The cast of Harold Pinter's *The Caretaker* arrived chez nous. Rosemary thought: "This was not really a suitable play for Isfahan, very 'kitchen sink', but the chance of a play with such a small and competent cast, and only one arranged set was too good to miss. We had all five (two wives – one for production, one for lights) staying in the house to save costs. It was great fun to have the house really used, and all such good company – two were at Tabriz with us. I had never before had to produce all meals for seven for several days – a mere bagatelle for Mum with our family. Some stayed on a day or two, enjoying our peace and quiet, and the escape from their young."

Tehran for a Directors' Conference: Gardens and flowers en route

"We left Isfahan early, as it was a holiday, and drove the old way to Tehran by Natanz to Kashan, a town on the edge of the desert, where we spent two nights in a fairly crummy hotel." [Where we were able to buy a very attractive and signed Kashan carpet.] "We are good at amusing ourselves with whatever we find. Kashan is no longer beautiful or famous, but it still has its wonderful Garden of Fin, all huge cypresses and water channels and pavilions; the forerunner of the Moghul gardens."

Thanks to our visit to Kashmir from our time in Rangoon, we had found delight in the Moghul Gardens, for instance the Shalimar and Nishat Bagh in Srinagar, and the Shalimar in Lahore. A garden in such a climate and landscape depends on shelter. Vita Sackville-West described the Persian walls of sun-baked mud which are common to all Persian villages and caravanserais and gardens – and pigeon towers.[20]

To many Westerners the Persian garden appears to be only a walled orchard. But there are many varieties of trees – especially the chenar. There is the poplar certainly, then the cypress, pine, ash, elm, lime, pistachio, walnut, chestnut, and myrtle. There are the fruit trees: orange, lemon, almond, plum, cherry, peach, apricot, and pomegranate. And as for flowers, they are carefully cultivated in a natural way under the trees, dotted about, as you can see in Persian miniatures or in mediaeval Books of Hours.

The rose is the flower most associated with Persia. It may be the national flower in Britain, but the Persian poets adopted the rose quite as early as we did. We admire the charming Persian unselfconscious love of flowers. I became aware how the love of flowers, to collect, to grow, to paint, and to use them, produces charming, sensitive personalities, such as Admiral Paul Furse and the warm-hearted Baxters.

Tehran was fun. As Rosemary said, "We had such nice British staff there and some we know well having been at Tabriz together. Good meals and a film in English are treats for us as well as 'shop', and lots of laughter. I was taken back one day to a former happy haunt, our ski spot at Ab Ali. Although the weather was sleety, it was fun to see the so-familiar road again. Michael was told in his annual interview not to be so kind to his staff!"

A pause for The Tombstoners, established in Tehran

Ever since being in U.S.A. 1943–1944 and enjoying Tucson, Arizona, and learning about the 'Wild West', and myself being interested in 'hand-guns', I have kept up my boyhood pistol shooting, and thoroughly enjoyed trying to improve my skill, not so much at deliberate target shooting but more in snap-shooting – self-defence or attack stuff. I found that many young men would have a go, and in Guyana one woman! In Iran the desert was a perfect place to shoot safely.

---

[20] Vita Sackville-West, 'Persian Gardens', *The Legacy of Persia* (OUP, 1963).

372

After our Tehran start five years earlier, it was easy to pick up again, and easier still with young Peace Corps Americans, who had been brought up on the background of the Goodies and Baddies of the West. It was one young Peace Corps (possibly Greg Brown) who designed my Tombstoners letter-head from Tombstone, Arizona, and its famous sheriff, Wyatt Earp. Empty beer tins made ideal targets in the desert sand.

I had plenty of good card targets. Mr Fatemian in our Tehran Office, was a printer at home, and did me very well. We also had wind-blown captive balloons as I had had at Oxford with the O.U.R.A. In Isfahan I went round the potters, and asked for old or spoiled pots (subu, or khomré) or vases (guldan). "What on earth for?" "For targets" (hadaf). "Ah," so it was easy.

One day I went to the airport to meet a thoracic surgeon, Mr Boulton from Bristol. He stepped off the 'plane wearing the tie of the British Pistol Club. He said he found the control needed to fire a pistol accurately helped his surgery skill. Of course he came out into the desert with us. I have kept his target for emulation. We never equalled his score.

Commuting the Isfahan way

Although from our new home I had to go a little further than downstairs each morning to my work, we were both glad not to be on top of it all the time. Now I could easily walk daily to and from the office with the greatest of pleasure, over the Si-o-Seh Pol, with the river below and the minarets and mountains near and far. It was always inspiring. If I was late or lazy or had a job to do in town first, I could always hail a keraiyeh – a shared taxi. It only cost me the equivalent of sixpence. I don't understand why the system isn't used in Britain, or in Europe as far as I can gather. It is so simple and cheap. If full, a driver won't stop, and one understands that.

21 March 1969

Now Ruz has come round again, and we are off to the south-west.[21]

---

[21] See Footnote 16, p. 356.

Easter 1969 and visitors

Easter weekend followed on our return to Isfahan, and we had a lot of people around: almost all the Council staff from the north, and Embassy and American friends. People came for drinks or meals every day. Now we had many official or V.I.P. visitors. A.V.M. Sir Edward Jones from Cyprus, came on his second visit asking to see us again. That was nice. We had to go twice to the airport all 'togged' up for 'the King of Malaysia'.

Rosemary got to Tehran friends for three days, happy to drive the Land Rover on a longer distance – 285 miles – more than she usually drove, accompanied by the reliable and competent John Gurney. Two art exhibitions and a ballet show and kind friends restored her. She returned to a merry-go-round. She immediately had to attend a dinner party for a professor of English literature. We then had Roy Flood, our Deputy-Director of Books from London – an excellent staff visit. Next came the pianist, John Clegg, followed by Albert Rowe, the forceful headmaster of a progressive comprehensive school in Hull giving lively lectures and having discussions all over the place! Finally, a delightful couple, Anne and Norman Loweth, a former V.S.O. girl from Fiji, and her forester husband. I was up at 5.15 am. to take them to the airport, after two hours at the airport with another visitor the night before!

5 May 1969

Since Now Ruz, we had had sixty visitors for drinks, eats or sleeps, and twenty-four to dinner for Roy Flood.

20 May – 22 September: Home leave

We flew to Beirut, which was very hot but vital shopping was achieved. We embarked on the Adriatica Line M/S Stelvio, and reached Famagusta next morning. Then we travelled on to Salamis, Nicosia (chez Everett from Tehran days in their holiday villa), Latakia, Krak des Chevaliers, Iskanderun, Antioch, Mersin, Izmir, Ephesus, Athens, and beyond. The Wilsons of Ethiopia days lent us a house in London: marvellous.

An enjoyable period of 'home-work' in June was a staff course at Sir Paul Sinker's Jesus College, Cambridge. It was heartening and valuable to meet staff from all over the world, and to take in talks by well-known personalities on aspects of life and trends in Britain. Roy Strong stood out! We greatly appreciated the Council's generous leave allowance.

Shiraz

We made several trips to the south, which more or less had to include visits to Shiraz, a very agreeable city, and which I thought of as a twin to Isfahan.

> Pleasant is the New Year's outing, especially in Shiraz
> Which turns aside the heart of the wanderer from his native land.
>   (Sa'adi)

For such a good reason, we went to Shiraz at Now Ruz. The above quotation from the Shiraz poet Sa'adi came from Edward Browne on his way to Shiraz from Isfahan.

The more I read Edward Browne and about him, the more I admire, and envy him. The special interest in *A Year Among the Persians* is E.G.B.'s deep knowledge of the Farsi language, and his ability to handle it which put him in close touch with the people. Then his hardiness, his patience, his putting up with discomforts, his method of travel on hired horses and his awareness of exactly where he was going and what he was doing, make him a man apart. What a contrast his experiences are to those travellers of a later date who, like ourselves, to my regret, remained apart from the local people and local life. We have felt sad everywhere about what we have perforce missed.

Browne's description of the village of Yazdikhast on his way to Shiraz from Isfahan intrigued us. So when we went to Shiraz comfortably and safely in our Land Rover we wondered what we would find. It was exactly as he described:

> While I was reflecting thus, and wondering if the muleteers had, for some object of their own, deceived me, we passed through the cemetery, and all at once I came upon one of the most remarkable sights I ever saw.
>
> Right across our path lay a mighty chasm, looking like the dry bed of some giant river of the past. In the middle of this stood what I can only describe as a long narrow island, with precipitous sides, the summit of which was crowned with tier upon tier of gray, flat-roofed dwellings, which even hung over the edge of the cliff, supported by beams and rafters.

The Gardens of Shiraz and a lot else.

I have come to the conclusion that despite Sir Roger Stevens, Robert Byron, Wilfred Blunt, and others, Vita Sackville-West wrote the most vivid pieces of all on Persia, which contain quotes from Edward Browne, of course!

We were lucky to make a friend of Ibrahim Khalili Shirazi, the owner of a lovely Shiraz garden. He was very generous, and used to bring presents up from Shiraz to his friends along his way. One day in May we received a second present from him with a letter, which I have kept. He was staying, good man, at the Iran-Tour Hotel:

> Dear Mr Halsted,
> Thank you very much for your kind letter appreciating my humble gift. I hope you will kindly excuse me for this humble gift of orange chocolates and a few grape-fruits from my garden. At this moment I am on my way to Tehran.
> Sincerely yours,
> signed (Ibrahim Khalili Shiraz)

(I adore orange chocolates!). Shiraz is in the province of Fars (Pars), the cradle of Persian history and poetry. This is the south and nomadic tribal land. There are mountains for water and pasture for flocks. The valleys provide corn and citrus fruits. The lower hillsides are terraced with vineyards.

The Arab conquest was not so complete here. The city escaped destruction by the Mongols and Timur, and flourished in the eighteenth century under Karim Khan Zend (1759–79). The city is fortunately sited, sheltered by pleasant hills from the north and the south, with fertile valleys to the west. It is a city of great gardens and mirror-decorated, tall houses, such as the Narangistan, the Bagh-i-Aram or the Garden of Dilgusha, each a paradise. No houris, alas.

The Shirazis are dotty about their city, which does not surprise me. As I am not a Sufi, nor a Persian, at least I agree with Hafez:

> Sweet is Shiraz, and its incomparable site!
> Oh God preserve it from decline.

Thus Edward Browne quotes Hafez at the start of his account of his three weeks in Shiraz, to which he looked back with pleasure. The tombs of both Hafez and Sa'adi are in Shiraz, and are quite different. Hafez lies under an ornate cupola in a garden and a lovely setting reached down a colonnade. Sa'adi's tomb is more modern; rebuilt alas in the 1950s, in a spectacular position at the base of the mountains, with a turquoise dome and red marble columns. The Reverend Norman Sharp produced a beautiful blue and white card showing the tomb of Sa'adi. It is cheering to read the first English sentence below:

All the great Persian poets have numerous references in appreciative terms to our Lord Jesus Christ.

Byron mentions the gardens of Hafez and Sa'adi, and others as "delicious for their cypresses, pines and orange trees aflutter with white pigeons and orchestras of sparrows".

We were very happy being able to stay centrally on the fine Avenue Zend stretching out to the west, at the British Council, the former British Consulate-General. It had an impressive gateway and garden, with one of the Judas trees of Shiraz noted by Vita, and stores, offices, and a Residence built by British Army Engineers from India in the time of the telegraph.

The wines in Iran went by numbers. In Shiraz we happily drank the 1001 red, which may have been Byron's "dry red claret". Our supplies were most courteously obtained for us by Mr Emami, a classic, nineteenth-century character, one-time Chief Consular Clerk, now the British Council's factotum. He brought us butter too. It was very hairy but we didn't say so.

It would have been pleasant to have been posted to Shiraz with such housing and surroundings, but none of the sights could compare with the jewels of Isfahan. For us, apart from the poets' tombs, there was only the Vakil Mosque of 1773 to see, and other little buildings here and there. What is fascinating is the fine, eighteenth-century Bazaar and its contents. The wares and buyers and sellers are largely tribal folk. The gelims were unsurpassed in quality, quantity, and design. Qashqai women were striding about with flashing eyes and glittering lurex. We bought what items we could afford.

When we think of Shiraz, it is of people. There was the generous Ibrahim Khalili Shirazi. There was Mr Nemazi, the creator of the admirably equipped Nemazi Hospital; he also had a zoo. There was the English Dr Coleman at the C.M.S. Hospital, who, as the whole medical profession seems to do, lived for his patients. He had time for visitors, and was kind to us. We were warned against his total dedication to his work. He gave us a slide show: "Here is my parents' garden in England:" and (next slide), "Here is a rather interesting case of anthrax." Horrible!

Another character was the saintly C.M.S. Reverend Norman Sharp. Sir Roger Stevens mentions the "remarkable Christian Church in Shiraz dedicated to St. Simon the Zealot." He continues:

This building which was erected shortly before World War II

under the personal supervision of the Reverend Norman Sharp, is a skilful blend of Christian and Islamic architectural forms. The cruciform ground plan is that of a Christian church, but many of the details, such as the geometrical stained glass windows, the brickwork and the tiled stalactite vaulting are borrowed from Islam.

I was in touch with Norman up to 1994 when he was ninety-seven and writing so well. This extract from a letter is typical of his character.
    Churches:

I don't think that anyone will be interested in anything that I did in Iran. I built several churches there, all constructed in Persian architecture, but my name is not recorded in any of them. I did not want it to be known that a foreigner had a hand in their construction. The most beautiful church is the Shiraz one. I do not know if you have seen it. It is regarded as one of the fine buildings of that city.

Norman prepared a card for the Queen on her four-day visit to Iran in March 1961. He wrote:

One of the days was a Sunday, and it was arranged that she should spend time at a service in the Shiraz Church, after which she was presented with a framed copy of the card which has come to you. For the Queen this line was appropriate – 'Monarch and minion alike are suppliants at His (God's) Gate'. But the words were originally chosen by me because of the blessed name of Jesus. 'Value, O friend, at the dawn the Jesus-like breath that blows.'

Norman Sharp told me: "I had 43 years in Iran (1924–1967) and could not leave as we were short of Persian clergy, and I had to serve Persian Christian congregations as well as English ones." He was happily married to Barbara Carden for 63 years until she died on 4 July 1993. Norman had had to look after her for a long time. He himself died at the age of 99 on 11 September 1995.
    Another time Norman wrote:

The Suez Canal was constructed in nine years by de Lesseps, and opened in 1869. But 2,500 years ago Darius, king of Persia, who had seized Egypt, ordered the construction of a canal from the Nile to the Red Sea: and four blocks of stone describing this event

378

were placed at different sites along the canal.

Fortunately one block survived, and is now in the Cairo Museum. I send you a copy of the original old Persian inscription of Darius with an English translation. I could of course supply you with an exact transliteration, if you wanted it, but as there are twelve lines, a typed copy would take some space.

For seven years I taught Persian students in the Faculty of Literature of the University of Shiraz, the old Persian cuneiform script and language. After studying in class one of the inscriptions to be seen at Persepolis, we went out there, and read the text from the stone.

It remains a pleasure re-reading Norman Sharp's letters; and especially his Christmas message to us in 1993.

It is no wonder that you came to love Iran, as of course I also do. Bishop Dehqani-Tafti and his wife were so happy to welcome you to services in St. Luke's Church, Isfahan.

I am afraid we did not attend very often because of many factors, such as Sunday in a Muslim country being a working day for me.

The next character is Paul Gotch, who, to my mind, was for all too short a time, our Regional Director, Shiraz, 1959–66. He fitted in completely with Shiraz and life in the city and region. He contributed to the study and recording of Persian ancient history and did an excellent British Council job. His enthusiasm for Persian history, for Shiraz and environs, even for his guests, official or on a jolly, became legendary which put an added burden upon him. Energy? He was inexhaustible. Research? His work is permanently recorded in the annals of the British Institute of Persian Studies. We were dilettanti – by make-up and opportunity, I suppose; but we loved Iran no less. Paul after being posted away to other worlds returned twice to his researches.

A character to whom Shiraz owes a debt was the American, Arthur Upham Pope. He had developed a certain reputation for his knowledge of Persian rugs in particular. He decided to visit the source, and wrote:

As a result of my first trip to Persia in 1925 I came back in quite a glow over the gorgeous architecture and beautiful interior wall decorations of the Isfahan palaces with their obvious association with carpet design . . .

Pope spent a good part of his life organizing international exhibitions of Persian art. In 1966 he founded in Shiraz the Asia Institute, an adjunct to

Pahlevi University. Here, after some twenty trips to Iran during his life-time, he finally decided to settle.

We were pleased to have, in a sense, followed Robert Byron:

> This time we stopped to see Upham Pope, who arrived yesterday. Some of my photographs and information may be useful to his forthcoming 'Survey of Persian Art' (his major contribution).

I quote part of a letter we received from Pope's assistant at the Pahlevi University, Asia Institute, written on 22 February 1967:

> Prof. Pope was extremely pleased to get your photographs of Bersian, just received. He says that it was the only monument in the Isfahan area that he never saw himself or therefore, photographed, and he immediately requested that I make a file for your pictures in order to complete our records . . .

Pope wished to be buried in Iran, and the Shah agreed. A mausoleum was designed and approved by Pope, and he was buried in it on September 1969 in Isfahan on the very spot which he had gazed upon at sunset on one of his first days in Iran.

5 October 1969: Back from home leave. All well.

Rosemary noted, "Michael was very pleased with the state of affairs in the office; the new registration system of students is going smoothly; alterations to make new class-rooms are finished at last. Our four young people who are freelance teaching arrived safely, and are doing very well and getting on with their own arrangements."

We had been warned at home to expect a visit from Princess Margaret and Lord Snowdon about now and to be ready to arrange a Reception for the British Community. This did obtrude a little on our peace of mind on leave. However, en route to Isfahan we had two days in Tehran, and we were thoroughly briefed by the Embassy. Rosemary wrote, "We are told to wear short gloves which looks mighty peculiar with a cocktail dress. The B.C. in Tehran have sent us lovely big invitation cards which have raised our morale. Now we are trying to smarten up our hall, think about flowers and tables and trays and dress, and so on. The party has had to be restricted to about thirty Iranians, as there are almost ninety British." (Very tricky.) "We have a new Governor-General, so have had to call on him and his wife. They are much more social than the former, which will help a lot. The G-G is so busy having arrived in Isfahan a day after us that we haven't yet received the Persian official details of the Princess's visit – such as, are we being invited to his dinner?"

13 October 1969

Rosemary described the occasion: "All went off well as far as the party was concerned, but Princess Margaret saw hardly anything of Isfahan (or us, and vice versa) as she was prostrated by migraine on arrival. We had turned out to the airport to meet her, with just a small group of top brass and I was surprised she was in sunglasses, cotton dress, and sandals, all ready for sightseeing. Me in hat and Liberty silk. Our Ambassador told us to follow to the hotel to go sightseeing with them, but after hanging around a bit we were told she'd gone to bed. H.E. said that the day before had been very busy and full, and she had done very well all through opening our day at the Trade Fair, visiting every one of our exhibits, with 2,000 guests there, lunch, cocktails with the staff, and stayed at his Embassy dinner till 12.30 a.m.!" This after a gruelling Japan visit.

"She didn't appear all day, even for the Governor-General's dinner, but Lord Snowdon was in good form and carried out the programme. There's something wrong about asking so much of such people, although it's only occasionally. Her Private Secretary also collapsed, due to overstrain and altitude."

"It was more fun just with Lord Snowdon. We joined on to Honarfar's afternoon tour, and were useful talking with the equerry. We went round the Ali Qapu and the Shah Mosque in the Maidan. We were only a small group, and passing tourists weren't excluded. Lord Snowdon amazed us by his thirst for detailed knowledge of construction techniques in mud and tiles, and asked very intelligent and perceptive questions throughout. He's very quick and bright. He was up all the ladders to see the restoration workers' techniques, but he took no photographs. He said he couldn't do two jobs at once."

"Then H.E., who loves diving into the back streets of Isfahan, whisked us off to a carpet dealer's wonderful old house. It has a dreary mud street frontage, but inside there was the most exquisitely decorated, eighteenth-century salon overlooking a lovely little courtyard. Here we admired paintings and carpets and drank tea and ate sweets. Although it was nearly six, when most work finishes because of the light, H.E. was determined to get into the bazaar, so we shot round there, and did a quick walk around a small area, and saw quite a bit although much was closed. It was all rather dramatic in the half-light, with the security officers getting less and less happy as I appeared to be guiding them into the tattier areas, but I assured them we were turning back into the carpet bazaar shortly! Lord Snowdon has a taste for very vivid colours. He bought a cotton carpet, and was with difficulty dissuaded from a red and yellow one. It was rather a long tour, but it was fun. It would never have been allowed for H.R.H. We were at the Governor-General's dinner that night."

"On the second day Princess Margaret only managed to visit the garden of their hotel later in the morning. We couldn't possibly have organized the whole event if John McDouall and his hotel hadn't been available, with every last thing to be brought in."

"As guests arrived, Michael got them into groups roughly by occupations, and we were to set off in opposite directions with our respective Royals, confident of getting round 120 people in forty-five minutes. But when the Royal Party arrived, the Iranian guests swooped down as soon as we and the Hamburgers had made our curtseys, and quite deprived us of the little chat we'd planned before introductions started! There really was a frightful five minutes when I thought all our plans were gone, but Margaret soon sat down, to our disappointment, but Michael was at least able to control the situation and bring people up just as H.E. had suggested."

"I carried on with Lord Snowdon as decided, quite a tricky job planning who to move on to next and how to get to them, when he'd finished talking with someone. He talked too much with people, and I couldn't move him on; but he was excellent, direct and interested, lively as well. It was a great help having met him the day before so that I could adapt to his style, and he was pleased I think. He had to be dragged away in the end."

"I have really even now no idea of what else was going on, but the service was better than before – everyone on their toes. John McDouall put all the waiters into new jackets with black bow ties, and all were very pleased with themselves. Smoked salmon and caviar, prawn patties by me, other things by Ellen, such as sausages. Rather a panic to get ginger ale for Tony's whisky, not normally available here." [Princess Margaret asked beforehand for Fernet Branca, and that fairly shook us all. But the Hotel Shah Abbas produced a bottle.]

"Alas, I had no conversation at all with H.R.H., nor did the Hamburgers. Michael didn't either as he was always introducing someone to her." [But I did tell her she was marvellous.]

"There were many amusing incidents, such as jockeyings for introductions. But the British are a comfort on these occasions, all perfectly happy whether they were introduced or not. H.E. said he and Tony were in the foyer of the hotel when an American woman tried to give Tony her camera so he could take a picture of Margaret for her!"

"Then the officials gave a quiet dinner at the Shah Abbas, and there was a special display of Iranian dancing and music. H.R.H. left that fairly quickly. Up we went to the airport next morning. It took us two days to recover!"

To Isfahan Iran 1966–1970

1 November: The passers-through via Kuché Bahrami

Rosemary wrote: "Life has been very full, but chiefly with visitors, not Council activities". [But we did have working visits by two very useful colleagues from the London Office, Mrs Lee Pledger, who was in charge of accommodation etc., and Harold Bell, the auditor. Accounts are not my strong suite but George and I survived his scrutiny.] "It is almost as bad as the Spring, the number of odd people floating around whom Michael wishes to entertain."

"Sir Denis and his wife came for two nights. We like them so much, and he greatly enjoys Isfahan, so it was very easy. They had been having a few days off on a shooting-trip camp, and came laden with partridge tiny, and grapes huge. They only left after we'd gone to the airport to meet friends – it was rather a scramble to change the beds!"

Rosemary had two really worthwhile friends to stay: Margaret Barbour, and her sister-in law, Edith, who was nursing in India. Their visit made such a difference to Rosemary's morale. They went to Persepolis by taxi, visited a caravanersai, and went gelim buying from the Qashqai nomads in the Shiraz bazaar. Then they had two national holidays, a happy, religious one and the Shah's Birthday. Rosemary noted, "The hall of one mosque was all decorated with carpets, right up the pillars, and happy crowds everywhere. Even in small villages there were carpets on the front of police stations, and singing and dancing going on. Margaret was a very satisfactory visitor, being genuinely intested in all she was shown, or whoever she met."

A discovery of the past!

On a country tracks trip west with Margaret we three went further than before, and came across a small fort. It was a hunting lodge of the former Zil-i-Sultan (Shadow of the Shah), once Governor of Isfahan, with courtyards and stables. It had been quite a residence at one time. Now it was ghostly, sad, but moving. The upper rooms had their walls still papered with pages from the *Illustrated London News* and the German and Russian equivalents, circa 1894–95. It made fascinating reading, on the edge of the Iranian desert, about the Cairo Racing Season and 'Fashionable Funerals at Moderate Prices'. Charles Gault (who had been the Consul in the thirties) told us a bit about the Zil, including the fact that he travelled about with 40 -um- 'women'. No wonder his hunting lodge was up to Highland castle size.

8 December 1969

Rosemary recorded: "Life has been fairly peaceful here, a few visitors but only for the day, but high-pressure guided tours were required. Ramadan is on, so we are not giving parties unless they are essential, but we are taking a deep breath for the Xmas rush. Last Friday we had a great day out shooting, leaving here at 6.30 a.m. and returning at 7 p.m. after 180 kilometres. We were with a large group of very cheerful and friendly Iranians, going after ibex (capra hircus). No ibex were shot, but we once glimpsed a group bounding along the skyline."

Christmas again

"We have had a very busy and happy Christmas, doing our best to provide something for the various young English around, only to find there are more parties on than usual including one given by our two elegant bachelors. We really are lucky, they are all extremely able and pleasant people and liven up the social scene a lot."

"As our student numbers are so large we did our usual Christmas show twice this year, and had tea, soft drinks, and cakes first so that the student audience, who were limited to a hundred could have a chance of conversation with European guests. There was quite a lot of organization involved with props for the show as well as food, etc. I have said either a party or a show next year, not both at once twice running! Michael is too keen. This year Santa Claus was not mobbed. Then the Monday before Christmas we had forty-two to buffet-dinner over which I took a lot of trouble; it was much appreciated. We tried to play the Bean game, but the guests got out of hand at once and rushed off before getting all the instructions, Michael foolishly having told them early what they were looking for – dried, white marrow seeds, sold salted as a nibble here. Chaos resulted!"

"Michael kept up traditions by going on a Boxing Day shoot, but I stayed to clear up a bit [Friday, no servants] as the drawing-room was knee-deep in paper."

1970
More peaceful lovely days

The entry in Rosemary's diary of 31 January 1970 reads, "Instead of presents to each other, we have been getting locally made items for the future; a set of tiles for a table larger than any we have. It is such fun choosing a design and then going back several times to check progress with our ideas. We have a lovely, flowing design. We also ordered a miniature painting from a dear little man called Omumi, who has his 'studio' on the Maidan-i-Shah. He chats away very pleasantly about his work: lots of cypresses blowing in the wind and blossom trees for me, and huntsmen in the foreground for Michael. This man is producing in quantity: over 2,000 miniature-type paintings on shell disc pendants for Israel. Also a set of twenty-four large paintings for reproduction for an establishment called the 'Persian Caravan' in Berkeley, California. The exports from this bazaar are amazing."

"Despite persistent low temperatures and hard frost every night – the snow of weeks ago hasn't all gone yet – we have had some really wonderful, clear, sunny days. I took a student of Mongol architecture and his wife on Thursday afternoon thirty-five kilometres down the river to a huge [160 ft.] minaret of the eleventh or twelth century. There was brilliant sun with jagged blue hills behind and a fine sunset."

"Then yesterday six of us went after duck and snipe. It was a lovely day with a picnic on a bund in the middle of the blue water, with red tipped willows behind. No luck again. No-one minded. Tea with pancakes at 7 p.m.!"

13 February: A fire!

Rosemary reported: "A rather distracting week started on Saturday lunch time with a fire in our fuel store. By the time we were alerted by a whooshing noise – the paraffin drum trying to blow out – the fire was well away. Luckily we were four in the house, and concentrated on emptying the storeroom next door in case its roof beams caught. Michael was incredibly rapid in getting the new extinguisher, a special all-purpose type suitable for paraffin as well, into action and did manage to put out the flames playing on top of our 200-litre drum but couldn't reach the firewood beyond it because of the heat."

"He was very brave because the drum could have blown up and he hates fire more than me, maybe a relic of the war and burning tanks. Then the extinguisher finished, and then the second one, and we were running back and forth with loads, breathless. I'd rung the fire service but hadn't known if they'd understood my panic-stricken Farsi, but they rang back to check it was not a hoax. They arrived in three minutes, astounding me and had enough hose for the long distance from the road to the back of the house. All was soon over and they pulled out smouldering rubbish."

"The next day I was out from 8.15 a.m. till 6.45 p.m. helping take round three M.P.s who were having a day off from their sub-committee on

Overseas Aid. They were to call on, and lunch with, the Governor General. Michael came some of the time, and Dr Honarfar was the main guide. But helping five people to shop in the bazaar! Andrew Faulds was one of them, a bearded actor, good value, and a very strong character. He decided to buy one of the wooden-handled chain (or metal strip) flails used in the mourning processions in Muhurram. He said he would present it to the Chief Whip!"

"The day after I tried hard to put my best culinary foot forward for a dinner for our new French colleague. They have just opened an institute. We included their Consul and two other French couples and others. They came one hour late and stayed till after midnight! I suddenly realized the name of one dish was 'Beef Wellington' – was I pleased? The four French women wore black and sat together all the time!"

A good play-reading

Rosemary wrote: "This past week has been quite busy with a staged play-reading of *Arms and the Man*, performed twice: once in a university hall as it is their set book, and once in the Council. We had excellent audiences and were very pleased. It is a good play, always amusing and interesting after many hearings."

We subsequently received a reassuring letter from the Director of International Relations at the University which stated:

> I am writing to say how much the University of Isfahan appreciated your courtesy in staging the famous play of "Arms and the Man" by Bernard Shaw at the University for the Faculty and students of the University. There is no doubt that the students of English who are studying "Arms and the Man" benefitted greatly from the performance. May I ask you to be good enough to convey our thanks and appreciation.

Tehran: Jewels and carpets

Just back from Tehran from the annual Directors' Conference, Rosemary wrote, "I was very tired the first day, but a round of meals in other people's houses soon revived me. We only bought ourselves three main meals in a week!"

We luckily got in for a lecture at the British Institute of Persian Studies by our friend David Stronach. We also took the opportunity to see the Crown Jewels again now that they had been re-set, displayed, and lit by

Cartier. There were some wonderful effects in the various precious stones illuminated by tiny, powerful, hidden beams, and all the vast assemblage had been tidied up in a precise modern manner. This was all a pity. The skilled work had removed the wonderfully haphazard, unselfconscious treasures of the Shahs' from their place in history, and turned them into museum pieces.

We also took the chance to rush round our old familiar carpet places and faces in order to buy ourselves a selection of rugs to take away with us for future ornamentation, pleasure, and evocation.

"Thick and fast, they came at last . . ."

By being in Isfahan we met and made other important friends – important in that they have become leading academics on Iran. Robert and Carole Hillenbrand, for instance, were around later and were great fun. They are both now professors in Edinburgh. John Gurney, who was with us a good long time, is now a don at Wadham College and the Oriental Institute, Oxford. James Allan is Dr James Allan of the Department of Eastern Art, the Ashmolean Museum, Oxford; and Teresa Fitzherbert, who was Lady Wright's secretary, is also in the Ashmolean. It was stimulating and fun knowing such talented young people, And it still is!

As Rosemary described, "This is the busy season: new faces nearly every day hoping for a drink or a meal, and mostly good value if one had time." Turning the pages of Rosemary's Guest Book (for meals) there are a very large number of names, both European and Iranian: such an exciting assembly of acquaintances. Alas, I cannot recall nor record them all. But some I can – such as John Julius Norwich who dropped in by 'plane with Darrell Blake, when filming the historical monuments of Iran, and their restoration. He bore off two of the English girl assistants at the Blind School, and took them round with him, lucky things.

There was one young visiting professor with whom I did not start so well, but he forgave me. I was driving him in from the airport and speaking lyrically of Isfahan and our delight at being there. "My goodness," I said, "supposing I was living in, say Wimbledon – what a come-down." "Not at all. I live in Wimbledon. It is a very pleasant place to live." I now know that it is, because Paul Gotch of Shiraz used to live there.

Work for Rosemary

On top of all her guiding and entertaining Rosemary became needed as the Council librarian – part-time. She was excellent. She prefered to be at home in the mornings, otherwise the servants did very little. She took on the job from 4.30 p.m. to 7.30 p.m. when classes were on and students thronged in, and "help, to them, is really needed," as she said. The pay-off, not the salary, was that she has a facility for contact with people, with the knack and ability to pass on information.

She needed a work permit, and I had to show that she had qualifications which no available Iranian had. I wrote to her University of St. Andrews, and their reply satisfied the authorities.

Our Now Ruz trip of March 1970 to Fars Province followed, and then we had a short Christian holiday.

The Easter break

This break gave us two days to visit Ardestan, north-east of Isfahan on the edge of the desert, to find one thirteenth-century and two twelfth-century mosques, two largely unknown Safavid buildings, and an incredible nineteenth-century hunting-box tucked away up a ravine. We picked up Sebastian Cleaver, and headed for Natanz – at last!

We turned east and drove towards mountains. Swinging into a pass we could see the village of Tarq and its great stone fort perched half-way up the opposite hillside, and lovely blossoming walled orchards spread over the valley below. Towering above this whole scene is Kuh-i-Khargiz, 12,793 ft. Behind its eastern shoulder lies Natanz at 5,000 ft.

Before the Natanz-Ardestan fork we turned south to the little hamlet of Tadjiabad, which was a skeleton of its former self because its water supply had almost dried up. But its remaining inhabitants can boast of a charming little Safavid summer-retreat with garden and adjoining bath-house. Enough remains to make it worth a visit especially as the locals are so pleasant.

Unfortunately, no water flowed along the channels of the miniature Moghul Kashmir Nishat Bagh, but each of the sloping stones down which the water cascaded from level to level, had a different pattern as in the great Moghul gardens. Nearby was the underground bath-house, very similar to the one in Shah Abbas' famous Garden of Fin near Kashan.

It was a satisfying surprise to find such an establishment in such a remote setting. No-one but the Safavids could build so practically, or in such an aesthetically pleasing manner. One marvels at the architectural skill and fitness of design and decoration for such landscape settings. Alas, this was not true in Persia in 1970. The arts were in limbo. Domestic architecture had little consideration for climate or idea of taste and harmony. The modern tomb in Hamadan of Avicenna, the great tenth-century Persian philosopher and medic, looked like a petrified rocket. But Persian craftsmen can still execute brilliantly all the styles of Safavid and Qajar interior decoration (1787–1925), as can be seen in the Shah Abbas Hotel, Isfahan, as it was then called. The same building was once a great caravanserai and we remember it as such in our Tehran days (1957–1961).[22]

In gratitude we handed money to our volunteer guides. It was not easy to get it accepted, but we took our tip from Robert Byron, which still works: "I gave him five crowns, which he was loath to accept, until I employed the unfailing formula, 'For your children'."

Then we drove north past Natanz and to Abbasabad. The eastern foothills of the high mountains between Natanz and Kashan, on the very edge of the desert, have always had an abundant water supply. How else could the region contain the once great Garden of Fin, or the rose-growing villages in which the traditional rose-water industry still flourishes, or the formerly beautiful and imposing estate of Abbasabad, and most of all, Tepe Sialk?

We believed that at Abbasabad there was a hunting-lodge of Shah Abbas. We could see a single cypress on a spur, and a pool, from which water-channels step down steeply into a high-walled garden, full of old shade trees. The garden encloses a remarkable building, with a striking east facade, similar in appearance to the upper rooms of the Ali Qapu, Shah Abbas' pavilion on the Maidan-i-Shah in Isfahan.

We carried our lunch up the hill beyond the garden, and picnicked by the falling stream below the cypress tree. After lunch we peeped through the heavy wooden garden gate and were delighted to watch a family of golden hamsters popping about in a most amusing manner.

Sebastian reached the upper storey, and found at the back corner a little room to which the only access was by a narrow, angled passage. This is similar to the built-in security of approach to the upper rooms of the Ali Qapu in Isfahan. Ergo, were these the Shah's quarters on hunting trips?

We could not go back through Natanz without showing Sebastian at least the main gateway of a religious building built next to the Friday mosque in A.D. 1304. It is the most satisfying Islamic entrance we know. The proportions are impeccable. Into the soft, sand-colour of the bricks is worked all manner of patterns and calligraphic designs in a basic turquoise glaze relieved with deep blue. One can sit on a wall nearby and gradually understand the skill and inspiration of those early fourteenth-century craftsmen who created to the glory of God this simple and beautiful gateway.

---

[22] This, and many other lovely buildings, can be seen in the wonderful engravings in Voyage en Perse (c. 1840) by Eugene Flandin (painter) and Pascal Coste (architect).

There is more than just the gateway. There is the mosque itself with an opening down to the underground qanat in which there are fish.[23] Natanz is another town with its own style of pottery. Before mass production they used to produce the most satisfying shapes with bird and animal designs.

Staying with Persians

In order to have somewhere to stay in Ardestan I had to rely on Colonel Assadollah Massoud, who gave me a letter to his friend Amir Hossein Ameri – without an address, of course. People in small towns don't have addresses, it is known where they live. We were looking forward to at last being in touch with Persians, and not isolated in our vehicle.

In the town I spotted an elderly man in a hat (always ask someone wearing a hat – it denotes status and reliability). He seemed unsure of the way to our host, so I told him that I had the best of intentions towards Mr Ameri and that I had actually brought a letter from Sarhang (Colonel) Massoud in Isfahan. Ah well, that made a difference. He summoned his brother, who knew the way. He agreed to come in our Land Rover to show us. So off we went out into the desert to the south and east. The cheerful brother told me to have confidence, and we finally re-entered the town and stopped in a very narrow kuche (lane). A son of the house, Mehdi, appeared and now I learned why we had taken such a route. It was because few streets in Ardestan are wide enough for motors.

Staying with a Persian family gives one an immediate feeling of security and belonging; but there is no hope of privacy. By the immemorial laws of hospitality, the guest comes first. One is treated royally but there is no escape from the treatment. Guests don't present the same problems as guests in European homes. For one thing, as I mentioned earlier, simple Persian homes have no beds and no bedrooms furnished as such. Furthermore, quantities of the staple diet of rice, bread, vegetable stews, kebabed meat or chicken, in the usual large household stretch to feed extra mouths. The flat slabs of bread serve as plates, and fingers for forks. There may be a queue for the courtyard lavatory, but washing is done in the pool, even for Rosemary, but only the minimum! The problem for a European lies in the layout of the house, for since each room leads off the next he cannot simply retire to "his" room, he hasn't one. In the living-room he is never left alone in silence, there's never any silence.

Luckily, Mr Ameri's house had a new front wing beginning with a grand wrought-iron and glass front door. We were shown into a room, and

[23] See Anthony Smith, *Blind White Fish in Persia* (George Allen and Unwin, 1953).

after removing our shoes, sat down on cloths on the carpets, against bolsters and velvet cushions.

We were brought iced fresh lime juice, and were grateful for it. We were joined by five young men, sons, and nephews, and for a short time by Mr Ameri himself. Plates of oranges and biscuits circulated and then tea, Persian style, in little straight-sided glasses (istikan) on saucers, with diminutive spoons, no milk. The Persians put lumps of sugar in their mouths and drink the tea through their teeth. We didn't, but we have learned to do without milk. Next, pyjamas were produced and we were urged to take off our trousers and relax in these. Persians already wear pyjamas under their trousers so that whenever they relax in living room or garden or on a picnic, they begin by removing their trousers. It's disconcerting until you know. We retained our trousers and were forgiven our foreign obstinacy.

Then I made noises about getting what we needed from the car, and after some protestation was allowed out with two of the boys. Persians never seem to travel with any luggage, and "anyway," said our host, "we can provide all you need". Indeed, he could according to his customs. Then we all settled down for a happy evening.

Sebastian was the star and Rosemary the supporting cast. They chattered away merrily in confident, if ungrammatical, Farsi, and Sebastian got the boys to play cards, vingt-et-un for matches. The ice was now broken to the extent that two young sisters in chadors, Shokuh (Blossom) and Firoozeh (Turquoise), who had been peeping in at the door, were induced to enter, mainly by Sebastian who made a great fuss of them. I had horrors of knives in the back from jealous men-folk, but the girls' modest giggles seemed within the bounds of convention. We were still being plied with fruit, biscuits and tea. What about leaving space for dinner? What about dinner?

To my relief, our host soon appeared and asked if we were ready for it. We nodded rather eagerly and were led across to the other room. A plastic cloth had been spread on the carpet and all the food laid on it by the women from across the courtyard, who had once more retired. We men, and Rosemary, disposed ourselves round the spread, sitting cross-legged. There was excellent mast (a creamy yogurt), grilled chicken and meat, a vegetable stew (khoresh), with slabs of an excellent rough local bread (lavash). We drank Pepsi or 'Canada', (their name for orange fizz bottled by Canada Dry,) or 'doogh' which is a diluted form of yoghurt (mast) with herbs in it. In towns you can buy it bottled in soda water, and it is a good, refreshing drink.

Mr Ameri ate with us briefly and then disappeared. In Persia, the close of the evening meal, which is served later than in England and eaten in relative silence, is the signal for the departure of guests, and bed for the household. I heard a bit of whispering going on, and then Sebastian asked us if he should sleep in our room or with the men. He was welcome to sleep with us, but he felt that the household might be shocked, so settled for the men. After the tablecloth had been removed, bedding rolls were laid out on the carpet and Sebastian plus three prepared for sleep.

Rosemary and I were given the first room to ourselves: (what upset did this create in the family?). We firmly put up our safari beds, with difficulty refusing the offer of bedding rolls, Then came the problem of what the army calls 'ablutions'. Visits to the Asian lavatory in the corner of the courtyard were successfully accomplished. Then Rosemary, prepared like us to do the minimum of washing, went to the pool. A boy servant put on an electric pump in the house. This made a pipe over the pool produce fresh water for washing and teeth cleaning. He did the same for each of us. I believe they thought Sebastian smashing in his best persimmon silk dressing-gown, and so did Sebastian. It was the least he could do for them.

When I announced that we were ready to put the light out the men retired. But we had to have a night light in the form of a tiny 15-watt red bulb in the corner – which I later removed. Was it for some reassurance for guests, or are Persians nervous of lurkers in dark rooms?

Next morning the reverse procedure was quite straightforward; and Sebastian and I obtained hot water for shaving without trouble. We propped up mirrors in the courtyard and Shokuh and Firoozeh came to watch us. We were far from embarrassed by now. Breakfast, in the other room again once the bedding had been neatly rolled, was tea and boiled eggs and bread, butter and jam. I always enjoy breakfasts in the country in Iran. The early mornings are lovely, and eggs are specially delicious in simple homes or in smoke-scented chaikhanes.

Off we went with Abbas Ameri and his friend, Hassan, to look at the Masjid-i-Jomeh (Friday or Public Mosque), which is a remarkably beautiful Seljuk brick mosque dated 1158, one of the earliest built. Here we found the brilliant stucco work of the period. This and the magic of the brickwork itself (as Sir Edwin Lutyens describes this Seljuk art) were wonderful to contemplate.

We launched out into the brown of the arid zone on the twenty kilometers to Zawareh. Zawareh is an ancient town which was very important in Seljuk times. It has water from a narrow canal, but the great bazaar is deserted and eerie. All the children it seemed came round the town with us to the Masjid-i-Jomeh, built A.D. 1136, even older than Ardestan. It contains some lovely brickwork and beautiful stucco Kufic lettering. As in Ardestan, the short stub of the minaret was easily climbed and gives a unique view over all the tightly packed, thickly built, mud houses and domed roofs of the town. The custodian of the mosque was a kindly old man in a long robe who took peaceful pride in showing us round, particularly the beautiful, cool, vaulted, underground prayer-chambers.

We bowed ourselves out and walked through the dusty kuchés to the eleventh-century Masjid-i-Parmenar.In a circular tour we saw no less than four great, square, brick-built Husseiniehs[24] which stood empty and silent.[25] Finally we had to see Sarhangabad reported to us by Sir Denis Wright.

Sarhangabad lay beyond Zawareh. We passed the tiny village of Mozdabad, and further on we met a gnarled old man stumping along in the middle of nowhere towards us. He told us the way, which was a relief.

Driving up the rocky river bed of the main valley we entered an S-bend and suddenly on the very edge of the river-bed was the amazing house of Sarhangabad!

The house itself was fabulous still, but it would not last much longer. We lunched on the verandah imagining life in its hey-day, aristocratic hunting parties: feasting and entertainment? How was it provisioned? How many servants? Who were the guests? How did they come? And when was it last fully used?

Our return to Isfahan was via Fashakhod, a pool and dwelling; one of the best places in the country for mountain partridge in late summer.

'My' golden hamsters

My izzat (C.O.D. = honour, reputation, self-respect) was and has remained unbounded when I received a detailed and helpful letter from Mr S. R. Hedges, of the Mammal Section, British Museum (Natural History) dated 26 September 1968, informing me that I appeared to have discovered the Persian golden hamster in a new location, Abbassabad. They haven't yet named it Halstedii, or whatever. Unfortunately, we were not around long enough to trap one, or put round the word for a corpse in a suitable state of preservation to be produced as proof.

---

[24] Places where the martyrdom of Imam Hussein is mourned or passion plays presented.
[25] See Sir Denis Wright, James Morris and Roger Wood (the photographer) who produced a magnificent book *Persia* (Thames and Hudson, 1969). Included are a number of places I mentioned: Mahyar, Yazdekhast, Sarvestan, Natanz (the minaret), and the filigree stucco of Ardestan.

We can be useful . . .

Rosemary wrote on 3 May 1970, "Our weather has gone right back to cool with the best rain yet – no complaints from me, it'll be hot enough later on. We have had some good trips, including one to the mountains to see the Crown Imperial Fritillaries growing wild in their thousands. There have been fewer official visitors this year, but many individuals really interested in Iranian architecture and 'monument hunting' so we had lots of happy exchanges of finds!"

"We now know the location of a number of the smaller places around Isfahan so we can be useful even to experts!"

16 May: Summer School preparations

"Now comes the end of term followed by the Summer School for Iranian teachers of English to be held here this year – much work for three hot weeks. There should be 150–180 teachers, which is a lot, and about 15 of our colleagues and others on the staff. Luckily, I had straightforward relations with our own Isfahan Education Department, which made sure of administrative success of this Summer School.

We were wondering where to take the teaching staff on their day off, and musing over our country trips, we decided that Qamishlu, which we knew, would be the best. Qamishlu was lovely. Rosemary wrote on the subject: "It was in an amazing situation some way off the main road through completely bare hills, no villages at all, and then this compound – several courtyards of housing, stables, and yards, a large garden of mature trees with fields below using the water, all in the midst of nothing. There was a large pond in the garden, a head of water for irrigation, where we sat and revelled in the dappled greenery and the birds and the fish rising." I wrote to the owner and I received such a nice letter back in Persian, which alas I could not read.

It was once a residence of the Zil-i-Sultan with quarters and stables for his troops and horses, and a whole village inside the walls. It was now the summer retreat of His Highness Sarem-ed-Dowleh, (Sword of the King), son of the Zil, and Jahangir's uncle. Sarem-ed-Dowleh, the G.O.M. of Isfahan – a really grand, old man full of sparkle and kindness. He was Iran's Foreign Minister in the 1920s, and was the oldest surviving Qajar of the dynasty overthrown by the late Reza Shah. He was treated with great courtesy by the Shah's representatives in Isfahan. H.H. seldom visits Qamishlu now, but his son, Prince Asghar Mirza, and all that Massoud generation made great use of it. What company they are out hunting! What hunters the old Massouds were! "How long did it used to take you

394

to get to Tehran, Jahangir?" "Oh, a fortnight, hunting all the way." But there is depressingly little game left today, owing to the opening up of the country, and depredations.

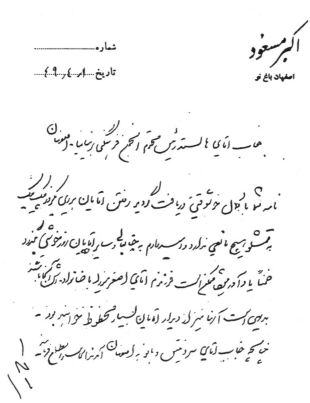

The letter reads:

June 1970   Bagh i No, Isfahan
Mr. Halsted – repected Head of the British Council in Isfahan
    Your letter has been received with great pleasure. There is no objection to the gentlemen going to Qamishlu for a picnic and a pleasant day. Incidentally I should mention that my son, Asghar Mirza, and his family will be there. Of course they will be very pleased to see the gentlemen. If Sir Denis and his wife should be coming to Isfahan please let me know.

Rosemary commented on Gulf news: "Now that the problem of Bahrain has passed off peacefully I'm not so nervous of being 'front-line troops'. You saw that the B.C. library in Rawalpindi was attacked?" What a shame! We were lucky throughout our career. Neither our offices nor homes were ever attacked – though we had anxious periods. One was always conscious of the risk.

19 June 1970

Term ended, and Rosemary gave a dinner for some fifty Cambridge Examination class students. Then after three days the Summer School in Isfahan was upon us.

It finished well at the end of July, and was reckoned to have been successful. Qamishlu had been perfect. The British Council party for about 250 people was in the Council garden. The local invited nobs were occupied elsewhere, but our Ambassador, Sir Denis Wright, who was staying with us, moved around a lot and was of course excellent. Rosemary wrote: "The Iran-Tour Hotel did all the food well. By having long tables on the drive and in the hall, all were served pretty fast. We had a band playing, so a few men (and Michael) did some local dances after supper, and the "horse" Michael had made for earlier student parties came in useful. Michael still has a bruise inside his thigh from his leg grip! We were absolutely whacked when they had all gone. We hadn't the energy to go away on holiday – it's all so far and so hot."

A reward we could not share with others

Whacked maybe, but I was very happy. Not only had everyone appeared satisfied, but whatever was the verdict on the academic side – which was not my responsibility, except my small share of class work – I received from the staff a copy of the book *The Traditional Crafts Of Persia* by Hans E. Wulff (M.I.T. Press, 1966).

Everything is to be found in the book! For instance, Rosemary and I were out for a little stroll in the neighbourhood, and we heard a very strange noise as we entered a kuché. It was a very light, rhythmic rumble, very quiet and even, and very persistent. We looked in at a doorway and saw a yard full of huge, unbaked Ali Baba jars; there was no sign of a person but no cessation of the little rumble. Until a head in its blue basin felt hat appeared out of the top of an enormous, beautifully swelling pot. I have consulted Wulff and seen it all in text and illustration. The head belonged to a coil potter, and he had produced an oven – on the age-old technique of rolling lumps of clay on a wooden board into coils, etc., etc. The noise we heard was the potter within, polishing the inside of his oven smooth with a sizeable polishing stone! Of course, going for bread we had often stood back from such ovens like tandoori ovens, waiting for our mouth-watering lavash. Now we knew.

4 August 1970
A memorable trip to Kuhrang, in the territory of the Bakhtiari tribe

West of Isfahan rise the Bakhtiari mountains, and in the area known as Kuhrang the great Bakhtiari tribe has one of its summer quarters. Here is the village of Chehelgerd, and towering behind is Zardeh Kuh, the 'yellow mountain'. Here is the source of the Kuhrang river which becomes the Karun as it flows south; and the source of the Zayandeh Rud, the river of Isfahan which flows east. This is what we had come to see.

The tribal areas were restricted, but General Zandiyeh, the area commander in Isfahan, gave us permission to enter. "No guns," said the general, and I obeyed.

We stayed the night at Hajiabad, the late Jahangir's hunting lodge, an hour west of Isfahan. His retainers were pleased to have guests again to serve. Further along the main road comes Tiran, with its beautiful dark-blue and green tiled mosque, and minarets. After the turning to Khonsar of happy botanical memories comes the area of the Chaharmahal of very fine carpets. Here are several Armenian farming communities, and back from the road a few surviving Georgian villages.

We were now up at 6,000ft. After two hours of cautious progress we came to the Zayandeh Rud valley itself. Pools in the winding river of ice-blue water sparkled in the sunlight. We stopped to eat lunch in a walled poplar grove out of the sun and wind.

In the far distance where peak piled upon peak, we could see, in August, a final snow-white ridge. Many miles further on we could see a vertical white streak in the face of an east-west ridge. This is what we had come to see, water from the south flowing Karun river, diverted into the east flowing Zayandeh Rud.

We reached the village of Chehelgerd supplying the Bakhtiaris in summer, as the winters would be too cold for village life. A figure approached us. "Iskander Faramazi?" "Bale". Yes. He was the caretaker of the Water Board Guest House. We were made welcome by Mrs Sehatpour who ran it. She and her family had left us the best rooms. In Persia, Hospitality has a capital H.

The river Zayandeh Rud came solely from a spring above Chehelgird, and flowed eastward as no more than a stream. That is until 20th Century!

We drove up to what seemed a bridge, a third of the way up along a low ridge at 9,000ft, with higher mountains behind.

At the far side of the ridge the Kuhrang river fed by long-lasting snow-fields on the Zardeh Kuh, at 15,000ft, begins its long journey southward with a constant great flow of water. It flows through a wild, rocky, useless world until it reaches the plains, and flows into the Gulf.

Shah Abbas the Great of Isfahan realised the wasted potential wealth for his capital because the Karun river source is at a higher level than the Zayandeh Rud's spring. It was he who started a dig through the ridge from the south side. The only result was a pitiful little trench which can be seen today.

Some three hundred years later, Alexander Gibb and Company were able to drive a six-foot tunnel through the ridge. They had tapped the source of the south-flowing Karun, and we were standing on a bridge over east-flowing roaring water, making the Zayandeh Rud into a permanently flowing river. This water has created a great rich valley as far as the city of Isfahan. The first of our objectives had been achieved.

We were looking down on the summer pastures of a section of the Bakhtiari tribe. Up here the tribe comes in the spring away from the parching sun of the Khuzistan plain, by way of tortuous mountain tracks and dangerous river crossings, right up through the highest range of the Zagros.

There was a lively scene below. Here and there were groups of black, open-sided, goat-hair tents with children and dogs playing, and a few sheep and goats grazing nearby. Bakhtiari women in their long bright, multi-petticoated dresses were preparing food over little smoking fires, or engaged in the back-breaking chore of fetching water from a long distance in wobbling, weighty skins. They came right up to the purest water at the tunnel mouth where pipes led off sideways above the spillway. Through these, water shot at some velocity into irrigation channels starting at this height in order to carry water to the furthest fields. Many men passed on foot, dressed in round black felt hats, and wide thin black cotton trousers, a shirt and a waistcoat. On top was a straight, open-fronted, sleeveless woollen coat, woven by their women in pleasant, vertical, blue and white varied patterns. Some were driving teams of donkeys in circles threshing corn; others tended large groups of bee-hives, because a certain mountain bush produces fine honey. Along the track and across the meadows, riders dashed up and down on their lovely little Arab-blooded horses with proud, arched necks and high-arched tails supported by special cruppers.

This was the season of weddings – after the harvest and before the winter migration to southern pastures – and many a marriage festival was in progress below us, hence all the galloping about.

We took a steep footpath down near one of the little, blue, bee-hive colonies and its owner's canvas tent. I suddenly saw a young figure running up towards us: "Mr Halsted! Mr Halsted!" I could hardly believe it, but I waved knowingly. The figure was young Najafy, one of our students of English in Isfahan. His father had retired from business and produced honey instead. When he wanted to move, he hired a lorry which took all his hives and his tent over the very road we had come, to Khonsar in the winter.

It was a lovely evening on the terrace with whisky and pistachios, and the company of Iskander Faramazi, and Cheragh Ali Khan, Iskander's uncle, who still used his black tent in summer. He produced honey himself. He very much appreciated whisky – who doesn't? He and Iskander kept us greatly interested recounting the seasonal life of Chehelgerd.

The early morning was fascinating. We sat and gazed at an animated Persian miniature on a tremendous scale.

Cheragh Ali Khan had invited us to breakfast in his tent. This is what Rosemary wrote home: " . . . breakfast in his tent, reclining against lovely, hand-woven saddle-bags, to have flat bread and honey and milk! They were very kind and took us to some wedding parties, great fun. This is the season, after the harvest. It was delightful to watch the procession of tiny brightly coloured figures move across the great, wide landscape to visit the bride's 'home'. There was lots of dancing, to trumpet and drum, the girls too, and men charging about on horses to pick up handkerchiefs."

Next morning we saw a wedding procession moving slowly on foot up the valley from the bride's to the bridegroom's tents. In the van were musicians with drums and long, bell-mouthed, brass trumpets, emitting typical mountain noises (I mean music). It was less sophisticated than the bag-pipe, but extraordinarily similar in sound to Baluch dance accompaniment. Then followed a grand swirl of petticoats, as the bride and her escort flowed along in flashes of green, pink, and gold in the soft sunlight. Up and down ran little boys and girls all in miniature Bakhtiari costume, and of course the dogs came too, around the heels of the horsemen tittuping along beside the swathe of colour.

Coming down to meet them, but taking care not to become involved, was the bridegroom on a lovely piebald horse (a rarity), with his best man also mounted. They put up a fine display of nonchalant horsemanship.

In the afternoon we went into Chehelgerd, where we were drawn by the smile of the man who made the black Bakhtiari pudding-basin felt hats and stiff-sleeved, felt coats which, as his small son demonstrated, stood up by themselves. I couldn't resist buying a felt hat to add to our Acting Box.

We wanted to buy at least one gelim and if possible a horjeen – a woven, woollen carpet saddle-bag. Iskander directed us to the tent of a well-known old Bakhtiari woman, at the top of the valley. We drove as far as we could, and then had to walk steeply up.

Fearsome dogs were beaten back for us as we approached, and we were made volubly welcome by a coven of hags, and younger offspring who clutched the next generation. We sat cross-legged as long as we could and searched among the woven coverings and embroidered cushions, but we were unlucky. All we got was sour sheep's milk. For this a young man had run the gauntlet of the next camp's dogs, and I feared for his safety. He came with one of those vast Persian tumblers called 'livan', brimming with milk; I found it tasted disgusting and the flies were sickening. Luckily one of the babies knocked it over when it was my turn, so I didn't have much to finish. I was therefore able to beam out my gratitude and then mumble about having to get back for a wedding party.

A local Khan had invited us all to return to his tents after dark. Three craggy Khans came to greet us. We were squeezed into a body of cross-legged, black-hatted men. We disposed ourselves onto portions of cushions or rugs between seemingly interlocking knees. The pressure-lamp was set down in the middle. Behind us women stooped over pots of rice and stew and turned skewered chicken over charcoal grills. Others slapped out unleavened bread, while their daughters in flowing skirts and petticoats dashed helpfully, and coquettishly I suspect, hither and thither among the guests. What a pleasure to be in a country where alcohol is far from the measure of a party's success. It is, of course, forbidden by the Prophet.

We conversed as best we could but we soon left them to their gossip and repartée. We enjoyed just looking and listening. I sat next to one of the rare outsiders, the young officer commanding the army's area detachment. He was accepted – as a neighbour; a remarkable change of role.

On the far side of the group, I could make out a crowd of younger faces standing behind their seniors, laughing and joking, shifting about. They were worth studying, for their sheer masculinity and dark, rugged features, with a few, round, fair ones. Settlement cannot come easily to such people. However, the Government of Iran is doing much to help the tribes to adjust to modern life, by providing schools, clinics, and wider medical services for those who wish to settle.

Before long, the women were at our backs passing the food to us from their open kitchens. Very shortly the musicians started up. The largest and most plaintive trumpet was opposite me. The volume was distinctly painful. I was taken by the reaction of the young. First of all, one of Iskander's very small daughters danced charmingly down the length of the table rugs. She stamped her little feet, dipped and swayed, moving her arms and neck and hips in contra- movement, to a strange and hesitant rhythm.

We saw the real thing when the unmarried girls danced in a dim-lit circle beyond the feast. The young men crowded round to appraise until they could bear it no longer and themselves jumped in. The girls stood aside with a good grace, and yet the animation of their innately striking features increased. There were beauties among them; but the intensity of those piercing eyes revealed a depth of passion which gave me a feeling of total inadequacy!

The men's dance was very different. There were just two in the ring for the stick dance: provocation or defence by one against attack by the other.

Since I obviously enjoyed every minute of it, I was prevailed upon to have a go. I could manage the movements and rhythm, but I simply could not grasp the conventions, and I was grateful to my opponent for his forbearance. How exciting it was to be encouraged to enter the ring, and I revelled in my last 'fling'. There were no protestations against guests' departure, and the same Khans readily escorted us with the pressure-lamp back to our vehicle.

Next day we left after lunch, but first we stopped at the tent of Mr Najafy, and bought two huge combs of honey in plastic bags. They remained intact when placed vertical behind our front seats.

We took the more direct route via Babar Haidari, Farsun, and Shahrkord. We halted briefly by a lovely fall on the river, by a rock known as the Elephant's Nose. We crossed the salt-pans which lay in a narrow, sunken valley, where women were cutting out blocks and loading them onto donkeys – a hot and messy business it looked, in the glare.

Reaching a small village, we found a tribal unit engaged in mounted sports as we had seen at Chehelgerd, no doubt as part of more wedding festivities. The men were galloping at red kerchiefs on short sticks snatching them up in marvellous displays of balance and agility.

There was still more to see and many familiar spots to say good-bye to. Across the next plain we passed the turning for Bagh Baderun, a riverside village, the home of Babai of our Tehran office. Here his family had entertained Sir Denis Wright, Stephen Bach, and me on my first week-end in Isfahan.

Then came the riverside village of Chamaseman, the home of Parveneh Chamasemani, our good friend and teacher of English in Isfahan. The Zayandeh Rud is beautiful here, for the valley is full of trees and rich gardens. The road returns to it at Pol-i-Qaleh (the Bridge by the Fort), a lovely old stone bridge with a popular tea-house on the east bank. At the thirty-kilometre sign out of Isfahan we waved to Bagh-i-Vash, where once the Zil-i-Sultan had a zoo; and where a great spring floods the land in winter. Here, with Reza Gholi and Colonel Massoud, we had sloshed through the bogs in vain attempts to close with the Siberian geese and various duck. But we did shoot snipe.

Sometimes at this point we would take visitors along a track to the beautiful fourteenth-century mosque of Ostorjan. This evening we could just see the broken minarets peeping through the trees against the hills beyond.

On the east bank of the river lies Lenjan. Here one finds a lovely example of Mongol architecture in the tomb and mosque of Pir Bakran.

We were becoming confident enough to start on a little guide-book on Isfahan and Environs, since I expected to remain another year. But I was suddenly ordered to take up the post of Representative, Guyana. It may have been promotion, but it was a shock to us both: our one heart-break.

We had two nights in Tehran before flying home. We cared too much for our friends there to pass them by, and we were rewarded unexpectedly by the Wrights very kindly inviting us to luncheon. That was the best way to leave the country we loved.

We were able to return to Isfahan in 1975 on our way on home leave from Karachi, and again in 1978 on leaving Karachi for Morocco. This visit was not so happy. The revolution led to the loss of two fine Christians whom we had admired: the brave and cheerful Revd Aristoo Sayyah in 1979 in Shiraz; and in Tehran in 1980, Bahram, aged twenty-four, the son of great promise of the indomitable Bishop Hassan and Margaret Dehqani-Tafti.

Both sacrifices are recorded in the *Book of Modern Martyrs* in the Martyrs Chapel in Canterbury Cathedral. Here are two verses of a poem in Bahram's memory written by Michael Burn.

> I never learned the language you returned to,
> Or saw the country you refused to flee.
> To me it just meant poverty, and domes, and princes
> Sauntering through the gardens among nightingales.
>
> The East that my imagination fed on
> I never dreamed would disquiet me with this death;
> Or show me Oxford's happy scholar lying
> Like a young saint in jewelled Isfahan.

We were lucky to have come to know a little of Bahram's wonderful country.

Interlude in Guyana
1970–1973

Our move from Isfahan to Georgetown would be our third jungle posting after Burma and Fiji. We still prefer deserts, but the Guyana experience was worthwhile. A Scot in 1760 wrote with lasting truth:

> The country round the Arinoco which we call Guyana
> seems another world: so splendid and remote, with huge
> mountains and fierce rivers in a continent that even now is
> scarcely known.

All life – I mean all the life Europeans brought there – clings to a fringe beside the sea. The islands can be penetrated and even mapped, but in Guyana, who knows what happens a few score miles inland. And of those who discover, how many have returned to tell? Luckily we have.

The Dutch took control in 1621; and then the French from 1782 to 1802. Only the Dutch with their experience and expertise in the Low Countries could have made a viable settlement on a miserable coastal strip some ten to twenty feet below sea level. Their extensive and expensive drainage systems remain vital, and so does the sea-wall, kept in repair in our day by Messrs. Halcrow.

The whole country was ceded to the British in 1814, to become British Guiana until 1966. The slaves, who did all the work, were freed in 1838. But their descendants didn't forget this degradation.

Our voyage

Off we sailed from Southampton on 24 September 1970 on the one-class Dutch 'Oranje Nassau'. Our heavy baggage hadn't caught up, but our new, white Hillman Hunter estate was on board.

We were lucky to travel to post by sea again. We enjoyed the rest after the force-8 gale, and especially the contact with the British and Guyanese bound for Georgetown. One table companion was Bella Datadin, a Guyanese staff-nurse based in Britain who was returning for a break at her home in Crabwood Creek, down on the Courentyne River, the border with

403

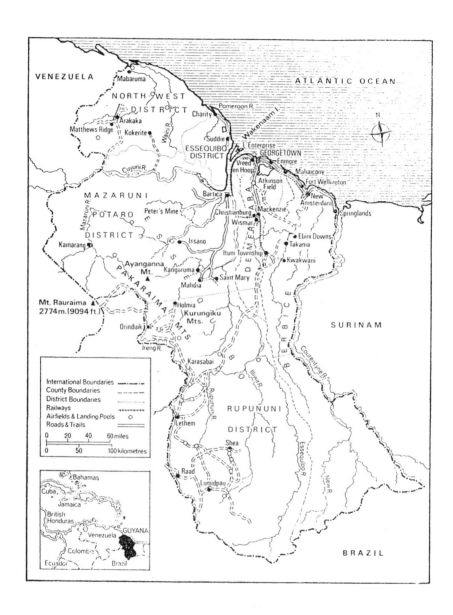

Surinam. She became a good friend. The crew spoke excellent English, were cheerful and friendly, and produced imaginative diversions. If only the purser hadn't been quite so assiduous in kissing the ladies!

The shore-line at Paramaribo, where we put off eighty-eight Dutch passengers, was not as forbidding as we expected. We got ashore and found the whole town to be attractive and individual with fine Dutch, brick buildings which gave Paramaribo a prosperous and welcoming air.

On we sailed through murky waters to arrive at Georgetown the next day. I quote Evelyn Waugh who sailed to Brazil via Guyana in 1932:

> Blue water ends at Trinidad; there and from there onwards the sea is murky, opaque, dingy stuff the colour of shabby stucco, thick with mud sweeping down from the great continental rivers, the Orinoco, the Essequibo, the Demerara, the Berbice, the Courentyne. All along the coast their huge mouths gape amidst dune and mangrove, pouring out into the blue Caribbean the waters of the remote highlands.

Yes, brilliant observation and description, as we found out, but we did not travel as far as the Orinoco in Venezuela.

Arrival

Georgetown, situated on low lying land up the muddy mouth of the Demerara river, did not look very exciting. There wasn't much colour about, but we had a fine welcome from the British Council admin. man, Brian Chan, and a British High Commission Representative, and by Jim and Dorothy Hardman. Jim was my A.C.E. (Aids to Commonwealth English). Both he and Dorothy have a great sense of humour and a lot of histrionic talent between them. I had no customs or immigration problems as I had diplomatic status. We were whisked off to the new B.O.A.C., Forte Guyana Pegasus Hotel, a round tower in which we had to stay until we could get into our house. It was a bit awkward having to live and sleep in a room the shape of a segment of a circle, but the facilities and service were very good. There was a large, sociable, swimming-pool area with eating and drinking surrounds, and constant warm outside air. We were plied with a variety of rum drinks, and assessed! The Guyanese of course pronounced the hotel name as Peg-arsus, which I'm afraid sometimes was referred to as the Pig's Ass. We retreated into our segment up in the Pegasus tower in a state of gloom. When I moaned in a letter to Papa, he replied in his wisdom: "It is the usual story of all who follow the drum round the world. The last place was paradise to this new one."

The Guyana Government required British Council London staff to be integrated into the British High Commission. So, after an interview in London, I was really rather pleased to find myself First Secretary, (British Council Representative) – I was number four in the batting order under Bill Bates, the High Commissioner, John Sankey his deputy, and the First Secretary, Political. I was newly responsible, in terms of the British Council, for some aspects of the Overseas Development Administration and its staff in the field. This gave me a wider and more interesting view of what Britain was trying to do for Guyana. The O.D.A. staff consisted of a number of congenial, qualified British men in diverse fields.

They were good company and good value. They could also be sharper towards the B.H.C. and the British Council than the equally stimulating seventeen V.S.O.s! As a first-time diplomat I found the post interesting and helpful because it allowed me to gain insight into the Foreign Office mind and work, especially when I was kindly invited to sit in at various meetings which did not wholly concern me.

The British Council office was in a pleasant, three-storey, wooden house on a wide, flame-tree-lined street with a wide trench (drainage ditch) down the middle allowing a dual carriageway with connecting bridges at intervals. The B.H.C. was just down the road. We had plenty of office space and room for a library, five staff, and three driver – projectionists, a gardener, and a night watchman. I gave the staff and myself more room by moving my office up to the top floor, which was still quite accessible, yet peaceful.

I was very lucky. I had as my P.A. a most congenial, helpful, and efficient Englishwoman, Marjorie Crombie, who was married to "B.L." a fine Guyanese athletics coach and administrator. They had a young son, Richard. I was happy to get on so well with such a 'local' person; and she was a great help to Rosemary. I had the beautiful Yvonne Ramsahoy as secretary. She was one of a very fine Indian-Guyanese family of distinction and service, and consequently she knew everybody, which was very useful. I had an admirable accountant in Jeanette Alexander, and it was essential to have such a person. She was one of six remarkable sisters in and out of Guyana. Jeanette later joined the British Council in London. Brian Chan also ran the record library. Being part Chinese he was efficient and very personable. I also had around the place ex-Cpl. Mohabir Singh, who had been in the British Army and served in Aden and Cyprus. He was smart and very useful. We understood each other, and got on fine. Mrs Phyllis Shepherd was our librarian, an absolutely charming, and very talented Guyanese. She welcomed everyone so well to the library, encouraging callers to read our books or papers and magazines. She was always at hand with help or advice. Phyllis was also a pillar of the local Theatre Guild, which achieved excellent popular productions of English and Guyanese drama or music in its little playhouse. The Guyanese and most of the Caribbean people are compulsive talkers and natural actors, and the Guild went along splendidly.

Luckily for us we arrived in time for a concert programme called 'Six Guitars and a Flute', which was terrific. The flute was played by Corporal Keith Waithe of the Guyana Police Force Band. He was not only brilliant but very funny. He was the first person in Guyana to be awarded the Licenciate Diploma of the Royal Schools. I was able to get him a scholarship to the Royal Military School of Music, Kneller Hall. He continues from strength to strength, but in Britain. From the music we heard in Georgetown I was most struck by his combination of flute (which he played perfectly), two guitars and a banjo. I would put money into the success of such a group called The Kisikisi.[1] Jim and Dorothy Hardman were much in demand by the Theatre Guild for production and performance. They helped our image greatly, and gave much pleasure.

The large part of our work seen by the Guyanese public was the showing of films to schools, clubs, the Services, etc. The projectionist team run by Messrs. Croall and Bollers in Land Rovers were out at all hours, and under all conditions of weather or travel, and they did a great job, almost entirely unaided.

In addition to normal liaison with the Guyanese Ministry of Education regarding courses in Guyana for teachers, I spent quite a lot of time on administering those going to Britain for training under Technical Assistance – as policemen, librarians, firemen, engineers, and the like. I first had to learn about their parent bodies, see where training would help, suggest courses, and note possible candidates. I was a link man putting Guyanese in touch with the right people in Britain. I could also advise potential visitors from Britain, through British Council departments, on what was needed, and what might be expected from Guyana. There were many other official visitors 'in their own right', Government invitees for instance. It was a pleasure to help them all, and I found it very interesting.

I also enjoyed being British Council within the High Commission, which made it easier for me to pass on to B.H.C. staff local background information which I may have obtained, or to join in the policy decisions which particular cases might require. Rosemary reported home: "Their staff always seem to have time to talk at length. They may not realise that Michael runs the whole show himself, and copes with London's flow of correspondence re accounts, furnishings, bursars, book exhibitions, etc!"

[1] See p. 439 The Zoo and Fauna.

As often happened in other postings, we were at first not too happy with the house on Church Street rented for us by the British Council. The Portuguese landlord Mr Gomes wasn't keen on spending money, and both the house and the British Council furnishings were somewhat dilapidated. Like most Georgetown houses it was built of wood, painted white, and raised on concrete stilts. We lived below sea-level! The area under the house was useful for drying laundry, or holding film shows or large parties. The Films Department did us very well, sending out, for instance, *The Go-Between, A Kind of Loving, Accident, Billy Liar*, and the hilarious, *Morgan, A Suitable Case for Treatment.*

Our closed-in stairs at the front of the house led to a large, L-shaped room which got all the sun but, unfortunately, none of the prevailing north-east breeze which was essential when living in high humidity. There was a long balcony at the breeze end, with two smaller rooms within. There was a garden below, with grass, but not a lawn. Our Indian gardener had to cut it by hand. The grass grew in very hard soil, deeply fissured despite the rains, and it was not easy to walk on. But the area was pleasantly edged by palms, an old mango, and a handsome breadfruit tree. Rosemary planted cannas at the far end, which could be seen from the balcony. There were also hibiscus, bougainvillea, ixora, flame-trees, and a royal palm. Next door was a little tin mosque, which with the sounds from within made us feel at home after Isfahan.

Indoors, up the back outside stairs, was an adequate kitchen with a very good gas cooker from our Supplies Department. We had two excellent maids, Sybil and Olga. Being Guyanese, English was their native tongue. Not only could Sybil read recipes, but she enjoyed looking at cookery books. Sybil was a treasure. She went up in my estimation when she told us she knew Clive Lloyd. She shone specially when we entertained such cricketers.

Going about the house we discovered little heaps of very fine, brown powder on the floor or in odd corners. "What is this, Sybil?" "Grammy sugar, Madam." It was the deposit from the depredations of termites. It was horrid to tread on, and had to be cleared up every day. We also had cockroaches, which are the most horrible of insects. They are intelligent, very fast movers, and alarmingly bold. I cannot cope with them. Margaret Bacon in her excellent book, *Journey to Guyana* (Dobson, 1970), tells the most horrifying story of meeting them. "Call Rentokil!" was our cry, and our salvation. Whenever I see one of their vans around, I think of those Guyana days.

Interlude in Guyana

Birds and James Bond!

The great joy of Guyana was the birds.[2] In Georgetown I was able to buy a copy of James Bond's *Birds of the West Indies* published by Collins in 1960. The author's name was taken by Ian Fleming for his hero. Collins' Bird Books are excellent.

'Manna' from Heaven – not for us

I am up after sunrise and whilst shaving I can just see the garden and the mango tree if I peer through a side window. Then I hear: Foomp! "Bloody hell!" I mutter and then cry, "Olga, Sybil, Rosemary, out in the garden quick, get the fallen mango before a parrot, kiskadee (a predator with an irritating call), a yawari (opossum), a small boy from over the fence, or our night watchman gets it!" Still half-soaped I get my catapult (made while a boy at Bradfield), and cursing away try to scare off the saucy little parrots who are nonchalantly edging either way up along a branch, helping themselves to this most delicious of fruits which we want for our breakfasts. But they are very funny.

Garden birds besides parrots!

I am afraid we have a skimpy knowledge of birds at home, let alone abroad; but thanks to *Birds of Surinam* (Oliver and Boyd, 1971), we were able to identify some which came into our garden. These included a fork-tailed flycatcher on 9 May 1991; and a yellow oriole in December 1992. Humming birds were common place and we didn't try to sort them out. The most common and regular birds, which were very likeable, were varieties of tanager: the blue-grey, palm and silver beaked kinds. They loved the showers of rain and gleamed in it! We even had a stray pearl kite in one day, and tropical king birds sometimes, which are reported to be common.

We had a joke bird too: the blue-black grass-quit or Johnny Jump-Up. After sitting on the fence minding its own business unlike the parrots, it suddenly leaps vertically up in the air uttering a sharp "pzeet!" and then shoots down again. It's as if it suddenly had a guilty conscience, or been bitten by an asp.

---

[2] See Book List.

The furnishing game

We had to make do at first with scrappy furniture. But after many months and thanks to the understanding, good taste, and procurement skill of Ken Reed in our Supplies and Despatch Department, we received exactly what seemed right and was strictly necessary for our type of house and social use.

We found we spent most of our time on the balcony, eating there as well. The need to live in a breeze was another novelty for us. But if we wanted to listen to records or the radio, we would have to sit indoors because of the frogs. Whatever kind, shape or size they were, or living style they preferred, they seemed to fill the surrounding air space with squeaks, whistles, peeps, and burps, FORTISSIMO. We had Western music on tap on the local radio, and the B.B.C. was clearly relayed – two more bonuses for us. But outside the frogs and cicadas drowned any music. Even Wagner could not compete. No similar sound heard since could be more evocative of Guyana nights.

We were in the Tropics for the first time. This meant an annual mean temperature of 84°F only descending to 74°F. It was always hot and humid, but never excessively so as in a monsoon climate. We had a high rainfall on the coast of eighty to a hundred inches annually. There was a fairly constant north-east trade-wind, which was a bore sometimes but it occasionally eased the temperature. There was a dry season from January to February, and from May to August, which was the planting season. Up in the Rupununi savannahs in the south, there was one long, dry season from October to March.

Our morale rose when our Hillman Hunter estate appeared at the office off our ship almost immediately – diplomacy has its points – and was ready to be driven to our home. It was a good buy and never gave us any trouble. But this reliability was also due to being put on to Cyrus, who was an independent mechanic only a few streets away.

We were given much advice and support by the British High Commission starting with Bill Bates, the High Commissioner and his sweet wife Susie, who was from the Service herself. John Sankey, Deputy High Commissioner, said to me: 'When you drive to the office be sure to keep your eyes on the road". I was a bit taken aback which he saw with a grin. "Have a look at the back of any car in Georgetown and I bet you find that most have dents in them. That is because the chaps driving to work will be looking at the girls' legs, and they usually bump into the car in front before long." Mini-skirts had just come in. I soon saw the sense of his warning. Of the large mixed population there were many attractive girls. The mixture does the trick. We knew some, such as the lovely and talented Hunter girls, Carrie and Felix. Many go to work on the cross-bar of their man's bicycle. One leg is crooked and the other out straight for the best balance, and ease for the pedaller. With a mini-skirt above, wow! "We felt the wrong colour," says Rosemary. "A pale skin in those parts is unattractive. Brown is just right in the strong light and with all the bright colours worn. I felt a revulsion at the white skins. The Amerindians are a perfect colour." It was a bit of a shock to find that the daily clouds of cyclists, who behaved sensibly on the whole, had rights over the motorist. We don't get the same status in Britain while we shop by bicycle in retirement.

The first few drives round about told us the Guyana story in brief. It seemed that the whole settlement was still precarious, protected only by a seawall. The coastline was below sea-level: ten to twenty feet, I believe, in some parts but by Georgetown only three feet. In central Georgetown there seemed to be more trenches, or water area, than streets. And just as well, for we were never flooded. In the suburbs the scene and conditions could be very unpleasant and grim. Behind the shore, below the high-tide level was a half-mile-wide strip of back-shore. This area contained housing which meant that quite an area of greater Georgetown was very prone to flooding. The houses, which were all on stilts, were sometimes isolated after heavy rain by water which took a long time to drain off.

We saw that inside the sea-wall the drainage channel network and the great sluices, which were a feature of the town and country, were vital for the towns, but even more so for agriculture along the entire length of the coastal strip. The responsibility for the whole system was with the Ministry of Works, Hydraulics and Supply. We never ceased to admire the work of the Dutch, who had been the first to tackle settlement on this coast. Even so, tides came up the trenches, and if these overflowed, sea-water would be deposited on the land. Where there wasn't sufficient drainage the back-shore became an unappealing, brackish swamp, of interest only to zoologists and botanists, and pleasant for amphibious creatures, but which was no good for food production.

The sea-bed off Guyana is a gently sloping shelf leading up to a shallow foreshore which is composed of thick deposits of shell, sand, and silt. This is backed by a belt of mangroves (*Rhizophora*, *Avicenna*, and *Laguucularia*). Owing to certain tide and current action, the mud or silt banks gradually shift from area to area, adding interest for those who frequent the shore as we did. Guyana in Amerindian means 'The Land of Many Waters'. The colour of the sea off the flat coast is largely the fault of the great rivers (as Evelyn Waugh described the scene). The coastline itself is not attractive, and the human habitations do not help. We found uninspiring sameness in the wooden houses of the settlements, and their almost contiguous siting along the one coast road, with sugar cane and rice fields stretching far behind, reached by unmetalled roads and tracks.

411

One was conscious of the powerful ocean just over the sea-wall, the upkeep of which required a considerable outlay in men and materials; almost too great a burden for such a little country. When we walked a little further east, always keeping a wary eye on any passing persons, we found that over eighteen months a shell bank was building up over the Kitty stone jetty that we would walk down. Further east, the sea was scouring away the shell base of a pleasant, green strip of coarse, salt-tolerant grass and sportina, and other thick-leafed plants. We often walked this way watching the sea-birds. There was the occasional elegant frigate-bird, various terns, and the black skimmer with its longer, lower mandible scooping up mud-hoppers as it almost hovered along. We were to find the birds of Guyana a joy and a revelation and a recompense.

Hot and cold shirts

While we were settling in it rained heavily every few days and the humidity was oppressive. We had sufficient light clothing until the baggage arrived, but we didn't know that the official formal garment was the tie-less shirt-jac: a long-sleeved shirt-coat with pockets. It was practical, and smart if well-tailored. And good tailors there were, Chinese or Indian. Ties, announced the Prime Minister, were vestiges of colonialism and were out. But not entirely for us. It was nice to dress on occasions in a smart tropical suit, shirt and tie, (Guyana Cricket Club tie later). But the Guyanese favoured 'hot' shirts of very brightly coloured even garish materials. I was shocked at first, but I came to enjoy my selection of 'hot' shirts and my usual more sober (cold?) shirts of lightly patterned material. Bookers Store had lovely materials, and much else. Bookers was an important element in Guyana's economy; I am sure that Guyana did not benefit from nationalising it. On the other hand, the paternal presence of Bookers wasn't altogether beneficial for Guyana. Bookers (Guyana) supplied absolutely everything, and in consequence there were no artisans in Guyana: everyone had always "got it from Bookers".

We personally owe a lot to Bookers because we found special friends in John and Maria Hudson, Booker hands of long-standing. They often took us out on fascinating short trips providing chances and choices of up-river locations by launch, which we needed to know. There was also bachelor Arthur Goodland, a Booker senior. He had a lovely house, was highly intelligent and very well read and a most able sculptor. He became a good friend. Then there was Ian MacDonald, whose evocative book on his childhood in Trinidad, *The Hummingbird Tree*, was televised by the B.B.C. and shown on 19 December 1992.

Bookers management made the swimming-pool in its attractive town estate, Colgrain, available to diplomats. This was a real boon for Rosemary. We kept to Bookers for all our shopping. It had a Diplomatic liquor store and, to my delight, I was allowed to choose my liquor. I went straight to a cache of fine wines remaining from the Grenadier Guards Mess of earlier, troubled times and was thus kept well supplied. Rosemary could buy our main food requirements from European or Indian stores, but she usually bought the fruit and vegetables in the crowded, hot and noisy pavement-level market, choosing from little piles brooded over with much cackling and wise-cracking by large mamas. This was fun in a way, but very wearing for Rosemary, and very hard for her to account accurately, as required for official entertainment returns.

Georgetown was well off for jewellers, and I enjoyed buying Guyanese gold nugget ear-rings for Rosemary, and gold, Amerindian-design cuff-links for myself. Of more use, were the Bata shoes which we encountered for the first time, and of which we bought several pairs They were cheap, long-lasting, and especially good for jungle conditions. Rosemary's real success was at an Indian pawnbroker's. In his inner sanctum the gentleman showed her a pile, (about two square feet) of unredeemed, beautiful silver bangles from Indian labourers' ladies ankles and wrists. She bought a few for nieces which were much appreciated. We should have bought many more at those very good prices.

Food and drink

I thought of writing a Guyana A.B.C. I have the ingredients on cards for a rainy day. Now I will give you F for Food, and mention Pepper Pot. This is a very ancient form of long-lasting stew. Meat of any kind, wild or tame, is added to the pot day by day, casareep as required, peppers, and black sugar according to taste.

Casareep is the poisonous by-product of cassava the staple food of the Amerindians when made into cassava bread. But the white root must be scraped and grated, and packed into a matapi, a long, cylindrical, woven basket, and the prussic acid squeezed out. The cassava can then be baked into big circles of (tasteless) bread. The poisonous liquid is boiled into a thick syrup. It is then safe, and becomes a house-keeper's blessing: a preservative for meat stews such as pepper pot. It is essential in a world without refrigeration. The Amerinidians are wizards at making beautiful, delicately woven containers.

D for Drink

Drink seemed to be a large part of life in Guyana, and rather a lot of alcohol was drunk per capita compared with many other countries. Rum is the drink; and it comes from sugar cane. Working sugar cane, as we had first seen in Fiji, is a very tough life. We passed the distilleries outside Georgetown on the way to the airport. From a 1970s Visitors' Guide we learned that the local rums were X.M., Russian Bear, El Dorado, and King of Diamonds. Other spirits made locally from sugar cane were Gilbey's Gin, Booth's High and Dry, Smirnoff Vodka, Diamond Club Gold Label Whisky, and Bardinet Brandy. The local whisky didn't agree with me but Banks beer was good.

The local rum agreed with everyone. Giving a party was no problem, once our Guyanese guests had got to know us. There was sadly, but understandably, an inner reserve – a reminder to us of their slave origin, and who had run the slave trade. But having got over that, the Guyanese were great ones for parties, for 'jump-ups' – rum and reggae being the catalysts! Their colonial status until independence in May 1966 was never mentioned.

An incentive for giving a party, and a considerable help at reasonable cost, was the existence of a 'corps of waiters'. They were employed by everybody and must have done very well. They were not only efficient but they soon got to know what people liked to drink, and how much. What else must they have learned (and been paid for)?

One drawback about Georgetown life then was the lawlessness mainly among the youth. Many youths had difficulty finding work; at the same time they were not terribly keen on work. They were very happy to laze around. It just comes naturally in the Caribbean: easy climate, easy food, easy pickings here and there if rum was cheap, reggae music was cheerful and so was the company. At the same time there was neither a high regard nor support for the law. Such attitudes do not always go down so well in England. No wonder our police became very suspicious (sometimes rightly) in the early days of immigrants, and not sympathetic to the lay-about attitude which struck them more like insolence or loitering with intent. It was very difficult for the police to know how to react, which the loiterers knew! I was very pleased to be able to help in a small way by finding suitable Guyanese family accommodation and contacts for two Metropolitan police officers who were wisely sent out from London to study the Guyanese and their way of life on the spot. It is a great pity that our English climate isn't suitable for the verandah life, and neighbourliness, which is an attractive custom of the Caribbean, and which is especially suitable for the happiness of the sociable, easy-going, less mobile elderly.

Away in this strange land which somehow involved one in its own problems, one felt in need of some protection, and this one got from being a diplomat in the British High Commission, whose concern for its staff gave us a feeling of security. We were immediately warned by the B.H.C. of the prevalent practice of 'choke and rob'. One chap gets you round the neck while the other picks what he can from you.

We never went out after dark by car or on foot without leaving behind anything we did not need for the occasion, such as a pocket knife, pens, diaries, watches, purses, etc. We often bought cinema tickets beforehand to avoid taking money along to buy them. It wasn't safe to walk along certain streets in the day-time, and practically nowhere at night. The airline which said it took 'good care of you' should not have suggested "a stroll down Water Street, teeming with life as in every busy sea port." At least one air tourist in our day spent time in hospital. My predecessor, David Lodge, was attacked in his bedroom (our bedroom!) by a man with a panga. He was saved from severe injury by his brave boxer dog which received a number of slashes itself.

Out and about

We had to learn quickly the area round Georgetown, to be ready for visitors. Unfortunately, the white sands region at the back of the coastal strip was rather horrible, but it did have the bonus of some afforestation, and it was the home of a large range of birds and animals. In one 'outgoing effort' we took Arthur Mee (Centre for Education Development and Vacation Courses) to St. Cuthbert's Mission in an Amerindian village on the Mahaica river, east of Georgetown. We went by borrowed Land Rover as we couldn't spare the boat time.

Our route was on the white sand, which makes a reasonable road even when wet. But driving through the low bush and faced with a number of possibly alternative tracks was tiring, and changes of direction were time-consuming. When we got near the river we were stuck in mud several times, and once I caused the engine to fail through flooding. Travel in these regions is by boat!

At the mission we met a very understanding and dedicated priest who showed us round the school. I hadn't the resources to offer the Mission actual aid, but we did enjoy feeding with sweets lots of delightful, little Amerindian boys – "such grins" wrote Rosemary. On our way back we saw an anteater and found a lovely orchid.

415

Better by boat

Another trip with John and Maria Hudson by launch up Kamuni Creek to an Amerindian village was a pleasant contrast. We embarked at the creek junction with the Demerara, just an hour's drive out of Georgetown.

It was perfect to nudge gently along in the deep shade with all kinds of plants, trees, lianas, and ferns reaching down into very dark, but clear, brown water, with perhaps anaconda and piranha lurking below! The pilot constantly had to watch for underwater tree obstacles, but we could relax. We saw no creature on shore but we were excited by the butterflies especially the great blue Morpho. And we saw a ringed kingfisher with a pale-blue head and wings, white throat, pink breast and narrow, black bars across a wide, white rump. However scenic, I now kept creeks and tea-coloured water strictly for visitors!

There were problems in the background all the time: and we felt them in our little lives. The following comes from a 1972 Survey of the East Indians in Guyana and Trinidad:

> ... the pattern of economic competition imposed on the African from an early date by the importation last century of Indian indentured labour, makes life hard for them [the African]. It was competition over land shortage that fed the hostility created by the arrival of the Indians in the first place ... the Indian could save more money than the African to buy land because he had not been brought up to accept western values and standards ... Urban development was first seized by the Portuguese and Chinese immigrants to the Africans' loss. The Indian population began to expand and overhaul the African, and also to move into the towns which had been the main African settlements. The African in the towns therefore tended to take power through Government jobs available preferentially to him ... the Indians came to dominate the labour market on the plantations even though the African still cut the cane, and also worked in skilled jobs in the estate factories.

This illustrates the nasty problem in Guyana of which one was always aware. The African, in his resentment of the current situation, still felt the wounds of slavery. The chip on the shoulder was there. But we found great warmth from everyone towards us personally; and outwardly, there was genuine appreciation of the work of the British Council.

But the other body with which we were concerned, V.S.O., was not so lucky. Shortly after my arrival I was summoned to the office of the Minister of Information, Culture and Youth. I was courteously received by the Minister, a young, highly competent, and clear-minded lady – whose origins I could not make out. She told me that the Government had decided to ask V.S.O. to close down at the end of the present group's contracts. This was sad but I understood. They wanted the positions for their own qualified young men and women from now on.

"Three returns to Adventure"

When Hugh Carey of V.S.O., whom we knew well from Fiji days, came to visit his seventeen lambs we began with a visit to three of them who were teaching at Anna Regina up the Essequibo Coast, west. And so Mr Bollers, our driver-projectionist with the Land Rover, bought us three return tickets to the township of Adventure. (Gerald Durrell's *Three Singles to Adventure*, Penguin 1969, is a joy.) We set off at 7.30 a.m. to catch the Georgetown-Vreed-en-Hoop car ferry across the great brown muddy Demerara river, from the stelling (landing stage) by the Starbroek Market. The market was a huge red corrugated-iron-roofed structure dominated by a clock-tower with a vast black and white face. The conditions in that market were dark, hot, and crammed, but cheerful and colourful. There one could buy anything from yams to nuggets of Guyana gold.

We were soon down the ramp and stowed among a variety of vehicles: station-wagons packed tight with cloth and hardware labelled 'Huckster'; taxis still labelled 'Hackney Carriage'; produce lorries; family saloons; and government Land Rovers.

Across the Demerara we drove twenty-five miles to another ferry, to cross the huge Essequibo estuary. It took the hefty ship three hours to thread its way among many islands. Ashore at Adventure all the sixteen miles to Anna Regina looked much the same on both banks with tatty villages, patches of scrub jungle, and endless rice fields. On arrival in Anna Regina we were made welcome, and found that our volunteers were well integrated and respected, and seemed to love it. But they were experiencing the same stultifying sameness in life and landscape, as we felt further east, therefore breaks for the V.S.O.s had to be planned. Our next visit to Anna Regina was in February 1971 with our Textbooks for Secondary Schools Exhibition. This was well put together by the London office, and worth all our efforts round the country with it. Here the V.S.O.s were a great help in staging it. Travelling by water in Guyana, as we could to Anna Regina and easily taking heavy loads, could be enjoyable if not faced with rocks or rapids.

Travelling by air in small aircraft is exciting, and it was fascinating at low altitude to be able to see the ground below clearly. But at the end of the flight being dumped in the interior left me with an unpleasant feeling of isolation, though out and back trips were great value. Sometimes we went by Canadian twin Otter, an amazingly useful, small, but multi-load-carrying, rear-loading aircraft, and with an astonishingly short take-off and landing. The first such flight we were on, carrying people, sacks, and boxes containing all kinds of necessities for jungle or savannah life, we flew over a hole in the jungle, and I said: "What a view. What goes on down there?" The answer was "us". In fact it was a small clearing in which we could easily land, off-load people, and supplies, and fly further south again.

On other occasions the ten or twelve-seater Norman-Britten Islander was an excellent aeroplane. But once I needed to go south urgently to see a V.S.O., and I was very anxious when I couldn't get on a scheduled flight. I shall never forget what Yvonne Ramsahoy in the office managed for me. "Oh, I'll get Eric Phillips to fly you up himself." "But he's the Director of Civil Aviation." "Yes, in his Cessna." He did! What a relief, and what a treat!

Language

One advantage of serving in Guyana is that the official language is English. And, of course, it makes Guyana an ideal country for English-speaking scientists, naturalists, and others because they can communicate and travel around easily. The Government Guide Book mentions Creolese, a sort of patois, which is widely used though it is "not at all popular among educationalists". I should think not, and I hope our V.S.O. teachers played their part in keeping their pupils on the right tongue at least at school. Creolese is a broken form of English with limitless and indefinable borrowings from other languages, and has an infinite variety of rhythms and inflections. I imagine Creolese is good for self-expression and relief at home, away from authority or foreigners. Among the East Indians Hindi and Urdu were sometimes used. The majority of Amerindian people in the interior still adhere to their own language, of which there are about ten recognized dialects.

Teachers of English, such as the admirable Lynette Dolphin, M.B.E. of the National History and Arts Council, and her sister, Celeste, who ran the Ministry of Education broadcasts to schools, spoke perfect English. But pupils who arrived at schools did not yet have good English. Teachers might understand: "She uses to have sat" but it is not the past continuous form of sit. It is a pity our language doesn't allow the following phrase, heard at a funeral: "The Lord said unto him: "Fight the good fight," and he fought the good fought." A little girl under stress in her anxiety to help two mourners, went straight into Creolese (I suppose) when she cried out: "Na go deh, cushi ants a tear dem ass"!

418

Interlude in Guyana

Jean Deas, a senior and charming lady visitor from the Overseas Development Administration, returned late to the Council office after a long day's drive. Driver: "Where's the boss?" Nightwatchman: "He's not here; he's had a drop." Consternation of visitor. Luckily, Bollers explained to her that I had been given a lift home.

One of the best illustrations of Guyanese English (Creole?) is given in the delightful songs by the Emmel Singers (Multi-Lateral T.T.C.) on a record called *Bamboo Fiah*, directed by Lynette Dolphin. There are eleven songs under the title of the first. Bamboo Fiah has a double meaning. The housewife blames the wood for not burning well as the reason for her husband's meal not being ready; but it is late because she has been dallying with a lover. Sancho (of the second song) is a caveman type of lover, who finds that his girl-friend shouts murder whatever he tries to do with her – beat her, hug her, kiss her. Her shouts alert the police, i.e.

> Sancho chase e lover pon de dam an'de gal ah halla murdah!
> Vip, vap, Police ah come, etc.

Other songs in the selection are about neighbourhood relations; but one, 'Itanami' is about the sometimes hazardous river journeys up or down the powerful, rock-strewn, white-water rapids such as the Itanami.

> Captain, captain, put me ashore,
> I don't want to go any more
> Itanami gon friken me.
> Itanami gon drownded me.

Eastward next – by road

We drove east on our own to New Amsterdam on the road to Surinam through open countryside; here were large areas of rice fields and sugar cane with higher trees to the south. Our objective was to visit the amusing, bright spark V.S.O., Graham Stratton in agriculture. When I got to know him, I sent him this poem:

Out At No Hope

> The farmers down at Mocca
> When life is really chokker,
> Ring for Stratton.

419

When the pigs have all got worms,
And milk turns in the churns,
Best ask Stratton.

When it's raining cats and dogs,
And the pasture turns to bogs,
Put your hat on,
And send for Stratton.

After our initial trip I found I could combine a visit to Graham with a bit of duck shooting, having somehow established a rapport with a like-minded guide, James Bishpat from the Ministry of Health. There were plenty of very destructive, whistling tree ducks (dendro cygnini), causing as the *Guyana Graphic and Evening Post* of May/June 1971 reported "untold damage to the rice crop." It was very wet at this time of the year. I noted: "4th June. Horrible thundery night. Poured all day. Let up at 7 p.m."

My Hillman Hunter couldn't get us very far off the road, but with Terence Mapp (from Construction) as picker-up we had a bash floundering about in the wet mud on the Burma Estate. We shot fifteen of these pathetic creatures. They were rather easy to shoot if one could get near them. They were not gun-shy, since the local Indian farmers had been forbidden to have firearms since the troubles in the sixties. But they desperately needed guns now to protect some of their crop.

We shot eight at De Hoop another day, but I gave up the game. There were far too many interesting birds to watch. Nevertheless, I accepted at once an invitation from the Attorney-General and Minister of State, S.S. (Sonny) Ramphal, to shoot on his country estate up the Abari river. This was thanks to Derek Jakeway in Fiji, who had admired Sonny in Guyana in the sixties, and described him as balanced, charming, well-informed and unflappable. Sonny certainly deserved his knighthood and shone as Secretary-General of the Commonwealth.

We went up-river in an open, outboard-powered boat, with a marvellous, old Indian named Labbi. We were excited by the huge muscovy duck moving about out of the forest to the south of us. A few were shot, but none hit the boat; such weight and velocity might have sunk us. But the very clear views of the extraordinary hoatzin were special. Hoatzin have been well-covered on television in nature programmes. As Rodney Dawson wrote in *Animals* "their reptilian affinities are unique among the birds of the world." It is the bird of Guyana, and on the country's coat-of-arms.

420

Barbados

Douglas McCreath of Collins from Barbados called on me one day, with a surprise. "I'm going to marry Yvonne". "Help! Oh no!" I protested. I couldn't spare her. After I became more civil, Douglas said he was returning to London for a while, and would lend us his flat in Christchurch, Barbados, with a secretary and a car. "Thank you," said Rosemary "but no secretary". We had a tremendous free time in Christchurch, including enjoying a flat full of new books.

What a lovely historic island to visit. Rosemary snorkled of course. One day the sea was very rough, and Rosemary was out in it from Crescent Beach, St. Lawrence Gap. I really thought she would be unable to make it to the shore, though she was very confident – afterwards. Thank God, Police Commissioner Farmer was passing by, and without hesitation went in and pulled her out. I was terribly grateful.

Have you tasted sugar-cane brandy? It is excellent ten-year-old rum. I took a Barbados bottle home to Papa, who loved it. He survived into his ninetieth year on rum and ginger wine taken liberally twice a day.

Back in Guyana – Buses Lust

Buses Lust was a Lot – a narrow strip of land bought by the early settlers for building and cultivation. The whole of Georgetown is divided into Lots. We kept a large-scale map of these in our Lot 298, which happened to be in Church Street. It was essential to know Lot numbers in order to find friends' houses for the first time.

The coastal and riverine Lots had names as well as numbers, and these names reflected the nationality and sometimes the aspirations of the original Dutch, French, Scots, and English owners. Along the Essequibo coast – between the Essequibo and the Pomeroon rivers, near the Venezuelan border, there were for instance Hackney, Enterprise, Land of Promise, Marlborough, down to Charity; below which was Somerset and Berks, La Resource, Better Hope, Better Success, Joanna Cecilia, Taymouth Manor, Golden Fleece, and of course Adventure.

Along the east coast (East Coast Demerara) there was Non Pareil next to Paradise, where Rosemary swears there was a signpost to Bachelors Adventure. Dantzig next to Fairfield; Inverness was not far from Burma, and so it went on and on. Between the Berbice river and the Courentyne river (the border with Surinam), Bohemia was a few miles from Hammersmith. Beyond Rotterdam were Brothers, Sisters, and Friends. These three 'Lots' happen to belong to a Nepali family, whose heir was our messenger, Mohabir Singh!

I wrote at the time: "There is plenty of work and plenty of social life so we don't get bored. It is only that getting even a few miles away is difficult at any time and doesn't give any pleasant contrast to our immediate surroundings which are pretty dull." But we were lucky in the mobility that was possible in my job, and the experiences we had.

Baggage at last

On our return from Barbados we found that our heavy baggage had arrived and we got it all out of the crates in a terrific burst the next morning. So the vital housewife was re-vitalized, and we could begin some real entertaining. Then we had the Guyana versus India cricket match to watch which was good value, with an enthusiastic crowd. Rosemary was in the Ladies Pavilion, sitting airily on the second floor, and had fun trying to understand the niceties of first-class cricket which she had hardly ever seen before.

Fort Island

We made a local trip to an island in the Essequibo which became a Dutch colony known as Flag Island. In the eighteenth and nineteenth centuries it became the capital of the colony for which a fort named Zeelandia was built by slave labour, and Britain renamed it Fort Island. Settlers moved in, but in the nineteenth century the centres of Guyana life shifted to the stable coast and by 1921 only about twenty families remained.

During our time there were some sixty families at Fort Island with a population of 600, and cattle, goats, sheep and poultry, and shops – three groceries, two 'cake shops' and a spirit shop – and a modern steamer stelling. There were also Hindu, Anglican, Congregation, Baptist and Pentecostal Churches. Rosemary wrote an account of the trip: We went up-river in a passenger launch specially hired, for one hour to Fort Island. It had rained all the time so far, unusual here where heavy showers are more normal, and our arrival was marked by a real downpour – so we ate lunch early on the boat. When it cleared a little, we 'paddled' along a grassy path to Fort Zeelandia."

"More impressive than expected, it's placed right on the river with low banks between brick walls as outlying protection. It's really very small, and diamond-shaped which I'd never seen, all built of brick brought from Holland as ballast, rather lovely, small, narrow bricks, and well laid. The wooden roof and insides are missing but the brickwork is fine, rather black than red now."

"All around has become a treasure trove of eighteenth-century bottles of all shapes and sizes flung into the surrounding mud by the military, with little else to do but drink. Today the bottles are industriously disinterred by the Indian children of a few farming families and sold in Georgetown where they are popular collectors' items. There was also a huge, barn-like, brick-walled church, with a few fine Dutch tombstones; presumably there were ordinary homes along the quarter of a mile path between church and fort as life wasn't always dangerous."

Oddly enough, Tradescant's Diary in *The Garden* of March 1995 contains this item: "The Gardeners Magazine of 1835 carried reports of orchids collected on the Spanish Main and adding "justly has Demerara been called the land of mud." The rain did stop for the boat trip back – a blue sky over such a wide river would have been lovely. Any expedition here involves rather a lot of effort and, or, money.

As Rosemary described: "On the return trip we stopped at a sandy beach, so I walked about while the children bathed, and was very lucky to spot a sloth, three-toed up a tree! He was rather exposed on top of a bare branch, so I think he was trying to dry off a bit. He never changed position, only waved his head slowly about."

Having seen the muddy fort area, I thought I would like to have a few of the old bottles Rosemary mentioned. They looked attractive. Without knowing anything about them I got in touch with the Guyanese historian, journalist, and film maker, Brian Stuart-Young. He provided a most informative article on these bottles and put me in touch with one Mohabir, who made a name and a profit by collecting such bottles with the aid of his scouts. Through him I have a small collection of dark-green glass bottles of satisfying shapes and sizes, but none with the glass seal which collectors go for. The abundance of principally eighteenth-century bottles of Dutch, French, and English origin are indicators of history.

Officially to Venezuela

I was asked to attend a Central American British Council Representatives' Conference in Caracas, Venezuela. New places, the climate, the company of colleagues, the scenery, and the food re-energised us. It was a sensible British Council policy to allow the interchange of experiences and ideas, which was especially useful for posts with only one London-appointed member of staff. I benefited from the advice of senior colleagues such as Dick du Vivier from Mexico, our hosts the de Saumarez, Paul Gotch from Colombia, Norman Sutcliffe from Peru, and J. D. Hughes from British Honduras. Rosemary came too, at my expense, and was very glad to meet older, experienced Council hands after our one-man-band stints.

It was a revelation and a shock to be in a high-rise, good-taste, fast-moving, modern city with whizzing traffic on wide roads which one was nervous to cross. Give me Georgetown; I couldn't have stood the frazzle of Caracas life. But it was good to meet dynamic people at a British Embassy luncheon, and to enjoy the odd reception or good restaurant meal. It was naturally a Hungarian who headed the Volkswagen Agency! Alas, we had little chance to understand anything of Venezuela and on our weekend off we had no hope of seeing some of the old Spanish towns, the architecture and the remaining culture. We were taken for lunch to a Bavarian colony!

Trinidad, more our scene

We learned a lot more when we stopped off in Port of Spain, Trinidad, facing the delta of the Orinoco. We stayed at the Queen's Hotel for a night, which was not far from the Test Ground.

The racial diversity struck one immediately. The first new settlers were French, and we found that a French patois was still spoken in places, and Roman Catholicism was the dominant religion. Today's Trinidadian is most likely to be African from the slaves (freed in 1833) or East Indian (Hindu and Moslem) descendants of indentured labour. The last shipload reached Trinidad in 1917. Other racial strains are Portuguese (who came as the first indentured labour in 1834), Chinese, Lebanese, Syrian, and British.

Trinidad and Tobago were united by the British in 1889. Tobago's population is overwhelmingly African. But the prettiest girls are some of the young, modern, 'liberated' Trinidad Indian girls. A British Council colleague married one. The city was cooler, brighter, and more cosmopolitan than Georgetown. The streets were vibrating with the events leading up to carnival, which we had to miss. But we much enjoyed sampling one of the 'Calypso tents' – a hall in which several groups were getting into training by putting on a show every night. These were calypsos being tried out on enthusiastic, happy, noisy, and critical audiences. The rhythms were compulsive, the words brash and basic sung by contestants such as Mighty Sparrow or Lord Canary. Steel bands were practicing too. One could hear them miles away. In the bar of our hotel sanctum I felt drab alongside an exquisitely turned-out Norman Parkinson in his own tropical style. We didn't speak. Rosemary and I managed a sea-bathe at the lovely Maraccas Bay. At Caroni Creek we had a glimpse of the wonderful scarlet ibis.

Interlude in Guyana

Even so, Guyana was best

The life-style, the customs, the folk-lore, the worship, the singing, and the music of the Guyanese were all a pleasure.

What was so refreshing and cheering was the religious tolerance throughout the country, and the delightful, highly vocal variations of the Christian faith. And I must emphasize that the verandah life of the older ladies, and all members of the family in the course of the day, and the lay-about street life of the men and lads were perfectly natural in such a climate in such a country.

We came to enjoy the steel bands greatly, which like the bag-pipes are best appreciated out-of-doors and at a distance. Unfortunately, we were often V.I.P. invitees and led to front seats at indoor functions. There we were fixed, right in the piercing batter of the pans, or near the buffeting of deep drum beats in a folk combo hired for the occasion. It could be terrible, but everyone was loving it all. I gave a certificate of the 'Order of the Pierced Ear-drum' to a poor visitor we dragged along to the Police Sports Club Boy Scouts' Dance. As for reggae, we both came to respond completely to this fascinating and very clever reverse beat rhythm. In the tropical climate, and with every window open, sounds carry far. I was lulled to sleep quite gently some nights to the sound of reggae from the neighbourhood.

Matthew's Ridge

The Easter break gave us a chance to visit a little township, which was once the operations' base for the extraction of manganese that had been opened up in the 1950s. It was now the base of an agricultural project managed by Ken Abraham, and his assistant Lyo Wong, with a residential Club under Carter Daniels in which one could stay. All were most cooperative. We flew one and a half hours north-west over jungle, and we were about thirty miles from the Venezuelan border. A Land Rover met us driven by a man named Jesus (actually Rudolf de Jesus). So I was able to write: "With Jesus in the Jungle."

Rosemary described the township: "All the houses, roads, village and plant are still there and the area is one of the first they are trying to develop agriculturally. The project houses, Club, and tennis court, are on two hilltops cleared of bush so there was a lovely view down across the trees to vast distances of jungle. What a variety of textures of trees! Every evening we sat on the hillside with binoculars watching for birds in the sunset – parrots, toucans, and especially macaws are thrilling to watch flying free. What a row the macaws make and how flamboyant they are!

425

There were wonderful jungle noises too, including deep, engine throbs of a howler monkey band. It was very cool at nights and so quiet – and hot baths too were a treat."

"The house was very spacious and comfortable and was maintained as a fancy guest house – awful food though. People were very friendly and took us around – even on a train trip on the single-track line down to the river thirty miles away – we sat in state in armchairs in a covered wagon with sliding doors! Two hours down and the same back, and a trip on the river as well. The two keen orchid collectors in a party which had come up, had a field day. We had some good walks on roads and trails, though very hilly, and we had a memorable confrontation along a narrow forest track with a great, iridescent blue Morpho butterfly."

"We saw the following while at Matthew's Ridge: a tiger-bird (bittern) which remained motionless beside the little railway, and kingfisher, cormorant, woodpecker, mocking-bird, vulture (grey?) hawk, fork-tailed hawk, red and blue macaws, toucans – ones with grey-green backs, white fronts and a red stripe. On a forest walk we were fascinated watching a colony of leaf-cutter ants on the job. And finally, very close-up on the floodlit tennis court, there sat a nightjar, a weird bird."

I was impressed by the schooling facilities in the capable hands of the Jesuits, who showed me what they were achieving. I told them what I might be able to offer.

Georgetown again: Birds, birds

Thanks to Bella Datadin, our staff-nurse companion voyager on the Oranje Nassau, we met Mr Naranjan O. Poonai, who was her uncle. In his little two-storey white wooden house near the City Hall he was a lawyer downstairs, and a naturalist of world-standing upstairs. Besides his wide scientific knowledge and experience which he was happy to pass on to us, he had the courage and energy to press for legislation to control hunting and trapping and to enforce measures of conservation.

The world and local governments are now aware, through the media, of the destruction of forests and the decimation of wild-life in South America; but greed, in the name of development, seems to be causing irreplaceable losses that are harmful to nature and mankind.

On a Saturday holiday N. O. Poonai took us an hour into the interior in his neat little open, army-type VW. The rainy season had started and it poured all the way there, but kindly let up for an hour and a half when we reached a clearing in the forest. Rosemary's big moment was watching two woodpeckers arriving at the same time on opposite sides of the same tree! We saw twenty different kinds of birds: ruff-winged swallow, a colony of yellow-rumped caciques, bunyas and orioles, bloody woodpecker, blue-headed parrot, green honey tree-creeper, channel-billed and white breasted toucans, lace-winged trogon, turkey vulture, magpie tanager, scaly-breasted ground dove, banana quit, paradise jacamar, tropical king bird, Cayenne tityra, Cayenne jay, plumbeous kite, and large-billed hawk! We also saw a funny little agouti, and at last (after Gerald Durrell's *Three Singles to Adventure*) a capybara.

We later had a unforgettable trip with Poonai to see a scarlet ibis breeding colony, some way east of Georgetown which we would never have found ourselves. Ibis are big birds, the size of heron. Here, against the green of young rice or the blue sky, they seemed unreal – so intense was the brilliance of their red plumage.

British Expedition to Mount Roraima. July – September 1971

We had a lucky break in being around to meet and entertain members of the British expedition to 'The Lost World', a legend which fascinated Sir Arthur Conan Doyle, and which he made famous. Roraima is real. It is a great plateau or mesa of twenty-five miles at a point where the borders of Guyana, Venezuela, and Brazil meet. It juts up out of the tropical rain-forest of the Pakaraima mountain range, and is isolated from the surrounding tableland by giant sandstone walls of sheer rock 2,000 ft. high.

The Amerindians call Roraima 'the Mother of the Waters' because the almost continual rainfall drains from the plateau on all sides, feeding the tributaries of the Amazon, Orinoco, Essequibo, Mazaruni, and Brano.

> The plateau is often swathed in unshifting cloud for weeks on end. When it does appear for a tantalising hour, it is possible to see the black-capped summit, scarred and eroded, from which vertical white columns of water plunge down the golden-red walls to the green forest below.
> (Roger Chapman, Deputy Leader).

The expedition, led by Adrian Warren of London University, hoped to carry out for the first time a thorough survey of the plateau's ecosystem. But the only way up was from the Venezuelan side which they were refused permission to use. However, they successfully carried out a zoological, botanical, and limnological survey of the unexplored northern ridge.

Here was El Dorado – for the botanists and other specialists. David Philcox of Kew Botanical Gardens brought back some 500 species for

Kew. Martin Lyes returned with over 200 reptiles, amphibians, bats, fish, and fifty large spiders. Our Guyanese friend, Adrian Thompson, was the expedition's scientific liaison member. He was invaluable for his years of experience as farmer, government servant, and jungle explorer. He was up Roraima in 1956 and 1966. David Attenborough was on the top, in one of his wonderful 1995 programmes on the *Life of Plants*. Hamish MacInnes' *Climb to the Lost World* (Hodder and Stoughton, 1974) truly describes what Roraima was like for the pioneers.

We learned a good deal about the jungle from Adrian Thompson; about the flora and fauna within, and how to behave as a human. "Look after your feet," he said. "Eat porridge, raisins, chocolate, limes and brown sugar. Take enterovioform and kaomycin. Leave the jungle alone, and it will leave you alone." For instance, never fight the jungle if you can't get through it, or if it gets one down, or if one is in a panic when lost. Then you would only do yourself damage, and striking out blindly you might upset a deadly tree-snake. If you are bitten by a snake, rest. Cut immediately, and squeeze out the bite area until the blood runs pure red. To find a means of following water down is the best way to safety. Adrian had nothing to say to us about vampires. As for survival, we never practiced that or had to survive. Nor did we learn to recognize the traces of creatures nor their sounds nor their habitats, nor the calls of birds or frogs – much as we would have loved to.

But we learnt how to sling a hammock, and how to enjoy sleeping in one. Hammocks are remarkably comfortable, and the best ones are made from a special quality cotton woven by the Wapishana tribe in and out of Brazil. Adrian taught us a knot to use to keep oneself safely suspended above wild pig or other creatures dashing about along the forest floor.

In Georgetown Adrian Thompson had created a farm with fruit trees, and continued to develop his property at Madewini in the bush near Timehri airfield. It had a creek nearby – a rather swampy area with the jungle intact all round. It was a lovely spot in which to find peace. As on Bishoftu lake outside Addis Ababa, we had the use of a canoe in which to paddle quietly and glide about among the reeds. The golden orioles were perfect.

Rosemary wrote home: "It was gorgeous to be on our own for the night there. We sat under the house (on stilts as all houses are) till dusk became dark, listening to the different forest noises and watching the fireflies, rather worrying Adrian's retainers who thought we didn't know how to light the pressure lamp! They were too helpful being rather drunkards. Drink is an awful blight in Guyana. As dusk faded we watched the parrots bombing in like Wellingtons to roost. We gave up sitting in the dark after a large hairy spider fell onto Michael's neck! I was up at 5.45 a.m. to walk round watching the toucans (white-throated and channel-billed), jays et al, feeding noisily among the tree tops."

The Amerindians in Guyana

We were very struck by the Amerindians. They had a marvellous physique, fine features, and a beautiful skin colour. They belonged to the forest, to the jungle where they were entirely at home. Whether it was right, or sensible, or beneficial to the Amerindians to drag them into our world, and convert them to Christianity, even to educate them were unanswerable questions. It is extremely sad to me that a wonderful people, with a unique and almost unbelieveably skilful mastery of their jungle world, were so treated. They fared the worst. Adrian Thompson understood them, and they him. The different tribes, I'm sorry to say, meant nothing to us: Akawaio, Arawak, Makushi, Wapishana, etc. No European can manage to emulate their knowledge of flora and fauna, and their ability to make full use of every living thing in order to survive. But in town, in what we call civilization, they were at a loss. They fell prey to the worst aspects of European life, particularly to alcohol. Those who could not cope fell to crime and even violence. One good young chap working for Adrian Thompson committed suicide while we were at Adrian's house. He shot himself through the stomach with a shotgun but, to our great distress, lingered on while we could do nothing for him, except send for the boss.

Roger Chapman on the Mount Roraima Expedition spoke very highly of Irvine George, No. 2 of the Akawayou tribe party. He wrote:

> All Amerindians are expert watermen, and Irvine was no exception . . . Irvine seemed part of the forest itself. To every call he could answer with an exact mimic. Occasionally he would point out a flat, greenish dun turtle basking on the bank, then burst into a frenzy of paddling to catch up with a couple of "waterdogs" – giant otters – whose white furry heads would appear some ten feet ahead of the bows of our canoes, playing and plunging until they were tired of our company. At one time he motioned to us to stop paddling and watch. He pointed to a black tube schnorkel pushing across the mirror-like waters. It reached the bank, a few feet ahead of us, then the whole elongated head emerged followed by a six-foot body covered in shaggy black and grey hair. The giant anteater gave a swish of its massive tail, turned its piggy eyes towards us, then lumbered into the darkness of the forest.
>
> Their Amerindian porters carried their equipment and stores in 80–100 lb. loads with comparative ease, so it seemed, in their 'waraishees' – strong, basketwork rucksacks woven from strips of the turu palm, bound with fibre made from the bark of the mamuri tree. Much of the weight is taken by straps, made from the karakalli bark, passed round the forehead. When the waraishees

were loaded and set in place on their backs, the porters would grin under their enormous loads and individually answer: "Good, all right, me!" Then they would burst into laughter before moving off down the trail which had been laboriously cut the day before.

Roger Chapman had reason later to be particularly grateful to the Amerindian porters who may have saved his life. Dr Henrik Forss, a Finnish doctor, diagnosed a stomach pain as acute appendicitis. They were seventy miles from the nearest airstrip, and 350 miles from the nearest hospital. The Amerindians cut a fourteen-foot pole, tied his hammock beneath it, and invited him to climb into it. His whole rescue journey became a fine, combined effort by companions and the Guyana Defence Force back-up.

February 1972 down to earth again

Republic Day was upon us. It began as an evening affair at the National Park. There was a speech by Prime Minister Burnham, followed by dancing and bands, a torchlight procession, and a re-enactment of the Cuffy Revolt of the late-eighteenth century. (I was given a Cuffy Medal one day). The next day was a parade of costumed bands and floats from 10 a.m. to 5 p.m., to be judged in the Park and all round the town. Their supporters kept dancing away – on rum. We went to the President's reception in the evening on the lawns of Government House, a charming site surrounded by palms. It was very hard to recognize dark-skinned people at night, when one is looking into the spotlights, and the guests come up to you.

Cricket

It gave us a boost to find that the Bourda Ground of the Georgetown Cricket Club (founded 1848) was just across from our house. We were lucky to become part of the scene because the President of the Club kindly made me an honorary member when he learned that I was a member of the M.C.C.

The Guyanese are mad about cricket. What an admirable trait! On any little street at any time of day a small boy is very likely to explode from up a side house-drive, and hurl a ball right across the road to a young batsman facing him at the rough distance of a cricket pitch. At any state of the tide where a firm beach remained, one would find boys doing just the same thing but at less danger to the passer-by or spectator.

When the John Player League Champions came to play Guyana in

January 1972, we were asked to entertain some of the J.P.L. party to supper. Our maid Sybil was in her element – she had been a neighbour of Clive Lloyd. I think we were a little out of ours!

Luckily, there was provision in the Club rules for ladies, in fact there was a separate, but contiguous, ladies pavilion – where men might enter, although ladies could not enter the men's pavilion! Rosemary reported home on the West Indies versus New Zealand match ". . . dreary cricket brings a strong reaction – a marked drop in attendance. A selfish performance by . . . a dearth of good West Indian bowlers." The most forbearing and courteous Guyanese spectators shouted: "We want cricket". On the fourth day the President of the G.C.C. invited me to lunch in the pavilion. Very kind, I thought, but I had to do my stuff as he had invited the President of Guyana too!

If one walked past the back of Bourda Ground during any match along the tall solid wooden fence, the trees close behind would be full of spectators in the 'birdie seats' who were vocally reacting to the game and giving one an idea whether it was worth watching or not.

The Guyana Graphic 6 April 1972 reported:

Another judge gives time-off for cricket

Mr Justice Frank Vieira yesterday told a Demerara High Court jury that he intended to see the first ball bowled in the Cricket Test match between New Zealand and the West Indies which opens at Bourda today.

His Court would sit from 8.30 a.m. to 10 a.m. today and only for the morning session on all other days of the Test, he declared.

In February 1973 when the Shell Shield matches were on, the Government gave all public servants time off to attend the matches, subject to the exigencies, etc.!

Some time later I found myself lecturing on cricket. Guyana was an American Foreign Service rest-post for diplomats between tough assignments. The American diplomats and some U.S. Aid staff very much joined in the spirit of life in Guyana. But they found that to be accepted and to enjoy life to the full they had to know something about cricket, and quickly. So I volunteered to run classes (of theory) at the British Council, and this was accepted. I thoroughly enjoyed it. I had to bone up a bit more on my subject than I had anticipated. I also enjoyed the setting and marking of their 'end of course Final Test', as supplied by Papa. I list it below; it is a well-known, of course. The Council thoughtfully sent out a delightful little cricket film called *The Summer Game*. The opening shots are of sandwich rubbish drifting about in the puddles of rainwater below the pavilion seats.

FINAL TEST
Cricket Course – Georgetown 1973

Turn the following into clear English in the light of knowledge gained:

CRICKET, described to an American by an enthusiast:

You have two sides, one out in the field and the other in. Each man in the side that's in goes out, and when he's out he comes in, and the next man goes out till he's out.

When the side that's in is all out, the side that's been out comes in, and the side that's been in comes out, and tries to get out the one that's coming in.

Sometimes you get men still in and not out when the side that's in is finally out.

When both sides have been in and out, including those that are in and not out, that's the end of the game.

J.G.H./J.M.G.H.
Certified Examiners.

17 March 1972

Official visitors kept coming: those in such fields as Merchant Marine training, the Overseas Development Authority and technical assistance, as well as British university librarians, Caribbean ministers of health, and the Inter-University Council of Vice-Chancellors. We were extremely lucky to have a really fine Vice-Chancellor of Georgetown University in Dennis Irvine.

Most welcome was Dr Hugh Jolly, from the Medical Research Council, a friend from Isfahan days. Guyanese medicine was sadly not following his sound advice. He was against putting all resources into a huge, expensive hospital in the capital – with attendant problems. He felt that the country would be much better off with a number of small, well-equipped and well-staffed regional hospitals. But few doctors were willing to work out in the sticks. I'm afraid I couldn't blame them.

On the education side, we were lucky to have a City and Guilds Administrator out. How sensible of the Guyanese to realise the inter-national value of C. & G. qualifications in a wide range of industrial or commercial subjects. I was glad to encourage examination entrants.

A wider appeal to Guyanese schools, and to us, were the Royal Schools of Music syllabi. We were very happy to welcome Hector McCurrach, who was undemanding, fond of cricket (for a Scot!), and generous of his time and energy. He was a British Council windfall because he was willing to give a free pianoforte recital at the Pegasus Hotel. Such events were few in Georgetown, and well attended.

Hurray! The Tombstoners were in business again!

Leaning on our balcony over Sunday morning drinks, I told Liam Sharkey I feared I had said 'Goodbye' to the Tombstoners in Isfahan. And Liam (of Halcrows) said he would love to shoot!

As I was a diplomat there was most understanding back-up from the B.H.C., whose administrative officer quickly had an application in to the Guyana M.F.A. for me to import my pistols and .222 rifle. I already had my shot-gun. It was like magic, in came pistols and automatics .22, .38 Special and 9mm., and ammo. We were off. The Guyana Defence Force let us use part of their range near the airport, and the police let us use their indoor range in town, which was very handy but very noisy. And there was a police station just down the road where I could put weapons into safe keeping. I was able to buy a large heavy, old, key-operated safe which my study floor would just bear, for the pistols and ammunition.

In Georgetown the Tombstoners flourished as nowhere before or after. What fun we had on Saturday afternoons! I loved the game of loading up the car with weapons, ammo, and targets – cardboard and small, angled, steel plates, and a table for the pistols. We couldn't have had a safer site in the desolate scrubland with a soft, sandy backstop. Guests came and one lady distinguished herself: Diane McTurk, daughter of the famous Tiny McTurk of Karanambo Ranch in the Rupununi. What a life the family had. In February 1995 Diane appeared on British television in a programme on the Giant Otter. Another lady willing to 'have a bash' was Afric de Freitas, wife of Paul de Freitas, from a well-known, old Portuguese family. Afric sent us a thank-you note signed Calamity Afric!

Close to nature

One feels pretty close to nature in Guyana, much of it menacing in various ways: the sea, the jungle, the snakes, the caymen, the rivers, and the terrain. We never felt quite at ease, though there was much to admire especially in the bird life. Guyana is ideal for English-speaking scientists to visit. One such whom we greatly enjoyed meeting was the Australian, Joseph M. Forshaw, who wrote *Parrots of the World*. Joe was a Churchill

Scholar. He and his book were mentioned by David Attenborough on his television programme *Portrait Painter to the Birds*, broadcast on 1 January 1993.

We felt at ease in the Botanical Gardens. What we particularly enjoyed seeing was a very special water-lily *victoria amazonica* (synonym *regia*), family *nymphaeaceae*. It is a remarkable plant which the Guyanese proudly consider their own. It appears in the national Coat of Arms: "On the shield a Victoria Regia open lily and a bird, the hoatzin, conjoin on two sides of a leaf". This lily is found throughout the Amazon basin. The *victoria regia* flourishes in two long pools down each side of the Gardens' main avenue. The leaves frequently grow to six-foot diameter; and leaf growth is very rapid. In its early stages the leaf can increase by four to five square feet per day.

We could often see the delightful little reddy-brown, voluble jacana or lily-trotter with its huge, splayed feet walking about on the leaves![3] But the jacana can equally well walk on an ordinary water-lily or water-hyacinth leaf. The underside of the *victoria regia* leaf is strengthened with a network of spiny veins containing air cavities which provide buoyancy; and leaves have frequently supported weights of up to 200 lbs. The under surface is a beautiful example of natural engineering. In fact, this lily inspired Sir Joseph Paxton's design for the Crystal Palace which was completed in 1851. It had a system of girders and supports modelled on the lily leaf.

The *Victoria Regia* is admirably displayed in the Edinburgh Botanical Gardens, for not only can you view it on its pond, but you can enter a glass-sided passage below and clearly see the underside of the leaves. It is grown in Kew as well. Sir Joseph first met the *victoria regia* through the Duke of Devonshire. After seeds had been introduced into Kew in 1846, the Duke commissioned Sir Joseph to design a special glass-house for it at Chatsworth where it first flowered in Britain in 1849.

In Guyana the lily flowers between June and October; and when the first buds open – in the late afternoon – they are creamy white and fragrant. They close the next morning. By the time they re-open again in the afternoon they have turned to pinkish purple. On the third day they begin to fade. The fruit is a prickly berry six inches across, which becomes submerged, and the mature seeds sink to the bottom. They are sometimes ground into flour, and give the plant its local name of water-maize.

I remember the Georgetown Botanical Gardens very well for two other encounters. We were learning a bit about the buttressed trees around us. Beyond was an open space of tall grass. Here we found a great, seated statue of Queen Victoria lying on her back with her crown on a peeling,

---

[3] It appeared on *The Really Wild Show* of 8 January 1993.

red cushion nearby. Sic transit . . . Walking away we suddenly felt the most terrible itchings on our legs. Getting home as quickly as possible and undressing we found our lower limbs were covered in tiny, bright-red spots. We had made the acquaintance of the 'bêtes rouges'.[4] Even after frequent applications of a variety of unguents, it was days before we ceased to feel these bites.

A break in the Rupununi

We flew south to Manari Ranch in one and a half hours by elderly Dakota, with twelve passengers and freight, roughly on the line of the Essequibo river, first to Annai, a settlement and local supply point on the edge of the savannah. We called at the McTurk's Ranch at Karanambo before flying twenty-five minutes on to tiny Lethem, the government centre on the Takatu river, which forms the border with Brazil.

"Everyone meets the 'plane," wrote Rosemary "like the boat at Carradale." Here were African teachers and administrators, an Indian vet, craggy-faced ranchers of mixed blood, and Amerindian cowboys. A truck from Manari took us the seven miles to the ranch, the only hotel-guesthouse in the interior offering holidays. The whole complex had been built up over forty-seven years by a family who were a mixture of Portuguese, Scottish, and Amerindian. We were in a very good spot, and on a real working ranch.

We went along with a keen American fisherman, Hank Bruns, who had an ideal craft for any nature activity – a collapsible canoe with a very light electric jet outboard. He could make silent approaches even through weed. We learned a little about the fish. First the seven to eight-foot arapaima, the largest river fish in the world (apart from the rare Amazonian laulau and pacumo); then the lokanani with a butterfly eye on its tail; the byara with very long lower front teeth; the bony, aggressive hori; the yarrow; the hassa; the patwa; and of course the deadly piranha or pirai. The stories about their activities made one's flesh creep and kept me out of South American waters!

---

[4] Since these were invisible we could not see or obtain a specimen for the Dept of Entomology, Natural History Museum, who think 'bêterouge' maybe a form of sand-fly.

Into Brazil

We were mindful of Evelyn Waugh's visit to Boa Vista, when Manari staff took a group of us over to Brazil. It was very tiring but worth the effort. We were off at 8.30 a.m. into Lethem to check with the police; and then we crossed the frontier river Ireng in an outboard dugout canoe. After lunch in a very simple restaurant, we 'did' the town.

Everyone is impressed by Brazil, including Tim Fison, our V.S.O., who appeared on the Ireng, back from his trip to Peru at the end of his Guyana stay. We too were impressed by the building and bustle and atmosphere of one of Brazil's remote northern centres.

21 April 1972: Georgetown again

We had heavy, continuous rain for a month. The children loved romping in the flooded streets – flooded until the tide went down and the sea-wall sluices could be opened. The heaviest rain was recorded on 4 May in the press 9.7 inches in a week. Herons and snowy egrets were stalking hopefully about our neighbour's lawn.

Civilisation

The most memorable cultural activity in which we were ever involved happened to take place in funny old Guyana. The people were bright and avid for the arts of the Western world. The British Council, to the delight of staff and centre visitors all over the world, had bought a set of Kenneth Clark's thirteen fifty-minute T V films entitled *Civilisation*.

We showed each film twice at the British Council, and once at the University and once at the Pegasus Hotel. The audience appreciated them as much as we did. It was a tribute to Council staff in London and in offices sharing these films all over the world that only three films arrived out of sequence. This didn't matter as they were about separate subjects. After the final showing we gave a party at the Pegasus for anyone who had come to a *Civilisation* film there. "What next please?" we were asked.

Our Chairman

Our admirable Chairman, Sir Leslie Rowan, who was only appointed in 1971 died in this year, 1972, at the age of 64. Lord Ballantrae was appointed to succeed him, this splendid figure was well known to Papa.

He had given me his signed autobiography *The Trumpet in the Hall* (Collins 1970/71); the title being a quote from the Scottish Psalter, paraphrase 18. I risked disciplinary action by sending him a cable based on five paraphrases (44, 18, 23, 50 and 67):

> Delighted appointment Lord Ballantrae Chairman. All old things
> now are passed away, and a new world begun.
> Although he has hung his trumpet in the hall,
> we trust the progress of his zeal and power.
> Steadfast let us still remain though dangers rise around,
> to ensure a rich inheritance rewards the conquests he has won.

I received a perfect put-down for insubordination by this reply: "Mock not his name with honours vain, but keep my holy laws." (Paraphrase 17.)

Timber

Guyana is a land of great woods. So the Council provided us with an 'Exhibition on the Modern Uses of Timber'. The Conservator of Forests opened it at the Council in front of Bill and Susie Bates and sixty other guests, such as furniture factory owners, cabinet makers, architects, saw-millers, artists, including Arthur Goodland, a carver himself who had suggested the exhibition, and our joiner-carpenter Mr Aldridge.

I am fascinated by woods, and enjoyed handling examples and learning about a number of Guyana's great woods, i.e. greenheart, which is tremendously strong and durable, for piers, docks, and locks, etc. To illustrate the nature of greenheart, my forestry brother-in-law tells this story. Years ago when British Columbia ordered greenheart from Guyana to replace some dock piers, a huge consignment was unloaded at the port. The Superintendent suddenly needed dock space to unload an unexpected ship. Therefore, accustomed as he was to British Columbia's softwoods floating, he ordered the greenheart to be pitched over the side, and secured. But it all sank!

Teak is the finest of Guyana's woods. Kabukalli is used for buildings; Simarupa for interior joinery; Dukali and Manni for general use; Wallaba for poles and posts; Wamara for floors and furniture; Manniballi for floors and furniture; Mora, Al at Lloyds for boat building; and Purpleheart, which true to its name and so hard that it can destroy saws, is employed for flooring, heavy construction, and decoration.

The Zoo and fauna

We were always conscious of birds, and such a pleasure they were. Not all the creatures were endearing. For instance, the heavy rain brought a visitor to the drain outside our front gate, an eight-foot anaconda – which was captured by a brave young man before it could hug anyone. Then there were poor comical manatees with old Bill phizes. When one surfaced in murky water, we got the odd curious look; we couldn't help smiling.

The capybaras and agoutis and such were not that attractive. The monkeys such as the howlers were so noisy. The smaller, more delicate monkeys were beautiful and the New World prehensile-tailed monkeys were marvellous gymnasts. These creatures were in the interior as well as squirrel and spider monkeys, marmosets and tamarins, and sakis and capuchins, who were especially attractive little chaps.

Thanks to Mr Lee, the director of the Zoo, we were able to make visits to the zoo as often as we liked, and he would give up time to talk about his work and his charges. The giant otter was as noisy as the howlers, and harsher. Of the large cats we luckily never met a jaguar, neither in the jungle nor on the road. In the local press we read that Donald Periana of Alcan hit a jaguar head-on while driving his Ford Capri from Mackenzie (Bauxite) one evening. It died on the spot. It was six-foot long and weighed some 250 lbs, but he was able to drive on.

We were glad never to meet a five-foot puma such as the one on a sugar estate track, which was about to attack a certain Mr Eugene Samuel's dog! The puma fled up a tree on seeing Mr Samuel and his friend; and Mr Samuel shot it. I suppose he needn't have done, but such powerful and dangerous carnivores represent a constant menace to country folk. The whole range of lovely smaller cats are a joy, but they could only be seen at the zoo.

We were much happier looking at the seemingly contented birds in the new aviary which was opened in 1971. We were over-awed by the vast harpy eagle (no longer under threat). It is seven-feet tall overall, and commands extreme circumspection and deference even when approaching its cage. The owls were wonderful, and in the wild were adjusting well to man's presence. The great horned owl of the coastal mangroves was impressive, and the mottled owl of the same habitat, was attractive with a fine presence. We saw a curassow, which Gerald Durrell described so amusingly (*Three Singles*).

The special bird of Guyana is the cock-of-the-rock (*rupicola rupicola*). It is seven inches high, bright orange all over with a large, compressed, fan-shaped crest which reaches from the top of the bill to the nape. It looks strange because its bill is hidden below the fan. The Pegasus Hotel had a caged one for all to admire. Guyana also has the *lipaugus vociferans,*

438

a sober little slate-grey bird, which is just over five-inches high and unfortunately called the screaming piha. But Haverschmidt says "it has a fine melodious call, with intermittent gurgling notes, and is the bird of our [Surinam] forests". We never heard one. The bird we loved was the sun parakeet, locally known as the kisi-kisi. We saw them in the aviary, close up together kissing away quite shamelessly. What an exhibition of love! Upon seeing Haverschmidt's *Birds of Surinam*, you will be amazed at the varieties, shapes and colours in the region and will want to visit Guyana just for the birds – to see the swallow-tailed kite, which to me is the most marvellous flyer of all.

Two one-man theatres!

Georgetown audiences had the experience and benefit of contrasting visitors: Emlyn Williams (sponsored) and Brian Barnes (free-lance). Both solo performers gave excellent performances and drew adequate audiences but young Brian came out the better, although Rosemary described him as "a small, active man with a snub nose and modest appearance." Emlyn was then sixty-seven years' old, and a Very Important Person with three fussy staff. They all had to be handled very carefully. They were tricky, and gave us anxious moments. Emlyn was very pleasant and sometimes amusing. He *was* Charles Dickens, whom he portrayed superbly; but he was just one character and his choice of items seemed disappointing to me.

Bill Bates and Susie took the heat off us one night by their hospitality for invitée diplomats, etc. The next night we hosted the stage crews and local actors too. Brian played many characters and moved about all over the stage. Rosemary wrote of him: "He gave a superb, fantastic performance of *Under Milk Wood* – more than twenty-five different voices, many acted out with full use of the whole stage. His second night was for children: called *Chestnuts for You*. He performed pieces from Edward Lear, *Alice in Wonderland, A Midsummer Night's Dream, The Pied Piper*, and they loved it. He's so good, also advising the young 'back-stage', telling them techniques and all that might be useful."

Wifely interlude

Rosemary wrote home: "Barnes has now left. Bed at 2 a.m. and woken at 6 a.m. by the army's bugle band. So what with running about during yesterday, pressing stage clothes, helping make scrolls, finding swords, etc. I've had it now, and I'm off for a nice refreshing swim – for a miracle it's sunny today."

It is marvellous having a wife who can and does take part in my work – and a vital part. How loyal she is; and how revealing I find her letters home which her parents kept. She could look at our work objectively. From then on, alas, we would not have any more of Rosemary's letters home to read in the future, because her father died on 8 October 1972. He had been so attuned to our life. He was so aware of our lives through his own experiences overseas, and from his friends who had met us here and there. It's worth just quoting a little more from Rosemary: "We haven't made any particular friends here – we are very fussy! One doesn't see enough of the very pleasant people around, once one has entertained those one ought. I miss social contact outside of evening parties. We used to go on picnics in Iran with chums. We miss our lively, young English there very much. Many of the Guyanese we enjoy having around, and one always has lots of easy happy talk at parties. Guyanese love talking, parties are no problem, unlike the Persians where everyone sat around formally and 'made' conversation."

Education

"Now I think about it," added Rosemary, "our Guyanese friends are more interesting than most of our British ones." Yes, in the Department of Education for instance, I had the most delightful talented Guyanese men and women as friends with whom to cooperate. For instance, there was the Jarvis family, one of whom was Carmen the headmistress of the excellent Bishop's High School for girls. I treasure a letter from her when we left: "The Bishop's High School has always been given much help and information by the British Council, but with very few Representatives have we enjoyed such friendly relations as we have enjoyed with you." "You have done so much," etc. The gratitude of such communities is rewarding: even for the very little which one is able to offer. Other pillars of society in various fields were the Pilgrims from the Civil Service, the Dolphins in music, the Campbells in broadcasting and the Pollards in higher education, all spring specially to mind.

Sharing experiences

After the effect which Iran had upon us, we were delighted to find that the international community of Georgetown, including bright Guyanese, were prepared to turn up and absorb what we had to say about Iran and show in the form of our slides. We had a hundred people at our first talk, and requests for a repeat. It was great fun, even if time-consuming, to work out together what we wanted to show and say. "We worked hard," wrote Rosemary, "on connecting themes and basic explanations. For instance, why the Persians had to use mud for building, hence the arches and domes; then to discuss the irrigation pattern and water problems. Guyana was such a contrast to Iran in every way."

We were later pleased to lecture on Iran to members of the Bahai community of Georgetown. We had admired them in Iran, where they suffered so much. I think their faith is a satisfactory bridge between Christianity and Islam. In Guyana they were enforced exiles. As our second lecture was to a general audience, we decided to focus on 'Art and Architecture in Iran'. We were asked why Rosemary hadn't spoken at the first lecture after it had been announced as being given by both of us. Rosemary explained that we only needed one speaker, and she had the major knowledge on this subject.

Sunset Inn, Tobago

Rosemary wrote: "How easy and cheap it is to pop off from Georgetown to the Caribbean; another plus against the odd moan." When we told Ena Burke, a nursing sister in the Christian Hospital, Isfahan, that we had been transferred to Guyana she told us that she had family in Tobago, and Grenada, and gave us an introduction. What a chance! Tobago was important to Rosemary because there is coral here, but none off Trinidad.

The history of beautiful Tobago is pretty violent with the French, Dutch, and English all having a go at possession. There had been privateers after plunder, and even American rebels with their warship, 'Oliver Cromwell', in 1777, but they didn't take Fort Mitford. There are several good forts to be seen, and an old cannon.

There were other pleasant daylight diversions: watching the pelicans diving so neatly despite appearing so ungainly. And we were able to visit the private bird sanctuary of an original English family the Alefounders.

July 1972: Georgetown

On our return to Georgetown we were plunged right into the merry-go-round. We gave a dinner for the Minister of Education, the head of a U.N. Mission, and the editor of the *Guyana Graphic*. This pulled us together smartly. Venezuela National Day (on my birthday) suited us very well: it was a good, free occasion. The Colombian National Day on 2 July gave us fun and a very good meal! The next day had less rain and was hotter than previously; we gave our first under-house party. Pel chairs from the office usefully increased our seating capacity. Rosemary made good use of her precious Chinese lanterns, and 'chilled' red hibiscus on thorn branches. She "had meant it to be a cocktail party with more food than usual, but the guests treated it as a dinner, queuing up at the table and scoffing the lot; the last doing very badly. You can't very well tell people they aren't meant to eat so much," Rosemary recorded.

Science teacher vacation courses

We had two crises. Firstly, nine teachers had been booked into the hotel which was now requisitioned by the Foreign Minister for Non-Aligned Conference Delegates. Oh well, it was the Ministry of Education's problem. The second crisis was caused by a ground staff strike at Heathrow airport which affected the plans of John Clegg, our pianist who had played for us in Isfahan and intended to perform in Georgetown. His concert was delayed for a day, but the audience responded sportingly, and to our relief, all went very well.

'The Prime Minister and I'

We were invited to a University cocktail party for a visiting English professor. "Groan": why do we have to go out so much? Shame on me. The P.M. was there, and I had had a scheme in my head ready for the right occasion. I felt that there should be in Georgetown a time-and-climate-proof repository for valuable documents; and that British know-how and some funding would make an ideal starter for such a project. "There are your speeches, Prime Minister, that form part of the history of Guyana." "Not all of them, I hope," he replied with a grimace. I thought it safer not to agree.

1 August 1972

Commonwealth Day was on 1 August and we had a cheerful, noisy beginning to the month with a steel-band competition, which involved a general public turnout to go 'tramping with the bands'. We happily joined in the steady plodding pace of the 'pans' round the streets of Georgetown.

Interlude in Guyana

Nine science tutors/lecturers on our hands!

We were visited by seven O.D.A.-funded tutors for teachers' vocation courses, and two funded by the Centre for Education Development Overseas. They were a grand lot: first-class in their fields, and so adaptable and appreciative. It was such fun helping to organize their spare time. And bless John Sankey for lending Rosemary his wife's Mini so together with our Hillman Estate we could transport them all.

Kaiteur Falls

One day of the tutors' spare time was one of the most memorable trips we ever made. We hired a Norman-Britten Islander (George Grandsoult was the pilot), and with seven teachers we flew to the Kaiteur Falls. These 741-foot falls are in a long deep gorge of the Potaro River, which flows into the great Essequibo from the north-west. Kaiteur means a lot to the Guyanese, hence the popularity of Arthur Seymour's *The Legend of Kaiteur*.[5] The Victoria Rainbow Falls are 326 ft., and the Niagara a mere 167 ft. The Angel Falls in Venezuela are of 3,212 ft., but they have much less water than the others. Kaiteur, of 741 ft., was terrific.

Before we took off from our base, several of our visitors expressed their keenness to see birds. George offered to do his best and flew as low as he was allowed over the forest. This was an experience in itself. We did indeed see birds, the tree-top characters, macaws and toucans flashing about in sparkling colours, free from any enemy or disturbance. They took no notice of us.

In due time we lost even more height (we were actually below ground level!) to fly up the Potaro Gorge, with Kaiteur suddenly ahead as George banked each way to show us what to expect. Then the great falls appeared in front of us, with a spray cloud rising, and up we shot straight above the falling water. George understood our excitement and carefully flew round in two circuits from either side so that we could get good photographs.

He landed near-by, and we could walk right up to the edge of the cliffs, and be suitably impressed by the roar of the water. Luckily there was plenty in the river. From Kaiteur George flew us to see falls of great contrast, the Orinduik Falls on the Ireng river in the savannah on the Brazilian border. Margaret Bacon described them beautifully:

> At Orinduik we came down on a little landing-strip like a red cricket pitch . . . The falls were wide and symmetrical and fell in

[5] The text of which is in Longman's Anthology of Guyana: *My Lovely Native Land*.

three great tiers like an amphi-theatre. The air was cool and light and we sat near the highest up in the Gods and breathed the intoxicating air. The one disadvantage of Orinduik was the Kaboura fly, a black, vicious, little creature whose bloodsucking activities leave some patches on the skin for many days afterwards.[6]

Fortunately we do not remember the Kaboura fly.

Georgetown, and 'Carifesta,' the 1972 First Caribbean Festival of Creative Arts

Guyana at this time scored an undoubted double for us: first the flight to Kaiteur, and now this festival from 25 August to 15 September which was the most exciting period of my career. It was an amazingly courageous, some thought foolhardy, undertaking by this little country of Guyana to decide to host the first occasion of this festival. Indeed, the organisers were taken aback when far more groups applied to come than expected. The festival was the brain-child of Sonny Ramphal. I know for sure that the man who bore the greatest burden was the festival secretary, Frank Pilgrim. He was a large, cheerful, friendly, unassuming, and imperturbable man, and was ideal for the job of which he made an enormous success.

I believe that the basic idea was a search for 'cultural identity', especially on the dramatic arts' side. This subject is often under discussion, for so many of the island and mainland African peoples are the descendants of slaves, and have only the faintest, handed-down ideas of tribal dances and rites, if any at all. Sadly, the people have practically no idea of their own roots; no knowledge of their original family names, hence the names their own slave ancestors took from the names of estates or of their masters. I was at first taken aback to meet a Mr Paris and a Mr London, and even a Mr Sholto-Douglas. Maybe it was this aspect which stimulated and inspired the spirits of all those concerned with Carifesta, led by the unremitting efforts of the Guyanese. But even their efforts could not get the great 1,000-seater Cultural Centre finished in time. There was only the roof lacking! But there was a miracle! The Americans flew down a huge canvas Big Top.

Guyana contributed some pretty good talent in music and art, beginning with 'All Kinds of Folk' a song and dance welcome to the Carifesta guests written by Frank Pilgrim. Celeste Dolphin directed the show. Guyana's greatest effort was the massive choral performance of 'The Legend of Kaiteur'. The author Arthur Seymour, Guyana's poet, man of letters, critic,

[6] Margaret Bacon, *Journey to Guyana* (Dobson Books, 1970).

and editor became a particular friend of ours. The music was by Philip Pilgrim, a scholar of the London Royal Schools of Music. He was awarded a British Council Music Scholarship for Further Studies, but unfortunately he died a few days before he was due to take it up.

There were, we were told, about eighty different contributions from - Venezuela, Brazil (Bahia), Cuba, Antigua, Barbados, Monserrat, Jamaica, Surinam, French Guiana, Guadaloupe, Dominica, the U.S. Virgin Islands, St. Kitts, Puerto Rico, St. Vincent, Netherland Antilles, Haiti, Belize, Colombia, Grenada, Trinidad and Tobago, and some local Indian Groups, for whom Carifesta didn't actually apply, but who couldn't be left out.

Later we were lucky to be invited to one of many Indian Government cultural tours, a performance by the Kathakali Dancers. They were of the class of the Kalekshetra Dancers whom we had been excited to see in Fiji. In Guyana earlier we had seen the dancers from Traveni Ballet from Manipur (near the Nagas), who were also wonderful.

I was in a dream-like state because I love folk-music, and here it all was from a wide region of the world performed by some of the finest exponents of rhythm and dance. I wish I then had a small portable tape-recorder. The Jamaican National Dance Theatre Company under their internationally famous Rex Nettleford was the most exciting and technically superb.[7] He was originally a Rhodes Scholar at Oxford (History and Politics) in the late 1950s. Another worthwhile Jamaican contribution was the play *Smile Orange* by Trevor D. Rhone. It was set in a third-rate Jamaican hotel at the start of the tourist season and was extremely funny. But we couldn't understand the dialect, nor could the Guyanese comprehend some of it. Equally entertaining was the *Mystic Revelation of Ras Tafari*. We who had actually served and met Ras Tafari Makonnen, Emperor of Ethiopia, fifteen years before, could appreciate what it was all about. The programme said:

> The music is immediately identifiable with the life styles of the Rastafari Brethren. It is a music of controlled anger and laughter. It is a music of love. Written on the skin of the bass drum are the palmist's words:
>
> "Behold how good and pleasant it is
> For brothers to dwell together in unity!
> It is as the precious ointment upon the
> head that ran down upon the beard."

I wish life in Africa truly means "brothers dwelling together in unity . . ." The Cubans were the very best contributors. A special 'plane-load of

---

[7] See Fiona Maddocks of *The Times* on Rex in Caribbean Focus of 1986.

seventy came, but they made a very short visit and too few people saw their sophisticated and admirably performed versions of their slave and religious dances. The Haitian Institute of Folklore and Classical Dance put on very powerful performances of voodoo chants and initiation ceremonies.

Trinidad and Tobago made a considerable impact (and noise) with their much sharpened, traditional steel-band music and light-hearted calypsos. They were always good value. The most interesting group was Viva Bahia, the Brazilian Folklore Group from the State of Bahia in the North-East, which contains a high proportion of West African people. The dancers were so original and primitive that they would not begin a performance without involving as many rows of audience as they could manage, in some form of pagan inclusion ceremony of chanting and the sprinkling of sacred water.

Nearer home, the Lauriers Roses Folk Group from French Guiana were interesting and evocative in their interpretation of the dance Lerole, which is an imitation of the Quadrille which the slaves had seen their masters performing. The simple basic dance patterns were like the Scottish, and we felt we could have joined in. Nearer still, an extraordinary item in the Surinam effort was a display of the incredibly bulky costumes the female slaves were made to wear so as not to attract their masters' attentions. There were several distinct styles – short, loose-sleeved jackets over layer upon layer of long skirts held up by a tape to make a great fold around the waist, plus a bustle, forming a grotesque total effect.

My favourite of all the Carifesta productions was *Banjo Man* by Roderick Walcott, from St. Lucia. (Derek Walcott is a Caribbean writer of world status, who won the Nobel Prize for Literature in 1992.) It was a charming operetta of haunting music and poetry sung in French patois. The programme notes tell one that *Banjo Man* had previously been banned by Rome as being contrary to the Roman Catholic Church. The theme is the rivalry between the annual Flower Festival Societies unique to the island. I still haven't been able to hear any of the music recorded, or to obtain the score. How I really needed my own recorder then. Unfortunately, the producer or prime mover of *Banjo Man* in the Carifesta production was killed in a car crash not long afterwards. I hope there may be a British production one day.

There were exhibitions of art all over the town including children's art. The art from Bahia was strikingly good and we have two examples of their bold, bright folk art at home. We were glad to see some of the work of the internationally know Guyanese artist, Aubrey Williams, who was a lecturer at Exeter and Camden. Guyanese Philip Moore's sculpture and paintings were also good to see. In America he had been Artist in Residence at Princeton University and Livingstone College. At Carifesta there were

446

discussion groups for writers and poets, and variety shows at the outdoor venues. And there were pre-view evenings: four different groups doing short versions of their shows for those who needed to decide which to see. Public response to Carifesta was pretty good and the participants seemed pleased at reactions. There were some people who would rather have seen the money spent on health services, etc. But how can one gauge the true value of such an event? We absolutely loved it. No complaints – but Rosemary said, "We are of course enjoying it thoroughly, right up our street, though I feel my head won't stand much more drumming."

22 September 1972

We were brought back to earth when we gave a party for fifty; sending off to Britain a number of scholars, technical assistance study fellows, and education study fellows; and welcoming others back.

October 1972: Work and play

In October I received a Commonwealth Parliamentary Association delegation in my office, asking questions. They enjoyed the iced lime juice supplied by Rosemary.

This was followed by an annual charity effort which, since the Guyanese are not afraid of a drink or two, was a profitable success. Each country taking part had to provide a complete national bar of food and drink, and if possible, entertainment too. Each bar was self-contained in rows of tents. The B.H.C. put on a London Pub with darts and songs to a piano. The Americans included a very fine barber's shop quartet in boaters and striped aprons. Everyone from Georgetown and beyond came – to be served happily by diplomats and their wives and staffs. Just imagine the variety of food and drink one could sample!

Our Commonwealth delegates were present but we never saw them. Maybe they had been laid out by the Canadian High Commissioner, (a super chap) doling out dollops of 'red-eye', a drink he extolled.

December 1972: Guyana scored a Christmas treble

Our Christmas was terrific. We had a staff party on 12 December and then on 22 December our own party for forty guests including two High Commissioners, the Chief Justice, and one or two other Government servants. We performed my version of the Mummers' play, *St. George and*

447

the Dragon, improved by the Minister of Transport, a Chinese who, of course, knew all about dragons. He was even able to produce a smoke-breathing dragon whose effect was spectacular, although his head was on backwards! Rosemary's Christmas pudding and mince pies were praised, and our joint decorations too. Departures were at 2 a.m. A day or two later, Rosemary gave a dinner for seven of us, and guests left for home from 2.30 a.m. Guyana is that sort of place!

What we loved was the cosmopolitan nature of the Guyanese, and everyone's jolly attitude to Christmas. We shall never forget the Barclays Bank carol group of charming little Chinese girls under their attractive part-Chinese Manager, Evadne Walker. The carols went with a Guyanese swing, and so did the dear little carollers' bodies, especially as seen from behind!

The highlight of our Christmas break was our invitation from the President, Arthur Chung, to join his family to listen to four specially selected carol groups: singers of the Blind Home; the Salvation Army; the police choir; and a country folk group from the Essequibo coast. There were twelve guests. The only other foreigners were the American Head of Aid and his wife of whom we were fond. We had an elegant and informal evening, and enjoyed being shown Christmas cards from the Queen, the Emperor of Ethiopia (there are many Rastafarians in Guyana – the stronghold I should think), and from Ted Heath.

1973

The year was well seen in by a party at the home of a U.N. English friend and his Parsee wife, who had invited an Indian couple, a Japanese and his American wife, a Bolivian and his Brazilian wife, another Brazilian, an English girl diplomat and two Russians. We danced a sort of reel together to the Demerara Tobacco Company Steel Band. It was a good start. But hold it! Orders now arrived from the British Council, London, for me to return to Karachi as Regional Representative.

We still saw some good cricket from the John Player League match: Kent (who were the current champions) versus Guyana. The match was all the more enjoyable after entertaining some of the players, and meeting more across the road in the pavilion. A handy spot, Georgetown!

To Imbaimadai

Adrian Thompson had told us about Imbaimadai and given us his usual sound advice. Now on 15 January, a Muslim holiday, we were able to make our long delayed trip to the area. The town is on the upper reaches of the Mazaruni river, a diamond and gold mining centre set in marvellous highland scenery, an hour's flight south-west.

"Get in touch with Peters," Adrian had told us. "He is a splendid man, very reliable. He can show you diamonds." Imbaimadai was only a collection of miners' tin huts and stores; it was very bleak-looking indeed. Peters, then the local agent for mining, the airline, postal services, etc. and a former pork knocker [prospector], had built a very adequate, wooden guest-house, and was a pleasant knowledgeable and sound chap. We took our own food and drink for a start and had a very good time.

We walked beside a tributary to the Partang rapids, and next day went by outboard up another tributary, walked past more rapids with Amerindians carrying the engine and fuel tank. Above these rapids we boarded another craft and went up to the very fine Maipuri Falls. Here the banks of the Mazaruni rise sheer on either side. Maipuri (Arawak for tapir), is a wall of water 80-foot high which thunders into a basin and produces a terrific roar. From there Rosemary and the Pims walked up for over an hour to see some ancient rock paintings, at the Tramar Cliffs.

One day we were taken downstream on the Mazaruni to the Amerindian settlement of Javalla. The weather was perfect, and we were able to spend some enjoyable hours walking through the forest, although I didn't like having to cross little creeks by log bridges! We were guided to a tributary on which we watched prospectors dredging for gold. They worked from rafts and went under water in diving-suits. They shifted sand and gravel with suction hoses driven by small diesel engines. We actually saw gold appearing in a wide, shallow pan, sifted gently by expert hands. There were no diamond shouts that day!

It is interesting to read Henry Kirke (in Guyana 1872–1897) on the gold industry, having seen the men on the ground and under the water! In 1887 it was found necessary to establish a town at the little settlement of Bartica at the junction of the Mazaruni and the Essequibo, because by then rumours of gold finds had been succeeded by the actual discovery of gold in paying quantities in the Essequibo region. A central depot was needed whence the gold industry could be regulated. This is what Bartica continues to do today. It occupies one of the greenest, choicest sites in Guyana, as Henry Kirke found. The British Commander-in-Chief based in Trinidad at the end of last century said to Guyana's Governor Scott, "Why don't you all go and live up the Mazaruni, and send the convicts from the penal settlement there to Georgetown. They are much better located at present than you are." I wonder why the move was not made? I wish it had been!

And Guyana?

"El Dorado" is still there, but no search has yet come up with treasure. But the country is rich in accessible and workable natural resources: sugar, rice, bauxite, alumina, timber, coconuts, manganese, gold, diamonds, fish, and all the secondary industries thereon. Yet Guyana, I felt, wasn't meant to be an independent country. It was still essentially an estate to be managed skilfully, requiring considerable cash input and expertise. The Dutch, French, and British had their chances and resources, and didn't do too badly. But they hardly did more than extract wealth through slavery, and then the new free African population were upset by the introduction of indentured labour from India. Independence under such conditions was not contemplated by statesmen outside Guyana. Instead, there seems to have been a somewhat cheese-paring colonisation.

I grant you that freedom and independence is dearly sought by states and citizens, but dogmatic independence regardless of prosperity and happiness doesn't seem to produce the expected standards and benefits. I was sad to see what was happening in Guyana just four years after independence. There was nationalisation of bauxite and trade (Alcan and Bookers), resulting in an immediate down-turn of prosperity and shortage of standard commodities and foodstuffs. There was no use for the old regime, and the consequent exodus of admirable men and women who could no longer find acceptance of their skills in fields in which they had formerly flourished and served. We saw them suffer and go. I am afraid we got the impression of general retrogression which I hope has since been reversed.

Goodbye

February was a loss for us, in that we had to spend time on the administration of getting our baggage packed and despatched, and our house steadily cleared. We went about sadly saying good-bye to a number of delightful Guyanese and international friends – too many to name.

A great jump-up

Our farewell party and welcome to our successors, the Fergusons, took the form of drinks and dancing to Keith Waithe and his Police Combo under our house; 150 out of 200 invited came. Keith and company were terrific. Hurray for the Guyanese music-makers everywhere!

The hardest part was saying goodbye to my office staff who had been faithful and admirable, though dear old Wiggins the night-watchman, had earlier died one night at post. Parting with our memorable servants Sybil and Olga was sad. They might or might not be (or might not want to be) taken on by our successors. Good servants are treasures, especially when one is in a job in which entertaining plays a part. It is perhaps they whom we remember best in all the countries, sometimes with real pangs of anxiety as to their future. Where are they all now? Some answers would be fairly easy to find if it weren't for the politics.

However, I am afraid I must truthfully say that in Guyana we never really felt at ease despite our lively, talented Guyanese friends. It was to do with the very nature of the country, and its history – of slavery and hardship – and present-day politics. Moves from 'our' countries have been hard, but this was the only time that Rosemary did not cry as we left a country. I was sad not to be able to achieve more. This was partly due to not being allowed to do so, and that is the business of the host country. But my staff and I and my wife believe we did achieve something. Certainly there was appreciation and kindness all round. A lot of things special to Guyana gave us novel interest and rare pleasure.

A letter from the Minister of Education left us encouraged:

Dear Mr Halsted,

Thank you for your kind letter of 6th March, 1973.
Please accept my appreciation for the ready help you have given while in Guyana. I thought that on the eve of your departure I should let you know that I feel that Guyana will have said goodbye to a good friend.

We were heartened by your genuine interest in things Guyanese and your many ways of helping.

I wish you all the best in your new life and look forward to a close cooperation with your successor.

With all good wishes,
Yours cooperatively,

Shirley Field-Ridley,
Minister.

Of all our memories, we found special enjoyment in the natural world of Guyana, thanks particularly to Adrian Thompson and to Naranjan Poonai. We owe much to both men, and so does Guyana.

Sind and the frontier 1973–1978

With the opening of Pakistan's new capital, Islamabad, we now had our Head Office there, with a Regional Centre in Lahore, and ours in Karachi.

My reaction to being posted back to Karachi after twenty-two years was one of "Oh, no!", but of course we went. The drabness of the desert of the southern part of Sind was as before, but life for me this time with Rosemary was very different and greatly rewarding. It was hard on Rosemary, who had to cope with heat and humidity, traffic chaos, crowded bazaars and pavements, and there was little of Islam to study locally. But she managed marvellously, and gave me the highest quality support, which was much appreciated by our Pakistani contacts among whom we made the best of friends.

Back in England, in a rented house in north Oxford, I ploughed through my essential reading of E.V. Hodson on Partition, *The Great Divide* (Hutchinson, 1969). In London, Mr College of Diplomatic Sales in Rootes, Piccadilly, was as helpful as ever in obtaining for me the latest Hillman Hunter estate in safari beige. It was sturdy and an easy car to maintain or repair, which is vital in remote places.

On our British Airways flight we found an Englishman to whom it was very useful to listen. He was Len Papworth, retired headmaster of Karachi Grammar School. After years in Pakistan he did not take to retirement in England. He badly missed his friends in Pakistan and the social life. He had done the right thing in returning to Karachi. The school was very good to him and gave him a flat in its compound. He was happy and never any trouble; and there he ended his days.

It was an odd feeling flying in to Karachi's Drigh Road Airport after twenty-two years. The scene was familiar and reassuring. The early morning sun's beautiful low light was still on the sand, and there were the same flat-topped, white-washed houses, and palm trees. I had quite a responsibility ahead but I could take it calmly. I had Rosemary with me, and I carried the lease of a fine change of premises for the Council, which had been achieved by my predecessor, Dan Somerville.

The original choice of Pakistan Chowk had been good in the early days; but now the Council found itself close upon an expanded bazaar area. We needed to be more accessible to students and teachers. Dan, a highly regarded and intelligent Wykhamist, was leaving me the very best of a going concern with high staff morale. One or two members already knew me from my bachelor days!

We were warmly welcomed without formality, into the Sind Club by the Secretary, Commander S. A. Waheed, P.N. retd. How pleasant it was to return to this admirable island refuge with every facility that a club should have. I was back at the long bar where with Roger Rigby I had just managed my beer and pink gin chasers before luncheon. We had even stood alongside the Auk and A.V. M. (Batchy) Atcherley. I enjoyed hearing Commander Seyed's macaronic telephone conversations part Urdu, part English. This proved to me that Urdu wasn't difficult if one knew when to break into English. Unfortunately, Rosemary and I were pretty soon laid flat by some horrible stomach 'bug'; but it gave us time to get over jet-lag and adjust a little before facing some forty-five staff, headed by my admirable second-in-command, Chris Chislett, and before setting about the big move.

The Somervilles first took us out north to the Council's beach hut at Bulegi. It was a pleasure to drive along part of the route taken by Alexander in 325 B.C., up the coast to the original four little kingdoms of Kalat, Kharan, Makran, and Las Bela. The twenty-one-mile journey passed first through the commercial centre of the city, then through Lyari, a district of closely-built, airless, fetid tenements, with the minimum of sanitation, sewage disposal, and rubbish collection; the area known to us as 'pooh corner'. But then came the interest, the oil-soaked, sandy area of repair shops and goods depots where a regular collection of highly decorated, long-distance trucks from the frontier and Afghanistan was on display.

The tarmac road continued through clean and quiet light industry, thence past the homes of fisherfolk. Vegetation now appeared: tamarisk, acacia thorn, and euphorbia – the cactus of Asia. Then we turned west towards the sea, to a loose circle of huts facing a sandy beach and an area of rocks.

Each hut had its own chowkidar from the nearby village. Ours would magically appear as we arrived, and help us unload everything. There was nearly always an agreeable breeze, and round our hut was a pleasant place to relax at week-ends, particularly with hard-working visitors, although the scenery was just desert. The rocks were disappointing for Rosemary, yielding few worthwhile shells; but for me the creatures at the sea surface were fun to watch: crabs, crustacea, urchins, and tiny fish. The sea was pretty safe except when it became rough in the monsoon period from April to October when Portuguese men-of-war were churned around and spewed ashore.

At some weekends we would stay the night; perhaps throw a party, or join one at another hut. We never had to contend with vandals or intruders (human or animal). We could sleep peacefully on our safari beds in a gentle breeze, listening to the sea, keeping the return journey and the rest of Karachi out of our minds. We blessed our donor.

My next priority was a visit to our sub-centre at Hyderabad, Sind, the old, pre-1846 capital up the Indus (as distinct from Hyderabad, Deccan, India). Pre-partition the population of Sind was roughly fifty percent Sindhis, who were mostly in Hyderabad. But at Partition came the Mohajirs, Muslim refugees from United Provinces (U.P.) who were mainly businessmen on the make rather than villagers; also Ismailis came, who were good providers of schools and hospitals; and about 10,000 Goans (Portuguese descendants) arrived; then Muslim Biharis, refugee people and civil servants; also Parsees; Bengalis; and Kuchi Memons from the Rann of Kutch, over the Indian border 100 miles or so south-east of Karachi.

I had to make frequent visits to Hyderabad during our five years. The journey was a hundred miles north-east along the edge of the Sind desert. Fortunately, the drive only took two hours and twenty minutes, along the recently completed Italian-built highway, on good tarmac, but even so, the journey was boring and grim in a bare, rocky land. We never had a break-down thanks to our drivers' maintenance. The main danger was the thundering flow of lorries whose drivers preferred the middle of the road by day and had poor lights at night.

Our man in charge at Hyderabad was the personable and conscientious Mr I. A. S. Bokhari, who with his three staff knew all about Hyderabad and was well known himself. He ran our centre and library and was most useful when our specialist visitors needed guidance and introductions to various educational establishments in the region.

Back in Karachi, the Somervilles had laid on a magnificent farewell and welcome party – in the great empty Mackinnon House which the Council would soon occupy. There were well over 200 guests, and Rosemary and I were under scrutiny! What a difference to my arrival in 1947! Now we had access to many senior Pakistani and foreign officials, and retired men of great experience and understanding. The support we needed came from H.M. Consul-General P. D. McEntee, his staff, and his wife Mary. They remain great friends.

I would like to pay tribute to the leaders of the new nation, Land of the Pure, and to the people themselves, having together triumphed in the early years over the desperate conditions and deprivations of four million refugees. And especially after the double blow of the death in 1947 of the country's founder, Qaid-i-Azam, Mohammed Ali Jinnah; and the treason-ous murder in October 1951 of the brilliant and charismatic Prime Minister, Liaquat Ali Khan. I was so glad to be able to meet Begum Liaquat Ali Khan again, now Governor of Sind. She was a dear person and so helpful and humble too. All the educated Hindus had left Pakistan.

It was the Hindus who had taken advantage of the British education policy laid down in 1833 by Lord Macaulay, leaving behind the Muslims who preferred firearms to type-writers. The Parsees remained in Karachi, the only port and the national commercial capital of a vast hinterland. They were congenial company. Though well placed under the British Raj they had lost much of their wealth and power through the Pakistan Government policy of nationalisation. This loss did not help the country.

Pakistan remained in need of funds to cope with never-ending problems. For instance, it needed a wide expansion of science and engineering training. In the days of the British Raj the sciences were largely neglected through Lord Macaulay's system of Civil Service-type education, which concentrated on excellence in English, the arts, and classical studies. The British were now criticised for this – quite fairly, I thought with hindsight. The British Government was in our day doing its best to help Pakistan to correct this imbalance, as were other European nations.

However, there was definitely new interest and new life in Karachi through the influx of Muslims from all over India. These 'Muhajirs' were now just in the majority, and they caused a great problem because there was confrontation, as well as co-operation, with the Sindhis. However, Karachi certainly generated forty-five per cent of the country's wealth. We found that many Karachi friends were broad-minded and highly intelligent Muslims from Lucknow. I wish I could have known the mixed communities of pre-Partition Lucknow.

By 1964 Pakistan had a newly-built capital, Islamabad, 1,000 miles to the north; but Karachi remained the international city. Life was lively and stimulating with friends of many nations. We were all the envy of people in Lahore or Islamabad, where life was almost wholly confined to the diplomatic enclave without the varieties of local life.

The standard of new housing development was high in Karachi, especially the Defence Housing Phases I-V, built for the Services and administrators. The whole area had been desert before, but we did very well in the Somerville's house and garden in Defence, 9B Fifth South Street. There was only air-conditioning in the bedrooms, but for most of the year we could entertain very well in the attractive garden, planted with frangi-pani, bougainvillea, hibiscus, gul mohr, plumbago, jasmine, yellow oleander, Indian laburnum and Rangoon creeper. We could run out standard lamps to light the tables, and have recorded music in the background.

We inherited excellent servants. Niaz Hussein, the bearer, was a refugee himself, after years of experience under his father in a British army mess in Jhansi. When he finally unpacked our household cases, he said: "Where are the port glasses, memsahib?" We hadn't any. Loss of face. How to retrieve it? Do *you* have port glasses?

The early part of these moves from country to country can be a trial to housewives. Transit delays did not allow us to operate at full efficiency for some time. For instance, our air freight (containing essentials) reached Karachi after us in reasonable time. But our heavy baggage (including warm clothes which we now needed) didn't arrive for *six months*.

Poor Niaz had a wife and eight children, whom we never saw. We felt awful about this but he didn't want us involved. He had an elder daughter to marry off at the time, and was very worried: "She is not a beauty girl," was the problem.

Ghaffar was cook; he was a small, monosyllabic man with a forceful personality. He could be touchy, and Rosemary was very clever with him. He was too good to lose, being competent and hard-working.

Rosemary: "Sahib is very fond of curry, Ghaffar." (A good opener, she thought.)

Ghaffar: "Memsahib, before here, I was the English food cook."

Rosemary: "Oh, very fine Ghaffar; but could you kindly oblige . . . dah di dah?"

He did and kept on doing fine curries. He ground up all his spices assiduously by hand on a rough, granite slab (like a local tombstone).

Michael: "Very nice, Ghaffar, thank you. What do you call this curry?"

Ghaffar: "Just curry, sahib." And so it remained.

His stuffed crab was also excellent.

Our chowkidar, (watchman) was Yar Khan, an ex-Punjabi regimental sepoy, vouched for by kind army friends, Colonel and Mrs Ali Asghar Agha, who were charming. (They have since moved to Lahore, but remain good friends.) Yar Khan was totally loyal and adequate despite his problems such as the expense and worry of absence from his family in the far north. He had quarters at the back of the house. He would help Rosemary by doing the watering; but when we realised the desperate shortage of water in the poorer areas, we cut this down.

Our dhobi (washerman) was a good man and a boon. He came twice a week, and washed our laundry in the bath, dried and ironed in the day. We also had a sweeper who came in daily: first William, a Christian who bettered himself, and then Sultan.

Rosemary could manage the garden on her own, but she got our Mackinnon House mali to help with some plants. She attended a municipal gardening course for memsahibs, run by the excellent A. K. Khan, Director of Parks and Gardens. He had to be a skilful martinet!

Rosemary couldn't stand the crows in the trees above. Their constant cawing and hanging around were the housewife's daily burden. But after a long time, just a menace by her with my catapult did assist in driving them away. I made little impression with my air-rifle or air-pistol. I couldn't get within range; the crows were too wary. One consolation was the occasional appearance of delicate, shapely hoopoes on the lawn.

Sind

Our French cultural colleague lived next door. He had two lovely cypress trees in his garden, which are rare in Sind; but his wife had them cut down because they reminded her of cemeteries at home. We 'culture wallahs', American, Japanese, German, French, and British met for a monthly luncheon in each others houses – without our wives. When it took place in our house poor Rosemary had her lunch delivered upstairs.

Karachi was drear: the population outside the original port, was plonked down in the sand of the Sind Desert. The Defence Housing Society phases were all in the sand right down to the sea. From Phase V we could (with nowhere else to go!) drive to the sand-hill edge above the beach, and walk a long way east, amused by the crabs, sometimes finding interesting desert plants.

This desert had oases – in our friends' houses and gardens, and in the clubs, and occasionally in the hotels. The walks round the streets of Phase V were a rather miserable form of exercise, past burning household rubbish, but the trees along the streets and plants in gardens or on walls were a pleasure. There were no buildings of historic or architectural interest.

It was hot and humid from March to June, but a constant sea-breeze helped, and blew away any smog. There was plenty of sport: sailing, tennis, swimming, and the bunder-boating was as good as it had ever been. I had the choice of three free tennis courts: Mackinnon House, the Sind Club and at the Consulate-General, thanks to the McEntees. Our house had double, sheet-metal gates leading into a short, paved drive up to a car port; and there was just room for a long-wise Scottish Country Dance set. Our friends and the activities they generated made up for a lot. Indeed, I was affectionately disposed towards Karachi.

We hadn't much local culture for our official or private visitors, but there was plenty of atmosphere on short trips. There were occasional, good, local art exhibitions; local handicrafts worth examining; and onyx from Baluchistan that was worth buying. There were Pakistani-made carpets of excellent value and wear, based on traditional Persian patterns. Local materials were good; and tailors and shoe-makers constitued real perks. There were visiting national cultural occasions to enjoy by invitation: film shows, musical events, and dance. There was amateur talent around for drama and musicals which were enormous fun.

Pakistan had much to offer. I had educational establishments, teachers and students all over Sind to visit; sometimes with a visitor. I had to get out and about, and I could take Rosemary. We had time to absorb history, architecture, life, and cultures in the course of my work. No wonder that I often say that in the British Council I could not distinguish work from play. From here my head office was 1,000 miles away in Islamabad, in a fascinating other world of rivers and mountains, and the distance had its advantages!

How to fill in five years in Karachi? Easy

In early August we had an important visitor for Karachi, Dr Smurfit, to the Pakistan College of Family Medicine. I was anxious about the medical training standards in Pakistan since classes were so large; and also because young doctors tended to leave for Britain.

26 August 1973: Hyderabad

Flood waters on the Indus threatened to cut off the return of three British science teachers who were running a teachers' vacation course. The airfield there might be flooded, so, with Chris in his car and Rosemary and I in ours, off we went to Hyderabad. The water was pretty high at the Kotri Barrage, but it had been very strongly built, and we got across to the town without qualms. We even got accommodation in the Sardinia Hotel before the course's official dinner, and the closing ceremony the following morning. The proceedings and my speech were on Karachi television that evening, providing useful publicity for our science in education approach. Then we ferried three relieved teachers back over the Lion River to Karachi.

All along I was very occupied with the furnishing, decorating, sign producing, and shelving for the move of our library and offices. I was greatly helped by our London-appointed librarian, Dennis Spiby. I had to beg London for money to bar the windows to prevent students throwing books out to accomplices. I knew this trick. It would have been a waste of valuable resources otherwise. I had to fight for more money for the whole move. London had written: "The state of the premises is not important in relation to our main effort: The Printed Word." Of course it all had to be first-class, especially the library. Peter McEntee supported me; and so did our Controller, Hugh Ellis, who came out from London and was so good. My confidence was restored.

On 17 November the office moved out of Pakistan Chowk; it was a great day. A speech of thanks was made to our landlord, the Shahani family of the Devan Metharam Trust, for their twenty-five-year support. Mr Siddiqui, our head librarian, gave the figures of 7,852 members, and 120,047 issues in 1972/73. Inam Ikramullah, assistant librarian, read a farewell poem. I removed the British Council brass-plate and carried it along to Mackinnon House.

By 18 December all the 54,000 books had been moved and were in place. Rosemary did the colour scheme throughout. Between us we worded all the notice-boards and they were well produced locally. Luckily, our Ambassador, Sir Laurence Pumphrey, was in Karachi at the right moment, and kindly came to open the Library.

Getting around Sind

We hadn't been able to get any useful provincial maps in London, but the Surveyor-General in Karachi kindly supplied what we needed, and enough for the McEntees too. Now we engaged I. U. Chowdhury, Professor of English, to teach us Urdu. I am afraid all I learned was enough to write a simple Urdu course from the notes I took. Luckily it was our spoken English that people wanted to hear.

In September we were quite busy meeting or sending off wives or children of staff, or caring for colleagues having to stop over en route to elsewhere in the world.

A great surprise

Later in the month we went to an excellent amateur production of the very funny play *Boeing, Boeing* by Marc Camoletti. The box and cox antics reminded me of Roger and me, and our air-hostesses stopping over.[1] When the lights went up we recognised in the audience the Burmese architect, Bilal Rashid, and his wife, Tin Lay, from Rangoon days. They had escaped after their father, a former Minister, had been put in detention. Through the Rashids we found that all the Ahmed family, Haji and Amina, their six girls and a son had also come out of Burma to Pakistan. It was fun to have them around.

Seeing nature in comfort

The McEntees took us and the Faggs (Australian Consul-General) to their beach hut along the coast. After an air-conditioned car-ride, there was a cook and a bearer fully installed with all forms of food and drink in a well-furnished concrete house. The air was balmy, as we waited for the high tide which occurred conveniently after dinner, at 10 p.m. We stalked along the beach, and were soon rewarded by seeing for the first time two turtles laying eggs in the sand.

October

We welcomed the so agreeable Professor Colum O'Flaherty (Transport Studies at Leeds University) and his wife Nola. His advice was very

[1] See Karachi, p. 68.

valuable to Pakistan's town planners and police in the main cities. The professor had met the man in charge of the new Calcutta Underground. "How much is it costing you?" "Oh, about three million." "You'll never do it for that." "I know; but if I had told them the truth they would never have let me start."

The French showed the unforgettable film, *Allez France* ,at the Sind Club. It portrayed a French Rugby team in Britain. At the start the screen appeared opaque. We were anxious, but then it cleared, and a voice said: "Le fog".

The London Shakespeare Group came with a production of *Macbeth*. It was fun for us, if alarming with regards to the venue and publicity. The group was a jolly lot, particularly Edward Jewesbury, a friend of Andrew Cruickshank. "They all love Harriet," he said of Andrew's daughter (Papa's god-daughter). We had something in common with three of the cast. Rosemary gave a happy party for forty-eight guests after the performance; and Hameed Zaman wrote a reflective and useful piece on the British Council in past and present Karachi in the *Morning News* (9 October 1973), supporting our move up-town.

November

After attending the English Teachers' Convention, a valuable meeting point for me, we had another very significant meeting. Our friend, Chris Savage, from Tehran days arrived in his wildlife role; and introduced us to Tom and Frances Roberts of F.A.O. They remain two of our dearest friends. The brilliant Tom has produced valuable, definitive works, such as the *Mammals of Pakistan*, and the *Birds of Pakistan*, which he himself illustrated. In 1994 he was awarded Pakistan's highest honour: Setare Pakistan (Star of Pakistan).

Cricket. Visit of the World XI to play Pakistan

When I arrived in Karachi I presented a letter of introduction from the Secretary of the M.C.C. to Zafar Altaf, Secretary, Board of Control of Cricket in Pakistan. His kind response was valuable.

There was no better start to the cricket side of life than the Sind Club Reception for the World Eleven. The team contained a number of well-known West Indians including Kanhai, Lloyd, and Gibbs from Guyana. I wore my Guyana C.C. tie which Kanhai spotted immediately. The next evening John Venning of the British Consulate-General gave a party for the team, and I took along my West Indian records. I had briefed John that a 'jump-up' might be popular. It was!

The cricketers behaved as the perfect gentlemen they were. They may have been bored stiff, but they were not a bit spoilt or blasé. They listened politely to all the inanities uttered and joined in whenever they could.

English

The speaking of English was my speciality in the field of English language teaching. The teaching included understanding, enjoying, and reciting poetry, which is a good way to help fluency in speaking the language. Hence it was a pleasure to be asked to judge school elocution competitions, such as at the B.V.S. Parsee High School and the Y.M. Zoroastrian Assocation; the very bright Parsees stress the vital value of English. They have high standards of education, and intend to succeed in life.

The Mama Parsee High School for Girls, and Rosemary invited to give the prizes

"How does one react to the Blue Bird Brownies all flapping their
elbows and going tu-whit tu-woo?"

29 November 1973: Al-Biruni

We became involved in a small way with the British delegates to an
international, Pakistani-run congress on the life and works of the great,
eastern scholar of 1,000 years ago, Al-Biruni. We met Dr David Bivar
from London, Professor Montgomery-Watt from Edinburgh, and a Persian
lecturer in Persian from Edinburgh. One visitor recognised me as his
English teacher in Tehran; and another delegate, the Persian teacher at the
Iran Institute in Karachi, had been a pupil of mine for English. We were
happily back in a Persian milieu. It was amusing hearing Rosemary
speaking Persian to the Russian Professor Gankovsky. He took to
Rosemary, who helped him a bit; and we took to him. He produced a
special, little 'Christmasy' box of Russian Troika cigarettes for me.

The ceremonies took up a lot of time, but it was worth being around
to pick up what one could. A speech by a professor from a Tehran
university struck me as a landmark. To all Muslims he spoke firmly
saying that to date most Muslim visitors to the West came back with the
worst aspects of Western life into which they were so easily drawn. This
was partly because they had set out with no confidence in their Islamic
faith and way of life. They did not speak out on their beliefs, but allowed
themselves to be brushed aside as mere foreigners. Now was the time,

he said, to stand up for Islam, and to carry forward the strength of their faith, and actively champion the achievements of their men of letters, architects, astronomers, and medical men. I think this speech stirred Islamic consciousness, and even contributed to the rise of the Fundamentalists.

Dr Bivar was particularly stimulating and interesting. He lectured on pre-Islamic contacts with Iran, and on the ancient Persian Hunting Manual. David B. told us about the science of topographical archaeology.[2] From the air it is possible to discern the outlines of Alexander's forts from their known shape, such as by Minagara, the Sythian capital.

S.C.D. once more

It was great to be back again in the Karachi Scottish country dance scene. The Caledonian Ball was the big social event in Karachi. Practices and the Ball were held at my 1949 original haunt, the Beach Luxury Hotel, thanks to the owner Byram D. Avari. After I had attended a practice or two and kept quiet and just danced, I was happy to be taken on as coach. Bed after the Ball was at 3.40 a.m.

December 1973

We were invited to the banquet of the All-Pakistan Medical Conference. Three jolly British doctors were attending, "I'm all for exploratory eating," said one, as he piled his plate with hot curry. We later discussed antidotes.

I had to give the Visitors Speech at the Karachi Grammar School Speech Day; an honour I much enjoyed. My subject was 'Choice'.

Christmas in Karachi was a very social festival. A number of couples were happy to give parties for many of the community. Life became wearing: but how could we have missed such occasions?

Bush Christmas

We had enjoyed escaping from the Christmas racket in Tehran, so we decided we'd escape out of Karachi. We took Tony Moggach of O.U.P. and his wife, Debbie, to the Waterworks Rest House at Halegi Lake, fifty miles east near the ancient town of Tatta. There was agreeable,

[2] See above, Tehran, p. 179.

semi-cultivated countryside with low hills in the background; and the area round the lake was a bird/wildlife sanctuary. The weather was clear, with a cold wind. There was a golden sunset on Christmas Eve. We were in a palatial, brick bungalow with beds and a bearer and a cook, with a local-type charcoal kitchen on which Rosemary did most of the cooking. It was cold enough to be glad of our sleeping bags and blankets. We had our radio to listen to the King's College Chapel service; and a good dinner!

Out on the shore of the attractive, tree-lined lake we had a picnic lunch, and the pleasure of spotting and identifying a number of birds: pochard duck, pied and blue kingfishers, a fish eagle, and a number of herons. Before returning to Karachi we took in the town of Tatta of the fourteenth to nineteenth centuries with the stone and brick tombs of the great in early Indian/Persian style. Then we returned home to a party at the McEntees. It was a perfect Christmas.

The McEntee's party was terrific:

Marvellous party,
Christmas spirit,
Everyone delighted,
Non-pareil hostess,
Thank you both,
Embraces earned,
Endearing effort.

Debbie is now a well-established writer. This is not surprising to us after she had showed such a keen, perceptive interest in Karachi life; for instance, the contrast with the appalling squalor around us which affected her deeply. Rosemary hoped she could help Debbie out of the disquiet in which she found herself in the circumstances of our lives in the sub-continent. The servant/master relationship worried her as it must worry many other wives today who had no servants at home, let alone being new to India or Pakistan. One solution to Debbie's problem was for her to give her servant a uniform, which Debbie had first recoiled against. But it is the uniform which gives a servant in the Indian sub-continent his dignity and his own private world.

Debbie wrote sensitively for *The Morning Herald* that December. She ended her article with "the sinister kites and black crows: omens of doom circling endlessly."

Jimmy and Tessa Midwood (Burma-Shell) old hands who helped us a lot also gave a memorable party:

464

Sind

Mellow matrons, merrymaking men,
Inescapable intoxication, idyllic indulgence.
Disturbing daughters, delightful dancing,
Warming whisky, worthy wassail.
Occidental oblivion, overwhelming occasion.
Orgiastic openings, opulent odours,
Delicious delicacies, diverting dalliance.

January 1974

Our tetanus, cholera, and small-pox 'jabs' were due. We were visited by
Dr Blakeborough, Professor of Chemical Engineering, with his wife and
daughter. At Bulegi they enjoyed pottering among the rock pools at low
tide under Rosemary's tutelage. Dr Blakeborough gave us a rotary spring-
acting bowl ashtray, which was ideal for the Bulegi hut, and known ever
after as 'The Blakeborough Bequest'.

A U.N. host gave a Bulegi New Year dinner party with ham and wine –
which were unobtainable by us. I did miss bacon for breakfast.

There was an Eid holiday. I went to the airport on impulse to welcome
to Pakistan the new headmistress for the British School, Islamabad. I'm
glad I went. Her connecting 'plane was cancelled over the holiday so I was
able to get her on to another. Peter McEntee was there meeting a friend.
He was more aware of the consequences of the oil price rise than I was,
and a chat with him was very useful. "Will we still be paid?" Peter asked!

We went exploring in the car – and survived. The more we drove – and
it was daily – in the shambles of this vast and swarming city, I realised the
perils Rosemary went through from impatient, mad, or egomanic drivers.
I felt what she also suffered from the heat and dust, taking me to and from
the office, or shopping in between. One day we tried to find a new road
out of the city. We had to proceed at a carriage pace in a welter of
victorias, donkeys and carts, buses, camel carts, motor-scooter taxis, and
goats being offered for sale after the Day of Sacrifice. We failed and had
to retreat through the crowds still in holiday garb. Nobody minded us.

As elsewhere, I made an offer to the police here, and gave a talk on
Good Driving. I think this was a new concept. I used material from my
cousin, Robert Peters, who then ran the British Institute of Advanced
Motorists.

The rest of January saw no complaints about life in Karachi. There was
a good value American dance group, and a dazzling Russian dance group
from Kazakstan. The Clifton Players performed an enjoyable *Arsenic and
Old Lace*; and Mac came from London and Tehran on his way to Cooper
Bros. Singapore, with whisky, cheese, sausages, caviar for us, and my

unobtainable Senior Service cigarettes. Rosemary had a gardening class and horticultural lesson. Then we had a moonlight search for shells on the reef as she initiated friends into conchology, and newcomers to safari meals.

Our Hyderabad

Hyderabad under the British Raj had its cantonment; its Circuit House and Civil Lines and hospital; a beautiful Victorian entrance-arch to the bazaar, with clock-tower above; a fine High School with clock-tower and crenellations. Some unkind observer wrote that neither clock worked. Unlike our main military and civil stations such as Peshawar or Rawalpindi, which still survive with their clubs and hotels, Hyderabad never had such a station life; and the cantonment had disappeared into commercial development.

There was no club for me to stay at but I was happy in Sainjee's Motel. I was given delicious porridge, but now and then I had an impression of the odd rat in the dining room, or actual cockroaches in the shower.

Hyderabad city streets were as colourful as ever; but unfortunately the picturesque, and any calm, disappeared long ago under the internal combustion engine in its wide and horrible variety. The town suffered from ear-splitting, vapourous motor-cycles and two-stroke motor rickshaws; ramshackle, untuned diesel trucks and buses, all pouring out noxious, black fumes. The hand-carts, donkey carts, camel carts, and push barrows stood little chance against such traffic. Overall there were horrid noises and smells mixed with dust and sand.

But the Sindhis themselves survived brilliantly. They got about in the finest of one-horse, two-wheeled, high-slung tongas driven with dash and bravado. The men had great moustaches and huge turbans and shawls of lovely red and blue patterned ajrak cotton cloth. The tongas were brightly painted and highly polished. It was a pleasure to see their spirited, high-stepping horses. The women clustered on backward-facing seats, dressed in black or white chadors. Whole families would be piled high in these 'carriages'. The little girls wore bright, patterned costumes, wearing the gararah – a full-length divided skirt.

There were some great forts in Sind. But, alas, erosion by the elements of neglected mudbrick was causing many to crumble fast. A typical ancient example was Ranikot Fort, some twenty miles beyond Jamshoro, the university suburb of Hyderabad. The fort was eighteen miles in circumference, contained in once magnificent walls twenty feet high. An army could march along their top, reminiscent of the Great Wall of China.

Hyderabad had two forts, the remains of which were not easily seen until one braved the old city. Here the main walls of the pukka qila (well-built fort) still towered above the street; and thanks to the local family of Kaders we were able to visit it easily. Rafia Kader[3] took Rosemary into the Bazaar and to one or two of the best stockists for the various very attractive Sindhi materials, such as ajrak as worn by the men. There were khes (double-woven bed-spreads); then rilli (cloth with appliqued patchwork); and sussi (striped cotton or silk mixed).[4]

We all enjoyed a tour round the tombs of the Kalhora Mirs and then the Talpur Mirs (1783–1843). Mir Nasir Khan, who came to the throne in 1840, was forced to abdicate by the British in 1843. After our Iran posting, it was exciting for us to visit these variations of Muslim mosque and tomb architecture. The physical composition of the region was a factor in its architectural evolution, and accounts for the type of building then prevalent in Sind. Also Sind was outside the main architectural Hindu and Muslim development of styles in the Punjab, Rajasthan, etc. Neither stone nor wood were readily available, so the architects tended to use brick as the principal building material. A special feature was the enrichment of the brickwork with brilliantly coloured tiles. It is probable that the monotonous surroundings of the Sind cities which border the great Indian Desert account for the particular arts of Sind, in cloth, wood, and superb tilework. The noted pottery of Hala, fifty miles north, and the textiles everywhere, and the enamelling and lacquer-work were all in brilliant colours.

The lack of large trees for furniture-making was visible in the household furniture of which Sindhis are proud. It was nearly all of brightly lacquered colours in small-gauge wood, ingeniously fitted together.

Even without academic knowledge, and even in the remains of cities and cemeteries where factual history was scarce, we found that our visitors were as excited as we were to walk around the cities of these ancient civilizations which flourished in such harsh, remote lands.

Dentistry!

The British Dental Surgeon, Dermot Strahan, was excellent value, besides being on the side of our well-being. It was a pleasure getting the dentists of Karachi together, making more friends; and then having a good reason to go with Dr Strahan to Hyderabad.

---

[3] We gave Rafia a scholarship to London University to study for a Ph.D. in education. Her impressive thesis went to the Pakistani Ministry of Education.
[4] *Threadlines Pakistan*, Ministry of Industries, (Pakistan, 1977). Colours of the Indus, Askari & Crill, V & A, 1997.

The Chaukundi Tombs: well worth visiting

Some eighteen miles on the old Hyderabad road was a great cemetery, a square mile in area of strangely shaped, tiered stone tombs, but still no-one knew to whom they belonged. We were lucky in having a particularly fine Sindhi couple as friends, Justice Feroze Nana Ghulam Ali and his wife Begum Shireen. They were proud of Sind and knowledgeable, but knew nothing of these people who had left no trace of their way of life, no names, few dates, and no signs of their dwellings.

4 February 1974: Birds with the Roberts

A memorable Ashura holiday of Muharram was a trip to the village of Wategi, off the old road to Hyderabad in the scrub desert. We bird-watched under the tutelage of Tom, and ate Rosemary's picnic. It is both of benefit and fun having the 'littles' identified, and being told what to look for. For instance, a splash of orange indicated a wandering minivet.

February life for the record

Rosemary was involved with the Karachi branch of the Horticultural Society's Flower Show.

Next we had a formal visit from the diplomatic inspectors, who wanted to know exactly what we spent on what; Rosemary was complimented on her detailed records. She wrote: "The whole Consulate-General has been in a tiz for weeks." Wives were comparing notes – "How many rolls of toilet paper do *you* use in a month?" The Inspectors went into the cost of everything: milk, mails, petrol, parties, drink and dusters, soap and shoe laces. I enjoyed the exercise involved. I was so pleased that they recommended an increase in local staff salaries. We depended so much on the qualities and loyalty of such men and women who receive no pension from us. It is always good to meet officials off-duty (balancing truth and discretion perhaps?)

We went to Hyderabad again, just for the night, to attend the closing ceremony and party of an Audio-Visual Teaching Course sponsored by the Council – which participants always enjoy. I was responsible for extracting our lady lecturer and putting her on a 'plane for Lahore to repeat her valuable dose.

I was at the time on a C.B.I. Scholarships Selection Board: seventeen graduate engineers were applying for further training.

I am leaving out the details of the business receptions to which we were kindly invited, and were pleased to accept. I took it that we were invited to give visitors another view of life in Pakistan, not just for ourselves. We were happy to speak of the British Council's work. I did so to a Russian diplomat once, who commented, "What a waste of money!"

Body and brain exercise

Rehearsing for Scottish country dance performances was as much fun as in my bachelor days. We soon had a very reliable set of eight led by Bill Drummond (of J. & P. Coats), who injected the vital sense of humour which let us enjoy ourselves. So many Scottish country dancers are so serious! We performed at a Boat Club's Scottish Night. It was very well organised and particularly well decorated. There were hundreds of people, two-thirds of whom were Pakistani. The Port Trust Pipes and Drums were splendid.

More flowers

The Karachi Floral Art Society laid on a flower show. This was inaugurated by the popular American Consul-General, Gordon Tiger, and his wife, Marion. They became special friends of ours and the McEntees. "How did you get your name?" "Well the family arrived from Central Europe with a long unpronounceable name with no vowels. It could sound like Tiger, so that is what we decided to call ourselves."

Visitors

A British Council Management Services Inspector, Brian Humphreys, arrived "only to look at jobs and who does them; not how well or how badly." What a relief! We tried to reach one of the Delta sites by launch, but the sea was too rough.

Another visitor was Peter Collister, O.D.A. Education Adviser. He was a great chap: Cheltenham, Cambridge, Gloucesters in the War, Headmaster, H.M.I. We had dinner for eighteen educational staff, after Peter had looked into the most suitable aid projects in Education in Karachi and Hyderabad.

How we suffered!

The French showed their classic film *Orfeo Nero* at the Sind Club. That is the way to see films, in an armchair with a whisky, and to be able to get another if needed. I never go to concerts, because I can't respond physically to the music when imprisoned in a row of seats. The Italian Ferris with the Drummonds gave a full moon party out at Bulegi – flares lit the route across the sand. Our beds were handy at 1 a.m. There followed in Karachi an Arts Council exhibition; a party for the Australian Ambassador; a dinner by the Ismaili community for the Minister of Education at the Sind Club. We had to drink for two hours before the dinner arrived. By 11 p.m. I had taken Rosemary home, and gone on to an evening of Pakistani music at the von Halems of the Goethe Institut. The audience were all sitting rapt and barefoot on a wholly carpeted floor. It was good, but not easy to understand. The Muslims found the fundamentals of north Indian music much like their own. And in due course from the fourteenth century they got away from the conventions and conservatism of Hindu music, simplifying it, and making it more secular and understandable to the ordinary people.

Korangi Creek

We stayed in town some weekends because of the fascination to be found in much of the local life connected with the sea. The fishing ports and creeks were as full of colour, activity, and odours as anywhere in the east. But Korangi was different. It was the site of the ancient craft of dhow building which continues today. It was satisfying to see lovely vessels in the course of construction, in the classic wood-working shaping and jointing methods, producing the style of ancient times.

Korangi had another life, not long passed away. Once upon a time, in my life-time, Korangi was a touch-down and mooring point for the Sunderlands of Imperial Airways on their four-day route to India. Southampton to Karachi was three days; with night stops in Corsica and next a houseboat on the Nile. What a shame that such a perfect way to travel – comfortable, insulated, leisurely and atmospheric – has been totally lost in favour of speed, and sameness. Travel should be an easy break into new surroundings, with interest and rest en route, thus providing heightened anticipation for gently treated travellers!

17–21 March 1974: The visit of our chairman, Lord Ballantrae

These were unforgettable days. Lord Ballantrae and Laura, Lady Ballantrae, were eagerly awaited. As we hardly doubted, they were full value, and a great stimulus to our work. They had perfect manners, total understanding, ready sympathy and co-operation; and were great fun.

470

Here came the famous monocled Chindit, Brigadier Fergusson, author of *The Wild Green Earth*, and *Beyond the Chindwin* – heart-rending and heartening stories of suffering, endurance, and victory. Apart from other achievements, Lord Ballantrae had been Governor-General of New Zealand. His autobiography, *The Trumpet in the Hall*, was published by Collins in 1971. Here he was, right on the ball, sharp as a needle, no half-measures; he had a fabulous memory of places and people (a recipe of a great leader), a lovely sense of humour in right measure, and was our Chairman He expected much of his men: us!

This visit required concentration and precision from the son of Lieutenant-Colonel J.G. Halsted, H.Q. Administration, Palestine 1936, when Lieutenant Fergusson was in the field! My Representative, David Reid, 1,000 miles away was naturally anxious beforehand, and understandably harried me a little from that distance. But when he received a copy of my Operation Order he relaxed. Peter McEntee smiled and accepted it after one or two changes. Peter and his staff gave us admirable back-up; including smoothing the Ballantraes' passage into and out of the country through the necessary protocol, which was not in our hands.

My staff, British and Pakistani, did splendidly – never leaving anything said to have been done without checking that it had been done and worked. They were all agog at what would happen when the Chairman and I met at the aircraft (a diplomatic facility fixed for me by Peter). Lord B. wore a clear, unattached, prescription monocle. I wore a dark one over my glass eye, on a cord. We met and shook hands. He looked at me hard – and said: "Chicken". I had been nervous as to how he would feel coming off a dry Saudi Airlines 'plane from Bombay, but he was fine, and pretty sunny after I had produced a whisky for him at the hotel. He was pleased that I had some pocket-money for him, but there was no ice in the room fridge. The best laid plans, even by . . .

The next scene took place in our Mackinnon House and garden: a great, long, two-storied, sandstone house and terrace with large lawn and trees around; an ideal venue for a 150-person reception for such a V.I.P. The old building was floodlit, and there were white fairy lights in the trees. Hidden behind a box tree in a corner of the terrace was a police piper. The gallant Lord and Lady shook hands and spoke cheerfully to everyone introduced up the assembly line. Finally, I called for a toast and then our secreted piper struck up with the regimental march of the Black Watch. Lord B. started, and turned, listened and left the throng for the terrace. He went up the steps and stood motionless, while the piper paced up and down before him. The music stopped at a discreet word from us; and Lord B. went to speak to the piper, who alas knew no English, but he was pleased when he understood the impression he had made.

All went well in Karachi, again thanks to Peter. We learned from

Islamabad later, from Lady Pumphrey (who was a cousin of Laura Ballantrae), that the trip to the Frontier went well – particularly well, since the bearer in charge of Lord Ballantrae was ready, whenever called, to slake his lordship's thirst in such a parched land, with a thermos kept handy. There was some beverage called Gordon's in it, I'm told.

News for me

David Reid in Islamabad was promoted to Director, S.E. Asia from the summer (1974), and I was to go up to Islamabad as Acting-Representative from May to October. What a chance, although it meant upheaval for Rosemary.

March 1974: Mohenjo Daro

Mohenjodaro, the huge city site of the Indo-Sumerian period (2500–1700 B.C.) represents the earliest civilisation of the Indus Valley. Mohenjo Daro is on the west bank of the Indus, some 200 miles from Karachi. Its buildings are of burnt brick, and today are unadorned. Yet the systems of the city, covered drainage, garbage, granary, public baths, religious buildings, etc. indicate a high standard of culture.

We were able to take a first-class visitor with us to this site. He was Dr David MacDowall, Master of University College, Durham; a member of our University Grants Committee, out advising Pakistan. His special interest was South Asia. He is also an antiquarian and numismatist, and most interesting. Such men give us great pleasure. What advantages we had in our way of life! David was able to give us a detailed, verbal picture of life at Mohenjo Daro as it might have been. The little museum there had a charming collection of utensils, toys, and ornaments providing an idea of domestic life.

April 1974: Baluchistan

I had to go to Islamabad, so I arranged to fly with Rosemary via Quetta to save spending on a separate trip. I needed to discover the state of English language teaching and of the teachers; the materials available, or lacking; the attitude to the English language, leading to contacts with Britain; and I visited the University. What an enjoyable work-holiday: coolness and greenery at 5,500 ft Rosemary wrote: "Small fields of brilliant green wheat, mud walls, and flat-roofed houses of mud, little orchards still with

472

some blossom and the fine, bare, craggy hills all around. The hotel has a pleasant lawn where you sit under the walnut and plane trees and entertain your friends and meet newcomers. It was fun to be back in the small-town atmosphere where an hour in the central position in the main hotel gives you all the information you need about people!"

"Michael made his calls while I wandered along the shopping streets gaping at the multitude of men in shaggy turbans and fierce whiskers. Pakistani friends of friends did us very well giving us drinks in their home and then dinner at the China Café, practically the only decent eating place. I was delighted to find Chinese shoemakers producing sturdy, rubber-soled sandals that I haven't seen before. So I got two pairs, made to measure in three days, the cost was under £2.00 per pair."

We achieved a visit to the hill station of Ziarat seventy-six miles away. It took over three hours winding through the mountains until the road reached a height where juniper trees grew tall. Ziarat is on a steep hillside, 8,050 ft at the bottom; it is not a big place but it has the usual Commissioner, Governor and C.O.'s houses, and a branch of the Quetta hotel.

The Quetta manager kindly agreed to have a room opened for us, and sent their young manager and a bearer up with us. It was all very simple: pleasant stone bungalows built by the British; junipers and apricots shading the little, terraced lawns; a chowkidar who made excellent brown chupatties; and nomads with masses of lambs and kids encamped just outside.

We saw chukor (partridge) on the way down, and nice fat little hamster/marmot things on our walk.[5] Chukor, poor creatures, are very popular pets and you often meet these fierce-looking Baluchis in the town tenderly carrying one along in a split-cane cage."

I was pleased to meet Ronnie Holland again: a fine ophthalmologist working in Pakistan in the steps of his father, Sir Henry. His wife Joan had been paralysed from the waist down ever since we first met. Ronnie carried her to cars, and everywhere, which was wonderful. Ronnie received a C.B.E., and I cheered at the news.

I wrote home: "Poor Rosemary doesn't have much energy in the tropics, but she comes to life in the cool upper air, and walks firmly for three hours, between 8 and 9,000 ft! She enjoyed the rather Persian mountain atmosphere – I enjoy and appreciate her interest in fauna and knowledge of flowers and plants."

[5] The hamsters that Rosemary referred to were pikas (known as chuas). They are in the order – Lagomorpha: Mouse-hare or Calling Hare – Ochotona. They are not a bit like a hare but six to seven inches long, fat, and sandy brown, with hairy soles for grip. They are well adapted to survive extreme cold and have been found living at 17,500ft. in the Himalayas, higher than any other mammal. See Burton's *Systematic Dictionary of Mammals of the World* (Museum Press, 1965).

23 April 1974: Karachi

We couldn't manage a St. George celebration this year. We worked flat out with Brice Bending, our English language specialist here at the invitation of the Pakistan Government to advise on future policy on the teaching of English and on the training of teachers of English. The project was just up my street. The main point being that the standard of English of the next generation was not up to the requirement for higher studies abroad. This had to be remedied.

On the speaking of English, I was happy to have been given an annual assignment to address the annual Cento Officers' Course at the Naval Staff College on this subject. Brice lectured to them on the 'Writing of English'.

May merry-go-round

The Ambassador came down for talks with the C-G, involving me; and we were invited to join a drinks party and a sit-down dinner the next evening for Pakistani Government officials. That kept us on our toes. I spoke with the Chief Minister on his Karachi transport plans, having learned a bit from our Professor of Transport Studies!

Then I was able to take our Ambassador in the Consul-General's air-conditioned car to Hyderabad with Alastair Baillie (Deputy C-G) for a tour of the University, and a luncheon for local dignitaries in the Sardinia Hotel (some Ismaili connection here), laid on by Mr Bokhari. Then H.E., went to see an Overseas Development project to make a double-track railway bridge over the Indus. A lovely girl, Irena, called on Alastair in his office one day, and he married her!

Next we had a Professor of Administrative Studies from Manchester visiting the Public Service Commission. Then the Hollands came to stay with us, especially to meet the Roberts. It was rewarding listening to two experts on their own jargon – as Kipling knew well from the Pig, the Lahore Club.

Finally, prior to our departure for Islamabad, Rosemary and I gave two sixty-guest farewell drinks parties, senior and junior. Rosemary's Hong Kong bought Chinese lanterns were fine in our garden. We used mosquito-coils, not force-blown insecticide, met at larger occasions; there were no complaints of mosquitos.

27 May 1974

We set off for Islamabad by train to Rawalpindi: 1,000 miles nearer the Frontier! We had an air-conditioned coupé with bathroom. The train was not as fast as in Britain, but smoother. Rosemary brought supper and lunch; the carriage-bearer produced chai (tea) and chota hazri (breakfast). We crossed the Indus at Hyderabad, and found our Mr Bokhari with charming loyalty standing on the platform as we drew in!

We saw Upper Sind unfold from Multan. The line followed the river Sutlej, but at night we missed seeing the crossing. We crossed the Ravi north of Lahore. After Wazirabad we crossed the Chenab. That amounts to four rivers of the Punjab (meaning five rivers). Which is the fifth we did not cross?[6]

I needed my car in Islamabad, so I had it put on the train from Karachi. Our splendid driver Mohammed Fazl accompanied the car all the way – not in a sleeper, but with the car itself on the flat railway wagon, living in, on, or under it, in temperatures hot by day and cold by night, and delivered it safely. What a chap! We remain in touch. He is now well set-up with an oil-field security firm in Dubai.

June – October 1974: Islamabad

I had two fine young men in the office as No. 2 and No. 3.: Dr John Hawkins and Malcolm Hardy. Malcolm had already written an excellent travel guide to the area, entitled *Between Indus and Jhelum*, published by the Asia Culture Study Group. It was very useful.

In spite of a letter from the Ministry of Education addressed to 'The Active-Representative', I had decided to lie low and not to innovate, but to face up to problems. I resolved to visit out-stations, to learn and to cheer.

Islamabad was a new government capital and diplomatic city.[7] It was bewildering to get around. As Malcolm noted in his book:

> One is really driven to distraction in trying to locate particular houses. Originally, each sector (of a basic grid) was divided up into numbered plots, e.g, F7/3 188. Then as streets and houses appeared and gaps were filled up, an alternative address system emerged, e.g. 23, 22 Street, Shalimar 7/3. Both address systems

---

[6] The Beas.
[7] Work started on the new capital in 1961. By 1964 2,000 civil servants were already established there.

are in simultaneous usage, and the numbering of the streets is not always sequential!

We found giant sign-boards here and there filled with letters and figures like abstruse equations, and as difficult to understand.

After two weeks Rosemary had the Reid's rather hot house in order with our belongings and soft furnishings – a few Persian rugs, etc. The servants after Karachi were a bit 'jungli', but she trained them patiently. Unfortunately, one Abdul was too keen and used brasso on our gold-leaf and black lacquer presentation box from Rangoon, wiping off much of the gold in a stroke. It is too expensive to re-gild.

We were in a new climate. By 15 June it was 98°F in the hall. The inconvenience of thunderstorms was off-set by their bringing the temperature down from 90°F to 80°F. The Embassy pool helped, but had little shade. The hills behind were soothing to walk in. We had been told that our Ambassador, Sir Laurence Pumphrey, was a fanatic walker. Lo and behold, on our first totter into the hills we met him striding along. The stern figure passed swiftly by with a polite response to our greeting and a sharp stare.

I had my first Saturday off since my arrival in Pakistan, there being a different working week in Islamabad. Thanks to the well-established Roberts, we were lent their dear little Rose Cottage and the faithful factotum, Kushal, at Dunga Gali, a little water-catchment hill-station at 7,747 ft. above Murree, short of the well-known old hill-station of Nathia Gali.

23 June 1974: Back to the Frontier

I went with Dennis Spiby, our librarian for Pakistan who was based in Lahore, and the office driver, Aurangzeb, to Peshawar to see Mr Qureshi and staff in our centre there. The library had had its share of attacks by easily swayed, and possibly paid, 'badmash'. But all were in good heart and the place was well-run and well patronised.

At the University I met a fine old Pathan, Vice-Chancellor Dr Yusuf, who was not afraid of his students or to wield his authority. I also met the greatly loved Professor Margaret Harbottle, who had taught English literature there for years. She much regretted the cuts in former B.C. British staff – a regional officer and a centre had ben abolished at the stroke of a pen. Our lack of presence was hurtful to all who knew the past, and had worked so hard for British-Pakistani relations.

The British have always had a strange relationship with the Frontier tribesmen: a mixture of admiration and respect, tinged with horror – and requiring enormous courage. Here I can tell my story of the very experienced Donald Makinson[8] in the South Waziristan Scouts. He was out on an exercise with a new, white-kneed Brigadier. The Brigadier outlined a nasty situation with the Scouts facing a large concentration of tribesmen in a strong position. "What would you do, Makinson?" "Run away, sir." The effect was a Bateman-like apoplexy on the senior officer's face, but Donald was right. Lives are not thrown away any more on antiquated canons of courage. We learned to apply the same principles in the Western Desert, in which we could move fast.

Shades of Alexander

Having had just a glimpse of the site with Roger Rigby in 1950, it was a welcome surprise to find that Alexander's university town of Taxila was only twenty miles away from Islamabad. One of the reasons for the site of Islamabad was that it was near an earlier main city.

We revisited Taxila twice before leaving Islamabad, once at leisure, thanks to the kindness of Pakistan's Director of Archeology, M. Ishtiaq Khan. When I applied to stay at the Taxila Rest House, he wrote such a warm letter of welcome, and gave orders to provide us with all facilities. This is typical of the attitude of officials to responsible visitors. The museum at Taxila contained some beautiful gold objects with designs which would surely be in demand if copied today.

The Grand Trunk Road

In 1950 I was lucky to drive with Roger Rigby from Karachi up the Grand Trunk Road to the Frontier. It was thrilling and we said: "Next time. Ah next time!"

Now it *was* 'Next Time' for me with Rosemary, and I was happy.

Back in Islamabad

Work was done and enjoyed, but people and places also meant very much to us. For instance, Sir Laurence and Lady Pumphrey were extremely kind. "Sir Laurie" was splendid, as I had told Papa in several letters. He replied: "Sir Pumphrey must be a very human H.E."

---

[8] See Tehran, p. 193.

July 1974

It was getting hotter but not raining. Islamabad is an all-year capital, unlike the old days. It is sad that the houses were modern and not all that suitable for the climate; air-conditioning was available but expensive to run and maintain, and a drain on power sources. We escaped at 4 p.m. on Friday 2 July for Dunga Gali. We were used to the road now. We had marvellous weather, and Kushal walked us 10,000 ft to the top of Mukshpuri, the hill behind. We had terrific views of the Jhelum to the north-east, and the snowy mountains to the north and north-west, although not Nanga Parbat. We saw few flowers, no animals and, sadly, few birds.

Lahore

I had to go to Lahore on official business and so we could take our nieces, who had come to stay, to this famous city. We could all stay with Dennis Spiby, who was an excellent fellow as I had learned from our Peshawar trip. I greatly valued his advice and company. Aurangzeb took us by car on the sections Rosemary had missed on the way up by train: Jhelum, Gujarat, and Gujranwala – not the tourist route! It was great to be able to take her to Lahore, of which she had heard so much from her father, J.G. Harley, who had been a college lecturer, and a much respected warden of the Student's Union Hostel from 1908 to 1912.

It was particularly interesting for Rosemary and I to see Moghul architecture and tile-work and to compare them with the Persian, which was much finer. Luckily, it was no longer swelteringly hot, as the rains had begun, but it was hot enough! The girls were not put off by the curiosity of the local menfolk who still found an unveiled European woman a novelty and a target.

No-one can put it better than Fodor:

> Lahore is the other end of the Moslem World, the counterpart of Istanbul. It is one of those swarming, confused cities where life embraces and swallows up the treasures bequeathed it by history. It is a melting pot of animated squalor adorned with pink sandstone and white marble. It is only when you enter the monuments conceived by Moslem abstraction that sanity returns. The paths of the marble gardens lead into an ordered world.[9]

[9] Fodor, *Islamic Asia* (revised 1973), p. 31.

478

In 1848 four strong rulers kept out the Sikhs, but they succumbed to the Persians under Nadir Shah, and then in 1749 to the Afghan Ahmed Shah Durrani. From 1767–1798 a Sikh coalition ruled under Ranjit Singh. The Moslem mosques and tombs deteriorated, and Sikh architecture and art appeared. The British efforts in 'the Sikh Wars' prevailed: and the appearance of Lahore changed for the worse.

I quote from Fodor again:

> Walls tumbled down, the moats were filled in and turned into lawns, and Anglo-Muslim or neo-gothic architecture sprouted along the wide boulevards. The mosques were used as railway depots or private residences. This dreadful vandalism and desecration was put to an end by Lord Curzon under a law of 1904 for the preservation of ancient monuments.

These monuments specially appeal to me: the wonderful tomb of Jahangir in its island of green; defaced by Sikhs, Afghans, and the British. Then the Mosque of Wazir Khan (1634) which contains decoration in the Persian style right in the heart of the old city. And the Tomb of Anarkali, 'pomegranate blossom'. Anarkali was a lovely girl in Akbar's harem who caught the attention of Prince Selim.[10] The Museum (in which Kipling's father J. Lockwood Kipling was once the Curator) is a must.

A writer in our time remarked in an issue of the excellent series of colour magazines *Focus on Pakistan* that the attention of Rudyard Kipling on Lahore "gave the city one of the best public relations' boosts vouchsafed to any city in the East." True. I always associate Kipling with Lahore, and vice versa. But a large number of his *Tales* are from 'the hills'; on life for the Anglo-Indian in the Hill Stations in the hot weather. There are two tales which especially appeal to me; the fascination in them is because the main characters behave 'differently' from the norm.

The stories concern two men in government service who were out of the ordinary, and therefore, in the very rigid social code of the time were not considered "quite, quite". In 'Miss Youghal's Sais' there is this early statement:

> "Strickland was in the Police, and people did not understand him: so they passed by on the other side. Strickland had himself to thank for this. He held the extraordinary theory that a Policeman in India should try to know as much about the natives as the natives themselves."

[10] See Karachi, p. 78

'Beyond the Pale' is a different sort of story. It starts:

"A man should, whatever happens keep to his own caste, race and breed, let the White go to the White and the Black to the Black. Then whatever trouble falls is in the ordinary course of things – neither sudden, alien, nor unexpected. This is a story of a man who wilfully stepped beyond the safe limits of decent everyday society, and paid for it heavily."

To Swat

I longed to see the land of the Akond, and find out for myself:

Who or which or why, or what
Is the Akond of Swat.[11]

and a lot more.

19 July 1974; to the North!

We drove up the G.T.R., past the town of really fine textiles, Laurencepur, forty-five miles on. The lengths of cloth which Rosemary and I had bought there were made up in Karachi and remain good today. We were to stop at the Tarbela Dam Guest House at the invitation of an English chum. This was situated on the Indus up-river from Attock Fort, the road and rail crossing, where the river comes out of the hills on to the Peshawar plain. We were extremely lucky to have this chance, and it was fascinating.

We were looking at the world's largest earth-filled dam. It was a vital construction because Partition had left the headwaters of all Pakistan's great rivers in India. The necessary Indus Water Treaty had taken the World Bank twelve long years to negotiate. The dam was actually completed this very year, 1974, by an international consortium. The lake behind was due to fill to fifty miles back in the Indus Valley.

On to Swat

To quote Winston Churchill: "Among Pathans it is a common saying "Swat is heaven, but the Swatis are hell fiends." We agreed with the first

---

[11] *The Faber Book of Comic Verse* compiled by Michael Roberts (Faber & Faber, 1948), Edward Lear, *Nonsense Songs,* pp. 168–177.

part, but not the second. The Swatis were very pleasant; but then we weren't Pathans.

In ten days, the four of us with all our baggage covered 691 miles in our good old Hillman Hunter Estate. We managed all the passes including the Khyber with only the rear window falling out from downward baggage pressure on the steep Ambela Pass. This was the scene of a very nasty campaign in 1863–64 against the Mohmands, inflamed by the intrigues of the Akhund of Swat.

Our route was over the Dam to Topi, on to Swabi, Shahbazgari, Rustum, the Ambela Pass, through the delightful Buner district, to Daggar, Jowra, the Karikai Pass, a breathless 'vertical' descent which was very beautiful; then on to Barikot, up the lovely main Swat valley to Madyan. Later on to Kalam, and a rest house for two nights. One morning we went up the Utrot Valley, and watched a police officer netting trout.

Thence down again to Saidu Sharif, the capital of Swat for one night. Next day out of Swat over the Malakand Pass, down to Nowshera, and right, up the G.T.R. to Peshawar.

Islamabad: Local Life

Sarah, a second- year medical student, had a week's trip in the Punjab with the excellent Kip Warr of Oxfam to visit hospitals. And later she had five days at the C.M.S. Hospital at Taxila, as an observer, particularly of cataract operations. After that she and Alison dashed off to India.

I tied for first prize in a limerick competition organised by the Embassy's weekly *Islamabad News*. Thereafter I have spent my time writing limericks whenever a new town name comes up, in any country. Local lore researched included:

> There was a young fellow from Murree
> Who took off his clothes in a hurry.
> > He said: "Sure the ants
> > May make free with my pants
> But where they go next is the worry."

> There was a young Scot at Taxila,
> Who smothered his wife with a 'pilla'.
> > Despite the delights
> > Of conjugal rights
> He preferred the full use of her 'siller'.

Now we had the pleasure of a visit from Stan Smith, Ron Barren, and

Derek Forbes, for Maths, Science, and English vacation courses for teachers. They were excellent chaps, as usual, well-chosen by London, humorous, adaptable and efficient. Their teacher-pupils were very responsive and pleased with them, and so were we: "They thoughtfully brought us cheese and chocolates!"

We spent enjoyable cultural evenings in Islamabad – either in an Embassy home or in ours. It was not easy to get together with senior Pakistanis, who were the Islamabad residents. Government Servants were not encouraged to accept invitations. We had Council films such as *A Midsummer Night's Dream* (of which I always have happy stage memories) and also play-readings of *Blithe Spirit* and *Twelfth Night*. Shakespeare's English frightened some of our recruits, but only at first. James and Kay Patterson were the Embassy bright sparks. Later posted to Trinidad, James kindly up-dated us on the Reggae we missed after leaving Guyana.

Internal upheavals

John Hawkins left us for Bogota. Malcolm married his Yugoslav girl-friend, Vesna, from his Zagreb days. She was another splendid example of her nation marrying into the British Council. There were initial problems: the Consul in Islamabad was not empowered to marry them but they could be married by the local licenced Christian marriage official. All went well, but it was very hot. H.E. and Lady P. came to the reception.

A sign-board in the new capital Islamabad.

482

Never again

The congenial Laurie Pumphrey invited us and our nieces to luncheon with his son Joe and friend Martin, (both Magdalen, Oxford). He announced he was prepared to add our nieces to his party on a walk from Kalam (the limit of our Swat trip) to Gilgit. This was no walk, it was an expedition. They were off on 22 August, over the Kachikhani Pass of 15,687ft.! We feel, from what we heard, that he took a risk, but they made it; and their pride of achievement was deserving of great admiration. We were relieved to greet them as planned on 29 August. H.E. wrote an account of this tremendous achievement, entitled *Never Again*.! However, for others with similar spirit, he added 'Eight Points' comprising advice on porters, tentage, food (they took too much!), medicaments, hobbies, fitness, and age. "Don't be too ambitious," he wrote, but "above all, have a go!" I quote:

> Never again? . . . Now, with the lapse of a few days, I think a question mark should take the place of the exclamation.
>
> I should welcome, and I hope I shall have, the opportunity of another expedition of this kind. But there are some points, I think, which should be borne in mind.

I keep the text as a reference for anyone so inclined to undertake such an enterprise!

28 September 1974: last lap

The new Representative, A. J. Herbert, and a new No. 2, John Dobson, arrived. There were hectic handovers. Then we gave an arrival and departure cocktail party: 66 guests out of 100 came. Of course, our packers had to be let in to upset the household; and two British Council auditors came from London. We had a dinner party for A.J.H. the next day.

After dinner I called for 'silence please!' and stood up. I could see H.E.'s face: "Oh lord, another speech . . ." I began heavily, and then I said: "Your Excellency, would you kindly step forward?" His expression changed. I then spoke of an intrepid traveller, beautiful heavenward land, etc., and invested him with the Kachikhani Pass Medal, (executed by the Rawalpindi Sports Shop and blue-ribboned by Rosemary), and H.E. embraced me Frontier style, left and right.

What could he do with the medal? The Pumphrey's small son had a large Teddy Bear who sat in their hall – as a chowkidar (watchman). Teddy proudly wore the medal!

From a Local Newspaper

Teachers bodies
dissolved
in Baluchistan

1.   We cannot recommend recruitment just at present.

Michael Halsted.

J M G Halsted
Acting Representative Pakistan

A roundabout way back to Sind

Rosemary suddenly said to me, "Having got this far, let's go further." In fact, we travelled to Samarkand, and on to see the glories of Persian Islamic architecture and design.

I was now temporarily free of responsibility, and there was a new Representative who was able to say: "Yes, take some leave". It was necessary for us to gain the British Government's permission to visit Russia at the time, and it was granted by an F.C.O. telegram signed 'Callaghan', which seemed awfully grand. Good old local travel-agent, Waljis, whom H.E. had used for his expedition, fixed us a tour of Kabul, Tashkent, Samarkand, Bokhara, Khiva, and back to Karachi.

We were driven to the Peshawar Club for the night in our car, by Aurangzeb. Next morning we went by bus to Kabul via Jalalabad, which was an agreeable little agricultural town situated in a fertile valley of the Kabul river, where sugar cane, orange trees, and pomegranates flourished. It was 4,000ft. lower than Kabul at 5,786ft., and was a fashionable winter resort for the rich, and also a nomad winter camp. We went up through the new tunnel in the Tang-i-Garo, cutting out a number of the gradients and bends, which were especially tough to negotiate in winter.

We stayed in Kabul at the Spinzar Hotel and got around by taxi. Our knowledge of Farsi helped and was remarked upon. In Afghanistan one of the languages is Dari-Farsi. The British Council man, Peter Connell, gave us confidence with his hospitality and help. Tony McNicoll of the British Institute of Afghan Studies was kindly informative. The Ambassador gave us permission to look over the excellent Embassy library, and the Oriental Secretary to whom we turned for all sorts of information was Catherine

Himsworth who had been at the Blind School, Isfahan while we were there. It was exciting to have a brief look at the great old fort, the Bala Hissar, but it was most rewarding to visit the beautiful, Persian-style Gardens of Babur, the progenitor of the Moghul Emperors, and stand at his tomb.

In the bazaar we were particularly impressed by the quality, designs and quantity of gelims. I was excited to find a very well preserved, brass-chambered, pepper-pot revolver (the old form in which the barrels revolved instead of the later cylinder). I should have bought it, but we were travelling on into Russia! We did so by Aeroflot, which was rather grim and crowded with large, stony-faced stewardesses. Our passports were taken away, which alarmed us. Russian waitresses in Tashkent were unpleasant. So was the bread.

Travel: The essentials

Wilfred Blunt, the Eton Art Master became a wonderful interpreter of Islamic Art. He was at first apprehensive about travel in the East. After arriving at the British Embassy in Tehran, he asked H.E.'s wife what he should take with him. "Whisky and lavatory paper" she replied briskly. She was quite right. I wrote an account of our trip, which was made in rather more austere, primitive days, and called it *The Land beyond the River*.

October 1974: To Karachi again – by Aeroflot!

It could have been a comedown, but it wasn't. The lift-van from Islamabad had arrived by lorry: and Niaz had emptied it and unpacked most of it, and put everything back where it should be, down to slippers by the bed. What value we had from our servants in our life.

It took Rosemary a week to get the household running again. We had an interesting visitor in Professor Stewart Bark, an analytical chemist from Salford University who was here to advise chemists and industry. He was in the hands of our new John Dobson from Islamabad who was in fact a Scientific officer, one of the Council's range of specialists posted to meet the needs of countries. The British officers and wives from Quetta were down; and Rosemary was able to repay hospitality by taking the ladies shopping, although this was very hot and tiring particularly in view of Karachi driving conditions. I got on with my homework for brush-up classes for the forth-coming Caledonian Ball.

Then Jim Herbert came down to meet us all. It took time and trouble to find the right people for him to meet, but it was fun and a good excuse to get them altogether. First we had a buffet-dinner for twenty-eight in the garden; and then a reception at the Council for 164. Rosemary managed all the catering and staffing. The next day was spent at Hyderabad in visiting the University and providing a Reception for sixty-three.

November 1974

Out at Bulegi one weekend we joined in an Italian-U.S-Scots farewell party for the popular Mike and Judy Sommers. U.S. whisky and Italian wine flowed. There was recorded music via a muffled portable petrol generator, but dancing on soft sand was quite tiring. I was inspired to write this early English parody:

> Sommers are a'going out
> Lhude cry 'Boo-hoo'.
> Tidings hurteth, naught averteth,
> What's left for us to do?
> Cry: 'Boo-hoo'.

We valued all our specialist visitors and each one made a contribution to the interest in our lives, for instance Dr Anthony Smith, Tropical Research, Edinburgh, made one lazy day at Bulegi absorbing for us by talking shop.

Then John Deakin of C.E.D.O. (Centre for Education Development Overseas) came. He was an examinations specialist. Just the scholar to advise on this contentious subject. I had been convinced for years that we tended to set papers requiring knowledge other than the answers to the questions. In fact, Professor C. B. Cox, Manchester (English) wrote so well on this subject in this same year 1974 in 'Encounter' which reinforced our views.

Mark Dodd, was our next visitor. He was Head of Eastern Services, B.B.C. and an old friend since his Isfahan stint. We liked him so much, and his attitude to the Burmese. He said: "Burma is shabby and in some ways chaotic, but the people are so very nice and the country so beautiful. I think it is perhaps my favourite country." We belonged to the B.B.C. panel of listeners who sent home reports on the reception of the World Service.

I would rather the British Council was cut than the B.B.C. World Service. Every nation has, I hope, millions of listeners to it, sometimes anxious to know exactly what was going on in their own country, revolution or disaster. I knew where to take our radio when things were tense in Karachi, up to the turn of the stairs for a clear reception. This is the spot where our dear little durzi, Siddiq, would sit sewing away so industriously and well. Sometimes I could hear the familiar voice of Pam Creighton, (who only retired from the World Service in 1994). She had been one of the 'delightful daughters' out in Karachi with her parents in those bachelor days.

It was essential to hear the truth while there was a crisis on, such as civil disorder – a favourite disorder being a 'wheel-strike' during which nothing on wheels was allowed to move. The city was thereby paralysed.

We had only one tense moment – for me at least. A group of students were on a roundabout to bar our way into town. Rosemary was driving. As it was open desert all round with good visibility, she approached as normal on the left, but went out of the roundabout right-handed!

I took Mark Dodd to Tatta, sixty miles up the Indus on the way to Hyderabad. There wasn't much charm in the arid, stony hinterland of Karachi; but there certainly was in the irrigated areas fed from the Indus, thanks to the great barrage at Sukkur. It was especially attractive beyond Hyderabad into the cotton-growing areas and beautiful mango trees; and of course here were the colourful Sindhis and their animals and conveyances.

From the early 17th Century: Tatta was a thriving port, with an English Trading Centre; until drought and plague, and the Indus changing course, left an almost dead city with only its tombs on Makli Hill.

Hyderabad we began to discover was a lovely, noisy, dirty, crowded shambles of a town, containing much of interest to admirers of great Islamic architecture. In Hyderabad one could see Hindu influence, and the development of Moghul styles.

The finest monument was the mosque started by Shah Jahan in 1647 and finished by Aurangzeb. It amazes me how effective was the power of those great rulers, considering the problems of communications, and how they were able to concern themselves with many of the intimate details of daily life in their domains.

Finally, in this perfect Indian winter climate, even in Karachi, came Dr E. Machin of Birmingham to help the authorities develop their Civil Service. In pre-partition India this was mainly in Hindu hands. Now the Muslims of Pakistan had to take on every form of civil role – as opposed to military which had been their forte – in order to face great internal problems in a nation only thirty years' old.

Remembrance Day 12 November 1974. Every year sees a very good turnout of British and Pakistanis, including some fine XIVth Army warriors.

The run up to Christmas 1974

We had the visit of H.M.S. Blake; in honour of which there was a great party at the C-Gs. We met captains of ships and nuclear submarines, helicopter pilots, divers, and fleet auxiliary captains. Three cheers for the Royal Navy – what a boost they gave us. We knew they would be around if needed.

The Caledonian Ball came round, of course, but it lasted too long. The Chieftain, or Committee, did not take a firm enough grip, and bed was not until 5 a.m., which was not funny.

Shikar for Rosemary

The charming French Consul M. Galas and his wife, took Rosemary shooting near Tatta. He had energy, experience, humour. But they got no pig only two partridges and one teal.

I was born too late for shooting in Sind. The Karachi Handbook of 1913 says:

> The small game shooting, duck, partridge and snipe etc. – near Karachi and all over Sind, is some of the finest in the world. The easiest arrangement is to engage a 'shikari', and go out on camels, either from Karachi direct, or from some station up the line. The charge for a camel and his driver is usually Rs. 4 per diem.

Christmas

We escaped, just us – for peace. We drove very easily to the fine, modern Cultural Rest-House outside the village of Bhit Shah in Sind, some thirty miles north of Hyderabad off the east bank road of the Indus, near the famous pottery town of Hala. The village which is perched on a rise above an ornamental lake is holy to all Sindhis because it contains the tomb of Shah Abdul Latif, the great poet Pir and Sufi saint (1689–1752) who taught and died there.

The rest-house had been built by a Trust set up in memory of Shah Abdul Latif, and was intended for V.I.P. pilgrims. The house had a long, arched verandah, a brick-paved courtyard, and a pleasant, tree-shaded garden. There were two factotums, whom we found useful. Luckily the whole building was ours. It made a welcome retreat from Karachi.

It was cold at nights: there were neither fireplaces nor heating in a house in so hot a region as Sind which has such a short winter. But we were fine in our Black's Icelandic sleeping bags. During the days we enjoyed pottering about the mosque and the shrine, mixing with the throngs of the devout, and talking to the various old birds with whom we could just communicate. There were some marvellous Sindhi costumes and moustaches. At one moment I found myself caught up in some little ceremony, and I had to eat rose-petals from a proffered bowl. The participants must have thought that I was a devotee. I suppose I was in a way – of Shah Abdul Latif.

According to the author of a long and informative article on the Pirs in *The Karachi Herald* of November 1977, the early Pirs were philosophers who followed one of the cardinal commands of the Holy Prophet, "Seek knowledge, along the line of spiritualism and thus to mysticism." But today there are spurious Pirs with buildings and elaborate un-Islamic ceremonies performed on a commercial basis. A senior Pakistani friend in Lakarna informed me, "If you would like to be a Pir, that is easily arranged." I thought this was a great compliment. All I had to do, he said, was to be around and make some wise utterances, and he could easily rustle up a couple of hundred followers. I was not tempted!

End of 1974: Reflection

It was most exciting having been within reach of the North-West Frontier again, last visited in 1963 on my way back to Burma. Now we were officially working 1,000 miles south in Karachi, but this had an unforeseen benefit. Sind had been more or less neglected by the British Government in India; and insulted by being for a time tacked on to the Bombay Presidency. It never became well-known to visitors. But from my post in Sind I developed an affection for the province, once I had become better acquainted with it, and accepted the drawbacks of its terrain and climate; it had had its anti-British fighters all right.[12] Sind had been annexed by Napier in 1843: and achieved its own status as a Province in 1936.

January 1975: The interior of Sind

Papa used to say that the Indian winter is the best climate in the world, and I agree. The sun warms up everything by midday; but the early mornings and nights are cold. Unfortunately there are Indian summers too! January

---

[12] Read H. T. Lambrick's, *The Terrorists* (Ernest Benn, 1972); and also his books on John Jacob of Jacobabad and *Sir Charles Napier and Sind* (1952).

was the best time for work and play. My aim, already stated, to visit all the major educational institutions could now be embarked upon to assess the numbers and the quality of students, the standards of English and other studies of both the teachers and those being taught; their needs for books and materials; and to find staff worthy of further training in Britain.

The interior of Sind was a pleasant surprise. Once away from the desert and into the land irrigated from the Rohri canal, the countryside viewed in January was charming. The main roads and high-banked canals were tree-lined. Broad, spreading acacias gave attractively arched shade to villages and settlements, which were often situated at canal crossings. Beyond the fields and orchards, clumps of vast mango trees sometimes merged into forest areas, breaking up the flat landscape, attracting the eye and strengthening the spirit.

There was constant activity everywhere, and just as in Hyderabad there were the Sindhi scenes we so much enjoyed: groups of white-turbaned figures striding along draped in ajrak, often sporting superb moustaches; or men on cycles wearing gold embroidered Sindhi caps with sometimes incongruously coloured, modern scarves.

Camels were frequently met; and so were lumbering bullock carts in convoys of four perhaps, creaking and squealing, piled high with produce (rice, oil-seed, cotton, wheat or sugar-cane according to season) drawn by determined-looking, conscientious, straining oxen. The characteristic noise of Sindhi bullock carts was caused by wheels being fixed to the rotating axles!

In winter or early spring there was an overall impression of green; but small areas of sand dunes in the south, broken up with tussock grass and white, glistening, salt-encrusted soil further north, reminded one of the two battles being constantly fought in Sind: one to provide water; and the other to remove an excess of it. Here the water table has been forced too close to the surface, resulting in seepage causing water-logging or salination.

Everywhere we went, we remained in awe of the proximity, and of the capriciousness of the river Indus which has changed its course or destructively overflowed at intervals of history and pre-history. Indeed, the major road repairs in certain sections were a reminder of the severe floods of 1973, despite the vast protective bunds that we could occasionally glimpse.

So far 144 sites of the early Indus civilizations had been located and no doubt there are others waiting to be revealed. But much still remains to be learned from major and minor sites. Unfortunately, the high water-table prevents deep excavation; and also causes the rapid decay of sun-dried brick.

Matiari

Seventeen miles north of Hyderabad is the little town of Matiari of some 5,000 souls. It derives its name (I quote the Official Gazetteer)

> from being the seat of the Matiari Saiyids. They are the descendents of the Holy Prophet's grandsons, and are regarded with enormously superstitious reverence. This fact has no doubt helped to bring these numbers of people together, Saiyids and Sheikhs predominating, and a good many Memons also.
>
> The place has a considerable trade, furthered by the fairs annually held at the tombs of Pir Hashim Shah and Pir Rukuu Shah, built in the years 1762 and 1765 A.D. respectively. There is also a Jama Masjid built in 1803.

Apart from the religious buildings we were unaware of the Saiyids. Matiari is a veritable warren of a town with 'streets' no wider than a donkey with two panniers. In it we found what we wanted: an establishment which dyed and hand-blocked the attractive ajrak cotton cloth, in soft reds and blues on white with patterns that varied according to the district.

Rosemary made me an admirable dressing-gown of ajrak. She was already quite knowledgeable on local materials and embroidery, and knew where the best examples could be found.

This brings me to David and Catherine Gerrard who were great acquisitions to Karachi society. David was Director of the Pak-Swiss Design Centre, and Catherine a teacher of art from Edinburgh College of Art. We owe much to their own creative skills and to their highly trained powers of observation and interpretation of local art forms.

It is worth repeating some observations from the local *Morning News* of 31 August 1975, which interviewed Catherine:

> Embroidery could be as complex, intriguing, easy and splendid as the life itself. A European woman is never so emotionally involved in her embroidery as a Sindhi woman, who takes years and years to complete a bed-cover or a 'rilli' ensemble. It took Catherine Gerrard a long time to comprehend the traditions of Sindhi Folk Art, particularly the wealth of the needlework. The lines, the curves, the colours and shades, the threads and shreds. This is a world by itself. The Sind desert is different from Arabia. The Sindhi village women who are secluded from modernity are still working under the thatched roof listening to the howling winds. Their miseries and mysteries, joys and glories are all there on the stitching frames.

Catherine found that Sindhi women know collage instinctively:

"just observe the boldness, imagination and fantastic sense of colour which she displays in her embroidery, patchwork and mirror work. Sindhi women are using colourful forms, glittering material and shining stuff to enrich their creations."

Rosemary brought home several lovely examples.

On past Sakrand we crossed the railway and the vital Rohri canal, to reach Nawabshah, a little agricultural town choked with people and vehicles, including tractors. It was once a village owned by a Saiyid zemindar (land owner) named Nawab Shah. The cantonment consisted of several very sad, neglected buildings in a miniature park. But along fine, wide roads we found the imposing houses of the administrators with large gardens planned for flowers and food.

We were kindly allotted by the D.C. the V.I.P. suite in the Irrigation Inspection Bungalow. The bathroom drains did not empty where they should; but the kitchen which we finally found was equipped with eight gas burners, and sets of heavy gauge stainless steel pans. In the garden of the Inspection Bungalow irrigation was done by means of a charkhi (lift), and the water raised by a hurlo, a wheel turned by one bullock. From here we set off to the People's Medical College for Women, in which we found immured 200 educated young ladies.

There were another 200 to come next year, and a yearly intake of the same number until four figures were reached. New hostels would be built each year. There were ample attractive grounds, but very little play facilities. There was no library, no film projector, no sports field, and only one television set. Until the inhabitants of Nawabshah would accept the fact that there were respectable girls who were not in purdah, none of the girls were ever allowed out of the compound on foot.

We knew one girl medical student, the niece of good friends in Sind, whom we were allowed to take out. The lowdown received from her was useful to me. We learned in the bygoing that the girls were very short of skulls. Attempts to obtain some of these reminded Rosemary of the Edinburgh body-snatchers Burke and Hare. The girls said they had engaged the services of an unscrupulous Hindu, but he had not been successful, so far!

Warning: it is not advisable when visiting Medical Colleges to stride cheerfully on, peering through every door proudly opened. I peered once too often – into the refrigeration room and on the whole prefer not to gaze on bits of people however neatly piled in muslin.

From Nawabshah, with permission, one can take the very pleasant, peaceful, tree-lined Rohri canal road. But we had been warned of the possibility of dacoits, so we went back to the National Highway at Sakrand.

At Moro (fifty-seven miles on) there was a road with a ferry across the Indus to Dadu. This access from the west to Moro, an important agricultural centre, may have accounted for some of the vast concourse we found gathered for an open market. The Sindhi visages, costumes and animals and their trappings, and the multitudinous activities were most exciting, but alas we could not stay. We went on beyond and found a lovely, Persian-style, walled orchard in which we were readily given permission to eat our lunch.

We passed through other smaller towns such as Nausharo Firoz, Kandiero, and Ranipur Riyasat and headed for Kot Diji, the fort which from the seventeenth century had been the stronghold of the Khairpur Mirs, and subsequently the Talpur Mirs.

Peter McEntee described the fort as being remarkably well preserved. We had not time to climb up to it but we saw the doors that had been built to be elephant-proof. They were about six inches thick with steel spikes a foot long protruding through great brass knobs.

Khairpur

Khairpur had a Nawab (or mir) and we had a look at his very Victorian-oriental guest-house, the Fais Mahal. It later became his residence, which we visited two years later.

I had a gruelling time in the Government College of Technology. I hadn't had time for any lunch but could say nothing. I was immediately shown every inch of the complex by proudly booming heads of departments (of the mechanical, civil, electrical, automotive and farm departments), until 3.30 p.m. when I was given tea with an egg. The College had produced 700 technicians since 1963: a magnificent and vital effort.

Sukkur

The town of Sukkur lay fourteen miles on. Here the great Guddu Barrage (formerly called Lloyd) across the mile-wide Indus was opened in 1932. The Barrage was brilliantly engineered, feeding into a series of canals, and transformed a huge area of desert into much needed, cultivatable land. One could contemplate the whole scene from the comfortable and well-run Inter-Pak Inn.

Sukkur was a grimy town; but there were many places of interest to see: such as Mir Ma'sum Shah jo Minar and Tomb (1618); the little island Hindu shrine of Sadh Bela; the midstream fort of Bakhar. From the comfortable Inter-Pak Inn we could enjoy watching the antique river craft and the people who lived on them; the great kauntails, used as ferries; and the more common carriers, the dhoodhis, and the bhatelas of the fishermen. We hired a well-furnished smaller dhondho, with upright, wooden chairs, for our trip to Sadh Bela with Mr Zahir Hussein, Principal of the Government Vocational Institute.

The construction of these various craft seems to have remained unchanged since man arrived on the Indus. There is a kauntail depicted on a seal at Mohenjo Daro. This craft has a flat bottom but a beautiful, almost regular, half-moon curve from bow to stern, with a high poop. It has rudimentary mast and sail; and for steering or manoeuvring a great sweep is manned from the flat roof of the cabin with a rotary motion. Often the wooden superstructure has fine carving or fretwork decoration.

Lakarna

The 48.5 mile-drive down the Rice Canal (1hr. 35min.) was delightful, early on a January morning. It was a beautifully shaded and well-maintained kaccha (unmetalled) road. We encountered the occasional camel or car; otherwise we had peace. We had the gradual revelation of the beautiful wooded countryside as the level changed. After the Khandero sugar-mill off to the east one could see clearly across the whole, vast, rich, cultivated land which was a balm after Karachi.

The old town of Larkana (Bhutto land) was extremely colourful and marvellously congested. It had an atmosphere of its own due to the high percentage of settled or transient Baluchis whose appearance and bearing lent a special air to the crowds.

The Sambara Inn was a pleasant surprise. It had a brick and tile exterior, and examples of the beautiful, black woodwork of Baluchistan within. On our last evening we were very pleased to be invited to dine with M. A. Khuro and his wife, the seniors of a very old Larkana family.

As the sun was setting, the son of the house, Mahmood Khuro, drove us round the old bazaars and east to the village of Akil which the family owned, past rice fields, and through their first crop of sugar-cane just being harvested.

To complete the picture, a string of unladen Baluchi camels emerged from the scrub and plodded up the steep Indus bank on their way to Larkana to pick up fresh loads. All was calm and serene – and beautiful. But a tall concrete post below us, with scribe marks on it, reminded us of the whim of the river of life beyond. We had partridge for dinner; and I was invited to shoot partridge and duck next season. Our driver Siddiq took us to Mohenjo Daro, from where we had air tickets. He then drove back to Karachi.

Thanks to Mr Ishtiaq Khan, the Pakistan Director of Archaeology, his curator at Mohenjo Daro, Mr A. A. Farooq, gave us a clear and comprehensive tour on a lovely cool morning.

When at lunch time we found that our 'plane was delayed, we ate our lunch in the garden of the Museum and Rest House, while half a dozen delightful, little, five-striped palm squirrels (*Funambulus pennanti*) skipped around us. They could move like lightening with an incredible agility and seemed to have a sense of fun.

Our 'plane was finally fixed and the pilot kindly flew us low in good light right over the Larkana and Sukkur areas we had just visited.

13 February 1975

We began our home leave with an air visit to Isfahan. Then in England we bought our Cheltenham house, and moved in in May. I soon had to leave Rosemary behind in England and return to Karachi taking an anti-crow air-rifle this time. She stayed until August making curtains and doing much else.

I returned to find the house and Niaz and Ghaffar in good order. I had been able to sub-let it with them included to a U.N. professor of English. Of course, this was to avoid – in 'Civil Service-ese' – "nugatory expenditure".

In early August I was surprised to find Parsee friends returning so early from England – escaping from the hottest August for 25 years: the night lowest temperature was 70.7°F in Cheltenham, and 92°F by day. They couldn't stand the heat, and rushed back to Karachi to their air-conditioned houses!

Rosemary returned on 17 August. I laid on a drinks party for sixty-four to celebrate. The garden looked good after the rains. The fairy lights, and Rosemary's dress were admired. An exhausted Rosemary was annoyed with me, but I think she came round. Karachi was a great place for camaraderie: one valuable compensation of overseas life.

Once back on the job again, Rosemary and I were cheered by a letter from a visiting British Oriental professor, which ended thus: "My best wishes to you and Rosemary, and congratulations on the finest cuisine in Pakistan."

Official visit by Guided Missile Destroyer, R.A.N.S. (H.M.A.S.) HOBART.

The ship had guns! I found the gunnery officer at the McEntee's party, and explained that I couldn't love a guided missile launcher, but I could love a gun. On board next day I was introduced to one of two turrets, each containing two, five-inch, rapid-fire, fully automatic guns. Each turret fired 40 17lb shells a minute, and could saturate a two hundred-yard spread at ten miles![13]

26 September 1975: A sign of winter

The rains were over. It was very hot and windless – until the cooling north wind came from the interior. It hadn't cooled in Sind, but there was a sign: the white pelicans arrived. It was a thrilling sight: a great flock of majestic birds with black wing tips leisurely soaring and wheeling high on a thermal over the Indus Delta.

October and November 1975

We received visitors: an expert in irrigation; another in local government; a member of staff from the B.C. Personnel Department; and an auditor. Chris Chislett, who loved Africa, was happy to be posted to Malawi. He was replaced by Edward David, a high-quality history lecturer from Bristol. He needed to be inducted into Council life, and we had to find a suitable house and furniture for him and his wife, Hazel, and his small daughter Caroline. Rosemary was very taken up with them.

Even 'bigger news' was that we had a new Consul-General: Maurice and Nellie Eaden replaced the McEntees. We found that they were keen bird-watchers at our level so we had a bond, as well as an introduction from Donald Makinson.

Busy times

One day whilst looking at the crowded letter-rack that I had made, I realised that for a whole month we would never go to bed on the same day that we had got up. Afternoons could be like this: back home for lunch at

---

[13] "That's nothing," say my Royal Artillery Rocket Launcher Battery friends of today. God help the human race!

1.40 p.m. until 2.40 p.m.; zizz till 4 p.m.; 5 p.m. leave for Arts Council Exhibition; 6.15 p.m. leave for farewell to an American colleague; 8.0 p.m. out to dinner with an ophthalmic surgeon. On another day Rosemary was speaking at a Women in Education symposium in the American Centre, while I was opening a Council book exhibition. But we were very cheerful; and the Indian winter had reached Sind.

The final hurdle before December was the Caledonian Ball. I quote Rosemary in a letter to Papa, which I only saw years later: "Michael had the satisfaction of seeing a whole hall full of people moving all together, and at least looking as if they knew what they were doing." I was very touched when they clapped as we left after 4 a.m.

Christmas 1975

On 12 December was the All-Nations Christmas Party (we were encouraged to take two presents and mince pies). I found myself appointed Father Christmas at the annual joint Consulate-Council staff children's party, held this year at the Consulate. There were at least fifty children and it was very well run. Being in Sind I decided that the going was a bit hard on reindeer so I arrived on a camel. I think this surprise was enjoyed. The camel was beautifully decorated with a gold tinsel bridle and a red saddle cover, and behaved very well; but I'm afraid I needed the aid of the camelteer.

The following Sunday there was a fine Nine Lessons Carol Service at Holy Trinity Church, and I was asked to read Lesson Eight, the Three Wise Men, which I enjoyed doing. I had last read a lesson in this church in 1950!

23–28 December

At Khanewal, Punjab.

We were invited by Tom and Frances Roberts to celebrations at Khanewal. On Christmas Eve the party boarded the Tezgam Night Express at Karachi Cantt Station. We had our own food and drink, and we sang carols as we rumbled along.

On Christmas morning it was a pleasure after leaving Sind to see a succession of small green fields, and tiny, mud-walled villages of farming families. Here and there singly or in clumps were the very attractive, dense, great mango trees.

Tom's father was Sir William Roberts formerly of the Indian Agricultural Service, who in the space of twenty years had turned 7,221 acres of wilderness into admirable, viable, cotton-growing land, even though the water supply had to come from the River Ravi, 140 miles away. This land had been leased by the Government, and became the investment of The British Cotton Growing Association run from Khanewal. As we looked at the sharp edge between B.C.G.A. land and the soft desert sand right beside it, we were amazed at what Sir William had done for Pakistan.

After an early lunch we drove out to attend a mela (a fair) in honour of Tom, and the Christian Tihwar (festival). We were shown into a shamiana (open awning) with armchairs and chairs, where a large reception committee greeted Tom. But first we had to move fast, over to the ox-ring where owners straining at ropes were being led, or even dragged round in the dust at a fast, shambling trot by the most magnificent, wild-looking oxen, either single or in pairs, sometimes scattering the eager spectators. Tom judged them all. He then went on to judge the horses which were more amenable. We then could stop spluttering and dust ourselves down and sink into our armchairs.

This mela was a competition between two villages, which still remained on B.C.G.A. land after the Pakistan Land Reform Act of 1959, which took five-sixths of private estates. We found the participants and local spectators more exciting than the events. These Aryan men, women, and children were very handsome.

The country folk wore becoming clothes in rich satisfying colours and the turban is a becoming headgear. Certain men were more handsome than others. The most striking were three brothers aged between fifty and sixty. They were mounted on fine mettled horses. The most handsome won the spectacular tent-pegging. I was apprehensive because Rosemary was crouching with her camera nearly up to the peg.

We next watched a fine tug-o-war. Both teams were bare except for a loin cloth wrapped tightly up between the legs. Then came a game of kabbadi which is a kind of tag in which the 'he' has to touch a member of the opposing team, and reach home base in the time limit of one held breath. This game was more violent than the tug-o-war. Tempers flared but there were no incidents.

Throughout the whole mela the village supporters swirled and eddied over the dusty ground like a flock of vociferous, multi-coloured starlings, rushing from event to event in a cloud which separated and settled at each spot leaving just enough room for the participants. Several venerable and conscientious marshals armed with light sticks finally achieved some order. But when dancers arrived, the marshals and everybody on the committee gave up. The performers were so hemmed in on all sides that we could hardly distinguish them from the spectators. The first group, men only of course, consisted of a drummer and a shenai (reed trumpet) player, and a one-man black and pink cow!

Next came the real dance troupe, dressed in yellow pugarees. Their vigorous playing of pipes and drums delighted the crowd even more.

Isfahan

British Council staff 1966–70, in front of the premises (office and library downstairs, flat upstairs, classrooms round the garden). In rear Prince Massoud and Eric Hamburger.

Leaving for the airport to meet the King & Queen of Thailand, only one top hat between us: M. H., Shazdeh (wearing it), Lt Col Eric Hamburger, Nasser, and Ellen Hamburger. Photo: Rosemary Halsted

H. I. M. the Shah's visit to Isfahan: the Armenian Archbishop, the French Consul and ourselves being presented – April 1969.

The great Isfahan caravanserai drawn by the French artist Eugene Flandin, c. 1840.

1

Isfahan

Seljuk period (AD 1098) mosque and minaret at Barsiun, 40km from Isfahan.
See page 380.

Typical travel scene between Hamadan and Kermanshah.
Photo: E Beazley

Rosemary, "I must see round the next corner."

Isfahan

Pigeon towers at Najafabad.
Photo: E. Beazley

Rosemary with Lord Snowden and H. E. Sir Denis Wright, in the Ali Qapu.

*Summer School, Isfahan 1970, Miss Teresina Saetti, one of the staff,
and some of the student teachers.*

Isfahan

Halsted dancing with teachers from Kurdistan.

Trying to stay on 'my' horse!

Coronation Day, November 1967, Isfahan – Salaam Ceremony in the Chehel Situn Palace, where the Safavid Kings used to receive in State.

Reza Gholi Massoud takes a nap after lunch on a summer bed platform in the garden, over the stream.

Isfahan

The Maidan-i-Shah as it was originally planned, photographed in 1931 by the Missionary Dr Schaffter. (An original kindly loaned by Charles Gault.)

Guyana

A small but possibly useful presentation of 'National Anthems of the World' to the Guyana Military Forces Bandmaster.

Particularly good Guyanese friends of distinction: Adrian Thompson, wide knowledge of the land; Frank Pilgrim, Carifesta Secretary; Mr Justice Bollers.

Dangers on the road at night; an Alcan executive in from Mackenzie, unfortunately kills a 6ft–250lb jaguar:

Sind

*The 1987 Chieftain of the Karachi Caledonian Society greets dear friends
Frances and Tom Roberts, followed by David Adeney, another stalwart
of the community.*

Sind

St Joseph's College for Women, Karachi, Annual Debating Competition.
Presenting the cup to the winning team leader.

The C-in-C, Major-General Sir Bindon Blood, and officers of the Malakand Field Force, 1897. ILN Library

Morocco

Fountain inside the Bab Guissa in Fes.
Photo: Alan Harley

Morocco

The end of 33 year's most enjoyable work and play; leaving my office and staff with the gift of an antique pistol – 4 July 1980.

Then, at a barely noticeable signal, all came to a sudden end. Everyone from 'Huzoor' (His Highness Tom Roberts) to the ox-tender was ready to go home. And so on to the prize-giving.

On the morning of Boxing Day village no. 85 was on show for us. We drove to the B.C.G.A. buildings where all the men and the children from the previous day were gathered in their best clothes.

We recognized several faces, particularly the three distinctive brothers, as they swarmed round to greet Tom. Opposite, beyond the stream, was a high bank on top of which was an ox-powered water-wheel of tin buckets. Here more villagers were gathered, mainly women and children. The variety of the colours they wore contrasted with the snowy white turbans, kurtas and lungis on either side of the track below.

Greetings concluded, the programme opened with a parade of stud bulls past Tom down between the spectators. It was a treat to see the same great oxen as the day before now beautifully groomed, unobscured by dust and less perturbed – but still proud and powerful. The horses followed; and then two lovely riding camels with very fine saddlery and trappings. There's a world of difference between these creatures and the average Karachi working or beach-plodding camel. They are taller and slimmer and move at a smooth fast trot giving a satisfying ride.

Lady Lawrence writing from Sind on Christmas Day 1917 said:

> The riding camels of Gul the camelman are the large light-coloured ones carrying their heads high and nobly. Gul prides himself on their smooth gait, and with justice. He lent one once to Henry (Sir Henry Lawrence, Commissioner in Sind) for a month or so, and Henry tells me how it was possible to read a book whilst padding noiselessly along, and how one night he had slept peacefully from nine o'clock till six the next morning wedged in behind Gul in the high peaked saddle.[14]

We were led away over the stream through the trees into the village itself. We watched a demonstration of bread-making, in a tall, fat, conical mud-oven fuelled by another old man with dried cotton. We moved on to watch three colourful and bashful ladies demonstrating with locally-made implements, spinning, weaving, and milk-churning. They never once looked at us.

Round the corner we found shoemakers sitting in the sun against a wall. They were making leather slippers, plain or decorated, with a narrow instep and pointed toes. The decorated ones were in red leather with patterns in silver.

[14] *Indian Embers.*

In a tiny room sat the village jeweller and his son, working in gold and silver and stones, producing chains, pendants, rings, and ear-rings.

A more original and interesting craftsman was the blacksmith (lohai) in another 'street'. We saw him turning out small, saw-toothed, wooden-handled sickles, as he sat on the mud floor of an open-fronted booth. He showed us samples of his own special padlock which had a concealed key-hole. Most of us failed to find the catch which released the cover to it; and we marvelled at the skill which could forge and assemble such relatively intricate mechanisms.

The last display of skills was by the village carpenters who were fashioning and repairing massive wooden ox ploughs and yokes, and items for water-wheels and grinding mills. Next door to them two oxen were plodding round in a circle turning the great beam and grind-stone of a flour mill, while a group of villagers sat around waiting for their measures of flour to be poured into bags.

To us it was an unfailingly beautiful scene; but perhaps not to those involved? For the majority there was unlikely to be change for many generations.

A final ceremony remained. In the centre of the great B.C.G.A. courtyard was a lonely looking table and chair, with a cloth, a book, and a vase of flowers. The book was a very battered Visitors Book from near the turn of the century. The signatures of long-departed governors and district commissioners, even a Viceroy, were followed by that of a burra sahib named Roberts.

The day of 27 December was idyllic. Tom and Frances took us for a picnic lunch at the Irrigation inspection bungalow at Jaimthal a few miles away. The entire countryside was criss-crossed by canals large and small. The little settlements at the major road/canal crossings were all attractive and had life about them. There might be a tea-house or a bicycle repair shop, and usually there were oxen or sheep or camels under shady shisham trees while their drivers were refreshing themselves and gossiping.

On our last morning Rosemary and I went off on our own canal walk. At one point on the road there was a harmonious group of houses and buildings round a simple, but striking little country mosque. It had a low, white dome and a high white mud-walled enclosure with low corner towers, and a heavy, green-painted wooden door. The scene was intimate and reminiscent of an English stream until one met turbaned passers-by or a flock of black and grey goats, and their bare-legged goat-herd with a long stick across his shoulders, followed by rough-coated black dogs. Buffaloes stood under enormous mango trees, and the occasional white-clad figure moved about against a background of vivid green rice.

We all left Khanewal by car that afternoon for Multan. We were excited at the prospect of visiting Multan at last, and at the only possible time of

500

year. In summer it would be insufferably hot. The city was once regarded by British troops as a punishment station. There was a Punjabi saying: "The four notable things in Multan are dust, heat, beggars, and tombs." Luckily for us the first two were absent, and the beggars who still congregate at the five great saints' tombs of early Islam – Shah Yusuf Gardizi, Shadna Shahid, Shamsuddin Tabrizi, Bak'ul-Haqq, and Rukn-i-Alam – were no problem.

Multan was the old capital of the lower Punjab even at the time of Alexander the Great (356–323 B.C.). It was exciting to walk in a city of such antiquity. We could see the magnificent mausoleum of Ruknuddin or Rukn-i-Alam (A.D. 1420) towering above the rooftops of Multan from some thirty miles away. It was of a pyramidal design, but its lowest storey, the tomb chamber, was octagonal. There was wonderful relief brick and tile-work, and superlative surface decorations. Sir John Marshall, the archaeologist, described it as "one of the most splendid memorials ever erected in honour of the dead."[15]

As an anti-climax we made a quick bazaar foray to the shop selling Multan's speciality – a halwa made with nuts and ginger. Then all eleven of us, and our baggage, piled into a small P.I.A. Fokker for a smooth two-hour flight back to Karachi.

22 January

We put a tremendous effort into a British Council-arranged visit of a Royal Shakespeare Company group of five actors and two stagers: John Bennett, Julian Curry, Ann Firbank, Adrian Herman, Charles Kay, and Ian Duke (Stage Manager), and Candy Baker. They performed two well-received compilations: *The Hollow Crown* (an entertainment about the Kings and Queens of England), and *Pleasure and Repentance* (a light-hearted look at love), at the Ebrahim Alibhai Auditorium, which was a well-designed Parsee Centre. The cast comprised the best possible types. I wrote home "Life is a riot: but what organization it all requires! The leading actor was John Bennett, who had been one of the finest boy actors ever at Bradfield, and one of my key commandos! He soon told everyone about his former teacher, Hank!" There was a bond between us, and it remains.

John Bennett gave several fascinating actors' workshop sessions in which we learnt the following: Every audience in 500 performances will be different, so you mustn't anticipate one night's reaction when in the next. Every professional has a sense of humility. Every new production throws you on the mercy of the public. On television you must be

[15] J. Burton-Page, *Splendours of the East*, ed. Mortimer Wheeler (Hamlyn, 1970).

absolutely honest. The camera immediately detects lies. Of first importance to actors is relaxation. Relax! And before you go on, relax voice, muscles, fingers, etc. The set must be as familiar to you as your home. There's no bumping into furniture or tripping on stairs at home. It is better to go too far in rehearsal and then pull back. There are no small parts, only small actors. Shakespeare's advice to the players has never been bettered. "Don't over-exaggerate reactions like listening. Anyone you meet who adopts a listening attitude, isn't!" Zia Moyaddin, a leading Pakistani actor who was humble and attended, said: "All Shakespeare is thinking aloud".

I am very fond of armchair games when relaxing, and I enjoyed getting the Shakespeare group to join in one evening. A game to which we were introduced was beyond our mental capacities when playing against the group. It was called "Bum, bum". The first caller "speaks" a line of verse or well-known line of prose, not in words but only with the sound "bum" representing a long or short stress in a word: i.e,

Q. Bum bum, bum bum bum bum. A. "To be, or not to be."

Anthony Thwaite, the poet, critic and lecturer was out with us in February. He was excellent value. His anthology which was especially written for the British Council was a very handy reference book for students of English literature. He had a game for us: each person writes a line of a sonnet, not necessarily a start line, the folded paper going round until the fourteen lines have been composed. Then, in committee, the players have to assemble them.

I couldn't resist composing this limerick for our visitor:

Our debonair lecturer Thwaite,
Embarked on what seemed a safe date,
With a beautiful student,
More eager than prudent,
And now they both share the same fate.

Into India

Our local leave allowed us time to visit India. We chose Rajasthan, the Land of the Princes, to fill in our knowledge of Moghul (Muslim) art, architecture and history, before, if ever, tackling the Hindu world.[16]

In Upper Sind in the district of Thar Parkar, we were in a former part of

---

[16] We found that the best factual introduction to the Moghuls is Bamber Gascoigne's *The Great Moghuls* (Jonathan Cape, 1971), which is beautifully illustrated, including photographs by his Persian wife Christina.

Rajasthan of unified India, at the western end of the Thar or Great Indian Desert. This desert stretches eastwards as far as the Aravalli Hills ending on the Delhi ridge.

My love of India springs from my admiration for the British Raj, built up, I suppose, from contact with my father and other officers who had served in India, and my meeting men and wives, such as Rosemary's parents, who devoted years to service in the sub-continent.

One aspect of India full of nostalgic interest and sadness to me are the native Princes, the Maharajahs – alas no longer in power.[17] The very essence of romantic Rajasthan is the Jagniwas, or Lake Palace Hotel, at Udaipur. The whole region round Udaipur is lovely, and a complete contrast to the desert further west. There are rolling hills, jungles, and lakes on an intimate scale: miniature landscapes which are beautifully depicted in Mewar miniatures. In the middle of blue Pichola Lake is the gleaming white marble palace built by Maharana Jagat Singh between 1628 and 1650 as his summer residence.

I took Rosemary for a quarter of an hour's row in a little boat to the other island palace of Jagmandir. It once gave shelter to Prince Khurrum, exiled after his unsuccessful revolt in 1623–24 against his father, Jahangir. From Udaipur, Prince Khurrum emerged as the Emperor Shah Jahan on Jahangir's death in 1627.

Jagmandir became a refuge again during the War of Independence (which we British insultingly call the Indian Mutiny) when Maharana Swaroop Singh lodged in the palace a number of British women and children refugees. As a local guide book describes:

> The palace on its lush, narrow, little island is not yet a ruin. The interior has some excellent early inlay designs of onyx, cornelian, jasper and agate. The building may well have influenced Shah Jahan when he created the Taj Mahal. Tie up your little boat by the four large white stone elephants. Wander round in peace amid the greenery and the bird life; and dream.

The Lake Palace Hotel is the finest place in India to relax and be uplifted by beauty and the fascination of one's entire surroundings.

One morning I left Rosemary in peace, and indulged in a taxi to take me to Chittorgarh, some seventy miles east, to visit the fort of Chittor having read Kipling's *A Little of the History of Chitor*. It was a ghoulish trip to make; but I went in memory of the wonderful wives and women of a succession of defeated defenders of Chittor, who in 1303 and 1533, and finally in 1567, suffered the fate of 'johar' (death before surrender). They

---

[17] See Charles Allen's *Lives of the Indian Princes* (Century: London, 1984).

were all burned alive in the great vaults. Some were able to press pathetic little handprints in red on the palace walls, which can still be seen. The final sack was by the Moghul Emperor Akbar (1556–1605) from which this great fortress never recovered. "A blot on the career of this otherwise humane and liberal ruler," says the writer of the official guidebook. Blots, even of such enormity, seem to make no difference to those in power.

We continued to Jodhpur staying at the Circuit House, and were not disappointed by the great fort. It towered above the old city. There was an interesting variety of cannon on the upper ramparts. I gazed down below at tiny streets, where Rosemary spent time looking for old silver jewellery. In her usual fashion she was able to find her way about with accuracy. We particularly enjoyed the atmosphere of this city. It seemed to have been created by pleasant people, despite the tough, precarious life they had always led. The Maharajah was a fine, modern soldier, who had distinguished himself in World War II.

We visited Jaipur next, the home of the brave, outspoken Maharanee. We stayed at the Rajasthan State Hotel, which was fairly simple despite its grand name and were glad to experience its local atmosphere. Jaipur City Palace has the finest collection of Rajput Rajasthan arms, and armour, and costumes that I have ever seen. One costumed figure was real! He remained incredibly still and deadpan; and caused much amusement to those who realised the joke. There is remarkable red stone architecture, giving the city the name 'Pink City'. We fell for some of the lovely Jaipur jewellery on show there, and looked for items of silver in the Johari Bazaar.

We went to Amber Fort by the local 'bus in twenty minutes, and ascended the wide, winding, elephant path on foot. We found this building full of beauty and amazingly delicate stone and plaster work. We hadn't time, alas, to visit Bundi of which Kipling wrote so amusingly, but we managed Alwar out of curiosity.

We took the 07.10 hrs Chatak Express, which was a good way of seeing city life. At Alwar station we had to take a cycle rickshaw a mile or two. We just managed to cram into it. As we went uphill a little I felt like jumping out to help the poor fellow on the pedals, but he wouldn't hear of a sahib doing that. A certain Maharajah of Alwar was rather a rotter: "He taxed his ryots (peasants) to the point of beggary; and was rumoured to have tied up old widows as tiger bait." One item of interest was the Maharajah's amazing custom-built Lanchester of 1925; I believe he was conveyed to his burial sitting up in it.[18]

Agra was a joy, especially the Fort, and of course the Taj Mahal, brilliantly saved from damage and desecration by Lord Curzon. When I

[18] Chas Allen, *Lives of the Indian Princes*, opposite p. 151.

went to the guichet to buy two ridiculously cheap Rs. 2 tickets to enter, I exclaimed so and added how wonderful it was to see so much beauty etc. for so little. A firm voice from inside said the unforgettable "Mention not," as he handed me the tickets. But as James Cameron wrote: "The Taj Mahal symbolises India to the West; but to the majority of Indians, the Hindus, etc., the Taj is an arrogant expression of conquerors."[19]

My favourite building was the 1628 tomb of Itmad-ud-Daula, the Persian father of the Empress Nur Jahan, and grandfather of Mumtaz Mahal for whom the Taj was built. It lies on the left bank of the Jumna, three miles north of the Taj. It is the first Moghul tomb in white marble, and fore-runner of the Taj. I love its modest size and the perfect proportions of the four minarets rising from the corners of the lower storey. The pietra dura decorations of flowers and patterns are exquisite. One day we also went to Fatepur Sikri by car, and to Sikandra, Akbar's tomb; there was so much to see and admire, and to learn.

In New Delhi (at the Janpath Hotel) I will only mention the Purana Qila, Homayun's Tomb, the Red Fort, and the Rastrapati Bhavan with its 'Moghul Gardens', once the residence of the Viceroy, which was built by Lutyens. Here there was much for us to reflect upon, from the past, up to the negotiations for Independence – and, alas, Partition.[20]

10 February 1976

We flew back to Karachi, by chance with the twenty-three members of the Sydney Conservatoire Chamber Orchestra. Then we had more culture: two brilliant but widely different performances, one by an Austrian classical guitarist, followed a week later by the Tadjik Dancers, who were absolutely up my street. I would never have had the chance to enjoy such enthusiastic dynamism if I hadn't been in Karachi.

February 1976 was very busy, with three visitors at once. Two Sundays involved me getting up at 4 a.m. to meet planes from London, but desert dawns even at Drigh Road are pleasant if spent outside the airport buildings. I certainly enjoyed of having such men on my hands as the well-known ophthalmologist Patrick Trevor-Roper. He was so kind to me when I had a bit of an eye problem. Two of the visitors involved us making trips to Hyderabad and staying overnight. Both wanted to see the ancient sites on route, which involved longer journeys and careful timing. They were delightful and stimulating people, who were most welcome (and of course it was part of my job to look after them) if only they would space

[19] James Cameron, *An Indian Summer* (Macmillan 1974), p. 162.
[20] See Cameron also on this subject.

themselves out! We had ten consecutive nights of entertaining.

Rosemary wrote of success in sowing some annuals at the right time and having quite a splash of colour: "just dianthus, phlox, and French marigolds but gay." Her pots of morning glory growing up a pyramid of canes were novel and successful.

Free entertainment

The ruler of Abu Dhabi came over annually for the hunting of bustard. He owned two sections of our Defence Phase V housing area: one for himself and his family and guests; the other for staff. At this period our neighbourhood was transformed into bedlam: with comings and goings, noise, smoke from cooking fires, and the strange cries of seated circles of falcon trainers. It would have been more fascinating if it hadn't all been quite so close. Fortunately, these Arabs were used to city life, and did not destroy their Western accomodation as earlier ones had done – out of ignorance.

From such bases in Karachi, the sheikhs would move to a desert palace in Upper Sind which Rosemary once inspected. It was fully furnished Western-style for men and women guests down to dressing table items and toiletries. Unfortunately, as the Conservator of Forests, Multan Circle, reported in 1984, those hunting Houbara bustard in Cholistan, Thal and Thar deserts massacred hundreds each year, totally ignoring official quotas. The bustard population, which is important in checking the locust swarms, is threatened with extinction. Also between twenty-five and thirty beautiful Chinkara deer were poached annually and are now an endangered species. After the whole entourage had returned to Karachi and packed up, they left behind a horrible stench of offal and rubbish on which masses of beastly crows descended and were for once welcome.

March 1976

We had visitors: the fascinating and charming Professor of Energy, G. R. Bainbridge, a Professor Keynes, and Professor Smart, an Edinburgh orthopaedic surgeon. His father had been a surgeon in India, and had operated on the Maharajah of Jodhpur, who had given him an early motorcar and driver as a reward. We enjoyed describing Jodhpur fort to our professor.

Visits to Sehwan

Reconnaissance

Sehwan was a little town some ninety-three miles up the Indus west bank road. The houses clustered below a great brick fort of ancient pre-Mohammedan origin. On the remaining mound of earth and bricks stood the Irrigation Department Rest House – of spacious imperial accommodation, which was kindly booked for us by the Deputy Commissioner, Dadu. We took the Gerrards with us, because they were highly intelligent, full of interest in all around them, and fun. The journey in perfect weather took us six hours including snack and lunch stops.

But Sehwan was no ordinary little town: it was famous for containing the tomb of Lal Shahbaz Kalandar, the most revered mystic poet-saint in Sind, who resided here in the thirteenth century. We owe our visit to our special, well-loved, and knowledgeable Sindhi friends, Justice Feroze Nana and Begum Shireen.[21]

The Pir's tomb was the shrine to which pilgrims came from all over Sind. It was a pleasure to be made welcome to watch the daily assembly of devotees, which meant the comings and goings of a fascinating cross-section of Sindhi men, women, and children.

With the Gerrards we drove the twelve miles to Manchar Lake, a great stretch of water and marsh up against the Kirthar Range of hills dividing Sind from Baluchistan. We hired a covered dhoondi, and were poled for a couple of hours by a fisherman and his son down the main reed-edged channel and back. We were in a wilder form of Norfolk Broads; but here we passed villages of boats moored at huts on tiny spits of land on which cows and donkeys could be kept, as well as chicken, ducks, and geese. We saw the winnowing of sarhai (mustard) seed for oil; but we had no time to look more closely into the people's way of life.

Among the devotees

In the following year (1977) we had a visit from our niece, Janet, who arrived sensibly dressed in the qameez[22] and shalwar. It was a good camouflage precaution in a Muslim country. And Rosemary got Siddiq to make a new outfit for herself. The day after Janet arrived she was plunged

---

[21] In 1994/5 the Victoria and Albert Museum put on a display of Sindhi Embroidery collected by Begum Shireen Nana, donated in memory of her husband Justice Feroz Nana Ghulam Ali. There was also a display of Sindhi Pottery. Alas, Shireen Nana is now dead.

[22] Tunic top; the man's long shirt is a Kurta.

into our second visit to Sehwan, which had to be in August, with David Latter, Jim Herbert's successor. It was exceedingly hot. We got through our two-day carried water supply in half-a-day. From then on we had to boil local water, and try not to drink the silt.

Roughly knowing the form from before, we were ready to take David and Janet into the thick of the evening assembly. The locals were very good about letting us in. They somehow found space for us to sit down on the floor of a huge rectangular court-yard in the Shrine complex among the crush of spectators and participants. It was a fantastic evening: especially of rhythm. Rhythm is within each one of us from babyhood as Robert Lynd wrote so discerningly many years ago on poetry. I am fascinated by rhythms. As we age we respond according to our souls and are moved in different ways by particular rhythms, so have Rosemary and I been moved as we went round the world.

The giant-size Sehwan drums were a mesmeric background to the horns, gongs, cymbals and bells. The drummers began in slow time: ti tum tum, ti tum tum. A group of long-haired devotees swung their hands and hair in a circular movement of no doubt muscular necks. The rhythm slowly accelerated, and the instrumental din, increased in volume. When the players reached crescendo, the drums beat out in fast time: 'ta, ta ta ta tum'. We were already captivated. Then we were shocked by the totally strange and deafening intensity of the music, and alarmed by the entranced state of the women revolving their heads with their swirling hair sweeping the ground as the ear-splitting cacophony continued.

We extracted ourselves at a moment of lull, in which we were motioned to leave if we wished. We tottered back to our comfortable rooms, but accommodation was short: and Janet slept on a camp bed at our feet. I never felt safer!

Before we left next morning we went to see the Shrine itself, then embellished with huge golden doors presented by Prime Minister Bhutto, a man of Sind. But the Saint did not save him.

April 1976: Sind is hotting up!

The excellent Stan Smith from York University was out planning this year's summer courses for teachers in maths, science, and English. He was totally reliable and a pleasure to welcome. He had run such courses for ten years. These courses provided good diversions for the teachers. But unfortunately in Karachi, in a Muslim country, the usual beneficial social occasions for staff and teacher-students were not possible. Muslim men and woman teachers do not mix and were unlikely to go to restaurants even on single-sex occasions, and they certainly would not have come to our house together for parties, more's the pity.

Another visitor was Dr Peter Hardy from SOAS, who was studying Muslim history in India. He was a historian who was illuminating to meet; and his subject was close to us all. In fact, we ourselves escaped over the Easter holiday, motivated by the history of Sind, to find the field of the Battle of Miani of 1843, after which General Sir Charles Napier annexed Sind. This was a vital factor in 'The Great Game'. Sir Charles is reputed to have sent back the signal "Peccavi," the Latin for 'I have sinned'. But I believe this was a joke in *Punch*. However, Sir Charles had sinned, as he admitted in his Journal:

> We have no right to seize Sind, yet we shall do so, and a very advantageous, useful, humane piece of rascality it will be . . .

He wrote to his brother Henry:

> They would not take quarter, but turned on us from behind when passed . . . I saw no safety but in butchery.

Poor, brave Baluchis.[23]

We were allowed to stay in the Forest Rest House in April when it was 10° hotter than Karachi. We were comfortable except for the rats at night. They even gnawed a hole in our neat, Persian, plastic sugar dispenser. We vowed to return to Isfahan to buy another. And we did!

We had to walk to reach Napier's monument to the fallen at Miani of 17 February 1843 against the Baluchis commanded by the Chief Mirs of Hyderabad and Khairpur. This monument was Napier's gesture. It is a simple, sandstone pyramid on a square base inset with marble plaques and surrounded by a wrought-iron fence. The deepest impressions which remain with me of Miani, having been on the spot, are of the endurance and supreme courage of British and native units, bearing in mind the climate, terrain, distances to march, their totally unsuitable uniforms, primitive equipment, and limited supplies.

Back in Karachi: Our tailor bird

A beautiful white bougainvillea was massed above the dining-room of our house, creeping towards the front door. A delicate, green, leafy tendril would curve down into the pathway, ending in a spray of shining

[23] See Lady Rosamund Lawrence (neé Napier), *Charles Napier, Friend and Fighter* (John Murray, 1952).

blossom which bobbed only five feet from the ground. We returned home cheerfully one night, slammed the car doors, said "Goodnight" to the chowkidar and walked up to the house. Then Rosemary noticed a blob of grey-brown fluff in the middle of a blossom, which itself was nodding and swaying, rising and falling quite roughly in the constant eddies of wind. Thinking it was yet another untidy piece of crow-dropped debris, she bent to remove it, then stopped and signed to me to approach quietly. The object was a ball of fluff indeed, soft and spherical. But out of it cocked up stiffly was a narrow edge of tail. The ball of fluff was a delightful little tailor bird.

I found myself fixed with a distinctly frosty look from an unwinking yellow eye behind a sharp little beak. Then our tailor bird took umbrage, flew upwards and perched stuffily in the main stem above. For nearly a week the bird returned every night to sleep on an eccentric perch; tossed about by the slightest ruffle of air and well lit. He did no more than grumpily wake up as we came and went.

Until the night when Jim Herbert left the front door and advanced on the circlet of blossom with a cry of admiration. It was too late to stop him. He gave the petals a big sniff; then recoiled with a start as our tailor bird flew out into his face, and never re-appeared.

Work-wise we had an excellent exhibition from London: Museums in Education. Pakistan then could not manage a sophisticated education policy. A nation-wide establishment even of libraries, librarians, let alone museums and staff, was financially unlikely in our day. We at least had good media coverage of our message.

Drama

As 23 April approached we decided to put on a show in the lovely garden of our Centre to celebrate St. George's Day and Shakespeare's birthday. Elsewhere in Karachi we had the pleasure of Jenny Habib's excellent local children's production of *Help! Help! The Globolinks* (Gian-Carlo Menotti), and then a wholly adequate *Jesus Christ, Superstar* by an inspired drama group.

We decided on a programme of excerpts, recitations, and songs. Our introduction to the items explains our way of going about it. The programme was really too long, but here was a chance to invite some of our Pakistani friends to take part. This required some tact.

I quote from the Programme note:

This evening on the occasion of his birthday, which is also St. George's Day, some of us are going to use Shakespeare's own

510

words to express that something of Shakespeare which belongs to our individual spirits.

Please remember that this is not a rehearsed performance. It is a combination of personal responses. If they are all too much for you, we shall not mind if you go home – because as I suspect in the words of Peter Quince on behalf of his players in M.N.D.: "All for your delight we are not here."

About 200 people came – and stayed for the entire programme.

On 24 April 1976 I recorded: "Tonight we are off to the wedding party of the Chief Justice's daughter (Qader Shaikh); and then to an All-Nations Club dinner of different national dishes. Rosemary is taking sole en evantail, and making it/them at the moment with Ghaffar. I went to the kitchen to enquire, and was chased out."

The following day we had a lovely outing with Tom and Frances Roberts to Sonmiani up the coast beyond Bulegi. It was our first visit there, and we experienced quite a different atmosphere being with Tom, who spoke perfect Urdu and had his own 'retainers' here and there. His boatman Bachoo Ali took us around the creeks and sand bars. Tom's bird count was eleven species: bar-tailed godwit, turnstone, reef heron, curlew, spoonbill, saunders tern, lesser crested tern, brahmini kite, slender billed gull, lugger falcon, and Chinese cormorant.

May

The month of May went fast, without fuss but it was hot: 84°F in the study with 86% humidity. However, we had fun and good audiences with our classic films *The Prime of Miss Jean Brodie*, and *The Importance of Being Earnest*. More seriously, we had our British Books for Children Exhibition, which we took on to Hyderabad in early June. Such books were really too expensive for Pakistan schools, and beyond most individuals. But the factual ones in particular were of good value. They showed the tools good teachers needed. But Pakistan is poor. There was as yet no lucrative source of revenue. There was oil all around, but Pakistan had none in our day.

June 1976

There was a water shortage. We needed a tanker of water to top up the ground tank of our house, so that our electric pump could fill our roof tanks. It took about a month, for different reasons, for a tanker to reach us.

Our Admin. Assistant, a good man, refused to shell out, but we just got a delivery in time!

Rosemary escaped the depressing no water no gardening period by accepting an invitation from our colleagues the Hardys in Islamabad, and going on to Dunga Gali to Pakistani friends, the Afsal Khans and Timmi Bokhari, who had a cottage next to the Roberts. On one of the lovely walks along tracks up there in a water catchment area she came across a Queen's Bays badge cut into the rocks – just like those other regimental badges in the Khyber Pass.

Interval: Verse

We had two charming and very amusing friends in Kaleem and Riffo Hagani. He was a Chartered Accountant and had an English mother. The name Kaleem just triggered off this:

> Have you seen Kaleem?
> Of what does he dream?
> On what theme
> Is the scheme of life
> For himself and his wife?
> Why:
> He does his best
> For every guest
> With utmost zest.
> The East and West
> Within him makes
> The perfect host for our sakes.
> And Riffo?
> She has what it takes!

15 July

We held an evening of Rudyard Kipling recitations and an evocative film of his life and work. Six of us recited, and it was a memorable occasion. The secret of "If' is not to declaim; it is a father speaking to his son. To have declaimed would have got the father nowhere.

Sind

Work

We were visited by Colin Fuller, lecturer in Administrative Studies, Manchester. Rosemary gave a dinner for twenty-three guests for the course he ran. Two tutors in English, John Morris and Bob Parkin, arrived for a teacher-training college staff seminar. It was most interesting and useful for me. They kindly asked me to handle 'The Speaking of English', as I was doing for the Naval CENTO staff course. Then Brian Hunter and Dennis Lee arrived as technical tutors.

The Gerrards' party

This party was the most memorable ever. The invitation said to come in "Black or White, or Black and White". The choice of costumes was marvellous. Someone arrived as a crossword puzzle; there were devils, jesters, and harlequins. I wasn't very original. It was easy for me to don my Hungarian peasant costume: black breeks, white shirt, black waistcoat, black hat. One of the best efforts was by a couple who both came under the same large white burqa . They were able to continue dancing as they were. A first glance on the dance floor below the voluminous garment revealed two pairs of feet and gave us a shock!

2 August 1976

I noted in my journal: "The koel is in the garden – and it is the end of the mango season." The koel is a bird of groves and gardens and never descends to the ground. It is found throughout India and Ceylon, but in the North-West Frontier Province and Sind it is only locally common. It is large, but secretive and cunning. It is parasitic on the common house crow, and in India is in a position analogous to the cuckoo in Europe. The call of the koel is known to everyone in India. It consists of two syllables 'ko-el' repeated several times, increasing in intensity and ascending in the scale, with an indefinable sound of excitement in it. The koel is sometimes confused with the common hawk-cuckoo, known as the brain-fever bird.[24]

---

[24] See Whistler, *Indian Birds*.

15 August 1976

We had six visitors to look after at once – juggling transport to meet all their requirements, there being no public transport. It meant giving up nearly all day and part of the night to them. We took two tutors and the Dalys, our new Consul and his wife, to some of the sites in Lower Sind. It was tiring, but fun, The tutors were good enough to pay for the petrol. Jim Daly, a keen pistol shot, became an instant Tombstoner when he beat me with my anti-crow air pistol, in the garden, and took the Cup home.

Rain

The monsoon arrived in August. The rain was very heavy when I had to fly to Islamabad. Driver Baboo Din did well to get me to the airport through flood water. Later, we passengers had to wade barefoot to the bus. Islamabad was green and 10° cooler. Rosemary stayed in Karachi and coped with the flooding caused by lack of drainage, and the wind driving rain under doors. The poor people have a really miserable time when it rains. Their houses are not waterproof and there are no drains round them.

2 September

The floods were worse than in 1973 but they were better handled despite cut communications. We had a cheering reward from the tutors on the earlier summer courses for teachers who wrote: "What an interesting and enjoyable month we spent with you – it really was a very pleasant sojourn and I am truly most grateful for all that you both did to make our stay so happy. I can quite honestly say that in all my six years of education seminars I have never been so well 'squired', looked after and generally coddled by such great people."

Birds

27 September was Id-ul-Fitr, the end of Ramzan, and so it was a holiday. The Roberts took us out on a marvellous circular tour and bird scan in the Delta.[25]

---

[25] I have Tom's beautifully written out Notes: 54 species, all with their Latin names: and some notes on when and where. We were very lucky.

Sind

October 1976

Rosemary and I went to the North-West Frontier Province to follow up Winston Churchill's *The Story of the Malakand Field Force* raised in 1879. Our Defence Attaché Brigadier George Powell of the Bays smoothed the way for us to go up to Mardan, the H.Q. of the famous Corps of Guides, and into Swat over the Malakand Pass to photograph the various landmarks and sites mentioned by Churchill. Luckily for us, Feroze Nana's son, Rohil, and family were posted to Mardan with the Khyber Tobacco Co., and they had us to stay. We flew to Rawalpindi, staying at Flashman's Hotel. There was a notice in the foyer which read:

> **PLEASE DEPOSIT YOUR WEAPONS**
> **WITH THE RECEPTIONIST**

Twenty-seven miles along the Peshawar road we saw the lovely little Moghul Gardens at Hassan Abdel, and a number of tombs, one of Lalla Rookh, the beautiful daughter of the Emperor Aurangzeb – perhaps. Then we crossed the Indus guarded by the great Attock Fort constructed by the Emperor Akbar in 1586 with a small harbour to protect the ferry crossing. A crossing was possible here where the violent upper course of the river becomes a 'stately flow'. But below Attock there are gorges for ninety miles. Alexander crossed the Indus at Hund, by a bridge of boats upstream from Attock, after the rajah Ambhi of Taxila had surrendered to him.[26]

The Nanas were great hosts with their four girls: Muna, Rima, Lena, and Lulu. We heard a lot about life in Mardan! Rohil told us that a fine old Pathan had said to him recently about Mardan in the season they call 'Wedding Time': "Things are very different now; times are hard and everything is very expensive. Ahmed Khan had another son the other day, and only bought 200 cartridges. In the past he would buy 1,000."

Mardan had been the base of Queen Victoria's own Corps of Guides from 1887. I have always had a great admiration for them. On 14 December 1846, Colonel Henry Lawrence, Agent for the Governor-General for the N.W.F.P., ordered Lieutenant Harry Lumsden to set up a Corps of men specially recruited for their local knowledge. Harry sounds just the man to have been the ancestor of the late Major-General Herbert Lumsden who commanded our Ist Armoured Division in the desert so well. Harry's unit was the first of any army to wear khaki (meaning mud or dust). They

[26] Robin Lane Fox, *Alexander the Great* (Penguin, 1986).

515

came to Mardan in 1853 under Lieutenant Hodson (who later formed Hodson's Horse).

It was exciting to be invited into the Guide's Mess with my wife, and to enjoy cool drinks in long chairs on the lawn. We later visited the Guides Church (1887) and their officers' graves. What history; what service! In Mardan Cantt. we saw the memorial to the Guides escort which had been massacred in the Residency at Kabul in 1879 together with Sir Louis Cavagnari and the entire British Mission.

The task of the Malakand Field Force was to deal with the rise of the so-called Mad Mullah, who rallied thousands of tribesmen for a jehad, a holy war, to prevent further British domination of the region, which would have been against the interests of the Mullah and his following. But these tribesmen had not the power to resist Russian or Afghani infiltration.

Sadly, they often fought among themselves, as did the Scottish clans, and so weakened their power. I quote from a local newspaper article that illustrates this point:

27 KILLED IN TRIBAL CLASH

Chakdara (Dir), June 10: Twenty-seven persons were killed in pitched battles and hand-to-hand fighting between two tribes over the ownership of Pass Karrodarra in Dir district.

The Deputy Commissioner of Dir told newsmen here yesterday that the tribes, Karrodarra and Niagdarra, fought for two days late last month and left 17 dead on one side and ten, on the other.

"Nevertheless the Mad Mullah's uniting influence with outside backing was exceedingly dangerous to us. We had to prevent at any cost the establishment within this outlying country of the political preponderance of any other power." (Government of India, Letter No. 49, 1879, to the Secretary of State).

I had read Churchill's description of the famous March of the Guides Infantry in 1879 from Mardan up into the Malakand Pass: thirty-two miles in seventeen and a half hours of intense heat and dust. Luckily for me we were able to follow the course of the campaign by camera using Churchill's account. Thanks to the Nanas, the Chief Justice Safdah Shah gave us his support, and lent us his son, Asif Shah, Assistant Political Agent, Malakand, to act as guide, taking one armed levy as escort.

Using my slides and Churchill's words which I recorded (but did not imitate his voice), I was able to make up an amateur sound and vision presentation of 'The Story of the Malakand Field Force'.

On the frontier, in the clear light of morning, when the mountainside is dotted with smoke puffs, and every ridge sparkles with bright sword blades, the spectator may observe and accurately appreciate all grades of human courage.

What a start to a story!

Back in Peshawar

H. E. very kindly allowed us to stay over in the Residence. Peshawar has a very ancient history: too long to tell here except that prior to Alexander's invasion in 327 B.C., Peshawar formed part of the ancient Kingdom of Gandhara. After Alexander the city became an important Buddhist centre, and Buddhism flourished in the area for some 900 years, until the rise of Islam in seventh century A.D. We saw in the museum priceless examples of Gandharan art, very beautiful Indo-Greek heads, or sections of friezes. Too much of it has been ruthlessly looted, for sale abroad.

At the University I lectured on 'The Speaking of English' while Rosemary enjoyed herself in the city's marvellous bazaar, looking for and buying several good examples of local copper-ware. She was unconcerned for her safety in the great throng, and so was I. We never gave it a thought. There is honour among the Pathans. The kidnapping of Mollie Ellis in the thirties was an exception.[27] The next day I was able to join Rosemary in the bazaar. I wish I could have spoken Pushto to make some colourful contacts.

One other visit we had to make in Peshawar, on our own account, was to the grave, in the Cantonment Church, of Wilfred Kirkpatrick, our gentle, sensitive, scholar friend and colleague. Wilfred had been murdered in the town in his hotel room. He had simply moved there from his house for one night before flying home on leave. I do not believe his murderer has ever been identified by the law. Wilfred had been at Mandalay University when we were in Rangoon. I had visited him there in April 1962. But politics intervened, and he was withdrawn and posted to Peshawar University. I last saw him in Peshawar in 1963 when I stopped off in Karachi for a few days on my way back to Rangoon from leave, as I mentioned in 'Burma'. What a loss Wilfred is to so many friends in many countries.

[27] See Arthur Swinson, *North-West Frontier* (Hutchinson, 1967), chapter 13, 'The Mollie Ellis Affair'.

Darra – guns

A special treat for me was to make a visit to the village of Darra on the road to Kohat. Darra is famous for its blacksmiths, who are in fact all armourers! They fashion rifles, revolvers, and pistols, excellent copies of the original makes: British, Spanish, Italian, Russian, etc. These work extremely well, but I wouldn't risk using any such weapon without a genuine, not forged, proof-mark on it. One little job fascinated me: a single shot .22 pistol in the form of a fountain pen with pocket clip. Just aim it at your enemy's most vital spot available, pull back the knob on the cap which is the end of a spring-loaded firing pin, let go and hey presto!

From Peshawar we were able to fly back to Karachi direct, in a Boeing 747 crowded with colourful Pathans in full costume with their padlocked tin boxes, off to the Gulf to seek their fortunes.

28 October 1976: Operation Sardine

H.M. (Submarine) Osiris arrived on a CENTO Exercise. We were invited on board for drinks. Fazl drove us, through the dock gates, into blazing lights ahead. Where on earth do we go? "Fazl," said Rosemary, "look for an empty space on the quayside" Sure enough a black gap in a row of ships disclosed a black whale-shape below: unmistakably a submarine and H.M.S. Osiris, we hoped. A light shone out, and a figure beckoned with a call of reassurance that we would fetch up safely. We walked down a sloping gangway, turned left onto a narrow walkway and reached the conning tower. Up and over went Rosemary with a welcome from a host on deck; straight on down with encouragement from below. Then down a narrower tube, by a not very accommodating ladder, certainly not for ladies in long dresses and high heels. The reception committee below were very funny in doing their best to encourage and help the ladies down without looking up their skirts. But the Navy are gentlemen and poodle-faking artistes.

We found ourselves in a very small space menaced all round by machinery. In the middle was a great round pillar of a periscope. Beyond the periscope was a tiny table, crammed with bottles and glasses, with grinning matelots behind it. All around was a crowd of slightly bewildered civilians standing guardedly hunched together so as not to bump their heads or elbows against solid steel. They were trying to take it all in; talking politely to each other and occasionally to a rare host of a naval officer who managed to insinuate himself close to their elbows.

Soon the strangeness and reserve were broken down, and rebounding sounds of cheerful hubbub followed. I could see that it wasn't easy for any perspiring matelot on duty to get hold of an empty glass to refill, let alone return it to the drinker. I was standing with my back to the periscope (the support was useful): and I suddenly found that I had a job. If I stretched my left arm out with an empty glass in it, it would immediately be refilled, and I could transfer the refill rapidly into my right hand, and extend my right arm out to the eager owner in the middle of the fray. I was encouraged by both hosts and guests to continue doing this, and I persisted for a time with my popular corvée. Then I went on a gentle sightseeing wander round the torpedo tubes and other armaments or pipes, tubes, and stop-cocks. Rosemary had already escaped, I noticed. I found her forrard in the Petty Officers' Mess, or whatever, having a very interesting and happy chat. I was glad to join in. In due course we said 'Thank you' to Lt. Cdr. Littlejohns, and found our way rather gingerly and gladly back to Fazl on the solid quay.

Next day we were able to invite two crew members L/S Hichman (Torps.) and L/S Arnold (Sonar) out to Bulegi. It was particularly interesting listening to L/S Arnold on the fish sounds he heard when at his station. Now he was excitedly wearing a snorkel and was able to meet some of the sound sources!

November 1976

A warm letter of thanks came from the Captain of Osiris to Twink Inglis, Chairman of United Kingdom Association of Pakistan. I quote just a little of Douglas Littlejohn's admirable composition:

> . . . I think we all approached harbour in two minds as to whether the mystic East would live up to its exotic reputation, or whether this would be just another port. However, we were immediately accepted, en bloc, into various families as though we were old friends, and shown sights and sounds which we could never have experienced in the time available without local knowledge . . .

Scottish country dancing

S.C.D. reached its zenith in our career for me 1973–78. It was not only the French expatriates who became keen to learn and join in reels, (if not strathspeys), on special occasions and at private parties. Our Italian friends, self-styled McFerris were the keenest. They were in New York on business in November 1976, so they sent a telegram of regrets in verse in astonishingly good English:

The fair memories never shall fade.
The short break we'd take to have just a sip,
Michael condemning the improper grip.
The feeling of shame, the sense of guilt for
disappointing the master kilt.

The Caledonian Ball duly took place on Saturday 27 November and I responded with a ballad, by letter to McFerri, Il Turbino di Vento (Whirlwind), with couplets such as:

Andrea McFerri: and Ginetta was his bride,
The only girl who stood the pace, and never left his side,
Except the one occasion at the Sindhi Highland Ball
When Andrea let go too soon, and threw her through the wall.

Then we had extra good news: Rosemary was elected Chieftain 1977/78 of the Caledonian Society, Karachi.

A producer at last

At last I had the time, the place, the climate, and the cast potential to produce something other than our Christmas 'The Holy Season'. I had a go at "Comus" – verse and incidental music only. Our Centre garden was ideal and the weather was perfect. I had adequate principals from the British community; and I had a particularly promising "rout" in the boys and girls of the British School, who were willing and allowed to take part. I had to be pretty rough in teaching them to move fast and whizz about, which surprisingly they seemed unable to do. When they could, the show went on.

We had a private visit from our friend Sylvia Matheson, the highly talented Persian archaeologist and authoress. The trouble was she transported us back to Persia!

Ava Boga, my super secretary was telling Rosemary with awe, how hard I worked. "She must keep up the figment," I wrote to Papa. This illustrates my early contention that it was really very hard to distinguish work from play.

December 1976

We were given Home Leave. The thought of spending Christmas with family for once, was so compelling that we cabled Chris, Rosemary's youngest brother in Strathpeffer, Ross-shire (where it would be very cold) as follows: "Overcome yearning bosom family may we join you over Christmas despite latitude?" The reply was: "Indigenous delighted intrepedist polar expedition share festive igloo add Hogmanay." It is sad that there are no longer telegrams in which to practice pithy telegramese English – to save money.

On our flight home we touched down at Jeddah, and took on board a crowd of boisterous, oily boys, happy to be able to drink again. One Brian Dale, a crane driver, sat with us and said that he earned £50,000 in two years, had a large house with swimming-pool, and could send his son to private school. Excellent! A litre of water in Jeddah he told us cost the equivalent of 50p. But 120 gallons of oil cost £3!

Once again we were met at Heathrow by our dear friends, the Wilsons from Ethiopia days. That was lovely. And so was 31 December staying with Elizabeth Beazley (Iran and Morocco days). She took us into the great Bell Tower of St. David's Cathedral, to watch and hear them ring in the New Year. The best celebration ever.

1977

I returned to Karachi on 18 April, and to political trouble: Martial Law . . . It was a bore being without servants. They couldn't get over from their homes and back for long enough to work; but the Consulate-General, and mon cher collègue (Alliance Francaise) Christian Damour and Madame next door were so kind.

Rosemary returned on 14 May at 04.35, a specially lovely dawn! She went straight to work on a piano concert by Anthony Peebles. Luckily the Buschmanns of the Goethe Institut, which of course had a fine piano, agreed to put him on 'in conjunction', and they fed us all afterwards.

Hurray! The Queen's Jubilee, 8 June 1977 – a celebration

The Consul-General gave a cocktail party first – in the lovely garden, all lit up; it was a beautiful evening, if humid. The British Community provided dinner on the spot. There was to be a Music Hall on the verandah steps, followed by dancing. I contributed as Major Gallstone, retd. (mythical) ex-Clifton[28] Squadron Camel Corps, living up-country and still in the Victorian era, and I was puzzled to be invited by a Consul-

---

[28] Clifton is a superior residential suburb of Karachi.

General. Exit at the end singing 'Soldiers of the Queen' with the audience joining in.

Rain

A fortnight later we had the heaviest rain since 1967, I was told. There was considerable suffering. The city drainage system couldn't cope. The great increase in population led to housing settlements being tolerated in unauthorised areas such as on natural drainage lines. These quickly filled, and the water swept along, tumbling debris and humans too. I managed to drive Niaz and Ghaffar some way home one night through light flooding down to where the buses could still run in deeper water.

11 July 1977

We had a new Representative, David Latter with his wife Alison. "David is academically bright and was back after a sabbatical year in Education," I wrote. "He is a sympathetic and kindly man, with good powers of analysis and judgment. As a start we happily agreed on policy and many matters."

Alison was born in Karachi, the younger daughter of Sir Sidney Ridley, one time Financial Secretary. Roger and I knew him from our Karachi days, and also Alison's mother and elder sister. Alison went to Karachi Grammar School at the time I was teaching there! Sir Sidney now returned, and out to Bulegi he went, where he was greeted with affectionate surprise by our chowkidar and a number of villagers. They knew that such men in the I.C.S. had cared for them – and had not forgotten them. They were delighted to be spoken with in Sindhi.[29]

Notes for Newcomers

I have written on the importance I attached to our British Council Record of Living Conditions being comprehensive and accurate. Now Rosemary, with several years experience of life in Karachi, could competently help a team compile an up-to-date British Wives Association (BWA) 'Notes for Newcomers' which evolved into a forty-page booklet!

One subject we had so far only encountered in Addis was rabies. For Karachi our Consulate-General produced an account from a wife who had

---

[29] See Sir Sidney's obituary in *The Times*, 16 October 1993.

had experience of this deadly disease. Rabies was unfortunately becoming an extra menace in Karachi – the pi dogs, strays which could be carriers. These dogs were beginning to unite and scavenge in packs, even tracking people walking the sandy desert streets of the suburbs.

I was pleased to find a copy of *The Karachi Handbook* for 1913. I quote:

... and the newcomer with letters of introduction to the right people can be sure of the warmest and heartiest of welcomes.

There is a whole page on 'Calling', and a good deal on 'Dining and Tea-Parties'.

India is the land of precedence, and woe betide the hostess who dares to disregard the Official Table of Precedence.

The B.W.A. 'Notes' of 1977 list and describe the following nine kinds of servant one could have: Cook, Bearer, Hamal (under-bearer), sweeper, Ayah (children's nanny), Dhobi (washerman), Chowkidar (watchman), Mali (gardener) and Driver.

The 1913 Notes list sixteen servants: including a dressing boy (odd title, described as a second under-butler), two syces (groom and footman), a chokra (message boy who carries the cook's bazaar purchases!), and a durzi (tailor and dressmaker). The durzi is not a house servant today, but he comes to the house complete with machine and also his pins and scissors. I have mentioned our durzi Siddiq, an excellent craftsman and a meticulous copier of men's shirts and pyjamas, and all forms of ladies garments. He worked and worked, and never seemed to need anything: but Niaz would give him tea. Siddiq was much in demand by 'senior' housewives, so that he was sometimes ruthlessly commandeered!

Some of the sports and activities of 1913 haven't changed much, but in 1913 the Handbook stated: "The Ladies Rifle Range has fallen into disuse during the past year, but will no doubt be revived." I don't think it was, but sailing and rowing flourished; as did amateur dramatics; the Clifton Players continued the great tradition from 1970 onwards.

The Handbook wrote: "Hunting for jackal used to be, until recently, one of the features of the cold weather, but hounds so constantly died that the finances of the Hunt were somewhat strained." So were the horses strained in the broken country, I read. There was riding and race meetings: "A lady is strongly advised to have her habit and saddle specially made for her at Home," the Handbook advised.

Local conveyances available in 1913 were one-horse victorias and buggies – a small, low, two-seated, two-wheeled cart, with a little step-like seat hanging down behind, on which the syce was precariously perched.

Also in 1913 "Motors are becoming very popular and numerous in Karachi. Only a small car is needed as the only run out of Karachi is the twelve miles to the tomb of Mungo Pir (where there are flesh-eating muggers and hot springs visited by lepers)!" Fascinating!

Abolish the British Council!

We now found ourselves, so to speak, in the thick of battle over the Berrill Report by the Central Policy Review Staff and its Think Tank. We had to rely on believers fighting for us, and just had to carry on with our work. I remain very grateful to Iris Murdoch who fired a fine salvo on our behalf in *The Times* of Saturday, 6 August 1977, viz:

> The suggestion that the British Council should be abolished will shock many who know the work of this extremely valuable body. Its offices abroad are full of people coming and going in an easy informal manner, eagerly seeking every kind of information about our life and culture: seeking books, seeking access to the best language and literature in the world. Satisfying these customers are a small, devoted and I should have thought comparatively inexpensive staff, who seem to exercise a great influence in their regions.
>
> This is an important and entirely good way to remind others of our continued existence and to satisfy their persisting interest in us; and no doubt this export of our language and our values is also "good for trade", which seems to be a prime consideration nowadays. It is a narrow view of greatness which says we are not still a great country.

I wrote to thank her and she kindly gave me a very useful piece of advice, roughly this: If you want to make a particular point, in print for instance, write calmly and cogently and do not fly off the handle. This will only negate your effort and stimulate any opposition.[30]

Towards the Roof of the World. We reach Gilgit.

Rosemary, Janet (our niece), and I met in Rawalpindi and stayed at Flashman's. The weather let us fly to Gilgit next day, past Nanga Parbat. The

---

[30] It was only recently, when I wrote to ask her if I might quote as above, that I learned of Iris' cruel mental incapacity (through Alzheimer's disease) from her saint-like husband, Professor John Bayley.

mountains were all around us. We flew above them smoothly in the blue sky, but not above the great massif away up on our 'starboard bow': Nanga Parbat in snow. This was a rare experience in the course of my service! In this small Fokker, and up with the pilot we did not feel apart. We felt we belonged to the scene; but we were filled with awe and respect for the vast, jagged landscape below us. When we began to descend, there spread below us was a superb aerial view of the great, wide, river valley of the Indus.

On our final descent at the foot of the Rakaposhi Range, we marvelled at the beauty of the colours of the rocks and of the area of cultivation. It was the immense scale of the mountains and valleys which took our breath away. But after all, we were near the Roof of the World.

We were very comfortable and at peace in the Chenar Inn (Pakistan Tourist Development Company). We were able to enjoy the scenery about and above us, and observe the way of life of fine people bred in such a world.

We were also able to visualise a bit of past history learned from the works of certain old hands such as Charles Chenevix-Trench. He had been on the Frontier himself and wrote a splendid book, *The Frontier Scouts* (O.U.P., 1986). Unfortunately I never had the chance to meet, for instance, the Gilgit Scouts. All I have is a postcard photograph of unusual quality, of the Memorial to their Fallen: a tall column on a five-step plinth, with a faithful representation of a very fine horned Ibex on the top in gold. The whole is set in the beautiful Chinar Bagh: green grass, and a wonderful variety of trees in front of a backdrop of bare mountains.

After taking in the sights and sounds of the town, we walked up and down the valley of the Gilgit river and greatly enjoyed the 'Persian' scene: streams and gardens and orchards; and the wind in the leaves; the cries of sheep and goats; and the carrying voices of the farmers and families in distant conversations.

One day the 'girls' went for a dizzy jeep drive to Naltar on the Hunza road. In the old days on foot even or by mule, one slip and you were 'a gonner'.

One evening we wandered amid the chatter and clutter of bazaar, and emerged to find a game of polo nearby. What a scene: the cheerful spectators; the hard-riding teams on the dusty ground; the planes and poplars behind; and the pleasant, low hills leading the eye up to the mountain above. In August 1993 the great annual polo match between Gilgit and Chitral was televised. It was played in the Shandur Pass, the only flat land between the teams. Imran Khan's commentary was excellent. So were the Pipes of the Chitral Scouts.[31] When we got back to the Inn, I

---

[31] See John Keay, *Where Man and Mountains Meet* (John Murray, 1977), and *The Gilgit Game* (Murray, 1979).

made a dreadful mistake, losing Janet a reel of unrepeatable photographs by putting the exposed film back in the camera!

We had flown into Gilgit in a bright, early light. We flew out later one morning when the day's 'plane was ready to return. Now the light was softer and the colours of the crops and the waters of the rivers more pronounced. A lovely contrast.

I was sad not to have time or opportunity to reach Chitral to the west, although I had all the right advice and contacts through our good friend, Colonel Ali Asghar Agha in Karachi. And I had John Harris' *Much Sounding of Bugles* (The Chitral Campaign 1895), Hutchison, 1975.

Janet was an ideal and appreciative traveller. We were glad to take her to Peshawar and the Khyber Pass from Jamrud Fort H.Q. of the Khyber Rifles. This time we went underground literally, into the market at Landi Kotal, and felt a bit of a thrill. Here a large variety of smuggled goods were sold. On our return to Jamrud we stopped at a vantage point from where we could see both the motor and hoof or pad roads. And lo! There was a string of donkeys coming up the animal track each with a household bath slung on either side. From whom, to whom?

Back then down the Grand Trunk Road as far as the Armoured Corps Base at Nowshera; over the pontoon bridge and up the valley as far as the old hotel at Saidu Sharif. It was good to return. One sees so much more on a second visit.

Next day we continued north as far as Bahrain with a picnic lunch down by the rushing Swat river. We put up again at the Mountain View Hotel, Madyan, a charming spot to rest. Next morning we went down the valley as far as Saidu Sharif to see the crumbling yet impressive Buddhist stupa of Butkara at Mingora. Nothing remained of a once great monastery. The stupa had obviously been largely vandalised and, no doubt, much lovely Gandharan art looted from the site. At Udegram nearby, Italian excavations in 1956 of what was the ancient city of Ora, produced a quantity of fine artefacts. Then we continued to Mardan, and found our way to the village of Takht-i-Bhai. The name means 'Spring on the Terrace' from the original spring on top of a ridge above, an important factor influencing a Buddhist settlement here which developed into a great monastery.

The ruins were extensive and spread over the steep hillside, and were very impressive. Sir Mortimer Wheeler made excavations here but large areas remained untouched. Round a central courtyard were empty niches, where the statues of Buddha once stood. A few of these statues were in the Peshawar Museum. Also in the courtyard were the bases of several stupas. This one of many such monasteries was probably founded at the beginning of the Christian era, reaching its peak of development under the Kushans during the first and second centuries. It was destroyed by the Huns in the fifth century. From the top of the ridge behind the monastery there was a marvellous view north to the mountains of Chitral, and south across the plain of Peshawar.

The history of the region is complicated.[32] In Saidhu Sharif was the tomb of the famous Swati saint, Saidu Baba. He was a true Muslim who left home to fight against Kafir superstition and ignorance, and revive the Faith. He returned to Swat in 1835, and rests inside the fine Jamia Masjid. *He* was the Akond!

To quote Churchill again: (what contempt he reveals here):

> The Ahkund [sic] of Swat was by origin a cowherd: an office considered most honourable in India. From such employment the future Ahkund received his inspiration. He sat for many years by the banks of the Indus, and meditated. Thus he became a saint. The fame of his holiness spread throughout all the region. The Swatis besought him to come and live in their village. He died in 1870, and sleeps in an odour of sanctity at Saidu, near Mingaora [sic].

Sharif means holy.

There is no Ahkund or Akond of Swat today. The current ruler, Wali Sahib of Swat, is very much the ruler and benefactor of a worthwhile people. We met him in Karachi.

Swat was heavenly – for us. Life was a struggle for existence for the Swatis. I don't blame anyone being resentful of rich and foreign infidel tourists intruding and prying into their 'picturesque' lives. But the foreigner can help by buying examples of lovely embroidery, and find real silver jewellery for sale. More practical, I think, is to buy some of the warmest and whitest woollen lengths found nowhere else in the world; produced from the hardiest, high-altitude sheep.

The Swatis claim descent from Alexander's soldiers, who not surprisingly chose to settle in their land. Here, and over the Afghan border in Nuristan, one can often see fair-haired young people with pink and white complexions, straight noses and green eyes. They are the Kalash, the Kafirs of Kafiristan, a branch living in the Chitral valley, infidels, unbelievers from Macedonia who carved wooden statues of knights to place over the tombs of warriors – which was very un-Islamic. The women were less shy than the Moslems, which was so pleasant for us.

From Peshawar I treasure this postcard, which gave us all in Karachi renewed faith in our work:

---

[32] See Francis Watson, *A Concise History of India* (Thames and Hudson, 1974).

Central Jail

Peshawar   N.W.F.P.

Dear Sir,
Keeping my humble spirit free and my soul unbiased from all
carved devices and devil's edifices, I wish the Muslim members
of your staff, your good self and all the others a very happy Id ul
Fitr! May God shower His blessings upon all humans and forgive
us for our failures and lurkings.

Others and your books helped me learn the duties and obliga-
tions of a human and the most I feel missing are the books. Even
prison could not deprive me of the zeal for learning – the only
light which uplifts man from his inferior tidings.

Thanking you and wishing all the best.

Yours ever sincerely
M. R. Sherwani
8.10.1975
A member of your library.

October 1977 to the year end:

Friends and acquaintances; work and play:

We were very busy with our new boss, David Latter, who came down
with Alison. A thousand miles between offices, and a very different scene
presents quite an administrative problem for the boss. We welcomed to
Karachi Hugh and Valerie Thwaites and family. They knew the Millars
from India, and we knew the Millars from Iran. Such is the pattern of our
friends, the most important element in life.

I asked the London office if I might go to Morocco as my last post,
because we wanted to make use of, and widen our knowledge of Islam.
This was the first preference I had ever given.

On 1 November H.M.S. Tiger came in. The Eadens gave a great party
and we met some 'good eggs': Lt. Fox of Helicopters; Lt. Cdr. Just; the
Captain; C.P.O. Smith, car mechanic and enthusiast.

Our last Caledonian Ball was on 30 November, which I missed as the
Council kindly flew me to Bristol for E.N.T. treatment. Our friends, the
Wilsons, met me; and the Gayfords, our predecessors in Isfahan now
Regional Officer, Bristol, put me up! Rosemary, who was Chieftain in
Karachi, did a great job. The Vice-Chancellor, Dr Ehsan Rashid, was her
chief guest. We had the greatest respect and affection for him. He was a
charming, straightforward, admirable man, typical of our best Pakistani

528

friends. Incidentally, we were lucky to strike it right in Karachi for the Council and for ourselves with the Secretary of Education, Panah Ali Shah and his Head of Planning, Ali Mohammed Mahar. We felt quite at home with such men; and they were very kind to us.

December 1977

Luckily I just got back from England in time to help cope with the London Shakespeare Group from Tokyo. They 'did' *Romeo and Juliet* all over Pakistan!

Next we received the noted physician Sir Graham Bull, who had been lecturing in China for the Council. He was such a good man; he was humble and very interesting at our small dinner for him. He was followed by the Council's language teaching specialist, Gareth Owen. Gareth was tremendously useful with advice and encouragement to the Government's Education Department staff on the training of teachers of English, and on the standard of English required. There had naturally been a decline in all this since Partition and as yet there was no firm Government policy – such as we felt there should be. But there must have been understandable opposition to the continual dominance of English over Urdu.

23 to 26 December: An unforgetable Christmas

We took Peter and Gabrielle Shoubridge and drove to Hyderabad to Sainjee's. After a breakfast of the usual porridge we set off on the 180-mile trip to Khairpur Mirs where we were to be under the hospitality of the Mir of Khairpur himself. This was arranged through a letter of introduction, posted ahead in good time, from our redoubtable friend Justice Feroze Nana Ghulam Ali. His Highness was no longer officially a Mir but the senior Talpur in receipt of a State pension. We stayed in the grand Circuit House, which used to be the Mir's guest house. In the days of the British Raj the Mir of Khairpur together with the Amir of Bahawalpur further north, and the Khan of Kalat to the west were the three independent rulers in this part of united India.

We unpacked a few decorations, crackers, a collapsible snowman, and other items for an instant Christmas, including the vital Butagaz cooker. We discovered that the Mir had given instructions to his Estates Manager, Serai Mohammed Hassan Khan, (formerly entitled the Wazir) to look after us.

Serai Sahib, a large and genial man, did us well. This time we got into the Palace which he showed us round, the Faiz Mahal, a tall, airy Victorian-style mansion with good, shady verandahs. The whole was charmingly intimate, compared with the grandeur of Jaipur for instance, but Khairpur had sets of silver furniture! There was also a highly decorated swing sofa in local style, on which Serai Sahib enjoyed sitting so that I could photograph him.

Serai Sahib told us that next morning, Christmas Day, we should be ready early for a day out, since His Highness was providing for us a day in his game reserve. He had some time previously ordered his former shikargar (hunting reserve) to be made into a well-protected game sanctuary.

Serai came for us in a blue Toyota jeep and drove us fast through the irrigated area of the Reserve, to a spot from which we crept up to strategically constructed reed hides. We saw hog deer, and a few wild pigs. This area was used for occasional duck and pig shoots. We extracted ourselves quietly, and were driven up and down the sand hills out to similar reed hides in the semi-desert. Here we had good views of several of H.H.'s beautiful black buck which he had imported from India. We were very pleased to see the creature so often painted in Moghul miniatures as symbols of the absent male lover.

We were driven back into a forest clearing to find it full of retainers setting up trestle tables, open fires, pots and pans, chairs, utensils, glasses, table-cloths, everything for an alfresco luncheon in style. We were glad to tell H.H. that we had managed to see quite a bit of Sind, over the years, and that our greatest impression was the Fort of Kot Diji. "Ah," said the Mir, "built by my great-grandfather". The final touch was when villagers came in carrying small, wild honey combs still on their branches. These were divided up for our plates, and were delicious.

After a pause, four of the Mir's own beautifully caparisoned riding camels appeared with their drivers. We were invited to mount behind the drivers. We had a marvellous scenic ride (one gets a fine view from a camel). We went on a reconnaissance with Serai Sahib, on behalf of H.H., looking for water, and migratory duck in two separate, seasonal lakes. We only saw a few duck in one lake; the other was dry. We were pretty tired when we got back at 6 p.m.

The 'girls' did us proud for Christmas Dinner although they hadn't had much time for preparation. We had had a wonderful time, but I was extremely upset to find WOL missing from my bedside, my clipped, woollen owl mascot who accompanies me (and then flies home to Edward Bear and tells him all the news). I suspected the cleaning woman's child: but no. I told Serai Sahib, who put me on to the District Commissioner. I had to tell the D.C. all, but I didn't mind. I offered a reward: and we left, for Bhit Shah again, for the night. I was a bit sad, but we enjoyed showing Peter and Gabrielle round the Shrine next morning.

Sind

In Karachi I wrote to H.H., and composed a Khairpur Carol:

Christmas 1977: for Serai Sahib:

Good Serai Sahib took us out
In the blue Toyota
Over sand dunes, round about
Teaching us to motor.
Off to machans[33] three we went
Viewing God's own creatures
Then some time at lunch was spent
One of the best features!
The best excursion ever yet
Serai Sahib then sent us.
On three camels off we set
Which His Highness lent us.
So we spent our Christmas Day
Thanks unto His Highness
Serai Sahib sent us on our way
We'll ne'er forget his kindness.

And Serai Sahib replied in a letter he wrote on 1 January 1978: as follows:

I do not find words best suited to express my gratitude for the beautifully worded letter of commendation sent by you for the very little efforts that I could make on your visit to our place. Although I tried my best to make the party feel easy and enjoy the outing, yet there may be certain shortcomings in the arrangements or any inconvenience caused during your stay for which I may please be excused. I hope I will be able to serve even better on your next visit for which you will be kind enough to give me advance information.

The verse written by you has greatly impressed me and for that I thank you very much . . .

Kindly pay my respects and good wishes to Mr and Mrs Peter and your Mrs.

I remained sad at the loss of WOL and thought of M. M. Kaye, and how she felt at the loss of her beloved Roller-Bear, as she related in *The Sun in the Morning* . But suddenly without explanation, WOL was returned! Al-hamdu li'lah! Whoever took him had roughly scratched the black off

[33] A hide from which to watch or shoot game.

his little eyes. But Rosemary gave him much better eyes. It's an ill wind . . .

1978: January to April

One reaction from London to my request for posting to Morocco was that our ambassador in Rabat was concerned at the standard of my French. But good old Christian Damour wrote with the authority of the Alliance Francaise that I would get by with hard work and six weeks' study in France.

New Year's Day

At a New Year party my boss referred to me as 'jungli' Halsted. I was offended! I soon put him right: 'jungli' means uncouth. He meant that I preferred country to town.

At home we entertained Justice Dorab Patel of the Supreme Court. He was a Parsee, and we admired him greatly.[34] He was very good to us. He insisted on calling round while he was down from Islamabad. He was such an honourable man that the Government gave him the job of Election Commissioner after the troubles the previous spring. Dorab sometimes talked quite a bit about the past, especially about how the little people had appreciated the fairness and justice they had received under the British Raj.

I had to go to the University at Tando Jam, Hyderabad, to see the Vice-Chancellor A. K. Ansari. I also met several of my friends on the staff who took me round their departments. The Department of Sind, for instance, had historical and cultural material more in my line than science.

We stayed at the little Central hotel where the M.C.C. teams put up, as did the *Sunday Times* reporter, Scyld Berry. He did not like Hyderabad! He unkindly called it 'One of the Seven Horrors of the World'. Perhaps he led a pampered life! He should live in Sind. Unfortunately, we had to miss the match, while I worked for a couple of days. Rosemary shopped by motor rickshaw for materials in the bazaar. Intrepid!

When I could escape we drove forty-two miles east to Mirpurkhas and had a picnic lunch in a mango orchard nearby. The Moghul artists appreciated the mango's decorativeness, and often painted it pretty faithfully.

We were aiming for Umarkot, almost on the desert frontier. We were

[34] He died on 15 March 1997 in Karachi.

well looked after by the servant, Kanrudden in the Circuit House: a good architectural example of its type, built in 1877. Umarkot was a medieval Rajput fort, but not oriental in design. It had an inner, central, round artillery tower ascended by a wide ramp. It is fascinating to think that the Emperor Akbar (1556–1605) was born in this fort. In 1540 the Emperor Humayun defeated by Sher Khan of Ghor fled west into the desert, and sought refuge with the Lord of Umarkot. Here he married Hamida Begum, and then departed. He returned to find that a son and heir had been born – and named Akbar!

We had a colourful time wandering about the little town, among the fascinating locals and all their occupations, photographing where possible, i.e. when the children didn't get into the scene first! Alas, we only had twenty-four hours in Umarkot. We had to be home the next evening, which meant travelling 200 miles in six hours.

Immediately upon our return the London Auditor arrived: a young Teddy Hall man, which was a pleasant surprise. Later in January our Controller came out from London to assess present and future work in terms of the Pakistani response; and next came our Regional Finance Officer. We were thus fully occupied.

But our next visitor was a specialist, far above our heads but of new interest: Professor Elfenbein of Goldsmith's College, studying the Burushaksi language of the north spoken in Hunza, Nagri, and Yasin.

He spoke of other local dialects: Shina spoken in Gilgit, Kowan in Chitral, and Burush Wakhi in Hunza – not to mention Baluchi and Pushto. He reminded us of Colonel Lorimer, the Political Agent in Hunza in the 1930s, who wrote a *Dictionary and Grammar of Burushaksi*.

10 February 1978

I had an excellent official Upper Sind visit, with much interest in the bygoing. I sent Mohammed Hussein up by car to Sukkur, and followed by air the next day. Here and at Khairpur again I spent two days in academic institutions. Then I reached Jacobabad at last, named after the famous General John Jacob, who took control of the Upper Sind frontier in 1847. Upper Sind had been in a state of anarchy, with bands of brigands ravaging the countryside. Both sides fought bravely, with no bitterness after Jacob's final victory. The General proceeded to found a city with a cantonment in which he settled, and made clocks in his retirement; even though Jacobabad was the hottest place in Pakistan: 100°F in the shade in June was not uncommon. Alas I didn't have time to see a clock of his which was still going, I was told.

Shikapur was once an important stop on the caravan route connecting

Central Asia with the Indian Ocean, via Kandahar and Quetta. The people of Shikapur were the famous merchants who held sway over the caravan-trails in Turkestan.

Following my return to Karachi I was much occupied work-wise: a week with an E.L.T. visitor; an F.O. property man looking at our premises: and an O.D.M. Aid Team involving me on their education funding side. I was interested to hear discussions on the various projects put up by the Government of Pakistan: water supply, tractors, agricultural research, roads and transport.

On the lighter side was the organisation of a piano recital by a really first-class, very pleasant and amusing young Englishman, Richard Deering, who was on a world tour and had never been to Pakistan. He wrote to me, and I arranged it with the co-operation of the Goethe Institut once again. They had a very good piano – and good hearts!

March 1978

My posting to Morocco was agreed. I was to depart Pakistan on 22 April for language training, a hospital visit (repair work), and Home Leave. The trip home being planned by us was via India, Afghanistan, and Iran. Then we had the usual game of packers, squaring up the office, selling the car, and so forth. There was one extra chore: the Moroccan Government's demand for a list of all our books, records, and tapes!

16 March 1978

We received our last and ideal visitor: Professor of Dentistry, Ray Duckworth, and his doctor wife, who was interested in family planning. Where has this got today in the sub-continent? The superabundant new generation requires a great body of teachers who hardly have time to be taught their own subjects, let alone how to teach them. Classes are so large that pupils cannot fully benefit. One medical college used to have classes of 150, but the same class of its year now has over 500 students.

We really took to the Duckworths, and we were happy to take them to Hyderabad. We were fond of our Karachi dental body and they were easy to get together. The following was well worth receiving from one of them:

> This is to say a special Thank You for all the good you both have done in Pakistan. The lives of many of us are certainly enriched to some extent because of the interest you have taken in our people during your stay here . . .

534

As Rosemary recorded on 26 March: "We took one last night off at the beach hut which was a little bit sad, as well as memorable. It nicely coincided with a full moon, and it was an ideal spot from which to watch the eclipse."

Then of course we were busy day and night. We had some lovely farewell parties to go to: including ones given by the Tapals; by the Adamjees; by Liaquat Ali Khan (fine son of the great Liaquat) with his mother, the Begum; by Javed Iqbal, formerly Lt. Colonel of Probyn's Horse, and his wife Joy; by Dorab Patel; and one by Dr Ehsan Rashid. How happy and sad we were.

April 1978

In the office we had an English language teaching book exhibition – which was most interesting to this 'old-stager'; but some of my long favourite 'tools of trade' which were not on show are still solidly useful.

We gave a farewell party for the staff, outdoors at Mackinnon House, and managed to get some of them to play more active games, such as the flower-pot race (using three pots). Their spokesman's farewell speech, in Urdu and translated into English, was very touching.

On 17 April we had our own official party in the Mackinnon House. This was my invitation:

> I am writing to tell you that I have been posted to Rabat, Morocco: and that my wife and I will be leaving Pakistan towards the end of April 1978.
>
> In case there is no chance of seeing you again I want you to know that I could not leave without at least getting in touch with you. We shall miss you: in no other country have we been able to make such good and kind friends.
>
> We take with us vivid memories of fascinating places we have visited: but above all of the welcome, hospitality and assistance we have received from everyone everywhere.
>
> Of course we are looking forward to Morocco: and the chance of becoming acquainted with the wealth of Islamic culture in the region.
>
> But we shall never forget Pakistan: and I envy my successor Lloyd Mullen and his wife, who will be coming from Colombo at the end of June. In the interval, Edward David will be in charge in Karachi.
>
> In order to say goodbye to as many of our friends as possible we are having a tea-reception at the British Council on Monday

Round the World in Forty Years

POEMS FROM WHICH TO CHOOSE ONE FOR EACH SECTION (CHORAL & SOLO)

UPPER SENIOR CHORAL:
    17-19 years

- The Listeners - Walter de la Mare
- Tarantella - Hilaire Belloc
- Pert of Many Ships - John Masefield
- The Golden Journey to Samarkand - James Elroy Flecker

UPPER SENIOR SOLO:

- The Express - Stephen Spender
- The Old Ships - James Elroy Flecter
- The Burning to the Leaves - Laurence Binyon
- I Think Continually of Those Who Were Truly Great - Stephen Spender

LOWER SENIOR CHORAL:
    15-16 years

- The Rolling English Road - G K Chesterton
- Santorin - James Elroy Flecker
- From My Diary, July 1914 - Wilfred Owen
- The British Museum Reading Room - MacNeice

LOWER SENIOR SOLO:

- A Thing of Beauty - John Keats
- The Solitary Reaper - William Wordsworth
- Music Comes - John Freeman
- Prospice - Róbert Browning

MIDDLE A CHORAL:
    13-14 years

- The White Birds - W B Yeats
- Fear - Rudyard Kipling
- Fairy Music - Rose Fyleman
- To a Poet a Thousand Years Hence - James Elroy Flecker

MIDDLE A SOLO

- Tartary - Walter de la Mare
- It Was the Lovely Moon - John Freeman
- Ozymandias - Percy Bysshe Shelley
- November Skies - John Freeman

MIDDLE B CHORAL:
    11-12 years

- Wander-Thirst - Gerald Gould
- The Tyger - William Blake
- If I Could Tell You - W H Auden
- Sea-Fever - John Masefield

MIDDLE B SOLO:

- The Donkey - G K Chesterton
- Five Eyes - Walter de la Mare
- Leisure - W H Davies
- Silver - Walter de la Mare

JUNIOR CHORAL:
    9-10 years

- Spells - James Reeves
- The Fairies - William Allingham
- The Brook - Alfred, Lord Tennyson
- From a Railway Carriage - R L Stevenson

JUNIOR SOLO:

- Night Song - Frances Cornford
- O Dreamy, Gloomy, Friendly Trees - Herbert Trench

- Broken Hearts - W H Davies
- Frolic - A E (George Russell)

I much enjoyed laying this on in my last year.
Would you have chosen differently?

Sind

CONTEST:	
	MARKS GAINED
	AGREED TOTAL OF MARKS
SPEAKER:	PLACING
Subject/Title	
Audibility	
Pronunciation	
Stress, Rhythm, Phrasing & Flow	
Intonation & Expression (Tone and Contrast)	
Understanding of Passage: and feeling of being with the poet/author	
Intelligibility and conveyance of sense	
Personality and general effect: (attitudes, mannerisms)	
GROUP Imaginative treatment	
COMMENTS:	
Date: Signature:	

537

the Seventeenth of April from 6 to 7.30 p.m. Should you be able to look in, we would be delighted to see you.

My staff were terrific. I only mention the following from the point of view of this happy British Council officer, and his pinch of salt. What was said at the end of the farewell speech, cheered me, especially "You have endeared yourself to us through your understanding and sympathetic approach to the various problems of each individual member of the staff."

And this: "Although Mrs Halsted has not been too directly involved with us, she has equally contributed towards the British Council . . . It is often said that behind every great man there is a woman." I needed my wife in order to achieve anything.

Justice H. T. Raymond was good enough to write: "Over the years I have received similar farewell communications from departing dignitaries but never have I had such a masterpiece like yours."

Last days in April 1978

I ran my British Council Poetry Recitation Competion, for eighteen English-medium colleges and schools, and helped to judge the finals.

We had the good, old annual beano: the Queen's Birthday Party, which was exactly the right day for us to say "Good-bye. See you again one day," to so many. Thank you, Consul-General Maurice and Nellie, for your support and friendship.

A surprise awaited us at Karachi Airport. Dr Ehsan Rashid was there to see us off to New Delhi from the V.I.P. Lounge, which he had booked! As a parting present he gave us a set of beautiful, mottled-brown onyx coasters from Baluchistan.

Home Leave: the best laid plans . . .

In New Delhi we had time for a quick visit to the tombs of the Lodi Sultans (1451–1526). We saw architectural styles to store in the mind's eye. Then we took the train to Bikaner, which was well worth-while.

Bikaner is a princely state 500 years old which had steadily progressed under Rao Rai, who received his title from Akbar in 1573. Rao Rai built Junegarh Fort, a handsome pile, between 1588 and 1593. It was he who helped Prince Selim to succeed to the Imperial Throne as Jahangir: a sensible and handy start!

In the nineteenth century Maharajah Ganga Singh succeeded his brother, Durgar Singh, at the age of seven. The Regency Council of Ministers did not achieve very much for the state: they only built Lalgarh Palace, it seemed, and apparently did nothing to improve the lot of the ryots (peasants). But Ganga, when he succeeded in 1898, was very progressive. He put Bikaner 'on the map'. He established proper administration, 800 miles of railways, and a canal system.

We stayed at the Circuit House and were very comfortable. It was a pleasure walking about the town and seeing the colours of the marvellously costumed Rajasthani women and men. We saw the houses here of the Havelis (the old-time merchants), and would love to have had the leisure to go inside.

My particular interest was the camel-breeding farm at Jorbia. It had been going for twenty-two years and was obviously 'a good thing' (under N. L. Sharma). In Rajasthan the camel is a very important element of life.

I shall always remember the Circuit House, and our bearer. I had left my jacket with pen and diary in the wardrobe. The bearer found them, and cycled with them to the station and caught us just before the train started. Marvellous, and vital.

We flew on to Srinagar where we were very happily settled into the houseboat 'Claremont' moored at the Garden of Chenars of Haji Butt. It was perfect, but not for long. We were suddenly asked to leave because of the arrival of an "important party" who had to be accommodated in an emergency. "Who is it?" "Mr Rockerfeller." "What is the emergency?" "A revolution in Kabul." We moved.

Now we couldn't reach Kabul or Herat, and go by road back to Meshed in Iran. We had to spend time getting ourselves re-routed to New Delhi, to Tehran, to Isfahan. I am afraid this means that we are unlikely ever to be able to visit Herat. We were so close! But we could continue to enjoy Kashmir from the houseboat 'The Lion of Kashmir'. For instance, we took a shikara to Cheshmi Shahi; a bus round Wular Lake; and a taxi up to Yusmarg for a picnic lunch.

Our last visit to Isfahan was on our journey home, and alas it was unpleasant. Worse was to follow. We never imagined that soon, not far from us in Rabat, would be an unhappy and sick refugee: the Shah of Iran.

And so, on to fresh woods and pastures new, for the last time under the British Council: to Morocco, where we wanted to go. We have no regrets, only gratitude.

AN APPRECIATION

Let it be known by all persons
for all time, that

MOHAMMED FAZL

IS HELD IN THE HIGHEST ESTEEM
by his former Director in Karachi,
for his years of faithful,
trustworthy service.
FAZL was always ready and willing
to undertake any duty
cheerfully and loyally, regardless of himself.

SUCH AN EXAMPLE OF SERVICE

has over years of interest and concern,
led to valued mutual friendship and
affection.

Signed

Moroccan Diary

Our last post: October 1978 – July 1980

In filling in my last Postings Preference Form while in Pakistan, I had for once specified a country: Morocco. Rosemary and I agreed that the Islamic world was our main interest. Morocco would allow us to attempt a reasonable job; and at the same time give us a valuable insight into an Islam of the 'far west'. I am most grateful to the Council for generously allowing us to serve here for such a short tour of only twenty-one months. I had to retire on my sixtieth birthday in July 1980. Nevertheless, we could not have had a more rewarding or exciting end to my thirty-three-year career. Morocco was a revelation.

Morocco is so much better known today that I am only going to give certain basic details whilst recommending two admirable writers: Christopher Kininmonth and Jane Holliday. Luckily for us there were a generous number of Moroccan national or religious holidays which we could take for short familiarisation trips, or add to further working visits with guide books in our hands.

Morocco is a magnificent country with a variety of remarkable scenery. There are fertile coastal plains on the Atlantic west, and some on the Mediterranean north. There are upland interior regions with great forests of cork oaks, and vast acres of orange orchards, and rich river valleys. The country is geographically dominated by the narrow Rif mountain range across the north, and by the Atlas mountain ranges – the Middle, High and Anti-Atlas – running north and south separating the coastal plain and forests from the desert: grand and beautiful with delightfully varied country in between the ranges. The land south-east of these mountains slides down into gravelly sands which become the Sahara Desert.

The climate varies with geography. In general there are two seasons: one is hot and dry, the other is cool and rainy. During the winter there is sufficient snow for ski-ing in the Rif and Middle and High Atlas. Coastal cities have a pleasant, temperate climate. The rainfall varies considerably between the coasts, the mountains, and the south.

The Berbers, the original inhabitants of Morocco, were isolated from Africa by the Atlas Mountains and the Sahara, and escaped the invasions, plunder, and conquest of the Mediterranean region. The Phoenicians, Romans, and Vandals reached Morocco's Mediterranean shores, and also

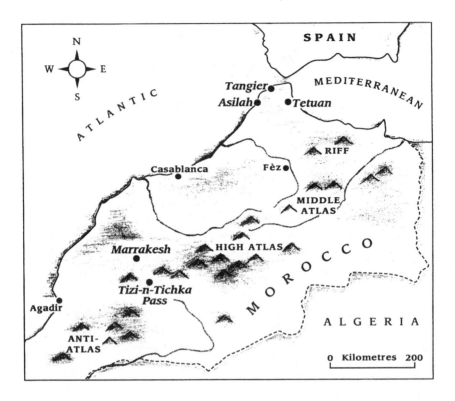

the Atlantic shore, via the Straits of Gibraltar. The Berbers of the north were influenced by the Romans, even adopting Latin and Christianity. But when the Arabs arrived in A.D. 681 the native population quickly accepted the new dynamic Islam, and the language in which the Prophet Mohammed proclaimed his faith. One faith and one language became common to all, but a separate, independent personality developed in Morocco.

Arab and Berber co-operated and quarrelled, fought together and against one another over the centuries. But at the height of their powers the Moroccan dynasties, the Almoravids (A.D. 1060 to 1147) and the Almohads (1147 to 1244), ruled much of Spain and as far as Egypt. Many of Morocco's most enduring monuments date from this era.

By the fifteenth century internal dissension and declining leadership resulted in a prolonged period of Portuguese, Spanish, and French occupation of areas right up to 1956, when Morocco regained her independence from being a protectorate, but not a colony, of France. The constitution promulgated and approved by referendum seems an admirable path for a country like Morocco to follow. The King is not only Head of

542

State and C. in C. of the Armed Forces, with extensive rights of action, he is also a direct descendent of the Prophet, and is therefore the religious leader, and Commander of the Faithful.

The Moroccans are Sunni Moslems. There is a small Jewish minority, and there are respected Christian communities. In our day the population was growing rapidly, over half being under twenty-one years old. There was an unfortunate steady drift to the towns since an agricultural life is pretty hard, especially in rugged areas with annual extremes of climate. The economy is based on minerals, agriculture, and fishing. Only one third of necessary foodstuffs was then produced.

Tourism is very important, but in our time foreigners could experience considerable hassle from the young. We lent our little voices whenever we met authority to beg the government to put an end to this for the sake of the country. The Moroccans are great people, much to be admired: they are hardy and proud, well aware of their rich and varied history and traditions. It is heartening and picturesque to see so many Moroccan men and women from all levels of society wearing the traditional djellabah – a full-length, sleeved gown with a hood; and the men often wearing the yellow leather slippers, called babouche. Underneath the djellabah of a court official or some local government dignitary, you may glimpse a smart shirt and suit. Some women prefer to continue with a nose-and-mouth veil, and many wear head-scarves.

The French protectorate, apart from the ignominy Morocco felt, had been beneficial to the country. The first French Resident-General was General Lyautey and his attitude to his tremendous responsibility to Morocco was wholly positive. Lyautey learned to love the country and was scrupulously careful not to undermine Islam, nor to destroy any of its monuments. He built the ports of Casablanca and Kenitra (further north), and the new towns of Rabat, Meknes, Fes (or Fez), and Marrakesh. He deliberately left the original medinas, the old towns, quite alone, and built outside these. It is a pleasure to stay in these new towns, and just totter down to the picturesque hurly-burly of medina and souk. Lyautey laid out excellent roads and rail links which were of tremendous benefit to modern development.

The British Council's main job in Morocco was to teach English, to support all teachers of English, and to arrange for those competent in English as much as possible of the mutually hoped-for professional interchange. The social and business language of Morocco is French. But France had to accept the finding of its own government's National Commission of Enquiry in 1979 that English, not French, is now the second language of the world. I was there at the time, and did my best not to talk or look as smug as I felt. The French wish to ensure their language remains the language of culture which I will not deny them! It was clear to

Moroccans that to conduct international business, or to continue with higher studies both inside Morocco and abroad, adequate English was required.

I found myself in a very efficient and agreeable set-up. Neville Townsend* was an excellent administrator with a command of French. I had a congenial P.A. in Emilina Oturno, who was Spanish, and I had a fine typist in Wendy Nast, wife of Tim in the Embassy. A Moroccan, Munira Dahmani, was our office strength. She and her husband, Miloud, were a great help to us in interpreting Moroccan life and customs. British Gretel Murray was our competent librarian. The office and library frontage was a double shop-window on the pleasant Avenue Moulay Youssef, and was good for the regular display of B.C. materials, publications, library books, and pictures illustrating aspects of Britain, etc.

Our main effort was our Language Centre, which was ten minutes walk away. Its Director was Tony O'Brien*, who was highly qualified and experienced in English teaching. He was firm and congenial, with a good command of French – an ideal choice. He had taught in Tabriz so we had the Persian scene in common. Here in Rabat, Tony and his assistant handled 700 adult students. There was no lack of qualified British teachers to call upon in Rabat, which made me envious after my problems in Isfahan. Also Tony could pay his teachers proper salaries; whereas in Isfahan I had only been able to pay recruited teachers for the hours they taught. Of the teachers of English whom we employed in Morocco some were from the English faculty in Rabat University, who could spare us a few hours. Others were freelance, qualified T.E.O.s (teachers of English overseas), either local residents or travellers willing to stay for a period.

We had great encouragement and support from our Ambassador, Simon Dawbarn (later knighted at post), and his wife Shelby, whom we had known in Tehran days. Simon wrote to me before we arrived, "Morocco seems to be full of delightful possibilities, and in many ways reminds me of Tehran when we were there". True. We didn't have a generous budget, but enough to keep the vital E.L.T. going; and the office staff were strong enough to cope with our fairly simple administration, and to welcome the procession of specialist visitors.

I found that my staff felt neglected, so I gave them my full support and encouragement. I gave them proper standing orders and procedures, so that they knew where they stood. Then I decided that I could confidently leave my base, and travel the country in support of teachers of English in schools, institutes (state or private), or groups (English clubs) outside the capital who might feel isolated.

For the first time we were in a country in which we had both Saturday

---

* Neville and Tony were British Council, London appointed staff.

and Sunday free, so it became easy to explore and enjoy the country in our free time as well as in the course of duty. Thanks to Simon, our first official appearance in Rabat was to attend an Embassy reception for Lord Limerick and his mission for Middle East Trade. Lord Limerick spoke excellent French but his team spoke hardly any. The mission therefore cut little ice. It is all very well for missions to say of their foreign counterparts: "But they all speak English," many don't. Even if some negotiators do, the British executive needs to know roughly what the hosts' reactions are in their own language, in which they probably feel more confident to negotiate. We must get the next generation to master European and Far-Eastern languages to a higher standard than appears today.

Our residence in Souissi, the Rabat garden suburb

The Townsends kindly put us up until we could move into our very spacious, five-bedroomed Villa El Fath in the pinéde, an area of pine trees. Our air-freight baggage came in our first week – a help to give us a quick start in our suitably prestigious base. The villa was 3.3 miles from the office, and only twelve to fifteen minutes easy drive by car. We enjoyed the space and quiet, and a large garden with lawn and pine trees and a paved terrace – we did not enjoy the miles to and from the kitchen.

We had a male factotum, Miloud, who came with the house as manservant and gardener. He was useful, cheerful, and co-operative. He dusted, cleaned, and gardened, and raised or lowered the numerous heavy, French-style, wooden roller-shutters. He brought our morning orange-juice to the bedroom at a quarter-to-seven, and made the breakfast table ready – on the terrace in summer. In winter he managed the antique central-heating system. There was a huge, voracious boiler in the basement, burning local coal. When Miloud was absent I had to cope. My heart would sink. I was terrified of the roars and rattles along the huge bore pipes in the cellar to the radiators above. I was convinced that the boiler's ancient wired-on safety-valve would cease to function and cause it to blow up and some of the house to collapse. Miloud just laughed. He also found for us Zohra, our daily maid, cook, and washerwoman. She had a pleasant temperament. I was amused to calculate that the whole area of our first little semi-detached bungalow home in Addis Ababa in 1953 would have fitted into just half of the sitting-room area of our Souissi villa! We must have made some progress in twenty-seven years.

Rosemary enjoyed the garden, but not its fifty pine trees which shed needles everywhere all year round. She wrote home: "The soil was light and easy to work, with plenty of manure available. It was a joy to have at last a rewarding garden after so many difficult ones, although alas for such a short time. The whole layout was painful, orange and medlar trees were dotted about with aimless, crazy-paving paths. There was a high hedge of purple bougainvillea on the road side, and hibiscus and plumbago along the side wall. Fine pots had fuchsias, clivia, and strawberries. By the second spring when I was getting the hang of the timing, we had a good show of calendulars, French marigolds, phlox, penstemon, dwarf delphiniums, godetias, pinks, antirrhinum, eschscholtzia, all from seed, with cannas, shasta daisies, arums, dimorpotheca perennial, and Miloud's nasturtiums . . . Not so bad?"

Out of town

On our first Sunday the Townsends took us up the coast to La Plage des Nations, a 'smart' resort on one of the main Atlantic coast beaches. It was a bit up on our Karachi beach-hut at Bulegi, but Bulegi had its own charm.

November 1978: getting mobile

I bought a Moroccan-assembled Renault 12 and never regretted it. We had to buy locally because the duty on an imported British car was prohibitive, and uneconomic for the Council. I didn't mind because Renault had good local service and spares, which gave me confidence. Also, thanks to the Council driver, Driss Bennour, we were able to buy a good, second-hand Renault 5 for Rosemary, and there was a double garage underneath the villa. At last, after all the years of having to share one car, and all the hassle, such as in Karachi, Rosemary was now independent.

We were keen to meet Moroccans, but this wasn't easy socially. We were seldom in a Moroccan home. Moroccans would come to our Council homes, and thus we staff met a number of charming people. Most of our contacts spoke English, or had foreign wives who did.

Our first British visitor was Dr Duncan Brown, a parasitologist (Kenya and Edinburgh), who was engaged in implementing the first-class idea of setting up a joint veterinary centre for the Maghreb (Morocco, Algeria, and Tunisia), from which, among many problems, a destructive tick-borne, cattle disease could be more easily combatted – the aim being to increase the meat supply to feed the growing population. I was very pleased to be associated even in a small way with such an important Aid-assisted project. At one small party for Dr Duncan Brown there was an Indian with a Belgian wife, a Moroccan with a Dutch wife, and a Frenchman with a Finnish wife. I was relieved that they all enjoyed using their English.

546

We had splendid cooperation from British Embassy staff. Peter Williams, Head of Chancery, soon organised a welcoming party for us, and a hundred came. Two particular and very useful friends we made at that party were Michael Peyron, part-English and a university lecturer, and his wife, Losiane. He was an experienced and knowledgeable traveller, who gave us excellent advice on where to go and what to do. The choice was tremendous.

On our first venture, in November, we drove eighty miles east to Meknes. It was through a varied countryside: largely rolling uplands and river valleys, and huge, beautiful, orange orchards. Meknes was once the capital of the Alouite King, Moulay Ismail, who reigned for fifty-five years, and died in 1727. He built an imperial city on a vast scale, trying to rival Louis XIV of France, with palaces, gardens, great reservoirs, stables for 12,000 horses, mosques and mausoleums, and huge, beautiful gateways. The remains of the city are fascinating. The modern town of Meknes, across a deep ravine, thrives on its agriculture.

The Romans and the Berbers

We had time to continue our 'explorations'. Twenty-eight kilometres north of Meknes along a little road lined with olive trees with views of patchwork plains are the remains of the most pleasant little Roman town of Volubilis, of the Province of Mauretania Tingitania, of the second or third century A.D. In Rabat Museum is the magnificent bronze head of the ruler King Juba II.

Quite near Volubilis is the beautifully sited, small town of Moulay Idriss, perched on its hill. This attractive town is a shrine to the beginnings of Islam, and to Sultan Moulay Idriss, founder of the first Arab dynasty in Morocco. We then went on for an hour south-east into the Middle Atlas to the French holiday town of Ifrane.

We were now in Berber sheep-rearing country: an area of folded mountains and high, windswept plateaux, of majestic cedar forests and Barbary macaques,[1] as there are in Gibraltar, and lakes and streams with trout. There are warm, dry summers but very cold, snowy winters. It is all very beautiful. The houses and villas, and gardens and restaurants make for ideal holiday surroundings. The King has a palace here.

We went on south-west to stay in Azrou, in the strange old, wooden Hotel Panorama with the rooms created by very high, wooden partitions along a passage with an even higher ceiling. Meals are taken in a great hall. Azrou is an attractive, old and new town with well developed, local

---

[1] Read about them in the Fauna and Flora Preservation Society's *ORYX* of June 1978.

woodworking skills in cedar wood. It is on a hillside reached through lovely oak forests. One memory of Azrou is of the delicious local form of sweet doughnut called 'svinge' sold in the cafés or on the street. Before returning to Rabat we had a quick look higher up in the cedar forests as far as the attractive village and market centre of Ain Leuh.

Back to Meknes

A couple of months later Tony O'Brien and I, with Mr Hajouji, an inspector of English, returned to Meknes, and put up at the Hotel de Nice. We had lunch at the Bar-Restaurant Novelty, and drank the Moroccan Vieux Papes Rouge, and then were ready to run a meeting of teachers of English at the Lycée Moulay Ismail. Over fifty teachers came, male and female, some Moroccan, some French, and some American Peace Corps. They were all marvellously attentive on their free Friday afternoon, Islam's day of rest. We applauded their choice of teaching subject!

We were very lucky in Morocco having easy access to teachers of English through the Education Department's organisation of regular Jours Pedagogiques at which we were welcomed. There was a very efficient French civil-service element remaining in Morocco in all departments, which we respected.

22 November 1978: North and south

Luckily, work took us north and south, with Tony and Yolanda. Our aim (which we achieved) was to assess the state of English teaching and at the same time savour exciting cities. We had a pleasant break over La Fête de l'Independence on 18 November. One could do worse than 'see the East' by just visiting Tangier.

The history of Tangier is exciting to read. Because of its position and port just across the Straits of Gibraltar, Tangier has formed a link between the continents since its foundation by the Phoenicians – and was fought over from 1000 B.C. to A.D. 1860. Of course the city and port is no longer what it was in the days of its international status from 1923 to 1956. From then on its fascination was its foreign residents and their society, until they 'faded away' – alas, before our time.

After 1956 Tangier went into decline, and has been swamped by that dreadful national 'asset': tourism. Very many of the tourists would go no further inland than the main shopping streets, which certainly are colourful and tempting. Some tourists may keep to the beaches beyond, backed by the incongruous great new hotels. I hope they see the lovely remains of the old city and the great souk. We penetrated the fusty, Miss Haversham atmosphere of the Continental Hotel, fixed at a point in history like Pompeii. It has produced a brochure since we left. The Continental will now be lovely or ruined. Which has it become?

After two nights we drove south-east to Tetouan, inland on the Rif river Martil. It is a fine, old city with a handsome modern town. I quote from Kininmonth with whom I entirely agree here:

> There are mosques, cult centres and markets behind the fine old walls, a Jewish quarter (mellah) and a casbah (citadel) too. The real interest of the town lies in its sophisticated domestic architecture and the delightful colours everywhere in the old quarter. There is nothing quite like it anywhere else, neither in Morocco nor in Spain, yet it belongs to both . . .[2]

Tetouan must give one the clearest impression of old Andalus (Moslem Spain). It is a town in which to walk about at random, to take in slowly all the views, scenes, and people in attractive and unusual costumes. The Rif women are unique to Morocco with their red-and-white-striped shawls and skirts, their gaiters and wide-brimmed hats with pompoms.

We next went south to Chechaouen (or Chaouen). It is the gem of Moroccan towns, high in the Rif mountains, an amalgam of Spanish and Moroccan architecture with local inspiration. It is dominated by a mediaeval fortress, with its ruins peacefully overgrown with trees and shrubs. There are tiny, whitewashed, stone houses with coral-red, blue, amber, and umber tiles. There is a large and beautifully arcaded market-square; minute streets winding in and out and round about, sometimes with steps leading to new corners, to mosques, and tombs and sanctuaries and giving new vistas of the mountains in the clear air and bright sun. The people were sheer delight to watch, or walk among with an intimate feeling, in this tiny town. So staunch and independent were the inhabitants that the Spanish could not enter Chaouen until 1920.

On to Fes (or Fez)

We drove east along the Rif ridge to Ketama (107 kilometres in two hours), and after lunch took the spectacular minor road south via Taounate, thence a lovely descent of 160 kilometres in three and three-quarter hours.

We stayed in the New Town, and we were able to meet several admirable teachers of English and to visit their schools. This trip gave us a number

---

[2] C. Kininmonth, *Travellers' Guide, Morocco* (Jonathan Cape, London, 1974), p. 295.

of contacts in each town we reached, and smoothed the way for future instructive visits. In Fes we were in one of the most exciting cities of the world; it was still mediaeval and fascinating.

Fes was founded by Moulay Idriss II in A.D. 800 on a stream in the foothills of the Middle Atlas. It was fortified and developed over the centuries to be more or less complete by A.D. 1276. Since then Fes right up to the 1990s has hardly changed. Enter Fes and you return to the Middle Ages.

30 November 1978: In Rabat

We had good news. We had a visit from John Kirby, a senior man from the Ministry of Overseas Development. He was able to recommend the supply of aid funds to Morocco for Embassy and Council use – such as training grants, and the cost of recruitment of English teachers.

Language

Occasionally I had to speak French, as with the Director of Planning, Ministry of Education, who did not speak English. Luckily, I had the French speaking second secretary of our Embassy to help me, on the subject of British construction teams. But when high-ups did speak English I found that they enjoyed doing so – to get practice. Of course, when presenting teacher-training films to the English department of the Teacher Training College I spoke English – although the director said he felt happier in French. I could end up sadly in Arabic: "Mafish flous". (No more money!)

The next event was an official invitation to a stag evening reception for visiting heads of agricultural establishments in a number of African countries. It was a pleasure to talk with my Moroccan hosts and to several delegates, despite the continuous noise of a troupe of musicians and 'Shih-hat' dancing girls from Meknes among us all the time. Now I understood the 'stag' reception! I was particularly happy to chum up with Professor Dr Ali El-Bassel, dean of the Faculty of Agriculture, Fayyum, Egypt. He spoke perfect English. The Egyptian gentry are delightful people. There were also entertainers who acted and sang. The girls were ready for the guests to join in and dance, which only Professor Ali and I did. The rest of the party hadn't the courage, or perhaps they disapproved of us?

5 December 1978: A United Arab Emirate (U.A.E.) party

The U.A.E. party proved to be good fun, and fortunately everyone wanted to speak English, because the tendency was to speak more English than French outside the Maghreb. Senior Moroccans told me they recognised the need for English to communicate with Arab neighbours, who spoke different dialects.

The following March this need was confirmed when an Arab League seminar on the writing of textbooks for Arabic learners was held in Rabat. We were pleased that the organisers, the Arab League educational office in Tunis, invited the British Council to take part, because of our E.L.T. expertise. There was a most agreeable collection of delegates from Egypt, Jordon, Kuwait and all round, and Britain. Professor Cowan (from Haddington) of SOAS (School of Oriental and African Studies) was one delegate, and Mr Dexter from our British Council Middle East department another. I was warned that I would be put at the Chairman's table on the opening morning, and asked to make a speech. I felt it was the most anxious moment of my career. But it wasn't. I heard later that no conclusion was reached because the participants were too disparate.

Under crossed swords – a great moment

December was decreed to be Le Mois de l'Artisanat (crafts and craftsmen). We were invited to the official theme exhibition, which was to be opened by Prince Sidi Mohammed. After his arrival all the guests followed along the route to the hall which was lined by the Royal Foot Guards in their red uniforms, baggy trousers, white spats, red and white cloaks, and black leather hats. They stood with their arch of drawn sabres glittering over us in the bright lights. That was an unforgettable thrill.

A sad blow

So far in our career we had lost very little of anything in the packing or unpacking, or in transit. But this time we found a disaster in our heavy baggage. A portion of our cases, all from Karachi by sea, had become waterlogged up to a foot and a half. We could see the line, and braced ourselves. It so happened that several waterlogged cases contained at the bottom a thousand or so of our precious, very carefully taken colour-slides of Iran. They all were ruined. We had hoped to use them for talks around Britain on retirement. One value of the collection was that we had had two tours in Iran, five years apart, and two other visits when going home on leave, during which we were able to fill in gaps or take new slides of some places in better light. The whole loss was irreplaceable. We also lost clothes and linen and a few, but not precious, books. Much else was damaged by damp.

Casablanca

Our first official visit to Casablanca, at the end of 1978, was cheering. It wasn't the city we needed to see, but I had to assess the teaching of English in the government schools, and in private institutes. We were made welcome everywhere, and I was encouraged to find that all classes seemed pretty effective.

We went down one fine day to lunch with old American friends from Iran, Tom and Margaret Greene. He had been Amercian Consul in Tabriz in 1960, and was now Consul-General here. They gave us a useful view of Casablanca.

Our third and final visit to Casablanca took advantage of the holiday Fête du Throne, before getting on to the job of meeting a Council-sponsored drama duo, consisting of Gareth Armstrong and Molly Williams. We had planned their Moroccan trip some time ago. They came to Rabat, and we went to Fes with them. They stayed in Casa to perform Shakespearean extracts at the Churchill Club. Then they entertained at a dinner-party at our Consul-General's. Gareth and Molly were a conscientious and talented couple who went down well with their verse-prose programme, *Mad Dogs and Englishmen*. They had arrived from Cameroon exhausted after many performances in the bush and journeys over rough roads. Morocco actually gave them a bit of a rest! They left by air for Tunis. Such competent duos, or very small groups, can be of great value in presenting vivid and vibrant extracts from English literature, which students find exciting and comprehensible. Our young Moroccans did.

We particularly wanted to visit the city's fine sea-water aquarium; and I was able to observe my favourite intelligent and talented squid family.

December 1978

The year ended very pleasantly. First of all we received a classic film from London, *Blithe Spirit*, which gave a lot of pleasure to many. Margaret Rutherford is my favourite pin-up girl.

Christmas in Rabat

Our Christmases abroad meant a lot to us. Having been an only child with rather dull Christmases at home, I was very happy with every variety of celebration which Rosemary and our friends provided. Yet Rosemary missed her large family occasions. Luckily for us in Rabat, the Dawbarns were good enough to treat us as family, and included us in their dinner and dance. And the very sweet Noreen Maxwell, retired from U.N., living down the coast at the attractive, little village of Temara Plage, invited us to lunch on 21 December. We don't forget that.

We gave a party for the B.C. staff and families, and English teachers who remained in Rabat, including Robin and Mandy Cooper, both D.Litt. I was very touched when they later asked me to be a godfather to their first-born, Joe.

Christmas Day was a day of rest for us. In the morning we drove a few miles south-east into a valley where we walked a little way up-stream spotting birds. We wished we knew enough to identify more easily. There were pre-lunch drinks with my No. 2, and an evening party chez my director of studies. A pretty happy, satisfactory Christmas, I thought, during which we heard the beautiful carol 'Tomorrow shall be my dancing day'.

28 December 1978

At last we got off to the famed Marrakesh. Our four-hour drive was easy on the excellent Moroccan roads. The flat coastland gradually gave way to low hills as we entered the drier region, and the view became more scenic. Soon we could see the snow-covered Atlas Mountains on the sky-line. We were lucky to find a hotel room, and a very comfortable one thanks to a contact in the tourist office.

We were pleased to be able to meet the young teachers of English at the university and to give them a bit of cheer. However lovely the scene, they experienced frustrations and drawbacks which we could discuss and possibly help to solve.

The other call we made was upon Field-Marshal Auchinleck. He had retired to a spacious, first-floor flat in the Villa Rikichem in a quiet green garden suburb, on le rue Hafid Ibrahim. Living alone, he was looked after by a Moroccan driver-factotum. He finally accepted a maidservant who was needed for the cleaning. He had never had a female around when he lived in India, he said. He possessed interesting books and many enviable mementoes of his service, in pictures, rugs, and silver. He loved the climate and didn't seem to be lonely. He was taken every day to the Hotel

Renaissance café at 11 a.m., where he would read *The New York Herald Tribune*.

He was an amazing ninety-four years old, but he did not remember things from one minute to another. We learned about his life from Lance Corporal Milward from Gibaraltar, who lived in the flat above with his Moroccan wife. Milward, who volunteered for the post of guardian to our hero, was an ideal person for our Ministry of Defence to find. The Field-Marshal did not realize this. He believed that Milward was our army liaison for the Service expeditions regularly run in the High Atlas, and this was true. These expeditions had various objectives covering ecology, topography, travel and weather conditions and ornithology. I am fortunate to have a copy of the 1979 expedition's bird-list.

Of course, the poor Field-Marshal had difficulty in making out who we were. But we knew he was most happy talking about India; and we had come from Karachi, and with greetings from many officers who remembered him with affection. I think he understood that my father and he knew each other, and that I had served in his Desert Army, of which I was very proud. I had known then how good the 'Auk' was, but he had been remote from my tank troop. Then I couldn't have known all that I have since learned about his admirable handling of so many different army commands, and what he had to face on taking over the Eighth Army, and also how he was later treated by Churchill and Montgomery. The dear, old Auk died in Marrakesh in 1981. Now, many of the valuable treasures which he had out in his room, would no longer be seen.

We returned to Rabat along the edge of the Atlas Mountains on the Fez road as far as Beni Mellal through a lovely agricultural region with vast olive-groves. We were very pleased with our Renault 12, which gave no trouble throughout our stay in Morocco, except a broken fan-belt in Rabat.

The New Year began well in the oldest part of Rabat. We explored the Kasbah (or Casbah) of the Oudaias, the citadel of one of the early Arab tribes that settled on the promontory on the south bank of the estuary of the Bou (River) Regreg. This area remains the most memorable of all our visits to old Morocco.

One resident of the Kasbah whom we came to know was Dr Kenneth Sinclair-Loutit, ex-U.N. He had a fund of information to give us on Morocco. He introduced us later that year to his house-guest, the Conservative M.P. for Beauly. It was Colonel Billy McLean, who had been at pre-prep school with me, whom I had last met in Ethiopia. We had a great natter one evening about Iran and Pakistan. Billy is one of those mysterious birds whose career took him to 'romantic' places such as Kashgar, for which we, particularly Rosemary, envied him.

From the top of the main street in the Oudaias one has a fine view of the open sea from the ramparts. Many Rabatis stroll here, watched by the comic storks from their nests high up on the walls. The storks are regarded with affection, wherever they choose to build their very untidy nests, even on top of minarets. I was very interested in two beautifully preserved cannon in the Oudaias, trained to cover the river mouth. The Curator of Artillery from the Tower of London Armouries gave me a detailed reply to my query as to their provenance, illustrative of the best of British scholarship, interest, and courtesy. His letter gave me an opening to speak of this British quality, while in Morocco.

And here are the parts of a cannon:

THE PARTS OF A GUN

From the Catalogue of Ordnance. HMSO, Vol. 1, 1976, by kind permission and assistance from the Curator of Artillery, Royal Armouries.

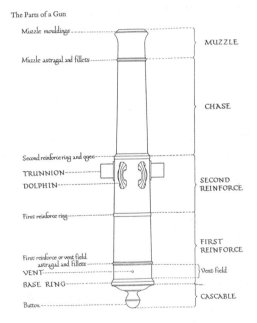

The Parts of a Gun

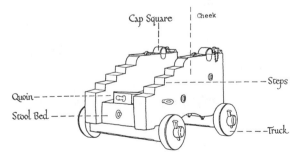

January 1979: libraries

The British Council's libraries around the world are a very important element of our work and it was a pleasure to have a visit from our regional librarian, Geoffrey Glaister, whom we shared with Algeria and Tunisia. He was a man of considerable knowledge and experience. He has, alas, died. We got on especially well as he had spent some years in Karachi, as librarian, and he had been an Eighth Army soldier. He is now famous as a 'mere' R.A.S.C. clerk, whose letter to Field-Marshal Montgomery is published in the Field-Marshall's memoirs.

In my book *Shots in the Sand* I described how we front-line troops suffered from complete lack of information as to how the desert war was being fought. Monty immediately saw this great weakness, regarding it as an enemy of morale and he put it right. Geoffrey Glaister wrote to thank him for his letter to the troops, and how much it and Monty meant to them.

We took Geoffrey up the coast and walked on top of high cliffs above great Atlantic breakers until we reached the Casbah de Mehdiya. This is a fine, old fort with guns still in place guarding the mouth of the river Sebou. It had been built by the Spanish after 1614, later taken by the renowned Moulay Ismail of Meknes. We marvelled at its original architectural strength after learning that the Americans had knocked it about a bit when they landed there in 1942, as part of TORCH.

English language

We had a boost to our morale from a visit by Peter Strevens, a renowned English-language and language-teaching expert from Cambridge whom we had first met in Tehran in 1960. Peter was mostly with Tony O'Brien and some of our adult students, and with the French/Moroccan E.L.T. staffs. H.E. and Shelby Dawbarn came to our buffet dinner for thirty English, French, and Moroccan English-language teachers, and were such good value at this worthwhile occasion. The Dawbarns said they enjoyed the chance of meeting people outside their normal circle,, who were important to the British effort.

Most local high-ups I met were pleased to practise their English, and I tried to give them a chance in order to hide my inadequate French. An Italian diplomat said to me: "Oh I prefer to speak English. I have come from Cairo. There one might start in French, but conversations usually continue in English."

Morocco

February 1979

Now came our chance to visit Salé (once Sala Colonia) across the river. At the time of Idriss I (late eighth century) the inhabitants were forced to flee from cruel, forced conversions to the new religion of Islam. They re-established themselves across the river on a better defended site which they called Sala. On the same site the Almohad Sultans of the eleventh and twelfth centuries built Salé, a city fortified by massive walls that still exist. The city became a thriving port and of greater economic importance than Rabat. A large number of mosques and medersas (theological colleges) were built as well as the trading markets, quays, and warehouses. The prosperity of Salé at this time was based on the export of goods from all over the country: skins, fabrics, carpets, spices, etc.; and ships bearing English, Italian, and Flemish merchants came into the port to receive the goods. The inevitable result was pirates – of all nationalities. Indeed, Salé became infamous for its pirates, and what a history they gave rise to! It is worth reading Kininmonth on the Corsairs of the Barbary Coast, the Sallee (or Sally) Rovers, as the English called them by tradition and in literature. The Rovers penetrated north to the English Channel and west as far as the Caribbean.

> They were the world's outcasts with nothing but their lives to lose, a desperate condition that rendered them almost invincible.[3]

Our introduction to Salé was at a curious, annual ceremony conducted by the boatmen in honour of their ancient Saint Abdullah, who was akin to our Saint Christopher. Thanks to Shelby Dawbarn we watched a procession of ancient mariners in costumes of some centuries back, carrying banners, candle lanterns, and painted, wooden emblems, encouraged along by a local band playing reed trumpets (rather like the Indian shenai) and percussion of tambourines and drums.

Entering Salé through the great water-gate, one notices its remarkable height which was to allow the Rovers' tall ships' masts to pass through into safety, after being chased in by European warships exasperated by the piracy. Salé is a blue-and-white town. The shadows are blue and the paint on the doors and windows is blue. The walls are of intense, blinding white. The whole is best seen from the roof of the famous Medersa.

---

[3] Kininmonth, p. 174.

Off to the Middle Atlas

In early February there was the Muslim Feast of Miloud, so we could get away to the hills and forests to the south-east. We went to Immouzer. We followed a sign to Chalet du Lac, Dayet (lake) Aoua, where we found accomodation. We were well heated and well fed, and found ourselves in the middle of a French hunting and fishing centre.

Our route home was through the cedar forests; the roads were rougher and took up precious time. However, we were very excited to see several Barbary macaques while Rosemary was collecting moss and lichen.

Useful films

The Films department gave us *Far from the Madding Crowd* which made a pleasant diversion for invited guests, as well as being specially useful for English literature students. We then received Wilfred Thesiger's *The Empty Quarter*, which was just right for a dinner showing which we laid on for eighteen special guests, British, French, American, Italian and Moroccan. The guests enjoyed both films, and especially Rosemary's steak and kidney pie.

February 1979: An English club

The English Club was formed by teachers of English. I hope it still exists – at El Jadida down the coast 195 kilometres, and two and a half hours beyond Casablanca. El Jadida (jadid means new in Persian and Arabic) was a perfect small previously fortified Portuguese sea-port, with a sea-moat all round, and a tasteful little modern town outside the walls. We found a fascinating fish market, where Rosemary obtained loup de mer, which we enjoy eating. It was a pleasure to meet all the members of the club and talk English, and to present them with a collection of English language and literature books as a nucleus for a small library. Just outside El Jadida lies the ancient, miniature fishing-port of Azzemour founded by the Carthaginians in the fourth century B.C.

Othello in Fes

I was asked over to Fes University as a special guest at a first performance of *Othello* in English, staged by a young English lecturer with an entirely Moroccan cast. It was a very good effort. Then I joined Tony and Yolanda at an evening with French teachers of English at the home of one of them. It was a kind gesture, and encouraging for us, since the teachers had asked for such contact.

Fes again

We were soon back again in Fes with a specialist visitor, John Heath-Stubbs, the poet and writer, to whom we much enjoyed listening. Here and in Rabat he lectured to students every day for a week, and they thought he was very good value. Unfortunately, we could never get him to ourselves at home. But he was a fine excuse for a party in a Fes hotel for the staff of the University's English department. James Glaze, Head of Chancery, joined in – with the funding – so as to include any British residents who cared to come too, and whom James might not know.

Friends to visit us

Very few friends or relatives had managed to visit us as we had always been so far away, but Morocco was the exception. David Walters, Sub-mariner, Capt. R.N. Retd., and his second wife, our Elizabeth Beazley of Isfahan days who wrote *Living with the Desert*, joined us for our local leave in April. We had to take local leave in each country, so as not to get stale, but also to become more familiar with the country. So we went off with the Walters on a 2000-kilometre tour over the Atlas by the Tiz n'Tichka Pass.

We returned to Azrou in the Middle Atlas via the Tizi-n-Talent Pass, where we stayed for three days for David to fish. To our consternation, David one day was stopped by a river bailiff and his rod impounded for not having a fishing licence. This had not been mentioned or printed in any pamphlet during Rosemary's prior research. It was Rosemary's spirit and command of French which got everything sorted out amicably by the Chief Conservator in Azrou.

Easter 1979: Ourgane

For our Easter holiday trip and a peaceful break for Rosemary, we drove to the great Tiz n'Test Pass in the High Atlas, as far as Ourgane, a caravanserai settlement. Our 'pull Inn' was the well-known, French-run hostelry called 'Le Sanglier qui Fume'. An added pleasure was the company of the Dawbarns and their young son, Nat. We had cheerful drives and walks, and chatter, good local eats and drinks, and for the Halsteds, lots of sleeps.

It was a relief sometimes, after rest-house travel in Pakistan, to end the Moroccan day in a well-run, small, country hotel, and drink a good glass of local wine. But, despite the basic provisions, it is the atmosphere and ambience of Pakistani rest-houses in ancient historic towns or settlements, which are remembered with the most nostalgic affection.

An added bonus was our memorable trip to the twelfth-century mosque at Tinmal, reached on foot from the main road since flood waters had destroyed the bridge on the approach road. There was little left of the bridge, but Rosemary unhesitatingly led the way over some remaining sloping girders, to the admiration of the young 'official' guide from the village, and an old man in his djellabah posing as a guide. It was well worth a visit, being so special and remote.[4]

April 1979

The first ten days were happily filled, first in Rabat by being invited to two concerts: an Italian trio with food and drink, and a French piano recital by Roland Proell. Of permanent interest to us was receiving the B.C. film *The Sounds of Islam*. We now have it on tape, an excellent reminder of that other world.

We showed *The Sounds of Islam* to the Ecole Normale Superieure. The British interest in Moroccan culture impressed the staff and pupils. For the last two days of the Easter break Rosemary and I got away to Fez and Sefrou on our own. We had a lovely time moving gently around the great bazaar area, and the mosques and medersas. We loved the souks or medinas, the old towns, of Morocco. There was so much going on, and such a marvellous variety of people, occupations, trades, and animals, and beautifully tiled fountains cum waterpoints. We even found a stall-holder who was a faithful supporter of Leeds United. Unfortunately, we had not got the Arabic as we had the Persian, but French and English would do in the shops. This time we bought some examples of local pottery. One would find unusual shapes and patterns that were nicely restrained. The crafts received government support, which helped to raise the standard of workmanship.

[4] See Kininmonth, p. 332.

May 1979

A very satisfactory official visitor and already a friend was Dr Duncan Brown, who had come in October the previous year and was now following up the veterinary centre project.

The Council film, *A Man for all Seasons*, proved excellent for home and university student study and entertainment. Our next effort was our own walking play-reading of Alan Bennett's *Habeas Corpus*. As elsewhere, I found this method of putting over some English literature and entertainment works extremely well. As long as there is live action, and costume and staging when possible, audiences will accept discreetly held parts, which our amateur actors simply didn't have time to learn.

June 1979: Rabat

We were lucky to get a glimpse 'behind the scenes' in Oudaias from an invitation by Countess Belleville, widow of a French engineer, to her fascinating old house. It had been perfectly restored and extended, and was full of carpets and valuable objets d'art, lovely wood-work, tasteful soft-furnishings, and all skilfully combined. The international conversation among the guests was informative! It says a great deal for the Moroccans allowing such an establishment among the native, white-washed houses that were sketchily plumbed and unheated.

An evening chez nous

Seven mixed couples, selected with care, fitted in well. We had steak and kidney pie again, which suited me. The guests stayed until after midnight. Official dinners were accountable to the audit department, and items had to be substantiated by bills. This accounting was an awful bore for the housewife, but essential because it involved public funds.

The garden

Rosemary wrote home: "I spend quite a lot of time on the garden as Miloud isn't a proper gardener, and he can only manage to keep the whole area tidy and watered, but the water is quickly lost in the light, sandy soil. There are lots of delays and disasters with my seedlings. The garden hadn't many perennial plants except geraniums, which flourish here, so I have been begging cuttings from friends, and nicking bits from hotel and public gardens. Everything seems to take root easily here, really an easy place to garden."

"Just now all the residential streets are at their best with hedges of pale-blue plumbago, red hibiscus or purple bougainvillea in full flower, and jacarandas in clouds of mauve above."

Contacts

As Rosemary recorded: "Slowly, slowly, we get to know more people. The Ambassador's wife (Shelby Dawbarn) kindly had a ladies' tea party for me to meet some senior foreign ministry and other wives. One guest was the Director of archaeology and curator of the museum, and I hope to see more of her as she needs English practice." Tony was running a one month's English-language course, for which Rosemary did her best to recruit. The director of archaeology was a very welcome contact for us.

Visit to Tunis

The Council kindly let me pay a visit to my colleague, John Lancaster, Representative Tunisia, and his Spanish wife, the delightful Anna. She was the result of an early posting to Barcelona. It was very useful for me to learn how things were going for the British Council in another Maghreb country. I was intrigued because Tunisia has been 'civilised' for a very long time. This is reflected in the people and their behaviour, and the obviously age-old mixture of races which one can discern in their features.

The British Council No. 2, Paul Howson, who had been in Islamabad when I was in charge in 1974, took me off John Lancaster's hands, and gave me an excellent conducted tour.

I met Dr Rais, the dean of English, at lunch one day at the restaurant Chez Slah; he was a charming, sophisticated Tunisian. I was surprised to hear bricks being ordered, but Brik de l'Oeuf is delicious. I was taken to the Phoenician/Punic town of Utica, to Bizerta, and to various war cemeteries including Massicault where I found the grave of Lt. W. A. Sandys-Clare, V.C. of my father's regiment, the Loyals (North Lancashire).

Then over by ferry to Cap Blanc, the most northerly tip of Africa, we visited the beautiful village of Sidi Bou Said and the Roman town of Thuburbo Majus, which began in 27 B.C. as a colony of veterans.

I had to see Carthage, but it had been well and truly 'delenda' by the Romans. I admire the Romans, but not their destruction of such an advanced civilization. Imagine, there is a Hotel Dido! However, my admiration for the Romans returned on seeing the most marvellous

562

collection of Roman mosaics in the Bardo in Tunis.

The month of June continued cheerfully. The Queen's Birthday Party was particularly pleasant, being held in the charming Residence garden, though late stayers were not eased out until 10 p.m. while the Bishop of Gibraltar waited patiently for his supper. Not many Moroccans on H.E.'s list or mine came, but the young teachers and other British lecturers and English girls married to Moroccans all enjoyed themselves. It was good to meet British residents from outside Rabat, such as Miss Dykes, working for the Save the Children Fund at Khemisset (on the way to Meknes); she was given the M.B.E. in the Birthday Honours.

Anyone for tennis?

Yes, we had a tennis tournament at the British Council Language Centre. Tony, who was a very good player, won with his charming student partner Mrs Ourgacem. Mrs Lahlou, wife of a ministry of education official, was unfortunate enough to partner me, and we lost in the first round. We had great playing support by the Dawbarns and James Glaze.

Sometime later we had the Ourgacems and the Lahlous to a party, and so met their other halves. We decided after supper to introduce them to Scrabble, and to be fair to the players, English, French, and Arabic words were allowed. It worked!

The month ended with the Cambridge Examinations in English. We had over a hundred entries, and some of the office staff were needed to help out. My Emilina administered very efficiently; Rosemary invigilated; and I conducted oral comprehension tests.

Phosphate exports

To see if I could help to spread our language efforts further, Driss drove me some two hundred kilometres south-west to Khouribga, the centre of the largest phosphate-mining area in Africa. It is the main source of wealth for Morocco after overseas workers' remittances. But, alas, they only needed occasional translations from English of instruction books of English equipment. Why weren't they supplied in French by our firms? This was typical, and I reported it.

Social life

The social side of our British Council life went on and on – purposefully. The Goethe Institut gave a party for a town-planning seminar. The Murrays (Gretel, our librarian) had us to supper in their attractive, but cold, little house deep in the Oudaias. The Herbert Evanses, B.C. contract teachers, had us to an English teachers' supper. The Canadians had us to their National Day: and the O'Briens gave a party for Tony's senior English proficiency class.

July 1979

I got home for a spell to see my specialist, and as it turned out, to see Papa for the last time. He was in good form, in his ninetieth year. I am heartened by reading the obituaries of many fine old soldiers, who all seem to have been unexpectedly long-lived – often into their ninetieth year, like Papa. Why? Papa said we were not to come home if anything should happen to him. Very good of him. His attitude to life and death, gave rise to the following verses composed between us:

Ill-Advised
Son: You are ill, father dear
His son Michael said.
It is clear to us all
That you should be in bed.
Father: Rubbish, young fellow,
The general replied.
Strode into the garden
Fell over and died.

I was so glad his was a sudden death, and not after being bed-ridden or suffering from some terrible disease. We were at the Hotel Panorama in Azrou in May the following year and there was a telephone call for me from the Embassy in Rabat. Rosemary took it, and as she came to tell me, I knew what it must be. I was kindly given permission to fly home.

4 July: U.S. Independence Day

In many countries in which Americans were so good as to invite us to their Independence Day occasion they unwittingly gave me a free pre-birthday party! Very kind of them! I would first thank the ambassador, or whoever the host was, for my birthday party, and he would be taken aback until I explained.

An earthquake

During the day we suddenly heard a very loud noise, like lorries arriving. Could it be an army coup? No, it was an earthquake. It shook the house, but it was only for five seconds, and caused no damage in Rabat or elsewhere. We were lucky to escape any earthquake damage or disaster in the countries we were in.

August 1979

The Pakistani Ambassador, whom we liked very much, gave a party with good friends of ours and the Rumanian Ambassador and his wife; all had excellent English (shaming really) and were very jolly. Our host was a find!

The Dutch Head of Chancery gave a party for a professional musician friend willing to give an impromptu piano recital, which was all too rare an occasion. Then an American military attaché invited us round to dinner. One of the guests was a retired German military attaché, once of the German 28th Infantry Brigade that was poised at Le Havre to take Brighton. What would have happened to us in Britain if the Germans had won?

The Dawbarns invited us to a small dinner for our new friend, the Pakistani Ambassador. He was a former civil servant, and was very interesting on the old days of the British Raj. Rosemary and I kept him talking. Simon didn't know India, and told Rosemary that all this reminiscing was pathetic!

24 August 1979

Ramadan was over. It was Eid el Seghir. The new moon was sighted at 0130 hours on 23 August. On the following night the Moroccan tradition took place, of staying up all night with candles and reading the Koran right through.

Administration

I discovered in Rabat, to my surprise, that new young British teachers didn't understand the need for an office. It was even suggested that I should be doing the work of the British Council, and not wasting time and money sitting in an office! They were not aware of office practice, or of the work of an executive or secretary. I think I understand what we look like to the outsider, but without administration there would be chaos. The Duke of Wellington insisted on good administration, which he said was essential to victory. His officers came to understand his point.

I wrote a paper describing how an idea or a project starts, and must be recorded, and new information also recorded under the same subject and added, and retrieved for discussion and action. Of course I may be wrong after the electronic progress of the last ten years, but the principles remain the same don't they? Efficiency, and the saving of frustration, time and money depends on retrieval – even when writing a book. I look forward to visiting an up-to-date British Council office.

Birds

We had no Tom Roberts as in Sind, but his tutelage helped. For instance we had two tawny owls in our garden. From the house we often heard a hoopoe, but never saw one; its cry 'hoo-hoo-hoo' is very far-carrying. The sound we liked best to hear was the delightful trilluping call of the bee-eaters, such as a little flock passing by. They are charmingly coloured and shaped.

September 1979: Family visitors

We were happy to be visited by two nieces who were at university: Christina at Edinburgh and Bertha at York. They were fun and no trouble and with them we made our first trip to the Spanish-held port of Ceuta, or Sebta. It was a little town crowded with Spaniards who were busy shopping due to the wider variety of goods available here than in mainland Spain; and the prices of food and drink were worth the effort. After a scrimmage we obtained tins of Walls sausages that were unobtainable in Rabat. From a high-vantage picnic spot above the town we could see Gibraltar.

Morocco

Moussems: Good for entertaining relatives!

September was the best period of the year for moussems – festivals held all over the country in honour of a saint or marabout (a teacher who is profoundly venerated and has a cult following). The name marabout, or koubba, is given to the saint's actual tomb building. At a moussem pilgrims gather round the shrine of their saint. Notables set up their tents to receive visitors, and also for deliberations on many matters such as local or national politics or the arrangement of marriages. There is the atmosphere of a fair, maybe with dancers and musicians.

A moussem will also attract people from the neighbourhood who have no connection with the saint, bringing food and goods to sell, and sometimes there are entertainers too. One can feel a religious atmosphere. They were exciting times for us because moussems, as with Moroccan national occasions, must have a *fantasia*. This is a charge in line by a group of horsemen brandishing arms which they discharge in the air in unison before coming to a spectacular halt before the notables' tents. We had no idea who each group was, but we knew that each performance would be critically judged. We seemed to have seen the same riders, charging and firing again and again. No matter, we had excellent, free excitement.

It was fun to go to an assembly of men and horses, both at the start of the fantasia and at the finish. Here we could see at close quarters the beautiful horses, which exist all over the country, and their richly decorated, colourful bridles and caparisons. The riders too were elegantly dressed, and at one with the horses. I was amused to see the feverish activities of the muzzle loaders of the muskets for the riders between each charge.

Islam

We judged this a good time to show the Council set of six films entitled 'The Traditional World of Islam' comprising:

Part 1. **Unity**. The overall spiritual cohesion of the Islamic world.
Part 2. **Nomad and the City**. It included scenes in Marrakesh, Fes, and Sanaa in the Yemen.
Part 3. **Man and Nature**. The Muslim's belief that man must never be in conflict with nature, but rather be as a partner or traveller passing through it.
Part 4. **The Pattern of Beauty**. Attempts to show some of the incredible richness and diversity of the Islamic arts as seen through the disciplines of architecture and abstract decoration.

Part 5. **Knowledge of the World**. The film demonstrates that many of the ideas and institutions now taken for granted came to Europe from Islam.

Part 6. **The Inner Life**. The film illustrates the way of life of the Sufis, and how some of Islam's finest musicians, architects and scientists have been Sufis or strongly influenced by Sufism.

We and our mixed audiences from East and West were impressed and grateful.

Scholars and fellows

Scholars are graduates funded by the British Council for Higher Studies. Fellows are professionals funded for association with a British body. The selection, advice, and despatch from our end of Scholars and Fellows, and the placing and welfare by our London office was a very satisfying part of our work. We gave a dinner for some Moroccans about to leave for the British academic year 1979/80. It was a cheerful occasion. Several wives came too. Our satisfaction was reinforced when we get letters such as this one:

> Mr Hassan Abou Abdelkader,
> Teacher of English,
> Lycée Omar Ibn El Khattab, Meknes
> 24th September 1979

Dear Mr A. J. O'Brien,
Dear Mr Michael Halsted,

I am writing to you to give you my impressions of the course I had in Leeds this summer, on the one hand, and to thank all of you who've offered me that gift of which I'll be grateful to you all my life. I'd have you thank all members of the British Council in Leeds for their efforts to make all of us comfortable.

In brief, the course was superb, the staff lovely and the atmosphere warm and friendly. I really fail to convey my feelings about it. I enjoyed it very much, and I "hope" that I've left a good record there.

I'll be glad to hear from you.

Yours sincerely and gratefully,
Hassan

568

October 1979

In the evening in Fes we were joined for dinner by eight young British E.L.T. staff at the adequate Restaurant des Voyageurs. Next day 'Aunt Rosemary' showed Fes to niece Alison and friend Joanna, who had joined us from Marrakesh. We were not usually bothered by local lads wanting to show us everything and take us to friends' shops. It was partly because we felt familiar and behaved so, but Rosemary's personality and purposeful progress helped a lot. Knowing the way is the secret. To hesitate causes hassle! Here and in other markets Rosemary found that carrying (and using) a shopping bag showed that one lived locally. Back in Rabat after a very wet and thereby a rather dangerous drive, Miloud awaited us with a warm house and whisky. What comfort – and more kindness. A friend who had heard about the girls' plans took them to Nouassar Airport (Casablanca) since he was also flying home – a typically kind, expatriate reaction.

19 October 1979: A delightful non-Council surprise

This materialized in the form of Anthony Rooley, lute-player, and Emma Kirkby, singer, both with international reputations. They were not officially sponsored by the British Council, but we were asked to help them all we could – nothing loth! They began by giving a recital in Rabat University's amphitheatre, Ed Idrissi. Luckily, niece Bertha, a musician and singer, had been around earlier when I was doing my reconnaissance and, after testing the venue with music and song, said that the acoustics were good. I was very relieved. An encouragingly large audience appeared (always my worry on such occasions), but there was not much reaction.

The next day we took them to Fes. I wanted Anthony and Emma to perform specially in Fes, an ancient cultural centre. I could not launch out into hiring a big hall, but fortunately the director of the French Cultural Centre was pleased with my suggestion of a joint effort, and Anthony's thesis appealed to him. The essence of this is that Europe in the Dark Ages only had rudimentary percussion and horn in addition to the harp. That is until other musical instruments reached Europe from the eighth and ninth centuries via Arab influences in the Iberian peninsular. By A.D. 1200 we in Europe had plucked and bowed strings, reed wind, whistle wind, and elaborate percussion. Anthony felt that he was bringing back the lute to its birthplace.

The venue was ideal. The Centre was in a beautiful, traditional, Moroccan-style house in the old city; a suitable ambience for such music. But, alas, the duo received no greater enthusiastic reception in Fes, not even from the well-known local musicians who were invited and fully briefed. They and many others received free copies of a beautifully printed and illustrated programme in English and Arabic, containing Anthony's scholarly thesis.

More catastrophic was what befell one of Anthony's precious lutes. In the afternoon we went into the souk to find a carpet for Emma. We succeeded, and took it back to the car, which was now in the shade. We opened the boot, and then the lute case. There was a terrific crack, and the lute sprang apart in a jangle of strings. The authentic glue hadn't withstood the heat. Anthony was very good about it: he said he would manage with alternative programmes for his other instruments until he got home.

To the Sahara

In response to my letters to Roger Rigby, my original Karachi friend of 1949, he and his wife Patricia wanted to explore Morocco. With them we set off in two cars over the High Atlas for Erfoud and the Hotel du Sud. We were not far from the Roman camp of Sigillum Massae (Sigilmassa).

The market square in Rissani was the furthest south we could go by car. Its size was an indication that here was an important souk of the Middle Ages, on the camel route between Fes and the sub-Saharan region. It was also the departure point for pilgrims crossing the desert on camels to visit Arabia. From here the twelfth-century rulers sent troops to the Niger. Rissani certainly had a new atmosphere for us, with men from different desert tribes in their flowing white robes and turbans bringing their wares to sell.

Returning to Erfoud we spent a very happy time looking into the whole process of date cultivation and harvest in the most picturesque surroundings and villages with very unusual and interesting mud architecture, and wonderful old men. Our way home was up the valley of the Ziz again – a truly memorable route. Up in the Middle Atlas we ate our lunch in wind and rain in the Col du Ziz. Then we travelled on through Midelt.

Over to Andalusia (Al Andalus)

Spain was not exactly 'local leave' in my country of posting, but visiting Moorish Spain would give us a wider grasp of Islamic art – and was my reason for asking to be posted to Morocco. Al Andalus was the Muslim name for all the territory of Spain brought under the control of Islam. It was exciting for us to cross over from Tangier to Algeciras in the steps of the Moorish conquerors who first arrived in A.D. 711. By starting in Morocco we were better able to appreciate the wonderful flowering of

Islamic artistry in Spain. It was a brilliant civilisation.

We drove along the south coast to Granada, the most brilliant under the Nasrids (circa A.D. 1232). The architectural style of the Nasrids, who were the last comers, was highly sophisticated, but not innovative. Its glory was in the ornament and decoration. The Nasrids lasted until 1492 when the Catholic King Ferdinand and his Queen Isabella finally took the last stronghold in the struggle, which was Granada.

We drove on to Cordoba, north-west via the lovely little town of Alcala La Real, with the Fort of Ben Said El Maghrebi, 1213–14. Of the three major cities we visited, Cordoba on the river Guadalquivir we found the most attractive with the strongest atmosphere of its great past. It became the capital of two civilisations.

We were overcome by the great Mosque of Abdu'r Rahman I (756–788), enlarged by successive rulers until Al Mansur in the tenth century nearly doubled its size. The gleaming, gold mihrab (niche in the quibla, or wall facing Mecca) and triple maksourah (enclosure reserved for the caliph) is breath-taking and unforgettable – such exquisite work, done by order of Caliph El Hakam II in A.D. 961.

With a car we were easily able to reach the Medina Azahara outside the city. This palace complex, begun by Abdu'r Rahman III in 936, was named after his favourite, but it was sacked by the Berbers in 1013 resulting in a terrible loss to civilisation and Islam. The palace was more of a township extending upwards in three tiers overlooking the river. It was in the process of being restored as far as possible.

We journeyed on to Seville, via Ecija founded by the Greeks, and Carmona on its hill with ancient walls, a Roman necropolis, and the double, Moorish arch of the Seville Gate.

Seville

Seville, also on the Guadalquivir, was reclaimed from the Moors on 19 November 1248 by King Fuad III of Castile, and therefore it was Christian at the time the Nasrids were building in Granada. But appreciation and pleasure in Arabic design remained in the minds of the rulers and nobles. Seville has lovely examples of what is known as the Mudejar (Moorish) style of architecture and design: Muslim work executed under the Christians according to their own traditions and techniques. These traditions under the Seville Almohads of the twelfth and thirteenth centuries are characterised by brick construction, with wide bands of decoration in relief. The finest example is Seville's Giralda Tower, 322-ft high, once a minaret. The Almohads were a dynasty of strict religious beliefs, so that their ornament was perfectly controlled and delicate, with no ostentation

571

but utter simplicity. It was most interesting to compare the Giralda with the twelfth-century Koutoubia minaret in Marrakesh, and the Tour Hassan in Rabat. All this was a special kind of pleasure for us in Seville.

We drove home via Jerez de la Frontera, by-passing Cadiz, but stopping at the lovely mediaeval town of Tarifa on the most southerly point of Spain, with the coast of Africa less than eight and a half miles away. There was very pleasant rolling wooded country on the road round to Algeciras in the bay opposite Gibraltar. The name Gibraltar comes from Jebel-el-Tarik, the mountain (jebel) seized by Tarik-ibn-Zeyed in A.D. 711, the date on which the Moors arrived in Andalusia.

It was rough on the crossing to Ceuta, so we kept our lunch to eat on the quay. We returned to Rabat via Tetuan and Larache.

17 November 1979: back to work in Fes

Soon after our return from Spain we went to Fes with Tony and one or two other staff, having arranged a meeting of teachers of English in the local high-school, Ecole Normale Superieure, taking them an exhibition of English-language teaching books, and showing them what we thought was a good (B.B.C. television) film of *Macbeth*. This was all great fun. Rosemary and I (yes, I'm afraid she was pressed into service once more) have had pretty good practice in putting up book exhibitions. One reward for us all was dinner in the medina house of Jacques Tual, the head-teacher.

Birds

A feature of Fes and Rabat and elsewhere were the swifts. They are the most aerobatic and competent flyers (the most aerial says our standby, Collins, *The Birds of Britain and Europe*). Their narrow, scythe-like wings, and short, forked tail are ideal for very fast flight. Our Moroccan bird is the plain swift (*apus*) which "has vigorous dashing flight. Wheeling excited squealing parties chase each other round the houses in towns and villages". They certainly do.

The swifts nest in holes or crevices in cliffs, and in Fes large numbers seem to be attracted to the great, crumbling and creviced walls of the medina. I loved to watch them and I marvel at their skill and life-style. Once on the Usk, a swift actually caught one of Papa's flies in the air as he cast. There was a to-do until it could be released. He was surprised at the lice it bore.

In November on a sunny and warm Sunday we went down to the sea at

Temara where we enjoyed watching little egrets, ringed plover, and knot along the shore, and the general, green shore- scene.

A social week

The Gattis, an Italian doctor and his Belgian wife who was a friend of Rosemary's, gave a dinner including a French medical couple and a Moroccan Frenchman and his Canadian wife. We don't have such sparkle at home! Nor the international flavour which our cultural lunches gave us, such as we had enjoyed in Karachi. Rosemary was allowed to host this one which, as a woman, she hadn't been allowed to do in Karachi. The guests were Spanish, German, Austrian, American, French, Italian, and Neville Townsend as a British re-inforcement. This camaraderie is very cheering, and good value for discussing our programmes and ideas.

Then the Swedish Ambassador included us at a buffet dinner with a variety of senior guests including Moroccans at chief secretary level. It was not exactly fun but was very useful. Many subjects were covered, French and Arabic flew around fast, with very little utterance by us. But when the subject of tourism came up after population, agriculture, and crime, we were able to mention the need to curb the very off-putting attitudes and actions towards tourists, causing possible financial loss to Morocco. We hope tourists fare better today.

December 1979: A trip to Taza

Rosemary and I had an interesting week starting with a trip to Taza, via Fes. Taza is a town of strategic importance in a gap in the mountains on the east-west route from Algeria. It had last been a French garrison town. We went with the O'Briens to meet teachers of English at another Jour Pedagogique, to talk to them about English-teaching techniques and to show an exhibition of English language teaching books (to bring them up-to-date), and to show films about teaching techniques and documentaries. Rosemary was very useful as usual, helping to put up and take down the exhibition and talking with the Moroccan teachers, and to American Peace Corps on the same job.

We then returned to Fes, and repeated the E.L.T. exhibition, and showed certain films for the English department of the University. In this department, as well as the British-born teachers on contract, there were a number of French, Americans, and Moroccans teaching English to some 2,000 Moroccan students.

573

A good 'Spec-Vis!'

These specialists are so cheering for us, and such good value for 'our' country, Morocco. The Moroccan and French mathematicians invited Professor Graham Vincent-Smith of Oriel College, Oxford, who was cheerful and friendly. We couldn't hope to understand why he had come. He appeared to be the last word on triangles, I think. We enjoyed a dinner put on for him by Mr Hamid Quessons, head of the mathematics department at the Univerisity, and his paediatrician, Tunisian wife.

Of course we gave a 'mathematical dinner'; and Professor Vincent-Smith had next day off. When we had pressed him earlier as to what he would like to do, he diffidently said that he would really like to go to the Roman town of Volubilis. We were very happy to take him, and Louise Phillips, H.E.'s P.A. too. What a pleasure and reward it was to have such diversions and peaceful talks with our eminent visitors whom we would never otherwise meet. We were lucky.

The weather was clear and sunny, and we had an idyllic picnic lunch in an olive grove (they are such attractive and sympathetic trees). We retired to Meknes for the night, and took them both round the old city next morning. Then we had another scenic picnic among olives on a hillside above a very English-looking valley, and then back to Rabat for tea and scones.

20 – 30 December 1979: Our last British Council Christmas.

Rosemary gave a Christmas Dinner on 20 December and planned for thirty-three guests, including the Dawbarns, the office staff, E.L.T. and Faculty staffs, and 'odds' such as Jenny and Camilla, British girls with adventure and expertise who were hired to manage the Prince's horses! But Rosemary had to cope with fifty-one guests. It was really great, except that I got two fingers of my left hand bent back at pat-balloon. They took years to recover.

On 22 December we got away down to El Jadida again. Before a good seafood lunch I popped through the walls to take a picture I had missed previously, and was assailed by a tiresome schoolboy who was determined to show me round. When it got through to him that I was not a stranger, and had nothing for him, he took off a shoe and threw it at me! I could have shopped him but . . .

We went on down the coast to Essaouira, the Mogador of the Portuguese, a really lovely sparkling fishing port, small but with everything: a fortress and ramparts lined with fine cannon of the 1780s; a medina and fishing harbour; white blue-doored houses in narrow winding streets; good food and adequate accommodation.

Next day we headed further south still: directly east at Ait Melloul to that fine old walled city of Taroudant, once the capital of Morocco until the Saadians (1554–1659) moved to Marrakesh.

Taroudant is a beautiful place in which to rest. There are no sights, but the whole atmosphere of the old town, the souks and the craftsmen in their workshops of a kind, all within the lovely, soft-pink, high-castellated, mud walls was most appealing. It was very hot in summer, but at Christmas it was pretty cold. We were within the walls of an old Sultan's palace, the delightful Hotel Salam, in room 207 off a tiny, tiled courtyard, with peacocks wandering about. By a huge fire in the main rooms we found Jean-Marie Houriez and his Bristolian wife, Jean. They were teachers of English whom we had met before and liked very much.

On our country drives through the desert and scrub, we passed through quite large areas of the feathery Argan tree (*argania spinosa*) which grows only in this part of Morocco. Also reared in this part are large flocks of predatory goats, which prefer to live off the argan leaves, and fruit, and climb up into the trees to do so! It is a unique and comic sight to see five or six goats up one tree at a time. The kernels of the fruit are crushed to produce a red oil.[5]

27 December 1979

On we went south-east via Ait Baha by an exciting, twisty, minor road through the Anti-Atlas mountains, lunching below Tioulet. Then on to the spectacular and highly individual town of Tafraoute in which the Hotel du Sud was good. The landscape was rugged. Kasbahs of red earth, some in painted ochre, were built high up on the rocks, with great, broken stone masses behind. There wasn't much cultivation, but there were flourishing almond trees, beautiful in the spring.

Close at hand to Tafraoute are some delightful little villages or townships such as Oumesnat and Tandalt. Here we found traces of ancient architecture, and had lovely walks up through tiny fields and orchards and streams. There were pleasant, cheerful girls about with round faces. Up and up we went within a red rock panorama, and we had tea and Christmas cake in the sunset.

[5] The rich oil is very good in salads. Kininmonth.

29 December 1979

It was time to head for home, alas. We couldn't manage to visit Goulimine, the red town with its blue men, so we had to make do with Tiznit, a pre-Saharan, walled town which we approached over a difficult and dramatic pass. We hoped to buy some good silver tribal jewellery, but we were disappointed. We drove north to Essaouira for the night. We shall never again have a Christmas like this one, which was perhaps the best of all throughout my British Council career.

1980

There were six months left until the end of my thirty-three years with the British Council, but there wasn't time to bother. We saw the New Year in chez Townsend – a very charming and appropriate occasion. Conrad de Planta de Wildenburg and Diana gave a number of us and Embassy staff a very good New Year lunch. The McMillans in the Embassy, who were being posted to Harare, Zimbabwe, gave a farewell party. As Rosemary put it: "I dragged Michael home at 1.30 a.m."

When the social whirl subsided, we took a new route up behind the Barrage inland, and found a huge egret roost, which was very amusing to watch. What a lot of yakkety-yak!

On 12 January our new-found, Turkish Counsellor friend, Mehmet Ezen, and his wife gave a jolly good New Year dance-party. We had never met any Turks before. I confess I had always imagined them to be dour and keen on massacre, but the Ezens were great fun. She had been a British Council scholar in town-planning, which gave us a bond. Could she continue her work? I don't know, but we soon learned the Turkish for good health: 'sherefé' (honour).

Travel agent – of a sort

Lord Ballantrae, our ex-Chairman,[6] wrote to say that he would like to have a holiday in Morocco with his son George, and what could we suggest? We did our best. Poor man, he had lost his wife, Laura, on 17 December last, in a tragic accident at home, and must have felt her loss terribly. We all did.

Duties now came thick and fast. First we gave a rather alarming dinner for eight, with our principal guest being one of the King's advisers,

[6] See Sind, p. 484

accompanied by his wife. Then we were invited to attend a French financial mission cocktail-party. I thought I made un Inspecteur de la Banque de France laugh, but Rosemary said: "He was laughing at your French".

Cultural conventions

The Council does not, nor cannot, function in a country unless by invitation, and such invitations are usually ratified. Rather embarrassingly, while we worked away I was beginning to notice a lack of enthusiasm towards us by the Moroccan authorities. I was now told that the British Council was still not officially recognised by Morocco, and I was asked to draft a Cultural Convention: a poser and a challenge. We managed with the help of the Embassy, of course, and sent a draft to London. I never heard the result. But what I did hear next was our Chairman, Sir Charles Troughton, speaking on the telephone from London! He was planning a two-day official tour with Lady Troughton and then a ten-day holiday. Morocco was ideal for this. He gave us time to make the necessary precise plans.

Temporary peace

"To Sidi Yayha des Zaers: perfect: larks, lambs, flowers and foals," wrote Rosemary. In Rabat we went to *The Devil's Disciple* produced by friend Murshed of the Pakistan Embassy: the cast was English, Moroccan, and German! It was very fine effort which we much enjoyed.

Still exploring – with time to do so

On an extra government holiday we took two of our young English bachelors from the Faculty of Letters to the farming area of Sidi Bettache, some forty kilometres south-east. It is a beautiful area where there are gorges one can suddenly come across. We picnicked by a stream with grassy slopes and sheep under the olive trees. No-one disturbed us.

10 February 1980: Off to Oujda

I went off with Tony one evening by train, with all our display and film equipment and ourselves in a couchette. We slept well until after dawn at 6.30 a.m. Then we enjoyed a perfect desert sunrise. Oujda is far to the east, close to the Algerian border. It has been fought over for centuries because of its position and the attempts of various dynasties and the Turks to edge further west into Morocco.

Oujda is a very French town because of its history of French occupations in the mid-nineteenth century and again in 1907 until the end of the Protectorate in 1956. Nevertheless, we were well received by a turn-out of eighty-two teachers of English from the area. We put out our E.L.T. books exhibition which was graced by the French Delégué, M. Idoub, a young, affable man with a goatee. Tony spoke on this and that, mainly on methodology. He showed *Great Expectations*, and invited the area inspectors of E.L.T. out to dinner.

The French like Oujda. The town is pleasant, the countryside is attractive, the Mediterranean is not far away and there is good bathing. They also have the little Spanish port of Melilla where they can buy goods cheaply. The sportsmen are happy. There are lakes around with enormous pike – the usual minimum length they indicated (in fishermen's style) is about 3 feet!

We returned to Rabat by day. I always enjoy train travel, and this journey allowed peaceful contemplation of the landscape which from Oujda to Taza was varied and wild.

Back in Rabat

Rosemary provided a dinner for the Pakistan Ambassador and his wife; an adviser to H.M.; the secretary to the Minister of Commerce and his English wife (who helped); an American, a lover of India, married to a Nepalese; the then Moroccan Ambassador to Iran; the head of U.S.I.S.; Dr Abdeljalil Lahjomri, director of the Ecole Normale Superieur, and his wife; the Turkish Ezens; and the Minister of Culture, Oudaias. It was a sparkling party. We showed our film *The Sounds of Islam* which covered Islamic music in Morocco, Turkey, Iran, and India with orchestras and famous exponents of the tabla, flute and lute. I loved it. The audience was polite. On another evening we showed the film *Desert Victory* at home to a group of mixed guests, a copy of which I had found in our Embassy in Tunis!

Marrakesh – E.L.T. and recce

Rosemary and I made a successful and enjoyable trip to Marrakesh. We drove ourselves, taking the usual four hours and enjoying the drive more, the more familiar it became, with its marked stages: agricultural coastal plain, small hilly area, stony plateau, little pass, etc., etc. We continued to have perfect weather – quite unlike the previous year which had been very wet and stormy at this time. Then we had gone to Ifrane in sunshine, and woken up in snow.

I was going down on a recce for the Chairman and Lord Ballantrae, and to assist Tony O'Brien with his meeting for teachers of English, to meet new English-born staff at the new university and to meet the dean, and to put up our E.L.T. book exhibition once again with dear Rosemary's assistance. It all went off very well with just over a hundred teachers participating, including a visit from the local Inspector General and the Delégué, very important persons in the French-orientated hierarchy! They both paid us the compliment of speaking a little English. On the two evenings we had some jolly company at dinner in pleasant, little restaurants, including the Field Marshal's guardian L/Cpl. Milward and his wife. The Auk was 95 and was persuaded into a new suit by Milward.

Back in Rabat we ran a rather special play-reading evening of W. Douglas Home's *The Reluctant Debutante*. Our readers were top class – viz. the Defence Attaché, the Head of Chancery, our Director of studies, and a delightful young English governess to the Italian Ambassador's family, named Pippa Watts. I wish we could have had a Moroccan audience, and not just ourselves. Well, one day . . .

The next evening we dined with the Chief Inspector of English, a charming, earnest Frenchman, André Menager. I think that we in the British Council had his support.

8 February 1980

Simon and Shelby Dawbarn helped to make the Ballantraes' stay enjoyable. They had been no problem, fully realising that our new Chairman's visit was looming large! They left Rabat by train for Tangier, and went on to stay with the Governor of Gibraltar, General Sir W. Jackson, R.E. He is a first-class military historian, who has been responsible for parts of the *Official History of the Second World War*, Vol: 6. 'Victory in the Mediterranean'. But he had not been popular in Rabat recently. When the Governor heard that the Consulate-General in Tangier was to close – a very sad move we felt – he wrote to the Consul-General and asked for the iron despatch chest from H.M.S. Victory, sent ashore at Tangier and never re-embarked, to be sent to Gibraltar, and also a beautiful painting of the Straits of Gibraltar, by J. Varley (circa 1810). But Her Majesty's Ambassador to Morocco replied that Gibraltar had no claim whatever to these items, and he swiftly installed them in the Embassy.

Our Chairman

Sir Charles Troughton, "call me Dicky", was a great chap who worked hard and successfully for the preservation and progress of the British Council. He was very thorough. He had been faced with an interview with the Prime Minister, Margaret Thatcher, who was fighting to save money and keen to reduce the British Council's budget.

Dicky got his wife to take the part of Margaret Thatcher and steadily fire at him all the questions or facts, true or false, which she could muster, which he had to answer satisfactorily. Our Chairman's interview resulted in no cuts to our budget.

Of course, the Chairman took on the matter of the Cultural Convention. He did not speak French, and although Simon Dawbarn did, he employed an interpreter, Bob Caspy, a retired British Consul. Simon had said "If I have to interpret, I shall not be able to think at the same time." This was a good lesson for me. I enjoyed being in on some high-level discussions with the Moroccan ministers concerned, and M. Bihareau, head of the French Cultural Mission to Morocco. His lady interpreter said that my French was quite good. How sporting of her!

Our Chairman was sporting too. He said in public that of the various countries he had visited, he had not found so vital an English-language teaching programme (well done, Tony)[7], nor so active a British Council Representative.

Fortunately, our programme for the Troughtons went off like clockwork. Emilina said to me next day, "It's all gone so quickly." I saw what she meant, after the weeks we had spent on it all, and I replied, "That is because we planned it so carefully".

The Dawbarns were especially supportive to us. Rosemary's buffet dinner for the Troughtons was the highest powered we would ever give: there were guests from the Cabinet Royale, foreign affairs, education, et cetera, and even from the Arab League.

Our specialist visitor

Added to all the goings on, Patrick Trevor-Roper, F.R.C.S., Ophth. arrived with Mrs Fleming, widow of Ian. Patrick had been one of our specialist visitors to Pakistan, and had been most kind professionally to both my father and to me at home, and in Karachi.

---

[7] Tony O'Brien went on to distinguish himself in E.L.T. elsewhere, in Hong Kong for instance. I was so pleased when he returned later to take my place as Director Morocco – the designation 'Representative' having been changed to 'Director'.

He spoke good French, and in response to my suggestion he had agreed to come out and visit the Moroccan ophthalmic fraternity whom I had already sounded out. They were very pleased with him. He spent quite a bit of his holiday on the job. He's a charming man and we were delighted by the success of his visit.

March to July 1980: The last run-down

30 March
Turned off the subterranean infernal heating-machine, thank goodness.
31 March
Changed into thin suits – note date!

Visitors

Dr Roger Wilkins, Reading University, Grassland Research. Mike Stimson, B.C. E.L.T. Staff, for a fortnight of lectures to teachers. Dr Clarke and his wife from Strathclyde, to lecture on English literature, and to try and create a link with Rabat University. All stimulating for us. The Clarkes were particularly good company.

April
3–7 April Easter holidays

After work, a few friends came in for a drink at lunch-time. But Rosemary and I managed to be off at 3.15 p.m. for Beni Mellal (three hours 248 km.). We saw a golden eagle as we went down into a ravine. I remember the moment clearly.

Beni Mellal is a town which sits up against the south-west end of the Middle Atlas, half-way on the road between Fes and Marrakesh.

Day one of the holiday: we spent the morning exploring Beni Mellal. Day two was a trip to El Kasbah, up the Tizi-n-Ait Ourira, an amazing little pass. Day three over an even higher and more spectacular little pass from Ouled M'barek, down into a valley, and thus enjoy the weekly souk in Bin-el-Widane, and come out over a third pass to Afourer.

We came back to Rabat by the same route via Kasbah Tadla. This was the French army base of operations in the twenties and thirties against the tribes who didn't want to be ruled by France. Home we went to Miloud on Monday 7 April. Of course, he immediately cleaned the car after helping us unload. I shall miss him, if Rosemary doesn't!

8 April

We parked the car in the shade for the first time this year. Some good films arrived from London: *Follow Me* from Peter Schaffer's play. It was first class, and thoroughly appreciated: charming, well-cast, well acted, good dialogue, and evocative scenes of London. Then *The Importance of Being Ernest* with the original superb cast. Next came *Animal Farm* followed by *Othello*, which I hate, especially with Laurence Olivier in the lead role. That casting didn't work.

9 April 1980: Safeguarding Fes, International Appeal Day

The week that followed began with a surprise. I hadn't been at my desk long on Tuesday morning before H.E. rang to ask me to represent him at a UNESCO conference in Fes on the preservation of Fes, in response to an invitation from the Prime Minister. There had only been twenty-four hours' notice from the Moroccans. The subject interested me, so I was very pleased to go.

I was off at 7 a.m. with driver Driss and we reached Fes in two hours, in time to join the other guests, who were mainly diplomats from countries expected to contribute to the Appeal, in the conference complex. Here we viewed a good exhibition of problems and plans before driving off to luncheon at the Palais Jamai Hotel – a former pasha's old palace on the edge of the medina.

We were served in the traditional manner: a flat, round, loaf of bread was issued to each of us as we sat at round tables, then three courses were brought in succession on round, flat dishes, about eighteen inches across, of roast mutton, followed by roast chicken and olives, followed by couscous and chicken – the couscous, was eaten with a spoon as a concession, the other dishes being eaten with the fingers. The roast mutton was burning mine!

There was a boring formal session of speeches which took over two hours – in Arabic or French. Then there was time for whisky at the bar of the Merenides Hotel, high-up above the old city, showing a wonderful panorama. Next we enjoyed a very good buffet dinner – western style and western dishes.

Afterwards we were all bidden to a family palace in the medina driving down in cavalcade behind motor-cycle police. It was rather fun. The palace was an amazing surprise, a huge, cathedral-like building in what one thought was another maze of small houses. Here we were waited on by relays of servants with mint tea and cakes and entertained by musicians and enactments of ancient (and modern!) Moroccan

582

customs such as circumcision and marriage. Bed was at 1 a.m. Apart from various Moroccan and foreign friends whom I was happy to be with, I was in the company of Ronald Bailey, a former ambassador of ours to Morocco who was good value – in knowing the form and so many people too.

Of course, I had to present H.E. with a report. This is its essence:

Briefly, the great mediaeval city of Fes has existed famously and unchanged for a thousand years – until today. Now its wealthier families have left their 'palaces' for commerce in Casablanca. The upper middle-classes have forsaken their highly decorated cold and inconvenient courtyards for modern housing. In their place have come country folk crowding in – eager to escape ceaseless drudgery on unyielding land or worse, no occupation at all.

One whole family per room is the new ratio for these old houses: and every other nook and cranny in Fes is filled with new bodies, seeking a new living. The services cannot cope. The restive young who form a majority of the population of Fes today do not want to be slaves of such antediluvian conditions – Tourism go hang. Can an ancient and fascinating Fes survive as a viable social and economic complex: and not be reduced to a museum or morgue such as Khiva, Uzbekistan, when we visited it in 1974 – very beautiful but dead and eerie?

Well, the (French?) experts of today hope to integrate this anachronism with new housing and new industrial regions built roundabout. Fes, they say, will then have a chance of survival.

Fes is certainly luckier than Isfahan, in that its great Medina and souks have not yet suffered from the megalomaniac depredations of a Reza Shah who drove incurably wounding, unrelating boulevards in his name through a glorious city.

18 April 1980: Practice in English

Up the coast to Kenitra itself this time – not the plage! We paid a visit to the Lycée Abdelmalik Es Saadia and to Mimosa College for young ladies, run by a bright, genial Madame Ben Salek. The heads of the two establishments were anxious for staff to make progress, both with the teaching of English and with the pupils' mastery of the language. Pupils at both schools were keen and a large number could communicate with us. English is an easy language for basic communication when possessing only a smattering of it.

23 April 1980

For the first and last time in our careers, two of Rosemary's brothers and their wives were able to join us at post, and what a posting for all to enjoy! First came Chris, once a war-time naval officer in Coastal Command, later development officer in the Highlands, and Mary, a very bright Oxford graduate, full of charm and humour, mother of four and a true lover of flowers.

May 1980

Next to come was Michael, Rosemary's eldest brother, a forester, and his wife, Unity, an artist. She became frustrated as we had to drive past so many scenes she longed to paint.

We all went off in our two cars down south. Out in the country beyond Said and Sidi Moussa (the mausoleum of a sixteenth-century ascetic), we stopped in the sandy, rushy countryside and found my delightful dung beetles. There they were industriously rolling along their large balls of dung. But they let me down and kept falling over on their backs, so Mary called them dissolute dung beetles, or hopeless rollers! I still cannot comprehend the thought processes of the Egyptians who treated the dung beetle, the scarab, as a life source. But I have much enjoyed every representation of the dung beetle I have come across.

We picnicked in an idyllic olive-grove some twenty kilometres outside Marrakesh before plunging into this city into the Djema El F'na, which was quite an experience. We noticed we had lost Chris and that somewhere not far away there were sounds of an altercation. Three mountebanks were protesting loudly that Chris owed them money. Tough Chris had called their bluff and picked up a 10 Dirham note (about £1) which they had let him win, but it was one of their decoys! Rosemary came over fast and sorted the gentlemen out, threatening to call the police – an idea of which they disapproved. They calmed down and Chris could walk off – with his stake. Warning often repeated: at the Djema El F'na don't have any money or valuables on you, only enough change to buy your mint tea in the café.

June 1980 Western Music and Eastern

In Rabat we welcomed our last visitor, the pianist Anthony Peebles, who had played so well for us in Karachi. He gave a recital in the Residence, to guests invited by the Dawbarns. It was a memorable occasion for what was to be almost our last British Council appearance. The last was in Fes, where we went back again with Anthony, for him to perform at the French Centre. It was lucky for us to be able to say au revoir to our kind French colleagues, and to our university friends, who gave us a lunch party.

Then we took Anthony to Marrakesh for Morocco's 21st National Festival of Popular Arts. I was ecstatic. There were evening performances on a most impressive, excellently-lit stage within the great walls of the El-Badi Palace, built by Achmed El Mansur from 1578–1602. The name Badi means 'incomparable' – as were the performances.

I think Moroccan music is great – in its place. I learned from Ali Bahaijoub, Ministry of Education and teacher of English, that most Moroccan music is 'trance' music with many variations between tribes or groups. It can go on for hours for the intended cumulative effect. The Moroccans are naturally musical people. To them making music is an important means of self-expression. Their traditional ceremonies and festivals require a musical accompaniment to which most Moroccans seem able to contribute either by song or rhythm on a drum or tambourine, or by hand-clapping, or with a simple, stringed instrument.

In the old days there was court music from the Arab school and rural music which was, and is, predominantly Berber. The Berber music is strongly under black African influence through their slaves. The purest Berber music is heard in the Rif mountains of the north where outside influence of any sort hardly penetrated. Unfortunately, this was our only good opportunity to hear the various types of Moroccan music, the Toqtoqa of the Rif with Arab influence, the Gnaou, the wild pure, black African men's drumming for festivals and exorcism. There's the Guedra dance of the blue-robed, kneeling women of the blue tribe, suitable in low tents. This is long drawn-out eroticism, and other dances were the same. All this made a very good send-off for us!

Winding down

We set up shop in the house, and disposed of numerous items 'not wanted in retirement', we hoped. We did very well. It's always hard to price one's own items let alone offer them for sale to friends. Then we packed, and in came the expert French packers, Bedel, who estimated almost exactly the 8 cubic metres which our baggage measured.

July 1980 diary

2nd. Ninety-one came to our farewell party – heartening.
3rd. The Glazes took us to luncheon at the Royal Golf Club.

       The Dawbarns gave us a farewell dinner. Delightful.

4th. Friday. 5.30p.m. PEN DOWN (literally).

       Walked out of the Office, never to return. Rather an odd feeling, but no regrets, The next day, a non-working day, would be my 60th birthday.

       Once again the American Ambassador in 'our country' gave me a very good, unintentional pre-birthday party, at which to enjoy the hospitality of Britain's lost colony.

7th. A week's leave by the Mediterranean, at Le Petit Merou, a very interesting holiday complex on Cabo Negro, south of Ceuta. Shining white, it looked from a distance like a higgledy-piggledy remains of a wasp's nest, but it was sheltered, comfortable, and ingeniously planned.

       On our way we passed the abandoned town of Thamusida, a fortified Roman camp of A.D. 200 on the river Sebou. But on the plain of Rharb further north we found Banasa, a beautiful site for a Roman colony established by Augustus within the Mauretanian Kingdom.

       We had several enjoyable drives around to Martil, Tetouan, and south-east to Oued Laou for the scenery, and then up the river at Amsa. Here we picnicked and Rosemary snorkled. Suddenly there was a tremendous kerfuffle under the water. It was Rosemary meeting a very small octopus. Shades of Arthur Grimble in the Gilberts, who met a very large octopus!

We went on to Tangier. Michael Scott a lecturer in Fes, had been at St Andrews in Rosemary's day. She had known of him as a badly wounded officer. He was still pretty battered. He was very kind to us, and let us stay in the house of his late father, Sir Basil Scott, at Dar El Quas, the House of the Arches, 43 Rue Shakespeare. Their grand old maid-servant, Alia, was at hand.

Back in Rabat we were allowed to sleep in our old house. We later sold our Renault 12 to my successor J. J. Dunn, who came from Tokyo where a car would have been a hopeless encumbrance. "Why should I need a car in Rabat?" he wrote. We told him he would need two.

Neville and Heidi Townsend gave us tea. Our kind Moroccan friends, the Moucines, gave us a surprise farewell evening. Next morning we said goodbye to the admirable Dawbarns, and Neville took us to Nouasser for the plane to Lisbon, where I ate pigs' ears by mistake (very leathery). Then we followed in the steps of Wellington: Sintra, Coimbra, Figuera da Foz, and Bucaco. We were really on our own now, and somewhat apprehensive.

FINIS

The Treasure of our Tongue

In 1971 the newly-appointed Chairman of the British Council, Sir Leslie Rowan, a distinguished civil servant, quoted the seventeeth-century poet and historian, Samuel Daniel:

> And who in time knows whither we may vent
> The treasure of our tongue? To what strange shores
> This gain of our best glory shall be sent
> To enrich unknowing nations with our stores?
> What worlds in the yet unformed occident
> May come refined with the accents which are ours?

Sir Leslie continued to remark: "Nearly 400 years later, the 'treasure of our tongue' still has new shores to reach, and this 'gain of our best glory' still has many riches to bestow, for it is now the key to both higher education and science. No political or other changes at home or abroad can slow this advance of the English language." Unfortunately, Sir Leslie died at the age of sixty-four, and so did not live to see the world-wide spread of English.

On 14 March 1994 our Vice-Patron, H.R.H. The Prince of Wales, came to our headquarters in Spring Gardens. Here once upon a time my father was taken by his nanny from 1 Cowley Street, Westminster, to see the milk-providing cow! H.R.H. launched the project 'Look Ahead', and praised the initiative of the British Council and the B.B.C. Then £4 million was available to expand the teaching of our tongue.

When I joined the British Council in 1947 its budget was £3.5 million. Today, 1999, the total is in the region of £424 million. the Government grant is £134 million, but the Council's income is £149 million: a triumph.

All the progress and development of such British Council's activities flourishing world-wide today with increased government support is most cheering. I was concerned with direct English-language teaching (E.L.T.); with the administration of English teaching institutes; and to my special satisfaction and Rosemary's too, assisting British tutors and teachers on their overseas assignments to 'teach teachers to teach teachers to teach'.

It was rewarding to be closely associated with such admirable men and women, and with their pupils in schools and colleges, or with mine in our institutes. English is an intriguing language. Teaching it is the quickest way to learn about it. One gets asked some tricky questions by eager pupils; and often there are no definitive answers. Teaching English is also a good way to make friends. It is particularly enjoyable teaching adults who have paid to learn, and of course, demand one's best. It is also fun with higher classes to range over subjects of mutual interest, and to indulge in some adult humour.

To-day English is the official, or semi-official, language in more than seventy countries: seventy per cent of the world's mail is written in English, and it is the first language of 350 million people. But world-wide English must be understood world-wide, despite the colourful variations in vocabulary and usage which I have come across, and which teachers are reluctant to discourage because they are the national idiom. When a senior British Education visitor was driven to my office in Georgetown after hours, she was told that I "had been given a drop". She was taken aback. The message I left was that I had been given a lift home! Let us leave that one. But it would not be right to let pass the English of this poster spotted in India: "BAN THE FAMILY FOR A BETTER FUTURE". English-teaching overseas must be tightened up, and at home also.

Finally, I am convinced that standard English must be firmly maintained in all our English-language teaching institutions, at home and overseas, including British schools abroad. I ask that all native speakers and teachers of English be encouraged to appreciate and practice the euphony of English vowel sounds; and to adhere to long-accepted patterns of stress, rhythm, and intonation. This will benefit the ears of all home and overseas listeners to English, and assist the success of universal understanding through the best use of "the treasure of our tongue".

Brief Narrative of our Voyage from Djibuti to Haifa, with the Abyssinian Royal Family and Staff on Board.

by Captain C.E. Morgan

H.M.S. Enterprise [1936]

... Early on Sunday morning, 3 May, H.M.S. Diana was ordered to proceed with all despatch to Djibuti to deliver a message to the Emperor when he arrived, to the effect that the British Government had agreed to convey him, his family and his staff in a British warship, and that H.M.S. Enterprise had been detailed for this duty. On Monday, 4 May at 0245 I was ordered to proceed to Djibuti, so as to arrive at 0800, embark the Royal Family and Staff and convey them to Haifa in Palestine.

I anchored at Djibuti at 0800, saluted the country and immediately landed, with the Captain of the Diana, to call on the Governor and have an audience with the Emperor ... After about half an hour's conversation with the French Governor of Djibuti, I was told that the Emperor was ready to receive me ...

My first impression on being presented to His Majesty on Monday morning was how very tired he looked. I felt somehow that he was almost at his last gasp, and from his first few remarks knew he was a very frightened man. He had a hunted look in his eye, and he seemed only too glad to sit down again as soon as the presentations were over. I was glad to notice that his hands were all right because we had heard a rumour that he had been gassed and that his hands were all bandaged from mustard gas burns. Such beautiful hands too; I have never seen such delicate hands on any man, and I should think his fingers must have been nearly twice as long as mine. As a matter of fact all the Royal Family had beautiful hands and I believe they take a great pride in them.

His first questions were about his own personal safety on board and I assured him at once that as soon as he stepped over my gangway, he would be as safe as the Bank of England. That was the first time I saw him smile, and I shall never forget it. There is something about his smile that you cannot resist, and you are always hoping that you will say something of which he approves, or do some little thing that will please him so that you can see him smile again.

He then asked if he would be escorted up the Red Sea, and I told him the escort was already waiting outside. I told him that it would consist of a cruiser and four destroyers, and although they would keep out of sight, they would be in close support. He then asked if he would be escorted up

589

the Gulf of Suez, and I told him a destroyer for that had been arranged. He then asked if arrangements had been made to escort him from Port Said to Haifa, and I told him a destroyer had already been told off for that duty. When he heard all that he seemed much happier.

The Emperor himself speaks his own language, of course; he speaks French well and he understands English. I found it was much the best and quickest to speak to him in English through his interpreter who was also his own private doctor and speaks English perfectly . . . The problem that I was immediately faced with was a request from the Emperor that I would take 150 persons, male and female, two lions, one dog, about 15 tons of baggage, and about 150 cases of Marie Theresa silver dollars, between 250,000 and 300,000 of them and valued at about £17,000.

. . . I had discussed it with the Commander before we landed. We had decided that in view of the fact that we might strike bad weather, in which event they would all have to be stowed down below, we could not possibly manage more than fifty bodies.

I therefore told the Emperor that I could not take the lions, but that I would accept a dog, the baggage and the bullion but that the party to embark must be cut down to fifty.

When this communication was communicated I thought the throne room in the Palace of Djibuti was going up in a cloud of smoke. They all held up their hands in horror and said it couldn't be done. I pointed out that H.M.S. Enterprise was not a passenger ship and that every person that came on board would displace an officer or man from his normal accommodation, and that as half the party would be females it would be extremely difficult to arrange for even 50.

I pointed out too that my Government had informed me that the party would probably consist of 12 and that 50 was the very maximum I could possibly take.

The Emperor looked so weary and fragile that I felt a perfect brute for screwing him down . . .

The next question to be discussed was the time he was to embark. I told him my orders were to leave at noon, that the escort was waiting outside, the Suez Canal would be kept clear of shipping, for our passage, from 0700 on Thursday 7 May and that the escort had been ordered to be at Port Said accordingly.

The Emperor said he was very sorry that he just couldn't do it. By then it was about 1030 and it was obviously quite impossible for him to settle up all his private affairs and the affairs of his country and embark in one and a half hours. Also, now that he knew that I could take only 50, he would have to go into conference with his Ministers to settle who was to go and who was to be left behind . . .

I pointed out that if we went at noon we could do the trip at 20 knots, but that every hour we delayed we should have to go faster and it would therefore be more uncomfortable for him living aft as I must be at the entrance to the Suez Canal at 0700 on Thursday . . . After a short conference with his Ministers he said he would embark . . . at 5.30 p.m., and I think it was rather marvellous that he walked over our starboard gangway at 5.29 p.m.

Actually the baggage and the bullion were the biggest problem, it took rather longer than we expected to load it into the lighter and hoist it all [on] board. So that finally we did not go ahead until 7.20. p.m. which meant a speed of 22 knots to adhere to our programme.

I don't mind saying that I did feel rather important when I had once got him on board and subsequent events were to prove that just for a few days the eyes of the world were upon us . . .

On leaving Djibuti I made a further signal reporting our departure and giving a nominal list of all the passengers.

. . . I received him [the Emperor] with a Royal Guard, the band playing the Ethiopian National Anthem. He walked down and inspected the front rank of the Guard. I then conducted him to the after end of the Quarter Deck which I had prepared as a sort of sitting-room with easy chairs, carpets and small tables with the awning curtains round to enclose it all in, if necessary.

I took him to the most comfortable chair, held the cushion up for him as he sat down he went fast asleep, and the awning curtain across the after end of the Quarter Deck fell on Act 1.

In Act 2 I include our trip from Djibuti to Haifa in Palestine.

According to the Empire Broadcast from the B.B.C., the journey was made without incident. This is certainly not a true statement . . . because every hour of the day and night was fully occupied from the moment we left Djibuti until 11.30 a.m. on Friday when His Majesty's train left for Jerusalem.

It was my intention that the Emperor should be worried as little as possible during the time he was on board and that he should do what he liked. I warned the Officers and Ship's Company that on no account was any attempt to be made to photograph the Emperor and that nobody was to visit the after part of the ship except on duty.

. . . The arrangements for messing and victualling the party were very thoroughly and efficiently carried out by the Accountant Branch under the direction of the Paymaster Commander.

. . . My idea was that my cabins were at the disposal of the Emperor and that . . . the after part of the ship should be isolated and screened off from view . . . The Gun room was used as a general sleeping space for all those Officers who had turned out of their cabins.

The Gun Room and Warrant Officers turned out of their Messes and lived in the Ward Room and No. 6 Gun Deck was reserved for the servants and retinue. Luckily they had no objection to males and females sleeping together in the same space, which helped a lot, but even so it was a tight fit. Luckily too, the weather remained fine, so that all those not supplied with cabins were able to sleep on deck. Service stretchers were used to make up the requisite number of beds.

It was my intention, if the weather turned bad, to clear the Marine Barracks so as to accommodate the party sleeping on deck. However, it would have been a very tight squeeze and I am very glad we did not have to put this plan into effect.

As far as messing was concerned, the following were included at my table:-

The Emperor and Empress, the Crown Prince and Crown Princess, the Duke of Harrar (2nd son of the Emperor), Isash Work (niece of the Emperor), Princess Sehaie (daughter of the Emperor), Haile Selassie (uncle of the Emperor), Ras Cassar (A.D.C.), Madame Cassar and Ras Guetatceou (2nd A.D.C.) = 11 in all.

The remaining 36 were victualled by the Ward Room and were divided into two groups. One, the Ministers, their wives and some of the children who messed in the Warrant Officers Mess and the other, the remainder of the children, nurses and servants, who had their meals at the forward end of the Quarter Deck on the Port side.

The Empress slept in my sleeping cabin, and the Emperor, the 2nd and 3rd son and one of the Princesses slept on the couch and on camp beds in my day cabin. The remainder of the Royal Family and most of the principal Ministers and members of the suite were provided with cabin accommodation . . .

The Warrant Officers' lavatories and bathroom were turned over for the use of the remainder of the party.

It can well be imagined what the after part of the ship was like at about 6 a.m. I went there only once at this time and found a seething mass of humanity consisting of Officers dressed, undressed or dressing, nurses, children dressed and naked. Abyssinian Generals in full uniform, sentries, Marine servants and Goanese Stewards taking round iced lemon-squashes. I only wish I could have had a photograph of it; it had to be seen to be believed, that you were really on board a British man-of-war . . .

I should like here to put in a word of praise for the Emperor's dog. My Coxswain told me that the Emperor always used to put him out every night before he went to bed, and that he never moved until the Emperor came out to him first thing in the morning. I used to go the rounds of the afterpart of the ship each night about 11 p.m., and I always found him lying in the Quarter Masters lobby. I used to pat him and tell he was a very good little dog and he just looked up and wagged his tail, but he never moved.

Incidentally, he was never observed to commit either the major or minor offences to us the whole time he was on board, perhaps he was like the proverbial canary.

Before leaving this country, the Emperor, so they said, spent the last three days in the front line trying to get shot. Eventually they dragged him out, unwounded, but his little dog was wounded by his side, and I should say for the look of his left eye, that he had lost the sight of it.

As far as the entertainment of the party was concerned, my hope that they would never have a dull moment on board was fully realised.

On Tuesday 5 May I presented all the Officers to the Emperor, and on Wednesday 6 May he inspected the Ship and the Ship's Company. During the inspection of the Ship he was accompanied by the Empress and all the Royal Family . . .

The Emperor had two officers to lunch and two officers to dine with him every day. The band generally twice a day and pictures when he wanted them . . .

During the trip from Djibuti to Haifa we were observed with the keenest interest by everyone. All ships going the same way and sighting us coming up astern hauled over, so that we should pass close to them and ships going in the opposite direction made a bold alteration in course as soon as they sighted us so that they should pass close.

Suez, Ismalia, Port Said and the banks of the Canal were crowded with people the whole way along and wherever the road runs close to the Canal, we were escorted by a force of police on motor cycles.

I think the Emperor was a little bit afraid of being potted at in the Canal. At Suez he was not on deck, but at Ismalia and Port Said he came and sat close to me on the compass platform.

Very nice for me if this was his idea, but as the eyes and glasses on shore were focussed on the Empress and the remainder of the Abyssinians sitting in chairs on the Quarter deck. It was perhaps rather clever of him.

The silver bullion was to have been landed at Port Said . . . However, one hour before leaving Port Said the Emperor got cold feet at the idea of losing sight of his money and decided that he would take it to Haifa with him. This meant cancelling all the arrangements for . . . landing the money and for taking in provisions and filling up with fresh water and I went straight through Port Said only slowing up to pick up our mails . . .

The destroyer H.M.S. Wolsey took up escorting duties after we had cleared the breakwater and we proceeded at 12 knots so as to arrive at Haifa in accordance with the wishes of the High Commissioner at 0830 on Friday 8 May. The night passed without incident; we arrived as requested exactly at 0830, and so ended Act 2.

Act 3

H.M.S. Enterprise had berthed alongside the Railway Pier at Haifa by 0900 and the Officer of the Guard came on board with the programme of the morning's events.

The Royal Train was drawn up alongside the ship and immediately on arrival we commenced hoisting out the baggage and bullion.

Incidentally, during the voyage the baggage was stowed on the port side of the ship. They were continually going to it to get things out and there was a lot of re-packing done during the time they were on board. There were about ten tons of it altogether and as it consisted mostly of old boxes and dilapidated suitcases with here and there a brand new one, it was lucky the weather remained fine.

At 10 a.m. I presented to his Majesty the High Officials of the Port after which he retired to his cabin to compose himself for the final ordeal of leaving the ship and entraining for Jerusalem . . .

During the voyage the Emperor received many messages of sympathy, congratulation, and condolence from all parts, and I am sure that he was greatly touched by them especially one saying "You put your faith in the Great White Nations and they have let you down. Sincerest sympathies and heartiest congratulations on your splendid efforts," handed in at Alexandra and signed 'A crowd of Britishers'.

. . . On the Friday morning . . . the captain of the Wolsey the destroyer which had escorted us from Port Said, came on board and behind him was an Able Seaman with an Engine Room glove carrying a large hawk and attached to the hawk's leg by a piece of string was a message for the Emperor written on a stiff piece of paper, like chart paper. I took it straight to the Emperor and he himself actually removed the message from the bird's leg . . . After that we released the hawk, but even then it was too far done to fly far.

I have many times seen birds, including hawks, on board a ship, but I have never seen one so exhausted that you could go to it and pick it up; and when this one fell on the deck of the Wolsey, it was so done that the Able Seaman went straight to it and after picking it up he put it in the meat safe.

. . . It has been suggested that it had flown from Abyssinia but I cannot believe this as it is 1500 miles from Haifa . . . The message was a 'welcome' message of three words written in French with a signature at the bottom, but I don't think that there is any doubt that it is meant for the Emperor.

The Royal Family and all the servants and valets left the ship at 11 a.m. walked over and took their seat in the train. At 11.15 a.m. the Emperor, the Crown Prince and the Emperor's second son left the ship. I paraded the Royal Guard and the band played the Ethiopian National Anthem.

The Party walked to the saluting base, took the salute from the British Regiment stationed at Haifa and the Emperor then inspected the guard.

After that he walked towards the train and all the local civilian officials including the Mayor of Haifa were presented to him by the District Commissioner.

An incident then took place which is typical of his Majesty's thoughtfulness and courtesy. After the final presentations were over he walked towards the train and stopping at the entrance to his saloon turned around and said, "I wish to speak to the captain of the Enterprise". I went up to him. He said what he had to say and I replied. The Emperor then said, "I wish to speak to my A.D.C.s Lieutenant Tillard and Mr James". He spoke to them and again thanked them and they replied. He then turned round, walked up into his carriage, the steps were removed and the train steamed out of [the] Station.

I have seldom been so impressed with any man, black or white and his consideration, courtesy, and above all his dignity has left a very deep impression on every officer and man in my ship.

The night before he left the ship he sent for me and gave me a replica, about the size of a five shilling piece, in pure gold, of his coronation medal. Handing it to me he said, "It is not the value of the thing that matters, it is the sentiment that counts". His two A.D.C.s were also presented with similar but smaller replicas.

Before he left the ship I presented His Majesty with a Roller Blotter . . . as a memento of his voyage . . . I explained how every department of the ship had helped towards the making of it . . . In accepting it His Majesty's extreme dignity seemed very surprised and touched.

I have referred elsewhere to His Majesty's extreme dignity but this applied to all the Royal Family. Princess Sehaie for instance, quite a good looker, educated in England and speaking perfect English could, had she wished, have mixed freely with the officers and have a wonderful time as far as I know, but she never once forgot herself, and her behaviour was at all times correct and dignified.

None of the party were any trouble or bother and the children were quiet and well looked after. Although the accommodation was crowded and far from ideal there were no complaints from any of them; as far as I know there was never a more happy or contented lot. They all thoroughly enjoyed the trip and their thanks at the end of it were moderate and genuine. They talked little and never got excited but they seemed able to convey appreciation without the use of words. Savages perhaps but well behaved and very attractive ones.

[Condensed version]

Appendix I

Supayalat – The Last Queen of Burma

On the cue 'Theebaw' I recall Rudyard Kipling's poem 'Mandalay'. 'There's a Burma girl a-settin' ' and all that, 'An' 'er name was Supi-yaw-lat jes' the same as Theebaw's Queen'. As an insight into the Burmese of old here is an article by my Controller and benefactor, A.J.S. White. 'A.J.' entered the Indian Civil Service in 1922 and was posted to Burma. After two years up-country he was appointed Under-Secretary in the Home and Political Departments in Rangoon.

"One of my minor duties" he writes

"was to look after the ex-Queen Supayalat (sic) and her daughters who lived in Rangoon . . .

Supayalat was the notorious Queen whose husband Thibaw ruled, (or rather badly misruled), Upper Burma from 1878 to 1886, when he was deposed by the British. Since the 1850s, Lower Burma had been ruled by the British, and Upper Burma by Burmese Kings in the capital of Mandalay.

King Mindon died in 1878. He had had fifty-three official wives, and by these wives had a hundred and ten children, of whom forty-eight were sons. Twenty-four of these sons were still then alive. There was no tradition that the eldest son should succeed, so there were twenty-four possible claimants to the throne. One of these sons, Thibaw, was only a younger son born of a lesser Queen. He was a very weak man, completely under the thumb of his wife Supayalat, but thanks to her intrigues and ruthlessness, he was able to seize the throne. As Mindon lay dying, a forged message had been sent to all the princes to come to the Palace in Mandalay to take leave of the King. At the instance of Supayalat, all these princes and their families were arrested when they arrived.

On many occasions in the past when a new king came to the throne, there had been a massacre of rival claimants. According to Sir George Scott, the writer of a classic book on Burma and the Burmese, 'many Burmans defend it (this custom) warmly on the plea that it secured the peace of the country'. It has been said that every Burmese has in him a streak of cruelty, and that this, although it rarely shows itself, slightly offsets the many good qualities which the Burmese have. But there was no doubt that Supayalat was an exceptionally cruel woman. When Thibaw had seized the throne, she organized the massacre of over 70 of those arrested, including women and children. Many were tortured, and most were trampled to death by the royal elephants. The slaughter took place over a period of three days in February 1880. According to Sir George Scott, 'All the three days, bands of music were playing, and dancers posturing, to divert attention from what was going on, and to drown the cries of the victims'.

This barbarous action caused a great shock in England and other countries, but another shock was in store for them thanks to the royal astrologers. When a new King came to the throne he would establish a new capital in the foundation of which a certain number of persons would be buried alive. This was on the advice of the astrologers, the idea being that those buried become spirits and protect the capital. The building of Mandalay was commenced in 1858, and according to Sir George Scott 'When the foundations of the city wall were laid, fifty-two persons of both sexes and of various ages and rank, were consigned to a living tomb. Three were buried under each of the twelve city gates, one at each of the four corners, one under each of the palace gates and four under the throne itself. Along with the four human beings buried at the four corners of the city were placed four jars full of oil. These were examined every seven years by the royal astrologers and as long as they remained intact the city was considered safe'.

At the examination in 1880 it was found that the oil in two of the jars was dried up. This discovery coincided with various other ill omens including an epidemic of smallpox. The astrologers advised a change of capital, but Thibaw rejected this. They then decided that the only alternative was the offering of propitiatory sacrifices and that this should consist of 100 men, 100 women, 100 boys and 100 girls and 100 foreigners. This the King, no doubt at the instance of Supayalat, accepted, and a royal mandate was signed and arrests commenced. A frightful panic spread in Mandalay and there was a general exodus from the town. Then Thibaw took fright at the indignation which the announced massacres caused in England, and the whole thing was counter-manded, though one report said that out of the 100 already arrested some were secretly buried alive under each of the posts at the twelve gates, 'as a compromise between the fear of the spirits and the fear that the English troops would cross the border."

A.J. continues:

"Thibaw's short reign, because of his weakness and hopeless incompetence and because of the evil influence of Supayalat, brought chaos throughout the Kingdom. Large numbers of people fled to Lower Burma to find security under British rule. Even Fielding Hall, most sympathetic of writers to the Burmese says 'it would be difficult to imagine anything worse than the government of Upper Burma in its later days'. Things finally came to a head towards the end of 1885 when Thibaw took action to break contracts with British firms, and was secretly negotiating with the French who were to be given trading rights in return for the supply of arms to Thibaw. After an ultimatum, a British force invaded Upper Burma in November 1885 and Thibaw surrendered.

The British were genuinely reluctant to annex Upper Burma; they would have preferred to see it established as a buffer state. But since the whole royal family (except Thibaw and Supayalat) had been massacred and there was no institution or individual to whom they could hand over control, they gave up the idea and Upper Burma was incorporated in British India in 1886 as part of a new province of Burma, and was administered on the British-Indian pattern. This was a great change from what one observer had described as the most complete of oriental despotisms.

Thibaw and Supayalat, (known to the British troops as 'Soup Plate'), were exiled to India, where Thibaw died in 1917. Supayalat was then allowed to live in Rangoon, and she died in 1926. Her daughters and the few others who attended her insisted that her body should not be touched in any way until the third Princess could arrive from India. Normally, in the tropics a corpse has to be interred within 24 hours or at most 48 hours, but the third Princess had a long journey to make. The result can be imagined. Fuller-Good, a doctor friend of mine who was Supayalat's doctor, told me the horrific effect of this delay. After some days, the Public Health authorities had to arrange for all people, mostly Europeans, living within a certain radius of the royal corpse, to be evacuated from their homes.

Some had thought that nationalist politicians would use the occasion of the Queen's death to make trouble by reminding the public that it was the British Government which had toppled the Queen from her throne. But these politicians knew what a wicked woman Supayalat had been, and they drew the line at exploiting her. Besides, their plans for a Burmese government, while no doubt including themselves, had no room for a monarchy.

However, the Burmese never miss an opportunity for festivity, and they decided that Supayalat should be given a royal funeral in the traditional Burmese style. They invited Government to send representatives and I was one of them, arrayed in my political uniform complete with a sword which hung almost horizontally and was apt to catch between my legs. We sat in a specially erected pavilion for VIPs and had a good view of the procession passing along the road below us. It was a magnificent spectacle – a large number of elephants with gorgeous trappings, groups of dancers, many Buddhist priests in their yellow robes, men bearing the white royal umbrellas and countless other groups and symbols of royalty. It was an unforgettable occasion, even if it was in honour of one of the world's most evil women."

Book List

Old Friends

Books, old friends that are always new,
Of all good things that we know, are best;
They never forsake us as others do,
And never disturb our inward rest.
Here is the truth in a world of lies,
And all that in man that is great or wise.
Better than men or women, friend,
That are dust, though dear in our joy and pain,
Are the books their cunning hands have penned.
For they depart, but the books remain;
Through these they speak to us what is best,
In the loving heart and the noble mind;
All that their royal souls possessed
Belongs for ever to all mankind.
When others fail him, the wise man looks
To the sure companionship of books.

Andrew Lang

Here are some tried OLD FRIENDS which have served us well, and which I am happy to have on my shelves for reference or to re-read. None will ever be wholly out-of-date. So over to you, the twenty-first century reader, if you care to make New Friends of Old!

My compilations have been very kindly checked by Roger Beacham of the Cheltenham Library.

Burma

Golden Earth: travels in Burma, Norman Lewis, Cape, 1954.
Railroad to Burma, James Boyle. Allen & Unwin (ex-prisoner on the Thailand-Burma Railway), 1991.
The Burma of 'A. J.', A. J. S. White, BACSA, 1991.
Burma. F. S. V. Donnison, Ernest Benn, 1970.

The Making of Burma, Dorothy Woodman, Cresset Press, 1962.

The Union of Burma, Hugh Tinker, OUP, 2rd ed., 1961.

Burma's Icy Mountains, F. Kingdon-Ward, Cape, 1949 & others by him.

The Lacquer Lady. F. T. Jesse, Heinemann, 1929; Virago, 1979.

She was a Queen/Siamese White etc. etc. by Maurice Collis, Faber 52/56.

Twilight Over Burma. My Life as a Shan Princess, Inge Sargent, University of Hawaii Press, 1994.

The Silken East, V. C. Scott O'Connor, Hutchinson, 1904. Reprinted Kiscadale, 1993, with colour and b/w illustrations.

Beyond the Chindwin, A. Mott, 1983/*The Wild Green Earth*, Bernard Fergusson 1951/54.

Burmese Days, George Orwell, Secker & Warburg, 1949 & Penguin, 1990.

Bandoola, 1953. *The Spotted Deer*, 1957. *In Quest of a Mermaid*, 1960. J. H. Williams, Hart Davis.

The Last Chukker, J. K. Stanford, Faber & Faber, 1951.

Ethiopia

The Fountain of the Sun, Douglas Busk, Parrish, 1957.

Desert and Forest, L. M. Nesbitt, Jonathan Cape, 1934.

Travels in Ethiopia, David Buxton, Ernest Benn, 1957.

The Abyssinians, David Buxton, Thames and Hudson, 1970.

Travellers in Ethiopia, J. H. A. Brown and Richard Pankhurst, Hakluyt Society, 1991.

The March to Magdala, Frederick Myatt, Leo Cooper, 1970.

The Abyssinian Campaigns, H.M.S.O., 1942.

Barefeet and Bandoliers, Wingate, Sandford and the Patriots, in the Liberation of Ethiopia, David Shirreff, Radcliffe Press, 1995.

The Incurable Optimists, Chris and Dan Sandford of Ethiopia, Eleanor Casbon, United Writers' Publications Ltd, Penzance, Cornwall, 1993.

The Mountains of Rasselas, Thomas Pakenham, Weidenfeld and Nicolson, 1959 and Weidenfeld & Nicholson, 1998.

Fiji and Islands

The Moon and Polynesia, C. W. Whonsbon-Aston, Society for the Propagation of the Gospel, 2nd edn., 1963.

Inoke Sails the South Seas, Ronald Rose, Collins, 1966.

A Guide to Pitcairn – South Pacific Office, Suva, 1963.

Fiji, Sir Alan Burns, H.M.S.O., 1963.

Islands of the South Pacific, Sir Harry Luke, Harrap, 1962.
A History of Fiji, R. A. Derrick, Government Press, Suva, 1963.
Isles of the South Pacific, Nat. Geog. Soc., 1968.
A Gift of Islands (and other titles), June Knox-Mawer, John Murray, 1965.
Marama, a Novel of 19th Century Fiji, June Knox-Mawer, Hamilton, 1972.
The Blue of Capricorn, Eugene Burdick, Riverside Press, Cambridge, Mass., 1961.
A Pattern of Islands, Arthur Grimble, John Murray, 1952.
Return to the Islands, Arthur Grimble, John Murray, 1957.
Best Stories of the South Seas, ed., Philip Snow, Faber & Faber, 1967.
Tales from the South Seas, Anne Gittins, Government Press, Suva, 1953.
Tales of the Fiji Islands, Anne Gittins, 14 Victoria Road, Fleet GW3 8DN, 1991.
The Fatal Impact, Alan Moorhead, Hamish Hamilton, 1966.
Return to Paradise, James Michener, Corgi Books, 1970.
Men Against the Sea, Charles Nordhoff & James Hall, Chapman and Hall, 1934.
Long Pig, Russell Forman, Pan.
An Island to Oneself, Tom Neale, Collins, 1966.

Guyana

Journey to Guyana, Margaret Bacon, Dobson, 1970.
Zoo Quest to Guiana, David Attenborough, Lutterworth, 1956.
Three Singles to Adventure, Gerald Durrell, Penguin, 1969.
British Guiana, the Land of Six Peoples, Michael Swan, H.M.S.O., 1957.
Don't Stop the Carnival, Herman Wouk, Collins, 1973.
Birds of Surinam, F. Haverschmidt, Oliver & Boyd, 1958.
The Naturalist on the River Amazon, H. W. Bates, Dent, 1969.
The World of the Jaguar, Richard Perry, David & Charles Newton Abbott, 1970.
Wai-Wai: through the forests of the Amazon, Nicolas Guppy, John Murray, 1958, Penguin Harmsworth, 1961.
The gentle people, Colin Henfrey, Hutchison, 1964 (Among the Indian tribes).
Black Midas, Jan Carew, Longman, 1969.
A Swarthy Boy (Autobiog), Edgar Mittelholzer, Putnam, 1963.
Parrots of the World, Joseph M. Forshaw, Blandford Press, 3rd ed., 1989.
Climb to the Lost World, Hamish McInnes, Hodder & Stoughton, 1974.

Hungary

No books in English by British or other European writers came my way while I was in Hungary 1947–1949, except some lovely books on costume, custom and dance. And nothing since, except Wayfarer in Hungary, George A. Birmingham, Methuen, 1925, and also Raggle-Taggle, Adventures with a Fiddle in Hungary and Roumania, Walter Starkie, John Murray, 1933.

Iran

The Land of the Great Sophy, Roger Stevens, Methuen, 1962.

The Road to Oxiana, Robert Byron, Macmillan, 1937; John Lehmann, 1950, Cape '57; Penguin, New ed., 1992; Picador Travel Classics, New ed., 1994.

A Persian Spring, Wilfred Blunt, Barrie, 1957.

Isfahan, Pearl of Persia, Wilfred Blunt, Elek Books, 1966.

Pietro's Pilgrimage, Wilfred Blunt, James Barrie, 1953.

Iran, Roman Ghirshman, Pelican, A239. English version, 1954, Penguin Books, Harmsworth.

The Legacy of Persia, A. J. Arberry, ed (Oxford Legacy Series), 1953. Thirteen Authors.

A Year Among the Persians, E. G. Browne, A. & C. Black, First edition, 1893. Reprinted, 1959.

Persia: An Archeological Guide, Sylvia Matheson, Faber & Faber, 1972.

Persia. James Morris, Roger Wood, Denis Wright, Thames and Hudson, 1969.

Living with the Desert, Beazley and Harverson, Aris and Phillips, 1982.

The Persian Carpet, A. Cecil Edwards, Duckworth, 1960.

Tribal Rugs, Jenny Housego, Scorpion, 1st ed., 1978; 2nd ed., 1991.

The Traditional Crafts of Persia, Hans E. Wulff, M. I. T. Press, 1966. Cambridge Mass. & London.

The English Amongst the Persians, Denis Wright, Heinemann, 1977.

The Persians Amongst the English, Denis Wright, I. B. Tauris, 1985.

Unofficial History, W. J. Slim, Field-Marshal, Cassell, 1959 (two chapters).

From a Persian Tea-House, Michael Carroll, John Murray, 1960.

The Last Migration, Vincent Cronin, Rupert Hart-Davis, 1957.

Daybreak in Iran, Bernhardt Schultzer-Holthus, Staples, 1954.

Four Studies in Loyalty, Christopher Sykes, Collins, 1946.

Twelve Days, Vita Sackville-West, Wulff, 1928, Michael Haag, 1987.

Iran, Anthony Hutt and Leonard Harrow, Scorpion, 1977. 1st ed., 1977, 2 ed., 1978.

The Valley of the Assassins, Freya Stark, John Murray, 1934, New ed., Arrow Books, 1991.

Lords of the Mountains, M. T. Ullens de Schooten, Chatto & Windus, 1956.

The Castles of the Assassins, Peter Willey, Harrap, 1963.

Persia and its People, Ella Sykes, Methuen, 1910.

A History of Persia, Vols 1 and 2. Percy Sykes, Macmillan, 1915, and later editions.

Touring Iran, Philip Ward, Faber & Faber, 1971.

Haji Baba, James Morier, John Murray, 1824 (and later editions).

To Persia for Flowers, Alice Fullerton, OUP, 1938.

Persia and the Persian Question, George, N. Curzon, 2 vols, Longman, Green, 1892 and 1996.

By Mountain, Lake and Plain, Lloyd Kennion, William Blackwood and Sons, 1911.

Persian Architecture, An Introduction by Arthur Upham Pope, The Asian Institute, Shiraz.

Persian Architecture, Upham Pope, Thames and Hudson, 1965.

Persian Cities, Laurence Lockhart, Luzac, 1960.

Persia, A. Costa and Laurence Lockhart, Thames and Hudson, 1957.

Blind White Fish in Persia, Anthony Smith, Geo Allen and Unwin, 1953.

The Influence of Islam on Medieval Europe, W. M. Watt, Edinburgh University Press, 1972.

Ancient Iran, E. Porada, Art of the World Series, Methuen, 1965.

The Golden Age of Persia, Richard N. Frye, Weidenfeld and Nicolson, New ed., 1993.

Through Persia in Disguise, Sarah Hobson, John Murray, 1973.

The Legendary Cuisine of Persia, Margaret Shaida, Penguin, 1994.

Persian Grammar, Professor A. K. S. Lambton, OUP, 1953.

Persian Vocabulary, Professor A. K. S. Lambton, OUP, 1953.

Beyond the Caspian, Douglas Carruthers, Oliver & Boyd, 1949.

Morocco

Lords of the Atlas, Gavin Maxwell, Longmans, 1966, New edition Arrow, 1991.

The Alleys of Marrakesh, Peter Mayne, John Murray, 1953.

The Traveller's Guide to Morocco, Christopher Kininmonth, Jonathan Cape, 1972.

Flowers of the Mediterranean, Oleg Polunin and Anthony Huxley, Chatto & Windus, 1965 (and later editions).

On Morocco, Edith Wharton, 1920; *The Century Travellers*, 1984.

Book List

Morocco that Was, Walter Harris, 1921; Blackwoods, Eland Books, 1983.
In the Lap of Atlas, Richard Hughes, Chatto & Windus, 1979.
North Africa, Islamic Architecture, Anthony Hutt, Scorpion, 1977.
Morocco: The Complete Guide, Jane Holliday, George Philip, 1974.
Morocco, James McBey's, Melville and Davidson, Harper-Collins, 1991.
Victory in the Mediterranean, vol 6: History of the 2nd World War by General Sir William Jackson, H.M.S.O. Parts 1–3, 1984; 1987; 1988.

Pakistan

Horned Moon, Ian Stephens, Chatto & Windus, 1953.
Pakistan – Old Country, New Nation, Ian Stephens, Penguin Harmsworth, 1964.
Pakistan: Nations of the Modern World Series, Benn, 1967, 3rd ed.
Islam, Alfred Guillaume, Penguin, Harmsworth, 1954 (and later editions).
Early India and Pakistan: Ancient People and Places, Mortimer Wheeler, Thames and Hudson, 2nd ed., 1969.
Between Oxus and Jumna, Arnold Toynbee, OUP, 1961.
The Lion River, (The Indus). Jean Fairlie, Allen Lane, 1975.
The Tigers of Baluchistan, Sylvia A. Matheson, Arthur Barker, 1967.
Saints of Sind, Peter Mayne, John Murray, 1956.
The Story of the Malakand Field Force, in Winston S. Churchill's Frontiers and Wars, Penguin, 1972.
To the Frontier, Geoffrey Moorhouse, Hodder & Stoughton, 1984.
Where the Indus is Young, Dervla Murphy, John Murray, 1977; New ed., Flamingo, 1995.
The Gilgit Game, John Keay, John Murray, 1979; New ed., OUP, (Pakistan) 1994.
When Men and Mountains Meet, John Keay, John Murray, 1977; New ed., OUP (Pakistan) 1994.
The Frontier Scouts, Charles Chevenix-Trench, J. Cape, 1985.
North-West Frontier, People and Events 1839–1947, Arthur Swinson, Hutchinson, 1967.
The Pathans, Olaf Caroe, OUP, New ed., 1977.
Much Sounding of Bugles, John Harris (Chitral Campaign '95), Hutchinson, 1975.
The Great Divide, H. V. Hodson, Hutchinson, 1969 (and later editions).
Sir Charles Napier and Sind, H. T. Lambrick, Clarendon Press, Oxford, 1952.
The Terrorist, H. T. Lambrick, Ernest Benn, 1972.
Indus Civilisation, Sir Mortimer Wheeler, OUP, 1968.

John Jacob of Jacobabad, H. T. Lambrick, Cassell, 1960.
Charles Napier: Friend and Fighter, Rosamund Napier Lawrence, Murray, 1952.
The Birds of Britain and Europe with North Africa and the Middle East, Helman Heinzel, Collins, 1979.
Popular Handbook of Indian Birds, Hugh Whistler, Oliver and Boyd, 1963.
Bowhani Junction, John Masters, Warner, London, 1953.
Chasing the Monsoon, (India and Pakistan), Alexander Frater, Viking, 1990, Penguin, 1991.
Punjabi Century 1857–1947, Tandon Prakesh, Chatto & Windus, London, 1961.

Central Asia

Beyond the Oxus, Archeology, Art and Architecture of Central Asia, Edgar Knobloch, Ernest Benn, 1972.

Index

Index

Budd, Bernard, 49
Buddhism, 218, 225–226, 239, 256, 517, 526
Bull, Sir Graham, 529
Bullard, Sir Reader, 138
Bumiphol, King of Thailand, 342
Burckhardt, Titus, 334
Burke, Ena, 335, 343, 441
Burma-Britain Association, 259
Burnham, Prime Minister (of Guyana), 430
Burns, Alan, 283
Burridge, Jack, 147
Burton-Brown, Christopher, 149
Burton-Brown, Theodore, 149–150
Busbridge, Raymond, 254
Buschmann, Mr and Mrs, 521
Busk, Lady Bridget, 119n.
Busk, Sir Douglas, 106, 113–114, 117n., 119
Butterworth, Jack and Doris, 339
Buxton, David, 100–101, 117
Byron, Robert, 180, 324, 326, 327, 376, 377, 380

Cakobau family, 286–287
Cakobau, King of Fiji, 269–270, 277, 300
Cakobau, Ratu Edward, 273, 275, 277, 283, 284
Calder, Ian, 209
Calder, Pat, 204, 209
Caledonian Balls, 253, 265, 463, 485, 488, 497, 520, 528
Caledonian Society (Karachi), 520
Callaghan, James 484
Came, Captain Peter, 80, 81
Cameron, James, 505
Campbell, Bill and Maria, 362
Carden, Barbara, 378
Carey, Hugh, 310, 417
Cargo Cult, 296
Caribbean Festival of Creative Arts, 444–447
Carr School (Isfahan), 335
Carthaginians, 558
Cartledge, Horace, 154
Casbon, Leslie, 104, 128, 131
Caspy, Bob, 580
Caten, Lt. A.W., 274
Cavagnari, Sir Louis, 516
Cerubino, Roberto, 336

Chalian, Mrs, 331
Chamasemani, Parveneh, 401
Chan, Brian, 405, 406
Chapman, Roger, 427, 429–430
Charles, Prince of Wales, 587
Charlton, Frankie, 283
Charlton, Ross, 119
Charman, Harry, 282, 316
Chenevix-Trench, Charles, 525
Cheragh Ali Khan, 399
Chindits, 237, 240
Chislett, Chris, 453, 458, 496
Chowdhury, I.U., 459
Christian, Mr and Mrs, 307–308
Christie, Dame Agatha, 353–354
Christmas Stocking, A, 185, 351–352, 368
Chugtai, 76
Chung, Arthur, 448
Church Missionary Society, 156, 328, 330, 334–335, 343, 377
Churchill Club (Casablanca), 552
Churchill, Sir Winston, 480, 515, 516–517, 527, 554
Clark, Adam, 16
Clark, Kenneth, 436
Clark, William, 317
Clarke, Dr and Mrs, 581
Cleaver, Sebastian, 331, 388–389, 391–393
Clegg, John, 374, 442
Clift, Bill, 116–117
Clifton Players (Karachi), 465, 523
Cloake, John and Molly, 366–367
Coke-Wallis, L.C., 69, 73
Coleman, Dr, 377
Collins, Mr, 7
Collins, Micky, 303
Collins, Lt. Col. Neville, 303
Collister, Peter, 469
Colwill, Col. Keith, 66, 253, 317
Communists, 13–15, 20–24, 25, 26, 29, 30–32, 33
Connell, Peter, 484
Coode, James and Charis, 289, 290
Cook, Captain James, 289, 296
Cooper, Robin and Mandy, 553
Cooper, Roger, 170, 182
Corbett, Jim, 43
Corona Society (Fiji), 281
Cowan, Professor, 551
Cox, Professor C.B., 486

609

Index

Index

Index

Index

Index

Index

621